THE LEGAL CHALLENGE
OF SUSTAINABLE
DEVELOPMENT

ESSAYS FROM THE FOURTH INSTITUTE

CONFERENCE ON NATURAL RESOURCES LAW

Edited by

J. OWEN SAUNDERS

Canadian Institute
of Resources Law

Calgary
1990

Canadian Cataloguing in Publication Data

Institute Conference on Natural Resources Law
  (4th : 1989 : Ottawa, Ont.)
    The legal challenge of sustainable development

  Conference held in Ottawa, May 10-12, 1989.
  Includes bibliographical references.
  ISBN 0-919269-32-X

  1. Economic development — Environmental aspects —
Congresses. 2. Canada — Economic policy — Environmental
aspects — Congresses. 3. Natural resources — Law and legislation —
Canada — Congresses. 4. International economic relations —
Environmental aspects — Congresses.
I. Saunders, J. Owen (John Owen), 1948-
II. Canadian Institute of Resources Law.
III. Title.
HD75.6.I58   1990   363.7   C90-091018-6

63,080

CONTRIBUTORS

Nigel Bankes, Associate Professor, Faculty of Law, The University of Calgary, Calgary, Alberta.

François Bregha, Director of Policy Studies, Rawson Academy of Aquatic Science, Ottawa, Ontario.

David B. Brooks, Coordinator, Environmental and Natural Resources Management Unit, International Development Research Centre, Ottawa, Ontario.

J. Anthony Cassils, Vice-President, C.F.G. Heward Management and Investments, Montréal, Québec.

Hélène Connor-Lajambe, Directrice générale, Centre d'analyse des politiques énergétiques, St. Bruno-de-Montarville, Québec.

Ray Cote, Assistant Director, School for Resource and Environmental Studies, Dalhousie University, Halifax, Nova Scotia.

P.S. Elder, Professor of Law and Associate Dean, Faculty of Environmental Design, The University of Calgary, Calgary, Alberta.

Jack O. Gibbons, Senior Economic Advisor, Canadian Institute for Environmental Law and Policy, Toronto, Ontario.

Andrew L. Hamilton, Senior Environmental Advisor, International Joint Commission, Ottawa, Ontario.

Constance D. Hunt, Dean, Faculty of Law, The University of Calgary, Calgary, Alberta.

Jay S. Johnson, Deputy General Counsel, National Oceanic and Atmospheric Administration, U.S. Department of Commerce, Washington, D.C.

David Johnston, Principal, McGill University, Montréal, Québec.

Janet Keeping, Research Associate, Canadian Institute of Resources Law, Calgary, Alberta.

Cynthia Lamson, Associate Director, Oceans Institute of Canada, Halifax, Nova Scotia.

Ann Leonard, U.S. Waste Trade Campaigner, Greenpeace International, Washington, D.C.

Paul Muldoon, Project Director, Program for Zero Discharge, Canadian Institute for Environmental Law and Policy, Toronto, Ontario.

Michael Pretes, Research Associate, Arctic Institute of North America, The University of Calgary, Calgary, Alberta.

Henry A. Regier, Professor, Department of Zoology, University of Toronto, Toronto, Ontario.

Michael Robinson, Executive Director, Arctic Institute of North America, and Adjunct Associate Professor, Department of Anthropology, The University of Calgary, Calgary, Alberta.

Nicholas A. Robinson, Professor, Pace University School of Law, White Plains, New York.

W.A. Ross, Professor of Environmental Science, Faculty of Environmental Design, The University of Calgary, Calgary, Alberta.

David Runnalls, Associate Director, Environment and Sustainable Development Programme, Institute for Research on Public Policy, Ottawa, Ontario.

J. Owen Saunders, Executive Director, Canadian Institute of Resources Law, and Adjunct Associate Professor, Faculty of Law, The University of Calgary, Calgary, Alberta.

Phillip M. Saunders, Field Representative (South Pacific), International Centre for Ocean Development, Suva, Fiji.

Peter G. Sly, Director, Aquatic Science Development Program, Rawson Academy of Aquatic Science, Ottawa, Ontario.

Peter Stokoe, Assistant Professor (Research), School for Resource and Environmental Studies, Dalhousie University, Halifax, Nova Scotia.

Adrian Tanner, Professor, Department of Anthropology, Memorial University, St. John's, Newfoundland.

Joseph P. Tomain, Professor, College of Law, University of Cincinnati, Cincinnati, Ohio.

Ralph D. Torrie, Torrie, Smith and Associates, Ottawa, Ontario.

Marcia Valiante, Research Associate, Canadian Institute for Environmental Law and Policy, Toronto, Ontario.

Jim Vallette, Director, Waste Trade Campaign, Greenpeace International, Washington, D.C.

David VanderZwaag, Assistant Professor, Dalhousie Law School, Halifax, Nova Scotia.

PREFACE

It is hard to imagine a cause that has more nominal friends and fewer declared enemies these days than environmentalism. No longer the primary preserve of a small core of activists, environmentalism today is fervently claimed as the true faith of politicians, businessmen, and public servants. And, at least within the Canadian environmental movement, no cause commands greater sympathy than that of sustainable development, a concept which, while familiar to some environmentalists, especially in the area of conservation, achieved public recognition only following the release of the report of the World Commission on Environment and Development (the Brundtland Commission), *Our Common Future*.

For a number of very particular political and personal reasons, the concept of sustainable development has probably found greater public acceptance in Canada than in any other country; certainly, the concept has found no comparable audience as yet in the United States. It is clear though, that, under whatever rubric, the underlying concerns of the Brundtland Report will occupy an important place on domestic and international policy agendas relating to both environment and development over the next few decades. A great conceptual advantage of sustainable development is that it embraces so many problems under one coherent structure. This breadth of vision that sustainable development offers is also arguably its greatest disadvantage. Because it is an extremely broad concept — reflecting more a theme than a set of specific policies — the substantive content of sustainable development is open to a wide range of interpretations, to the point where adversarial constituencies feel free to cite the principle in support of apparently contradictory policy positions. Thus, those who are attracted to such traditional environmental concepts as "small is beautiful" will emphasize the sustainable aspect of the concept; those who are uncomfortable with traditional environmental reservations about economic growth may note with approval the objective of development. Whether these views represent an accurate reading of the concept, at least as it was anticipated in the Brundtland Report, is of course quite another matter. Nor is it clear that the full implications of the Brundtland Report are yet fully recognized by any of the groups that have so readily taken the concept to heart. For example, there has been relatively little attention paid (by the traditional environmental community or other constituencies) to the Report's implications with respect to the need for a significant transfer of resources from industrialized states to the Third World — a course that would suggest declining (and quite possibly negative) economic growth for industrialized states, so as to allow some measure of growth in developing nations. Not surprisingly, few political leaders have been willing to put the case for sustainable development in quite such blunt terms.

While it is still unclear whether there is really widespread support as yet for acceptance of the full implications of sustainable development, it does seem that the concept will at least be influential in shaping a new approach to environmental problems — one that will reflect the changing nature of environmental concerns. More than ever before, environmental problems are being seen not as merely national or regional issues, but as truly global in scope — whether the issue concerns the greenhouse effect, the depletion of the ozone layer, the disposal of toxic substances, or the extinction of entire species of flora and fauna. This new generation of problems will call not only for new technical solutions, but also for a fundamental rethinking of the appropriate legal principles and mechanisms to engage these challenges (a rethinking that must be carried out within other disciplines as well). Domestically, for example, to what extent must "traditional" approaches to environmental law be amended to deal with the new agenda of sustainable development? Similarly, how can an international legal order founded on the principle of state sovereignty accommodate the constraints on that sovereignty that will be necessary to protect the global commons? It is these types of problems that this volume of essays attempts to address.

The essays are arranged thematically under five major headings. Although the general orientation of the volume is a legal one, the very nature of the concept of sustainable development militates against a narrowly legal focus. As a result, a number of essays from other disciplinary perspectives have been included to provide a context for the legal principles. The first group of essays presents an overview of the concept of sustainable development from differing disciplinary perspectives. Obviously, one of those perspectives is a legal one; however, the section also includes contributions from two disciplines that are crucial to any discussion of sustainable development — science and economics.

The second section deals with the challenge of implementing sustainable development, both domestically and internationally. This begins with a discussion of an area of resource management where there has been perhaps the most experience — both domestic and international — with concepts analogous to sustainable development: fisheries management. It then goes on to consider how both "traditional" and nontraditional instruments of domestic environmental law might be applied to the specific objective of sustainable development. Finally, the section includes papers on the problems of implementing sustainable development as a matter of international law, drawing on both bilateral and multilateral experience.

The third and fourth parts of the volume address the question of sustainable development in the context of two specific areas where it has been of special importance — energy policy and northern development. In both cases, there is an emphasis on Canadian experience, but with some additional material dealing with the United States, which shares similar problems in both areas.

Finally, the last section deals with an area of inquiry that has not traditionally been treated as falling within the province of environmental concerns, but that has important implications for the future of sustainable development. This is the question of international economic relations, which comprises for the purposes of this volume both foreign aid and international trade. This topic brings together the concerns of both developing and industrialized states, and describes not only the challenges that the current structure of international economic relations poses for the attainment of sustainable development, but also the opportunities it presents with respect to potential levers for encouraging environmentally appropriate behavior.

These essays arise out of the fourth biennial conference on natural resources law sponsored by the Canadian Institute of Resources Law, held in Ottawa, May 10–12, 1989, and, with the exception of some minor updating, generally reflect the law as of that date. For the first time, the Institute had as a co-sponsor of the Conference the Faculty of Law (Common Law) at the University of Ottawa. In chairing the advisory committee that planned the Conference, I benefited greatly from the advice provided by the other committee members: Dean Donald McRae and Jamie Benedickson of the Faculty of Law, University of Ottawa; Barry Barton and Janet Keeping of the Institute; Alastair Lucas of the Faculty of Law, University of Calgary; and Jonathan Scarth, then Special Assistant to the Minister of Natural Resources, Province of Manitoba.

Financial support for the Conference was provided by the Department of Justice (Canada), the Department of the Secretary of State of Canada, Ontario Environment, MacMillan Bloedel Ltd., Noranda Forest Inc., Dow Chemical Canada Inc., Dofasco Inc., Inco Ltd., the Social Sciences & Humanities Research Council, the Helen McCrea Peacock Foundation, the Walter & Duncan Gordon Charitable Foundation, and an anonymous donor. Environment Canada and the Alberta Law Foundation generously provided grants to assist with the publication of this volume of essays.

During the editing of the papers, I was assisted on the footnoting by Evangeline Case, the Institute's Publications Officer, and by Pat Osoko, a student in the Faculty of Law at the University of Victoria who served as a summer Research Assistant at the Institute. Susan Parsons of the Institute also assisted with the typing of certain parts of the manuscript.

Finally, I owe special thanks to Terry Teskey and Therese Goulet for their contributions to the technical editing, layout, and production of the volume.

J. Owen Saunders
Calgary, Alberta
October 15, 1989

TABLE OF CONTENTS

THE PATH TO SUSTAINABLE DEVELOPMENT: A ROLE FOR LAW

J. Owen Saunders

Although the concept of sustainable development, in one form or another, has been used by environmental policy analysts for many years, only with the release of the 1987 report of the World Commission on Environment and Development, *Our Common Future* (the Brundtland Report) did the term begin to gain some public currency. In Canada this was partly owing to the initiative of the Canadian government, which had been a major supporter of the Commission's work, and which embraced the concept, at least notionally, as a goal towards which public policy should be directed. However, public interest in the concept was undoubtedly affected also by the concomitant emergence of certain global environmental problems on the front pages of daily newspapers. These included especially the announcement of the serious threat to the ozone layer, which received particular attention in Canada because of the Montreal Protocol, and the growing awareness of the dangers posed by the "greenhouse effect", which achieved prominence as a public concern largely because of the widespread and serious drought in North America in the summer of 1988.

While the term "sustainable development" is now a familiar one, the substantive content of the concept is another matter. Beyond a rather generalized impression that we should be burning fewer fossil fuels, and perhaps engaging in more recycling of materials, the actual measures that need to be taken to move towards sustainable development — as well as the associated costs and benefits of such measures — are not well understood. Sustainable development is open to a wide range of interpretations, not all of them compatible. Not surprisingly, the particular interpretation chosen tends to vary according to the interests of the group identifying itself with the concept. For example, on the issue of nuclear energy, the implications of sustainability may be read much differently by the nuclear industry than by groups advancing a "soft" energy future. Similarly, while some constituencies might accept the environmental implications of the Brundtland Report, they may place far less emphasis on the question of economic development, especially to the extent that the Report may be taken as implying a significant transfer of resources from the industrialized to the developing world.

However one chooses to interpret the Brundtland Report or the concept of sustainable development, it is clear that the concerns raised by the concept will be of continuing importance over the next few decades. This fact is reflected both in the increased significance that all public opinion polls now attribute to environmental issues, and in the heightened profile that most governments have given to such concerns in the past few years. Even if one were to take the position that such a governmental stance is nothing more than an attempt to appease public opinion (and it cannot be denied that the environment has found an extraordinary number of new friends remarkably quickly), it is at least the case that governments feel they must *respond* to such issues, with all the public scrutiny that entails, in a way that arguably was not politically necessary in the past.

Fashioning a significant change in public policy with respect to the environment — which is nothing less than what is required by a move to sustainable development, however interpreted — necessarily involves the consideration of legal implications. This is obviously true in the mechanistic sense that new statutes and regulations must be drafted, passed, and interpreted if society is to move beyond the present substance of environmental law. While these aspects are not unimportant, however, lawyers should bring more to the public policy debate than narrow technical skills. At the heart of the coming discussion on the implementation of sustainable development are some difficult choices, choices that will almost inevitably involve, at least in the short run, winners and losers. In a word, like any other major change in the direction of public policy, these choices will involve conflict. The resolution of such conflict is something that must be accomplished on the basis of legal principles; the articulation of such principles is therefore a primary task that must be carried out before we can talk realistically about implementing a new generation of environmental law.

As Nicholas Robinson argues in his paper in this volume, law is more than a complicated set of rules to which we turn only when compelled. Law is a force in itself, capable equally of promoting values that will preserve and protect the environmental interests of future generations or of insisting on the economic interests of present society, regardless of the cost to those who follow. Put differently, as David Johnston states in his paper, law mirrors a society's values. How law articulates fundamental values can therefore significantly influence a society's view of itself and of the broad social policies that it considers appropriate, not only with respect to regulating conduct within the society itself, but also with respect to guiding the conduct of that society within the wider global community.

To focus, however, merely on the legal aspect of sustainable development would, at least at this stage, be an empty exercise. Much of the legal content of this subject is necessarily dependent on our assumptions about the substantive meaning of sustainable development, and the implications that flow from failing to meet this goal. For just as the concept of sustainable development arguably portends important changes in both domestic and international legal regimes, so too it holds far-reaching implications for other disciplines, with respect to both their assumptions and the tasks that may be required of them. Understanding the implications of sustainable development for these other disciplines is therefore a precondition of understanding the policy environment in which law and lawyers must operate.

Perhaps the discipline that will be called upon to carry the heaviest burden in shaping a future consistent with sustainable development is science. This is true most obviously in the sense that science will be asked to provide the technological solutions necessary to make sustainable development achievable. As Peter Sly argues in his paper, however, more than this traditional "problem-solver" role will be expected from science in the future. Science must not only *provide* solutions; it must also increasingly *justify* these solutions, whether by explaining how the solutions interrelate with and affect other, socio-economic and environmental, factors, or by framing these solutions in the context of models that are understandable to the wider population, yet rigorous enough to substantiate meaningful policies. This is not a role with which all scientists will be comfortable. Nevertheless, it is a role that is necessary if one accepts the value of the principles of participatory decision-making that are discussed and recommended in a number of papers in this volume.

If Sly challenges scientists to take on a new role in the move towards sustainable development, Hélène Connor-Lajambe, writing from the perspective of an economist, issues an even bolder challenge to her discipline — in effect, to take on a new paradigm. Connor-Lajambe argues that the very foundations of traditional neoclassical economics are called into question by the requirements of a world that would commit itself to sustainable development. She questions, for example, the assumptions about "rational economic man" that underlie the discipline, suggesting nothing less than the need for the development of a new type of individual, one who sees himself in a fundamentally different relationship with his environment than has been true in the past. Such a reassessment has obvious and dramatic implications, especially in areas such as economic growth theory, where it has always been at least an implicit assumption that growth as measured by material output is desirable — an assumption that has characterized both capitalist and socialist economic systems.

Even assuming some shared understanding of the goals inherent in the concept of sustainable development, it is impossible to emphasize too strongly the extremely difficult technical problems that may await us. Taking, for example, those areas of resource management where there has been some extensive experience with concepts analogous to sustainable development, we can see continuing difficulties with the specific realization of the generally agreed-upon goals. This becomes apparent when one considers an example of resource management that has been the subject of perhaps the longest and broadest efforts at cooperative regulation of a common resource — fisheries management.

Some of the problems confronting any attempt to frame even a coherent *domestic* fisheries policy are discussed in the paper by VanderZwaag *et al.* in the context of one Canadian province, Nova Scotia. As the authors demonstrate, the range of conflicts that are possible, and indeed likely, includes both the conflicting interests of different groups of fishermen (most notably, near-shore as opposed to off-shore), and those of fisheries as opposed to other ocean "users" (for example, aquaculture and tourism). Ocean-use strategies that encompass the interests of all such constituencies are yet in their infancy in Canada, and the difficulties they pose for both negotiation and implementation are obvious. When we move beyond the regional to the national and international levels, such an approach will clearly take a very long time to evolve.

The difficulties that attend the negotiation of an international fisheries management regime are described with respect to the Canada-United States west coast in the paper by Jay Johnson. As Johnson notes, even when there is agreement on a concept such as maximum sustainable yield to guide fisheries negotiations, the actual attempts to implement this principle soon encounter some important real-world obstacles, whether economic, environmental, or political. These include not only the barriers that might commonly be expected when nations compete for scarce resources, but also very often some important domestic limitations that as a matter of practice constrain what can be achieved. These latter may involve, for example, competing interests within the nation, such as those that arose between Alaska and the lower forty-eight states in the context of the Pacific Salmon Treaty negotiations or, for that matter, the special concerns of Alaskan natives as opposed to those in other states. What is more, fisheries is in many ways the "easy" case; at least for this resource there is a long history of cooperation and a number of fundamental principles with respect to resource harvesting that are agreed upon by most states (as well as some technical expertise to guide their implementation and monitoring). In other areas of resource and environmental management there is not yet nearly such a strong foundation to build upon.

We are not, however, left without any instruments to begin a movement towards the goal of sustainable development now. At the national level, perhaps the best building block in this respect is the model provided by Environmental Impact Assessment (EIA), a tool that has achieved widespread acceptance, and with which there has been considerable experience, at least in the industrialized world. Elder and Ross argue in their paper that EIA is precisely the vehicle that offers the best immediate possibility for addressing some of the pressing concerns raised with respect to sustainable development; their suggestion in this respect is to legislate the criterion of "maximum feasible sustainability" as a precondition for approving new project proposals. This might be supplemented by the additional adoption of an "environmental bill of rights," which would impose certain duties on decision-makers regardless of any EIA process; certainly this or some equivalent step would be necessary to address comprehensively those environmental problems that did not arise in the context of new project proposals.

Despite the undoubted value of EIA as a tool to protect the environment, the broad vision of sustainable development in the Brundtland Report suggests the need for more instruments than those provided by "traditional" environmental law. Just as the notion of sustainability implies far-reaching changes in many aspects of our society, so too it implies the need for other policy instruments to influence individual and corporate behaviour. One example of such an instrument is the tax system, a vehicle that has historically been much used to influence the social choices of both individuals (as, for example, with taxes on cigarettes and alcohol) and corporations (as with the special incentives that have been afforded the Canadian resource industries over the years). While the tax system is not normally thought of as a tool of environmental policy, it is nevertheless true that the taxation regime that we choose as a society has inevitable effects, for better or worse, on the nature of our economic development. As Anthony Cassils suggests in his paper, there is a strong argument that the taxation policies Canada has pursued in the past have encouraged unsustainable practices in the agriculture, forestry, and mining sectors. Cassils' suggestion that we should use the tax system actively to pursue a goal of sustainable development echoes some of the proposals made over the past few years for what has sometimes been referred to as an "ecology tax"; however, his approach clearly has more sweeping implications and touches on a broader range of tax levers.

As noted earlier, whatever the problems that may arise with respect to the implementation of sustainable development as a matter of domestic policy, the difficulties are obviously magnified when the policy arena is an international one. As Nigel Bankes notes in his paper, although the Brundtland Report identified a range of important global problems in the area of environment and development, it offered relatively little with respect to the specific international legal means that might be available to address these problems, other than a few general principles such as the equitable distribution of benefits and the full internalization of costs. Selecting as an example the currently prominent issue of global atmospheric protection, Bankes suggests how existing treaties in this area might be improved by the inclusion of principles that address the problems of global interdependencies and inequities, which the Brundtland Commission identified as being central to the resolution of many global environmental challenges. Specifically, for example, Bankes asks how the principle of intergenerational equity might be incorporated into conventions dealing with atmospheric protection.

In this regard, it might be useful to contrast some of the comprehensive, and even radical, suggestions of the Brundtland Report with the rather modest legal principles proposed by the legal experts group convened to advise the Brundtland Commission. This is not to suggest these principles represent an overly conservative view of the state of international law; on the contrary, what is suggested is that customary international law cannot be expected to develop principles in this area with any degree of timeliness unless positive treaty obligations are first negotiated.

If specific international obligations reflecting the principles of the Brundtland Commission are to be enshrined in treaties, this will often happen initially at the regional or bilateral level. One example of this can be found in the bilateral management regime that has evolved between Canada and the United States for the Great Lakes. This regime predates the Brundtland Commission, of course, but some of its most important principles are in many ways consonant with the thinking that underlies the Commission's Report, and draw upon similar environmental thinking. One of the major concepts that has been introduced into this regime (although it was not a part of the original Great Lakes Water Quality Agreement), as discussed in the paper by Regier and Hamilton, is the notion of ecosystem integrity. This is a concept that has its roots in federal legislation in the United States, and has since been adopted by the International Joint Commission (ICJ).

The concept of focusing on and preserving an international ecosystem is to some extent in contradistinction to traditional concepts of international law that focus on the sovereign rights of national entities. It might be, then, that in the articulation of global environmental norms this bilateral experience can provide some valuable insights; moreover, it also provides examples of state practice from which one may be able to argue for the evolution of new norms of customary international law. In this respect, it is instructive to note that the case frequently cited as marking the beginning of international environmental law — the *Trail Smelter* arbitration — began precisely as the resolution of a Canada–U.S. bilateral dispute, and one in which the tribunal drew explicitly upon principles from the inter-state law of the United States. One would hope that bilateral institutions such as the ICJ will continue to serve as crucibles for forging solutions to environmental problems, which solutions may eventually be adopted by the international community as a whole. (Similar comments could be made about other areas of resource management, such as the case of fisheries, noted earlier.)

Despite the value of such regional and bilateral measures, it is nevertheless clear that international law suffers from significant practical disadvantages as a vehicle for responding to many environmental threats. In the result, the primary responsibility for action in many areas of environmental degradation must lie with individual states, and especially those states that bear primary responsibility for the harm and/or are in the best position (technically and financially) to repair the damage. On both counts, this typically describes the community of developed nations, particularly as regards the environmental consequences of intensive consumption of particular forms of energy. In this respect, one can further distinguish between the consumptive practices of North Americans and those of other industrialized nations. A striking aspect of North American patterns of energy consumption is not only their high levels, but also the extent to which they are a creation of policy. The fact that Canadian per capita consumption of electricity is so dramatically higher than Europe's, for example, cannot be explained away merely by pointing to differences in climate or industrialization. Canadians have used energy with such profligacy because it has been cheap and readily available, and this has been so because of conscious policy decisions — by both federal and provincial governments of all political stripes — that energy *should* be cheap and readily available.

As Brooks and Torrie point out in their paper, much of the underlying appeal of cheap energy is built on a rather naive understanding of both economics and ecology. As to the former, it is clear now that the once-assumed identification of energy consumption and economic growth is overly simplistic. As to the latter, while economists for many years have recognized externalities and social costs as theoretical concepts, until recent years this realization has not penetrated energy policy in any fundamental way. It is true that the recent report of the Energy Options Advisory Committee (set up by the federal government in Canada) does recognize the need to internalize fully the costs of energy development in energy prices, as well as to include environmental quality as a fundamental and important factor in the assessment of living standards. However, in the view of writers such as Gibbons *et al.* these policies are not in themselves enough to implement a policy of sustainable development in energy. They may be a first step (and Brooks and Torrie similarly argue that even conventional economic objectives are not met by traditional energy policy), but they are by no means sufficient to meet the goals set out in the Brundtland Report.

Most fundamentally, there is arguably a basic difference between the objectives of energy policy in the Brundtland Report and those in the Energy Options Report. As pointed out by Gibbons *et al.,* the Brundtland Report implies a reduction of energy consumption by the industrialized states if developing nations are to be able to increase energy consumption, and at the same time pursue development that is sustainable; such a policy almost inevitably implies substantial government intervention in the energy marketplace. By contrast, while the Energy Options Report breaks with much of past Canadian energy policy in recommending that the energy sector bear its full share of *all* costs associated with it, the Report nevertheless argues for a pre-eminent role for market forces, and specifically rejects the concept of artificially induced constraints on energy consumption. Especially given the political climate in many Western nations today with respect to the iniquities of government intervention, this raises serious questions about the willingness of industrialized countries to accept the full consequences of the Brundtland recommendations.

Governmental reluctance to employ interventionist tactics to affect energy choices is perhaps somewhat ironic, given the strong evidence suggesting that existing patterns of energy consumption — both in total and as between different forms of energy — have been largely the result of active government intervention in the energy sector. Gibbons *et al.,* for example, show how the built-in biases of the legislative/regulatory structure governing Ontario Hydro operate in such a way as to favour coal and nuclear generation rather than energy-conserving, small-scale hydro and natural gas. As a result, the authors conclude that, at least in the short run, the introduction of the market-oriented reforms suggested in the Energy Options Report would move Hydro in the direction of sustainable development; in effect, then, less intervention is seen as preferable to the type of intervention now practised.

Nor is the artificial nature of the present structure of energy patterns unique to Canada. Joseph Tomain describes in some detail how the nuclear industry in the United States achieved its growth largely because of a favourable and highly artificial regulatory environment. Nuclear power, in Tomain's view, is a classic illustration of "big science", an approach that inevitably requires a government/industry partnership of some kind. (This partnership need not involve direct investment on the part of government, as was true in the Canadian nuclear industry; it could consist of the provision of a regulatory climate in which the industry can thrive, as, for example, with the limitation of liability for nuclear power operators under federal legislation in the United States and Canada.)

The love of bigness for the sake of bigness (although the rationale may be dressed in the disguise of economies of scale) has, of course, been a consistent element of the environmentalist critique (or at least the dominant environmentalist critique) of energy policy for many years in both Canada and the United States. This does leave us with at least one unanswered — and to date, largely unasked — question: To what extent must we look to "big science" to develop and implement at least part of a programme of sustainable development? And if "big science" is a necessary recourse, how do we manage it so as to avoid the problems of the past? The answer again probably lies in improving the decision-making process to increase the number and effectiveness of voices brought to bear on policy-making and implementation. Structuring these processes to accommodate more effective input from actors outside the constituencies of industry and government will be an important challenge to both lawyers and scientists — a challenge that harks back to the papers by Elder and Ross and by Peter Sly, referred to earlier.

The domestic arena not only poses *challenges* with respect to the implementation of sustainable development, however; it may also offer some valuable *lessons.* For example, many of the problems posed by the Brundtland Commission with respect to balancing development and environmental considerations are similar to those encountered by Canada and the United States in frontier regions, and especially in northern regions, which have unique and fragile environmental conditions, as well as aboriginal populations who are particularly sensitive to the impact of development on traditional lifestyles. The problem in the North, then, has not been merely one of how to stimulate economic development, even environmentally appropriate development, but also of how to accommodate such development to the particular needs of the indigenous community. This task is inevitably an extremely challenging one, to the point where Adrian Tanner questions the very possibility of sustainable development; for Tanner, nonsustainability is virtually inherent in the notion of development itself. This view is reinforced if one looks at the experience of cultures predicated on sustainability (such as aboriginal cultures in the North) when they come into contact with cultures predicated on economic growth (such as European colonizers). The evidence hardly supports an optimistic view of the latter's ability to accommodate the needs of the former.

Nevertheless, given the inevitability of some degree of development in such regions, one can at least distinguish between more and less destructive intrusions by southern influences. In this respect, Hunt's paper is a useful reminder of the extent to which legal structures may contribute to the effectiveness of resource management regimes. For example, she contrasts the disappointing experience of the Migratory Birds Convention, which was negotiated early in this century without reference to the opinions or needs of user groups in the North, with the much more satisfactory experience of the Porcupine Caribou Treaty, where the needs and goals were identified by northern user groups themselves. Not surprisingly, the key to the success of the latter treaty seems to lie in the much greater voice given to those most concerned with the management of the resource. The implication that one can draw from this with respect to the procedures likely to encourage optimum use of resources is not dissimilar to a recommendation frequently made in other areas of resource management and environmental policy, and one that has been noted in the earlier discussion: those most affected by resource exploitation must be given an effective voice in the management regime.

This emphasis on participation in the decision-making process is reiterated in the paper by Pretes and Robinson on the use of trust funds as a possible vehicle for the implementation of sustainable development in Alaska and the Canadian North. In the view of Pretes and Robinson, the beneficiaries of these trusts are in the best position to determine how the monies should be used, although they should be guided in this respect by the experience — not all of it favourable — with other resource-based trust funds. (Interestingly, one of the lessons that comes out of this experience seems to be the emphasis on avoiding investment in the large megaprojects that have been the hallmark of many northern development efforts, especially in the natural resources sector, over the past two decades.)

The discussion above has focused largely on the measures that might be taken to move towards a goal of sustainable development within or amongst industrialized nations. However, as discussed earlier, the essence of the challenge posed by sustainable development is that the problems it raises are ultimately global in scope. They are, moreover, problems that raise in a very fundamental way the question of how the benefits and burdens of development should be shared. It is not surprising, then, that there has emerged increasingly in the past few years the issue of the link between foreign development assistance and environmental health. This linkage of environment and development can be observed both multilaterally in the actions taken by such agencies as the World Bank and International Monetary Fund (as discussed in the paper by David Runnalls), and bilaterally in such initiatives as the adoption of the Official Development Charter by the Canadian International Development Agency (discussed in the paper by François Bregha).

As both Runnalls and Bregha suggest, these efforts have not been wholly successful, for a number of reasons. To take just two of the examples cited, it is unlikely that the directors of intergovernmental development agencies (who are generally representatives of national finance ministries), let alone the private banks that ultimately put up the loans, will be sensitive by nature to environmental concerns associated with development projects. Similarly, even in bilateral agencies such as CIDA, that evince a clear willingness to incorporate environmental factors into decisions on foreign assistance, there may still be lacking the requisite technical expertise — for example, with respect to the unique environmental problems of tropical or semi-tropical countries.

As we move beyond traditional considerations to the adoption of the wider goal of sustainable development, we will require an even more basic rethinking of our development assistance policy. As Bregha notes, the traditional objective of foreign development assistance has been framed in terms of reducing the economic disparities between developing and developed countries, so that the former can achieve the living standards of the latter. This strategy is usually conceived of in terms of increasing the economic growth of the developing nations so as to replicate the experience of industrialized countries. Obviously, insofar as one assumes that the present nature of economic growth in the developed countries is not sustainable, this calls into question the essential thrust of development strategy as it has been articulated over the past several decades.

The search for new models of development raises another issue for aid agencies in the industrialized world: the extent to which such agencies should require a clean environmental bill of health as a prerequisite to approval of particular projects. There is presumably broad support, for example, for the proposition that industrialized nations should not be engaged in the financing of environmental disasters in the Third World. It is unlikely, however, that development proposals will be this clear-cut in their effects. We must ask, then, to what extent developed countries should impose the same stringent environmental standards on developing countries that they (ideally) impose on their own domestic industries, even granted that such demands are likely to be for the long-run benefits of the recipient country.

The problems associated with imposing the norms of industrialized nations on developing states in the course of providing foreign assistance is well-illustrated, with specific respect to legal principles, in the paper by Phillip Saunders. As Saunders reminds us, law may play a critical role in the implementation of development assistance. Just as mistaken assumptions about the technical and administrative capacities of a recipient state may cause serious implementation problems (for example, in environmental monitoring) for a development project, so too can mistaken assumptions about the applicability of fundamental legal concepts result in inappropriate legal structures and unintended consequences. Perhaps the best example of this with respect to sustainable development is the legal baggage that natural resource managers carry with them when they move from Western nations, which share a more-or-less common view of the institution of private property, to societies where customary land-tenure systems reflect an emphasis on the rights of different groups and communities. Not only does the assumption of a common view of the nature of property result in a likelihood that the imported management concepts will be inappropriate; it also means that the possibility of actually building on traditional norms, for which there may be a substantial degree of community support, is obviated. This is particularly unfortunate — and some-what ironic — in the context of an aid programme that has as one of its goals sustainable development; as noted earlier with reference to Adrian Tanner's work, and as Phillip Saunders suggests implicitly, traditional non-industrialized societies have at the least developed a facility for managing their economies on a sustainable basis.

Another aspect of international economic relations that holds important implications for sustainable development — and one that similarly is of concern to both developed and developing nations — is the structure of international trade. Again, this is not an area that has typically been thought of as coming within the province of traditional environmental concerns. Nevertheless, as the global economy grows increasingly interdependent, the inquiry into the linkages between economic growth and environmental health must inevitably include a discussion of the role of the world trading system. As I suggest in my paper, the link between environment and trade has been recognized for some time in international organizations; however, the perspective has usually been that of trade-oriented bodies, which were primarily interested, at least originally, in the possible distortions to free commerce posed by environmental measures. This concern could be found not only in industrialized nations, but also amongst developing states, who were concerned that stringent and "inappropriate" environmental safeguards in the developed nations might be used as barriers to their own economic growth.

Clearly, both groups of states have become more sophisticated in the way they perceive the environmental implications of trade today. For example, the horrific environmental consequences that may result from the trade in hazardous wastes have become apparent to developing nations following several recent incidents described in the paper by Leonard and Vallette. As a result of this experience, a number of Third World states have taken measures to ban the import of hazardous wastes altogether, a measure that may force industrialized countries to face more directly the full costs of economic development. The recent actions of Kenya in destroying large stocks of elephant ivory indicate, in another context, the new priority that the Third World is giving to the protection of the environment over the dictates of short-run economic gain. (It is true that the Kenyan actions have not met with uniform approval from all African states — most notably Zimbabwe; however, it is clear that what differences exist are with respect to the effectiveness of the strategy being pursued and not the ultimate objective of wildlife conservation.)

Just as the environmental implications of certain types of trade are becoming clear to more and more countries, so there is an emerging recognition that the international trading system may in some circumstances be a useful means of encouraging environmentally desirable conduct. An early example of this is the international convention to protect endangered species; a more recent, and in some ways more powerful, example that I discuss in my paper is a trade-based approach to sanctions adopted in the recent Montreal Protocol for the protection of the ozone layer. The potential leverage of the international trading system as a tool for moving towards sustainable development is, however, a long way from being recognized; nor is it clear that those international organizations with primary responsibility for international trade (particularly the GATT) will be particularly receptive to such utilization of the system.

Such concerns do not, of course, preclude bilateral trade measures directed towards this end. Janet Keeping suggests in her paper, for example, that in the specific case of natural gas exports, consideration should be given to the possibility of including sustainable development as a criterion in the export approval process. In her view, then, the extent to which the use of exported gas enhances (or detracts from) the goal of sustainable development would be a relevant factor in granting or withholding export approvals. This view, at first blush, seems strikingly at odds with the current trend towards deregulation in the natural gas industry. It should be noted, however, that while one of the common complaints in the past with respect to gas export regulation was that it impeded the development of export markets, the result of the regulatory criterion suggested by Keeping might well be (at least in the short to medium term) a greater, not lesser, emphasis on exports to the United States, on the rationale that they would replace the more environmentally harmful fuels.

In summary, what do the essays in this volume tell us about the likely role that law will be asked to assume if we move, both domestically and internationally, towards a world characterized by sustainable development? Perhaps the first lesson is that the role will be an integrated one; that is to say, law (and lawyers) must more than ever be aware of the findings and contributions of other disciplines, especially in the physical and social sciences. This is not an entirely new development, of course. "Good" law-making has always been informed by such perspectives, which, after all, are nothing more than a means of achieving a fuller understanding of societal values and goals. Certainly the development of environmental law over the past two decades has been heavily marked by this interdisciplinary fertilization. What is really being asked for, then, is an intensification — and, in some sense, a "normalization" — of the links between law and such extra-legal influences.

Second, and as a concomitant to the expanded interaction of law and other disciplines, law must become more creative in the instruments it brings to bear on issues of sustainable development. To some extent, this involves improving and extending existing techniques that have been developed by "traditional" environmental law. However, given the pervasive and complex nature of the problems raised by sustainable development, it will also involve turning to other legal techniques not normally associated with environmental policy — for example, the tax system. Nor is the need for creativity in instrument choice a purely domestic challenge. If anything, this need is even greater in the realm of international law, where the instruments realistically available are not nearly as varied or as powerful as those within the domestic setting. This constraint is aggravated by the traditional reluctance of states to surrender their "sovereignty" to the will of the wider world community, a reluctance reflected in the relative conservatism of the principles suggested by the Brundtland group of legal experts when compared to the far-reaching recommendations of the Brundtland Report itself. Nevertheless, while this international legal conservatism is unlikely to give way easily, there is evidence of some ingenuity in current international approaches to certain environmental problems — for example, the earlier-noted use of trade sanctions to encourage appropriate environmental conduct in the context of both species and atmospheric protection.

A final important aspect of the role of law that is implicit in many of the essays in this volume concerns what might be called law's "translation" function. This function is reflected in a number of tasks, none of which are new, but some of which will take on a new importance in the context of sustainable development. Fundamentally, of course, law translates general policy into specific action; this role has been discussed above in the context of the need for increased creativity of lawyers in addressing the new environmental agenda. It need only be added here that in articulating the norms of sustainable development, law also facilitates the circulation of ideas amongst disciplines; to a degree, then, the common vocabulary in which the objectives of sustainable development will be discussed will be the legal language and principles that give voice to them.

Law serves other translation needs as well, however. Of special relevance with respect to the implementation of sustainable development, it provides an important role in communicating between the national and international arenas. This involves, first, translating norms that have developed out of domestic experience into principles that have global application and validity. One can cite a number of principles of domestic environmental practice that have over time been translated in this way, both through the evolution of customary international law and through the conclusion of treaties. An important example of a domestic norm that increasingly appears to be accepted as part of the international legal vocabulary is Environmental Impact Assessment, a technique that has special relevance for sustainable development.

A similar legal task that will become steadily more important over the next few decades involves the domestic implementation of internationally accepted principles relating to sustainable development. As noted, the corpus of international legal obligations relating to the environment is as yet in its infancy. However, as indicated by such developments as the Montreal Protocol, as well as the growing volume of work being done in international organizations such as UNEP and the OECD, this body of law is likely to expand rapidly in coming years. The bulk of such new international obligations will almost certainly be in the form of international conventions, but one can perceive, even in such documents as that produced by the legal experts advisory group to the Brundtland Commission, some significant changes in customary international law as well. If in fact there do emerge new and definite obligations with respect to the protection of the global commons, these may well have significant implications for the duties that are cast upon governments domestically.

1
SUSTAINABLE DEVELOPMENT: AN INTRODUCTION TO THE CONCEPT

A LEGAL PERSPECTIVE ON SUSTAINABLE DEVELOPMENT

Nicholas A. Robinson

Society charges the law today with tasks reminiscent of those ancient Roman mythology assigned to Janus, the doorkeeper of heaven. As guardians of doors and gates, Janus presided over the beginning of new ventures. Sculptors portray Janus' head with one face looking forward and the other looking to the past. The law, like Janus, is forever conservatively upholding the past and progressively ushering in the future.

Law serves policies that either shape new ventures or preserve older established rules. Since law orders a society's social relationships, it employs a powerful array of statutes, courts, police, and devices such as taxes, permits, insurance, subsidies, and, ultimately, criminal sanctions, to serve social policies. These instruments can retard "progress" or stimulate "reform." Law is capable both of maintaining traditional liberties or values, and of propping up dictatorial systems and unethical exploitation of humans and ecosystems.

The Janus-like role of law is frequently overlooked by scientists, policy-makers, and government administrators. Law is perceived as an often excessively complicated set of rules — boring in its detail, necessary, but worth avoiding whenever convenient. The law's role as itself a force molding conduct is over-looked. However, it is a mistake to discount the dynamics of the law by paying them little heed.

No contemporary issue better illustrates the need to understand the role of law than do the challenges of achieving sustainable development throughout this planet. "Sustainable development" is the emerging cluster of policies by which we manage the use of Earth's environment and natural resources to ensure the optimal level of sustainable benefits for present and succeeding generations. We do not achieve these management objectives at present, and indeed have never done so consistently for all Earth's peoples. Nonetheless, our world community aspires to such a goal, as is evidenced by the Universal Declaration of Human Rights[1] and the more recently adopted World Charter of Nature.[2]

THE THREATS TO SUSTAINABLE DEVELOPMENT

There is a new urgency for us to redouble and better coordinate our global effort for sustainable development. Global degradation of the natural environment threatens to undermine past development and deny us the ability to provide for the needs of our planet's rapidly growing population. Each day forty thousand children die around the world, the equivalent of the Hiroshima deaths each week. Escalating desertification, forest and wetland losses, pollution, depletion of finite mineral reserves and renewable resources, declines in ecological communities, and erosion of stratospheric ozone now portend disruption of our planet's fundamental biogeochemical cycles and climate.[3] Most of these trends result from the accumulation of many discrete adverse environmental impacts, some set in motion by persons intent on their immediate developments and unaware of their contribution to the trends. The United Nations' World Commission on Environment and Development (WCED) summed up the global challenge for sustainable development: "The next few decades are crucial for the future of humanity. Pressures on the planet are now unprecedented and are accelerating at rates and scales new to human experience."[4]

Over the next decade, we shall receive one billion new neighbors on Earth, as many as today live in China alone, and as many as were added to our ranks since 1970. If accommodating the last one billion additional human beings stressed our biosphere to the point that we are now perceiving peril, how will we greet the next billion newcomers? These new inhabitants will live largely in cities in developing

1   Universal Declaration of Human Rights, UNGA Res. 217 (1948).

2   World Charter of Nature, UNGA Res. 37/7 (1982).

3   These trends are well summarized in a journalistic setting in "Planet of the Year: Endangered Earth" 133(1) *Time* (2 January 1989). See also the earlier evaluations in M.W. Holdgate, M. Kassas & G.F. White, eds., *The World Environment 1972–1982: A Report by UNEP* (Dublin: Tycooly International, 1982); Council on Environmental Quality and State Department, *The Global 2000 Report to the President* (Washington: U.S. Government Printing Office, 1980); and the "early" warnings in D.H. Meadows *et al., The Limits to Growth* (New York: Universe Books, 1972) and M. Mesarovic & E. Pestel, *Mankind At The Turning Point* (2d Report to the Club of Rome) (New York: Dutton, 1974).

4   World Commission on Environment and Development, *Our Common Future* (Oxford: Oxford University Press, 1987) (Chair: G.H. Brundtland) at 310.

nations, drawn there by recent investments in industry and transportation that were made sincerely but without much forethought. Urban sprawl, the side-effect of these investments, has left these urban megacities without sewage treatment or potable water, much less decent housing, schools, or public safety law enforcement.[5]

If the challenges posed by these trends are to be met, law must be more than a Janus-like gatekeeper. Law cannot restrain change by perpetuating old legal norms: it must assume a proactive role, shaping the portal itself. To determine how law can provide for sustainable development, we must re-evaluate the law's present roles.

Our global society invests a great deal in development. Law today sustains a continued flow of investments from bilateral aid programs, the UN Development Programme (UNDP), the World Bank and other multilateral development banks, and the private sector. Our policies still favor investment in an urbanized and industrialized world, which exacerbates many of today's adverse environmental trends. As a result, we are enacting new laws to cope with some of the side-effects of economic investment. As water or air pollution grows, we adopt new environmental laws to manage these consequences. As people need more recreational space, we establish parks. Indeed, we have established over 150 ministries of the environment in countries around the world to manage pollution, and still more to manage parks. We have begun to assume a proactive role in fashioning legal tools to handle the excesses of development.

New environmental laws today represent the fastest growing body of legislation in virtually every nation. These laws address what the WCED has called "the effects-oriented 'standard agenda' [that] has tended to predominate as a result of growing concerns about the dramatic decline in environmental quality that the industrialized world suffered during the 1950s and 1960s."[6] In fact, the newness of this 'standard agenda' makes it hardly very standard and renders these laws as yet minimally effective; in most instances environmental law lacks sufficient trained legal and scientific personnel, equipment, and refined procedures to be very effective.

In addition, the older institutions resist the changes required by the new environmental protection agencies; these pre-existing authorities, both private and public, ably use their prior accretions of power to resist assuming responsibility for environmental protection. For instance, the Soviet Forestry Ministry won exclusion from the establishment of the new State Committee on Environment Protection, GOSKOMPRIRODA, in 1988,[7] and the U.S. Environmental Protection Agency has

---

5   See generally L.R. Brown & L.L. Jacobson, *The Future of Urbanization: Facing the Ecological and Economic Constraints* (Worldwatch Paper 77) (Washington: Worldwatch Institute, 1987).

6   See *Our Common Future, supra,* note 4 at 310–311.

7   On the establishment of GOSKOMPRIRODA, see generally N.A. Robinson, "Perestroika and Piroda: Environmental Protection in the USSR" (1988) 5 Pace Env. L.R. 351.

existed since 1970 as a sub-cabinet service, eclipsed by bureaucrats hostile to its mandate in older ministries such as the Interior Department or the Office of Management and Budget.[8]

Notwithstanding the rapid emergence of this still-fragile "standard agenda" of environmental law, the WCED has called for even more systemic reform of our environmental policy, laws, and institutions. The WCED notes that most environmental agencies

> have been confined by their own mandates to focusing almost exclusively on the effects. Today, the sources of these effects must be tackled.... Environmental protection and sustainable development must be an integral part of the mandates of all agencies of governments, of international organizations, and of major private-sector institutions.... They must be given a mandate to pursue their traditional goals in such a way that those goals are reinforced by a steady enhancement of the environmental resource base of their own national community and of the small planet we all share.[9]

In its assessment of how we should provide the legal means to advance environmentally sound development, the WCED observed that

> [n]ational and international law has traditionally lagged behind events. Today, legal regimes are being rapidly outdistanced by the accelerating pace and expanding scale of impacts on the environmental base of development. Human laws must be reformulated to keep human activities in harmony with the unchanging and universal laws of nature.[10]

THE JANUS-LIKE FUNCTIONING OF LAW

It is easier to call for this radical restructuring of law than it is either to identify specific proposals for law reform, or to persuade legislators, administrators, and judges to muster the political courage and intellectual wit to make those reforms. We can point to instances where the law has provided the sort of forward-thinking, fundamental reforms required. We can, however, just as readily identify instances where the law has contributed to or perpetuated problems while facing backward.

Illustrative of the first sort of reforms are the laws creating environmental impact assessment and those governing national parks and preserves. The type of

---

8   On some of the patterns of entrenched "turf" protection by established agencies, see generally J. Baden & R.L. Stroup, eds., *Bureaucracy vs. Environment: The Environmental Costs of Bureaucratic Governance* (Ann Arbor: University of Michigan Press, 1981).

9   See *Our Common Future, supra,* note 4 at 311–312.

10   *Id.* at 330. The WCED continued to propose four priorities for law as follows:
     - To recognize and respect the reciprocal rights and responsibilities of individuals and states regarding sustainable development
     - To establish and apply new norms for state and interstate behavior to achieve sustainable development
     - To strengthen and extend the application of existing laws and international agreements in support of sustainable development
     - To reinforce existing methods and develop new procedures for avoiding and resolving environmental disputes.

law that exacerbates environmental problems is exemplified by certain land tenure rules in Latin America, the divided water jurisdiction of the Ganges River Basin, and the regime of suburban land development in much of North America. There are, of course, many other examples. Law reform commissions, legislative committees, law schools, and grant-making institutions such as foundations should devote substantial effort to identifying such opportunities for law reform. Relatively little attention is now given to the study of these issues and their resolution.

Turning first to the Janus face of the past, we can note that many laws reaffirm the *status quo,* or at least perpetuate the *status* at the time the laws were enacted. Perfectly honest people obey these laws and often unknowingly cause environmental damage. For instance, many developing areas have a policy of encouraging expansion of agricultural capacity by allowing farmers to clear undeveloped land and obtain title to it once it has been farmed for a period of time.[11] This leads in Latin America to a process of nibbling away at tropical forests near already-cleared land. The incremental slash and burn of forests near farmsteads can be seen widely even in a nation such as Costa Rica, which has the most advanced environmental protection laws in Latin America.[12] Such laws encourage the destruction of rain forest, without any consideration of the effect of loss of habitat on biological diversity or the ability of the watershed to conserve water or avert erosion and sedimentation.

A regional example is the River Ganges, the "Ganga" shared by Nepal, India, and Bangladesh. Timber cutting in the mountains has led to landslides, erosion, increased run-off, flooding, and resultant downstream problems. In 1980, B.B. Vohra put the problem succinctly:

> The only way to tackle the growing menace of flood is to control deforestation, denudation and soil erosion in the watersheds of rivers. Such a task must be undertaken on the most urgent basis particularly in the case of the Himalayan Rivers, if certain disaster is to be avoided.... The key to the problem of soil erosion obviously is in the effective use of adequate legal and executive powers to provide the necessary protection to the land till it can be restored to health.[13]

The Indian Constitution assigns responsibility for most water law to its constituent states,[14] which guard their prerogatives; neither the federal nor the state governments curb the incremental increases in siltation and pollution as the Ganga passes through. Even if they wanted to act, neither India nor any of her states could

---

11 Typical of this procedure was the Homestead Act of 1862 in the United States, repealed in 1976 (formerly 43 U.S.C. 161). Resources still "given away" in the United States are some minerals. See the General Mining Law of 1872, 30 U.S.C. 22.

12 See G. Hartshorn *et al., Costa Rica — Country Environmental Profile: A Field Study* (San Jose: Tropical Science Center, 1982).

13 B.B. Vohra, "A Policy for Land and Water" (Sardar Patel Memorial Lecture) (New Delhi: India Department of Environment, 1980).

14 Constitution of India (1950), amended in 1976 (edition of 18 May, 1981, Part IV). Also see Water (Prevention and Control of Pollution) Act, 1974.

prevent the severe flooding and erosion caused by Himalayan misuse in Nepal. Bangladesh receives the brunt of all these problems.[15] India could establish a conservation regime for the Ganga through a treaty with her neighbors,[16] but her political disputes with each make it unlikely (absent the use of good offices from the United Nations) that such will be negotiated soon. And no outside agency in the UN family has any reason to pressure India to act.

Just as nations are unable to coordinate their disparate environmental policies regionally, so too the divided realm of suburbia. The area around most large cities in North America is divided into smaller townships, villages, or other municipal authorities. The local authorities are assigned principal responsibility for land often used by the provinces or states in which they are situated. As the cities grow, private owners of this land see their property's market value rise as nearby real estate develops more intensely. Open land or farms are converted to shopping centers or residential developments.[17] New suburban land development exacerbates demands on infrastructure for water supply, sewage treatment, and transportation; eliminates wildlife habitat; and cumulatively adds to regional pollution. If one municipality seeks to limit growth to avert these trends,[18] land developers invariably oppose these limits politically and in court actions. The property owners assert a legally recognized right to develop their land to maximize their economic return, regardless of the consequences or externalities. Even where one municipality acts to conserve open space, a neighboring government may fail to act in the same way; development then concentrates "next door," producing environmental problems regionally.[19]

These examples reveal how even mundane legal questions, such as the area of jurisdiction assigned to government (whether local or national), can be the systemic cause of environmental problems. Internationally, laws allowing transboundary air pollution, whether as acid precipitation or Arctic haze, attest to the same sort of difficulty.

What can be done to resolve such intransigent problems? Obviously, new

---

15   See generally J.D. Ives & P. Ives, ed., "The Himalaya–Ganges Problem" (1987) 7(3) Mountain Research and Development.

16   See N.A. Robinson, "Marshalling Environmental Law To Resolve The Himalaya–Ganges Problem" (1987) 7(3) Mountain Research and Development 305.

17   A. Leopold describes this process critically in *Sand Country Almanac* (Oxford: Oxford University Press, 1949).

18   Municipal law techniques to protect nature in the United States are reviewed in N.A. Robinson, *Environmental Regulation of Real Property* (New York: N.Y. Law Journal - Seminars Press, 1982).

19   For instance, in *Golden* v. *Planning Board of Town of Ramapo* (1972) 30 NY 2d 359, 285 NE 2d 291, 334 NYS 2d 138, app. dismissed 409 US 1003. The courts upheld a municipal plan to phase development over time to keep pace with infrastructure. While this stabilized land uses in the town of Ramapo, heavy commercial and residential development increased around the town. Traffic, localized pollution, demands in regional water, and sewage all increased nonetheless.

institutions can be created, such as a possible U.S.A.-U.S.S.R. Joint Commission for the Bering Sea, based on the precedent of the Canada-U.S.A. International Joint Commission. Regional cooperation pacts are also possible. The Association of South-East Asian Nations (ASEAN) has prepared a comprehensive Agreement on the Conservation of Nature and Natural Resources,[20] the goal of which is sustainable development via concerted action to maintain ecological systems and ensure sustainable utilization of natural resources; to this end, a joint secretariat is to be established. Substantial numbers of new personnel and amounts of money will, however, be required to implement the Agreement (which is not yet fully ratified). The regional seas conventions sponsored by the UN Environment Programme (UNEP) similarly constitute brilliant measures toward building new regional institutions and coordinating national laws to protect the shared marine environment, although few have as yet had a marked effect in achieving their goals.

A FORWARD VIEW – ENVIRONMENTAL IMPACT ASSESSMENT

New institutions alone cannot do the job. A more pervasive method to bring human conduct rapidly into harmony with natural systems is the law of environmental impact assessment (EIA). Twenty years ago, the U.S. Congress pioneered this approach in adopting the National Environmental Policy Act (NEPA).[21] Section 102(2)(C) of NEPA required all federal agencies to prepare a detailed written statement about the impacts of all their actions that significantly affected the environment. Agencies today make a threshold environmental evaluation, and seek to redesign a project to avoid or mitigate any environmental impact to the fullest extent possible. If impacts are likely, an environmental impact statement is prepared and widely circulated for comment by other agencies and the public.[22]

NEPA's innovation has worked extremely well; half the states have emulated the federal process, and a standard discipline of techniques for preparing the statements now exists.[23] More important, EIA is now an established legal process around the world. In nations such as Australia[24] and Canada[25] it is well developed, both at the federal level and in constituent states. In the European Community,

---

20 Reprinted in 15(2) Environmental Policy and Law (November 1985) at 64.

21 42 U.S.C. 4321.

22 See the Council on Environmental Quality's regulations set forth in 40 C.F.R. Part 1500.

23 See N.A. Robinson, ed., *Environmental Impact Assessment* (Proceedings of a Conference on the Preparation and Review of Environmental Impact Statements) (Albany: New York State Bar Association and Council on Environmental Quality, 1989).

24 Environment Protection (Impact of Proposals) Act, No. 164 of 1974.

25 Government Organization Act, 1979 S.C. 1978-79, c. 13; P.C. 1984–2132 (21 June 1984) Environmental Assessment and Review Process Guidelines Order (EARP) established first Cabinet Decisions 20 December 1973 and 15 February 1977; four of the ten provinces have enacted EIA legislation, while three use other provincial statutes and two use policy directives for EIA.

which requires EIA for large projects (by a directive adopted in 1985[26]), some states such as The Netherlands[27] have a strong EIA process, while in others it is embryonic. The Soviet Union has assigned its EIA process, known as "Ecological Expertise," to GOSKOMPRIRODA, but has not yet required each government agency to undertake its own EIA.[28] Several other nations also have established EIA procedures, usually for major new projects.[29]

Thus, jurisdictions in some thirty-five major geographic regions are today covered by EIA procedures. These governments are re-tooling their decision-making to encourage ecologically sound development. In the words of Professor Lynton K. Caldwell, a political scientist who advised Congress on the content of NEPA:

> The EIS process institutionalizes patience, caution and looking before leaping. Few if any among the critics of NEPA would act in their personal affairs in the manner that government decision makers formerly acted in relation to the environment. Legislation such as NEPA has been accepted because we are environment-shaping animals, sufficiently intelligent to recognize that our survival requires self discipline. In this perception of our need to supplement our inherent nature with social inventions designed to protect us against our susceptibility to error may lie our best hope.[30]

EIA is also a pragmatic method of implementing two of the basic principals of international law embodied in the 1972 Stockholm Declaration on The Human Environment. First, Principle 21 restates the rule of good neighbors *(droit de voisinage)* and the maxim *sic utere tuo ut alienum non laedas:* "States have ... the responsibility to ensure that activities within their jurisdiction or control do not cause damage to the environment of other States or areas beyond the limits of national jurisdiction."[31] Second, the Declaration goes on to declare Principles 13 and 17 as necessary corollaries to Principle 21:[32]

26 EEC Council Directive of 27 June 1985; 85/337/EEC; OJL 7 July 1985.

27 See Ministry of Housing, Physical Planning and Environment, *Environmental Impact Assessment in the Netherlands* (The Hague, March 1984).

28 See "On a Radical Reorganization of Environmental Protection in the Country" (Decree of the Communist Party of the Soviet Union Central Committee and of the U.S.S.R. Council of Ministers) *Moscow Pravda* (17 January 1988).

29 For examples, see:
    (a) Indonesia, 1982 Act on "Basic Provisions for the Management of the Living Environment," Article 16.
    (b) Japan, Cabinet Decision, "On Implementation of Environmental Impact Assessment," 28 August 1984.
    (c) Thailand, National Environmental Quality Act, 1975; proclamations on major industrial, mining, dams, irrigation, airports, large hotels/resorts.
    (d) New Zealand, Cabinet Decision of 7 August 1972, and EIA procedures effective 1 March 1974 promulgated by the Commission for the Environment.

30 L.K. Caldwell, *Science and the National Environmental Policy Act* (Alabama: University of Alabama Press, 1982).

31 "Declaration of the UN Conference on the Human Environment" reprinted in L. Sohn, "The Stockholm Declaration on the Human Environment" (1973) 14(3) Harv. Int'l. L.J. 423 at 484.

32 *Id.* at 472, 477.

In order to achieve a more rational management of resources and thus improve the environment, States should adopt an integrated and co-ordinated approach to their development planning so as to ensure that development is compatible with the need to protect and improve the human environment for the benefit of their population....

Appropriate national institutions must be entrusted with the task of planning, managing or controlling the environmental resources of States with a view of enhancing environmental quality.

EIA has proven its value through widespread application, and so it is remarkable that many still oppose it, distrust it, or are indifferent. For instance, although in California and New York the courts[33] uphold the rule that adverse environmental impacts must be mitigated, or avoided by the use of alternative actions, at the federal level the U.S. Supreme Court has refused to require that, after scrutiny of the impacts, the least harmful alternative be selected.[34] Similarly, the Governors of the World Bank currently resist incorporating widespread use of EIA into the Bank's decision-making.[35] As another recent example, during its first one hundred days the Bush Administration, acting through the new U.S. Secretary of the Interior, removed an experienced senior civil servant, Bruce Blanchard, from his post of directing that Department's EIA compliance: to avoid hearing any "bad news," the Department killed off the messenger. Whether the result of ecological illiteracy, knee-jerk traditionalism, or departmental defense of "turf," opposition to EIA is a reality. Laws establishing EIA must therefore be strongly worded in order to compensate for this inbred opposition.

Experience with EIA indicates that, at least initially, busy administrators rarely see environmental protection as a part of their primary mission. They view the legal requirement with hostility, and seek to avoid rigorous use of the technique. In jurisdictions in the United States, the judicial review of administrative action is crucial to making administrators take EIA seriously.[36] Where agencies become familiar with EIA, they eventually see its benefits.[37]

---

33 *Friends of Mammoth* v. *Board of Supervisors* (1972) 8 Calif. 3d 247, 104 Calif. Rep. 761 (S.C.); *Village of Laguna Beach* v. *Board of Supervisors* (1982) 134 Calif. App. 3d 1022, 185 Calif. Rep. 41 (C.A.); *Webster Associates* v. *Town of Webster* (1983) 59 NY 2d 220; *H.O.M.E.S.* v. *N.Y.S. Urban Development Corp.* (1979) 69 A.D. 2d 222.

34 *Vermont Yankee Nuclear Power Corp.* v. *Natural Resources Defense Council* (1978) 435 US 519.

35 See B. Rich, "Funding Deforestation: Conservation Woes at the World Bank," *The Nation* (23 January 1989) 1; B. Stokes, "Storming the Bank," *National Journal* (31 December 1988) 3250.

36 F.R. Anderson, *NEPA in the Courts: A Legal Analysis of the National Environmental Policy Act* (Baltimore: Johns Hopkins University Press, 1973).

37 See J.S. Doyle, "The Department of the Army and NEPA" in Robinson, *supra,* note 23 at 19. "Implementation of the environmental assessment process required by NEPA has been a learning experience for the Army, and what we have learned is that the NEPA process is a valuable tool to decision making. The Army leadership views the environment as a resource, equal to manpower and money, that we can ill afford to squander. That is not to say that we have perfected the process. There are those who continue to view the Environmental Impact Statement as a burden. But their

To be fully effective, agency use of EIA needs to be overseen, whether by courts or by an independent executive agency. There should also be an opportunity for other agencies and the general public to participate in the EIA process. Both of these measures encourage effective analysis. Whenever EIA is established, there is a delay in its implementation, because of political and bureaucratic resistance to what is mistakenly viewed as an unnecessary intrusion on otherwise capable, responsible, and important decision-makers. For instance, the U.S. State Department still resists the disciplined analysis that EIA produces; it rarely uses EIA, and actively opposes an extraterritorial use of NEPA because of fears that EIA fetters its discretion.[38] This bureaucratic mindset has also been criticized in India, which has no EIA legislation (but whose Environment Ministry does conduct environmental reviews of some major power plants and of new major industrial or mining ventures). B.B. Vohra suggests that

> there is ... little awareness of the seriousness of the situation which faces us. A surprisingly large number of our planners, politicians, policy makers and economists still believe there is nothing very much wrong in the manner in which we have managed our land resources all these years. This complacency is born out of sheer ignorance and a genuine unfamiliarity with the subject — what my friend Dr. Sudhirfen calls "resource illiteracy."[39]

In the face of today's abundant ecological illiteracy, the law can be effective only if it is rigorously enforced. EIA laws require supervision and enforcement to counter both political hostility and bureaucratic avoidance or lethargy.

A FORWARD VIEW — PARKLANDS

A second model of successful environmental law, albeit one not without problems, is the dedication of natural areas as parks. National parks have proliferated since their establishment in the nineteenth century. As a matter of national pride, few nations today neglect to set aside such parks. While a pattern of national laws and treaties establishing parks and preserves exists, much remains to be done to strengthen and maintain the juridical foundation for these areas.

National parks have been used to preserve extraordinary natural and geological sites and to protect the habitat of various important or representative flora and fauna. Areas meriting protection as a matter of international concern are listed on the UN List of National Parks and Equivalent Reserves[40] and are protected through the UNESCO World Heritage Convention.[41] A range of treaties, statutes, and decrees

---

number becomes fewer as we learn more about the process, and as the process itself continues to demonstrate its usefulness on making smart decisions."

38 See U.S. Senate Hearings, Subcommittee on Hazardous Waste and Toxic Substances, Committee on Environment and Public Works (16 June 1988).

39 See Vohra, *supra*, note 13.

40 International Union for Conservation of Nature and Natural Resources, "United Nations List of National Parks and Protected Areas" (Gland: IUCN — UNEP, 1982).

41 UNESCO Convention for the Protection of the World Cultural and Natural Heritage (1972) 11 Int'l. Leg. Materials 1358.

are in use today to establish these preserves, which amount to more than four hundred million hectares globally.[42]

Protected areas do not exist in isolation. They are subject to traditional problems such as poaching of wildlife, invasion by livestock, and timbering, among other economic activities. They are also subject to air or water pollution, whether by local activities or by long-distance contaminants such as acid rain. As population grows, the areas adjacent to preserved lands come under more intense uses, with adverse effects that spill over the border into the protected areas.

These threats to protected areas are "effects" that police controls can regulate only through major allocations of money and personnel. The legal framework for parks needs to employ some systemic reforms that are less costly to implement and can be more routinely effective. Protected areas need buffer zones around them. Their management and conservation should become part of the routine of the people living around them. And the laws government areas around a park must be integrated with the laws establishing the park; few are so coordinated at present.

One increasingly recognized rationale for protecting areas is the conservation *in situ* of genetic resources. The maintenance of biological diversity is becoming a matter of international concern.[43] Data collection to determine scientifically the minimum viable populations and habitats of species is required,[44] followed by institution of a legal regime. The law will be crucial to defining a park's relationship to the growing population around it.[45] The International Union for Conservation of Nature and Natural Resources (IUCN) has prepared a draft treaty on maintaining biological diversity with *in situ* preservation, the provisions of which propose that a fund be derived from fees on profits made from plant materials initially obtained in the wild. Such a fund could help to meet the needs of people around such protected areas and to involve them in activity that respects the need to conserve.

INTEGRATING NATIONAL AND INTERNATIONAL ENVIRONMENTAL LAW

These illustrations of how law either reaffirms the status quo or molds change and reform have cut across local, provincial, national, and international lines. In

---

42 K.R. Miller, "The Natural Protected Areas of the World" in J.A. McNeely & K.R. Miller, eds., *National Parks, Conservation and Development: The Role of Protected Areas in Sustaining Society* (Washington: Smithsonian Institution Press, 1984) at 20. See also the Convention on the Conservation of European Wildlife and Natural Habitats (Berne, 1979).

43 See "European Network of Biogenetic Reserves" (The Council of Europe's Resolution (79)9).

44 B.A. Wilcox, "In Situ Conservation of Genetic Resources: Determinants of Minimum Area Requirements" in McNeely & Miller, *supra,* note 42 at 639.

45 As N. Myers puts it, "If, then, local people are intimately involved in a protected area's welfare from the start, and if they can sometimes prove the main determinant in its survival, how can we recruit them in support of our cause? Answer: enable the park to respond to their needs — as they

environmental law, the dichotomy between municipal law and international law cannot be sustained. The biosphere can be scientifically analyzed as a single, interrelated system, and the historically derived nation-state system must adapt its behavior to correspond to scientific understanding. Today's framework treaties, such as the Convention on The Law of The Sea,[46] establish a global structure of environmental protection duties that must be implemented nationally. The International Meeting of Legal and Policy Experts in Ottawa on Protection of The Atmosphere concluded that an "umbrella" convention on protection of the atmosphere was needed.[47] Yet the duty to prevent, reduce, and control interferences with the international atmosphere can only be fulfilled through local actions to curb or eliminate air pollution.

Without local law, international law can have no effectiveness. Since natural systems are interdependent, the law must shape the many local patterns of conduct into one coherent system of social behavior. New York State banned chlorofluorocarbon (CFC) use in spray cans in 1975,[48] but that legislation alone made no serious contribution to saving the stratospheric ozone; it was merely symbolic. The 1985 Vienna Convention for the Protection of the Ozone Layer[49] and the 1987 Montreal Protocol on Substances that Deplete the Ozone Layer[50] did make a serious start at saving the stratospheric ozone, but they alone may not be sufficient. Until local law regulates the use, recapture, and disposition of CFCs, these international laws are of no benefit, and if any major area continues to use CFCs, the harm to the stratospheric ozone can continue.

What is needed is a more complete integration of the international and national framework of environmental law. UNEP is working on EIA guidelines, and the UN Economic Commission for Europe is preparing a draft treaty on transfrontier EIA. Much unintended environmental harm could be avoided if all private and public development had to undertake EIA.

Similarly, a set of standard environmental laws needs to be established in each nation. A pattern of such laws already exists;[51] it must more quickly be made

perceive their needs." See "Eternal Values of the Parks Movement and the Monday Morning World" in McNeely & Miller, *supra,* note 42, 656 at 659.

46 Convention of the Law of the Sea (1982) UNCLOS A/CONF 62/122.

47 See Experts on Protection of the Atmosphere, The Meeting of Legal and Policy (Ottawa: Department of External Affairs and Department of Environment, 1989).

48 Environmental Conservation Law, NYS, 17 1/2 McKinney's Consolidated Laws of NY, Article 38; L. 1975, c. 713.

49 United Nations, Vienna Convention for the Protection of the Ozone Layer (September 1985) in (1987) 26 Int'l. Leg. Materials 1516.

50 United Nations, Protocol on Substances That Deplete the Ozone Layer (16 September 1987) in (1987) 26 Int'l. Leg. Materials 1541.

51 See the common pattern of American and Soviet laws, noted in note 41 to N.A. Robinson, *supra,* note 7.

universal. The comprehensive chemical regulation of the Canadian Environmental Protection Act[52] is an excellent model in this regard. When one reads that Act together with the 1975 European Economic Community Waste Directive[53] and the U.S. chemical regulation laws,[54] a pattern of state practice emerges. A UNEP treaty on transfrontier transport of hazardous waste, now under negotiation, can help tie these practices into an international framework.

However rapidly international environmental law is taking shape, it is not keeping pace with the deterioriating conditions of those natural systems which sustain our human societies throughout the biosphere. More needs to be done, and law has a role.

There must be a radical restructuring of the international legal institutions that guide collective national policies around the world. UNEP has only some two hundred professional staff. Most national environmental ministries are too new, inexperienced, and lacking in personnel to have achieved much protection. In the short term, these agencies are unlikely to have the staffing their tasks require. Moreover, since all human endeavors entail some environmental consequences, the goal should be to make each social unit responsible for ensuring appropriate environmental protection.

AN AGENDA FOR LAW REFORM TO SUSTAIN ECOLOGICALLY SOUND DEVELOPMENT

Promoting universal environmental stewardship is as daunting a task as promoting universal respect for human rights. Law has been instrumental in the latter and will increasingly be critical for the former. The following elements of restructuring need to be considered.

Environmental Priority

A high-level policy commitment to protection of the environment needs to be made visibly and repeatedly. In private enterprise, the establishment of a corporate vice presidency for environment and a written board corporate policy are standard in multinational companies.[55] In governments, a cabinet post for environment, together with a basic legislative mandate to all agencies to adhere to environmental policies, works well.[56] Since issues of environmental protection are as continuing as environmental impacts, the role of these entities must be ongoing. When laws

---

52 Canadian Environmental Protection Act, S.C. 1988, c. 22.

53 EEC Directive 75/442 of 15 July 1975 on disposal of waste.

54 On American laws see D.W. Stever, *Law of Chemical Regulation and Hazardous Waste* (New York: Clark, Boardman, 1986).

55 The 3M Corporation, headquartered in Minneapolis, Minn., provides a good example.

56 The establishment of a Council on Environmental Policy in the United States through Sub-chapter II of the National Environmental Policy Act, 42 U.S.C. 4321, illustrates this approach.

require public disclosure, senior officials tend to pay closer attention to environmental matters; some laws even make a specific officer responsible for the accuracy of the disclosure. Examples of laws requiring public disclosures can be found in provisions relating to the inclusion of environmental costs in financial reporting,[57] environmental impact assessment,[58] or monitoring reports for all forms of waste management.[59] There is no focal point for such a high-level commitment at the international level as yet.

Global Perspective

The WCED report *Our Common Future*[60] provides a global view. The United Nations General Assembly's World Charter on Nature[61] establishes an integrated set of norms for human conduct, from the local through national, regional, and international levels. UNEP, UNDP, the World Meteorological Organization (WMO), IUCN, UNESCO, The Food and Agricultural Organization (FAO), and other multilateral agencies all have environmental programs; some defend their "turf" as an exclusive mandate rather than collaborating on common undertakings. A new international institution is needed to provide a sustained focus and to accord priority to a common global perspective. Leaders as diverse as British prime minister Margaret Thatcher and Soviet president Mikhail Gorbachev have recognized the need for a top-level international environmental forum that could set priorities for establishing and maintaining concerted action to cope with Earth's growing environmental problems. The Soviet proposal to convert the UN Trusteeship Council into an "Environmental Trusteeship Council" or an "Ecological Security Council" should be seriously studied.

Legal reform of the UN Charter could be undertaken between now and the twentieth anniversary of the Stockholm Conference on the Human Environment in 1992. At a minimum, the UN General Assembly could create a new committee to focus exclusively and annually on the Earth's environmental problems.

Public Understanding

If universal acceptance of environmental stewardship is to be promoted and secured, all levels of the public need to understand how nature works and what constitutes acceptable standards of public health and conservation of nature. There

---

57 See, for example, the Securities and Exchange Act rules on environmental disclosures in the United States.

58 On EIA, see notes 21-38, *supra*.

59 Emitters of wastes into air and water and the generators and handlers of solid and hazardous wastes must keep records of their discharges and waste-handling. In many nations these constitute public documents, available to the press and anyone else. Public exposure of violations has been an important force in promoting adherence to these pollution control laws.

60 See *Our Common Future, supra,* note 4.

61 See World Charter of Nature, *supra,* note 2.

can be no secrets about the environment, since adverse effects eventually reveal their causes, as surely as the contents of a drum of buried waste leach into groundwater and turn up in a well. Therefore, the tendency of some agencies to favor administrative secrecy must be replaced with open disclosure of all data collection, reporting, EIA, and other information. Education about environmental problems should be an integral part of all formal and continuing education. Legislation affecting these issues needs to be reviewed and revised accordingly.

Technology Transfer

Most large corporations operating in North America have developed advanced systems for minimizing waste and controlling pollution. A number of companies now assist manufacturing ventures in developing countries in adopting similar technologies, through the International Environment Development Service of the World Environment Center.[62] There is also a need to promote research and development in intermediate technologies such as those sponsored by the UN University.[63] Given high rates of population growth, and consequent urbanization and industrialization, a more rapid introduction of environmental protection technology is required. The substitution of CFC use in all nations will require a rapid mobilization of efforts at licensing new technology that is now proprietary, and increased aid in converting to new processes with new procedures. Law has many roles to play in this process, not the least of which will be to structure income tax provisions and other incentives so as to encourage corporations to assist in both technology transfers and research and development.

National Environmental Law

A system of national environmental law is emerging in most countries. Not surprisingly, these laws look very similar. They deal with the same natural phenomena and very similar effects from industrial, agricultural, or other anthropogenic behavior. Nations share data and management expertise, which practice reinforces the tendency to adopt similar environmental protection programs. Finally, the system of framework treaties previously noted promotes this harmonization of practices and procedures. Naturally, local political and cultural traditions govern the form these environmental laws take, but their operational or functional aspects are more than merely comparable. Environmental law is coming to have much the same content from nation to nation. As all nations adopted their criminal code over many decades, so today all nations are assembling their environmental law in a matter of months or years.

---

62   The IEDS of the WEC is a non-profit program of sending environmental engineers on loan from companies participating with WEC to developing countries on request. The engineers' expenses are covered by government aid grants. WEC was started by UNEP in 1974 and is located in the city of New York.

63   See the natural resources programs of the UN University, headquartered in Tokyo.

The rapid emergence of environmental law does pose difficulties. Relatively few experienced specialists exist in each nation; at present North America has the largest group of practising environmental lawyers, and all North American law schools teach courses in the field. In Europe the field is only now being recognized, and, prompted by the directives of the European Economic Community, is growing rapidly. In socialist nations the field has been taught at Moscow State University and L'vov State University, and courses on the subject are being established in all law schools. In developing nations some expertise exists, as is illustrated by the work of Professor Jariwala at the Faculty of Law of Benares Hindu University in Vanarasi, India, or of Professor Jin, Rui lin at Peking University in Beijing, China, but such examples are scarce.

National law-making tends to be concentrated within the new environmental protection and older natural resources ministries. In addition, legislative committees have increasingly acquired an environmental specialization. One result of environmental law-making is a large body of statutes. The generic pattern of these laws can be discerned by comparing environmental laws from representative nations in each geographic region.[64] Not all nations have enacted each component of the pattern, but the harmonizing tendencies noted earlier do eventually result in such legislation; for instance, UNEP has endorsed the use of EIA in all developing countries,[65] but many lack the trained personnel to establish EIA at present.

Certain efficient legal tools can be employed nationally to promote ecologically sound, sustainable development. Most nations, especially developing ones, will not, however, be in a position to enact the sort of extensive administrative law system that exists in the United States. A more streamlined set of laws must be prepared. The international comunity needs to focus aid on developing

1. *model laws* that build on the same scientific data base (to avoid national duplication of scientific tests on chemical risk);

2. *administrative law proposals for* streamlined personnel assignments in *implementing, administering, and enforcing environmental laws* (both doubling up on functions, as when customs inspectors enforce the Convention on International Trade in Endangered Species,[66] and coordinating roles, as in the port controls of the sixteen European states from Finland around the European coast to Greece[67];

---

64   The Center of Environmental Legal Studies at Pace University School of Law has a comparative law research project currently studying Canada, the United States, Mexico, Costa Rica, Brazil, France, Netherlands, the United Kingdom, the Federal Republic of Germany, Poland, the Soviet Union, China, Japan, Thailand, Australia, New Zealand, Kenya, India, Tunisia, and Saudi Arabia. The tutorials and seminars in international and comparative environmental law have reviewed developments in these nations' systems since 1980.

65   Agenda Item 10, UNEP Governing Council, 14th Session, June 1987.

66   CITES (Washington, D.C.).

67   *Memorandum of Understanding on Port State Control,* 1 July 1982, in ALI-ABA Course of Study

3. *new framework agreements on the trade aspects of environmental protection,* to ensure commercial trade parity in protecting the environment and to prevent nations from seeking unfair trade advantages by avoiding environmental protection measures (this provision would also involve, for example, measures to eliminate unnecessary friction caused by differing methods for testing for chemical residues in foods) — just as we have an international economy in our shared biosphere, so we must promote a common process of costing into that economy the environmental externalities;

4. *improved comparable liability and insurance rules,* to cover such major accidents as the Exxon Valdez, Amoco Cadiz, and Ashland oil spills; the Sandoz fire on the Rhine at Bern; the Bhopal tragedy and Seveso; and the Chernobyl accident — incidents that have exposed the inadequacy of current laws governing the establishment of liability, human compensation, and remediation of the damage to natural resources.

5. *rapid and effective means to transfer pollution control technological knowledge,* including the revision of trade secret rules, intellectual property rights, and other possible proprietary impediments to installing pollution controls (the implications of plant patents for enhancement of biological diversity furnish an important example of an area where law is undergoing scrutiny);

6. *waste minimization and materials recycling/reuse,* where it is essential that the "polluter pays principle" be observed along with the practice that "pollution prevention pays,"[68] and where law should promote the most efficient use of energy in the least polluting fashion, through utility rate reforms, siting and operation laws, and so forth; and

7. *mechanisms for conflict resolution,* including the opening of administrative and judicial tribunals to citizens and groups from other countries seeking to have environmental laws observed and enforced.

Nongovernmental Sector Involvement

For environmental protection to be effective, there must be active participation from all private-sector groups, including corporations, citizen associations, professional societies, universities, and religious communities. Some legal techniques, such as EIA and the disclosure of information on pollution discharges, are already made effective by nongovernmental involvement. Law needs to emphasize, protect, and encourage the procedures for such civic involvement.

Materials on Environmental Law (Philadelphia: ALI-ABA Committee on Continuing Professional Education, 1989) at 453.

68   See "La prévention de la pollution paie: vue d'ensemble d'une technologie non polluante ou peu polluante par la société 3M" (New York: WED IEDS, 1985).

CONCLUSIONS

Law can and must be conceptualized in terms of general principles of justice. It is a part of the human experience with nature that every religion and every cultural tradition celebrates nature and would have us sustain life. The "reverence for life" articulated by Dr. Albert Schweitzer[69] provides a broad base for much of environmental law today. It is in the concrete and practical application of these principles, however, that the human effort to safeguard the planet will prevail or fail. The minutiae of procedures for convening a scoping meeting for an environmental impact statement may be dull. The inclusion of environmental protection costs in a base for establishing water or electricity rates may seem ponderously bureaucratic. Moreover, the absence of either activity may never be noted popularly, at least until that future moment when it is too late because environmental damage has taken place.

Law is a web of interrelated social constructs. Its aspects can be mutually reinforcing or can work at cross-purposes. To protect the environment, to advance ecologically sound development internationally, we need a concerted effort to cull the dysfunctional legal strands that served Janus when facing the past, but that frustrate our future goals. All legal systems should embark on major new ventures. Some great strides have been made, as is illustrated by the work of such bodies as the Sector on Ecological Law of the Institute of State and Law in the U.S.S.R. Academy of Sciences in Moscow, and the Environmental Law Institute in Washington, D.C.[70] The UN Institute on Training and Research (UNITAR) has conducted some early legal studies.[71] But even these steps are not enough if we are to take the task of law reform seriously.

The WCED convened an experts group to frame a set of legal principles for environmental protection and sustainable development.[72] Its report does a fine job of synthesizing the general legal principles to be derived from state practice and from pronouncements such as the Stockholm Declaration.[73] The "emergency of transnational environmental law,"[74] however, requires a more focused response

---

69 A. Schweitzer, *Out of My Life and Thought,* trans. C.T. Campion (New York: Henry Holt, 1948) at 185.

70 See essays in the symposium on Soviet Environmental Law in (1988) 5 Pace Env. L.R. 345–541.

71 A.L. Levin, *Protecting the Human Environment: Procedures and Principles for Preventing and Resolving International Controversies* (New York: UNITAR, 1977).

72 See *Our Common Future, supra,* note 4 at Annexe 1.

73 The full text of the experts' report appears with annotations in Experts Group on Environmental Law of the WCED, *Environmental Protection and Sustainable Development: Legal Principles and Recommendations* (London: Graham & Trotman/Martinus Nijhoff, 1987) (Chair: R.D. Munro).

74 N.A. Robinson, "The Emergency of Transnational Environmental Law" in ALI-ABA, *supra,* note 67.

than this set of general principles permits. Even the WCED seemed to acknowledge that the time had come to focus on the details of law reform, in declaring the "urgent need" to "reformulate" law necessary to contain "the accelerating pace and expanding scale of impacts on the environmental base of development."[75]

A more precise formulation of the new laws is found in the World Charter of Nature.[76] As a working agenda for the more precise goal of law reform needed at present, the World Charter of Nature provides an important start. Only by advancing this agenda can the environmental base of development be adequately managed so as to sustain that development itself. The World Charter did not follow the traditional rules of language for statements of international state responsibility. It speaks of general principles, and then of functions, and even of implementation. It states mandates in terms of what "shall" be done. Finally, it speaks of all persons as well as of governments and nature itself. It may well be that the General Assembly delegates were more inclined to move on immediately to the necessary agenda of progressive law reform than were the experts assembled by the WCED. Nonetheless, the WCED experts' set of principles is compatible with the Charter, and both provide a sound policy foundation for reforms with respect to the structuring of functions and the techniques for implementation.

The legal perspective on sustainable development, in sum, is the view of Janus looking forward. The tasks are great, but many of the necessary legal reforms are known, and it is only the will to act and the work to do that await us. Unlike Janus in ancient Rome, the law will not usher us through the gates of heaven. Our enthusiastic undertaking to reformulate the legal basis for sustainable development can, however, assure us a home for Earth's children for as far as we can foresee.

---

75   "Towards Common Action: Proposals for Institutional and Legal Change" in *Our Common Future*, *supra*, note 4, 308 at 330.

76   See World Charter of Nature, *supra*, note 2.

SUSTAINABLE DEVELOPMENT: THE SCIENTIFIC DIMENSION

Peter G. Sly

Since the early 1960s there has been a steadily growing awareness of the nature and extent of human impacts on the environment, and the public has increasingly been exposed to a series of concerns about global change. These concerns include overpopulation, contaminants, deforestation, desertification, the energy crisis, species loss, global warming, and ozone depletion.

Although science has contributed enormous quantities of information and knowledge about these concerns, there can be little doubt that public awareness would not have risen to current levels without media support and interest. Public appreciation of environmental issues is a strong indication of the success of both journalistic and documentary reporting. In no small way, political acceptance of environmental concerns has been driven by public awareness and understanding; thus, for the future, it is essential that science and the media retain effective working relationships, even though many topics will not make headlines suitable for exhaustive discussion or long-term exposure.

The causes of global change derive from three major factors: rapidly increasing human populations, growth in technological abilities, and long-term (geological) alteration in the natural environment (such as climatic variation). The extent to which human impact, both in numbers and in technology, is changing the natural environment cannot be overstated. In many ways, humanity has reached the limit of environmental ability to support existing cultural activities. Science has contributed significantly to this state, while simultaneously knowledge and information have been used to impart both benefits and disbenefits. In particular, and in many societies, the roles of science and technology have been marked by short-term expedience. For the future, it will be difficult to ignore the significance of such actions, especially where previous short-comings sharpen the focus of evaluation.

Science cannot escape the responsibilities that knowledge brings. Whether because of ethics or out of necessity, there is wide recognition of responsibilities to change many past and present practices and to seek alternatives that avoid the scenarios of "gloom and doom." To a considerable extent, opportunities exist to support attractive future scenarios.[1]

---

[1]   *The Global Possible: Resources, Development, and the Next Century* (New Haven: Yale University Press, 1985).

The report of the World Commission on Environment and Development (WCED), *Our Common Future*,[2] recognizes the extent of numerous environmental problems, but presents a positive strategy to address global change. This report demonstrates that economic development, the use of natural resources, and the quality of the environment are all directly linked and closely interrelated. The report describes its strategy as "sustainable development"; that is, developing the ability of present generations to meet their needs and aspirations without prejudice to the options of future generations.

To achieve sustainable development, decision-making must change, and in particular it must place far greater emphasis on the long-term viability of goals and objectives. Further, management must make the best use of available knowledge and understanding, however limited those may be. The challenge to science and engineering is to describe and understand how the social (human) and environmental (non-human) systems interrelate, and to provide indicators and models that are simple enough for most people to understand, and yet rigorous enough to defeat the arguments of short-term interests where these do not support the public good. As stated by Thomas Malone, President of Sigma Xi:

> A new partnership of effort among disciplines and between these disciplines and political decision makers is required to identify the driving forces of change, assess the impact of this change, analyze policy options, and achieve international consensus on public policy.
>
> Science and technology as well as society are, then, approaching a watershed. Successfully traversing this watershed in human affairs is crucial to society and to science and technology.[3]

Although many issues and problems are of both national and global concern, this paper discusses sustainable development primarily in the context of Canadian examples and Canadian science. The following points are addressed: the meaning and implications of sustainable development; past and present concerns, including what has been learned; examples of sustainable development; the information and knowledge required; and the scientific resources available.

SUSTAINABLE DEVELOPMENT

From the WCED's discussion of mankind's global future, one key theme emerged: sustainability. The conclusions of the Commission can be summarized as follows:

1. Although there are limits to cultural growth and development, they are not absolute in nature. Limits will differ. They are set by the biosphere's ability to absorb human impacts, globally and locally; the impacts of technology

---

2   World Commission on Environment and Development, *Our Common Future* (Oxford: Oxford University Press, 1987) (Chair: G.H. Brundtland).

3   T.F. Malone, "Toward A Watershed: Society, Science and Technology" (1989) 77(2) Amer. Sci. 119.

are linked to those of social structure as an integrated effect, and this differs both within and between biogeographic regions. It is possible to meet present needs without compromising the ability of future generations to meet their needs.

2. The option of sustainable development exists. However, the ability to achieve it depends on political will. Because sustainable development is a global concept, it requires greater democracy in international decision-making. Policies must seek a much greater degree of international equity; societal structures and economies are continuously destabilized where poverty is endemic and natural ecologies are impoverished.

3. Sustainable development is only achievable if the size and rate of growth of human population are compatible, locally and globally, with the productive capacity of the ecosystem. Neither sustainable development nor productive capacity is represented by fixed states. To achieve a balance between these two, the exploitation of resources, the forms of technological development and institutional change, and the direction of investments must be consistent with long-term needs.

4. Sustainable development requires that the more affluent societies confine their life-styles within the ecological means of the planet; this applies particularly to the use of energy.

Based on the works of the Stockholm Group for Studies on Natural Resources Management, including Ackefors's, Bengtsson's, Bojo's, Jansson's, Soderbaum's, and Svedin's research,[4] the meanings and implications of sustainable development can be further summarized as follows:

1. Sustainable development is an option that still exists for much of human-kind.

2. The frightening alternatives presented in the Club of Rome's *Limits to Growth*[5] equally exist.

3. There must be political will to achieve sustainable development.

4. The size and rate of human population growth constitute the single most important environmental stress to be addressed.

---

4   H. Ackefors, "The Food Resources of the World"; B. Bengtsson, "The Brundtland Report and Research in Developing Countries"; J. Bojo, "Sustainable Use of Land in Developing Countries"; A.M. Jansson, "The Ecological Economics of Sustainable Development — Environmental Conservation Reconsidered"; P. Soderbaum, "Sustainable Development — A Challenge To Our World Views and Ideas of Economics"; U. Svedin, "The Concept of Sustainability" in *Perspectives of Sustainable Development: Some Critical Issues Related to the Brundtland Report* (Stockholm: Stockholm Group for Studies on Natural Resources Management, 1988).

5.   Science and technology must be applied to build political will, to reduce population growth, to reduce the integrated effects of human impact on the environment, and to preserve as much as possible of the remaining global ecosystem.

PAST AND PRESENT CONCERNS:
WHAT HAS BEEN LEARNED

Discussing amendments to the Fisheries Act then before Parliament, Chant noted in 1970:

> There was a very adequate bill passed in 1843 which prohibited putting anything in the waters of Canada that is harmful to fish. It would have done the job very well if we had chosen to make it effective.[6]

This statement sums up much of the North American attitude to environmental concerns prior to the mid-1960s, an attitude that Canada has generally shared with the United States.

The situation, however, was not simply that governments did not wish to take action, but rather that, for various reasons, either the public was not sufficiently supportive of remedial measures or the measures could not be justified in the light of other interests. For example, in the early 1900s, bacterial contamination of water supplies was a widespread problem, and typhoid was a major concern for many Great Lakes communities that took water from the lakes. The causes of the problem were well understood, but its extent and the means of remedial action were not. A bilateral group of medical and sanitary engineering specialists carried out an extremely extensive bacteriological examination of Great Lakes waters. The scope of the problem was well established by this study, and in 1916, following detailed technical assessment, the International Joint Commission (IJC) recommended to both U.S. and Canadian federal governments that all municipal and other sewage should be treated, and that discharge of industrial wastes should be prohibited.[7] There is no doubt that such actions would have been enormously costly, and neither federal government followed this advice. The general response of most jurisdictions around the Great Lakes was to ignore the study, and, instead, to employ chlorination as a means of purifying their water supplies.

The technique of chlorination became available at about the time that this IJC study was completed. Had the technique not been developed at that time, government decisions might have been very different. These decisions were based largely

---

5   D.H. Meadows *et al., The Limits to Growth* (Report for the Club of Rome) (New York: Universe Books, 1972).

6   "Environment: While There Is Still Time" 95(26) *Time* (29 June 1970) 6 at 11.

7   National Research Council of the United States and the Royal Society of Canada (NRCUS-RSC), The Great Lakes Water Quality Agreement (Washington, D.C.: Acad. Sci. Press, 1985).

on expedience — that is, addressing the symptoms but not the cause. As it was, chlorination allowed management to forget the underlying problems for nearly another half century.

On the other hand, governments have responded rapidly and effectively where the course of actions is in the public good, and where actions can be clearly and well substantiated — even though they might not be supported by some of the more influential sectors of society. This was particularly so in dealing with the problems of "cultural eutrophication" in the Great Lakes. Put simply, cultural eutrophication generally results from excessive nutrient loadings, which in turn derives from inadequate sewage treatment, industrial effluent discharge, and poor agricultural practices. Typically, lake systems' response to elevated nutrient concentrations is increased production at the base of the food-web. But, with large increases, major species-shifts occur and food-web structures become severely distorted. Complex interactions, such as dissolved oxygen depletion caused by the degradation of underutilized plankton, also result in major changes in water quality, which, in turn, feed back into the biological system. The changes involve at least four major nutrient elements and numerous trace nutrients. In addressing the problem, science provided two key pieces of information: first, that of all the nutrient elements involved, only phosphorus could be readily controlled through regulation; and, second, that based on worldwide as well as North American data, reduction in phosphorus loadings would result in significantly improved water quality. Despite the gross oversimplification inherent in these two statements, and despite strong resistance from many special-interest groups and the very high costs of the proposed phosphorus reductions, Canadian and U.S. federal governments both supported the necessary research and quickly applied its findings. To what extent the slogan "Lake Erie is dead" may have influenced political response remains unknown, but it undoubtedly introduced an element of fear and uncertainty that worked to the benefit of environmental interests.

Environmental problems arise as much from conflicting use of resources as they do from contamination or spills, and this is particularly well illustrated by the case of the Baltic seal. For comparison, the Baltic Sea covers an area of about 370,000 km² whereas the combined areas of all the Great Lakes total about 240,000 km²; the human population surrounding the Baltic Sea is about 90 million while that surrounding the Great Lakes is just under 40 million. The following passage is taken from Jansson, and is directly relevant to Canadian experience:

> As an illustration of the difficulties to safeguard an endangered organism by only focusing on the natural stock, let us consider the problem of the common seal in the Baltic Sea. Since the beginning of this century the number of seals has decreased from about 100,000 to less than 1,500 individuals.... In 1968 a new ban came into force in order to restrict the hunting of seals, then regarded as the main cause of the population decrease. But the numbers of seals continued to decrease and eventually the poisoning by DDT and PCB was proved to severely impair the reproductive capacity of female seals.... Attempts to save the seals by establishing sanctuaries

were commendable but insufficient. What had to be tackled was the spreading of organochloric substances in the environment and the bioaccumulation in the marine food chain.

But, even a complete ban on the use of DDT and PCB in all sectors of the economy may not noticeably improve the situation, because stable toxic substances tend to accumulate in the Baltic for several decades. In the meantime the seal's life support system has been diminished even more due to an increased competition from commercial fisheries. Estimates indicate that the present fishery exploitation requires a much greater support from the marine food chain than did the one hundred thousand seals that used to be the dominating top predators of the Baltic Sea. If the seal population starts to recover at a fast rate, which has been the case with the monk seal in the North Atlantic, there is a risk that its food resource of herring, cod and salmon in the Baltic is too limited due to heavy exploitation by commercial fisheries. It can be feared that starving seals will gather on fishing grounds and attempt to remove fish from nets. This might cause a similar conflict between conservation interests and the commercial fisheries as the one raging in the North Atlantic region.... In fact, many Baltic fishermen have already started to complain loudly about damages from a large number of seals gathering in certain coastal areas.

Thus the future of the Baltic seal as well as many other living resources is perhaps not primarily determined by preservation and pollution control but rather by profound changes in economic activities or the ability to balance ecological and economic interests.[8]

Ignorance of problems is also a major factor; not until the publication of Rachel Carson's *Silent Spring*[9] did the public, or in fact much of science, begin to appreciate the hazards associated with DDT and other pesticides whose use had become widespread, particularly in agriculture and forestry. Despite earlier work outside North America, it was not until Norvald Fimreite's work in the early 1970s that it became clear that mercury could be a hazard in the Great Lakes and, shortly thereafter, the English–Wabigoon river system. Few people had any idea that metallic mercury would become highly toxic as a result of bacterial processes naturally occurring in surface waters. Later still, it was recognized that mercury contamination could also arise in newly created reservoirs, where flooded soils and wetlands released organic matter that stimulated bacterial processes, which again methylated mercury (although, in this case, the mercury was most often derived from natural sources).

Individually, there have been numerous examples of both government decisions that have supported and ones that have defeated environmental objectives. From the environmentalist point of view, the Garrison diversion, Great Lakes winter navigation, and South Moresby Island national park may be seen as episodes with a positive outcome; the Mactaquac Dam, the Nelson–Churchill diversion, and the Rafferty and Alameda Dams as episodes with a negative outcome. Governments have openly deferred decisions in recognition of inappropriate timing, as, for example, with the Berger Commission hearings on the Mackenzie Valley pipeline during the late 1970s. Governments have also used other means of delay, such as

8   See Jansson, *supra,* note 4 at 32–33.

9   R.L. Carson, *Silent Spring* (Boston: Houghton Mifflin, 1962).

an extension of studies and investigations well beyond the point necessary for decision-making — a situation typified by the "acid rain" issue in North America. Most recently, decisions to greatly reduce the use and production of CFCs reflect the influence of strong scientific evidence but, also, a real fear of the potential effects of significantly increased ultraviolet radiation; this was a case in which uncontrollable risk became an overriding concern.

It is evident, then, that government concern for the environment is real. However, the difficulty confronting decision-making with respect to sustainable development is that the benefits and disbenefits of particular decisions may be neither clearly resolved nor of immediate concern. In such cases, experience suggests that apparent (and often short-term) gains receive support, even though decision-makers themselves often doubt the long-term wisdom of their choices.

The insidious nature of many concerns related to sustainable development is vividly illustrated by the following passage from a recent report by the Science Council of Canada:

> In the mind of the general public soil degradation is most often associated with drifting soils on the Prairies during the 'dirty thirties.' However, soil degradation poses a much greater threat to Canadian agriculture today than it ever has in the past. Headlines ... publicize only the sensational events or disclosures that capture the media's imagination. They leave the impression that the problem is episodic. In fact, soil degradation is an ongoing, insidious problem that occurs in all parts of the country at a cost of over $3.0 million per day or $1.3 billion annually. Losses associated with soil degradation now exceed $20–25 per hectare of agricultural land in Canada, or 38 percent of net farm income. For many farmers, the cost of soil degradation represents the difference between profit and loss....
>
> The economic viability of agriculture in all regions of the country depends upon the productivity of the top 10 centimetres of topsoil. While topsoil is constantly being formed, it is also constantly being depleted. Under present farming practices this depletion can far outstrip the rate of formation....
>
> The contamination of topsoil with salt, or salinization, is another form of degradation. In Alberta it has been estimated that crop land affected by salinity loses from 50-100 per cent of its normal productive potential and costs farmers $80 million per year in lost yields. As already noted, the total cost of soil degradation across Canada, not including off-farm costs, is $1.3 billion annually. If these losses are allowed to continue, the cumulative cost of soil degradation to the Canadian economy could be enormous by the turn of the century.[10]

Around the lower Great Lakes, agricultural run-off was seen to be an important source of nutrients adding to the problems of municipal and industrial effluent, and problems with soil management and agricultural practice were identified in the Pollution from Land Use Reference Group (PLUARG) reports to the IJC in the early 1970s. Only recently, however, have there been significant steps to improve

---

10   Science Council of Canada, *A Growing Concern: Soil Degradation in Canada* (Council Statement) (Ottawa: Minister of Supply and Services, 1986) (Chair: S.L. Smith) at 7.

agricultural activities in this area.[11] A soil-and-water-enhancement plan (SWEEP) has been prepared for southwestern Ontario, to be effective by 1990. The plan involves the use of conservation tillage, crop rotation, and wise fertilizer use; grassed waterways and buffer strips; and livestock waste management. It will make a major contribution to Canadian soil conservation, but it also illustrates how long it can take to implement decisions, even where there is already substantial agreement. Since PLUARG was enormously successful in developing public support through local hearings and participation, the slowness of this response is of concern.

Although most of the examples presented so far refer to decision-making at senior levels of government, the same general characteristics seem to hold for all levels of governance. Decision-making favours expedience, and this, in turn, favours short-term rather than long-term gains. Governments generally act responsibly in crises, but problems associated with cumulative impacts may become effectively insoluble (at least within desired time frames) if not addressed within critical windows of opportunity. None of these traits are conducive to sustainable development, which requires that all levels of government management emphasize long-term rather than short-term effects. Sustainable development also requires an integrated approach to economic and environmental planning and management. Most of all, sustainable development requires compliance with variously assigned land-, water-, and air-use practices, and deference to clearly established and publicly supported goals and objectives (assuming always, of course, that the areas and time frames selected are appropriate to sustain such use).

EXAMPLES OF SUSTAINABLE DEVELOPMENT

Before we consider the role of science in sustainable development, it is useful to illustrate the concept with real examples. Two such examples are discussed below, one emphasizing the "ecosystem approach," and the other dealing more specifically with sustainable development. Both examples are drawn from understandings that have evolved in the aquatic domain.

The concept of the ecosystem approach was first introduced in the 1978 Great Lakes Water Quality Agreement (GLWQA) between Canada and the United States. Scientifically, the idea was not new: ecological theory had been evolving towards it for at least a century. What was new, however, was the concept's status as a basis for management. It is true that many managers responsible for use of Great Lakes resources still do not have a clear idea of what is meant by the ecosystem approach, and it is similarly true that most management practice only goes part-way towards the concept's basic objective (which may be restated as "sustainable development"). The GLWQA ecosystem approach requires recognition that everything is

---

11   G.J. Wall, T.J. Logan & J.L. Ballantine, "Pollution Control in the Great Lakes Basin: An International Effort" (1989) 44(1) J. Soil and Water Conserv. 12.

linked to everything else, and that decisions made for one purpose in the Great Lakes, to a greater or lesser degree affect other uses. The approach was certainly intended to link socio-economic and environmental factors in decision-making, but, because of the difficulties in actually doing this, it has more often been used to characterize an approach to the management of integrated environmental processes, rather than their further integration with socio-economic factors.

The concept of sustainable development drives towards the same general objectives, but perhaps more from the standpoint of socio-economic interests than of environmental interests. Certainly, neither government nor industry sees sustainable development as an impediment to the cultural evolution of society — at least not yet. For the most part, it is business as usual, but with more careful attention to environmental concerns. Conditions are changing, however, and it will not be possible to ignore indefinitely the irrevocable interrelation between environmental and socio-economic factors. A merging of the ecosystem approach and sustainable development lies ahead.

An Example of the Ecosystem Approach

The Bay of Quinte is a small body of water that receives most of its inflow from the Trent River, which drains much of central southern Ontario. The bay is connected to the main part of Lake Ontario through a series of channels, west of the city of Kingston. This bay supports a major fishery and delineates an area of growing urbanization and shoreline development. Major improvements in the area's municipal sewage treatment plants have been required to meet water-quality criteria (as part of the GLWQA). A research study known as Project Quinte[12] was begun in 1972 to characterize the quality and biota of what was then an extremely degraded body of water. The study continued through the period of sewage treatment plant improvements; during periods of extremely high and low flows caused by natural climatic variation; at a time of slowly changing agricultural practices; and during an explosive recovery of the fishery.

The Bay of Quinte was a classic study of cultural eutrophication in which nutrient loadings to the bay caused huge algal blooms from late spring to late fall. Much of this material degraded within the bay and, in the process, depleted the water of oxygen. This effect not only reduced the total area of the bay in which fish could survive but, more important, it also destabilized the size and composition of the various biological communities that formed a continuous food chain, from the smallest algal particle to the largest fish. A major reduction in the phosphorus loadings from sewage treatment plants was thought to be the most effective remedy

---

12   C.K. Minns, D.A. Hurley & K.H. Nicholls, eds., *Project Quinte: Point-source Phosphorus Control and Ecosystem Response in the Bay of Quinte, Lake Ontario* (1986) 86 Can. Spec. Publ. Fish. Aquat. Sci.

possible. Indeed, this strategy for abatement has worked well. Environmental data are not available to characterize early conditions (before the 1940s) in the Bay of Quinte or those prior to the effects of cultural eutrophication, which became most dramatic during the 1950s (in response to the use of detergent phosphates). However, inferences can be drawn from sediment-core data and from fisheries records, and these suggest that water quality now approaches pre-1940 conditions, although the biological communities are somewhat changed. The manipulation of phosphorus loadings to achieve water-quality objectives and, to a lesser extent, desired biological community structures, is known as a bottom-up control.

Biological particle-size theory[13] states simply that, allowing for energy conversion efficiencies, there is a consistent relationship between the number of large animals in an ecosystem and the number of smaller animals upon which they feed. The biomass of piscivors (top-predator fish), therefore, cannot exceed the biomass of their food base (mostly planktivorous fish). By analogy, the biomass of zooplankton cannot exceed phytoplankton support. Interestingly, there is also a top-down control known as the cascade effect. Thus, if too many predator fish are removed from the system (for example, by harvesting), their food base is no longer limited by predation. Greatly increased predation by this intermediate level in the food chain, on that immediately below it, causes major reductions in the size of the zooplankton biomass. Finally, relaxed grazing pressures on the phytoplankton allow it to develop an excessively large biomass. Large quantities of phytoplankton produced as a result of reduced top-down control have much the same effect on water quality as excessive growth caused by nutrient enrichment.

The Project Quinte study analysed the water-quality and food-chain data, and compared potential effects of nutrient control and predator biomass (bottom-up versus top-down). A recent study has concluded that top-down effects, particularly through a benthic link, could provide an important control on phytoplankton abundance associated with cultural eutrophication in the bay.[14]

Since significant costs are involved in both sewage treatment and lake-water treatment for drinking-water supplies, it is essential to recognize that the maintenance of a healthy population of top-predator fish represents a major credit to both financial and environmental accounts. The top predators (walleye) have a large catch value, especially when economic multipliers are factored in. Given that sewage-treatment plants are already operating at close to optimum efficiency, these and other species of fish may be providing a measurable though uncertain amount

---

13 R.W. Sheldon & T.R. Parsons, "A Continuous Size Spectrum for Particulate Matter in the Sea" (1967) 24 Can. Fish. Research Board J. 909.

14 K.H. Nicholls & D.A. Hurley, "Recent Changes in the Phytoplankton of the Bay of Quinte, Lake Ontario: The Relative Importance of Fish, Nutrients, and Other Factors" (1989) 46(5) Can. J. Fish. Aquat. Sci. 770.

of extra treatment capacity in the bay. As human populations continue to grow in this area, the fish will represent an important buffer, providing a natural control on environmental quality. Sustainable development has yet to factor in such values, which include not only the fishery itself but also sewage treatment, water treatment, shoreline development (spawning and nursery areas for fish), and other forms of water recreation.

An Example of Sustainable Development

The Fish Habitat Policy of the federal Department of Fisheries and Oceans[15] is possibly the first known example of a sustainable development policy in Canada. The Policy, which was introduced in 1986, has two major objectives: first, no net loss of productive capacity of fish habitat; and, second, net gain in productive capacity, relative to 1986. The Policy takes a long-term view of both habitat and productive capacity; further, as part of its method of implementation, it requires assessment of the financial benefits or disbenefits that result. The Policy is subject to evaluation, which will take place in two phases — Tier 1 and Tier 2. Tier 2 will begin in 1990–91; Tier 1, which will be substantially more difficult to undertake, will begin some years later. It is the evaluatory process that makes this policy so interesting as a study of sustainable development. It not only challenges the management's ability to implement the policy, but also poses difficult questions regarding the means by which success or failure may be measured.

In very simple terms, the Fish Habitat Policy is designed to help increase stocks of economically desirable fish. Although it is a major move towards sustainable development, it represents only one part of a more comprehensive approach, which should include more effective regulation of quota and catch (recognizing the significance of natural predation) and the preservation of diverse genetic stocks.

Life histories of many fish species have in common one particular feature, namely, that the size of adult stocks is largely determined by the size of the juvenile population from which they are drawn. In many species, this implies that adult stocks are greatly influenced by the quality and quantity of their spawning and nursery habitats. Fish habitats differ from species to species, and sometimes from stock to stock within species. But although it is relatively easy to characterize the general requirements appropriate to different life stages, simple addition of all such characteristics (even if this were possible with available human resources) does not necessarily equal actual productive capacity of habitat. The integration of all such characteristics is usually governed, not by the sum of the parts, but by select controls that collectively define critical habitat. It is this, as yet specifically undefined, critical habitat that largely controls productive capacity within various biogeographic zones.

---

15 Department of Fisheries and Oceans, *Policy for the Management of Fish Habitat* (Ottawa: Department of Fisheries and Oceans, 1986).

Field management cannot wait for the definition of critical habitat (a definition that may never be widely established), but must instead proceed on a site-specific basis, attempting always to optimize available fish habitat. In this, it will follow existing principles or will develop new principles of habitat engineering for conservation, rehabilitation, enhancement, and creation of new habitat. Evaluation, however, must seek to provide a bigger picture — at the level of an entire lake, a watershed, or even an oceanic region. Integrated models describing habitat productivity, such as Ryder's morphoedaphic index (MEI),[16] have proven remarkably successful in estimating long-term fish yields from discrete water bodies, and other techniques are available for application to anadromous and open-sea species. If habitat inventory is charted against fish yield, long-term records may be used to establish relational trends, especially those differentiated by events or cumulative effects. Within such data, it will be necessary to further resolve the signatures of natural variability and the effects of human activities. It is the refinement of these data (for example, by estimating returning spawners instead of quantifying gross catch) that will essentially define the success or failure of the Fish Habitat Policy.

The evaluatory process is designed to address two issues:

1.   To what extent have conservation, restoration, and development of fish habitat resulted in a net gain of habitat productive capacity?

2.   What economic and social benefits have resulted from increased productive capacity, and how are such benefits distributed?

Tier 1 will use environmental data to quantify habitat and its productive capacity. Tier 2 will rely heavily on surrogate data and will use records of impacts in all major types of referrals (for example, protection, conservation, restoration, and enhancement). The economic value of the fisheries must account for several different variables, such as harvest value, multiplier effects, environmental benefits in terms of other water use activities, regional differences, preference shifts, health consumptive advisories, and departmental costs involved in enactment of the policy.

The Fish Habitat Policy is set within a context where global fish yields from natural stocks are already close to, or perhaps above, long-term sustainable yields;[17] where only limited additional production from mariculture is likely; and where there is increasing demand for product, yet also increasing competition for habitat use (for example, shoreline development, dam construction, and timber removal).

16   R.A. Ryder, "A Method for Estimating the Potential Fish Production of North-temperate Lakes" (1965) 94 Amer. Fish. Soc. Trans. 214.

17   W.J. Christie *et al.,* "Early Thoughts on Fisheries Futures and Sustainable Development" in *Proceeding of National Forum on Sustainable Development* (Peterborough: Harmony Foundation, 1988).

If the Policy is advanced as sustaining fisheries, it must be demonstrated that it sustains productive capacity (as fish yield), and that the practice is economically sound.

INFORMATION AND KNOWLEDGE REQUIRED

The ecosystem approach and sustainable development both require a holistic approach to management, thereby recognizing the interconnectedness of the component systems subject to decision-making. As the size and number of component systems increase, the complexity of the entire structure also increases. Science has a major role to play in finding the means by which such structures, their interconnectedness, and the effects of decision-making can be presented in a relatively simple but meaningful way. In effect, science is being asked to come to terms with the thermodynamic effects of entropy. This is a measure of the amount of disorder in any closed system, in which any changes of state increase entropy. In small systems, entropy can be ignored; in large systems (including combined groups of small systems) it cannot. Sustainable development will not displace the familiar roles of science but, rather, will focus attention on synthesis rather than reduction and, in particular, on many recently developed and exciting means of model analysis and graphic presentation (including GIS, or geographic information systems). The following topics provide a representative insight into the new roles to be played in this form of science; these include the scientific approach, scale effects, global systems, and intermediate and small-scale systems.

Scientific Approach

The scientific approach will differ, depending upon the characteristics of the process or processes under study. Processes such as wave formation in response to wind stress, or current flow in response to channelization, can be predicted through precise quantification of the bounding conditions and the forcing and response functions. This is known as a deterministic approach. Often, however, environmental data reflect the interactions of multiple stimuli, and are subject to considerable variability; it is therefore necessary to integrate them before seeking comparison with additional variables. The phosphorus-loadings model,[18] which related phosphorus concentrations to mean water-basin depth and algal chlorophyll concentration, was of this type. Models like this work on the basis of general quantitative relationships between principal variables, but without following the exact and often highly complex pathways that generate the relationships, and are termed empirical.

Many natural processes are controlled less by some form of continuous

18   R.A. Vollenweider, *Scientific Fundamentals of the Eutrophication of Lakes and Flowing Water, With Particular Reference to Nitrogen and Phosphorus as Factors in Eutrophication* (Paris: Organisation for Economic Co-operation and Development, 1968).

response than by events or thresholds. The simplest analogy to this can be seen by filling a bucket with water; nothing happens until the bucket overflows and the water escapes. These conditions are said to be probabilistic in nature and are frequently found in climatological studies where there is a high degree of "patchyness" in the data. Water-quality models developed for surface waters in temperate regions, for example, may not be applicable in arid or semi-arid regions subject to intermittent flooding coupled with high run-off nutrient loads that rapidly increase in concentration as evaporation occurs. The biota native to such ecosystems have evolved special techniques to survive and benefit from such conditions, and the use of standard water-quality criteria derived from other climatic zones is not appropriate under these circumstances. Rather, water quality and the planned use of waters in arid zones should be adjusted to probabilistic functions.

When the impact of toxic substances is considered, risk models provide another example of probabilistic modelling, in which risk results from a combination of exposure and toxicity. Common salt, for example, is widely used to improve driving conditions in winter, and thus is widely exposed in the environment. To much of the environment, salt is moderately toxic. By contrast, while hydrochloric acid can be considered highly toxic, its environmental exposure (mostly due to spills) is fortunately very limited. Based on probability models, therefore, the environmental risk of salt is probably greater than that of hydrochloric acid, even though the latter is much more toxic. Analyses of this type are required as a prime substantiation for product controls under the new Canadian Environmental Protection Act.[19]

Environmental data are frequently collected in a form that is already naturally integrated; for example, tree growth measured as ring width represents a response to available nutrients and local exposure and climatic factors, the significance of which can be determined (at least in part) through observation. On the other hand, data may be collected without clear knowledge of association. For example, sediment samples collected from the bed of a lake or river contain a record of formative conditions that people cannot directly sense. The effects of metal scavenging, or contaminant associations with the transport of particulate materials, is not something that people knowingly experience. Nevertheless, the end product of contaminated sediment represents another form of integration. Working in the dark, as it were, statistics enables science to emulate the observed data and, in fact, recreates a comparable but purely mathematical integration of the sediment data; in the process of doing this, statistics also quantifies the degree of association between different types of data and may make it possible to define corrective measures, selective to particular types of source contamination.

Model simulations variously combine analytical structures to develop

---

19   S.C. 1988, c. 22.

most-probable mathematical constructs of actual processes, and then use such constructs to hindcast (as a means of verification) or forecast (as a means of prediction).

Scale Effects

Scale effects represent a major problem in environmental science, particularly when the relationships between variables are non-conservative—that is, when they are not approachable by means of deterministic analysis. Typically, research is thought of as a mechanism through which more and more detail is established via the process of reductionist science, looking through the microscope at ever more minute components. Reductionism is an extremely valuable tool that makes it possible to define exactly which variable, or set of variables, is responsible for which cause-and-effect relationships, and to specify and quantify the exact processes by which some particular response occurs. In agriculture, for example, it is largely through the use of such techniques that it has become possible to offer selection of the most appropriate crops, and fertilizer and pesticide applications, for given soil types and climatic locations.

There is another side to science, which, instead of taking things apart, puts them together; this is termed synthesis. The science of synthesis, in one way or another, underlies most of the requirements of management for sustainable development. When environmental data are used to construct the "big picture" through the process of synthesis, there are usually two problems: the quantity of data involved, and the lack of compatible scale. It is this latter problem that is of such great importance when models are used in an attempt to duplicate natural processes.

When, for example, data are addressed from top-down (reduction), decisions are made at various hierarchical points to determine the pathways to follow at successively greater levels of resolution. For the most part, it is easy to follow this direction and to pass through each level of natural integration. When one moves in the opposite direction, however, the same decision point now presents itself as a probability function. Scale is represented, therefore, not just by the concentration of data points per unit area or unit time, but also by the number of distinct systems or subsystems that become connected through the process of synthesis. Thus, for example, if we average the data from a number of lake sampling stations to derive input to the Vollenweider[20] phosphorus model, we are already using naturally integrated data. Should we wish to derive each data point from a bottom-up analysis, it would be necessary to consider the probabilities of numerous interacting functions that will cumulatively produce the space-time history of that point. Even if this were possible, it would represent a ridiculous amount of work to establish point data, but the example illustrates the potential problems; fortunately, it is much less difficult to produce an "average" value for the full set of data points.

---

20   See Vollenweider, *supra,* note 17.

There are well-developed techniques to smooth scalar differences due to different concentrations of data points. There are also means available that will allow crossing of the structural barriers of hierarchical scale. For example, rather than measuring descriptive parameters of stream habitat throughout the length of a stream, one can measure them at a series of type locations and then, by comparing them with a more stable variable such as stream slope, can estimate overall quantities of some habitat type throughout the stream.

In synthesis, applied systems analysis looks at a wide range of scientific approaches, including those summarized here, and selects an approach that will be most likely to produce useful results; the approach must be appropriate to the process characteristics of the system, and to the scale effects controlled by data densities and the hierarchical order of component systems. In the following sections, the shifts in complexity dominate the selection and development of scientific technique, and illustrate the real changes being brought about as science begins to address sustainable development.

Global Systems

Ecosystem research — that is, the study of natural systems, including interactions between the human component and such systems — has been evolving for many decades. There are numerous publications describing the atmospheric, terrestrial, and aquatic components of the global ecosystem and their process interactions, and the effects of climatic variability and human activities such as the extraction and use of nonrenewable resources, agriculture, fisheries, forestry, urbanization, and water use. Possibly one of the most comprehensive summaries describing current understandings of the global ecosystem and the effects of human interactions with it may be found in *Sustainable Development of the Biosphere*.[21] The products of large-scale research have been very effective in leading to the recent public and political awareness of potential global crises and the need for concerted actions at the national and international level. Research into environmental problems (such as the studies proposed by the International Council of Scientific Unions under the International Geosphere-Biosphere Program) will continue at the global level, seeking to develop greater understanding of these same issues and to improve predictive and remedial abilities.

Future scenarios of climatic change resulting, for example, in sea-level rise; drought; shifts in energy consumption, agricultural productivity, and distribution of fisheries resources; and demotechnic growth (a term coined by J.R. Vallentyne to describe the combination of population increase and technological change) raise problems of staggering social and economic dimensions. Thus, at this time, it may

---

21   W.C. Clark & R.E. Munn, eds., *Sustainable Development of the Biosphere* (Cambridge: Cambridge University Press, 1986).

be that large-scale research can do little more than provide advance warning, since the time required to derive and implement solutions can be equivalent to that over which the problems have arisen as a result of cumulative impact. Leaving aside, however, the political and ethical concerns that lie ahead, science can contribute greatly to a more effective understanding of linkages between socio-economic structures and the environment.[22] This fact is important not only because of a lack of confidence in various economic models, and the fact that, for the most part, depletion of natural resources (both renewable and nonrenewable) is not factored into the accounts, but also because of the relatively short response times of economic systems and the social structures that they support.

Two of the more interesting recent developments in systems analysis are the Socio-Economic Resource Framework (SERF) model and the subsequent development of the Sustainable Development Demonstration Framework (SDDF) by Hoffman and McInnis.[23] The SDDF represents the physical basis of a socio-economy and contains only the minimum number of inputs required to simulate environment–economy linkages. The five subcomponents of the SDDF are demography, infrastructure, consumption, production, and resources — and computations follow this sequence. Demography tracks population growth and the availability of labour. The infrastructure registers societal decisions to invest in pollution treatment and waste recycling, to produce energy from renewable resources, and to upgrade technology. Consumption tracks a population's material wealth in terms of consumable goods, possessions, and facilities. Production includes both the transformation of raw materials and energy into finished goods, and the operation of pollution-treatment and waste-recycling processes. Finally, resources track the harvesting and husbanding of renewable resources and the depletion of nonrenewable resources. Although feedback is not built into the model and responsibility for ensuring that the scenarios are feasible and realistic rests with the users, the model has particular benefits in that it directs attention to select points of tension. For example, labour may be unavailable or, conversely, underemployed; or land availability may force agricultural or forestry collapse in the face of urban development.

Model approaches such as the SERF/SDDF are particularly important because they operate independently of artificially induced forcing functions. They can operate at different scales of application (global to regional) and, potentially, can be interfaced with economic models in which the addition of time-varying monetary

---

22   T.D. Crocker, "On Measurement and Value in Environmental Economics" in A. Davidson & M. Dence, eds., *The Brundtland Challenge and the Cost of Inaction* (Halifax: Institute for Research on Public Policy, 1988).

23   R.B. Hoffman & B.C. McInnis, "The Evolution of Socio-economic Modeling in Canada" (1988) 33(4) Technol. Forecast. and Social Change 311.

values can be incorporated. There is room for considerable research development in this field.

Intermediate and Small-Scale Systems

While it is acknowledged that it will not be possible to resolve most large-scale environmental problems by immediate and simultaneous global actions, other responses are necessary and possible. For convenience, these are considered in relation to prevention, remediation, and (in the following section) attitudinal change.

Prevention is an action taken now to avoid an additional burden on present or future generations, and largely involves careful assessment of existing or proposed development activities. In particular, prevention requires a full assessment of environmental impacts by all stakeholders, whether directly or indirectly involved. Environmental impact studies have become a part of doing business only in the past ten to fifteen years; they are not yet generally applied at the level of regional or local government, and even now they often lack objective assessment. Not only does science need to provide the best possible information for such assessments; it should also be used far more effectively to evaluate the impacts of decision-making: Did development follow its proposed outline? Was its impact well predicted? What type of indicators most usefully defines a healthy environment? What changes are now required, and how can future decision-making be improved? The science of evaluation is poorly developed as a support to either the socio-economic or the environmental aspects of sustainable development.

Science is equally a tool of remedial actions, which seek to recover formerly productive components of the ecosystem. Probably the largest single example of this type of use is the effort to clean up more than forty specific problem sites of environmental degradation and contamination in the Great Lakes.[24] Large as this problem is, it pales in comparison with the widespread contamination of groundwater supplies or the degradation and contamination of estuarine systems (generally the most productive regions of the marine ecosystem, and critical to the natural reproductive cycle of many commercial fish and other wildlife species).

Just as there is a need to understand the links between socio-economic and environmental systems at the global scale, so too there is a need for such understandings at regional and local levels, and for the ability to relate between different levels of scale. The need to develop such models is perhaps most urgent at the local scale, since it is this level where most development decisions are made, and from which most cumulative impacts derive. For example, while shoreline, wetland, and

---

24 Great Lakes Water Quality Board, *Report on Great Lakes Water Quality* (Windsor: International Joint Commission, 1985).

near-shore habitats are crucial to the survival of many populations of fish and wildfowl, shoreline development to house people seeking access to those very resources continues to deplete them. With more careful planning, and a better grasp of long-term socio-economic and environmental costs, it should be possible to accommodate both interests. The use of SERF- and SDDF-type models, tailored to these interests, could have a profound influence on local developments.

The following comments by Robert Adams, Secretary of the Smithsonian Institution, provide a useful summary and emphasize the importance of many of the ideas presented in this section:

> There is, in short, another axis of differentiation within the sciences that does not place physics at one extremity and the social sciences at the opposite one. Instead it runs from parsimony to complexity, from predictable, uniform, determinate outcomes to indeterminancy—perhaps even to chaos, which I am told is currently a field of great theoretical interest in mathematics and physics. This one cross-cuts all the usual disciplinary lines, based instead on an ascending scale of complexity and non-linear response. The properties of all systems, including social systems, change fundamentally under the impact of these variables, as well as in some dependent relationship to a third variable, the scale of their occurrences.[25]

Changing Attitudes

At first glance, the task of changing attitudes may seem inappropriate to science, yet it can be argued that it is one of the most immediate concerns that should be addressed. The old adage that "you can lead a horse to water but you can't make it drink" is, unfortunately, all too true. Already there are more than enough data and understanding to vastly improve socio-economic and environmental decision-making. The question is, how can attitudinal change be accelerated in all levels of government and in the public, so that necessary changes are quickly accomplished?

These comments apply not just to the preventative and remedial actions that must accompany the concept of sustainable development. They also apply to the establishment of clear, long-term objectives for both socio-economy and the environment. In other words, will society harvest all the available fish in the sea or shall some portion be left for the seals and whales? Will there be room for the caribou and, if so, how large a territory are we willing to leave unstressed by northern development? Or, closer to hand, how are we to resolve pressures for water diversion from the Great Lakes? (Future water-use objectives for these lakes will have to be accepted by a much larger group of stakeholders than just those of the basin.) As the percentage of Canada's working population decreases in the years ahead, how will the country afford future sustainable development? Should we modify immigration requirements? Sustainable development demands honest recognition of problems and objectives, and behavioural science has an important

---

25   R. Adams, "The Social Matrix of Science" (Address to the Centennial Meeting of Sigma Xi, Washington, October 1986).

role to play in guiding society to acceptance of this responsibility. Whether society likes it or not, society will play god.

SCIENTIFIC RESOURCES

The following information is drawn largely from the Professional Institute of the Public Service of Canada[26] and, although it primarily reflects the state of funding available from the Canadian federal government, it is a forceful indicator of the severe resource constraints faced by Canadian science.

Canada spends proportionally less on science and technology than other developed nations, and ranks about ninth among members of the Organisation for Economic Co-operation and Development (OECD). Expenditures on research and development have been about 1.2 percent of gross domestic product over most of the past decade and a half, and were 1.31 percent in 1987 (down from 1.35 percent in 1985). This represents less than 3.6 percent of the federal budget. Other indicia also reflect a weak investment in science and technology:

- Canada has 90 scientists and researchers per 100,000 of population, while Japan has 240 and the United States has 280.

- Canadian industry is not adapting to new technologies as rapidly as its competitors.

- Venture capital investment in start-up situations is only one-sixth of the rate in the United States.

- Government funding for post-secondary education has declined steadily in constant dollars over the past decade.

- Government investment in its own in-house research has declined steadily since the early 1970s.

- During 1987–88, support of in-house federal research represented 46 percent of the total funding for Canadian research and development (exclusive of provincial funding), while the federal government's commitment to the private sector accounted for another 35 percent, support for university research accounted for 12.7 percent, and independent contributions by the private sector accounted for the remaining 6.3 percent.

The accompanying table provides a selective summary of federal funding for government departments (1987–88).

---

26 Professional Institute of the Public Service of Canada (PIPS), *The Essential Role of Federal Scientists and Engineers: Their Role in the National Economy* (Ottawa: PIPS, 1988).

Federal Funding of Selected Departments With A
Significant Role in Sustainable Development

Department	Billions of Dollars (1987–88)	Percent of Total Net Expenditure
Agriculture	3.4	2.96
Indian Affairs and N. Devel.	2.8	2.43
Sec. of State (Post-second. ed.)	2.2	1.91
External Affairs (CIDA)	2.1	1.82
Regional Industrial Expansion	1.4	1.22
Energy, Mines and Resources	1.3	1.13
Environment	0.8	0.70
Science and Technology	0.8	0.70
Fisheries and Oceans	0.6	0.52
(Interest on public debt)	29.0	25.17

Of total federal government revenues (approximately $96 billion) in 1987–88, 46 percent was derived from personal income tax, 23 percent from sales and excise tax, and 12 percent from corporate tax. Given these figures, and the size of the public debt, increased support cannot be expected from federal government sources. Whether industry will take a more supportive role remains uncertain, but it is clear that, with substantial foreign ownership of Canadian industry (particularly in areas of high technology and resource development), Canadian interests are not necessarily of prime concern to this sector of the economy.

Many recent publications[27] have substantiated the excellence of scientific contributions made by the Canadian research and technology community; scientific competence is not in question. However, support and management of science is in question. The following passage from the Science Council report, *Environmental Peacekeepers*,[28] places the ability of Canadian research to support sustainable development in sharp perspective:

> Several recent reports have also noted the pervasive uncertainty inherent in current scientific knowledge of environmental effects and causes. There is a lack of basic knowledge of physical, chemical, and biological processes related to ecosystem disturbance and recovery. Environmental science is still developing and scientists have widely different views about the nature and magnitude of environmental problems. Although there are various multidisciplinary programs of environmental research in Canada, no one organization coordinates them all or has the critical mass of multidisciplinary scientific personnel necessary to undertake broad-based research. Responsibilities for different stages of research, or even for different aspects of the same stage,

---

27   For example, see P.H. Pearse, F. Bertrand & J.W. MacLaren, *Currents of Change: Final Report — Inquiry on Federal Water Policy* (Ottawa: Environment Canada, 1985); Science Council of Canada, *Environmental Peacekeepers: Science, Technology, and Sustainable Development in Canada* (Council Statement) (Ottawa: Ministry of Supply and Services, 1988) (Chair: G.A. Kenney-Wallace).

28   See Science Council of Canada, *id.* at 18.

are shared between departments of different levels of government and the private sector, without any effective overall coordination or setting of priorities. Recent government spending restraints have dimmed the prospects for enhanced scientific investigation of ecosystem dynamics. With few exceptions, fundamental environmental research is being reduced, not increased.

Damage to the environmental resource base in Canada is occurring more rapidly than scientists can measure and understand it. The money devoted to science for assessing the state of the environment is a tiny fraction of that spent on the actions that damage it. To assess and understand the impact of human activity on the environment is going to require a sustained research commitment. We must not be swayed by arguments that we cannot afford to put money into research that will not yield commercial applications. We must be prepared to pay science to investigate the state of the environment so as to provide the sorts of answers needed for informed public and private sector actions.

In all honesty, perhaps we are destined to be hewers of wood and drawers of water whether we like it or not. If so, let us at least do these tasks well.

ECONOMICS AND SUSTAINABLE DEVELOPMENT

Hélène Connor-Lajambe

Harmoniser l'environnement et le développement social et économique, c'est définir une autre modernité.

—Ignacy Sachs[1]

The unforgettable vision of Earth from outer space and the disturbance of its climatic cycles challenge humanity more directly than any other event of our times. The one fascinates, the other frightens. Both remind us that the peoples of the earth now have a common destiny, that of their planet. The magnitude and seriousness of ecological problems has finally resulted in the globalization of human consciousness, a process that owes its beginnings to scientific enthusiasm.

It seems only yesterday that we Western nations did not have much in common with the countries of the Third World. We now know that they face the same future — and neither will be able to pull through without the other. Remarkably, this awareness coincides with the unexpected rapprochement in 1988 of the Soviet Union and the United States, the two nations that for so long have allowed the threat of total war to weigh upon us. Is it, however, so strange to witness two tenants' discovery that they inhabit the same planet and that both have plundered it, each moved by conquistadores' ideals?

Both the liberal system, as exemplified by the United States, and the socialist system have been totalitarian in their approach to nature, if not humanity. Their development models, based on the blind exploitation of natural resources that were once plentiful and inexpensive, can no longer function as before. It is imperative that these models not be reproduced in the Third World, now that the state of the environment has become a matter of global concern. But what do we say to these countries, to which we have held out the bright prospects of a Western style of economic development?

As a species, humanity has no choice: it must not only survive, but also live to its maximum and evolve. The time has come to place a bet such as that once made by Pascal. The human race must *believe* in a possible future, and, in pursuing its own development, attain new heights.

The recent Report of the World Commission on Environment and Development (the Brundtland Report)[2] places such a bet, albeit in an almost clandestine

---

1   I. Sachs, "Notre avenir à tous" in *Futuribles* (March 1988).

2   World Commission on Environment and Development, *Our Common Future* (Oxford: Oxford University Press, 1987) (Chair: G.H. Brundtland).

fashion, by suggesting that humanity should embark with firm resolve on the path of long-term sustainable development. The Report manages to crystallize several recent trends in thinking that are already of considerable influence throughout the world. It paints a startling fresco of the state of humanity and its environment. In this respect, it points a finger at the numerous shortcomings of those economic theories that have contributed to the creation of a Gordian knot of problems — a knot that must be severed. Very few economists, however, are willing to play the role of an Alexander. We might as well admit the truth: economic theory, in its present framework, has very little to say about long-term sustainable development.[3]

The long-decried inability of conventional economic theories to resolve, or even simply explain, such problems as the coexistence of unemployment and inflation or the growing gap between the rich and the poor (a problem intensified by the accelerating and perhaps irreversible destruction of the environment) leaves the economic profession in a complete theoretical vacuum. The entire conceptual structure of the discipline must be rebuilt to reflect a living reality, the substance and dynamics of which cannot be grasped by traditionally reductionist and mechanist reasoning. This is why we cannot simply elaborate a new economic theory that takes the environment into account. We need a new paradigm, a fresh interpretation of the world.

A new generation of economists is asking itself what could replace the conventional economic approach. Already, a consensus based on a new vision appears to be evolving, as a prelude to the formulation of a more realistic paradigm. This thinking is, of course, focused on the same critical issues that confronted early economists: Where does wealth come from and what is the role of humanity in nature? However, it draws its inspiration from a spectrum of sources beyond economics, and the profession is opening up, in spite of itself, to the influence of other disciplines — ecology, health, physics, agriculture, geography, and psychology.

In this paper, I will first attempt to set the parameters of the vision that is emerging from this rethinking as well as the change in attitudes already being effected. I will then examine how the concept of sustainable development can become operational.

THE NEW VISION

At the root of research so ambitious as to aim at the goal of long-term sustainable development is a dramatic prospect: the spectre of, quite literally, the end of the world. We have recently entered an era of ecological and technological catastrophes, and both liberal systems and planned economies seem powerless to control the state of their physical and social environment. From belugas threatened

---

3   J.M. Keynes' jest, "In the long term we are all dead," has been taken literally.

by aluminum smelters to rhinoceroses and elephants threatened by surreptitious trade, many species face extinction. Nor does our civilization provide enough opportunity for our own young, who, in despair, turn to alcohol and drugs. The inability of economic systems to protect and perpetuate life condemns not only other species on this planet; it also condemns humanity.

Hencefore, the orientation of social and economic policies must be directed towards preserving life, rather than simply paying lip service to such a goal — as has been the case until now. This new imperative implies a fundamental questioning of life and of humanity's role in the environment. But life does not allow itself to be reduced to a material or economic logic: we have scarcely studied life and, as yet, we seem powerless to understand and perpetuate it.

In the same way as Man is within Nature, explains René Passet, Nature itself is within Man:

> Mankind and Nature are one: we represent the end of a long evolution that started with a process through which matter became increasingly complex, and resulted in the progressive development of life capable of organization and conscience, and then to a self-awareness (consciousness of one's own conscience), that is the most essential characteristic of mankind; ... thus, at this point, the human species represents the pinnacle of a process of evolution that has affected the entire universe from the very beginning.[4] (translation)

Passet's vision is akin to that of Teilhard de Chardin, for whom access to reflection has allowed humankind to establish its own place across and above the whole biosphere[5] through waves of "Hominisation." These successive waves of socialization (Populating, Civilisation, and Individuation) — after having spread out in a process of Cosmogenesis and covered the Earth with a cerebral web (the "Noosphere" or thinking sphere on the surface of the globe) — are now converging (through the forces of Totalisation and finally of Personalisation) towards the Omega point[6]:

> From now on (that is, since hominisation entered its convergent phase) it is becoming clear that, on the contrary, it is only as a result of synthesis, i.e. through personalisation, that we can preserve the truly sacred core hidden deep within our egoism. The ultimate centre of each one of us is not to be found at the term of an isolated, divergent, trajectory: rather, it coincides with (though it is not lost in) the point of confluence of a human multitude, freely gathered in tension, in reflection and in one common mind, upon itself.[7]

4   R. Passet, *L'économique et le vivant,* Payot, 1979 at 13.

5   P. Teilhard de Chardin, *Man's Place in Nature: The Human Zoological Group,* trans. R. Hague (London: Collins, 1966).

6   *Id.* at 115–116. As things now stand, modern astronomers have no hesitation in envisaging the existence of a sort of primitive atom in which the entire mass of the sidereal world, if we took it back several thousands of millions of years, would be found to be included. Somewhat similarly, it is not odd that if biology is extrapolated to its extreme point (and this time ahead of us), it leads us to an analogous hypothesis: the hypothesis of a universal focus (I have called it Omega), no longer one of physical expansion and exteriorization, but of psychic interiorization — and it is in that direction that the terrestrial Noosphere in process of concentration (through complexification) seems to be destined, in some millions of years, to reach its term.

7   *Id.* at 115.

The vision of Teilhard de Chardin, detached and cold like the temporal spaces he forces us to visualize, explains some of the phenomena that trouble us nowadays: wars, political and social conflicts, impoverishment of the Third World, and endemic unemployment. All are attributable to the effort of recentring effected during the process of convergence:

> Surely the basic cause of our distress must be sought precisely in the change of curve which is suddenly obliging us to move from a universe in which the divergence, and hence the spacing out, of the containing lines still seemed the most important feature, into another type of universe which, in pace with time, is rapidly folding-in upon itself. This brings with it a radical structural and climatic change that at one blow deeply influences and re-shapes our whole outlook and activity.... At this decisive moment when for the first time he (man, that is, man as such) is becoming scientifically aware of the general pattern of his future on earth, what he needs before anything else, perhaps, is to be quite certain, on cogent experimental grounds that the sort of temporo-spatial dome (or cone) into which his destiny is leading him is not a blind alley where the earth's life-flow will shatter and stifle itself. Man is now realising that this cosmic spindle corresponds, on the contrary, to the concentration upon itself of a force that is destined to find in the very heat released by its convergence sufficient strength to burst through all the barriers that lie ahead of it — whatever they may be.[8]

Even if he attempts to explain in only pure scientific terms, Teilhard de Chardin has nevertheless posited a few guidelines for the direction in which solutions should eventually be oriented. That direction is evolution, which is to say, a rise of consciousness fostering general unification:

> Fuller being is closer union.... But ... union increases only through an increase in consciousness, that is to say in vision.... To see or to perish is the very condition laid upon everything that makes up the universe, by reason of the mysterious gift of existence. And this, in superior measure, is man's condition.[9]

Because this direction is awareness itself, humanity seems to be progressing, as if by trial and error, from wars to comprehensive humanitarian movements, from crises to discoveries. However, an ever-increasing number of points of view evolve and unify. The ineffable vision of the Earth, for the first time seen from outer space, continues to affect us and, it seems, to bring us closer. The Brundtland Report has managed to give that vision some sense, and has revitalized and generalized the ecological movement that is capable of saving our planetary vessel. Humankind better understands its own nature, and is beginning to unify.[10] Who would have thought that the two major geo-political blocs would draw closer in the way they have recently? Apprenticeship is difficult, and there is no guarantee insofar as the

---

8   *Id.* at 103–104.

9   P. Teilhard de Chardin, *The Phenomenon of Man,* trans. B. Wall (New York: Harper & Row, 1959) at 31.

10   Major international solidarity movements have begun to emerge in favour of oppressed peoples in South Africa and Latin America, and in support of refugees and victims of earthquakes and famine. Research institutes such as the Rocky Mountain Institute in Colorado specialize in developing techniques of consultation and peaceful conflict resolution. See *New Options* (30 April 1987).

process of ultimate unification is concerned.[11] Humanity is the guardian of the right to freedom, and everything remains possible — even irreversible failure, if we choose a mode of unsustainable development.

Likewise, the Teilhardian rationalization of unemployment does not diminish its seriousness, but, by explaining its inevitability, suggests how to face it:

> We are now faced by the torrents of unapplied power already released by the convergence (little advanced though the process be as yet) of the human mass. A too common reaction — and an absurd and unnatural way to behave it is — is to try to force back this disconcerting outburst: the right action to take is surely to direct the flood along the slope to which its natural inclination is clearly leading it — and by that I mean the direction of research.[12]

Teilhard looked at macroeconomic units; yet it is certain that research directed towards reabsorbing excess labour capacity, or correcting its poor allocation, could help resolve problems posed by freeing the servants of the machine. In his vision of the world, unemployment was foreseeable at this stage of the development of the Cosmogenesis, and his thoughts stimulate the redefinition of full employment rather than deny it as a social objective: fewer hours of work and more self-managed activities for which individuals qualify themselves through personal development.

Thus far, the vision of Teilhard de Chardin appears easy to share, all the more so as it seems to verify itself. The role he assigns to research in achieving the Cosmogenesis may be more difficult to endorse because of the blind confidence he places in science and scientists, a confidence that is often undeserved, especially with respect to research that, however justifiable globally, destroys or manipulates life.

Research that has now become planetary — that is, collective — constitutes the human revival of evolution:

> Points involved are: the distribution of the resources of the globe; the control of the trek towards unpopulated areas; the optimum use of the powers set free by mechanisation; the physiology of nations and races; geo-economy, geo-politics, geo-demography; the organisation of research developing into a reasoned organisation of earth.... We need and are irresistibly being led to create, by means of and beyond all physics, all biology and all psychology, a *science of human energetics*.[13]

Our survival as a species, and the organization towards which we must aspire, should be considered in these terms. Since the Brundtland Report, it is essentially

---

11 Teilhard de Chardin indicates certain conditions that are necessary for the planetary evolution of consciousness in ultra-Hominisation through Noospheric metabolism. First, the planet must remain habitable, and possess enough material and cerebral high-quality reserves to maintain the collective germ of the Noosphere. Second, we will need *know-how* in order to avoid traps set against our freedom in the process of Totalisation (blind alleys, administrative bottlenecks). Finally, we require a *will to do*, an internal polarization in the depths of the human soul or a strengthening of the reasons and the appetite for living. See *Man's Place in Nature, supra,* note 5 at 117–120.

12 *Id.* at 105.

13 See *The Phenomenon of Man, supra,* note 9 at 283.

this approach that has been termed sustainable development — that is, a thoughtful development of the planet according to the degree of evolution attained by humankind.

Why should Teilhard de Chardin's attempt at explaining the world be accepted? First, because his explanation is global, and explains the world coherently and comprehensively. Second, as has been shown, because his explanation seems to be substantiated by certain trends and major events of our time. And finally, because his explanation encompasses, possibly by sublimation, most of the new visions of the world that are akin to it.

Teilhard has integrated the potential Carnotian counterargument, as formulated, for example, in the writings of Nicolas Georgescu-Roegen, by answering optimistically the question: "Does the universe concentrate itself above as assuredly and infallibly as it 'entropises' itself below?"[14] Teilhard's vision can also be reconciled with Ilya Prigogine's work on dissipative structures,[15] in which the latter suggests the spontaneous appearance of order and organization, within disorder and chaos, through a process of self-organization. Paradoxically, such a global, systemic vision is also foreshadowed by Marx, according to whom human beings act upon nature, transform it, and become themselves transformed by it.[16]

The most seductive attempt to explain the world, very close to that of Teilhard, is perhaps also the most recent: the Gaia hypothesis of James Lovelock. According to this hypothesis, "all living beings on earth, from whales to viruses, and from oak trees to algae, can be viewed as forming part of a single living entity that is capable of manipulating the earth's atmosphere in order to meet its general needs, and is endowed with faculties and powers that are greater than those of its component parts."[17] (translation)

But the analysis that most resembles Teilhard's seems to be that of René Passet. Passet has drawn conclusions based on Teilhard's theories by advocating, in particular, an "economics of being" that may no longer be only "economics," but also biology, sociology, and ethics:

At the national, and consequently at the planetary scale, no elements that touch upon the physical or biological equilibrium of the world can remain unaffected by production activities or fail in turn to have an effect upon them. Thus, economics, far from being discussed as an end in itself, should

---

14 See *Man's Place in Nature, supra*, note 5 at 117.

15 I. Prigogine & I. Stengers, *Order Out of Chaos: Man's New Dialogue With Nature* (New York: Bantam, 1984).

16 K. Marx, *Capital*, as quoted by P.A. Victor in "Economics and the Challenge of Environmental Issues" in W. Leiss, ed., *Ecology Versus Politics in Canada* (Toronto: University of Toronto Press, 1979) 34 at 39.

17 J. Lovelock, *The Ages of Gaia: A Biography of Our Living Earth* (New York: W.W. Norton, 1988) at 30.

be reconsidered as a function of its participation in a whole range of mechanisms that it cannot upset without being itself destroyed.[18] (translation)

Thus, at the end of the twentieth century the environment, which consists of a thin layer of life on the surface of the earth, is finally "recognized"; as a result, respect for major natural cycles will become the main constraint on all human activity. *Life* replaces growth or conquest of new physical frontiers as the ultimate value of a humanity now conscious of both its unity and the necessary morality of its acts.[19] This mega-systemic vision of the world will serve as the working hypothesis that enables us to propose the outline of a paradigm capable — through the new science of human energetics — of promoting a sustainable development mode in the twenty-first century.

TOWARDS A NEW PARADIGM OF DEVELOPMENT

Scarcely a quarter of a century ago, the concern with ensuring long-term sustainable development and respect for life was rooted in the ecological and human-rights movements. The impetus for overcoming the last vestiges of resistance to change, however, was provided by the international political community, in the form of the Brundtland Report. Although the Report has defined as "sustainable" that which does not compromise the potential for future generations, it has not defined the process of sustainable development. In reality, what is development?

An organism develops as it advances toward its biological maturity ... development is the process of realizing what is latent, the passage from *dunamis* to *energeia,* from *potentia* to *actus.* Evidently, this implies that there is an *energeia* or an *actus* that can be determined, defined, and made fast; that there is a standard that belongs to the essence of that which is developing; or, in the words of Aristotle, that this essence is becoming — in accordance with a standard defined by its "final form": *entelecheia.*

In this sense, development implies the definition of "maturity", and beyond that of a "natural standard": thus, development is but another name for Aristotelian *phasis.* Since nature has its own standards, in terms of the purpose for which beings develop or the goals that they effectively attain ... there is a natural state, a standard, a boundary (*peras*), an incarnate canon ... that, once it is reached, cannot be overstepped (for to go beyond it would mean a step backwards).[20] (translation)

Development therefore implies an opening up of potential, together with the knowledge that this accomplishment is also the norm proper to that condition. Throughout our history, a number of rural, agrarian, or tribal communities have known, or still know, such a state of stability. In such societies, people have an

18 See Passet, *supra,* note 4 at 13.

19 René Dubos emphasized the intrinsic value of nature, which position is superior to one that only recognizes its utilitarian value. See "A Theology of the Earth" in I.G. Barbour, ed. *Western Man and Environmental Ethics: Attitudes Toward Nature and Technology* (Reading: Addison-Wesley, 1973) at 43. This line of thought is in the tradition of St. Francis and Henry David Thoreau. See also A. Leopold, *Sand County Almanac* (Oxford: Oxford University Press, 1949).

20 C. Castoriadis, Domains de l'homme, *Les carrefours du labyrinthe II* at 139.

intimate knowledge of their physical and social environment. Such knowledge allows them to organize themselves according to what G. Bateson called the "systemic wisdom," or ecological consciousness, which recognizes the non-linear nature of all dynamic systems — a consciousness that is neglected in mechanistic and excessively rationalist societies.

Such communities are characterized by an optimal size as circumscribed by readily accessible and/or recycled resources. They use little energy; more often than not, only fire supplements biological (human and animal) and inorganic (wind) energy sources. Exchanges occur freely or through bartering rather than with currency, and speculation is nonexistent; indeed, it is held in contempt. Tradition and honour appear to be respected more than wealth and novelty. Equilibrium with the environment is preserved through socio-religious structures, which evolve over the centuries in order to maintain this ecological harmony.

These societies, which have developed in an authentic manner, were labeled as underdeveloped until the time that we recognized our own overdevelopment. Should those societies not serve as examples for our planetary civilization, given that the coincidence between the values adopted by individuals and the requirements of their environment appears to be a key to a society's viability? This recourse seems difficult, however, since in highly energistic societies, the consumption unit (the family) no longer coincides with the production unit, and for physical and historical reasons we will never know this coextensivity.

Such a divergence also affects the value system, and has given rise to numerous control bodies. According to Fred Cottrell, "The number of situations that demand this growth of groups and codes increases with the increasing use of energy, and this growth in turn presents new problems solved neither by the omnipotent state nor by the free market."[21] We must return to self-sufficiency or cast elsewhere for Sachs' *another modernity*.

Having reached the limits of its physical territory, humankind is confronted with itself and is forced to question its goals. Humanity is now compelled to reflect on its very essence in order to change its orientation and take a different path — one of a qualitative rather than quantitative nature. The impetus behind this reflection is the consciousness propelling us ever forward "for the simple reason that every increase of internal vision is essentially the germ of a further vision which includes all the others and carries still farther on."[22] We are probably in the process of taking a qualitative turn leading from material to spiritual growth, growth that knows no bounds and effaces all others.

---

21 F. Cottrell, *Energy and Society: The Relation Between Energy, Social Change, and Economic Development* (New York: McGraw-Hill, 1955) at 255.

22 See *The Phenomenon of Man, supra,* note 9 at 231.

In the reorientation, or recentring, in which we are presently engaged as a species, we as complete human individuals are committing ourselves, with our social, ecological, philosophical, and moral dimensions, and not merely as *Homo oeconomicus*. According to Fritjof Capra:

> This implies that the task of organizing the economy requires a multidimensional approach.... The need for a multidisciplinary approach to deal with our present economic problems implies an end to the preeminence of economics as the basis for national policy.[23] (translation)

By putting economics into perspective in all human activities, the systemic approach may constitute the most important advance in economics since the Physiocrats. François Quesnay and Cantillon were the first to conceive a theory of the general interdependence of all sectors of activity and of all elements in the economic process — where nothing happens in isolation, and where everything binds together. Their Tableau économique schematized these interactions. These early (eighteenth-century) writers had already devised theories of the origin of wealth,[24] the importance of the condition of lands,[25] and the dangers of underconsumption.[26] Since that time, however, little if anything has been said about nature in economic theory.[27]

Whereas early economists emphasized the importance of nature in the economy, the adherents to ecodevelopment broaden and reinterpret Quesnay's Tableau in modern problematics, situating the environment as the pivotal factor in development. Their message is that humanity must strive to live off the interest of this "Capital-Nature"[28] without reducing it. The proponents of sustainable development go one step further, by integrating the social, intertemporal, and interspatial dimensions, and by introducing the notion of solidarity between generations and peoples, particularly the most deprived.

---

23 F. Capra, *Le temps du changement: science, société et nouvelle culture,* Le Rocher, 1982 at 378.

24 "In order that the land should yield a revenue, work in the countryside must render a net product over and above the wages paid to the workmen, for it is this net product which enables the other classes of men who are necessary in a state to subsist." M. Kuczynski & R. Meek, eds., *Quesnay's tableau économique* (London: Macmillan, 1972) at 20.

25 "For land deteriorates, and the proprietors lose on the market value of their landed property, to the extent that the wealth of their farmers is wasted away." *Id.* at viii.

26 "That the proprietors and those engaged in remunerative occupations are not led by any anxiety, unforeseen by the Government, to give themselves over to sterile saving, which would deduct from circulation and distribution a portion of their revenues or gains." *Id.* at 4.

27 For example, in neoclassical theory ecological issues have been disposed of in externalities, with the impacts borne by people who do not make the decisions. Consequently, ecological problems are not considered in traditional cost-benefit analyses. Current cost-benefit and multi-criteria analyses are beginning to take them into account. Their real importance is more obvious in environmental assessment studies, but such practice is still far from universal.

28 The term is from Saint-Marc. The parameters to be used in evaluating this capital have been defined in particular by Michel Jurdant in *L'inventaire du capital-nature: méthode de classification et de cartographie écologique du territoire,* Ottawa, Pêches et Environment-Canada, 1977.

The initial test of viability for a new mode of development will obviously be the manner in which it deals with human resources. Unemployment, as the stigma of the failure of Western-style development, raises questions about the very concept of work itself. In his presentation at "The Other Economic Summit" in 1988, James Robertson suggested that the economic age coincided with the age of employment for the two hundred years when employment was the principal form of organization of work. It remains to be seen whether or not economists will be capable of broadening their horizons in order to encourage decisions reflecting the needs and activities of real individuals, and not only those of *Homo oeconomicus*.[29] A move in the direction of sustainable development requires individuals who are themselves well-adapted, stable, and mature. This implies that they have a certain degree of control over their own lives.

As yet our institutions have been unable to consider such novel concerns, which are both global in nature and disruptive. This inability explains the increase in all kinds of tensions, experienced by a world whose very survival appears to be more and more problematic. At the same time, however, a sign of convergence is that the community of living things seems suddenly to be coming together, with differences between species becoming relative, and even undistinguishable. The victims — human and non-human — of the Valdez accident concern us. The fate of the beluga whales in the St. Lawrence River worries us as much as that of the workers in aluminum smelters. A few months ago, in — by past standards — an incomprehensible, unwarranted action, nations united in order to save three whales trapped in ice. New priorities emerge without our being aware of them — anthropomorphic concerns of course, but already less exclusively anthropocentric, and even openly systemic, since humanity no longer thinks of itself without taking into account its environment.

Vivo: vivanti nihil a me alienum est[30] appears to be becoming the motto of our time. Consciousness has already taken a qualitative and quantitative jump that is enormous, unexpected, unhoped for, and essential. If the internationalization of economics has led to both the multiplication and the enormous proportions of ecological problems, the solutions to these problems must be of the same order. Be it monetary assistance, sharing of resources, research, or exchanges, nothing will be spared by this worldwide awakening of planetary consciousness. Some who refuse to change, their eyes riveted on profit, their hands clutching at power, will soon find themselves ridiculous in the face of coming crises. Centralized power structures that have furthered excessive and harmful growth will be compelled to break into a

---

29 The proceedings of this alternative economic conference are published in the September 1988 issue of *The Human Economy Newsletter*.

30 *"Homo sum: nihil humani a me alienum est"* (I am a man: nothing human is foreign to me). See Terence, *The Man Who Punished Himself*, I.I. 25. This expression of human solidarity has been adapted here to reflect the new solidarity with all life.

myriad of participative management centres. These new units, in which people have responsibilities, rights and duties, will further the revitalization and renewal of interest in the maintenance of life.

Having reached the limits of its material patrimony, humanity is beginning to realize that it has in fact only this patrimony to manage, in an adaptive rather than manipulative manner. Humanity will only be able to organize its environment if the latter lends itself to such organization, that is to say, if humanity thoroughly understands its environment and the importance of each of its components. The phase into which we are entering will reflect only our own qualities, rather than the quality of our technical or geographical discoveries — thus the reappearance of ethical concerns in principal areas of human endeavour.

Roszak summed up this interdependence between the well-being of the individual person and that of the planetary ecosystem:

> *The needs of the planet are the needs of the person .... The rights of the person are the rights of the planet....* The shift to a balanced social and economic system will require a corresponding shift in values — from self-assertion and competition to cooperation and social justice, from expansion to conservation, from material acquisition to inner growth. Those who have begun to make this shift have discovered that it is not restrictive but, on the contrary, liberating and enriching..[31] (translation)

This last point is critical. The systemic paradigm of the Teilhardian vision, through an awakening of consciousness, may supplant the paradigm of material growth — with the former accepted because life would be more livable, more understandable. If a good deed is its own reward, is there a more beautiful[32] undertaking than that of the well-thought-out organization of our passage on earth? Indeed, such an undertaking is sufficient to "give/give again a meaning to the human adventure. Find/find again a meaning. For there, probably, is the key," in the words of the Groupe de Vézelay.[33]

ANOTHER DEVELOPMENT: PRINCIPLES AND METHODOLOGY

During the phase of Personalisation or synthesis in which the Noosphere is formed, the preservation of life and the quality of human life demand intensive efforts in order to foster the development of the new science that Teilhard referred to as "human energetics." This is the science that, by means of internal reflection,

---

31 See Capra, *supra,* note 23 at 382.

32 As well as useful and satisfying.

33 Groupe de Vézelay, *Journées de Vézelay sur les risques technologiques majeurs,* 31 March 1988 at 31. The Vézelay Group, France, describes itself as a collectivity of "people who through their own fields of work and responsibility are responsible for the future of the world and our societies." This group has just launched an *Appel pour des Etats Généraux de la Planète,* which will be a "decisive step in the process through which humanity will take charge of its own destiny" (translation).

humanity applies to itself and uses to create institutions capable of piloting itself along the path of sustainable development — the product of this new systemic discipline.

A policy of sustainable development relies upon adherence to several principles already evident in the ethico-religious sphere. They are being progressively rediscovered, although this may be occurring only because of a perspective of the end of the world,[34] at the limit of the Cosmogenesis. Such principles pertain to our *knowledge, management,* and *control* of the environment, and constitute the main prerequisites for sustainable development as they now appear to us.

1. *Humanity must better know itself and its environment.* Sustainable development begins with a heightened sense of awareness, in that individuals who implement it are in symbiosis with their environment. The human race is becoming aware of itself and its wholeness through a broadening of its visual horizons. Seen from outer space, Earth has a harmony that is not apparent from the surface alone. Earth must now command a loyalty once reserved for the tribe or homeland.

Research in ecology and synecology is still insufficient and too compartmentalized. Moreover, as ecological problems become progressively more formidable, it is imperative to establish a proactive and collective system of intervention in order to ensure the safeguarding of the spaceship[35] and the evolution of humanity. Everyone must be able to contribute to this research and developmental process.

It is significant that these fundamental issues have probably never been debated as much as today.[36] This acceleration is owing in part to concern over the physical condition of the planet and the apparent increase in natural disasters. Interest in research on the origins of the world and the appearance of life and humanity has intensified. Ideally, this research should be structured along broad lines in order to provide a framework for the sort of convergence discussed in this paper.

If we are to develop the new science of human energetics, *new tools* must be created — tools that are more comprehensive than those presently available to the proponents of development. Our universe cannot be managed with instruments and indicators as narrow and restrictive as cost-benefit analysis or variations on the gross national product. Economists will remain relevant if they adapt their discipline to the new systemic vision and, together with other researchers and analysts, contribute to the identification of actual costs and the formulation of decisions based

---

34 Even more unifying than the prospect of war.

35 Image from K.E. Boulding, "The Economics of the Coming Spaceship Earth" in H.E. Jarrett, ed., *Environmental Quality in a Growing Economy* (Baltimore: Johns Hopkins Press, 1966) at 3.

36 Except perhaps at the time of the Gauls, who were afraid that the sky might literally fall on their heads. Victims of great natural disasters such as earthquakes harbour the same kind of fear long afterwards.

on criteria other than the strictly monetary. Even with new hypotheses, however, some microeconomic tools may continue to be useful.

We already report on the state of the environment and sometimes assess specific projects from an ecological perspective. Further, we can utilize certain indicators (such as those used by UNESCO to study the situation of children in the world[37]) that assist in evaluating the degree of economic,[38] and sometimes social, development. However, a considerable amount of research remains to be done, especially with respect to the ability to define thresholds of tolerance and avoid overstepping them. Moreover, such research is a fundamental precondition to intelligent decision-making and action; it is indeed a social responsibility. (Similarly, the results of such research should be viewed as "social assets," to be held in common and available to society as a whole.)

2. *Sustainable development depends on Capital-Nature and may only use the interest (flux). Sustainable development must respect life and the major natural cycles.* The implicit hypothesis that resources are unlimited is now unacceptable. Having understood that the real source of all riches is the Earth in its interaction with its inhabitant, humanity, in restoring the environment to the centre of its value system, will exercise as much care in maintaining its Capital-Nature as in generating its financial capital. Nature, in a way, is being emancipated, and its roles and rights — particularly the right to exist and to perpetuate itself — are finally being recognized.

Our industrial civilizations, which are based on continuing supplies of fossil energy and raw materials, are not really sustainable and are becoming unlivable. They should not only cease expanding (that is, achieve steady-state[39]), but should also decrease to an ecologically and humanly acceptable level — that is, quantitatively decrease (or rather, shed the fat) in order to allow the planet to accommodate the legitimate growth of Third World countries. The economic theory of sustainable development will emphasize primarily sharing. Both direct implementation of the theory (for example, the twinning of underprivileged and overdeveloped communities) and its indirect reinforcement (reassertion of the value of natural resources

---

37 Rate of decline in the mortality of children less than five years old; life expectancy at birth; literacy rate; income distribution in households; percentage of children whose weight at birth is insufficient; average index of food production per inhabitant; percentage of population with access to a drinking water source and to health services; comparison of the central administration expenditures for the health, education, and defense sectors; payment of the debt as a percentage of exports of goods and services. UNICEF, *La situation des enfants dans le monde* (1989).

38 Some researchers have suggested ways of improving the formula of the gross national product in order to accurately measure the flux of material well-being, which, as Nicolas Georgescu-Roegen pointed out, is the real purpose of production.

39 H.E. Daly, *Steady-state Economics: The Economics of Biophysical Equilibrium and Moral Growth* (San Francisco: W.W. Freeman, 1977).

and raw materials) are among the methods to be employed to re-establish an equilibrium.[40]

Given the planet's present state of deterioration, priority will logically be given to

- the struggle against pollution;
- the restoration of conditions facilitating the continuation of life on earth; and
- the creation of life-styles that conform to the three main themes of sustainable development: self-sufficiency, diversity, and equity.[41]

By ensuring responsibility for the life-span of products, humans will implement the major principles of management for sustainability (the Five R's): reflection (in order to foresee and readjust), reduction, reuse, restoration, and recycling. Indeed, there is no use in contemplating sustainable development unless those existing pollution sources and life-styles that contribute to the planet's degradation are eliminated. Suffice it to add that, at the present time, the developed countries would be entirely responsible for this great cleansing.

The theory of sustainable development is therefore bio-global, multidisciplinary, and, especially, normative: contrary to traditional economic theories, which claim to be objective, sustainable development has a specific goal. Consequently, its approach and methodology will be completely different,[42] and will permit the incorporation of other fields of study. In order to ensure intergenerational equity, the

---

40 See M. Roseland, *Social Equity and Sustainable Development: Uncommon Future* (Prepared for the Conference on Sustainable Development) (Vancouver: University of Vancouver, 25 November 1988). One of the more difficult problems that must be addressed in an economic theory of sustainable development is that of unemployment. On the one hand, in a society where unemployment carries with it a social stigma, having a job must be considered a right. On the other, it makes little sense to accomplish full employment at the cost of destroying the environment: work, after all, must have meaning (see Center for Reflection on the Second Law, *Trees, Work, Jobs, Income, and a New Approach to Economics* (Bulletin #109) (Raleigh, North Carolina, 29 March 1989)). The illusory nature of prosperity that is achieved at the expense of "bankrupting" our biosphere is discussed by W.E. Rees, "Sustainable Development: Economic Myths and Ecological Realities" (1988) 5(4) *Trumpeter* 136.

41 M. Redclift & J. Porritt, *Why Bankrupt the Earth? An Exploration into International Economics and the Environment* (Paper presented at the Conference entitled The Other Economic Summit) (TOES) (1986) at 41.

42 Important research is being conducted on this topic at the University of Waterloo's "Sustainable Society Project" under the direction of John Robinson. As a practical matter, the exercise of moving towards sustainable development should start with the definition of long-term objectives. The actual achievement of an ecologically healthy management model will require a transition period of several decades, in order to accommodate both a change in management styles and a turnover in capital stock. Given the agreed-upon objectives, planners will use backcasting (feedback planning) to ensure a smooth transition to this goal. This is in accordance with the approach that has been advocated for soft energy paths: for an explanation of the methodology of achieving

theory of sustainable development will have to answer questions that are ignored by the present-day science of economics, and formulate hypotheses as to the evolution of technological progress and the needs of future generations[43] (to say nothing of the present generation). It might, for example, be necessary to use a negative discount rate.

In order to ensure interspatial equity, we must create analytical tools to continuously rotate between the local and the global, to evaluate our legitimate needs[44] and compare them with available resources.[45] In affluent countries, at the local or microeconomic level, sustainable development and self-sufficiency may appear to be synonymous, but we should not forget that less-developed countries require foreign markets for their products if they are to move towards autonomy.

3. *"L'obligation de subir nous donne le droit de savoir"* (the obligation to endure gives us the right to know), wrote Rostand. And regarding our survival, let us add that it should also give us *the right to decide*. As the stakes have become planetary, so too should the responsibilities. Although our institutions as yet fail to reflect this reality, many people perceive that a redistribution of power — and, one hopes, an orderly and harmonious one — is necessary. Each individual has become responsible for all of humanity, since one person's act may imply risks to everyone's life (for example, sabotage of large systems, or nuclear terrorism[46]). Civic responsibility must regain a place of honour, so that each individual understands and exercises his or her responsibilities in the best interests of all. As a result, it is crucial that both neighbours and countries increasingly develop a common vision and common interests. Ultimately this implies that sustainable development requires concrete steps to diminish differences between and within countries. As a logical priority, then, remedial efforts should be first directed at the most deprived.

The systemic vision expands and globalizes the range of analytical inquiry. But action remains local, implying the implementation of new institutional links between levels of decision and those of enforcement. The motto "Think globally,

---

sustainable long-term development with respect to energy, see the work of A. Lovins, *Soft Energy Paths. Towards a Durable Peace* (San Francisco: Friends of the Earth International, 1977); and D.B. Brooks, J.B. Robinson & R.D. Torrie, eds., *2025: Soft Energy Futures for Canada* (Report prepared on behalf of Friends of the Earth Canada) (Ottawa: Energy, Mines and Resources and Environment Canada, February 1983).

43 According to J. Rawls in *A Theory of Justice* (Cambridge: Belknap, 1971), all generations should theoretically be brought together, with each person placed in an identical initial position behind a "veil of ignorance," which prevents knowledge of which generation one belongs to; thus the principles of justice would be defined between generations.

44 That is to say, needs that correspond to climatic and cultural necessities and do not deprive others.

45 That is to say, ecologically acceptable and essentially renewable resources.

46 See A.B. Lovins & L.H. Lovins, *Brittle Power: Energy Strategy for National Security* (Andover: Brick House, 1982).

act locally" requires institutional changes at both ends of the ladder (as well as in between) in order to accommodate both of the following needs.

(a) A true *democracy at work* is essential in order to protect the environment, rebuild local and regional economies,[47] and revitalize small human units such as families, villages, and urban neighbourhoods. Through the impetus provided by motivated citizens, numerous changes are occurring in many countries. One of the best organized appears to be the consumer group "Seikatsu Club,"[48] which, while it bans unhealthy foods, sets up cooperative systems at the citizen's level to stimulate the local economy and promote a non-centralist and globalist political option of solidarity with the Third World.

The strengthening of local institutions and the creation of necessary innovative ones will depend on the involvement of both informed individuals and central governments. This seems to be the only way to redistribute power in order to eventually short-circuit the present structures of management, which lack accountability. Such involvement corresponds to a major cultural change in each individual, who must be encouraged to redefine his or her own place in the universe.[49]

(b) Responsible national governments must, through concerted efforts, implement a *world-wide development strategy* that ensures coordinated standards and legislation. The Montreal Protocol was one of the first of a necessary series of agreements to this end.

Canada has already started its economic redeployment by creating a Cabinet committee on the environment. Most recently, the National Round Table on Economics and the Environment was established in order to foster this broader vision of the future, from which the strategies of various government departments may draw inspiration. The provinces of Quebec, Ontario, Manitoba, Nova Scotia, New Brunswick, Saskatchewan, and Prince Edward Island have taken the same initiative and are combining their efforts to start in Canada what will have to be done on a world-wide scale: that is, to live in harmony with nature and with one another on an equal and fraternal footing while managing the heritage of future generations.

CONCLUSION

"C'est une triste chose de songer que la nature parle et que le genre humain n'écoute pas" (It is sad to think that nature speaks and humanity does not listen),

---

47 The Rocky Mountain Institute is developing such local strategies at the request of concerned communities. See also J. Robertson, *The Economics of Local Recovery* presented at TOES, 1986.

48 *New Options,* 25 July 1988.

49 W.E. Rees, "Defining Sustainable Development" in *Planning for Sustainable Development* (Symposium Background Papers) (Vancouver: University of British Columbia, School of Community and Regional Planning, 1989) at 7.

wrote Victor Hugo more than a century ago. In recent years nature has spoken so loudly that it is no longer possible to ignore it. Now, it is not only poets or philosophers who listen, but also biologists, ecologists, urban planners, lawyers, and even economists.

All is therefore not lost. However, humanity needs a vision, an explanation of itself. It needs to "envision itself" accomplishing its own development in the universe, if it is to understand the changes that must take place in its economic development. Events of recent years suggest that this process of development, of a new modernity, has begun, on the impetus of thousands of dedicated participants throughout the world who are determined to preserve life on earth. Of late, this effort has been translated into a multiplicity of events organized with regard to the environment. This incipient consensus is a clear sign of the contagious effect of a vision of salvation, raising each of us to a level of consciousness that would make its accomplishment possible. It matters little that we are unable to precisely define sustainable development, as long as, united, we know how to live it.

SUSTAINABLE DEVELOPMENT: AN AGENDA FOR THE 1990s

David Johnston

In this paper I will discuss some aspects of the agenda for sustainable development in the 1990s, insofar as they relate to the role of the National Round Table on the Environment and the Economy, and will attempt to describe some of the challenges that face all of us in embracing and implementing the concept of sustainable development. I will also bring to bear my initial reactions as a lawyer, as an educator, and as Principal of McGill University for the last ten years.

I will begin with several personal comments that come to mind when I look at my own background and think about sustainable development. I was born in Sudbury, where my father managed a local hardware store, and we lived above the store in the shadow of the smokestack from Inco's Coppercliff smelter. At that time, it was the largest smokestack in the western world and, subsequently, perhaps the largest smokestack in the world. The results of the smelting of nickel and copper are pollution and its fallout over a wide area. Recently, Inco embarked on a program to reduce the level of air pollution by 1992 to one-tenth of its 1965 levels; I might add that air pollution was certainly even greater in 1941, when I was born.

The other part of my background of some relevance is that my father earned his living as a merchant in a community whose major customers were, of course, the International Nickel Company and all of its customers. Therefore, from the very beginning, I was confronted with the dual challenge of sustainable development. How could one maintain economic prosperity, and at the same time function in a way that protects and enhances the environment?

I moved from Sudbury at the age of seven to Sault Sainte Marie, where I grew to maturity. Once again, there were some interesting examples of sustainable development. Sault Sainte Marie lies on a river that links the city to both Lake Superior and Lake Huron. The river has a twenty-six-foot drop (called "rapids" or "sault") from the largest body of fresh water in the world down to Lake Huron.

Local legend tells us that, 350 years before Europeans came to Sault Sainte Marie, these rapids were the focal point of the largest gathering of native peoples in all of North America. They would come at a particular time of the year and wade into the rapids to net the white fish, dry them, and store them for food for the entire year — a striking example of nature's bounty. Around the turn of the century, entrepreneurs saw the potential of that twenty-six-foot drop and diverted the water from the rapids, mostly for hydroelectric power. This diversion produced an integrated power supply for the steelworks and a major newsprint mill; both of these endeavours are still functioning and, at the present time, flourishing.

Although my father regularly swam in that water, my brothers and sister and I could not because of pollution from the steel company, the newsprint industry, and municipal sewage drains. (Unfortunately, there were no sewage-disposal plants at that time.) Within the space of several decades, these industries had made it impossible for us to swim in the very waters where, a few hundred years before, native people came in massive numbers year after year to net the white fish in huge quantities — without even denting the fish stocks.

Another experience of my childhood was the building of the St. Lawrence Seaway. The seaway introduced ocean-going freighters, which subsequently introduced the lamprey eel, an ocean-going fish. Lamprey eels came into the seaway attached to the bottom of tankers, and were then transported into the Great Lakes and, in particular, Lake Superior. They almost succeeded in extinguishing the white fish population, with the resulting local impact of closing down entirely the commercial fisheries. White fish had been one of the great delicacies of Northern Ontario. Since then, through enormous effort and a great deal of scientific support, considerable progress has been made in reversing the lamprey eel problem. The white fish has returned to Lake Superior, but not yet in the numbers we saw in previous years.

I share these stories because they mean a great deal to me. I have also discussed them with my children, one of my most important audiences, because the challenges of sustainable development, including the question of how we face sustainable development meaningfully as individuals in our daily lives, are just as meaningful to my family as to environmental professionals and economists.

We are all experiencing a shift in public attitudes these days towards a "greening of the environment," or, in other words, towards environmental progress. It is heartening to see the desire growing by the day; it is clear that the green revolution has gained considerable momentum amongst the Canadian public. For example, four years ago rarely more than 3 percent of Canadians asked to name the most important problem facing Canada would answer "environmental issues." Those who have studied public-opinion sampling over the past couple of years have observed that there is a peaking phenomenon, with environmental issues gradually climbing to a place of prominence and then dwindling down to lesser significance. What is interesting about current polling is that the environment consistently heads the list, and that there appears to be a greater degree of *sustainability* or durability in that interest. For example, last year pollsters found that the environment ranked higher as a matter of public concern than any other quality-of-life issue in the history of polling in Canada. The environment is now the number *one* issue among four in ten Canadians who have some post-secondary education. Regionally, it is the primary concern of both Ontario and Quebec residents.

Numerous media reports reflect this growing phenomenon. Moreover, negative effects of unsustainable practices are depicted in strong visual and descriptive terms. The criticisms are numerous; one hears the cries of alarm and the castigation of both government and industry for inaction. I believe, however, that the challenge facing all of us is to ensure that these emotions are channelled into sustained action, aimed at ensuring that future generations have the necessary capital of water, earth, and air in which to live healthy and productive lives. Meanwhile, though, prospects of economic growth are being taken for granted. The practical and immediate necessities of economic activity and competitiveness, and their widely accepted benefits, cannot be ignored. The last thing we want is a backlash from the Canadian public. A crucial component of a move towards sustainable development is the public's desire for change. I believe the will for change also exists within Canadian governments and the business community. Now that the need for change is widely accepted, leadership is needed to show the way.

The Brundtland Report gave the initial impetus for the change that I am attempting to describe. It has brought the concept of sustainable development to the fore and has eloquently convinced us that today's course is not sustainable. It has challenged every nation and every one of us to redress that course with an optimism that I, and all those who have agreed to serve at the National Round Table, fully share.

There are at least three approaches we could take. The first one may be unduly idealistic — the exclusive pursuit of a wholly pollution-free environment at the cost of excluding economic interests. This might only succeed in blocking economic growth, and may force us to relinquish much of the economic freedom on which we have come to rely and to which less-developed countries aspire. If we attempt a second approach, whose objective might be to strike an exact balance between economic growth and environmental protection, we run the risk of inordinate difficulties in implementing it on a case-by-case basis. We may miss a desirable long-term goal by insisting on short-term perfection.

I suggest a third approach, aimed not at a perfect balance, but at a process of integration. This more realistic path might involve shifting from a situation of conflicting economic and environmental concerns to the integration of environmental needs with economic development. Or, to put it colloquially, "Let's run in the same direction rather than come to a head-on crash."

My own view about the necessity of adopting sustainable development is, first and foremost, that this is simply common sense — but also, how challenging it is! It will require all of our resources, ingenuity, and skill. Therefore, the agenda I see for the 1990s includes, first, corporate willingness to adapt, as a necessary precondition for any move towards the path to sustainable development; second, legal reform, as a very powerful instrument of change; and third, education, as a long-term factor of change. I will deal briefly with each of these three challenges.

With respect to business, it has been said that the concept of the environment as a dump with a zero-price is no longer tenable. David Buzzelli, President of Dow Chemical and one of the business members of the Round Table, clearly sees and worries about growing "public mistrust" of the corporate role in environmental protection. As a recent example, it may well be that the Valdez case, and Exxon's response to it, will serve to reinforce that mistrust. What is so intriguing and perhaps illustrative about that disaster is that it seems to demonstrate the simplest of human frailties, on both an individual and an intra-company basis.

I believe in sustainable development that presents a new challenge for industry: to adapt to environmental needs while remaining competitive. The business community will, of course, look for a level playing field, with adoption of the same or similar rules worldwide. This harmony of framework is going to require unprecedented levels of international economic cooperation. I suggest that, before this can come about, several traditionally conflicting notions have to be reconciled, such as short-term profit versus long-term environmental soundness, and short-term profit versus long-term losses. These tensions raise a number of issues, among them questions regarding environmental accountability and the full allocation of environmental costs to production.

Business must understand, and I believe that businesses are starting to comprehend, that poor environmental management is unsound, and that good environmental management is good business. Governments must, in turn, find a balance between providing financial incentives and strengthening regulations that are often ineffective and unresponsive to economic and technological changes. One of the dangers, in the words of Ian Smyth, President of the Canadian Petroleum Association, is that "regulations tend to regulate everyone to the lowest common denominator."

Let me turn from that brief discussion of business challenges to some legal challenges. Many of the papers in this volume provide a menu of legal issues related to sustainable development. Part of the global challenge will be met through law, both international and domestic. International environmental treaties, for example, are clearly necessary to overcome some of the transnational problems of environmental degradation. In many respects, there has been exciting progress on this front in the last two or three years, but horror stories continue to emerge, often of frightening proportions. International trade rules may also have to be scrutinized to ensure that export sales capture the fully allocated costs of production, including environmental costs.

Most important, domestic legal issues must be pursued actively, and lawyers, as individuals, should demonstrate leadership in these endeavours. For example, the Law Reform Commission of Canada has taken on a substantial agenda of environmental law. It includes sustainable development, questions of insurance, issues relating to criminality of polluters, the balance and spectrum of sanctions and rewards, the renewed challenge of private property versus public interest, and many other issues that require resolution.

Another initiative that encourages me is the establishment of the Canadian Institute for Advanced Research. This magnificent vehicle, launched six and a half years ago by Fraser Mustard and his colleagues, is one of the most interesting and successful forums for academic research that I have ever seen. One of the undertakings developed by the Institute is the Law and Society Project, which is attempting to implement several of the recommendations of the Arthurs Report.[1] These include ensuring that the law makes greater use of empirical evidence and that law as a discipline places greater reliance upon other disciplines in the social sciences and beyond. This broader compass could influence the choices and rules that help to evaluate the effectiveness and practice of law, and could, I suppose, bring into the Canadian mosaic the kind of philosophy of social engineering that Roscoe Pound, the Dean of Harvard Law School, preached fifty years ago.

The Law and Society Project has had a number of individual research endeavours, one of which was accomplished several years ago by Murray Rankin and Rick Brown in British Columbia.[2] It involved the comparison of two sets of statutes and regulations and their administration, to see how sanctions and rewards for work produce appropriate social and economic behaviour. They compared British Columbia's occupational health and safety legislation with the Environmental Act and, in particular, the penalties meted out for polluting. What they found was that the administration of the environmental legislation was quite immature, and that the compensation legislation and its administration were very mature; the latter worked much better than the former. One reason for the success of the compensation regime was that it contained a range of sanctions and rewards. The reward for an employer with a low incidence of workplace accidents (and even when those accidents occurred, they tended to be of a minor variety) was the payment of rather low premiums to the Workman's Compensation Fund. One could correlate employers' premiums with their performance with respect to workforce safety. There was, therefore, a very clear incentive for certain employers to adjust their practices to reduce injury; and where employers did not respond to incentives, the penalties were correspondingly severe.

The administration of the compensation regime was also tied to sanctions and

---

1 Consultative Group on Research and Education in Law, *Law and Learning* (Report to the Social Sciences and Humanities Research Council of Canada) (Ottawa: Minister of Supply and Services, 1983) (Chair: H.W. Arthurs).

2 R.M. Brown & T.M. Rankin, "Persuasion, Penalties and Prosecution: The Treatment of Repeat Offenders Under British Columbia's Legislation" (Research Report for the Canadian Institute of Advanced Research).

rewards. Where an employer consistently demonstrated bad industrial practices, with high rates of injury and fataility, the penalties as well as the premiums were very high, and penalties were applied in a way that curbed that behaviour immediately and significantly.

By contrast, the provisions applying to environmental pollution were entirely punitive in nature; the legislation was poorly administered and there was very little follow-up for second and third offenders. Moreover, when second and third and fourth offences were prosecuted, there was little escalation in fines. The pollution legislation was, therefore, no better than a licence to pollute, and continue current practices with minimum disruption.

The foregoing is a simplistic summary of the sophisticated study by Rankin and Brown. What it illustrates, however, is the importance for scholars of evaluating legislative interventions and their administration, and of establishing very clearly when they do work and when they do not. When they do not work in a clear and constructive fashion, we should suggest measures to make them work. This is precisely what the Rankin and Brown study did. It was one of the few academic publications of this kind that attracted attention in the newspapers; it actually made headlines in one section of the Sunday Toronto Star. But, more importantly, it made headlines in newspapers in British Columbia. The first response of the appropriate authorities was to dismiss the study as esoteric and lacking in understanding of British Columbian realities, but upon examination it is clear that the study did indeed draw very carefully from empirical evidence. The study later received a substantial response from the Ministry of Environment, which increased considerably the number of investigators and inspectors and raised the penalties for second, third, and fourth offenders. There is still a considerable way to go, but the initial response has been good, and the study has influenced the legislation.

This brings me to the third of the three topics in this section: sustainable development as part of the education curriculum. We want education to be one-half science and technology and one-half ethics. It will not be sufficient in the long run, however, to teach the "how to" of environmental consciousness in the form of memorized recipes. It is more important to teach the "why" and the "who" — in other words, the urgent need, and the individual and collective responsibility, for such consciousness. As an example of one small step to this end, my personal dream is that every schoolchild in this country will have the opportunity to plant a tree (and, as a symbol, to plant it in a field fertile for sustainable development). Of course, this exercise will require significant funds to have seedlings prepared and delivered to the schools, and to have teachers lead youngsters out on a rainy day in May to plant trees on the schoolgrounds beside the asphalt playing fields, or at the outskirts of the village, town, or city. It becomes one more exercise that, if simply a required chore, will not have much significance. If the act is to have meaning, a child will have to understand what a tree represents, not only to the balance of nature generally but to our own welfare specifically. This is what the Indians in Sault Sainte Marie intuitively understood when they went into the rapids of Saint Mary's and took those fish out, harvest after harvest, season after season.

A proverb I often use in finishing addresses to McGill alumnae is this: Blessed is the man who plants a tree knowing he will not be there to enjoy the shade. Of course, that is very applicable to a university, where there is a responsibility both to the past and to the future. It is similarly important that we engage the imagination of our young people to both plant the tree and, at the same time, appreciate the significance of the shade that will be there for generations to come.

The ethical aspect of sustainable development must, however, be studied in conjunction with the scientific aspect. Scientific evidence has played a key role in raising many environmental concerns and producing early successes. Examples include the case of mercury contamination, which in Canada was reduced by 90 percent in just over three years. Once the scientific evidence was clear, we knew that we had major problems and that something had to be done. Another example is the effort to reduce CFC emissions, as provided for in the Montreal Protocol of 1987. I remember stating, within two or three days of that announcement in Montreal, that here was something in the headlines we could all understand. In this case, a number of eminent scientists studying the Antarctic atmosphere noticed that there was a "tear" in the ozone layer — indeed, an enormous gap — and that through that gap was coming ultraviolet radiation, with the potential of causing dramatic increases in skin cancer and associated diseases. When these facts were understood, in a matter of days or weeks — rather than months or years — a group of scientists and public representatives gathered in Montreal and put together a protocol designed to respond immediately with solutions to the problem.

A strong scientific culture is needed to balance the understanding of environmental threats and the power of technological solutions. Once again, this understanding must be built on facts rather than on fears and emotions. Children must be given the tools to collect and interpret scientific evidence so that they can measure change for themselves. The school and home can offer the requisite testing ground for children to experiment; these contexts will influence both values and behaviour, and it is this fundamental change at which we are aiming. In sum, fields of science, technology, and ethics must be strengthened in the school curriculum and presented with the objective of mobilizing successive generations.

To conclude, the National Round Table on the Environment and the Economy has twenty-four members and was established by the Prime Minister. It creates a multidisciplinary forum for reconciling diverse views and stimulating the implementation of sustainable development in Canada. The Round Table has been likened to a crucible in which different values and interests, ideals and ideologies can come together. I also hope that we will be a catalyst for action.

The National Round Table will focus on three objectives. The first is to promote changes in attitudes towards environmental issues, from the boardroom to the classroom. The second is to create new partnerships, because partnerships of traditionally competing interests are necessary to give truly national attention to the priorities and issues we are dealing with; to this end, business, government, environmental groups, scientists, and other policy experts will be brought together at the Round Table. The third objective is to encourage a new form of institutional practice, one that would include a broad agreement on the kind of information required to make better judgements about sustainability and the stimulation of the work of key groups, with the aim of ensuring that sustainable development becomes an integral part of both our professional methodology and our daily lives.

I am enthusiastic about this process, but we must be realistic; even though seven provinces have now established round tables, we are not going to have all the answers in one or two years. We do hope, however, that we will make some ripples, ripples that may become waves, and that we may achieve common goals through the creation of new partnerships between economic and environmental interests. Change will come through patience, work, and creativity. Jim MacNeill, the Secretary-General to the Brundtland Commission and a member of the Round Table, has said, "If you change the way you make decisions, you change the decisions that are made." This significant change in societal attitudes must come about rationally if it is to endure; it has to be built on facts. Similarly, it will depend on legal reform that is sensitively attuned to environmental needs and institutional realities. Law mirrors the crystallized values of a society. Therefore, our responsibilities as professionals, as scholars interested in the law, are to ensure that we understand how attitudes are formed and changed, and to provide the ideas — the intellectual leadership — for that change.

2

IMPLEMENTATION OF SUSTAINABLE DEVELOPMENT

INTERNATIONAL MANAGEMENT OF LIVING MARINE RESOURCES TO ACHIEVE SUSTAINABLE YIELDS: THE PACIFIC NORTHWEST

*Jay S. Johnson**

In 1976, the United States established its two-hundred-nautical mile fishery conservation zone; in 1983, that zone was renamed the exclusive economic zone (EEZ).[1] The United States' EEZ, by some estimates, contains from 15 to 20 percent of the world's fish supply. It also supports large populations of marine mammals, some of which have been harvested commercially. With proper harvest management, and other conservation efforts, these resources may continue to be harvested on a sustainable basis in perpetuity. Unfortunately, as the disastrous oil spill from the recent grounding of the T/V Exxon Valdez amply demonstrates, protecting living marine resources from damage by external forces is just as important as protecting them from over-harvest.

---

* The author is the Deputy General Counsel of the National Oceanic and Atmospheric Administration, U.S. Department of Commerce, Washington, D.C. The views expressed in this paper do not necessarily reflect those of any government agency.

1 The Fishery Conservation and Management Act of 1976, 16 U.S.C. §§1801–1882, established the U.S. fishery conservation zone (FCZ) effective 1 March 1977. The FCZ became the U.S. exclusive economic zone by President Reagan's Proclamation No. 5030, 10 March 1983. The Act was later renamed the Magnuson Fishery Conservation and Management Act after the senator from Washington who was its principal author.

Proper harvest management and other conservation efforts are complicated by the fact that many of our fish and marine mammals do not remain within the United States' EEZ for major portions of their life cycles. Both fish and marine mammals are subject to capture in other nations' economic zones and on the high seas beyond. Many of these marine resources are shared between the United States and Canada, and several of the examples referred to in this paper represent joint efforts to maintain sustainable yields.

Canada and the United States currently participate in several bilateral and multilateral international arrangements designed to conserve renewable marine resources. Among these are the Pacific Salmon Commission, the International Pacific Halibut Commission, and the International North Pacific Fisheries Commission. The United States has withdrawn from or refused to join Canada in other organizations, such as the North Pacific Fur Seal Convention, the International Convention for the Northwest Atlantic Fisheries, and its successor, the Northwest Atlantic Fisheries Organization. Further on in this paper, I will discuss some of the reasons for the United States' unwillingness to participate in these arrangements.

Finally, two areas beyond the two-hundred-mile limit are of immediate concern to the United States, due to their rapidly expanding fisheries: the Central Bering Sea and the North Pacific Ocean. While fisheries in these areas focus on pollock and squid, they also take some resources whose migratory range includes Canadian waters. Canadian authorities have not yet participated extensively in this issue, although greater Canadian involvement might be welcomed.

MAXIMUM SUSTAINABLE YIELD

Most international conservation programs for living marine resources are based in some manner on the biologist's concept of maximum sustainable yield (MSY) — that there is, for each stock of fish or sea mammal, some maximum level of harvest that can be permanently maintained without destroying the resource's ability to reproduce itself. The resource manager's goal under this standard is to regulate the harvest and, where practicable, the other sources of mortality in a manner that ensures MSY will be achieved on a continuing basis.

In its simplest form, MSY management of a single species of fish or marine mammal requires information about the abundance of the resource, its reproductive capabilities, and the effect on that abundance and reproduction of various harvest techniques and efforts. Using strictly biological information, the resource manager will set harvesting restrictions to ensure that only that portion of the resource will be harvested that is not needed to maintain the population at a level allowing continued harvests at that rate. MSY management, therefore, maximizes the harvest available from the resource, not the abundance of the resource in the wild state, although the latter will, of course, be an important consideration.

OTHER MANAGEMENT CONSIDERATIONS

As biologists attempted to impose MSY-based restrictions on the harvesting sector, they quickly learned that economic, ecological, sociological, and political considerations are also very important in determining allowable harvest levels.

Economic considerations include harvesting costs, price fluctuations, and the fact that maximizing the harvest — or the harvest efficiency — for some species will inevitably produce smaller or less efficient harvests of other species.

Ecological considerations include, *inter alia,* the chemical and physiological properties of the ocean, the supply of available nutrients, predator-prey relationships, and, as evidenced by the Exxon Valdez disaster, the effects of pollutants and habitat destruction.

Sociological considerations include protection of aboriginal subsistence lifestyles, stability of employment in coastal communities, and even issues of morality, as evidenced by strong protest movements intended to stop commercial sealing in both Canada and the United States.

Political considerations include relations between nations that harvest the same stocks, relations between the national governments and the states or provinces, and strong regional differences of opinion as to how conservation and management programs should function.

As I discuss the various living marine resource management programs, these other considerations will become more evident.

NORTH PACIFIC FUR SEALS

The North Pacific Fur Seal is a pelagic species that ranges throughout the North Pacific. There are now essentially only two major stocks of these seals — one that breeds on the Pribilof Islands off Alaska, and another that breeds on several small islands off the Soviet Union. Historically, the fur seal stocks were among the most valuable resources to be found in the North Pacific, and they have been exploited accordingly.

Early commercial sealing was indiscriminate: animals of all sizes and sexes were taken, whenever and wherever found. The stocks soon collapsed. In response, the principal sealing nations — the United States, Great Britain, Japan, and Russia — signed the Fur Seal Treaty of 1911. The stocks recovered promptly, and so successfully that Japan abrogated the treaty in 1941 out of fear that the seal herds were harming its fisheries. In 1957, the Fur Seal Treaty was replaced by the Interim Convention for the Conservation of North Pacific Fur Seals,[2] with Canada replacing Great Britain.

---

2   8 U.S.T. 2283; T.I.A.S. 3948; 314 U.N.T.S. 105.

The concept of maximum sustainable yield is embedded in the preamble to the Convention in classical, if somewhat redundant, terminology:

> The Governments of Canada, Japan, the Union of Soviet Socialist Republics, and the United States of America,
>
> Desiring to take effective measures towards achieving the maximum sustainable productivity of the fur seal resources of the North Pacific Ocean so that the fur seal population can be brought to and maintained at the levels which will provide the greatest harvest year after year, with due regard to their relation to the productivity of other living marine resources of the area, ... Agree as follows:

The principal features of the Convention are:

1. The prohibition of "pelagic sealing" (the practice of killing seals while they are at sea, which had resulted in high juvenile and female mortality)

2. The institution of scientific resource management to determine the age, sex, and numbers of animals to be harvested

3. The establishment of marking requirements to ensure that all sealskins placed in international commerce had been legally harvested in either the United States or the Soviet Union

4. The formation of an international commission to oversee the management program

5. The provision of compensation to Canada and Japan for their abandonment of rights to harvest seals commercially in Japanese or Canadian waters or on the high seas.

The Convention provided that the harvest of fur seals would be conducted exclusively on the island breeding grounds in the United States and the Soviet Union, where animals could be identified by size and sex before they were harvested. Both the United States and the Soviet Union agreed to provide 15 percent of their harvests to Japan and 15 percent to Canada.

Under scientific management, the fur seal stocks recovered rapidly. The population on the U.S. Pribilof Islands rebounded from a low of three hundred thousand animals in the early 1900s to almost two million animals in the 1950s. Throughout the world the Fur Seal Convention was considered to be the model scientifically sound conservation program. No doubt it would have remained so, had it not come under intense pressure from the international animal protection movement.

Canada is very familiar with animal protection groups' opposition to commercial sealing. The U.S. government has encountered similar problems, although in the United States the Convention's demise can be traced partly to its title — it was an "interim" convention that required periodic renewal, with each renewal requiring the U.S. Senate's "advice and consent" to its ratification.

In the United States, as in Canada, a small sector of the population was economically dependent on commercial sealing. All of the American sealers were Alaskan natives employed on a part-time basis by the government. The natives were the descendants of Aleuts who had been forcibly relocated to the Pribilof Islands when Alaska was a Russian territory. As part of the United States' treaty obligations to Canada and Japan, the National Oceanic and Atmospheric Administration (NOAA) had been responsible for employing the Aleut sealers, supervising the annual seal hunt, and even conducting annual auctions of the sealskins to tanneries and furriers.

Animal protection groups found this level of U.S. government participation in seal killing particularly appalling; nor did the publicity surrounding the Canadian seal hunt help. The animal protection groups lobbied hard in Congress to "get the U.S. government out of the business of killing seals." In 1983, Congress established a trust fund to be used to train the Pribilof Islanders as commercial fishermen and to improve the port facilities in that remote area.[3] This fund served to lessen the islanders' economic dependence on commercial sealing. Animal protection groups then worked on the Senate to oppose ratification of the 1984 extension of the "interim" Convention. That tactic also succeeded, with the consequence that the Fur Seal Convention no longer exists; no commercial seal harvest may be conducted anywhere in the United States,[4] and neither Canada nor Japan receives any benefit for abstaining from seal harvests within their waters or on the high seas.

It remains to be seen what will happen to the seals. The elaborate scientific apparatus set up to maintain the maximum productivity of sealskins is no longer available. The seal population, at least on the Pribilof Islands, has declined substantially from peak population levels to about eight hundred thousand animals, and the fur seal is now listed as a depleted species under the U.S. Marine Mammal Protection Act. There is some speculation that a great number of seals are being killed at sea, not by commercial sealers, but perhaps by the rapidly expanding foreign drift-gillnet fleet from Japan, Korea, and Taiwan. In the absence of the Convention, these killings by the gillnet fleets are perfectly legal under international law.

---

3   Fur Seal Act Amendments of 1983, Public Law 98-129.

4   The Marine Mammal Protection Act of 1972 (MMPA), 16 U.S.C. §§1361–1407, generally prohibits U.S. citizens from taking or importing marine mammals except pursuant to a permit issued by the Secretary of Commerce. Takings allowed under international agreements such as the Fur Seal Convention and subsistence takings by Alaskan natives do not require permits and are not prohibited. Upon the lapse of that Convention, the MMPA came into full force on the Pribilof Islands, and the islanders' rights to continue killing seals has been reduced to a subsistence right enjoyed by all Alaskan native populations. Under this right, approximately 1,800 seals are killed annually.

PACIFIC HALIBUT

The United States and Canada are parties to a number of bilateral and multilateral fishery management conventions. One of the most successful has been the Convention for the Preservation of the Halibut Fishery of the Northern Pacific Ocean and Bering Sea, which dates from 1923.[5] Pacific halibut, like the fur seals, range widely from the Bering Sea southward to California. The Convention established the International Pacific Halibut Commission and empowered the Commission to adopt regulations designed "to permit the maximum sustainable yield from the fishery and for maintaining the stocks at those levels."

In 1978, Canada and the United State renegotiated the Halibut Convention in recognition of the fact that areas formerly defined as high seas, and open to either nation's fishing vessels, had since been designated as within the two-hundred-mile fishing zones. The 1978 protocol to the Convention substituted the term "optimum yield" for the earlier "maximum sustainable yield," and provided for a phase-out of Canadian halibut fishing in the U.S. EEZ in return for 60 percent of the overall harvest if that could be taken in Canadian waters. The term "optimum yield" acknowledges that the optimal result may not always be secured by maintaining the maximum harvest of a resource (in this case, halibut), because other ecological factors, as well as economic, sociological, and political ones, may be involved.

From a biological perspective, the Halibut Convention has been a success. The stocks of Pacific halibut reached all-time highs several years ago, and the industry in both countries prospered. The 1988 harvest was the second highest in history. There are, however, some dark clouds on the horizon.

One issue centers on the by-catch of juvenile halibut by rapidly expanding U.S. bottom fish fisheries in the Bering Sea. Another arises through the U.S. fishery management institutions' continuing inability to take advantage of the Halibut Convention's new management standard — "optimum yield." Both of these issues should be of some concern to Canadian fishermen and fishery managers.

When the United States extended its fisheries jurisdiction in 1976, Congress directed the NOAA "to encourage the development of fisheries which are currently underutilized or not utilized by United States fishermen, *including bottom fish off Alaska.*"[6] That development has occurred. Foreign markets, principally in Japan, have been generated; foreign fishing has been terminated; and a new fleet of sophisticated, U.S.-built and -owned factory-trawlers has been put into operation.

While many of the new factory-trawlers focus on Alaskan pollock — a midwater species that can be used for filleting or for minced fish products — some

---

5   5 U.S.T. 5; T.I.A.S. 2900; 222 U.N.T.S. 77.

6   16 U.S.C. §1801(b)(6).

of the vessels also fish for yellowfin sole and other flounders that are most abundant in areas where juvenile halibut are also present. Although U.S. regulations do not allow factory-trawlers to retain halibut, they do not limit the amount of damage that the groundfish fleet can do to the halibut resource.[7]

One of the proposals now before the Secretary of Commerce would impose limits on the halibut by-catch similar to those imposed on foreign trawl operations in earlier years. There is, however, widespread acknowledgment that these limits would be very difficult to enforce. Unlike the foreign fleets, which paid for full observer coverage, the domestic fleet is not required to bear these expenses, and the National Marine Fisheries Service does not have funding to provide more than a few observers for this purpose.

Without observers, the estimate of the juvenile halibut losses caused by the U.S. groundfish fleet will continue to be in doubt, and much of the fleet will be beyond the reach of enforcement measures. Since Canada does not fish for Bering Sea groundfish, but does fish for Pacific halibut, this lack of observer coverage will continue to disrupt our bilateral fisheries relations.

A problem internal to the United States, but whose lack of resolution continues to benefit Canada, is the lack of access control to the U.S. Pacific halibut fishery. Access control, or limited entry, is a means of obtaining increased economic benefits from a fixed natural resource. In land-based enterprises such as forestry, access control is provided by the need to purchase not only the equipment to harvest timber, but also either the land or the rights to cut the trees. In most fisheries, unless the government has instituted a limited-access system, only the equipment must be purchased to begin fishing. In economic terms, the consequence (particularly for very valuable species such as halibut) is that more fishermen will invest in equipment than are necessary to harvest the available resource. If it does not limit access, the government must limit harvests by imposing short seasons or quotas to preserve the resource for future use.

The U.S. Pacific halibut fishery is a classic example of failure to obtain the potential economic benefits of a sound management program. In U.S. waters, there are now over 6,000 vessels licensed to fish Pacific halibut, up from only 2,000 in 1982. In contrast, there were only 403 Canadian vessels licensed in 1987. The seasons in the U.S. statistical areas are exceptionally short — only three or four 2- or 3-day openings each year. The seasons are longer and more numerous in the Canadian statistical areas. All of the U.S. share of the halibut quota is landed at the same time, resulting in overburdened processing facilities, low prices to the

---

7   Regulations for the Bering Sea and Aleutian Islands Groundfish Fishery are set out at Title 50, Code of Federal Regulations (C.F.R.), Part 675. The prohibition against retention of halibut may be found at 50 C.F.R. §675.20(c).

fishermen, and lower quality to the consumer. Throughout most of the year, U.S. consumers who want fresh Pacific halibut have to buy it from Canadian fishermen, whose government instituted limited access to stretch out the seasons and obtain greater economic benefits.

Several years ago, the North Pacific Fishery Management Council proposed a limited-access system for the U.S. Pacific halibut fishery. Public comment was roughly equally divided for and against; ultimately, the proposal was shelved under intense political pressure. This year, the North Pacific Fishery Management Council is considering limited entry in some of the Alaskan fisheries, but not yet for Pacific halibut.

PACIFIC SALMON

The management of Pacific salmon is an exceptionally complex task that requires an unprecedented level of scientific understanding and international cooperation. There are five species of Pacific salmon caught in U.S. and Canadian waters: chinook, coho, pink, chum, and sockeye. The alternative, popular names for these species are king, silver, humpback, dog, and red salmon, respectively. The eggs of each species hatch in fresh-water streams, lakes, or rivers. Young salmon, depending on the species, may remain in fresh water anywhere from a few days to several years before migrating to the ocean, where they grow rapidly. As they approach sexual maturity, they return to their natal waters to lay their eggs. Most Pacific salmon fisheries harvest the returning spawning runs, either from a short distance offshore or when the salmon finally enter the rivers. Unlike Atlantic salmon, almost all Pacific salmon spawn only once and die soon after. The manager's task is to decide how many fish can be harvested, and where those harvests may occur, so as to allow both economically sound fisheries and continued sustainable reproduction.

In the United States, this task is made yet more difficult by the number of management institutions. No less than five states, three interstate compacts, two regional fishery management councils, at least ten federal agencies, and numerous sovereign Indian tribes have some responsibility for Pacific salmon. The United States also participates in a number of international agreements or continuing negotiations concerning Pacific salmon. Among these are the Pacific Salmon Treaty between the United States and Canada; the International North Pacific Fisheries Commission (INPFC), which includes the United States, Canada, and Japan; the new U.S.–U.S.S.R. Reciprocal Fishing Agreement; and continuing negotiations between the United States, the Republic of Korea, and the Taiwanese authorities.

Between the United States, Canada, and Japan, the major issue for nearly twenty years has been allocation. To simplify to a degree: the Alaskans thought that the Japanese caught too many Alaskan-origin — "their" — salmon in the North Pacific and the Bering Sea. The Canadians thought the Alaskans caught— or, in the vernacular of the negotiations, "intercepted" — too many of "their" salmon. And Washingtonians and Oregonians believed the Canadians caught too many of "their" salmon before those salmon returned to the streams and rivers of the "lower forty-eight."

While the United States and Canada struggled to reach agreement, Indian, non-Indian, sport, and commercial fishermen mounted a steady barrage of litigation in U.S. courts over who should get what share of a steadily declining resource. State and federal relations were also extremely poor, with the federal government representing the Indians in litigation against both Washington and Oregon.[8] The federal government twice took action to preempt Oregon salmon jurisdiction, and on several occasions threatened to take similar measures against California.

More than fifteen years of negotiation were required to solve at least some of the problems between the United States and Canada. By treaty, the two countries agreed to share the Pacific salmon resource according to each nation's production.[9] With minor deviations for transboundary rivers (other than the Yukon), the two sides agreed to balance interceptions so that the benefits of conservation would accrue to the nation willing to protect its stocks from over-harvest and its river systems from pollution or hydropower development. By another treaty,[10] the two nations brought pressure on Japan to further reduce high-seas gillnetting that intercepted North American–origin salmon in the Bering Sea and the North Pacific.

Negotiation of the Pacific Salmon Treaty was exceptionally difficult for the United States because of Alaska's separation from the lower forty-eight states. In effect, the treaty asked Alaska to reduce harvests of Canadian and lower-U.S. fish in order that Canada might reduce harvests of predominantly lower-U.S. fish. After a long period of stalemate within the U.S. delegation, the Indians threatened litigation against the State of Alaska, invoking their 1850s treaties that had proved so effective against Washington and Oregon. Ultimately, this litigation was settled on the condition that the United States ratify the Pacific Salmon Treaty. Companion legislation provided a balance on the U.S. section of the Pacific Salmon Commission between Alaskans and lower forty-eight interests, including the Indian tribes, that has stood the test of time.[11] The United States is extremely pleased that the treaty

8   The list of citations to all of the U.S. litigation concerning Pacific salmon is too lengthy to include in this paper. Those interested in the subject should start with the U.S. Supreme Court's decision in *Washington* v. *Washington Commercial Passenger Fishing Vessel Assn.*, 443 U.S. 658 (1979).

9   Treaty between the Government of the United States of America and the Government of Canada Concerning Pacific Salmon, signed at Ottawa, 28 January 1985.

10   International Convention for the High Seas Fisheries of the North Pacific Ocean, signed at Tokyo, 9 March 1952; 4 U.S.T. 380; T.I.A.S. 2786; 205 U.N.T.S. 65.

11   The Pacific Salmon Treaty Act is codified at 16 U.S.C. §§3631–3644.

has helped rebuild the important Columbia River stocks and offers hope for other stressed stocks.

There are, of course, many problems remaining between the United States and Canada concerning Pacific salmon. There is still no long-term agreement on sharing formulas for the important Taku and Stikine rivers, which flow from British Columbia through Alaska. Nor is there a hint of a sharing formula for the Yukon River, which originates in Canada but flows more than a thousand miles through Alaska, and supports extensive Alaskan subsistence fisheries. Finally, there is a major trade dispute concerning Canadian laws that benefit Canadian fish processors in violation of the General Agreement on Tariffs and Trade (GATT) and that, in the American view at least, are inconsistent with the new Free Trade Agreement. Although I will not dwell on this dispute, it illustrates some of the problems that must be addressed in the fishery management area.

Briefly, the dispute concerns Canadian laws that required pink and sockeye salmon — the mainstay of the canning industry — to be processed in Canada before they could be exported. The United States contended that these laws unfairly burdened international trade, and GATT agreed. From the U.S. perspective, this is a simple case of providing an open market for U.S. processors to buy Canadian fish, just as Canadian processors have been freely able to buy U.S.-harvested fish. From the Canadian perspective, however, one of the major economic benefits of the Pacific Salmon Treaty, which was concluded before the trade issue arose, was that both Canadian fishermen and Canadian processors would benefit from the improved conservation provided by the treaty. A major part of that benefit, which would have supported further Canadian funding of fishways and hatcheries on Canadian rivers, may be lost if U.S. processors can outbid their Canadian competition. Negotiations are now underway to resolve this dispute. The prospects are not particularly good, however, and the United States may be forced to retaliate by closing its market to certain Canadian fisheries products.

HIGH-SEAS GILLNETS

One of the unfortunate but predictable results of both U.S. and Canadian efforts to develop domestic fisheries in their EEZs has been the exclusion of large foreign fleets that formerly fished in those zones. Many of these vessels have been converted for use in the new squid-gillnet fisheries that have begun in areas of the North Pacific beyond the two-hundred-mile limits. The National Marine Fisheries Service estimates that over nine hundred Japanese, Korean, and Taiwanese vessels are now engaged in these fisheries, and that they each deploy as much as thirty miles of monofilament gillnet each night.

The northern end of the squid-fishing grounds contains significant numbers of juvenile Pacific salmon and steelhead. Under international law — specifically,

Article 66 of the Law of the Sea Convention — a high-seas salmon fishery is prohibited, except by agreement with the state of origin. In addition, the domestic laws of both Taiwan and Japan proscribe the retention of salmon by their high-seas driftnet vessels. Nevertheless, the evidence is now overwhelming that driftnet vessels from those two nations, as well as from the Republic of Korea, are taking substantial quantities of Pacific salmon, much of which is of North American origin.

In recent days, the U.S. Coast Guard detected eight Taiwanese driftnet vessels conducting what appeared to be an illegal salmon fishery far to the north of the authorized squid-fishing area. Last summer, the Soviets seized three Taiwanese vessels for doing the same thing, and tracked a number of other Taiwanese vessels that were transferring salmon to a Japanese refrigerator transport for delivery to Singapore. Some Southeast Asian countries have canneries willing to process this illegal harvest for sale in Europe. The profits in this illegal trade are immense. One Taiwanese group went so far as to import its illegal catch into the U.S., so that the catch could be reshipped under U.S. labels to avoid Japanese laws prohibiting the import of salmon from Taiwan.

For its part, the United States has recently agreed to cooperate with the Soviet Union in high-seas salmon enforcement measures.[12] We have suggested that all Pacific salmon–producing countries cooperate in ending this illegal trade, and are negotiating with Japan, Korea, and Taiwan to take greater enforcement action against the squid fishery. In June 1989, all three nations will face trade sanctions if they do not address conservation concerns.[13]

This is an area where greater Canadian effort would be most appreciated. Canada, for example, may wish to enact legislation similar to the U.S. Lacey Act and the Pelly Amendment. The former prohibits imports of fish that have been taken in violation of foreign law. The latter permits embargoes of fish products from

---

12   Agreement between the Government of the United States of America and the Government of the Union of Soviet Socialist Republics on Mutual Fisheries Relations, signed at Moscow, 31 May 1988.

13   Under the Driftnet Impact Monitoring, Assessment and Control Act of 1987, Title IV of Public Law 100-220, the Secretary of Commerce is required to certify to the President by 29 June 1989 if any nation conducting a high-seas driftnet fishery in the North Pacific Ocean has failed to reach and implement an agreement with the United States to provide for statistically reliable data collection and effective enforcement of the driftnet fisheries. Such a certification permits the President to restrict imports of fish or fish products from that nation.

The Secretary of Commerce announced on 23 June 1989 that Japan had agreed to implement such an agreement. Canada is participating with the United States and Japan under the auspices of the International Convention for the High Seas Fisheries of the North Pacific Ocean. Negotiations are continuing with the authorities of Taiwan and the Republic of Korea. Canada is not participating in these negotiations, but is expected to play a significant role in any future multilateral arrangements to regulate the high-seas driftnet fisheries.

nations whose fishing activities are found to diminish the effectiveness of international fishery conservation programs.

BERING SEA "DONUT HOLE" FISHERIES

One of the more important international fisheries issues that the United States is now addressing does not concern Canada directly, but is likely to have some spillover effects, either economically or politically. The "donut hole" is that portion of the central Bering Sea that is entirely surrounded by the two-hundred-mile economic zones of the United States and the Soviet Union. In response to the phase-out of foreign fishing within the U.S. EEZ, and similar developments in Canada and the Soviet Union, the large foreign factory fleets developed a new pollock fishery in the donut hole. The harvest increased very rapidly, from 93 thousand metric tons in 1980 to nearly 1.3 million metric tons in 1987. The nations known to be participating in this fishery are Japan, the Republic of Korea, Poland, and the People's Republic of China. The Soviets report that vessels from North Korea and Taiwan may also be involved.

The United States has two reasons for concern. First, in early 1988, a private plane chartered by a U.S. fishermen's association videotaped eight modern Japanese trawler-processors illegally fishing on Bower's Ridge, one of the most productive fishing areas in the U.S. EEZ, and one that is quite close to the donut hole. This videotape confirmed industry suspicions that some foreign vessels were using the donut hole as a sanctuary from which to stage illegal fishing forays into the U.S. EEZ. Second, the Alaska pollock being taken is believed to be from a single stock that spends part of its life cycle in the donut hole and the rest within the U.S. and Soviet economic zones. Thus, in the absence of any internationally agreed limits on foreign fishing in the donut hole, the pollock fishery within the U.S. EEZ could be harmed.

To address the data problems, the United States sponsored a scientific symposium in Sitka, Alaska, in July 1988, attended by scientists from all nations known to fish the donut hole; a Canadian scientist also attended. The United States is also supporting the Canadian-led effort to form a multilateral scientific organization to deal with all North Pacific environmental science issues.

To address the political problem, the United States has met with the Soviet Union several times to discuss various options under international law that may be used to bring the other nations to the bargaining table. One of the options would recognize the Bering Sea's status under the Law of the Sea Convention as a semi-enclosed sea for which coastal nations have special responsibility.[14] Interestingly,

---

14   Articles 122 and 123 of the United Nations Convention of the Law of the Sea, final text, Montego Bay, 10 December 1982.

one of the precedents examined in this respect involved Canada's assertion of special rights over the Gulf of St. Lawrence before the extension of its two-hundred-mile limit.

To address the illegal fishing, the United States is also considering some new measures, such as the use of satellite navigational transponders, and some new restrictions on foreign fishing vessels, including gear stowage requirements. Canadian precedent was used to support the latter requirements.

REVIEW AND CONCLUSIONS

This paper has reviewed some of the joint efforts between the United States and Canada to achieve, through international agreements, sustainable yields of living marine resources in the Pacific Ocean. Two of these arrangements have fully met expectations, one has failed, and two have produced only limited results.

Both the Pacific Salmon Treaty and the International Pacific Halibut Convention have been successful thus far, but there are still serious problems to be resolved. The salmon treaty may be successful because its goal of balancing interceptions between the two nations is quite limited. Since both nations share this objective, each is free to rebuild its stocks in confidence that its own fishermen will benefit. The problem to be resolved is the current trade dispute.

The halibut convention has been very successful in rebuilding the stocks. However, because it focuses only on a single species, it cannot address the dispute between the United States and Canada concerning the levels of by-catch to be allowed in the Alaskan groundfisheries. Moreover, and again because of political constraints, the United States has not realized the full economic benefits available from its share of the halibut resource.

The Fur Seal Convention, once the model for international management of natural resources, failed because public opposition to commercial sealing prevented the United States from ratifying an extension of the treaty. This failure, regrettably, has left the seals unprotected throughout much of their migratory range.

The INPFC has relocated the Japanese salmon fishery westward, to the benefit of U.S. and Canadian stocks. However, the development of major squid-driftnet fisheries beyond the two-hundred-mile limits threatens those stocks. U.S. economic sanctions may be used to address this problem in the future.

Finally, the United States and the Soviet Union have thus far failed to obtain international cooperation in regulating the expanding third-party fisheries in the Bering Sea donut hole. With the elimination of foreign fishing within its EEZ, the United States has little leverage, other than trade sanctions, to bring the other parties to the bargaining table.

IN SEARCH OF
SUSTAINABLE DEVELOPMENT
IN NOVA SCOTIA'S FISHERIES

David VanderZwaag, Peter Stokoe, Cynthia Lamson, and Ray Cote*

Jigging in a raging sea! That is the way politicians, bureaucrats, and academics may often feel when confronted with fisheries management issues, for the social, economic, scientific, and legal complexities are overwhelming. The fishing industry is difficult to understand because of its "spread-out" nature. In Nova Scotia alone there are nearly 16,000 fishermen, over 9,000 fish plant workers, over 350 licensed processing plants,[1] and about 400 fishing ports.[2] The Atlantic Fishery Regulations, 1985 list thirty groundfish species, such as cod, haddock, and pollock, and five pelagic fish, such as capelin, herring, and mackerel, not to mention crabs, scallops, shrimp, lobsters, and squid, as subject to regulation.[3] Waves of conflict abound in the industry: conflicts between inshore and offshore fisheries, fixed and mobile gear, recreational and commercial, domestic and foreign. Scientific uncertainties provide an unstable undercurrent. Stock assessments are given without confidence levels and are often perceived by fishermen as "mathematical fictions." Migratory patterns of fish stocks and ecological relationships in the marine environment are still not well understood. For example, the dependence of inshore lobster stocks on offshore stocks is unknown,[4] and the increased landings of lobsters in the 1980s is believed to be caused by an unidentified, widespread environmental change.[5]

This paper takes the reader on a "jigging journey," testing the Nova Scotia waters for sustainable development by drifting across six topics. The first section provides an overview of Nova Scotia's fisheries and highlights the growing awareness that "small is okay." A second section discusses the resource status of, and the regulatory frameworks for, the four major Nova Scotian marine fisheries — lobsters, groundfish, scallops, and herring[6] — and raises the need for creative

---

*   The authors would like to acknowledge the assistance of Neil Stalport, Research Assistant, Oceans Institute of Canada, the information provided by John Angel and Greg Peacock (Department of Fisheries and Oceans) and Peter Underwood (Nova Scotia Department of Fisheries), and the financial support of the Donner Canadian Foundation.

1   Nova Scotia Department of Fisheries, *Fisheries: A Policy for Nova Scotia, 1989* (Halifax: Government Printer, 1989) at 5.

2   *Id.* at 13.

3   Atlantic Fishery Regulations, 1985, SOR/86-21, Schedule 1.

4   *The Scotia-Fundy Lobster Fishery: Phase I — Issues and Considerations Summary Report* (Working Committee Draft Report for Industry Consultation, February 1989) (unpublished) at 18.

5   *Id.* at 21.

6   In 1987 lobster landings in Nova Scotia totalled 18,423 tonnes worth $160,341,000; cod landings totalled 132,493 tonnes worth $120,747,000; scallop landings were 66,295 tonnes valued at

experimentation in lessening regulatory complexity, reducing over-capacity, and forging new forms of co-management. The third section provides examples of recent conflicts between fisheries and other ocean users — for example, between aquaculture and recreational users — and examines the existing legal regime's inability to foster integrated ocean management. This is followed by a brief discussion of the dependency of fisheries sustainability on other economic sectors, such as tourism and forestry, and on environmental quality. Another section highlights the need to consider international impacts on sustainable fisheries development, such as the accessibility of export markets and the effects of sea-level rise on coastal communities. The final section summarizes recent policy and program initiatives that promise to further sustainable development.

NOVA SCOTIA'S FISHERIES: "SMALL IS OKAY"

Historically, Atlantic fishing communities have been at the periphery of economic and political power, owing largely to geographic and associated demographic factors. However, the dawning of Marshall McLuhan's era of the "global village" has eradicated most traditional barriers to societal integration; instantaneous communications and modern transportation networks, for example, now enable residents of "rural" fishing communities to enjoy relatively cosmopolitan lifestyles, with access to services once restricted to urban centres.

Fishing, which was once regarded as "employment of last resort," has been radically transformed in the decade since Canada declared a two-hundred-nautical mile zone of exclusive fisheries jurisdiction in 1977. With the proliferation of regulations to ensure resource protection and control harvesting, together with rapid technological advances, escalating costs, and intensified market competition, participants must apparently see major offsetting benefits to remain in the occupation.[7] Given the physical and economic risks associated with fishing, the question "Why do people continue to fish and live in small communities?" is a conundrum to many analysts. The answer, however, is straightforward: fishing ranks highly in two key dimensions — job satisfaction (indices include independence, earnings, variety, adventure, quality of the work environment, time available with family) and community attachment (frequent and continuous interaction with a network of kin and neighbours).[8]

Recent statistics reveal that, on average, Atlantic fishermen spend 17.5 weeks

---

$83,463,000. Following other groundfish species—haddock and pollock—herring ranked sixth in value at $18,868,000 for 98,392 tonnes. See Nova Scotia Department of Fisheries, *supra*, note 1 at 6.

7   C. Lamson & A.J. Hanson, eds., *Atlantic Fisheries and Coastal Communities: Fisheries Decision-Making Case Studies* (Halifax: Dalhousie Ocean Studies Programme, 1984).

8   R. Apostle, L. Kasdan & A. Hanson, "Work Satisfaction and Community Attachment Among Fishermen in Southwest Nova Scotia" (1985) 42 Can. J. Fish. Aquat. Sci. 256.

fishing, 6 weeks preparing for the fishery, 4 weeks in other income-earning employment, 17 weeks collecting unemployment insurance benefits, and 5 weeks in other activities. Fishermen in southwest Nova Scotia enjoyed the longest season in Atlantic Canada (averaging 26.1 weeks). In addition, their incomes were generally higher than average because of access to lobster and scallop resources. The average income of Nova Scotia fishermen from all sources was $19,459 (with 10.2 weeks of UIC benefits), compared to average incomes of $13,893 for Atlantic fishermen.[9]

Seasonality, resource dependency, small-scale, uncertainty: such labels were once used to explain the ills and inherent weaknesses of the Atlantic fishing industry. However, these same factors are now being described as strengths, as illustrated by the 1986 Report of Newfoundland's Royal Commission on Employment and Unemployment, *Building On Our Strengths:*

> The title of our Report asserts that, in working towards a post-industrial society, we have strengths — not just social strengths but economic strengths as well — that have been too little recognized. Flexibility, adaptability, occupational pluralism, home production, the rhythm of a seasonal lifestyle, household self-reliance.... In almost all the blueprints offered us for industrialization, these have been seen as barriers to economic development.[10]

Whereas Nova Scotia's 1989 Fisheries Policy also makes a commitment to maintaining diversity and the small and semi-rural character of the industry, the document fails to identify specific strategies whereby policy objectives might be implemented:

> The small port and semi-rural character of much of our province is deemed a desirable quality by Nova Scotians and must be preserved. Priority will be given to maintaining existing jobs, fishing communities and traditional life styles. At the same time, the province will continue to encourage and support technical innovations or developments which display clear advantages in economic return, market access and resource conservation.[11]

In March 1989, the Atlantic Environmental Network sponsored a conference entitled "Sustaining Our Communities" at the Memramcook Institute in St. Joseph, New Brunswick. A Conference Working Group suggested that "developing sustainability" was an appropriate goal (as opposed to promoting "sustainable development"), since flexibility and communications are important attributes for small communities facing uncertainty and change.[12] Thus, although few prescriptions about *how* to approach these objectives are yet in circulation, there is growing consensus that small is both "okay" and desirable.

---

9   Canada, Department of Fisheries and Oceans, *1984 Survey of Atlantic Fishermen* (Ottawa: Department of Supply and Services, 1987).

10   Newfoundland, Royal Commission on Employment and Unemployment, *Building on Our Strengths* (St. John's: Queen's Printer, 1986) (Chair: D. House) at 24.

11   See Nova Scotia Department of Fisheries, *supra*, note 1.

12   F. Sloan, "Sustaining our Communities" (1989) 7(2) Between the Issues (Newsletter of the Ecology Action Centre, Halifax) 26.

FISHERIES RESOURCE STATUS AND REGULATORY FRAMEWORK

Constitutional and Regulatory Overview

"Complexity within simplicity" describes the Canadian approach to fisheries management. The overall legal framework is quite simple. Section 91(12) of the Constitution Act 1867 grants the federal government legislative jurisdiction over sea coast and inland fisheries, while provinces have jurisdiction over fisheries insofar as "property and civil rights" and "the management and sale of public lands" are involved — for example, the licensing of fish plants on provincial lands.[13] The Fisheries Act[14] is the fountainhead of federal regulatory control over domestic fishing. Section 7 grants the Minister of Fisheries and Oceans the "absolute discretion" to issue fishing licences, while Section 9 allows for licence cancellation if licence conditions are not followed. Section 43 grants Cabinet the power to regulate almost all aspects of fisheries, from fishing gear to protection of spawning grounds.

Complexity enters through the hundreds of pages making up the Atlantic Fishery Regulations, 1985 (as amended), the detailed conditions of individual licences, and the managerial abilities to suddenly vary fishing quotas and closed seasons. Section 33 of the Atlantic Fishery Regulations spells out the kinds of licence conditions, which may include species and quantity of fish, type of vessel, gear type, fishing location, and timing. Section 4 of the Regulations allows a Regional Director-General to vary by order any fishing quota or close-time.

The actual setting and allocating of quotas is carried out through consultation with industry advisory committees after the Canadian Atlantic Fisheries Scientific Advisory Committee, a peer review group of scientists, provides advice on stock status. For example, the yearly Atlantic Groundfish Management Plan involves major consultations with the fishing industry in June (Atlantic Groundfish Advisory Committee) and in October (Offshore Vessel Owners Working Group, Independent Offshore Group, and the Atlantic Groundfish Advisory Committee), as well as various governmental reviews.

Case law has largely upheld federal jurisdiction over fisheries. In the well-known 1898 Fisheries Reference (*Attorney-General for the Dominion of Canada* v. *Attorneys-General for the Provinces of Ontario, Quebec and Nova Scotia*[15]), Lord

---

13   For further discussion of the Constitution and fisheries, see H.S. Fairley, "Canadian Federalism, Fisheries and the Constitution: External Constraints on Internal Ordering" (1980) 12 Ottawa L. Rev. 257; and D.L. VanderZwaag, *The Fish Feud: The U.S. and Canadian Boundary Dispute* (Toronto: Lexington Books, 1983) at 63.

14   R.S.C. 1985, c. F-14.

15   [1898] A.C. 700 (P.C.).

Herschell indicated that federal regulatory power over fisheries is exceedingly broad, even though the federal government has no proprietary rights in fisheries:

> [T]he power to legislate in relation to fisheries does necessarily to a certain extent enable the Legislature so empowered to affect proprietary rights. An enactment, for example, prescribing the times of the year during which fishing is to be allowed, or the instruments which may be employed for the purpose ... might very seriously touch the exercise of proprietary rights, and the extent, character, and scope of such legislation is left entirely to the Dominion Legislature.... The supreme legislative power in relation to any subject-matter is always capable of abuse, but it is not to be assumed that it will be improperly used; if it is, the only remedy is an appeal to those by whom the legislature is elected.[16]

In a more recent case, *Re Minister of Fisheries and Oceans and Gulf Trollers Association,*[17] the Federal Court of Appeal upheld the federal government's power to manage the fisheries for not just *conservation* purposes but also *socio-economic* reasons. In that case, Gulf Trollers, the owners and operators of commercial fishing vessels, contested the federal government's regulatory power to favour sport fishermen over commercial fishermen, which it did by closing the Chinook salmon fishery in the Strait of Georgia and the Strait of Juan de Fuca for only one hour per year for sport fishing, but for nearly ten months for commercial fishing. The Court concluded that federal fishery officers could vary the salmon fishing close-time for socio-economic reasons as well as for conservation purposes.[18]

The Canadian Charter of Rights and Freedoms[19] has opened new doors for fishermen to challenge regulations, based on such arguments as equality and mobility rights, but thus far courts (perhaps to the benefit of sustainable development) have largely upheld government regulations. In *MacKinnon* v. *Canada (Fisheries and Oceans)*[20] a Nova Scotia fisherman whose vessel had been arrested for fishing off Newfoundland argued that the federal government's Sector Management Plan, which limited the inshore groundfish fleet of vessels under 65 feet (some 15,000 vessels) to home port sectors (Scotia-Fundy, Newfoundland, Gulf of St. Lawrence) where fishing had traditionally occurred, violated his equality and mobility rights. The Federal Court, Trial Division, however, found that the Plan did not discriminate against him on the basis of any personal characteristic, such as race or national origin, and that the limitation of small fishing vessels to sectors had a rational basis of fairly allocating fish stock quotas and assisting in vessel monitoring. The Court also found that his mobility rights were not violated, since the geographical restrictions imposed on the inshore fishing fleet were of general application and were based, not on provincial residence, but on the areas historically fished.

---

16   *Id.* at 712–713.

17   (1986), 32 D.L.R. (4th) 737 (F.C.A.D.).

18   *Id.* at 747.

19   Canadian Charter of Rights and Freedoms, Part I of the Constitution Act, 1982, being Schedule B of the Canada Act 1982 (U.K.), 1982, c. 11.

20   [1987] 1 F.C. 490 (F.C.T.D.).

In *Munroe* v. *Canada*[21] the Court similarly upheld the federal licensing policy of restricting lobster fishing in District 4A off Nova Scotia to vessels under 45 feet in length. Munroe, who wanted to fish lobsters with a 59-foot vessel, argued that his right to equality was violated, since fishermen in other districts could fish lobster from larger vessels. Perhaps because the plaintiff's lawyer did not submit a legal brief on the Charter argument, the Court rather summarily rejected the equality argument, but the judge was probably influenced by the conservation rationale for the vessel length restriction. If large vessels were kept out of the fishery, fishing would for practical purposes be restricted to inshore grounds, leaving the larger lobsters in middle grounds as a spawning stock supporting the inshore lobster fishery.

A few cases have upheld Charter arguments in the fisheries area. In *R.* v. *D'Entremont*,[22] a Nova Scotia County Court judge upheld the defendant's argument that 1978 Atlantic Fishery Regulations (since repealed) discriminated against operators of big vessels (over 65 feet) fishing for scallops. Even though small and big vessels might fish side by side in some areas, and even though the same gear was used, federal regulations imposed a stricter "meat count" (39 meats per 500 grams) on the larger vessels. The court found such a requirement without rational basis and violative of the defendant's right to equality under the Charter. In another Nova Scotia case, a fisherman who was arrested for exceeding his catch limit argued that the variation order decreasing allowable catches by 2,000 kilograms was of no effect since it had been broadcast only in English and not in his language of preference, French. The county court's ruling in the fisherman's favour, according to a recent newspaper report,[23] will be appealed by the Crown prosecutor.

A further constitutional issue, on which provinces may disagree as to implications for sustainable development, is the possibility of rearranging federal-provincial powers over fisheries. Section 50(1) of The Meech Lake Accord calls for a constitutional conference at least once each year, and one of the agenda items is to be "roles and responsibilities in relation to fisheries" (Section 50(2)(b)). Nova Scotia is worried that provincial vessels may be excluded from fishing off Newfoundland, and thus, as recently stated in the 1989 Fisheries Policy, has favoured continued federal jurisdiction over fisheries:

> Nova Scotia deems it essential that the federal government retain exclusive jurisdiction over management of the marine fisheries, especially stocks which migrate or which are harvested by fishermen from several provinces. Viewed as a "Canadian resource" the marine fisheries must not be subject to trends towards provincial quota allocations, provincial "territorial waters" or undue barriers to the mobility of fishing fleets. In addition shared jurisdiction between provincial and

---

21   (1987) 6 F.T.R. 149 (F.C.T.D.).

22   (1988) 81 N.S.R. (2d) 134, 203 A.P.R. 134 (N.S. Co. Ct.).

23   R. Gorham, "Broadcast in Both Languages—Judge" *The [Halifax] Chronicle-Herald* (12 April 1989) 25.

federal governments is not desirable. The views of the province, however, must be considered in the management of these fisheries stocks, especially regarding socio-economic matters.[24]

As the following review of specific fisheries — lobster, groundfish, scallop, and herring — will show, Canada has had a track record of strictly regulating and restoring fish stocks since extending its jurisdiction in 1977, but innovative changes still need to be examined if sustainable fisheries development is to be achieved.

The "Big Four" Fisheries: Resource Status and Regulatory Framework

Lobster

While the Canadian Atlantic Fisheries Scientific Advisory Committee (CAFSAC) in 1987 concluded that inshore lobster resources were being exploited at a rate higher than maximum yield,[25] inshore lobster landings have shown steady growth. Scotia-Fundy region landings in 1987 were 14,700 tonnes compared to 4,500 tonnes in 1978, and the value of landings has increased from $25 million in 1978 to $139 million in 1987.[26] Offshore lobster catches have also shown an overall increase. In 1981, 572 tonnes were landed, compared to 779 tonnes in 1986 and 609 tonnes in 1987.[27]

Canada has tightly regulated both the inshore and offshore fisheries. The offshore fishery, conducted by eight vessels operating in lobster fishing area 41, located fifty miles from the coast,[28] has been subject to an overall quota (720 tonnes for 1988) with individual vessels receiving specific quota allocations through an Enterprise Allocation Program.[29] Each offshore vessel is restricted to a maximum of 1,000 traps.[30] Both offshore and inshore lobster fisheries are forbidden to keep undersize lobsters (81 millimetres for most areas)[31] and to possess any female lobster with eggs attached.[32] Inshore fishermen have been subject to limited-entry licensing and trap limits since the late 1960s, and a government-funded buy-back program took 1,300 licences out of service between 1978 and 1981, leaving about 3,100 licences since 1982 and approximately 7,000 fishermen participating as

---

24   See Nova Scotia Department of Fisheries, *supra,* note 1 at 8.

25   Canadian Atlantic Fisheries Scientific Advisory Committee (CAFSAC), *Annual Report, Volume 10* (1987) at 9.

26   *The Scotia-Fundy Lobster Fishery, supra,* note 4 at 29.

27   Canada, Department of Fisheries and Oceans, *1988 Offshore Lobster Fishery Management Plan* (Halifax: Department of Fisheries and Oceans, 1989) at 8.

28   Atlantic Fishery Regulations, 1985, SOR/86-21, Schedule XIII, Part II.

29   *1988 Offshore Lobster Fishery Management Plan, supra,* note 27 at 4, 7, 8.

30   *Id.* at 11.

31   Atlantic Fishery Regulations, 1985, SOR/86-21, Schedule XIV.

32   *Id.,* s. 59(3).

owners, captains, or crew.[33] Closed seasons are in effect for all inshore lobster fishing areas; for example, for area 33[34] the close time is June 1 to the last Monday in November.[35]

On April 29, 1988, Fisheries and Oceans Minister Tom Siddon announced an in-depth study of the Scotia-Fundy lobster fishery, and a February 1989 Draft Report[36] has raised a number of issues related to sustainability of the fishery that will be further discussed in Phase II of the study, through consultations with the Scotia-Fundy Regional Lobster Committee and Lobster Fishing Area Committees. Most fishermen agree that existing penalties for exceeding trap limits are not severe enough[37] and enforcement is inadequate; the question raised is whether industry can do more to police itself. A critical and controversial question is whether new lobster licences should be issued for the inshore or offshore. Additional licences would allow more persons to "make a living," but would probably reduce overall net incomes. Inshore fishermen worry about the offshore lobster fishery's negative effects on the inshore, and have opposed any new licences. Debate also continues over the appropriate minimum size for lobsters and the appropriate trap limit.[38]

The Department of Fisheries and Oceans (DFO) plans to enact new regulations in 1989, a number of which promise to strengthen sustainability in the lobster fishery. The minimum legal lobster carapace size may be increased by 1.5 millimetres and an amendment in 1991 may increase the minimum size to 84 millimetres.[39] The size increase is expected to increase the long-term yield, as more lobsters will survive to spawning age. Mechanisms to permit the escape of small lobsters will be required on all lobster traps.[40] Wire lobster traps, which if lost may undertake "ghost fishing," will be required to have decomposable escape panels.[41]

The Working Committee on the Scotia-Fundy Lobster Fishery has also questioned the adequacy of the consultation regime, and two previous incidents do raise the question of the appropriate institutional framework for lobster management. In 1983, when lobster trap limits were decreased, two fishery patrol vessels were burned in West Pubnico, Nova Scotia. Another highly publicized fishery protest

---

33   *The Scotia-Fundy Lobster Fishery, supra,* note 4 at 25, 52, 53.

34   Atlantic Fishery Regulations, 1985, Schedule XIII, Part V, as am. SOR/87-468.

35   *Id.,* Schedule XIV.

36   *The Scotia-Fundy Lobster Fishery, supra,* note 4.

37   Section 79(1) of the Fisheries Act, *supra,* note 14, provides that anyone who contravenes provisions of the Act or Regulations is subject to a $5,000 fine or to imprisonment up to twelve months or both.

38   *The Scotia-Fundy Lobster Fishery, supra,* note 4 at 61.

39   Canada, Office of Privatization and Regulatory Affairs, *Federal Regulatory Plan 1989* (Ottawa: Department of Supply and Service, 1988) at 168.

40   *Id.*

41   *Id.*

was triggered when the Minister announced on December 31, 1987, that he was issuing four licences to develop an experimental offshore lobster fishery. This controversy was fuelled by three factors: surprise (there was no prior announcement of the plan), charges of political favouritism (the firms involved were known to have strong ties with the incumbent government), and the Minister's deliberate or accidental misreading of scientific advice provided by CAFSAC. Initially, no information was released to explain the issuance of the new licences or the mechanics of the selection process.[42] For nearly four months, fishermen tried to persuade the Minister's Office to suspend the licences. Ultimately, fourteen members of the District 34 Lobster Advisory Committee resigned, citing objections that the new licences could threaten the existing inshore fishery. Eventually, on April 29, the Minister retreated, and announced that he was suspending the licences pending a report on the socio-economic conditions within the industry.

Groundfish

A crisis in the groundfish industry has been created by the decline in stocks, particularly of cod and haddock, on the Scotian Shelf and Grand Banks. Although the total Canadian quota for all Atlantic groundfish species dropped from 1,012,254 tonnes in 1984 to 972,965 tonnes in 1986, for an overall reduction of 39,289 tonnes,[43] in 1989 the Fisheries and Oceans Minister announced a drastic decrease in the northern cod stock quota alone, from 266,000 to 235,000 tonnes. In March 1989, three Nova Scotia processing plants announced closures — including the Clearwater Fine Foods, Inc. plant in Port Mouton, which provided about 40 full-time and 110 seasonal jobs — and eight or nine additional closings were predicted because of a shortage of fish.[44]

A complex management system has been imposed to control fishing of Atlantic groundfish, only the basics of which can be summarized here. The two key regulatory levers are close-times/areas and quotas. The Atlantic Fishery Regulations, 1985 adopt the area-zoning system of the Convention on Future Multilateral Cooperation in the Northwest Atlantic Fisheries,[45] and establish close-times in zoned areas for twenty-four classes of vessels.[46] Vessels are classed according to length and gear-type: for example, a Class A-1 vessel is less than 45 feet in length using fixed gear; a Class C-1 vessel is under 45 feet using mobile gear; a Class

---

42   R. Gorham, "Fishermen's Paranoia Over Offshore Lobster Licences Justifiable" *The [Halifax] Chronicle-Herald* (27 January 1988) 7.

43   Canada, Department of Fisheries and Oceans, *1986 Atlantic Groundfish Management Plan* (Ottawa: Department of Fisheries and Oceans, 1985) at 13; *1988 Atlantic Groundfish Management Plan* (Ottawa: Department of Fisheries and Oceans, 1987) at 18.

44   B. Ward, "Fish Plant Closures Predicted: Hundreds Will Lose Jobs in 1989 — Clearwater Head" *The [Halifax] Chronicle-Herald* (29 March 1989) 1.

45   Atlantic Fishery Regulations, 1985 SOR/86-21, Schedule III.

46   *Id.,* Schedule XXIII, as am. SOR/88-141.

A-2 is between 45 and 65 feet and uses fixed gear; and a Class C-2 vessel is 45–65 feet and uses mobile gear.[47] The Atlantic Groundfish Plan sets overall quotas for each stock area, with the area quotas allocated among the vessel classes. Considerable complexity is introduced by Section 4 of the Regulations, which allows sudden variation of close-times and fishing quotas. Even when an area is closed to a prohibited species, a vessel is allowed to fish for other groundfish species and to retain a 10 percent by-catch,[48] and some vessels are allowed to catch up to 1,500 kilograms of a prohibited species per fishing trip,[49] which limit may also be varied. The Regulations thus create a constantly shifting system of closed areas, seasonal quotas, and trip limits, in addition to imposing size requirements on both mesh[50] and fish.[51]

A program of specific company quotas, called enterprise allocations, was introduced for large vessels in 1984 and has proven successful in stabilizing harvesting and processing for large companies. No longer forced to grab for a share of a global quota, companies have been able to pace catches throughout the year. On December 20, 1988, the Minister of Fisheries and Oceans announced continuation of the program on a permanent basis.

The recent crisis in the groundfish industry is blamed on fishing over-capacity (particularly of the inshore fleet's 45–65 foot vessels), previous catch misreporting, and processing over-capacity. The groundfish fleet, if all vessels are active, has the potential to exert four times the sustainable fishing effort.[52] Misreporting of catch level by almost one-third is shown by 1985 inconsistencies between fishermen's reports and plant production: Nova Scotia cod, haddock, and pollock landings were reported at 227,000 tonnes, yet plant production converted to round weight (before gutting) was 304,000 tonnes.[53] Recognizing the problem of "too many processors for too few fish," the provincial Minister of Fisheries, on March 30, 1989, announced a moratorium on new fish plant and fish buyer licences.[54]

Calls for management changes to assure greater sustainability in the fisheries

---

47   *Id.*, s. 2(1), as am. SOR/88-141.

48   *Id.*, s. 88(1).

49   *Id.*, s. 88(2), as am. SOR/88-141.

50   For example, no one is allowed to fish for groundfish with an otter trawl having a mesh size less than 130 millimetres or to use a gill net with a mesh size less than 140 millimetres. *Id.*, ss. 91, 92.

51   Minimum lengths have been set for cod, haddock, halibut, and pollock. For example, for cod the minimum length is 41 centimetres, and 31 centimetres if the head and tail are removed. *Id.*, s. 92.1, as am. SOR/88-231.

52   *Report of the Scotia-Fundy Groundfish Industry Capacity Advisory Committee* (November 1988) at 2.

53   Personal communication with P. Underwood, Groundfish Advisor, Nova Scotia Department of Fisheries (20 April 1989).

54   L. Legge, "Fish Licence Moratorium Issued: Indefinite Freeze Covers New Fish Plant, Buyer Licences" *The [Halifax] Chronicle-Herald* (31 March 1989) 1.

are coming from numerous sources. In Nova Scotia's 1989 Fisheries Policy, the province suggests that alternatives to the complex quota management system be developed, particularly for the inshore fleet, and advocates numerous measures to this end.[55] Conversion to hook-and-line fishing might be encouraged through financial incentives, and would lessen the wasteful catching and discarding of immature fish. Regulations might prohibit not only the catching and retaining on board of undersized fish, but also the landing of such fish. Mandatory gutting and icing of groundfish at sea would promote fishing for dollars rather than tonnes.[56] Development of nontraditional fisheries (such as silver hake) or underutilized species (such as mackerel) might divert excess fishing pressures.

In June 1987, a Groundfish Industry Capacity Advisory Committee, with federal, provincial, and industry representatives, was established to identify and evaluate options for long-term capacity control on the inshore groundfish sector. Recommendations in a November 1988 Report[57] include an industry-funded buy-back of licences over a five-year period, an increase in trawl and gillnet mesh sizes, and further investigation of individual transferrable catch quotas (ITQs) — that is, individual boat quotas that can be transferred to other fishermen. Other suggestions include higher penalties for violators and mandatory reporting of catches before vessels land.[58]

Scallops

While supplementary fishing of scallops occurs on the Scotian Shelf,[59] the most productive fishing occurs on Georges Bank and in the Bay of Fundy. Following overfishing by U.S. and Canadian vessels in the disputed zone of Georges Bank, Canadian catches plummeted to 1,945 tonnes in 1984 (the lowest since 1959), but improved after the World Court's boundary decision, with catches of 7,812 tonnes recorded in 1985, 4,670 tonnes in 1986, and 6,800 tonnes in 1987.[60] In the Bay of

55   Nova Scotia Department of Fisheries, *supra,* note 1 at 16–17.

56   See P. Underwood, *supra,* note 53.

57   *Report, supra,* note 52 at 6.

58   Three government-industry working groups have subsequently been established to further develop recommendations and assist in consultation. One committee is looking at separation of licences into two major categories, specialist for those fishing only groundfish and generalist for those fishing species other than groundfish. A second committee is exploring a licence buy-back program for the mobile dragger fleet, and a third is examining gear and management changes such as increasing mesh size and banning the use of two sizes of net on a boat. (Boats can now carry one size of mesh net for catching cod and another, smaller mesh net for catching silver hake.) See R. Gorham, "Ottawa to Discuss Overfishing Problem with N.S. Communities" *The [Halifax] Chronicle-Herald* (22 March 1989) 23.

59   Canadian Atlantic Fisheries Scientific Advisory Committee, "The Status of Scallop Resources on the Scotian Shelf" CAFSAC Advisory Doc. 88/14 at 7.

60   Canadian Atlantic Fisheries Advisory Committee, "Advice on the Management of Scallop Resources on Georges Bank" CAFSAC Advisory Doc. 88/10 at 1. The 1987 catch is based on provisional statistics.

Fundy, scallop catches have fluctuated sharply since commercial fishing began in the 1920s, with the most recent peak in landings in the 1982–83 season, when about 1,050 tonnes were caught. Catches fell to 130 tonnes in 1986–87, but have since been recovering.[61]

A multifaceted regulatory regime has continued to conserve stocks and maintain a successful industry of about 384 licensed vessels in the Bay of Fundy, 342 along the coast east of Baccaro,[62] and about 60 vessels fishing the offshore.[63] Following disputes among inshore and offshore fishermen in 1985–86, representatives of the region's scallop fleets met at a scallop seminar in September 1986, where they agreed to separate the fleets. Inshore vessels from the Bay of Fundy were to be phased out of the offshore Georges Bank fishery by 1989 by receiving reduced quota allotments,[64] and the offshore fleet agreed to stay out of the Bay of Fundy north of the 43 40' line. The Atlantic Fishery Regulations, 1985 establish scallop fishery areas[65] and corresponding close-times. Additional controls on Bay of Fundy vessels include a minimum shell height of 76 millimetres,[66] a meat count of 72 meats per 500 grams in most of the zone,[67] and gear restrictions such as a maximum scallop drag width of 5.5 metres.[68] Offshore vessels, which have been subject to an enterprise allocation program, are also subject to meat counts (for example, 33 meats per 500 grams for Georges Bank[69]) and trip limits (twelve days dock-to-dock) of 13,700 kilograms per trip.[70] To aid enforcement, offshore fishing operators are under a "hail requirement"; they must notify a fishery officer of their place and time of landing at least twelve hours before they arrive in port.[71]

A number of issues concerning the long-term sustainability of scallop resources are being debated. CAFSAC has recommended a much more moderate exploitation level of Bay of Fundy scallops ranging from 40 meats per 500 grams

61   Canadian Atlantic Fisheries Scientific Advisory Committee, "Advice on the Management of Scallops in the Bay of Fundy" CAFSAC Advisory Doc. 88/13 at 1.

62   Canada, Department of Fisheries and Oceans, *1987 Inshore Scallop Fishery Management Plan* (Halifax: Department of Fisheries and Oceans, 1987) at 4.

63   Canada, Department of Fisheries and Oceans, *1987 Offshore Scallop Fishery Management Plan* (Halifax: Department of Fisheries and Oceans, 1987) at 7.

64   The inshore fleet was to receive 548 tonnes in 1987 (8 percent of the Georges Bank TAC of 6,850 tonnes) and a decrease to 4 percent in 1988. See Canadian Atlantic Fisheries Scientific Advisory Committee, *supra*, note 59 at 1.

65   Atlantic Fishery Regulations, 1985 SOR/86-21, Schedule XV, Part II, as am. SOR/87-672, s. 9.

66   *Id.*, s. 64(5), as added SOR/87-672, s. 5(2).

67   *Id.*, s. 64(1), as am. SOR/87-672, s. 5(1). In an eight-mile conservation zone off Annapolis and Digby counties, the meat count is 55 meats per 500 grams.

68   *Id.*, s. 71, as am. SOR/87-672, s. 7.

69   *Id.*, s. 64(1), as am. SOR/87-672, s. 5(1).

70   *Id.*, s. 65(1).

71   *Id.*, s. 67(1), as added SOR/87-672, s. 6.

(outside zone) to 33 per 500 grams (inside zone within an eight-mile conservation area of the coast).[72] Licence buy-back programs to reduce over-capacity have been discussed.[73]

Herring

Overall, the picture for herring stocks seems quite positive. For the stock off southern Nova Scotia (Area 4WX), catches averaged above 100,000 tonnes throughout the 1970s.[74] Following a decline to 74,000 tonnes in 1986, the catch rebounded in 1987 to about 101,200.[75]

There have, however, been some problem areas. The Georges Bank herring fishery has suffered the tragedy of the commons. After peaking at 374,000 tonnes in 1968, the Georges Bank fishery disappeared by 1977, following excessive foreign fishing. In 1984 some one-year-old herring were found in a research survey, and spawning seems to have occurred in 1986 and 1987. The fishery remains closed and its future resurgence remains uncertain.[76] The catches of herring stocks off northern Nova Scotia have declined from 27,000 tonnes in 1973 to less than 5,000 since 1979. The 2,370 tonnes reported in 1987–88 was the lowest catch in twenty years.[77]

Besides limited entry, the key to controlling herring fisheries has been quota management. Herring fishing areas have been established by regulation.[78] The 1989 Scotia-Fundy Herring Management Plan, developed in consultation with the Scotia Fundy Herring Advisory Committee, set an overall herring quota of 151,200 tonnes.[79] The quota is further broken down among purse seiners (132,450 tonnes), trawlers (850), and fixed gear (gillnets, traps, and weirs: 17,900). The purse seiner quota is further divided according to season and area.

Managing For Sustainability

Social scientists have collected massive files of ethnographic data to document the existence of local-level resource management systems. Davis and Thiessen argue that effective management of the small-boat fishery in Atlantic Canada requires recognition of local concerns, knowledge, and practice:

---

72   See Canadian Atlantic Fisheries Scientific Advisory Committee, *supra,* note 60 at 2.

73   See Department of Fisheries and Oceans, *supra,* note 62 at 10.

74   The exception was 1979, when only 77,500 tonnes were caught. See Canadian Atlantic Fisheries Scientific Advisory Committee, "Advice and Management of Herring in Divisions 4VWX and 5 in 1989," CAFSAC Advisory DOC. 88/21 at 1.

75   *Id.*

76   *Id.* at 5.

77   *Id.* at 3.

78   Atlantic Fishery Regulations, 1985, SOR/86-21, Schedule VI, Part II, as am. SOR/87-265.

79   Department of Fisheries and Oceans, *1989 Scotia–Fundy Herring Management Plan* (Halifax: Department of Fisheries and Oceans, 1989).

The livelihood motive behind participation for most produces a recognition that exploitation must be conducted in a fashion that leaves sufficient ocean resources for the next fishing trip, fishing season, and generation. This ethos, while disrupted by state policies, has demonstrated that it can underwrite responsible, effective management practices.[80]

For years, such arguments were dismissed as "unscientific" or unworkable; thus, the option of local-level management was slow to gain legitimacy, particularly in scientific and administrative quarters, where professionals are trained to collect and apply quantitative and verifiable data. However, the inability of scientific approaches to realize resource protection objectives, combined with inefficiencies associated with protests and political intervention, has opened the door for changes in decision-making procedures.

Two examples from Nova Scotia illustrate fishermen's willingness to cooperate and/or initiate management activities when certain conditions exist: (1) when fishermen perceive that resources are threatened, and/or (2) when decision-making circumvents established procedures or principles.

On May 11, 1983, two fisheries patrol boats stationed in West Pubnico were burned by angry fishermen. Fishermen resented the imposition of new management measures by external authorities, and vented their frustrations on the vessels assigned to enforce the unpopular regulations. The escalation of civil protest to violence was unprecedented on the East Coast, and government eventually recognized that changes were necessary if regulatory compliance was ever to be restored. Thus, in June 1983, a District 4A Working Group was convened to negotiate a new trap limit system. Although fishermen and government officials disagreed over the total number of traps individuals could set during the spring and fall seasons, the immediate stalemate was resolved by a government proposal to introduce a flexible trap limit. Under this system, fishermen could elect to set more traps in the fall than in the spring, providing their combined total did not exceed 750 traps.[81]

An example of fishermen initiating management measures is provided by members of Maritime Fishermen's Union Local 4, who in spring 1989 launched a campaign to reduce littering of marine plastics at sea. Fishermen are major consumers of plastic products, including engine oil containers, packaging, and gear (for example, lines and nets, floats, buoys). The campaign is intended to raise public awareness about the adverse environmental impacts associated with discarding large quantities of plastics in the marine environment. One tangible result of the project to date has been publicity about the lack of adequate onshore waste-disposal facilities.[82]

---

80   A. Davis & V. Thiessen, "Public Policy and Social Control in the Atlantic Fisheries" (1988) 14 Can. Pub. Pol. 66 at 75.

81   J.F. Kearney, *Working Together: A Study of Fishermen's Response to Government Management of the District 4A Lobster Fishery* (Point-de-l'Eglise, N.E., 1984).

82   J. MacArthur, "Fishermen Campaign to Stop Litter at Sea" *Atlantic Fisherman* (21 April 1989) at 8.

In a seminal article entitled "A Ladder of Citizen Participation," Sherry Arnstein discusses eight categories of participation, ranging from non-participation to tokenism and degrees of citizen control.[83] Arnstein describes "consultation," a favourite term of resource policy-makers and managers throughout the 1970s, as tokenism, and argues that partnerships, delegated power, and citizen control are vital components of citizen power. Parenteau examined Canadian public participation models and concluded that, within the context of environmental decision-making, consultation has taken extreme forms: at one end of the continuum, consultation "brings together citizens expressing their views and a proponent trying to persuade them. At the other extreme, it brings together two partners, one of whom plays the role of opponent."[84] Although both models have occurred in fishery decision-making, the first type has been more prevalent.

Nearly twenty years later, the Brundtland Commission Report *Our Common Future* catapulted the two formerly "radical" concepts, local-level management and citizen control and power, into the sphere of international politics:

> The law alone cannot enforce the common interest. It principally needs community knowledge and support, which entails greater public participation in the decisions that affect the environment. This is best secured by decentralizing the management of resources upon which local communities depend, and giving these communities an effective say over the use of these resources. It will also require promoting citizen's initiatives, empowering people's organizations, and strengthening local democracy.[85]

In Canada, delegation of management authority to fishermen would probably require a legislative amendment and is unlikely to occur, given that the federal government bears responsibility for protecting marine resources on behalf of multiple, sometimes competing, stakeholders. However, a middle option, "co-management," is being tested in several countries, including Norway, the United States, the United Kingdom, and parts of Canada. Jentoft describes co-management as

> a meeting point between overall government concerns for efficient resource utilization and protection, and local concerns for equal opportunities, self-determination and self-control. The responsibility for initiating regulations is shared.[86]

The rationale for exploring co-management options for the Atlantic and Nova Scotia fisheries is gaining support from diverse sectors, including provincial legislators. For example, Jim Barkhouse, MLA (Nova Scotia) for Lunenburg East,

---

83   S.R. Arnstein, "The Ladder of Citizen Participation" (1969) 35(4) J. of Amer. Inst. of Planners 216.

84   R. Parenteau, *Public Participation in Environmental Decision-Making* (Ottawa: Federal Environmental Assessment Review Office, 1988) at 9–10.

85   World Commission on Environment and Development, *Our Common Future* (Oxford: Oxford University Press, 1987) (Chair: G.H. Brundtland) at 63.

86   S. Jentoft, "Fisheries Co-Management: Delegating Government Responsibility to Fishermen's Organizations" (1989) 13(2) Marine Policy 137 at 144.

introduced a House Resolution on March 3, 1989, with specific reference to revised management procedures:

> Whereas the looming crisis in Nova Scotia's small fishing villages is reaching a climax with the closure of fishing grounds; and
>
> Whereas the difficulties experienced in hundreds of small fishing villages will have disastrous widespread economic effect on the commerce throughout Nova Scotia; and
>
> Whereas the livelihood of the fishermen in these communities has prospered through self-management practices which has been disrupted by federal and provincial policies;
>
> Therefore be it resolved that in the opinion of the members of this House, effective management of the fisheries will be resolved when discussions on allocations are made as a result of input from all fishermen in the region.[87]

Recurrence of protests and mounting evidence that existing approaches have failed to achieve acceptable levels of resource protection — at least for some species — or to sustain community viability should be compelling reasons to reassess management practices. To date, protests by fishermen and coastal communities have been among the most effective means of gaining government attention. Responses have included temporary adjustments to fish quotas, licence suspensions, and the establishment of new advisory committees.

Protests have been highly effective communication mechanisms, enabling fishermen to penetrate the faceless fisheries bureaucracy and gain access to the pinnacle of management authority, the Minister of Fisheries and Oceans. In addition, protest activities have accelerated the broadening of management decision-making to community levels and have, through grievance articulation, opened doors of opportunity to alternative resource-management and conflict-resolution systems.

In the long run, however, protests cannot be relied upon to resolve fundamental structural problems in resource management, nor will they restore confidence between fishermen and managers. Open and continuous communications are critical and, as Pringle argues, the first step is for government personnel to "approach fishermen with the philosophy that the latter care for their resource .... It takes time for each to gain the confidence of the others. The scientist must present data in a format understandable to the layman; he must 'come clean' and admit a lack of knowledge where appropriate."[88]

Developing sustainability, therefore, must begin with broadening participation in resource decision-making. Participation must also be meaningful; the tokenism associated with "consultation" is no longer tenable. Since the concept of shared

---

87   Nova Scotia, House of Assembly, *Debates,* Res. No. 167 at 449–450 (3 March 1989).

88   J.D. Pringle, "The Human Factor in Fishery Resource Management" (1985) 42 Can. J. Fish. Aquat. Sci. 389 at 392.

resource management rights and responsibilities has been introduced in Canada through the DFO Arctic Marine Conservation Strategy Discussion Paper,[89] a precedent has been set, and the time to lobby for co-management in the Atlantic fisheries has finally arrived.

FISHERIES AND OCEAN USE CONFLICTS

The romantic vision of fisheries is the small boat on a tranquil sea silhouetted in the peaceful sunset. However, as three recent examples from Nova Scotia show, ocean use conflicts are on the rise, and the legal framework appears inadequate to the task of balancing ocean users' clashing values and interests. Examples of such resource-use conflicts include provincial aquaculture conflicts; a contentious ocean-mining proposal near Lunenburg, Nova Scotia; and opposition to Texaco's proposal to drill on Georges Bank.

Aquaculture

At first glance, aquaculture seems like a fishery's godsend. Aquaculture offers one of the few opportunities to expand fisheries, as "wild stocks" are presently over-harvested or pressed to their maximum sustainable yield. Aquaculture can be a marketer's dream, allowing the cultivation of high-value species that can be delivered at a pre-specified quantity and quality, and when market demand is most favourable. Aquaculture's need for clean marine waters may add an incentive to protect coastal environmental quality.

Aquaculture is already a rapidly growing industry in Nova Scotia, with some 400 active sites. Commercial facilities produce salmon, trout, mussels, oysters, and Irish Moss. Potential cultivations of the bay scallop, sea scallop, quahog and bar clam are being evaluated, and halibut, cod, and other species may be the subject of future aquaculture projects.[90]

A legal framework for aquaculture has even been sorted out between the federal and provincial governments. While the Fisheries Act (Section 58) gives the federal government power to issue licences for oyster beds, that government in 1986 signed an Agreement for Commercial Aquaculture Development with Nova Scotia to clarify responsibilities and coordinate activities. Nova Scotia is to administer licensing and leasing of aquaculture facilities; existing federal oyster licenses (about 230) are to remain valid[91]; and Nova Scotia is to take the lead in aquaculture education and training, as well as in identifying suitable sites. Canada will continue to conduct research into such areas as fish disease prevention, diet formulations, and

---

89   Canada, Department of Fisheries and Oceans, *Canadian Arctic Marine Conservation Strategy* (Ottawa: Department of Supply and Service, 1987).

90   Nova Scotia Department of Fisheries, *supra*, note 1 at 19.

91   Previously, licensing occurred pursuant to a 1936 federal-provincial agreement. See Oyster Fisheries Act, R.S.N.S. 1967, c. 220, Part II Schedule.

genetic selection. To foster cooperation, an Aquaculture Coordinating Committee of Nova Scotia has been established (as required by the Agreement), with representation from the aquaculture industry and the federal and provincial governments. The Aquaculture Act,[92] passed by Nova Scotia in 1983, sets out licensing and leasing requirements, with the key provision being Section 7(1): "No person shall carry on aquaculture without an aquaculture licence from the Minister." Section 9 requires the Minister of Fisheries to consult with other departments (such as the Department of Agriculture and the Department of the Environment) before granting an aquaculture licence, and a public hearing must be held to determine any objections.

And objections there have been! In late April 1989, the province turned down two aquaculture proposals for areas approximately twenty-five kilometres south of Halifax because of major opposition from residents. A recent headline in a Halifax newspaper read "Decisions 'Stagnate' Aquaculture."[93] The reasons residents gave for their strong opposition were varied: the unsightliness of aquaculture equipment such as floats, hazards to navigation, interference with traditional fishing areas, and loss of property values.[94] Statistics from the Nova Scotia Department of Fisheries show that of 282 long-term licence/lease applications received by April 28, 1989, 33 had been issued, 71 were approved pending a return of seabed surveys, 112 were under review, and 37 had been rejected.[95]

Criticisms of Nova Scotia's decision-making process for aquaculture operations has focused on the weakness of the public hearing process and on the lack of an appeal procedure for closure decisions. Section 5(3) of the Aquaculture Act leaves the conduct of public hearings to an appointed official from the Department of Fisheries. No legislative criteria for determining the acceptability of an aquaculture proposal are provided and there is no formal requirement to provide reasons for rejection. Rod McFarlane, treasurer of the Aquacultural Association of Nova Scotia, summed up industry dissatisfaction with the decision-making framework in these words:

> We fear that these decisions set a precedent that will lead to the stagnation of the aquaculture industry in Nova Scotia....
>
> The only reason given (for the refusal on water leases) is a political one. There is a need for a non-political, objective analysis done for contentious issues.[96]

---

92 S.N.S. 1983, c. 2.

93 R. Gorham, "Decisions 'Stagnate' Aquaculture" The [Halifax] Chronicle-Herald (29 April 1989) 33.

94 D. Sullivan, "Province Turns Down Two Aquaculture Applications" The [Halifax] Chronicle-Herald (26 April 1989) 3.

95 In addition, 15 applications were withdrawn, and 14 are on hold.

96 See Gorham, supra, note 93.

While numerous changes to the decision-making process for aquaculture siting are possible, at least four seem worth considering. First, an independent panel should be delegated the responsibility for conducting public hearings and advising or deciding on licence applications. The existing system leaves the Department of Fisheries in the rather awkward position of a promoter of aquaculture yet a protector of traditional fisheries, and the public may perceive a developmental bias. Second, clear criteria for acceptance or rejection of aquaculture sites should be set forth. For example, the State of Maine requires the Commissioner responsible for granting aquaculture licences to consider whether there is unreasonable interference with ingress and egress by riparian owners and unreasonable interference with navigation, fishing, ecologically significant flora and fauna, public beaches and parks, or public docking facilities.[97] Third, a social and environmental review should be required for proposed sites and made available to interested parties.[98] Fourth, provision should be made for alternative dispute resolution — for example, direct negotiation between the conflicting parties or mediation — to see if creative accommodations can be fostered.

An overall control and estuary management framework might also be looked to. Rather than deal with aquaculture requests one by one, decision-makers might initiate a long-range planning process for coastal areas facing or likely to face developmental pressures, whereby local residents could be involved in setting ocean use priorities. The seeds of such an approach appear in the Nova Scotia Aquaculture Act itself, for the provincial Cabinet, upon ministerial recommendation, can designate aquaculture development areas, where other activities can be restricted and where water-quality standards can be imposed not just for marine waters but also for watershed drainage areas.[99] The public is to be involved in such area designation through "public hearings, advisory committees or other opportunities for the expression of public opinion...."[100] The difficulty with such an approach is the fragmented nature of the planning envisaged — the public gets to be involved, albeit with aquaculture breathing down its collective neck. To date, no aquaculture development areas have yet been designated in Nova Scotia.

Ocean Mining and Fisheries

While offshore mining might be described as an "activity of the future," the experiences of a proposed offshore mineral exploration operation in 1988 raise the continued need to develop an adequate decision-making process for resolving ocean

---

97   Me. Rev. Stat. Ann. tit. 12 §6072(7-A) (West. Supp. 1988).

98   A related issue, of course, is who should be responsible for the review. The State of Maine requires the Department of Marine Resources to undertake an independent site review before the holding of public hearings.

99   Aquaculture Act, *supra*, note 92, s. 5.

100   *Id.*, s. 5(2)(b).

use conflicts. In 1988 geologist Dr. Terrence Day proposed to dredge, in search of gold deposits, off the shore area of the Ovens Park near Lunenburg, Nova Scotia. Following loud protests from lobster fishermen, who worried about interference with lobster habitat, and from the adjacent park owner, the provincial Department of Lands and Forests refused to allow the exploration activity to take place.[101]

The proposal's fate highlights the existing legal inadequacies. Federal offshore mining legislation is still under preparation and review. Provincial statutes, which could indirectly cover the activity through leasing requirements for provincial lands, provided no guarantee of public participation, nor any mechanism for dispute resolution. The province's Environmental Assessment Act[102] (as yet unproclaimed) holds some promise of filling the "process gap" by subjecting undertakings that might significantly affect the environment to environmental assessment review. However, the Act leaves a broad discretion in the Minister of Environment to choose the level of public review. The Minister can appoint an advisory committee to make recommendations,[103] or can refer an environmental assessment report to the Environmental Control Council, which has *options* available as to how to consult with the public — through written submission, a public hearing, or some other manner.[104]

The Fisheries and Georges Bank Hydrocarbon Exploration

Following the resolution of the ocean boundary dispute between the United States and Canada in 1984, Texaco Canada Resources Ltd. proposed to drill two exploratory holes on Georges Bank. The company's rough ride through regulatory uncertainty again calls into question the adequacy of the present legal framework for addressing ocean use conflicts.

While some form of "objective" review of Texaco's proposal might have been useful in ascertaining its environmental risks, knowledge gaps, and technological capabilities, the decision-making framework left a broad discretion as to whether a formal review would occur. The *Canada–Nova Scotia Offshore Petroleum Resources Accord* of 1986, wherein the federal and provincial governments agreed to cooperate in developing offshore oil and gas, granted the Canada–Nova Scotia Offshore Oil and Gas Board discretion to conduct a public review of prospective

---

101 The Department had a number of possible levers to halt the project, including a lease requirement under the Beaches and Foreshores Act, R.S.N.S. 1967, c. 19, or a lease of Crown lands under the Crown Lands Act, S.N.S. 1987, c. 5. For further background to the dispute, see J. James, "Dredge First — Consult Second" *[Lunenburg] Progress Enterprise* (12 October 1988) 1; and "Local Concerns Block Project Near the Ovens" *[Halifax] Mail Star* (12 October 1988) 9.

102 Bill 10, Environmental Assessment Act, 4th Sess., 54th Leg. N.S., 1988.

103 *Id.*, s. 14(b).

104 *Id.*, s. 15(1), 16(1).

projects and to require an environmental and socio-economic impact statement.[105] Formal public review under the federal Environmental Assessment Review Process might also have applied, but in the end political lobbying decided the project's fate.

The Nova Scotia fishing industry, viewing the project as a risk to the Bank's fish stocks, which are worth more than $100 million annually to the provincial economy, formed a lobby organization and successfully blocked the project. NORIG (No Rigs on Georges Bank), an association of fishing interests, lobbied both federal and provincial politicians, and on April 18, 1988, federal Energy Minister Marcel Masse announced a twelve-year ban on Georges Bank drilling.[106] While one may agree or disagree with the result, the decision highlights the uncertainties faced by proponents of offshore projects where decision-making hoops are cloaked in ministerial discretion.

FISHERIES AMID ECONOMIC AND ENVIRONMENTAL CURRENTS

Intersectoral Economic Dependencies

Sustainable fisheries may be dependent on other economic sectors. A sector of growing importance in helping to sustain fisheries communities is tourism. As well as providing general employment in services, tourism and fisheries can be mutually supportive. Many tourists are attracted to Atlantic Canada by its marine and coastal amenities. Visits to fishing villages and lobster suppers figure prominently among the region's attractions. Fishing trips — especially deep-sea fishing — sea-bird watching, and whale-watching are examples of activities that can attract well-to-do visitors, and directly supplement fishermen's incomes. The freshwater sport fisheries have also been important tourist and recreational attractions. The decline of these fisheries as a result of fishing pressure and environmental degradation — especially habitat destruction and acid rain — is only gradually being arrested, but hardly yet reversed.

Many coastal communities also derive some of their employment in other resource sectors, especially forestry. Forestry, not fisheries, is actually the largest resource industry in the Maritime Provinces, and tourism is fast outpacing fisheries for second place. Forestry far exceeds the fisheries in economic importance on the West Coast, but even there, tourism is challenging for the position of leading

---

105 *Canada–Nova Scotia Offshore Petroleum Resources Accord* (Halifax: Province of Nova Scotia, 1986) art. 24.

106 The law was subsequently formalized in mirror legislation. The Canada–Nova Scotia Offshore Petroleum Resources Accord Implementation Act, S.C. 1988, c. 28, passed by Parliament in July 1988, prohibits offshore hydrocarbon exploration or production until 1 January 2000, requires initiation of an environmental and socio-economic review by 1 January 1996, and allows the federal and provincial energy ministers to jointly extend the prohibition.

industry. The major problem with tourism as an industry, especially in eastern Canada, is that it is concentrated within a very short summer season.

Environmental Currents

Habitat protection and restoration are essential components of management strategies for all fisheries. Interspecies interactions (such as increases in cod parasites because of increases in populations of seals, which are intermediate hosts of the parasites) must also be taken into account. The issues of marine environmental quality in general, and water quality in particular, are crucial to the future of aquaculture. Environmental quality is a factor of growing importance for tourism and recreation. The Atlantic provinces still offer a relatively pristine environment, compared with more populous and industrialized areas, but aroused publics are demanding attention to a growing number of local scars. Tourism, rather than public health or fisheries, is cited as the main reason for plans to install treatment facilities for sewage discharged into Halifax Harbour. This will be one of the largest environmental protection projects ever undertaken in the region.

Like economic considerations, many environmental considerations are intersectoral. Forestry practices can have major impacts on fish habitat. Lay-offs in the forestry sector or other industries can increase pressure on the fisheries, as unemployed workers seek employment in the fisheries to replace their lost income. Aquaculture and the activities and residuals of tourism may conflict. Pollution from municipal, industrial, and agricultural sources may also threaten aquaculture operations and fisheries generally.

These considerations, as well as other interactions, such as multispecies fisheries relationships and competition between inshore and offshore fisheries, suggest a growing need for an ecosystem framework for management. This framework should take account both of ecological interactions and of the effects of harvesting and other environmental impacts on these interactions. It should consider how ecological interactions in the sea relate with economic interactions on the sea and on shore. Only by taking account of both sets of interactions can strategies hope to sustain both renewable resources in the ocean and human communities on land.

INTERNATIONAL RIPPLES OF SUSTAINABLE FISHERIES

Globalization of Trade

Contrary to the romantic conception of the history of the fisheries industries, stability appears to be more the exception than the rule. The speed with which the fortunes of individual fisheries change appears to have been accelerating in recent years. Thus, application of concepts of sustainability to the fisheries industries becomes increasingly difficult, as these industries are constantly in flux, with new products and new technologies — each subject to their own changing circumstances.

A major factor in the acceleration of change has been the advent of global markets in fish products. In these global markets, the marketing functions within fisheries industries assume an ever greater importance. Much of the recent history of the fisheries industries is one of creating and responding to new market opportunities.

This pre-eminence of the marketing function has in turn been a major factor in the emergence of the large, vertically integrated fishing companies on the East Coast, notably National Sea Products Limited, Fishery Products International (FPI) Limited, and Clearwater Fine Foods Incorporated. National Sea Products is based in Nova Scotia and has sales of over $500 million per year, mostly in groundfish products to Canada and the United States. FPI is based in Newfoundland and has sales of over $400 million per year, mostly to the United States and Europe. Together, National Sea and FPI hold over 80 percent of the "enterprise allocations" or quotas of offshore cod, or somewhat less than 40 percent of the total allowable catch of cod. Clearwater has recently grown rapidly into a company of comparable size, with annual sales of about $500 million. In its original major business, Clearwater became the world's largest exporter of lobster (between seven million and eight million pounds per year), although this now represents only 10 percent of its total revenue. More recently, Clearwater has expanded with the help of investments from the British food conglomerate Hillsdown Holdings Limited, buying up fish companies in Canada and abroad.[107] All three companies are becoming multinational conglomerates, with subsidiaries and affiliated businesses in the United States, Latin America, Europe, and the Far East.

No doubt these companies have a long-term interest in the stability and reliability of fish supply to their operations, and to this extent have a stake in the sustainability of the Atlantic fisheries — although their diversification into foreign fisheries could make them less dependent on this. This long-term interest does not, however, necessarily translate into greater sustainability for jobs and communities, as evidenced by a recent series of abrupt processing plant closures.

One of the manifestations of a responsiveness to the global market has been the introduction of new products and production technologies in the fisheries industries. New products, directed to specialized niches of the global market, can enhance revenues and profitability. However, they can also be more vulnerable to the vagaries of market conditions. For example, the herring roe industry has undergone rapid expansion in recent years, catering primarily to the Japanese market. The illness and subsequent death of the former Japanese emperor practically halted Japanese consumption of herring roe (considered there as a festive food), and resulted in a substantial, if temporary, setback for the roe industry.

---

107   J. Henderson, "Vision Steers Canada's New Sea King" *Financial Post* (8 September 1988) 17.

A new opportunity that arises in the global market can sometimes put overwhelming pressure on a local resource. From almost nothing at the beginning of the 1980s, the Queen crab fishery, centred in Shippegan, New Brunswick, grew to be the dominant fishery in the area by mid-decade. This growth resulted from a decline in the Alaskan crab fishery, which forced buyers, especially in the United States, to find new sources of supply. The strength of demand and prices was enough to make millionaires of some of the thirty or so fishermen who held crabfishing licences. Some observers believe that another result was illicit fishing, in excess of quotas. Whatever the cause, catches have declined rapidly over the last few years. Now, the question is only whether stocks and catches will stabilize, or whether more stringent control of fishing effort will be required. The hardest hit by these changes are the processing plant workers, who constitute a large fraction of the total labour force around Shippegan.

The opportunities and vulnerabilities of participation in global fisheries markets will probably increase with further trade liberalization. The great question of the moment is whether this liberalization in general, and the Free Trade Agreement with the United States in particular, will require changes to the federal government's roles in the fisheries and precipitate major structural changes in these industries. The major topical concern in this regard is the fate of unemployment insurance, which supplements the incomes of many workers in the fisheries industries, although other programs could also be affected.

Climate Change and Coastal Communities

Even if international efforts are successful in reducing atmospheric emissions and delaying greenhouse warming, some climate warming is still probable. While it is difficult to anticipate all of the paths whereby climate change could affect a region and a society, some potential impacts could have important socio-economic implications.

A warmer climate could induce a northward shift in the geographic range of fish species on the continental shelf, and therefore also require shifts in harvesting patterns. Climate warming should generally have a beneficial effect on aquaculture, increasing fish growth rates and expanding the geographic range of suitable sites for aquaculture, especially finfish aquaculture.

Another major potential concern for fisheries is the effects of reduced stratospheric ozone, and consequently increased ultraviolet radiation, on phytoplankton, and on the whole marine food chain that is based on the primary production of phytoplankton. Some experiments suggest that phytoplankton growth and production is greatly suppressed by increased ultraviolet radiation.

A warmer climate would probably encourage greater tourism over a longer summer season, not only because conditions in Nova Scotia would be more pleasant, but also because a warmer climate would increase both the frequency and the severity of summer heat waves in central Canada and the United States, while Atlantic Canada would retain a relatively moderate summer climate.

On the negative side, a rising sea level, concomitant with climate change, may threaten coastal infrastructure, including most fisheries infrastructure, such as wharves and processing plants. If there is no increase in precipitation, increased evaporation as a consequence of higher temperatures could reduce the fresh-water supply available to communities and their processing plants. Lower water levels in rivers and streams could also impede anadromous fish and reduce their habitats.

POLICIES AND PROGRAMS;
DRIFTING TOWARDS A CONSERVATION ETHIC

While legislation is a necessary basis for regulatory authority, governmental and departmental policies and programs could also have significant impacts on the nature and scope of fisheries conservation, protection, and management. In the past ten years, there has been a shift in policy statements away from resource inexhaustibility and towards the need for conservation. Clearly, some stakeholders have realized the fisheries cannot be regarded as a "commons" that all can exploit, but for which no one has responsibility.

Federal marine fisheries policy and programs were reviewed in considerable detail by the Task Force on Atlantic Fisheries, otherwise known as the Kirby Task Force. Its report, released in December 1982, discussed the economic condition of fishing communities, the processing sector, marketing, quality control, the inshore-versus-offshore issue, management plans, and the problems in individual sectors and stocks. The Task Force recognized that conservation was necessary:

> It seems evident that the 'common property' nature of the fishery is the fundamental cause.... Here it is only necessary to point out that when everyone competes for a share of a common but limited resource, the result is a zero-sum game; one man's gain is always another's loss. All the conflicts over allocations — whether between provinces, between inshore and offshore fleets, or between individual fishermen — are of this type. And the conflict will become more intense when there is no longer any new growth to allocate.[108]

Unfortunately, the message that sustainable development strategies were needed was not conveyed strongly enough, nor does it appear to have been heeded by all stakeholders. On the one hand, the degree of research and monitoring has been inadequate to permit calculation of accurate Total Allowable Catches and quotas or enterprise allocations (as exemplified by the recent controversy over the Northern Cod stock). On the other hand, some fishermen and fishing companies retain the attitude that if they don't get there first, someone else will catch the fish. The fishery

---

108 Canada, Task Force on Atlantic Fisheries, *Navigating Troubled Waters: A New Policy for the Atlantic Fisheries — Highlights and Recommendations* (Ottawa: Department of Supply and Services, 1982) (Chair: M.J.L. Kirby) at 14.

has become more technologically complex, market prices have generally been higher, and other threats to the quality of the marine environment have increased. All these pressures, and the current problems of the fishery, indicate that the federal government has not yet been able to establish, unilaterally or cooperatively, a sustainable approach to fisheries management.

The recently released "Oceans Strategy for Canada" states as one of four goals: "oceans resources and an ocean environment soundly managed and protected for future generations of Canadians." Among other approaches, the strategy suggests that this will be achieved by "conserving and managing the living resources of Canada's oceans through prudent stewardship," and by "promoting development and exploitation of the non-living resources of our oceans in an environmentally acceptable manner."[109] Neither the goal nor the approaches are delineated further, but clearly these statements must be rationalized with fishery management policies.

The Arctic Marine Conservation Strategy, led by DFO, is an attempt to place fisheries utilization into a broader context for that region, recognizing that traditional uses will continue while there is an intensification of commercial fisheries and other developments.[110] No similar exercise has been attempted in the marine environment off Nova Scotia, although Environment Canada in the early 1980s recognized the need for such a strategic assessment.[111]

In 1989 the Province of Nova Scotia issued a new fisheries policy, a policy that emphasizes the delicate balancing of interests and values necessary for achieving sustainable development:

> Departmental policies and objectives must represent all aspects of the fishery, reflecting a reasonable balance of economic, social and recreational interests. The pursuit of purely economic objectives may result in undue social disruption and concentration of wealth. De-emphasizing social objectives and stability however, can result in a non-competitive and unprofitable industry. Industry must be allowed to grow and profit, while communities traditionally involved with the fishery continue to benefit from the resource.[112]

In 1987 a nongovernment group, the Canadian Wildlife Federation, initiated a policy study of its own into Canada's freshwater fisheries.[113] The purpose of the review was "to assess the situation, document problems, propose solutions, and

---

109 Canada, Department of Fisheries and Oceans, *Oceans Policy for Canada: A Strategy to Meet the Challenges and Opportunities on the Oceans Frontier* (Ottawa: Department of Supply and Services, 1987) at 15.

110 Canada, Department of Fisheries and Oceans, *Canadian Arctic Marine Conservation Strategy* (Ottawa: Supply and Services, 1987).

111 D. Kelly *et al.,* "Developing a Strategic Assessment and Planning Framework for the Marine Environment" (1987) 25 J. Env. Mgmt. 219.

112 Nova Scotia Department of Fisheries, *supra,* note 1 at 24.

113 P.H. Pearse, *Rising to the Challenge: A New Policy for Canada's Freshwater Fisheries* (Ottawa: Canadian Wildlife Federation, 1988).

draw attention of the fishing community, management agencies, and the general public to the need for action." While the study has little to do with marine fisheries, it is noteworthy that such an investigation was initiated by a group other than government. The other significant point is that the study was heavily oriented to conservation of the resource and the need for a participatory approach to its management. While there are many nongovernment organizations with special interests in freshwater resources, wildlife, land stewardship, air quality, and nature in general, there are few if any such organizations with a special concern for the quality of the marine environment and the conservation of marine resources.

The DFO policy for the management of fish habitat was announced in 1986 after an extensive consultation process.[114] While it has long been stated that the Fisheries Act is Canada's toughest piece of water-pollution-control legislation, the habitat protection provision has the potential to be more restrictive as a result of the "no net loss" principle. The way in which DFO applies the policy will determine the nature and the degree of conflict with other sectors. DFO is aware of the policy's implications and is spending a considerable amount of time on internal meetings and workshops at which implementation is discussed. However, those discussions must also occur in a multisectoral setting. Before DFO can proceed to resolve conflicts with other sectors, it should ensure that the best habitat protection strategies and practices are applied within the sector by the department's Small Craft Harbours Branch, by fishing companies, by processors, and by fishermen themselves. A combination of regulatory initiatives, educational programs, and incentives should be developed, aimed specifically at the fisheries sector.

The Department of Environment appears to have come to grips with the need for a statement to guide it and others in maintaining and enhancing the quality of the marine environment so as to "allow for sustained resource development and other benefits for the enjoyment and use of existing and future generations." The result is the Marine Environmental Quality Policy Framework.[115] The guiding principles on which the policy framework is built include the following:

1. Marine environmental quality is of national importance.

2. Canadians have a right to a safe marine environment and to a healthy economy based on that safe environment.

3. Knowledge of the marine environment and its timely application is critical to solving and preventing problems.

---

114 Canada, Department of Fisheries and Oceans, *A Policy for the Management of Fish Habitat* (Ottawa: Department of Supply and Services, 1986).

115 Environment Canada, *Marine Environmental Quality Management Framework* (Working Document) (1987).

4. The preservation and maintenance of marine environmental quality is a shared responsibility.

5. Consultation and cooperation with other governments is crucial to delivering a marine environment of acceptable quality.

It is significant that the need for a national framework to maintain an acceptable level of marine environmental quality has been recognized in the Multi-Year Marine Science Plan,[116] released by the Interdepartmental Committee on Oceans led by DFO. This fact indicates that the two departments may have finally reached an accommodation of their respective roles in the marine environment — an accommodation that can only be of benefit to all parties.

In addition, the Department of Environment, at both the national and the regional level, has initiated the preparation and distribution of reports on the state of the environment. A section on the Atlantic marine ecosystem[117] described the status of certain fisheries and discussed the major influences on the marine ecosystem. The latter included harvesting, pollution, physical restructuring, the introduction of exotics, and climate change. While the authors caution the reader to be careful in interpreting statistics, the report does state that "[t]rends in the harvest of important species are in themselves a reflection of the capability of the ecosystem to provide sustainable yields of valued renewable resources." Landings of a number of species — notably, herring, lobster, scallop, and salmon — are down from their peaks, though the report acknowledges that these statistics do not necessarily translate into an unsustainable situation. The reports on the state of the environment being initiated in a number of jurisdictions are meant to provide a point of comparison for the future, but they are also designed to educate and inform. Efforts must be made to distribute this information throughout the fisheries sector.

More recently, the notion of conservation strategies has been gaining momentum at the provincial level. These strategies, first proposed by the International Union for Conservation of Nature and Natural Resources (IUCN), are plans for the wise use of resources, clearly recognizing both the limits and the opportunities. Prince Edward Island adopted the first such strategy in Canada[118] and other provinces have now followed. Nova Scotia has initiated the process to build such a plan. The degree to which the strategy will address marine fisheries is debatable given the federal government's jurisdictional responsibilities for east coast

---

116 Canada, Department of Fisheries and Oceans, *Multi-Year Marine Science Plan* (Ottawa: Department of Supply and Services, 1988).

117 Environment Canada, *State of the Environment Report for Canada,* P.M. Bird & D.J. Rapport, eds. (Ottawa: Department of Supply and Services, 1986) at 77.

118 Coordinating Committee for Conservation, *A Conservation Strategy for Prince Edward Island* (1987).

fisheries. It would be beneficial if a way could be found to discuss conservation apart from issues of jurisdiction. Once the issues and possible solutions are on the table, then and only then should responsibilities be assigned.

At yet a more local level, cooperative efforts have been mounted between DFO and the provincial Department of Lands and Forests on the preparation of guidelines for constructing woodland roads,[119] and between DFO and the provincial Department of Transportation on environmental construction practice specifications for highways and related matters. These initiatives are important as they provide some protection for anadromous species and nursery areas along the coasts and in estuaries.

Finally, a national initiative, termed the Sustainable Fisheries Network, is being forged. The Network will link industry, governments, academics, other users such as Native peoples, and nongovernment organizations, in an effort to promote the sustainable use of Canada's recreational and commercial fisheries. Members of the Network are intended to operate at the national, regional, provincial, and local levels to study, promote, and implement an integrated, ecosystem approach to the management of fish stocks and habitat.[120]

CONCLUSION

Sustainability in Nova Scotia's fisheries is both a reality and a vision. Coastal communities in harmony with the seasons and the sea do exist and, while wages in some fisheries are rather low, there is a sense of lifestyle "wealth." While the status of many fish stocks is relatively stable, the recent groundfish crisis calls for a re-examination of fisheries management measures and the need for "tough decisions," such as the buy-back of vessel licences and perhaps even a "slaughter of the sacred fisheries cow"—quota management for the inshore sector. Incidents of fishermen's dissatisfaction with governmental management measures, and the growing literature on public participation, raise the need to explore new co-management arrangements. Conflict between fisheries and other ocean users is likely to increase, as recent aquaculture conflicts illustrate; appropriate decision-making processes must therefore be forged, involving long-range planning and a willingness to accommodate conflicting values and interests through negotiation and/or mediation. Sustainability of fisheries may also depend on appropriate policy choices in other sectors of the economy, such as tourism, forestry, agriculture, and energy. International instabilities of export markets and global climate change raise special

---

119 Nova Scotia, Department of Environment, and Canada, Department of Fisheries and Oceans, *Environmental Standards for the Construction of Forest Roads and Fire Ponds in Nova Scotia* (Halifax: Department of Environment, 1983).

120 W.J. Christie *et al.,* "Early Thoughts on Fisheries Futures and Sustainable Development" in *Proceeding of National Forum on Sustainable Development* (Peterborough: Harmony Foundation, 1988).

challenges for coastal communities. Public concern for the environment and quality of life is pushing government managers towards a new conservation ethic.

Jigging for new directions in ocean law and policy is required if the "big one" is going to be caught — a sustainable ocean environment with enough fish for all.

HOW TO ENSURE THAT DEVELOPMENTS ARE ENVIRONMENTALLY SUSTAINABLE

P.S. Elder and W.A. Ross

Sustainable development is described in the Brundtland Commission Report as "development that meets the needs of the present without compromising the ability of future generations to meet their own needs."[1] It is

> a process of change in which the exploitation of resources, the direction of investments, the orientation of technological development, and institutional change are made consistent with future as well as present needs.[2]

Of course, both local and global environmental implications must be considered before development proceeds. But the Brundtland notion is far richer than this; it implies consideration of economic and social sustainability as well. It also encompasses a concern for economic redistribution so that essential needs of the poor are satisfied first (internationally as well as nationally). It specifically applies to non-renewable resources: they may be used, but the rate of depletion should consider their criticality, technological means of reducing depletion, and the likelihood and possible timing of substitutes.[3]

The Report tells us that

> environmental regulation must move beyond the usual menu of safety regulations, zoning laws, and pollution control enactments; environmental objectives must be built into taxation, prior approval procedures for investment and technology choice, foreign trade incentives, and all components of development policy.[4]

Indeed, ensuring that ecological dimensions are considered at the same time and in the same institutions as all relevant policy "is the chief institutional challenge of the 1990s."[5] Concurrently, we must realize that governments alone cannot do it all: "Ecologically sustainable development requires ecologically sustainable

---

1   World Commission on Environment and Development, *Our Common Future* (Oxford: Oxford University Press, 1987) (Chair: G.H. Brundtland) at 43. See also at 8. Another useful formulation is provided by Liverman *et al.*:

> the indefinite survival of the human species (with a quality of life beyond mere biological survival) through the maintenance of basic life support systems (air, water, land, biota) and the existence of infrastructure and institutions which distribute and protect the components of these systems.

D.M. Liverman *et al.*, "Global Sustainability: Toward Measurement" (1988) 12 Env. Mgmt. 133.

2   See *Our Common Future, id.* at 9. See also at 46.
3   *Id.* at 45–46.
4   *Id.* at 64.
5   *Id.* at 313.

behaviour on the part of all people involved, and of whatever culture, station, or political persuasion."[6]

The challenge facing us is how to implement sustainable development. Assuming for the moment the will (both in a strong political constituency and in government) to implement this rigorous concept, we ask in this paper whether environmental impact assessment (EIA), alone or combined with an "environmental bill of rights," can ensure that Canadian development is sustainable. Following Brundtland,[7] we will argue that even this combination is inadequate. It seems to us that more is required than evaluating new projects and leaving it to private initiatives to force review of questionable continuing activities. We also think that both nonrenewable and renewable resource management need re-examination, in spite of claims that "sustained yield" criteria are already used for renewable resources. We will, however, incorporate EIA and a type of bill of rights into a package of proposals that could help us to favour long-term sustainability over short-term benefits. Failure to extend our time horizon will be a disaster.

It should be noted that sustainable development is a normative, not a technical, concept; this implies that assessments of sustainability must be viewed as politically accountable, rather than merely technical, exercises. The concept also begs the question: What are "basic needs"? Canadians define these far more broadly than do starving peoples in other lands. Yet Brundtland tells us that

> many of us live beyond the world's ecological means ... [S]ustainable development requires the promotion of values ... that are within the bounds of the ecological possible and to which all can reasonably aspire.[8]

A second issue is whether the rapid global economic growth called for by Brundtland[9] is compatible with the "ecological possible." The Report argues that it is, perhaps because it sees such growth as the only feasible way of abolishing poverty. But if the industrialized world is already living "beyond the world's ecological means," it seems overly optimistic to think that a switch to living within our means can be combined with a 3–4 percent annual growth rate in the industrial countries,[10] merely through improvements in efficiency. Of course, this support for

---

6   L.K. Caldwell, "Political Aspects of Ecologically Sustainable Development" (1984) 11 Env. Conserv. 299 at 306.

7   See *Our Common Future, supra,* note 4 and accompanying text.

8   See *Our Common Future, supra,* note 1 at 44. Rees claims that "on a per capita basis, Canadians are among the world's greatest contributors to global environmental deterioration, and have a corresponding obligation to lead in the search for solutions." W.E. Rees, *The Global Context for Sustainable Development* (Vancouver: University of British Columbia, School of Community and Regional Planning Symposium, 1988) at 2.

9   For example, see *Our Common Future, supra,* note 1 at 50 and 89–90. Part of the reason for the Report's apparent skirting of some important issues is no doubt the difficulty of attracting a consensus of the Commissioners on contentious questions.

10   *Id.* at 51.

continued growth may help explain the Report's rapid acceptance within business and government. Yet if the earth cannot support the increase in global energy consumption and chemical production implied by all countries' achieving our standard of living, a profound moral and physical challenge is presented, to which Brundtland has no reply.

Another question begged by sustainability concerns the impossibility of predicting future social or technological change. A technological optimist might accept the need for sustainable development but argue that we can go on largely as we have because future solutions will be found for the problems that we create. Burning all our fossil fuels does not prevent future generations from meeting their energy needs. They just have to be smart enough. And, if asked about the greenhouse effect,[11] the optimist might reply that technology will help us there too.

Therefore, accepting the concept of sustainable development still leaves open the possibility of significant disagreement over its specific implications. In deciding on an energy development proposal, for example, what weight should we give to reducing the greenhouse effect by minimizing the burning of coal for electricity,[12] as opposed to increasing nuclear power or building more hydroelectric dams? All three options have considerable environmental and socio-economic implications. One might intuitively feel that hydroelectric developments are much more benign than the other two options. It must be recalled, however, that the Churchill-Nelson project in Manitoba, the Baie-James development in Quebec, and the Xingu River proposal on the Amazon in Brazil all involved major controversy over the potential destruction of aboriginal territory and ways of life. The survival of indigenous cultures was an urgent concern of the Brundtland Commission.[13]

While others have argued that renewable energy options exist,[14] the above

---

11   The greenhouse effect involves global climate change caused by "greenhouse gases," mainly carbon dioxide, which accumulate in the atmosphere and reduce the rate at which the earth emits energy. This in turn affects the earth's energy balance and hence the global climate. The outcomes of the greenhouse effect are generally expected to be quite damaging to society; for example, see S.H. Schneider, "The Greenhouse Effect: Science and Policy" (1989) 243 Science 771; F.K. Hare, "The Global Greenhouse Effect" (Address to the World Conference on the Changing Atmosphere, 27 June 1988) (Ottawa: Environment Canada, 1988).

12   K.M. Sullivan, A.M., President of the Clean Air Society of Australia and New Zealand, pointed out in a report for the International Coal Development Institute that burning coal to generate electricity contributes only about 6 percent of the radiative gases produced by humans. He therefore concluded that a significant increase in the use of coal for power generation will have a virtually negligible impact on the greenhouse effect. See K.M. Sullivan, *The Effect of CO_2 Emissions From Coal Fired Power Plants: A Review in Perspective* (London: International Coal Development Institute, 1988) at 15. Of course, virtually every economic sector or source of greenhouse gases could say the same thing, leading to a prescription that nothing needs to be done. Such fallacious logic leads to environmental "death by a thousand cuts."

13   See *Our Common Future, supra,* note 1 at 12 and 114–116.

14   D.B. Brooks, J.B. Robinson & R.D. Torrie, eds., *2025: Soft Energy Futures for Canada,* vol. 1 (Report prepared on behalf of Friends of the Earth Canada) (Ottawa: Department of Energy, Mines

example at least illustrates that there will be considerable room for disagreement, even if the concept of sustainable development is accepted. In this paper, we will offer a limited version of sustainability to illustrate this indeterminacy, but will not argue the details. We base it on Brundtland's view[15] that industrialized nations are living beyond their ecological means and must become more efficient in their use of materials and energy. We have added to this the objective of safeguarding human and ecological health by minimizing the emission of toxic and carcinogenic chemicals. The complexity of the concept has led us to suggest legislation that establishes criteria for consideration and procedures to be followed, rather than pretending that a hard-edged definition of sustainability can be applied by technicians. At the same time, we believe that a combination of rigorous analysis and public debate will lead us to more detailed understanding of sustainability in the future.

ENVIRONMENTAL IMPACT ASSESSMENT

If EIA were done as well as we know how, would it ensure sustainability of new developments or activities? If we are to examine the role EIA can play in determining the sustainability of developments, we must first agree on a definition of EIA. Although a more complete set of definitions is available,[16] the following will be suitable for our purpose:

> EIA is a process which attempts to identify and predict the impacts of legislative proposals, policies, programs, projects and operational procedures on the biogeophysical environment and on human health and well-being. It also interprets and communicates information about those impacts and investigates and proposes means for their management.[17]

In order to determine the sustainability of a development, one must understand clearly its effect on the biophysical environment and on human health and well-being. It is for this very reason that advocates of sustainable development have indicated EIA should be used to promote sustainability.[18] But EIA, in itself, is not

and Resources and Environment Canada, February 1983); R. Bott, D. Brooks & J. Robinson, *Life After Oil: A Renewable Energy Policy for Canada* (Edmonton: Hurtig, 1983).

15 See *Our Common Future, supra,* note 1 at 44 and 51.

16 Alberta Department of the Environment, *Environmental Impact Assessment Guidelines* (Edmonton: Department of the Environment, 1985); Federal Environmental Assessment Review Office, *The Federal Environmental Assessment and Review Process* (Ottawa: Department of Supply and Services, 1987); United Nations, *Seminar Report* (Economic Commission for Europe, 1987).

17 Canadian Environmental Assessment Research Council, *Evaluating Environmental Impact Assessment: An Action Prospectus* (Ottawa: Department of Supply and Services, 1988) at 1.

18 The National Task Force on Environment and Economy, for example, suggested "increased use of environmental impact assessment" as one means of enhancing the understanding of linkages between the environment and the economy. See Canadian Council of Resource and Environment Ministers, *Report of the National Task Force on Environment and Economy* (1987) at 5.

> An increasing number of countries require that certain major investments be subject to an environmental impact assessment. A broader environmental assessment should be applied not only to products and projects, but also to policies and programmes, especially major

enough to ensure sustainability, for three reasons. First, EIA applies only to new, and not existing, activities. Second, EIA processes have some flaws that, critics argue, prevent them from being fully effective. Third, while EIA can certainly be effective in identifying and even dealing with some undesirable impacts, the fact that an activity has been reviewed under an EIA process is not an assurance of its sustainability. These three factors will be dealt with in turn.

EIA is intended as a means of anticipating and preventing environmental problems at the planning stage of an activity, as opposed to much more expensive and damaging "react and cure" strategies. All EIA processes are applied only to new proposals. Thus, even if EIA were completely effective in determining and assuring sustainability of proposals reviewed, there would still be problems regarding the sustainability of existing activities. These problems would need to be dealt with in other ways. (Of course, all existing activities will eventually be replaced with new activities, but the environmental damage and consequent unsustainability of present practices may be unacceptable.) One could apply EIA processes to major changes to existing projects, thus expanding the applicability of sustainability-based EIA.

There are, as several critics have pointed out, particular problems with EIA processes that make them less than fully effective.[19] These problems may affect EIA generally, insofar as they prevent the processes from meeting the goals of EIA, or they may specifically make it difficult for EIA to deal with sustainability.[20] The problems associated with EIA relate to authority and accountability, the scope of the EIA process, poor or inadequate science, a lack of opportunities for public involvement, weak links between the EIA process and the decision taken about the proposed activity, and inadequate post-project analysis. These problems are summarized in Table 1. These features of EIA need improvement in order to increase EIA's effectiveness as a means for determining the sustainability of proposals. In

---

macroeconomic, finance, and sectoral policies that induce significant impacts on the environment.

Our Common Future, supra, note 1 at 222.

19 G.E. Beanlands & P.N. Duinker, *An Ecological Framework for Environmental Impact Assessment in Canada* (Hull: Federal Environmental Assessment Review Office, 1983); M. Bowden & F. Curtis, "Federal EIA in Canada: EARP As An Evolving Process" (1988) 8 Env. Imp. Ass. Rev. 97; R.B. Gibson, "Tinkering is not Enough" (University of Waterloo: Environment and Resource Studies, 1988); T. Fenge & L.G. Smith, "Reforming the Federal Environmental Assessment and Review Process" (1986) Can. Pub. Pol. 596; W.E. Rees, "A Role for Environmental Assessment in Achieving Sustainable Development" (1988) 8 Env. Imp. Ass. Rev. 273; P.S. Elder, "Environmental Impact Assessment in Alberta" (1985) 23 Alta. L. Rev. 286; Federal Environmental Assessment Review Office, *The National Consultation Workshop on Federal Environmental Assessment Reform: Report of Proceedings* (Ottawa: Department of Supply and Services, 1988); D. Suzuki, "Leaders Heeding Ecology Advice Just A Dream," *Globe and Mail* (5 November 1988) D4.

20 Of the references given above, Rees is the only one that deals explicitly with the issue of EIA and sustainability, but some of the problems identified by others also relate to the issue of how EIA may be prevented from dealing with sustainability.

particular, it is important to apply EIA to all activities that have significant impacts on the environment — not just projects, but also policies, programs, new products, and new manufacturing technologies.

The main problem with using EIA to ensure the sustainability of proposed activities is both the simplest and the most fundamental. EIA is now used to identify environmental impacts so that decisions about proposals can be taken in the knowledge of their environmental consequences. No assurance is provided that

TABLE 1
Problems of EIA Processes

CLASS OF PROBLEM	EXAMPLES	SUSTAINABILITY
Authority and accountability	Legislation of process; enforceable by public	Problem for EIA generally
Scope of EIA process	Need to deal with all proposals of concern; need for broad definition of environment	Major concern as applied to sustainable development
Adequacy of scientific studies	Scientific studies claimed to be of little predictive value; must deal with cumulative effects	Problem for EIA generally
Public access to EIA process	Inadequate access to EIA process for public; lack of funding for public; EIA procedures discourage public involvement	Problem for EIA and for EIA and sustainability
Effect of EIA on decision	EIA takes place too late to affect decision; inability to decide against proposal	Problem for EIA and for EIA and sustainability
Post-project analysis	Need feedback from project for project management; need feedback from project to improve future projects	Problem for EIA generally

proposals will be free of environmental problems — only that, to the extent reasonably possible, the consequences will have been considered in making decisions about proposals.[21] If EIA is to be used to ensure sustainability, the EIA process must include the requirement that proposals be consistent with the principles of sustainable development, and with their corollary, that environment is as important as economics.

The political decision to establish such a requirement is essential. There is virtually no point in discussing how to attain sustainability unless the people and their government are committed to it. Even so, the EIA process would need more; it would require some explicit statutory guidance, presumably an operational definition of sustainability or the criteria implied by it. In the early years of EIA, questions such as what constitutes a "significant" impact or how best to conduct public hearings were hotly debated. There is now good documentation that addresses these questions operationally, and this has made a big difference to the conduct of EIA.[22]

The same sort of documentation is needed for a good understanding of what is sustainable. Because the concept is normative, however, the expertise that has been developed regarding sustainable development must be supplemented very significantly by the input of Canadian citizens.[23] The most difficult task will be to develop a working definition of sustainability that accords with what the people understand and want. In order to be useful, the definition must be shared and accepted by the many decision-makers, both public and private.

The determination of constraints must remain a democratic process, even if expertise can help in their specific application. The contrary view would be naive; if a majority in any country cannot be persuaded that sustainability is necessary,[24]

21 When significant information gaps are identified, it is important that either the "worst-case" scenario be used to assess the acceptability of the project or the decision be postponed until the information is available. One of society's problems is the urge to move too quickly on inadequate information. Saying "no" is almost always reversible; saying "yes" is too often irrevocable.

22 Federal Environmental Assessment Review Office, P.J.B. Duffy, ed., *Initial Assessment Guide: Federal Environmental Assessment and Review Process* (Ottawa: Department of Supply and Services, 1986); R. Roberts, "Public Involvement: A Canadian Government Manual For Planning and Implementing Public Involvement Programs" (1988) Env. Imp. Ass. Rev. 3; Federal Environmental Assessment Review Office, *Public Review: Neither Judicial, Nor Political, But an Essential Forum for the Future of the Environment* (Ottawa: Department of Supply and Services, 1988), *Public Participation in Environmental Decision-making* (Ottawa: Department of Supply and Services, 1988) (Compiled by R. Parenteau); *Environmental Assessment Panels: Procedures and Rules for Public Meetings* (Ottawa: Department of Suppy and Services, 1985).

23 Among other mechanisms such as White (or perhaps Green) Papers and national hearings, the Round Tables called for by the National Task Force on Environment and the Economy, *supra*, note 18 at 10–11, would serve a very useful role here.

24 The Brundtland Report suggests that the answer to persuading or making people act in the common interest "lies partly in education, institutional development, and law enforcement." See *Our Common Future, supra*, note 1 at 46.

we see no way out — unless a world authority could be created to deal with recalcitrant nations.[25] Certainly Brundtland argues that the transition to sustainable development must "be managed jointly by all nations."[26]

Because of the need for political consensus, we are reluctant to prescribe precise wording for a statutory definition of sustainability. Nevertheless, we offer a specific example of how our approach might work. Decision-makers could be required to reject any proposal that does not achieve "maximum feasible sustainability," however defined, or be allowed to reject even a proposal that meets this criterion on the ground that the "maximum feasible sustainability" in the particular case is not sustainable enough. Given our version of sustainability,[27] we might expect that a definition would require maximum energy efficiency (or at least minimum use of nonrenewable energy sources); minimum (or zero) emissions of environmentally hazardous materials; and maximum recycling of resources, or, to put this in another way, minimum exploitation of virgin resources. Thus, it might be expected that before any new pulp mills are approved (to pick a current example from Alberta), a rigorous inquiry into the possibility of using much more recycled newsprint would be required. (The United States recycles about 25 percent of its newsprint, while Canada reuses only 5 percent.[28]) It might be provided, for example, that virgin resources could not be used unless they were at least a specified percentage cheaper than recycled ones.

This example points out that legislation requiring the assessment of alternatives should explicitly include even those possibilities beyond the authority of the particular approval agency, as long as the alternatives might reasonably be achieved by the level of government involved, or are within the scope of intergovernmental cooperative possibilities. It should be possible for the governments of Alberta and Ontario, for example, to discuss whether the trees of the former need to be processed for newsprint when hundreds of thousands of tonnes of newsprint are landfilled in the latter every year. We shall discuss imposing further duties upon agencies to ensure sustainability when we have considered the desirability of an environmental bill of rights.

AN ADAPTED ENVIRONMENTAL BILL OF RIGHTS

The idea of an environmental bill of rights has been with us for about twenty

---

25   We should at least acknowledge, with Adler, the possibility that some form of
          world government is necessary for the control of technology itself, as well as for the
          establishment of world peace. The biosphere is global not local; its protection from
          pollution ... cannot be effectuated by the best efforts of local governments.
     Adler believes we need a "post-parochial" world. See M.J. Adler, *The Common Sense of Politics*
     (New York: Holt, Rinehart and Winston, 1971) at 176.
26   See *Our Common Future, supra,* note 1 at 41. See also at 46–49.
27   See *Our Common Future, supra,* note 15 and accompanying text.
28   "U.S. May Cut Use of Canadian Newsprint," *Globe and Mail* (18 March 1989) B18.

years. Its stimulus came from Michigan's legislation, drafted by Joseph Sax.[29] The basic concept of a bill of rights is to allow all citizens in the jurisdiction both standing and a substantive right to sue anyone — private citizen or public official — to prevent certain kinds of environmental harm. What this right should comprise, however, is a difficult question. Sax used the concept of the "public trust,"[30] but, for the following reasons, we will couch citizens' rights in the more familiar (to Canadians) language of administrative law. First, there is confusion about how the public trust concept relates to traditional notions of trust law. Second, the success of the public trust approach has been questioned.[31] Third, it is not clear that the idea supports sustainability, although it may seem to initially. Finally, we think that greater guidance must be provided to judges.

There would be no strong call for a bill of rights in Canada if people were satisfied with the results of governments' environmental protection activities. The most frequent criticisms of government are that:

1. Effluent standards on authorized installations are too permissive — exemplified by the fact that the 1971 Pulp and Paper Effluent Regulations[32] under the Fisheries Act exempted "existing mills" and that, eighteen years later, spokespersons for these mills say they still need time to comply.[33]

2. Sanctions for exceeding these standards are not imposed.

3. There is no sense of urgency in correcting known hazards, such as old toxic-waste dumps or depositories.

4. The use of many chemicals is permitted without rigorous assessment of risk.

5. EIA processes ignore incremental increases in environmental degradation, so that we are more apt to lose a healthy environment through many small developments than through a handful of big ones.

6. We seem incapable of looking ahead and regulating major technologies or industries that may pose risks of systemic environmental harm (for example, those that use gases damaging to the ozone layer or practices resulting in greenhouse gases).

7. All proposals are innocent until proven guilty (i.e., the presumption is that

---

29 Rockwell-Anderson Environmental Protection Act of 1970, Mich. Comp. Laws Ann. 691 §§1201–1207 (Supp. 1973).

30 See C.D. Hunt, "The Public Trust Doctrine in Canada" in J. Swaigen, ed., *Environmental Rights in Canada* (Toronto: Butterworths, 1981) at 151.

31 For discussion of these two points, see Hunt, *id.;* J. Swaigen & R.E. Woods, "A Substantive Right to Environmental Quality," in Swaigen, *id.* at 195.

32 SOR/71-578.

33 Canadian Broadcasting Corporation Radio News, 15 March 1989.

they will proceed unless they are clearly too damaging), although the harm they cause may be virtually irreversible by the time "guilt" is demonstrated.

Without entering the realm of political economy (which is vitally important here, but beyond our expertise), we suggest that these complaints stem at least partly from the disparities of economic and political power in our society.[34] The call for a bill of rights should be considered in this context (as should any claim that sustainability can be achieved without conflict). Depending on the extent of the rights given therein, such a measure would be at least a modest step towards enabling citizens to participate in decisions of great importance to them. Indeed, a bill of rights might even give citizens, through the courts, the right to obtain a veto of certain kinds of actions. More fundamental remedies for the disparity of power, however, cannot be provided adequately through the judicial process, which, we shall argue, should largely review, and not replace, the regulatory process.

Some see a bill of rights merely as requiring certain procedures to be followed before environmentally significant projects or developments proceed. They might be content to receive the right to information about a proposal (perhaps, for example, to force the preparation and publication of an EIA), to be heard before approval, and to receive compensation for reasonably incurred costs in the process.[35] If, in addition, a new right were created for private citizens to sue in public nuisance, without having to show "particular direct and substantial"[36] damage above that suffered by the public at large, it might be thought that most of the benefits of a bill of rights could be achieved without doctrinal difficulty.

At least two difficulties, however, would remain. In this instance, as with the common law generally, *ex post* clean-up, or even an injunction to halt an activity, is often a poor second-best. Environmentalists want to prevent damage, not ameliorate it. The common law's *quia timet* action is a weak substitute because of the very heavy onus of proof in Canadian courts upon someone who fears potential harm.[37] Second, the notion of a bill of rights implies, for us, more than merely the rights to proper procedures and to sue to protect Crown land and resources.[38] It

---

34 See *Our Common Future, supra,* note 1 at 38 and 46.

35 It is clear that the Bill of Rights is, in part, very closely linked to EIA; while we have separated the two for convenience of presentation, we see them as working together to help achieve environmental sustainability.

36 *Benjamin* v. *Storr* (1874), L.T. 30 C.P. 362 at 364.

37 In Canada the plaintiff's traditional burden has been to show either virtual inevitability of a nuisance or the high probability of one whose damage will be irreparable. See P.S. Elder, "Environmental Protection Through the Common Law" (1973) 12 Western Ont. L. Rev. 107 at 169–170, where at least two cases are argued to presage a possible easing of this burden. In the United States the burden appears to be lighter: the high probability of a nuisance suffices. See W.L. Prosser, *Handbook of the Law of Torts* (4th ed.; St. Paul: West, 1971) at 603.

38 We acknowledge that public nuisance can be used against widespread pollution damaging private

should also mean that people could sue, for environmental reasons, to force public officials to enforce the law,[39] or even to refuse permission for a project on private land. In the present context, then, a bill of rights would supplement the EIA and approval processes as well as add to common law remedies against existing activities. To achieve these ends, new duties need to be imposed upon bureaucrats and made enforceable in the courts.

It can be asked whether, in our democratic society, we wish to assign the balancing of these various interests to the courts instead of to the political process. This is an important question, and our desire that the political forum make value trade-offs was the main reason why we originally doubted the wisdom of a bill of rights. Now, however, we believe that well-crafted criteria and decision-making procedures can be established by the legislature for public officials to follow, subject to court supervision on administrative law principles and the requirements that reasons for agency decisions be articulated and that the decisions be "reasonable" (a test we think should be easier for a plaintiff to meet than the "arbitrary or capricious" one). At the same time, the criteria would not be detailed enough to allow detailed supervision of all activities. We do not propose administration or "substantive revision of majoritarian choices"[40] by the courts on an unclear "public trust" mandate. Detailed schemes for other policies thought desirable, such as automobile emission standards and tax and financial incentives, would be left to the legislature, since "[t]he judiciary does not appear to be the most appropriate arbiter for..."

> complex issues of resource allocation, distribution of society's environmental amenities, and methodology of protection efforts.[41]

Our courts almost always defer to agency decisions unless the statute's purpose is being frustrated, there is corruption, there is no evidence to justify a finding of fact, there is an error of law on the face of the record, or the rules of fairness (or natural justice, if applicable) have been violated.[42] The idea that a court would replace an agency's decision simply because it disagrees with it seems to negate an important reason for the legislature's having delegated the powers in the first place.[43] We

---

property *Attorney General* v. *P.Y.A. Quarries Ltd.* (1957), [1957] 2 Q.B. 169 (C.A.), but the owners can still sue in private nuisance.

39 See, for example, the recent *Canadian Wildlife Federation* v. *Minister of the Environment* (10 April 1989), Regina T-80-89 (F.C.T.D.), affirmed by Fed. C.A. (A-228-89).

40 L.H. Tribe, "Structural Due Process" (1975) 10 Harvard Civ. Rights Civ. Lib. L. Rev. 269 at 301.

41 M. Fisher, "The CEQ Regulations: New Stage in the Evolution of NEPA" (1979) 3 Harvard Env. L. Rev. 347 at 377. The words enclosed in quotation marks are actually in the sentence following the set-off quotation.

42 See D.P. Jones & A.S. de Villars, *Principles of Administrative Law* (Toronto: Carswell, 1985).

43 There is some indication that a court will substitute its opinion on a matter ostensibly within the discretion of an official if no reasonable official could reach a particular conclusion. See *Secretary of State for Education and Science* v. *Tameside Metropolitan Borough Council* (1977), [1977] A.C. 1014 (H.L.). See also *Friends of the Oldman River Society* v. *Minister of the Environment*

would therefore expect that the courts would approach their proposed task with great care.

Our modified approach to a bill of rights would work as follows. The legislation would create general criteria for sustainability, and would require *all* government decision-makers (not just those involved in EIA and project-approval decisions) to apply them in fulfilling their duties. We acknowledge that it is difficult to express clearly the circumstances where environmental considerations should be determinative. The common law, however, was able to develop and evolve such open-ended doctrines as negligence and nuisance, and we may hope that today's needs can evoke similar creativity within legislators. Examples of possible criteria for sustainability to be applied by decision-makers include avoidance of unreasonable risk to human health and security of the person; minimization of material throughput; minimization of emissions of environmentally damaging materials; maximization of reuse and recycling; "sustained yield" management of renewable resources; and conservation of habitat, species, and natural areas required for "re-creation." Indeed, if it proves desirable to eliminate essentially all emissions of persistent toxic chemicals, approval legislation could adapt the approach of the new Canadian Environmental Protection Act (CEPA) section on ocean dumping.[44] Here, the presumption is against issuing the permit:

> No permit may be granted in respect of any substance unless, in the opinion of the Minister, (a) the substance is rapidly rendered harmless by physical, chemical or biological process ... and does not render normally edible ... organisms inedible or unpalatable or endanger human health or the health of animals.

We might add the requirement that the opinion be "reasonable," and also that total emissions of the substance must be unlikely to threaten (singly or in combination with other chemicals) human or animal health, or other significant harm to the environment, whether through accumulation or through any chemical or physical processes. This rather verbose suggestion would encompass threats like greenhouse gases and chlorofluorocarbons.

Our proposed bill of rights would first permit any two residents in the jurisdiction to require the head of a department or agency — and possibly a Crown corporation — to explain and justify within a specified time limit[45] how sustainability will be achieved in a particular decision. If the applicant finds the answer unsatisfactory, recourse could be had to a superior court, which would be empowered to adjudicate the statutory meaning of sustainability in the particular context, determine whether the decision-maker's assessment was reasonable, and provide

---

of Alberta (1988), 2 C.E.L.R. (N.S.) 234 at 239 (Alta. Q.B.) , where Moore C.J.Q.B., in spite of wording allowing the Minister to waive public notice requirements "if he considers it expedient and fit and proper to do so," decided to substitute his own judgement that the waiver was improper.

44   Canadian Environmental Protection Act, S.C. 1988, c. 22, s. 71(3) (hereinafter "CEPA").

45   This idea is based on s. 12(5) of CEPA, *id.*

"such remedy as the court considers appropriate and just in the circumstances."[46] Such remedy might be the remitting back of the decision for reconsideration based upon the proper law, but, depending on that law, the court might order, for example, that a permit for a proposed industrial plant limit emission of dangerous toxic or carcinogenic chemicals to "essentially zero."[47] A court might also order that certain conditions be attached to a project's approval.

This "free enterprise" litigation approach, however, must fit into a regulatory context. In the first instance, we should rely on governments and negotiation. A bill of rights is a back-up, not a primary tool.

In order to reduce the difficulty in any environmental lawsuit of proving causation and the probability of future harm, we would also legislate the approach of the U.S. Court of Appeals in *Reserve Mining Co.* v. *Environmental Protection Agency.*[48] Although the evidence in that case did not show that the probability of harm (cancer) was greater than not (which would have doomed the case in Canada), a reasonable medical concern for public health was held to justify an injunction requiring abatement as a precautionary measure. Thus, in our scheme, the court would be required to weigh both the probability of harm and the consequences should it occur. In short, scientific uncertainty would be resolved in favour of prevention of possible harm, which is a way of putting the onus of proof on a project proponent.

Although recent measures against the emission of gases threatening the ozone layer may provide grounds for optimism, we find this issue illustrative of the need for the innovation just described. Fifteen years ago, one of the authors wrote the Minister of National Health and Welfare to recommend the elimination of chlorofluorocarbons (CFCs) where possible. The Minister replied that there was no proof that the ozone layer was at risk or CFCs were a problem.

Another provision in our proposed bill of rights would be a discretion in the court to award partial compensation for costs incurred by an unsuccessful plaintiff, if the case involved a reasonable claim that was in the public interest to pursue. As well, we would provide solicitor-client (full) costs as a matter of right to successful plaintiffs. This would be in accord with Section 136(1) of CEPA:

> Any person who has suffered loss or damage as a result of conduct ... contrary to ... this Act or the regulations may ... recover from the person who engaged in the conduct an amount equal to the loss or damage ... and ... the costs of any investigation in connection with the matter.[49]

---

46   Canadian Charter of Rights and Freedoms, Part I of the Constitution Act, 1982, being Schedule B of the Canada Act 1982 (U.K.), 1982, c. 11, s. 24(1).

47   This is the ultimate objective of the Ontario Government. See Department of the Environment, *Municipal-Industrial Sewage Strategy for Abatement (MISA) A Policy and Program Statement of the Government of Ontario on Controlling Municipal and Industrial Discharges into Surface Waters* (Toronto: Department of the Environment, 1986).

48   514 F.2d 492 (8th Cir. 1975).

49   See CEPA, *supra*, note 44.

Finally, we think there should be *some* rights to question proposed actions of private citizens if those actions threaten sustainability. Where any ten persons think an activity or proposal threatens the legislated sustainability criteria, we would allow them to require the proponent of the activity to negotiate the means of meeting the sustainability criteria. (It might be recalled here that defendants in lawsuits under Michigan's legislation may argue that there is no "feasible and prudent alternative" to the proposal and that the latter is in the public interest.[50]) If no agreement can be reached, anyone would have standing to intervene in the approval process, and any two residents could challenge any relevant government decision.[51] If the activity is unregulated, the ten could ask the appropriate Minister to intervene in order to ensure that the sustainability criteria are met.[52] Thereupon, the proponent would be barred from taking any further action until the Minister notified the ten of his or her decision, with reasons. The ten, if unsatisfied, could ask the court to review (as already described) compliance with the sustainability criteria.

As can be seen, we think a detailed proposal in this area should build in formal negotiating measures and strong incentives to maximize the opportunity to reach agreement without involving the courts. Through means such as these, we believe that the judicial role can be minimized and the satisfaction of those involved in the process can be correspondingly maximized. In order to avoid mere obstructionism or "environmental blackmail," however, we would retain the judicial power to order dismissal, with costs, of lawsuits found to be frivolous or vexatious.

Ultimately, though, we do not believe that private lawsuits are likely to form a coherent and sufficient strategy for handling global problems. Certainly they cannot "in the midst of a statutory vacuum."[53] Even in the context of legislation as suggested here, and given the existence of environmental public-interest groups, it cannot be assumed that plaintiffs with the requisite knowledge, determination, and money will always come forward — and in the proper order — to ensure orderly evolution of the law. Creating strong legislative duties upon decision-makers is necessary as well.

WHAT ELSE IS NEEDED?

The integrated and interdependent nature of the new challenges ... contrasts sharply with the nature of the institutions.... These institutions tend to be independent, fragmented, and working to relatively narrow mandates with closed decision processes. Those responsible for managing natural resources and protecting the environment are institutionally separated from those responsible for managing the economy.[54]

Because of this institutional separation, our proposed bill of rights imposes

---

50 See Rockwell-Anderson Environmental Protection Act of 1970, *supra*, note 29, s. 3(1).
51 See CEPA, *supra*, note 44 and text accompanying note 45.
52 This process is loosely based on CEPA, *supra*, note 44, ss. 12(4) and 108.
53 *Tanner* v. *Armco Steel Corp.*, 340 F. Supp. 532 at 537 (S.D. Tex. 1972).
54 See *Our Common Future*, *supra*, note 1 at 310.

positive duties upon all decision-makers, whether or not an EIA is required. As well as allowing the courts to review compliance with these general duties, we might want to develop more detailed, binding policies for all relevant government departments and policy issues (including population policy). For example, the Council of Provincial Energy Ministers is in the midst of a study to evaluate "techniques for reducing or eliminating energy-related atmospheric greenhouse gas emissions."[55] This may be only one aspect of sustainability in energy policy, but the decision to consider such issues is a positive development. Given the need for broad consensus, we would consider legislating such policy reviews, and would certainly recommend that such a process be participatory.

It may not be enough, however, to create legal duties. Given the complexity of organizations and decision-making, it would also be necessary to include, as part of public servants' performance evaluations for pay and promotion, assessments of their success in furthering sustainability. Moreover, analytical tools for measuring sustainability must be refined. For example, it might be possible for economic measures of sustainability to be included in macro-economic budget and financial analyses. Tax policy must also be looked at.

Once rigorous policies to achieve sustainability have been developed, many implementation techniques will be considered. Public involvement and education (including academic curriculum development) will be an important component. Programs such as the new federal "Environmentally Friendly Products Program" may be helpful, although there will be difficult decisions to be made about many products; moreover, bulk, non-retail items (for example, newsprint and primary metals) should also be covered. In some cases, taxes (for example, a CO_2 tax on fuels, and taxes on consumption of virgin resources or on disposal of many goods) or incentives may be most effective. Sometimes the command-penalty model will seem most practical. New techniques of environmental mediation or negotiation will probably also be tried.[56] Whatever the technique, however, unless individual Canadians are committed to the idea of sustainability and voluntarily try their best to effect it, the efforts of governments are doomed to failure.

Approval agencies will no doubt experiment with new techniques of environmental monitoring, including the use of resource-risk indicators, risk analysis, and technology assessment. Useful intellectual breakthroughs will be made. The fundamental problem, however, of assessing incommensurables will continue to require case-by-case judgment. On this latter point, we would suggest an adaptation of a power given to the Minister of the Environment by CEPA: where the parts of the Act or Regulations dealing with toxic substances are contravened (substitute,

55   Department of Energy, *Request for Proposals: Study on the Reduction of Energy-Related Atmospheric Greenhouse Gas Emissions* (Toronto: Ministry of Energy, 1988).
56   See, for example, Canadian Environmental Assessment Research Council, *The Place of Negotiation in Environmental Assessment*.

where the sustainability criteria are threatened), the Minister may direct a manufacturer or vendor of the offending substance or product to replace it "with one that does not pose a danger to the environment or to human life or health."[57]

Finally, Canadian policy-makers might wish to assess New Zealand's experience with a newly created Parliamentary Commissioner for the Environment.[58] An environmental ombudsperson with power to initiate investigations, and to advise other governmental bodies and Parliament of their results, might avoid some of the bureaucratic inertia and defensiveness that have characterized many environmental controversies.

CONCLUSION

To recapitulate, we have suggested the need for

1. extensive public involvement in the development of the working definition of sustainability and in the approval process;

2. assurance that normative judgments remain accountable to the political process;

3. dissemination of a clear understanding of sustainability's implications among both government officials and the public;

4. EIA of new proposals (including policy and plan review), with explicit consideration of sustainability, and rejection of proposals that militate against it;

5. some provision for review of the sustainability of all activities, relying both on government policy-makers and on court review initiated through our version of an environmental bill of rights; and

6. creation of new legal mandates to provide the power necessary for implementation of sustainability. (We have not addressed in this paper the respective constitutional powers of federal and provincial governments. It is clear, however, that all governments in Canada could do a great deal towards ensuring the economic, environmental, and social sustainability of the activities within their jurisdiction.)

"[I]n the final analysis," Brundtland tells us, "sustainable development must rest on political will."[59] It was suggested earlier that Canadians have a significantly broader definition of basic needs than do inhabitants of less-developed countries. Even if most Canadians accepted the Brundtland Report, it is doubtful that they would support a government that defined basic needs and then ensured that no

---

57 See CEPA, *supra*, note 44, s. 40(b)(i).
58 Environment Act 1986, S.N.Z. 1986, c. 127 (Pub. Law No. 127).
59 See *Our Common Future, supra*, note 1 at 9.

Canadians had anything beyond these until all developing nations had such needs satisfied. Canadian governments probably see sustainable development much more as a means of minimizing ecological, and consequent social, impacts than of implementing a radical redistribution of world income. Redistribution is more likely to be left to such traditional vehicles as freer trade and international development projects. It is for this reason that we eschewed the temptation to suggest changes in Canada's political and economic systems. We believe, however, that serious problems of distributive justice lurk just below the surface, and we predict significant conflict, at home and abroad, in implementing sustainability. We are not sanguine about the ultimate outcome, especially if Canadians begin to feel constraints on economic growth. Let us give Brundtland the last word on this:

> If ... the aim is to ensure that the world is well on its way towards sustainable development by the beginning of the next century, it is necessary to aim at a minimum of 3 per cent per capita national income growth *and* to pursue vigorous redistributive policies.[60]

---

60 *Id.* at 51.

STRUCTURING THE TAX SYSTEM FOR SUSTAINABLE DEVELOPMENT

J. Anthony Cassils

It has long been a source of wonder to me that the human population should press against the limits of our administrative ability and the carrying capacity of the planet. If we could stand back from the abyss, reduce our population and pollution, all people could have plenty and we could live in balance. Perhaps we are part of an experiment to see whether there really is intelligent life on Earth, or are we destined, as termites, to build our mounds in darkness? We have reached a turning point.

Throughout history, we have focussed our values and institutions inward on ourselves. No major turn in human history has occurred without our first changing the way we view the world. New knowledge leads the change. Recently, we have begun to recognize some of the appalling environmental consequences of our actions. As a result, we may be changing our primary goal from growth without end, to the maintenance of life on this planet so that we can continue to flourish. This environmental awareness explodes our existing habits and institutions, and we will need to rebuild all that we do in light of this new understanding. It appears that we are moving from one age to another, from the age of heroic materialism to the age of ecology. Such transitions are never easy.

As a necessary part of this transition, we will have to re-examine our structures and institutions. This paper considers some changes in the tax structure for the purpose of accelerating the implementation of sustainable development. The tax system can help us to set new parameters for the marketplace, raise financing, and move into a new age. This paper will set the historical context, review the role of taxation in the marketplace, consider a tax policy for sustainable development, examine some options, and touch on international competition, leadership, and the process of change.

As a preliminary point in this paper, development is understood to be sustainable when it meets the needs of the present without compromising the ability of future generations to meet their own needs. In the short term, it requires rapid and cleaner growth worldwide in order to meet the basic needs of all people, with the expectation that this will bring the population and our demands upon the planet into true balance sometime in the next century.

The concept of sustainable development was proposed by the report of the

World Commission on Environment and Development,[1] which recognized that developed nations cannot sustain many of their current practices, that poverty is environmentally damaging (for example, when the poor cut and burn forests or overgraze land), and that we can continue to have growth of a different quality although there are absolute limits to it. The report assumes that we will attain sustainable development by meeting the basic needs of all people, and by promoting values that encourage standards of consumption within the bounds of the ecologically possible, to which all can reasonably aspire.

We have two choices. We can do little, and our economy will stall and go into a free fall; or we can move towards sustainable development. Sustainable development is the only acceptable option. It is based on common sense. It is inevitable.

Government must continue to lead the drive towards sustainable development. As the need for change is urgent, we must be practical and use all available tools. This requires reshaping laws and institutions in order to nurture sustainable development. Each action sends a vital signal of change and moulds public opinion and personal habits. Government at all levels in Canada has introduced tougher legislation to protect the environment. This is a good start, but government has a unique opportunity to create a tax system favouring the environment, particularly through an expanded sales tax. Unfortunately, the current tax system encourages many unsustainable practices — for example, in agriculture, forestry, and mining. To make matters worse, most of our existing infrastructure of roads and buildings was built on the assumption of cheap natural resources and is expensive to operate. The extravagant abuse of the environment and large government deficits find common roots in values lodged in the short term; the tax system can be designed to resolve both problems. During this time of crisis, we cannot remain neutral, and neither can the tax system until we have achieved sustainable development. Otherwise, we may not have an economy worth taxing. At the same time, government must raise sufficient revenue to reduce deficits; all suggestions in this paper are made with this need firmly in mind.

Some people are uncomfortable with the idea of designing the tax system for purposes other than raising revenue with a minimum of disruption to the market economy. The tax system has been the subject of assaults in the past by various special-interest groups. However, the environmental crisis is unlike anything we have confronted before. It is not the concern of one special-interest group— it is our common future. The tax system can be designed to help diminish and recapture some of the environmental costs. The measures must, however, be well thought out and clearly focussed.

---

1   World Commission on Environment and Development, *Our Common Future* (Oxford: Oxford University Press, 1987) (Chair: G.H. Brundtland).

Once we agree that the tax structure is a useful mechanism for implementing sustainable development, the number of things we can do is almost infinite. The ideas developed in this paper are not intended to be prescriptive. As the concept of sustainable development is a new departure for us, we must think it through together, for it is in the process of developing and pursuing ideas that we come to understand what is practical, possible, and worthy.

TAXATION: A HISTORICAL PERSPECTIVE

While government in Canada has often been bold in public policy — as with the construction of the transcontinental railway in the last century and the development of the welfare system in the decades following the Second World War — it has been more circumspect in designing the tax system to attain important goals of public policy. There are good reasons for this. Taxes are not only as certain as death, but rank at the same low level of popularity. As taxing can be hazardous to the health of governments, it is not surprising that governments have approached it with a high degree of caution. As a result, taxes were added piecemeal, and, wherever possible, were indirect.

In Canada, during the period preceding the First World War, over 70 percent of federal revenue was raised by customs duties, and 14 percent by excise taxes. Most direct taxes were levied at the provincial and municipal levels in the form of sales and property taxes. It took the darkest year of the First World War, 1917, for the Government of Canada to gain enough courage to introduce, as a "temporary measure," direct taxes on personal income and corporate profits. (As an aside, the highest tax bracket for income tax in 1917 was 13 percent, and was intended as a tax on the elite.)

The depression of the 1930s and the Second World War gave rise to the perception that government should become more involved in stabilizing the economy and regulating the marketplace. By 1945, the Government of Canada had moved into a broadly based income tax. During the post-war boom, government expanded public services and taxes with the consent of the public; after two world wars and a great depression, people wanted to be protected from hardship. In the late 1960s, we embarked on a consumption binge. As we consumed more, we invested less, and our growth in productivity fell.

Policy-makers realize that, faced with intense international competition, Canada will have some difficult adjustments to make, and the emphasis on fairness in the tax system has been displaced to a considerable degree by the need for economic efficiency. The tax structure has become a politically attractive issue because many Canadians find the system complex, business recognizes the need for tax reform, and the government desperately needs more revenue.

The recent White Paper on tax reform had five broad objectives: fairness, competitiveness, simplicity, consistency, and reliability. These are the classic objectives of tax policy; they focus on the relationships among people and their institutions. It is often said that the greatest threat to an industry or a system comes from outside the system. The environmental imperative explodes our structures and practices by adding another dimension, the relationship of human society to all living things. This opens a whole new realm of possibilities for the tax structure.

In 1986–87, income tax contributed 45 percent of federal revenue; corporate tax, 11 percent; and unemployment insurance premiums, 10 percent; with most of the remainder coming from sales taxes, customs and excise duties, and return on investment. Since then, two profound changes have begun to rise to the surface of tax policy: first, the burden of taxation is shifting from income to sales taxation; and, second, policy-makers are recognizing the need to encourage savings and investment in order to reduce the cost of capital or interest rates, and to increase national productivity.

TAX AND THE MARKETPLACE

The accepted economics of the day always seems to be fighting the last war. Friedrich Hayek, the economist, is ninety years old this year, and journalists are extolling the victory of his theories over the evils of collectivism in the socialist mould. It appears that people can best deal with scarcity when production is in private hands, when the consumer has the freedom to choose what to buy, and when there is open competition in the marketplace. The less-encumbered marketplace has clearly outperformed the controlled economies of eastern Europe, and some leaders of Communist countries are acknowledging this fact. Many people speak of "market forces" in reverent tones. However, the marketplaces of states such as Japan and Korea have a high degree of government involvement, and the freedom of the consumer is constrained by cultural values. No one would argue with the international success of the constrained marketplace called Japan. Meanwhile, modern industrial countries have dealt so effectively with the scarcity of food, manufactured goods, and services that they have created new scarcities of clean earth, clean air, and clean water. Therefore, future economic growth will depend on the environment's capacity to absorb it. We need new theories of economics, for the old ones are past their prime.

Market forces have met some individual wants quite well, but they have also created great poverty. These forces have an opportunistic quality that, over time, often seems to push beyond the limits of the acceptable — as, for example, with the sale of oil products contaminated with PCBs. Economic theories usually take for granted the importance of cultural norms in determining the economic success or failure of nations. Both Brazil and the United States had access to the resources of continents; cultural values made the difference between them. Individual self-discipline and shared values seem to be critical determinants of a society's economic success. The health of the environment is an issue in which all people can find common cause. Therefore, all people should instill the environmental ethic into their young; the health of the economy, and their lives, depend upon it.

The tax system can help to set the parameters for the marketplace and guide the behaviour of individuals. The core challenge is to move from an economy that has not considered the environmental costs of its actions to one that does. This will require major restructuring and a redirection of financial and intellectual capital.

Any tax is an interference with the marketplace. If government could operate businesses itself and make a profit, it would not need taxes. It is not, however, in the nature of government to run profitable businesses, but rather to provide leadership and operating parameters for the marketplace. The marketplace, like all economic tools, is a means to an end, and the term itself changes in accordance with whether we sanction the activity. If we do not like what it does, we call it the underground economy, the black market, or the drug trade. The marketplace operates with a degree of anarchy that allows participants to feel pleasure or pain, depending on the size of their profits or losses. This dynamic process allows economies to adapt quickly, but the marketplace has no sense of direction or values beyond the bottom line. It is the duty of government to set goals.

Tax policy tends to fluctuate between the concepts of a neutral tax and a just tax. The neutral tax seeks to have the hand of government take only what is needed to maintain itself, and to tax evenly, so as to cause a minimum of disruption to the free market. The just tax is based upon the need to achieve some agreed-upon social ends, and the amount of tax is determined by the ability to pay. The neutral tax has much to commend it, and is clearly superior to the current tax incentives for unsustainable practices. As we are short of time, we must use the tax system to encourage companies to introduce more efficient and less pollution-prone technologies, and to change the habits of most consumers. The tax pendulum must swing from supporting unsustainable development to supporting sustainable development before we can achieve tax neutrality. The challenge will be to set new parameters for the marketplace without burying it in bureaucracy, to channel market forces rather than stifling them, and to build environmental standards and self-discipline into our culture.

SUSTAINABLE DEVELOPMENT AND TAX POLICY: THE DESIGN

By reforming our structures, whether these be the way we collect garbage or the way we collect taxes, we can create a climate that provides more opportunities for business to practise sustainable development at a profit. As we design a tax system for sustainable development, we must keep our goals clearly in mind. We must increase productivity, because there is a huge demand for necessities in the developing nations. We will need to achieve fairness by ensuring that the means of production, and the products, reach those in need. We must produce more, while using fewer natural resources and generating much less pollution. The tax system should reward individual initiative, but discourage environmentally harmful practices. Finally, government will require sufficient revenue to run its operations without incurring huge deficits.

Environmental needs and the concept of sustainable development are catalysts that will encourage both a shift in the tax burden from income to sales taxes and the creation of more incentives to save, just as, earlier in this century, war and social change compelled the development of taxes on personal and corporate income. These trends will become apparent with each federal budget, and are already more advanced in countries such as France, where the value-added tax collects twice as much revenue as personal income taxes. (The value-added tax is a type of sales tax levied at each stage of production.)

The beauty of the tax system is its pervasiveness. It can reach almost everybody on a daily basis. It can address the core challenge of moving from an economy that has not considered the environmental costs of its actions to one that does. Our economy has operated on a linear basis, taking in raw materials that are refined and processed, manufactured and consumed — leaving a trail of waste at each stage of production and after consumption. Now, we recognize that the biosphere is a closed system that can no longer tolerate our current business methods and life-styles. We need to reshape the economy from the linear to the circular, whereby there is little pollution and extensive recycling. Taxes can make it more expensive to pollute, cheaper to invest in more efficient methods of production. Taxes can expose the environmental costs of the convenience of throwing away, and the true costs of our love affair with the automobile.

The expanded sales tax offers government a wonderful opportunity to affect the day-to-day behaviour of consumers. It can be designed to favour environmentally beneficial products and services. By thus reshaping the behaviour of the consumer, it can reorient the production of companies. The sales tax could be progressive: for example, people buying cars could pay a 10 percent tax on the first $10,000 of the price. Any amount over that would be subject to a rising scale that might be as much as 100 percent for a $100,000 car, thereby including in the sales tax the "ability to pay" principle. A higher tax could be levied on cars that are not fuel efficient.

The sales tax has other advantages. It is voluntary above a certain level of subsistence, it encourages savings, it is easier to enforce than the income tax, and the burden of administration is passed from the public sector to the private sector. There is an element of privatization in it, although this will not be welcomed by business. Many European countries have already made the adjustment.

The government may wish to render taxes on personal and corporate income much less significant, given the amount of energy needed to collect (and avoid) these taxes. For example, a flat 10 percent tax (federal and provincial combined) could be levied on all income from whatever source. The tax would raise a considerable amount of revenue, would be very simple, would not be so high as to encourage elaborate plans for tax avoidance, and would recapture some of the underground economy. Additional revenue would be raised by the expanded sales tax. The nominal income tax would allow government to identify those people requiring assistance, and they could be given a rebate to compensate them for any regressive aspects of the sales tax.

Moving from an economy that is not sustainable to one that is will require large amounts of capital. It is imperative that the tax structure provide incentives to increase savings or capital. As the supply of capital increases, interest rates fall. Lower interest rates will encourage new investment worldwide and speed the economic restructuring essential for the implementation of sustainable development. Increased savings will supply the financing necessary to eliminate deficits, reduce pollution, provide care for the aging population in the developed countries, and assist the developing countries, which will experience a rapid increase in growth and demand. Investments in developing countries have the potential to provide huge returns. The challenge is to put purchasing power in the hands of those who need it on a global scale, in the same way that purchasing power was put in the hands of the poor in many developed nations during the depression of the 1930s. We need a "New Deal." One challenge will be to provide a reliable, well-administered international securities commission that will permit people to invest with confidence in countries located in the less-developed regions of the world. This will permit the next major flow of capital to developing countries to be delivered in the form of equity, not debt. Equity has the advantage of distributing risk among the shareholders, and, unlike debt, does not carry high and fixed costs.

SOME SPECIFIC ENVIRONMENTAL MEASURES

As we develop our thoughts on designing a tax structure for sustainable development, it is useful to consider some specific proposals. Each step, taken successfully, will build momentum and signal change.

An *emergency environmental fund* could be established and financed by a one-time levy on corporate profits or by an individual surtax. The cost would then be charged back to the polluters, representing a liability in financial statements. As science identifies, in increasingly specific terms, the sources and total costs of different types of pollution, the standards will rise and polluters will face not only high fines, but also the costs of cleaning up — costs with the potential to put them out of business. Over the longer term, a sustainable business will be one producing few, if any, pollutants.

A *disposal sales tax* could be applied to certain products that are inherently wasteful (such as paper diapers) or difficult to dispose of (such as tires and large home appliances). The disposal sales tax on difficult items would be refunded at the end of the product's useful life. These taxes would reduce the amount of waste — which is a concern for all three levels of government — and would produce a surge of revenue.

Some *tax-assisted investment products* could be created in order to redirect capital quickly, and then phased out after a predetermined time period — for example, of five years. While tax incentives are sometimes criticized because they are a type of public expenditure not subject to the close scrutiny of the budgeting process, supporters argue that they provide more scope for entrepreneurial action than, for example, a government grant, which involves more bureaucratic procedures. Undoubtedly, tax incentives distort the market, undermine the reliability of revenue collection, and often reward effort rather than profitability. Some tax incentives have been used to promote growth in established industries. In the following examples, they would be applied to speed the integration of the environment and the economy, and would act as catalysts for change. It is likely that some tax incentives will remain as long as we have high levels of tax on corporate and personal income.

The following *investment incentives* would encourage both the participation of individual investors, and savings. As people participate, they will gain a greater understanding of the issues; this will reinforce the shift to sustainable development.

New businesses are a major source of jobs. However, it is difficult to raise venture capital in Canada. Many expect the integration of the environment and the economy to give rise to a new wave of industries. This new wave will require large amounts of capital, and to increase the supply, government could give tax incentives to investors in *environmental venture capital funds.* At present, most investors in venture capital in Canada are corporations, but environmental venture capital funds could be sold in smaller units so that more individual investors could participate. The need for venture capital is evident. The challenge will be to shake it free from a society that has become risk-averse. Venture capitalists will have many business opportunities as the cause and effect of pollutants become more clearly understood. For example, epidemiologists are beginning to identify certain types of pollution as carcinogenic. Those who develop products to remove damaging particles from air or water will help polluters meet and exceed rising standards, and, over the longer term, will reduce the costs of health care.

Tax-free environmental bonds could be issued by municipalities to raise money for the construction, renovation, or improvement of infrastructure essential to a healthy environment, such as sewage and water systems. This measure would permit municipalities to raise funds at rates considerably below the market rate of interest. The tax-free status of these bonds would constitute a transfer of funds from the federal and provincial levels of government to the municipalities. However, these transfers occur in any event, and the funds are not always well spent (as, for example, with the Olympic Stadium in Montreal). The issuance of the environmental bonds could be tied to specific projects such as sewage systems, which are often ignored by the public and by politicians because they are not visible, and special provisions could be attached to reinforce spending discipline. As some people might object that the tax-free feature unduly benefits people in the highest tax brackets, tax credits could be offered instead.

Investment products could be created to reward companies with good environmental records and to punish others. For example, *flow through shares* could be adapted for environmental ends. In the last five years, this vehicle has raised over a billion dollars for the mining and oil and gas industries, which pass on their tax deductions for exploration to individual investors. The investors buy units in a partnership, which, in turn, invests in companies undertaking activities that qualify for the favourable tax treatment. By adapting this vehicle to environmental goals, companies investing in pollution-abatement equipment could be given substantial tax deductions, which would then flow through a partnership to the individual investors. The net effect would be to provide capital at a discount to companies, and tax credits to their investors. The largest companies can probably look after themselves. It is the medium-sized and smaller companies that might benefit the most from this vehicle, as they are often short of capital. As medium and small companies are also the major source of new jobs, and many of these companies pollute, the government may want to consider this and other tax options in order to help them adapt. To a considerable degree, an investment in pollution abatement will involve upgrading manufacturing equipment, and this should increase productivity, the value of assets, and share prices. Another positive factor for share prices is that the investment in pollution-abatement equipment would reduce exposure to penalties, which could loom quite large in the balance sheets of laggard companies in the future.

Provincial stock savings plans with an environmental twist could be created to help finance new companies associated with sustainable development, such as those pioneering new dimensions for recycling or creating environmentally friendly products or services. The Quebec Stock Savings Plan captured the imagination of Quebec, generated a surge of growth, and capitalized many small companies. The Plan gives deductions from Quebec taxable income, ranging from 50 percent to 150 percent of the amount invested in Quebec-based companies, with the larger deductions applied to investments in companies with small capitalization. The Plan has been viewed less positively following the stock market plunge of October 19, 1987, when many small companies were particularly hard hit. As well, some companies included in the Plan went public prematurely. However, the Plan's overall effect has been positive, and after the next economic slowdown rising stock markets will be more supportive of small companies seeking financing.

To move briefly to tax-related investment incentives for manufacturers, the *accelerated capital cost allowance* should be expanded to apply to investment in recycling technology as well as in pollution-control equipment. Some applications under this provision have been refused because the investments recaptured useful products from the waste, and were deemed to be investments for economic efficiency. The distinction does not make a great deal of sense in light of the goal of sustainable development.

Turning from tax-assisted investments to other tax and financial incentives, let us begin with agriculture. Most developed nations subsidize unsustainable agriculture that erodes the soil and poisons the water. Since 1945, agriculture has moved from a "soil base" to an "oil base." Oil-based machinery, fertilizers, and insecticides dominate the industry, creating such familiar problems as the level of pesticides on fruits and vegetables and the loss of top-quality farmland. Subsidies and tax incentives should be redirected in order to finance the transition to sustainable practices, such as *organic farming*. The science of biotechnology is placing a high priority on developing crops resistant to disease and insects. Organic farming is becoming a viable alternative. If it results in slightly higher food prices, an environmentally aware public will be willing to pay the price. The subsidies should be phased out as the transition occurs, so that farmers in poorer countries will be able to compete.

Taxes on energy consumption are an obvious source of new revenue. Canada is one of the least-efficient energy users in the world. The standard excuses for this wasteful behaviour are that Canada is a cold, sparsely populated country requiring the use of more energy, and that we have many industries that are heavy users of energy. There is a measure of truth to these explanations, but anyone who has been trapped in rush-hour traffic knows that we can improve our use of energy.

When energy prices fell in the early 1980s, many governments considered that the energy crisis had ended. In Canada, government reduced support for renewable energy and let some of the reduction in the price of fuel flow through to the public. This makes sense from the perspective of the market economy, but the greenhouse effect adds an entirely new dimension. Until we develop a substitute for fossil fuels, energy conservation is a matter of life or death. Highly polluting fuels such as coal and oil should be taxed more heavily than natural gas, and tax incentives could be reintroduced to encourage the insulation of buildings and the development of renewable energy.

The *forest products industry* is a major source of wealth and employment in

Canada, yet we are cutting four times as many trees as we are planting. Practices in many other parts of the world are even more destructive. This is clearly unsustainable, and the effect will be to drive up the value of forested land in the next ten or twenty years. It makes excellent ecological and economic sense to plant many more trees now, because it takes from forty to sixty years to grow a forest in Canada. Stumpage fees and leases of Crown lands to industries producing forest products must reflect this reality.

Pension funds constitute the fastest growing source of capital. Governments should consider changing legislation governing investments by pension funds to allow greater flows to environmentally beneficial investment vehicles or businesses. Investments by pension funds are subject to restrictions; for example, investments in common stock can include only companies that have paid dividends during at least four of the past five years or have had earnings of at least 4 percent of the average book value of the capital stock over a specified number of years. Seven percent of the portfolio may be invested in such vehicles as venture capital, warrants, rights, and stock options, which fall within a "basket clause." Companies addressing issues relating to the environment and the economy are sufficiently important to warrant the creation of an "environmental clause" that would permit pension funds to invest, say, up to 5 percent of their holdings in environmentally friendly corporations. Many incentives could be provided; for example, a pension fund might be allowed to invest two dollars outside Canada for every dollar spent inside Canada in an "environmental investment." Some people might object to this proposal on the basis that the managers of pension funds have a fiduciary responsibility to obtain the greatest return they can for their investors. This ignores the fact that, in Quebec, the Caisse de Dépôt has been a vehicle of provincial policy for many years, has been well managed, and has delivered good performance. Moreover, as conceived, the "environmental clause" would offer an opportunity, but not an obligation. It is worth noting that in recent years, many waste-management stocks have outperformed the general market by a considerable amount. Given the obvious need, and helped by financial incentives, environmental investments will provide many growth opportunities. Additionally, it is important to keep in mind that the proposed "environmental clause" would be another important signal of change.

Every country wants to transfer into new technology. The tax structure could encourage this by providing favourable tax treatment to foreign companies that bring environmentally beneficial technologies into the country. For example, Wellman Inc. is a medium-sized American company that for years has been recycling plastic materials and producing end products that are not only usable, but also highly profitable. They have proprietary processes and undertake continuing research. A recent investment report on Wellman commented on its subsidiary in Ireland, where the tax rate on its operations will not exceed 10 percent until the year 2000. Giving tax breaks or grants to encourage innovative companies to bring their environmentally beneficial technologies to Canada may be cheaper than paying for places to dump the waste.

MEASURING POLLUTION AND THE MARGIN OF SAFETY

In order to create tax-related investment incentives for sustainable development, one must distinguish between those investments to be rewarded and those to be punished. One of the main concerns of regulators is that they do not monitor or measure pollution extensively enough, and when they do identify polluters it is often difficult to assess the damage. This uncertainty creates a formidable barrier defended by scientists, lawyers, and accountants, and makes it difficult to distinguish between the environmental offender and the model citizen. As a further complication, numbers can mean different things to scientists on the one hand and lawyers and accountants on the other. For example, scientists may use numbers as indicators of probability, while lawyers and accountants expect them to be exact and accurate, giving rise to a potential for litigation. Government will need to monitor the sources of pollution much more closely in the future, and tighter regulation, based on a profound public concern, should make compliance the norm. Given the immediacy of the threat to the environment, we may need to act without the benefit of precise measurement. This has already begun to happen in the case of CFC production. We may need to move beyond reason and analysis to judgement and intuition, which implies adherence to the principle of a margin of safety. For example, a container of insecticide recently sank in the North Sea. Journalists noted that if the container opened, it would cause an unprecedented environmental disaster by destroying ocean life over a wide area, and would also put many fishermen out of work. The insecticide in question, however, was produced in order to be sprayed over land, whereupon it would flow into underground water tables and come into contact with numerous life forms. The question arises, then, whether we should be using these chemicals at all, if we believe in the need to maintain a margin of safety.

Government can apply the margin-of-safety principle by levying fines against those who pollute. In this way, government will be able to behave in a more arbitrary manner, insofar as it will only have to prove that the act of pollution occurred, and not the amount of pollution or the precise costs. Not only can such fines act as effective financial incentives for compliance, they also provide government with another source of revenue.

Where government does closely measure and monitor pollution from certain industries, it can tax more heavily those that fail to meet the standards, and give tax credits to those that do. The effect would be to drive out the inefficient operator — where inefficiency is determined by both the price of the finished product and the cost to the environment.

On a variation of this theme, Senators John Heinz and Timothy Wirth of the United States have, in a report entitled "Project 88,"[2] suggested some market incentives to both keep the environment clean and simplify regulations. Under their proposals, government would set the total amounts of emissions permitted for certain types of pollution, with permits available up to those limits. Companies would buy and sell these permits as needed, and the price would rise with demand to the point where it would be cheaper to reduce emissions. This scheme has promise, but would require close monitoring in order to ensure compliance.

INTERNATIONAL COMPETITION

The world economy is more interdependent than ever before. As some pollution-abatement costs may result in higher prices for some products in the international marketplace, there is a danger that the product with the lowest price will also become the lowest common denominator in terms of the environment. We will need to think of ways to resolve problems of this nature. Perhaps we could address the question of environmental standards within the General Agreement on Tariffs and Trade (GATT), so that products of heavy polluters would be subject to high tariffs, forcing those firms to comply with international standards. The World Bank is already beginning to tie environmental conditions to some of its loans. If we put our minds to it, there will be many solutions.

LEADERSHIP AND THE PROCESS OF CHANGE

The rate of change depends on the quality of leadership. At times of crisis, we need leaders, and we need to be leaders, with the courage to shape the consensus. Those who wait for the consensus to form are followers. We must remember that when something becomes common knowledge, it may be too late.

At this stage, it is important to stand back and assess the tax system in the context of the process of change. Change is first sensed, then articulated, at which point groups of supporters begin to cluster — as with the environmental movement of the 1960s. Politicians catch the scent and weigh the potential of the issue for attracting votes. Then change begins to encounter barriers created by those firmly attached to the existing structures. As change by its very definition begins outside established institutions, those who support it are looked upon as misguided idealists by those who say "show me how to make a buck out of it." If the issues are real, then public support grows, and government is forced to act. In the case of the environment, there was a period of "phoney war" in the 1970s. Government paid lip service to the issues by passing environmental protection and assessment acts, which were not really applied. With the sequence of environmental bad news in the 1980s, government bared its teeth with the threat of serious penalties. However, offences

---

2   T.E. Wirth & J. Heinz, *Project 88, Harnessing Market Forces to Protect Our Environment: Initiatives for the New President* (Washington: December 1988).

are not always detected, and are sometimes overlooked. Increasing the penalties for polluters was a good start; but legislators would create the critical mass necessary for profound change by designing the tax structure for sustainable development. This would create more opportunities for business, and the phenomenon of "swarming" would begin, as people rush to join the trend before they are left behind. This time, environmental concern will be more than a fad, and changed structures, such as the legal and tax systems, must anchor it.

As the momentum for sustainable development builds, financial institutions will need to fund extensive restructuring and many new companies. Clients of banks will begin to request that their deposits be used for environmentally positive ends; this could give rise, for example, to demands for environmental mutual funds and environmental deposit accounts. It is a matter of signalling change. As the issue becomes widely adopted, companies will indicate by means of new products and public statements that they are aware of the need to change. As capital flows into the new channels, customs and habits will eventually reform, until sustainable development becomes part of the mainstream.

CONCLUSION

Many people have accepted the concept of sustainable development, which is both inevitable and based on common sense. Its implementation requires a profound restructuring of our habits and institutions. Environmental crises have created a high level of public concern, and this has led to new and stricter legislation relating to the environment. At the same time, large governmental deficits and a complicated tax system have given rise to a cry for tax reform. The trends of tax policy are shifting the burden of taxation from income to sales taxation, and are encouraging savings. These changes should be designed to accelerate the implementation of sustainable development. By embodying the concept of sustainable development in a structure as pervasive as the tax system, and eventually in all our structures and institutions, government will build momentum for positive environmental change in Canada. We have started a voyage into a new age. It will shake our assumptions, offer great challenges, and provide many opportunities to improve the state of the environment and the quality of our own lives.

LEGAL PRESCRIPTIONS FOR AN ATMOSPHERE THAT WILL SUSTAIN THE EARTH

Nigel Bankes

The appropriate starting point for this paper, which deals with the development of a law of the atmosphere that will sustain the earth, is the report of the World Commission on Environment and Development, *Our Common Future*.[1] What problems did it identify with respect to the atmosphere? How did the Commission propose to deal with these problems in order to ensure that the atmosphere is capable of supporting sustainable development? And, in particular, did the Commission offer any guidance as to the legal tools to be adopted to ensure sustainable development?

After reviewing these matters, the paper proceeds to describe and analyze some of the more important legal steps taken to deal with problems related to the atmosphere. These include the Economic Commission for Europe's (ECE) Long Range Transboundary Air Pollution (LRTAP) Convention and protocols, the Ozone Convention and protocol, and various proposals for global atmosphere conventions.

The paper concludes by suggesting that proposals to develop a convention on the atmosphere would benefit from a more rigorous application of principle. Particular attention is given to the principles of intergenerational equity and equitable utilization of the atmosphere. As will become apparent, this paper is primarily concerned with developments in conventional law. This focus is not intended in any way to downplay the developments in customary law or the interesting theoretical work on liability being undertaken by the International Law Commission.[2]

---

1   World Commission on Environment and Development, *Our Common Future* (Oxford: Oxford University Press, 1987) (Chair: G.H. Brundtland).

2   State Liability for Injurious Consequences of Acts not Prohibited by International Law. The ILC's work on this topic was led by Quentin-Baxter until his death and subsequently by Barboza as the Commission's special rapporteurs. Their reports, and the subsequent discussions in the Commission, are reproduced in the various yearbooks of the ILC from 1980 to the present. For commentary on these matters the interested reader is referred to the writings of three authors: in particular, G. Handl, "Liability as an Obligation Established by a Primary Rule of International Law" (1985) 16 Netherlands Yrbk. Int'l Law 49; "International Liability of States for Marine Pollution" (1983) 21 Cdn. Yrbk. Int'l Law 85; "State Liability for Accidental Transnational Environmental Damage by Private Persons" (1980) 74 Am. J. Int'l Law 535; "The Principle of 'Equitable Use' Applied to Internationally Shared Natural Resources: Its Role in Resolving Potential International Disputes over Transfrontier Pollution" (1978-79) 14 Rev. Belge de droit int'l 40; L.F.E. Goldie, "Liability for Damage and Progressive Development of International Law" (1965) 14 I.C.L.Q. 1189; "Transfrontier Pollution — From Concepts of Liability to Administrative Conciliation" (1985) 12 Syr. J. Int'l Law & Comm. 185; "International Principles of Responsibility for Pollution" (1970)

THE REPORT OF THE BRUNDTLAND COMMISSION

References to the atmosphere are scattered throughout the Brundtland Report, with the most coherent analysis found in the chapter entitled "Energy: Choices for Environment and Development."[3] Other sections of the Report allude to the problems posed by the destruction of the ozone layer. Throughout, the Report emphasizes that problems of the atmosphere are interlinked with broad social and economic problems.

The Problems Stated

The Problem of Global Warming and Climate Change

By far the most serious atmospheric problems identified by the Commission were global warming and climate change. The Commission relied upon the Villach, Austria, workshop[4] for its conclusion that we face global temperature rises of between 1.5 and 4.5 degrees Celsius, with greater increases at the poles, along with a rise in sea levels of 25 to 140 centimeters. The Commission did concede, however, that there "is no way to prove that any of this will happen until it actually occurs."[5] The primary culprit in global warming was identified as the accumulation of carbon dioxide in the atmosphere through the burning of fossil fuels, and to a lesser extent through the loss of vegetative cover. The Commission believed that global warming of this magnitude would "inundate many low-lying coastal cities and river deltas. It could also drastically upset national and international agricultural production and trade systems."[6]

Among the more dire consequences were those referred to in the Commission's chapter on "Peace, Security, Development and the Environment." The Commission noted that climate changes might trigger mass population movements in areas where hunger is already endemic,[7] while rising sea levels might affect frontiers and strategic international waterways, as well as have a significant impact on fish breeding grounds.

Ozone Depletion

The problem of ozone depletion is perhaps the best known of the atmospheric problems facing the globe, and the Commission noted that the production and

9 Columbia J. Transnational Law 283; "Concepts of Strict and Absolute Liability and the Ranking of Liability in Terms of Relative Exposure to Risk" (1985) 16 Netherlands Yrbk. Int'l Law 175; D.B. Magraw, "Transboundary Harm: The International Law Commission's Study of International Liability" (1986) 80 Am. J. Int'l Law 305.

3   See *Our Common Future, supra,* note 1 at ch. 7.

4   Technical Workshop on Developing Policies for Responding to Future Climate Change, Villach, Austria, 28 September–2 October 1987, sponsored by the Beijer Institute, Stockholm, Sweden.

5   See *Our Common Future, supra,* note 1 at 176.

6   *Id.* at 33.

7   *Id.* at 294.

liberation of gases such as chlorofluorocarbons (CFCs) and halons would deplete the atmospheric ozone layer. "A substantial loss of such ozone could have catastrophic effects on human and livestock health and on some life forms at the base of the marine food chain."[8] The Commission was also aware that ozone-depleting gases contributed, as greenhouse gases (GHGs),[9] to global warming.

Other Atmospheric Problems

Other atmospheric problems identified included air pollution from the combustion of fossil fuels,[10] acidification of the environment from the same causes,[11] and the damages resulting from nuclear accidents (such as Chernobyl).[12] The Commission noted also that toxics released or used in one country might have significant effects in other countries as a result of, *inter alia,* atmospheric transport of those toxics. Finally, the Commission noted that the danger of nuclear war continued to constitute a major threat to the atmosphere. Nuclear war could result in a nuclear winter[13] — enough smoke and dust ejected into the atmosphere to absorb solar radiation and prevent sunlight from reaching the surface of the earth for a sufficiently long period of time to cause a widespread and prolonged cooling of land areas.

The Commission's Proposals

Emphasis on Linkages and a Restructuring of Global Society

Having identified the primary source of global warming as the burning of fossil fuels, the Commission suggested that the solution was to be found primarily in the development of an acceptable pathway to a safe and sustainable energy future, while at the same time protecting opportunities for economic growth, especially within developing countries.[14] In the Commission's view, the development of a sustainable energy path would have to be attained through a variety of methods, including a dramatic increase in the efficiency of end-users and a reallocation of capital investment to that end; the development and implementation of technologies and associated policies to reduce the emissions of GHGs; adoption of other fuels, such as natural gas and renewable energy sources; the development of fuel-wood sources in a manner compatible with societal and environmental needs; and the

---

8   *Id.* at 33.

9   A full list of GHGs would include carbon dioxide, methane, CFCs, and nitrous oxide. Technically, the term "heat-absorbing gases" (or HAGs) is preferable to "GHGs."

10   See *Our Common Future, supra,* note 1 at 178.

11   *Id.* at 178.

12   *Id.* at 172; for a review of Chernobyl's legal significance, see G. Handl, "Transboundary Nuclear Accidents: The Post-Chernobyl Multilateral Legislative Agenda" (1988) 15 Ecol. L.Q. 203.

13   See *Our Common Future, supra,* note 1 at 295.

14   *Id.* at 196.

development of general energy conservation measures and policies. The Commission was somewhat equivocal on a number of matters in the energy chapter, but nowhere more so than on the subject of nuclear power. While recognizing that nuclear power might help resolve the GHG problem, the Commission concluded that the "generation of nuclear power is only justifiable if there are solid solutions to the presently unsolved problems to which it gives rise,"[15] such as the risk of accidents, the high capital costs, and the disposal of radioactive wastes.

Obviously, any policy that brought about a reduction in the consumption of fossil fuels would not only help resolve the GHG problem; it would also address some of the other atmospheric problems identified by the Commission, such as increased air pollution and acidification. On other problems, the Commission made specific proposals, including the development and adoption of replacements for CFCs and halons, and the development and adoption of replacements for toxins currently in use.

The Commission also offered general advice that was less technical and more directed to social and economic policies. Several general themes run throughout the Report. These include:

1. A call to recognize the myriad interdependencies between environment and development. An example of a complex interrelationship would be that between the debt status of developing countries and the terms of trade between developing and developed nations; this linkage might in turn encourage deforestation and, consequently, the loss of species diversity, as well as global warming.

2. A call to redress the inequitable distribution of benefits between developing and developed nations, a call that is for social justice in global terms.

3. A suggestion that states and actors generally should internalize or fully account for the costs of their actions, *wherever* or *whenever* those costs might be incurred. This proposal was effectively a call for both nondiscrimination[16] and intergenerational equity.

The Legal Tools

References to some of these general themes make it clear that the Report is a radical social document, with its radicalism inspired by a perception of the crisis facing the globe. That sense of radicalism is reinforced by the Report's emphasis on

---

15 *Id.* at 189.

16 I use the term "non-discrimination" here in the sense coined by various reports of the OECD; a state should not treat negative project impacts outside its territory differently from those within its territory when carrying out project assessments: *Recommendations on Implementing a Regime of Equal Rights of Access and Non-discrimination in Relation to Transfrontier Pollution*, 17 May 1977, (1977) 16 Int'l Leg. Mat. 977.

redistribution, equitable access to resources, and equity in general, and by its preference for local democracy and decentralization in order to meet local needs.

It is true that the Report, no doubt in order to maintain consensus, contains caveats. To give but one example, the Commission, in its discussions of energy conservation measures,[17] referred to "conservation pricing" as one possible means of encouraging efficiency, but indicated "no preference." This ambivalence was doubtless due to a conflict between Commission members who preferred to rely upon the market to achieve social goals and those who favored government intervention. Nevertheless, the basic thrust of the Report is clear — the market cannot be relied upon, and government intervention will be required in order to establish the conditions and priorities for sustainable development.

What does all this have to do with law, and with the law of the atmosphere in particular? Quite a bit, I think. The very radicalism of these proposals portends problems of implementation, for law tends to be a reflection of society's most deeply held values rather than an instrument of social change. This is especially the case for international law, rooted as it is in the customs and practices of nations and in the principle of consent. By its nature, international law tends to lag behind social needs.

The Commission clearly recognized both the importance and the conservative tendencies of international law, and convoked a group of international legal experts to advise it. This initiative resulted in the preparation and publication of a separate report entitled *Environmental Protection and Sustainable Development: Legal Principles and Recommendations*.[18] Both the terms of reference of the expert advisors and their conclusions are instructive. The guidelines given to that body emphasized that it should formulate new principles of law; give attention to those principles that should be put in place to support sustainable development; and consider the responsibilities of states to future generations, other species, ecosystems of international significance, and the global commons. In formulating its responses, the group endeavored to distinguish between principles that already constituted customary international law and those that were merely *lex ferenda*.[19] Given the radicalism of some of the group of experts' proposals, it is hardly surprising that not all of them were able to command the status of customary law.

The Commission itself rarely felt able to advocate specific legal responses to the problems of the atmosphere. Thus, on the subject of global warming,[20] the

---

17 See *Our Common Future, supra,* note 1 at 200–220.

18 Experts Group on Environmental Law of the WCED, *Environmental Protection and Sustainable Development: Legal Principles and Recommendations* (London: Graham & Trotman/Martinus Nijhoff, 1987) (Chair: R.D. Munro).

19 *Id.* With respect to Article 1 (Fundamental Human Rights) at 40; with respect to Article 13 (Non-discrimination) at 88–89.

Commission merely called for a four-track strategy consisting in improved monitoring, increased research, the development of internationally agreed policies for the reduction of GHGs, and the adoption of coping strategies. Recent initiatives permitted the Commission to be more specific on the subjects of CFCs and nuclear accidents: the Report called upon states to ratify the Ozone Convention and develop related protocols,[21] and also to ratify the notice and assistance conventions developed as a direct result of the Chernobyl accident.[22] At a more general level, the Commission, in its chapter on "Institutional and Legal Change," called upon states to develop conventional environmental laws.[23]

Somewhat surprising was the Commission's failure to consider the status of the atmosphere as a "global commons" along with the oceans, Antarctica, and space. This was notwithstanding the Commission's analysis of the problems of the commons, which seem to apply equally to the atmosphere as well as to what the Commission describes as "shared ecosystems":

> The traditional forms of national sovereignty are increasingly challenged by the realities of ecological and economic interdependence. Nowhere is this more true than in shared ecosystems and in 'the global commons' — those parts of the planet that fall outside national jurisdictions. Here, sustainable development can be secured only through international co-operation and agreed regimes for surveillance, development, and management in the common interest....[24]

> By the same token, without agreed, equitable, and enforceable rules governing the rights and duties of states in respect of the global commons, the pressure of demands on finite resources will destroy their ecological integrity over time.[25]

I now turn from the Commission's analysis to consider the developing law of the atmosphere, and what needs to be done to achieve an atmospheric regime that will meet the goal of sustainable development. Particular attention will be given to developments since the Brundtland Report. Before doing so, however, I shall briefly consider the specific and unusual problems confronted by those who would develop a new law of the atmosphere.

1. The activities that cause atmospheric problems, and especially the problem of global warming, are pervasive in an industrial and post-industrial society. Hitherto, those activities have, by and large, been considered both *desirable* and *lawful*. The precise point at which such activities become unlawful is a matter of great debate and is one of the conundrums facing the International

---

20   See *Our Common Future, supra,* note 1 at 176.

21   *Id.* at 177.

22   Convention on Early Notification of a Nuclear Accident, Vienna, 26 September 1986, (1986) 25 Int'l Leg. Mat. 1370; Convention on Assistance in the Case of a Nuclear Accident or Radiological Emergency, Vienna, 26 September 1986, (1986) 25 Int'l Leg. Mat. 1377.

23   See *Our Common Future, supra,* note 1 at 333.

24   *Id.* at 261.

25   *Id.*

Law Commission in its work on liability.[26] Problematic activities include:

- Energy generation and consumption
- Transportation
- Manufacturing of cement
- Clearing of forests

These activities will not suddenly become illegal.

2. With respect to global warming (as opposed to, for example, ultra-hazardous activities), it is the pervasive effect of certain activities that causes the problem. This raises difficult questions of apportionment of both liability and the continued freedom to carry on the activities.

3. The harm that may be caused through global warming and ozone depletion is indirect, resulting from changes in the chemical composition of the upper atmosphere. For other pollution problems the causal chain may often be more direct.

4. There are tremendous problems of uncertainty and proof, although one should not underestimate the remarkable degree of consensus within the international scientific community as to the existence of a problem. Any attempt to resolve the remaining uncertainties will require a high degree of scientific cooperation and uniformity of standards.

5. The effects of activities are so widespread that the involvement of permanent international organizations must be central to the success of any international agreement. The global nature of the effects also requires that solutions be global rather than bilateral or regional.

6. The legal status of the atmosphere is uncertain, and use of the atmosphere to justify an international interest in domestic activities will undoubtedly be perceived as a threat to sovereignty and the principle of permanent sovereignty over natural resources. (It is perhaps this concern that prevented the Commission from dealing with the atmosphere as a global commons.)

Given this context, I now turn to the development of conventional law.

INTERNATIONAL AGREEMENTS DEALING WITH ATMOSPHERIC PROBLEMS

The condition of the atmosphere is most directly addressed by the Ozone Convention and protocol, and somewhat less directly by air pollution conventions and agreements. The most notable of the latter is the 1979 ECE LRTAP and its

---

26 Quentin-Baxter referred to this as the point of intersection between harm and wrong: *Third Report on International Liability for Injurious Consequences Arising Out of Acts Not Prohibited by International Law* (1982), [1982] 2(1) Yrbk. Int'l L. Comm. 51 at 54.

accompanying protocols. The details of these agreements have been analyzed by others elsewhere[27]; I shall consider them here primarily for the guidance they offer as techniques for developing a comprehensive law of the atmosphere, to deal with problems such as global warming. I then refer to some general conventional developments, and conclude by reviewing the proposals that have been made for a framework law of the atmosphere.

The Vienna Ozone Convention and Montreal Protocol

The Vienna Ozone Convention[28] and accompanying Montreal Protocol[29] represent the first set of global international instruments designed to deal with an atmospheric environmental problem. Although perhaps the primary impetus for the initiative was the effect of ozone depletion on human health (every 1 percent decline in the ozone layer may mean a 4–6 percent increase in certain skin cancers), both the preamble to the Convention and Article 1 (the general obligation clause) require parties to protect human health and the environment.

The Convention is effectively a framework agreement that envisages the imposition of particular obligations by means of protocols. To that end, the parties agreed in Article 2(2) to "[c]o-operate in the formulation of agreed measures, procedures and standards for the implementation of this Convention, with a view to the adoption of protocols...."

In order to facilitate that process, Article 6 established a Conference of the Parties and Article 7, a secretariat — a role filled on a temporary basis by the United Nations Environment Program (UNEP). Further support for the development of protocols was given by various articles providing for further research and systematic observation, further cooperation, and the transmission of information.

As it happened, negotiations proceeded simultaneously on the subject of a protocol to prescribe specific CFC and halon reductions. Those efforts came to fruition thirty months later, at a diplomatic conference in Montreal in September 1987. The details of the Protocol need not concern us, but the techniques adopted are certainly of note. The Protocol calls for a staged reduction in the level of consumption of controlled substances (using a 1986 base year) of, first, 20 percent, and then 50 percent. The second cut will take effect unless a meeting of the parties decides otherwise.[30] The parties may make further reductions at ensuing meetings

---

27 On the ECE Convention and Protocol, see especially the successive reports of the rapporteurs and chairpersons of the International Law Association's Committee on the Legal Aspects of Long Distance Air Pollution (Paris: 61st Conference, 1984) at 377; (Seoul: 62d Conference, 1986) at 198; (Warsaw: 63d Conference, 1988); A. Rosencranz, "The ECE Convention of 1979 on Long-Range Transboundary Air Pollution" (1981) 75 Am. J. Int'l Law 975.

28 Vienna, 22 March 1985, (1987) 26 Int'l Leg. Mat. 1516, in force 22 September 1988.

29 Montreal, 16 September 1987, (1987) 26 Int'l Leg. Mat. 1541.

30 This is an unusual "law-making" provision. On the problems of law-making by vote rather than consensus, see P. Kirsche & D. McRae, "Law-making Through International Institutions" in

(which are to be convened at regular intervals), with decisions taken on the basis of either consensus or, failing that, a two-thirds majority. These decisions are to be based upon available scientific, environmental, technical, and economic information. Article 6 provides for the regular assessment, at least every four years, of the effectiveness of the control measures adopted. The parties are to have the benefit of the opinions of panels of experts convened for this specific purpose. Special provision is made in the Protocol to deal with the situation of developing countries, and with temporary adjustments and transfers of production to assist in rationalizing the impact of the prescribed reductions. Finally, in an attempt to ensure the efficacy of the Protocol, there are measures dealing with the control of trade with non-parties.

The provisions in the Protocol that allow more stringent measures to be adopted have already proven their worth, insofar as new scientific evidence suggests that the depletion of the ozone layer is more significant than was thought at the time the Protocol was negotiated. For example,[31] scientists now believe that there is potential for significant ozone depletion in the Arctic as well as the Antarctic. These developments have led many countries (including Canada, the United States, and members of the European Community) to unilaterally adopt more stringent reductions (with a complete phase-out by the end of the century) than those called for by the Protocol. The regular review provided for by the Protocol admits of the possibility that more stringent international standards will also be adopted by a conference of the parties.[32]

Nevertheless, the Protocol does seem to have at least one significant problem in gaining acceptance, related to the concerns of developing countries.[33] The case for the developing countries, who are only now receiving the benefit of CFC technology, is being made most vociferously by China and India, both of whom have significant productive capacity. China participated in the Vienna Convention conference as an observer and accepted full participation in the Montreal meeting. India did not participate at all in Vienna and attended the Montreal meeting as an observer.

The difference of opinion between developed and developing countries was forcefully articulated at an international meeting hosted by the British government in March 1989 for the express purpose of building a wider basis of support for the

---

International Law: Critical Choices for Canada 1985–2000 (Kingston: Queen's Law Journal, 1986) at 1.

31 *Globe and Mail,* 11 February 1989.

32 Note at (1989) 28 Int'l Leg. Mat. 574. At the first meeting of the parties in Helsinki, May 1989, a resolution was adopted calling for a ban on ozone-depleting substances by the year 2000, see *Globe and Mail,* 4 May 1989.

33 On some of the legal problems associated with environmental standards and developing countries, see D.B. Magraw, "The International Law Commission's Study of International Liability for Non-prohibited Acts as it Relates to Developing States" (1986) 61 Wash. L. Rev. 1041.

Montreal Protocol, and for even deeper cuts. Spokespersons for China and India pointed out[34] that the basic CFC production level guaranteed to developing countries[35] was significantly less than that available to developed countries, even after the cuts called for by the Protocol. They also argued that the Protocol had to be amended to provide for more generous technological assistance to developing countries. For these two countries, the problem of ozone depletion and its solutions had to be seen against the background of a profound imbalance in the world's economic structure.[36] On this point, they would find substantial support in the Brundtland Report.

The ECE LRTAP Convention and Protocols

The ECE Convention[37] is not a global convention, but its ambit does extend to the Soviet Union, eastern and western Europe, and North America. The Convention grew out of the Helsinki Conference on Security and Co-operation in Europe and has spawned a series of protocols. Unlike the Vienna Convention, the LRTAP Convention did not make clear that it was to be used as a framework for the development of future protocols imposing specific reduction requirements. Nevertheless, the Convention, through the meetings of the Executive Body established by Article 10, has proven itself to be an effective forum. Essentially, the parties have chosen to "implement" their obligations under the Convention by the negotiation of protocols.

The Convention has been criticized by this[38] and other writers[39] for the generality of its fundamental principles, notably Article 2:

> The Contracting Parties, taking due account of the facts and problems involved, are determined to protect man and his environment against air pollution and shall endeavor to limit and, as far as possible, gradually reduce and prevent air pollution including long-range transboundary air pollution.

However, the Convention's real achievements lie in the procedural clauses, which have resulted in the creation of an information base that has justified and supported the negotiation of the sulfur and nitrogen oxide protocols.

Although the Convention did not refer specifically to protocols, it did make it clear in several places that programs for monitoring and evaluating long-range air

---

34   J. Gray, "Third World Finds Ally in Prince on Cost of Saving Ozone Layer," *Globe and Mail* (7 March 1989) A1–2.

35   Article 5 entitles them to delay compliance with control measures provided that calculated level of consumption is less than 0.3 kilograms per capita.

36   See Gray, *supra,* note 34.

37   Geneva, 1979, (1979) 18 Int'l Leg. Mat. 1442, in force March 1983.

38   N.D. Bankes & J.O. Saunders, "Acid Rain: Multilateral and Bilateral Approaches to Transboundary Pollution Under International Law" (1984) 33 Univ. N.B. L.J. 155.

39   See Rosencranz, *supra,* note 27 at 480.

pollution should start with sulphur dioxide, and then possibly be extended to other pollutants (preamble, Articles 8(a) and 9(a)(e)). Responding to pressure from, among others, the Nordic countries,[40] Canada, and West Germany, the second meeting of the Executive Body in September 1984 established an *ad hoc* working group to draft a protocol on sulphur dioxide emissions. The resulting protocol was signed at the third meeting in Helsinki in July 1985 and entered into force on September 2, 1987. The same meeting of the Executive Body established a working group on nitrogen oxides.[41] The mandate of that working group was expanded by the fourth meeting of the Executive Body, allowing it to elaborate a draft protocol[42]; the protocol was signed at the Executive Body's November 1988 session in Sofia, Bulgaria.[43] Of great practical significance to the future implementation of the Convention was the negotiation in 1984 of a protocol on the long-term financing of EMEP,[44] a data-collection program that provides the necessary information base for the negotiation of further substantive protocols.

The Helsinki (Sulphur) Protocol

The Helsinki Protocol[45] has the great merit of simplicity. Its main operative provisions state that the parties shall reduce their annual sulphur emissions or their transboundary fluxes by at least 30 percent of their 1980 levels by 1993. The Protocol also deals with the provision of information on emissions and contemplates the development of amendments for consideration by the Executive Body of the Convention. Although the Protocol has entered into force, there remain some notable dissentients, including Poland, Spain, the United Kingdom, and the United States. According to Dr. Lammers,[46] Poland has not signed because it lacks adequate technology, whereas the United States and the United Kingdom (especially the former) have not become parties because they believe that the use of 1980 as the base date does not give them sufficient credit for reductions already achieved. This problem of "credit" will likely prove to be a contentious matter in the negotiation of specific reductions for other gases under this and other agreements.

The problem of sulphur dioxide emissions is probably easier to address than that of nitrogen oxide emissions, because the cutbacks can be attained by imposing restrictions on generating plants and metal smelters without having to deal with myriad mobile point sources.

---

40   See ILA Committee, *Legal Aspects of Long Distance Air Pollution* (Interim Report) (Seoul: 62d Conference, 1986) at para. 4.

41   *Id.*

42   ILA Committee, *Legal Aspects of Long Distance Air Pollution* (Warsaw: 63d Conference, 1988) at para. 10.

43   Sophia, 31 October 1988, (1989) 28 Int'l Leg. Mat. 212.

44   Geneva, 24 September 1984, (1988) 27 Int'l Leg. Mat. 698, in force 28 January 1988.

45   Helsinki, 8 July 1985, (1988) 27 Int'l Leg. Mat. 707, in force 2 September 1987.

46   See ILA Committee, *supra,* note 42 at 4.

The Sofia (Nitrogen Oxides) Protocol

The Sofia Protocol[47] is significantly more complex than its Helsinki counterpart for several reasons. First, it was recognized that any attempt to reduce nitrogen oxide emissions would require the reduction of emissions from both stationary and mobile sources (preamble). Second, it was decided that any approach to reduction should be based upon the notion of critical loads, which would provide a scientific basis for proposing specific levels of reductions.

The Sofia Protocol provides for two steps in its basic obligations. At the first stage, parties must control or reduce their emissions of nitrogen oxides so that by 1994 they do not exceed their emission levels for 1987, or for any previous year specified by the party concerned. This clause (Article 2(1)) does not refer to the source of the emission and is, in effect, a stabilization rather than a reduction. However, within two years of entry into force, national emissions standards must be applied to new mobile sources and major new stationary sources (as well as substantially modified major sources). These standards must be based upon the "best available technologies which are economically feasible." Parties must make existing plants subject to pollution control measures, but taking into consideration "the need to avoid undue operational disruption," as well as the age and rate of utilization of the plant.

The second step calls on parties to commence negotiations to reduce emissions further, based upon scientific and technological development, critical loads, and the result of work programs undertaken pursuant to the protocol. In order to establish a sound scientific basis for further reductions, the parties agreed to give high priority to developing the criterion of critical loads.

In order to facilitate nitrogen oxide reductions from mobile sources, the parties also agreed to make unleaded fuel available on international transportation routes. Unlike the parties to the sulphur protocol, those in Sofia saw the need for a specific provision that would encourage technological exchanges to reduce nitrogen oxide emissions. The provision included a clause requiring the parties to consider the establishment of specific procedures to create favorable conditions for such exchanges.

The nitrogen oxide protocol is more forward looking than the sulfur protocol. Whereas the latter addressed the need for further reductions indirectly, in the context of a general amendment clause, several articles in the former envisage regular review and the continuation of the process. Article 5 requires a regular review based upon "scientific substantiation and technological development." Both protocols require annual reporting. Neither goes as far as the Montreal ozone protocol,

---

47   See Protocol, *supra,* note 43.

however, in providing an institutionalized law-making procedure by investing a conference of the parties with the power to bind a party to new reductions, even if that party does not specifically consent.

In the opinion of some states (notably the Federal Republic of Germany, Austria, the Netherlands, Sweden, Denmark, Switzerland, and Liechtenstein), the nitrogen oxide protocol did not go nearly far enough. They would have preferred an obligation to reduce nitrogen oxide emissions by 30 percent by 1998. As it stands, the Protocol has been drafted in a way that may achieve a broad consensus, and also pave the way for further reductions. At the same time, the Protocol accommodates states who insist upon receiving credit for steps already undertaken, by allowing parties to specify, upon signature or accession, an earlier year than 1987 as their base year.

Other International Agreements

In addition to the two agreements specifically discussed to this point, there are, of course, other agreements that bear on problems of the atmosphere and global warming, or that could be used to ameliorate atmospheric problems. The most obvious examples are bilateral and regional agreements dealing with air pollution, or, more generally, with environmental quality. Specific examples include the Nordic Environment Convention,[48] the rather limited steps taken by the United States and Canada towards the negotiation of a bilateral agreement on air pollution and acid precipitation,[49] and the U.S.–Mexico agreement on transboundary air pollution caused by copper smelters.[50] In addition, multilateral treaties such as the Law of the Sea Convention (LOS) also contain provisions dealing with atmospheric problems,[51] and the Test Ban Treaty[52] and recent International Atomic Energy Authority (IAEA) agreements on nuclear accidents[53] are of direct significance. One of the most notable recent examples is the Antarctic Minerals Convention,[54] which establishes the special responsibility of the Antarctic Treaty consultative parties to "respect Antarctic's significance for, and influence on the global environment" (Article 2(3)(b)). The Convention goes on to provide (Article 4(3)) that

---

48 Stockholm, 19 February 1974 in B. Ruster & B. Simma, eds., *International Protection of the Environment*, vol. 1 (Dobbs Ferry: Oceana, 1975) at 70.

49 *Memorandum of Intent Concerning Transboundary Air Pollution*, Washington, 5 August 1980 in Ruster & Simma, *id.*, vol. 28 at 352; D. Lewis & W. Davis, *Joint Report of the Special Envoys on Acid Rain* (January 1986).

50 Washington, 29 January 1987, (1987) 26 Int'l Leg. Mat. 33.

51 Montego Bay, 10 December 1982, (1982) 21 Int'l Leg. Mat. 1261, Part XII, "Preservation of the Marine Environment."

52 Moscow, 5 August 1963 in Ruster & Simma, *supra,* note 48, vol. 1 at 422.

53 See IAEA Agreements on Nuclear Accidents, *supra,* note 22.

54 Wellington, 2 June 1988, (1988) 27 Int'l Leg. Mat. 859.

[n]o Antarctic mineral resource activity shall take place until it is judged, based upon assessment of its possible impacts, that the activity in question would not cause significant adverse effects on global or regional climate or weather patterns.

Other agreements may have a positive impact upon atmospheric quality by encouraging the preservation of the globe's natural heritage. For example, protection of forest areas might be fostered by the UNESCO World Heritage Convention,[55] and damage to wetland areas may be slowed or halted by the Ramsar Convention.[56]

More recently, a commodities agreement, the International Tropical Timber Agreement,[57] has been hailed as an attempt to recognize some of the interdependencies on which the quality of the atmosphere depends. The Agreement called for the creation of the International Tropical Timber Organization (ITTO). The ITTO through its Council and committee will, *inter alia,* review projects in various fields, including reforestation and forest management, and seek financing for approved projects. Projects will be examined (Article 23(2)) in order to determine whether they further the objectives set out in Article 1, which include the following:

(f) To encourage members to support and develop industrial tropical timber reforestation and forest management activities....

(h) To encourage the development of national policies aimed at sustainable utilization and conservation of tropical forests and their genetic resources, and at maintaining the ecological balance in the regions concerned.

While this particular convention does not go nearly far enough, it does recognize some of the linkages with which the Brundtland Commission was so concerned.

At a more abstract level, one can also see in modern international environmental agreements a common concern with globalization.[58] While at one time environmental problems might have been conceived of and dealt with at a regional or bilateral level, it is now recognized that only global conventions and instruments will suffice. Perhaps the best analogy here is with international human rights instruments. This tendency towards globalization is illustrated by a number of agreements already referred to, but additional reference might be made to the Convention on International Trade in Endangered Species[59] and the Migratory Species Convention.[60]

---

55 Paris, 16 November 1972 in Ruster & Simma, *supra,* note 48, vol. 14 at 7238.

56 Convention on Wetlands of International Importance, Ramsar, 3 February 1971 in Ruster & Simma, *supra,* note 48, vol. 5 at 2161.

57 Geneva, 18 November 1983, UNCTAD, TD/Timber/11/Rev. 1.

58 See A. Kiss, "The International Protection of the Environment" in R. St. J. Macdonald & D.M. Johnston, eds., *The Structure and Process of International Law: Essays in Legal Philosophy, Doctrine and Theory* (The Hague: Martinus Nijhoff, 1983) at 1069.

59 Washington, 3 March 1973 in Ruster & Simma, *supra,* note 48, vol. 5 at 2228.

60 Bonn, 23 June 1979, (1980) 19 Int'l Leg. Mat. 15.

Evaluation

The framework convention approach, supplemented by protocols designed to implement broad statements of principle or aspirations, seems to have worked well. The approach requires two forms of institutional support: first, an international monitoring and data-gathering capability, and second, a procedure for convoking regular meetings of the high contracting parties that can be used to evaluate the data and develop protocols. The framework approach is ideally suited to dealing with uncertainty and changing circumstances, and can be used to build consensus on an incremental basis.

The prescription of specific targeted reductions by way of protocol also seems to have worked well, although some concerns must be expressed. First, the targeted reduction tends to be the lowest common denominator. Second, the base on which the target is calculated has been adjusted in some circumstances to give prior credit, although the principle that would justify this is not apparent. Related to the last point is the failure of recent conventions to deal with the question of liability.[61] Success has been achieved, but difficult questions have been sloughed off.

Finally, it should be emphasized that global conventions must be drafted in a way that takes full account of the special needs and aspirations of developing countries.

PROPOSALS FOR A GLOBAL FRAMEWORK CONVENTION ON THE ATMOSPHERE AND/OR CLIMATE CHANGE

Background

It is apparent that the multilateral agreements in force at this time do not in themselves provide an adequate framework for a legal regime for the atmosphere. They do not, for example, explicitly deal with global warming (although CFCs are certainly a significant contributor to the GHG problem). Moreover, not all of the conventions are global, and regional solutions alone will not suffice.

During the past eighteen months to two years, the consensus has grown that

---

61 The LRTAP Convention is not the only international agreement to sidestep the question of liability. The full list is quite depressing. For other examples, see Regional Convention for Co-operation on the Protection of the Marine Environment from Pollution, Kuwait, 24 April 1978 in Ruster & Simma, *supra,* note 48, vol. 19 at 9551 (Article 13); Convention for the Protection of the Mediterranean Sea Against Pollution, Barcelona, 16 February 1976 in Ruster & Simma, *supra,* note 48, vol. 19 at 9497 (Article 12); UNCLOS III, *supra,* note 51, Articles 235, 263, 134(2) (in which some attempt is made to deal with the problem); Convention for the Protection of the Natural Resources and Environment of the South Pacific Region, Noumea, 25 November 1986, (1987) 26 Int'l Leg. Mat. 41 (Article 20); Convention on the Control of Transboundary Movement of Hazardous Wastes and their Disposal, Basel, 22 March 1989, (1989) 28 Int'l Leg. Mat. 649 (Article 12).

states should endeavor to formulate a framework convention for a law of the atmosphere. To this there might be added a further framework convention on climate change or a series of protocols dealing with specific atmospheric problems, much like the ECE LRTAP Convention and protocols. To some degree, the debate is complicated by the existence of the LRTAP and Ozone Conventions themselves, insofar as they effectively constitute "frameworks" on specific atmospheric problems. This might in future generate some nice questions of consistency, but that fact should not undermine the validity of the approach.

The idea of a global convention was adopted in June 1988 by the Toronto Conference on the Changing Atmosphere, hosted by the Canadian government and co-sponsored by UNEP and the World Meteorological Organization (WMO). The conference statement called on the international community to "initiate the development of a comprehensive global convention as a framework for protocols on the protection of the atmosphere."[62] That initiative was followed up in February 1989 at a meeting of environmental law and policy experts in Ottawa, hosted by the Canadian government.[63] Perhaps of greatest significance, however, was the introduction of the idea in the General Assembly of the United Nations in December 1988.[64] The preamble to Resolution 43/53 noted that "climate change affects humanity as a whole and should be confronted within a global framework so as to take into account the vital interest of all mankind." The preamble also called on UNEP and WMO, through the recently established joint Intergovernmental Panel on Climate Change, to consider how international instruments on climate might be strengthened and to identify "elements for inclusion in a possible future international convention on climate."

The most commonly adopted model for a framework for a law of the atmosphere has been Part XII of LOS III,[65] which deals with the environment. For example, this formed the basis of the draft convention adopted at the meeting of the Institut International de Gestion et de Genie de l'Environment at Aix-les-Bains in 1988.[66] The LOS also underlay the "Comprehensive Global Framework Convention for Protection of the Atmosphere" prepared by Dr. Johan Lammers for the Ottawa meeting of law and policy experts. This general approach has not been challenged, although, as noted above, questions have been raised as to the precise "fit" between a global atmospheric convention and other framework conventions.

62 *The Changing Atmosphere: Implications for Global Security* (Conference Statement) (Toronto: June 1988) at 6.

63 Protection of the Atmosphere, Meeting of Legal and Policy Experts (Ottawa, February 1989). The final report of the meeting contains the text of draft atmosphere and climate change conventions discussed *infra*.

64 UNGA Res. 43/53, 27 January 1989.

65 See Law of the Sea Convention, *supra*, note 51.

66 16–29 May 1988.

The Aix-les-Bains and Ottawa Draft Conventions

The Aix-les-Bains and Ottawa drafting initiatives are not truly comparable. The Aix-les-Bains document deals with long-distance transfrontier air pollution and is very skeletal. The Ottawa initiative is much more comprehensive and provides a useful basis for further discussion. There was some confusion at the Ottawa conference, however, as to the subject of the framework convention and the number of framework conventions required. Hence, the final document of the conference contains "elements" for an "umbrella" convention on the protection of the atmosphere and "elements" for a convention on climate change. In the following discussion I shall draw, where appropriate, on both portions of the document.

The Ottawa conference proposed a framework convention that provides for states' obligation to protect and preserve the atmosphere, which obligation would be implemented through the negotiation of protocols. In addition, however, the convention contains what is in effect a free-standing obligation on states to "prevent, reduce or control any international atmospheric interference or significant risk thereof arising from activities under their jurisdiction or control." "Atmospheric interference" is defined as

> any change in the physical or chemical condition of the atmosphere resulting directly or indirectly from human activities and producing effects of such a nature as to appreciably endanger human health, harm living resources, ecosystems and material property, impair amenities or interfere with other legitimate uses of the environment....

The utility of the free-standing obligation is probably dramatically reduced by the need to establish a causal connection between an interference and its alleged effects. The present status of the science makes any exercise of causal judgement extremely speculative. One might ask, for example: What is it that is causing the climate changes? Are they linked to the emission of GHGs, or are they "natural" climate changes such as have occurred in the past? Can there be said to be an atmospheric interference by state Y when state Y contributes less than 1 percent of global GHG emissions?

In addition to this free-standing obligation, the draft convention envisages that the parties would endeavor to enter into protocols to implement the convention. The text of the "elements for a convention on climate change" indicates that protocols on the following subjects might be considered: carbon dioxide, methane, CFCs and halons, nitrous oxide, tropospheric ozone, deforestation/reforestation, and a World Climate Trust Fund. The same text further suggests that a Conference of the Parties should be established, to be supported by a secretariat. Finally, on substantive matters, the climate framework convention calls for the establishment of a World Climate Trust Fund, the beneficiaries of which would be developing countries. To further take account of the special concerns of developing countries, the conference proposed that states "co-operate in providing the development and transfer of relevant technologies and the provision of technical assistance."

The procedural sections of the draft convention are extensive. They include general obligations to cooperate, to coordinate policies and strategies, and to exchange information. More specifically, the draft calls upon parties to promote and cooperate in research and the systematic collection of data on the state of the atmosphere, activities leading to atmosphere interference, prevention techniques, and the nature and extent of harm. More radical is the scope of the proposed paragraph 16, requiring states to give notice of and conduct an impact assessment of planned activities that "may cause an atmospheric interference." Notice is to be given to competent international organizations as well as to states concerned, and may be followed up, upon request, by consultation. The procedural package is completed by a clause dealing with emergency situations, which would extend to natural incidents as well as to events such as Chernobyl.

The meeting of experts made no progress with the contentious subject of liability, owing in part, no doubt, to uncertainty amongst the various working groups as to where the threshold for harm was to be fixed. As drafted, the relevant clause seems to envisage that a liability clause will be included in each protocol.

Assessment In The Light of Brundtland

When the tentative steps taken thus far to develop a law of the atmosphere are measured against the prescriptions of the Brundtland Report, the result is not very satisfying. Where the Report called for radical solutions, the initiatives to date reflect only incrementalism. Where the Report called for redistribution of global benefits and burdens, the initiatives tend to protect the status quo. Where the Report called for the adoption by the developed world of a new ethic of asceticism, the initiatives to date have tended to confirm the "have" status of the developed world and the "have-not" status of the developing nations.

The Relationship Between Developing and Developed Countries

The ECE Convention and protocols have nothing at all to say on the subject of the relationship between developing and developed countries. This is not surprising in view of their provenance; more surprising is that they have so little to say on the subject of technology transfer. Only the nitrogen oxide protocol addresses this matter in any detail, in order to meet the concerns of southern and eastern European countries. The regional nature of the ECE Convention and protocols is a serious problem for the long term, for studies suggest that significant increases in energy consumption will likely continue in non–OECD countries.[67] ECE-driven solutions can be only partial, and their benefits must be extended globally, along with developments in technology.

---

67   United States Environmental Protection Agency, *Policy Options for Stabilizing Global Climate* (Report to Congress) (1989).

The Ozone Convention and protocol have made some attempt to deal with the special situations of developing countries but, as noted, they have been less than completely successful. Neither group of conventions or protocols has anything to say, of course, on the subject of the redistribution of wealth between developing and developed countries.

Protection of the Status Quo

Both the ECE and Ozone Conventions tend to protect the status quo, insofar as the cutbacks are structured in ways that bear no clear relationship to the amount of damage a particular state is causing or has caused. In all cases, flat percentage cuts have been imposed, based simply upon present or prior production levels. This approach tends to emphasize the value of minimizing the economic dislocation to the countries concerned, at the expense of de-emphasizing the harm done to other states. This is particularly apparent in cases such as the nitrogen oxide protocol, where states have demanded that credit be given for clean-up steps already taken, with no apparent regard for either the relative or the absolute historic contributions of those states to the harm caused.

ALTERNATIVE APPROACHES: A REASSERTION OF PRINCIPLE

Equitable Allocation

Unfortunately, space does not allow more than an outline of a suggested alternative approach that is more likely to achieve the goals of the Brundtland Commission — the goals of sustainable development and equitable redistribution. The suggestion is simply that there should be an equitable allocation of utilization of the continued freedom to emit GHGs.[68] This freedom would not be so great as to cause appreciable/significant harm to another state.[69] Other factors could also be taken into account in determining an equitable utilization, such as relative historical contribution to the problem; extent to which the affected state benefits from activities in the source state; contributions to abatement; some notion of proportionality, using criteria such as land mass or population; and relative level of development and/or ability to deal with the problem.

This approach to the problem of GHG emissions is modelled upon approaches to the allocation of international watercourses, and has been adopted by some authors in relation to transboundary air pollution.[70] A proposal based simply on

---

68   See G. Handl, "National Uses of Transboundary Air Resources: The International Entitlement Issue Reconsidered" (1986) 26 Nat. Res. J. 405. The terms "equitable allocation" and "equitable utilization" have both been used in the context of international watercourses, with the latter now being the term preferred by the ILC.

69   The criterion is effectively a liability criterion and the choice of "appreciable" or "significant" continues to be debated by the ILC in its work on liability and on international watercourses.

70   For example, see Handl, *supra,* note 68.

equitable utilization is, of course, naive. It is undoubtedly a long-term goal; in the short run, it is probably essential that states adopt the simpler solution of across-the-board reductions, but this tactic should not be seen as a final solution, or one that in any way precludes the adoption of an equitable utilization formula based upon the criterion of harm.[71]

The current emphasis on the avoidance of economic dislocation rather than the prevention of harm is a reflection of practical politics and of the difficulties associated with retrofitting existing plants. Across-the-board cutbacks also have the virtues of administrative simplicity and low transaction costs.[72] Perhaps, however, the current approach also owes something to the tendency of the international community to ignore, or at least refuse to address, questions of liability for harm caused by ordinary industrial activities that are not ultra-hazardous. This tendency may have serious long-term consequences for the development of the law. It is possible that the international community's failure to develop the customary law on liability is having an unfortunate effect on the way reductions are negotiated. In the absence of liability, there is little incentive for the major producing states to shoulder their proportionate share of the cutbacks. Furthermore, the existence of flat-rate negotiated reductions may make it extremely difficult to establish liability in the future. Is not a state entitled to say that its conduct is reasonable, or complies with a standard of due diligence, or is in accordance with the shared expectations[73] of parties, where it is acting in accordance with multilateral agreements to which the other parties have assented?

Intergenerational Equity

The second part of an alternative approach would see the adoption of the principle of intergenerational equity. None of the existing formulations of a law of the atmosphere has explicitly adopted this principle. Potentially, however, the principle is a powerful norm, which may be tailored specifically to the atmosphere and may, at the same time, prove to be a touchstone for assessing the effectiveness of international agreements — the test being the extent to which the agreement

---

71   Conceptually, I believe that adoption of an equitable utilization approach would be facilitated by a recognition that the atmosphere is a "shared resource." Physically, this is undoubtedly the case, but the appellation "shared resource" has a checkered history, especially in the context of international watercourses, where upstream states view the term as being inconsistent with permanent sovereignty over natural resources. In the case of the atmosphere, opposition to the "shared resources" appellation would no doubt focus on the fact that the sovereignty of a state extends to the air mass above the land territory of the state. It is, however, possible to adopt an equitable utilization approach without forcing the view, as the ILC itself has done in the context of international watercourses.

72   See Handl, *supra,* note 68 at 440.

73   The language of Quentin-Baxter. See his schematic outline in his *Third Report, supra,* note 26 at 62.

generations. The principle of intergenerational equity was specifically considered by the Brundtland experts group, and, although perhaps not expressly articulated, it does lie behind the Brundtland Commission's comments on the importance of species diversity and the implications of a nuclear winter. Concern with intergenerational equity can also be seen in the Commission's adoption of the term "sustainable development" to describe "development that meets the needs of the present without compromising the ability of future generations to meet their own needs."[74]

The experts group thought that the principle was important enough to be placed immediately after the statement of the human right to an adequate environment. Article 2, entitled "Conservation for Present and Future Generations," provides that "States shall ensure that the environment and natural resources are conserved and used for the benefit of present and future generations." The experts group also indicated in its commentary that this "basic obligation ... is further elaborated in the following articles,"[75] which dealt with such things as the management of stocks on a sustained-yield basis.

As used here, the term "intergenerational equity" has several aspects. It suggests, first, that subsequent generations should have as broad a range of options available to them as we have now. In a second sense, it requires that options of future generations should be at least as practical and realistic as present options. Third, the term is used in a specific sense to require that the present beneficiaries of a project, activity, or policy bear its full cost, unless there are corresponding benefits to future generations.

Intergenerational equity has been interpreted[76] as imposing a more or less formal trust on the present generation, but the principle has important applications even if one cannot accept the trust approach. It is closely allied to the principle of nondiscrimination and its corollary of internalizing costs. It may be, however, that intergenerational equity has greater substantive content than the principle of nondiscrimination. The latter principle calls for "no less favorable" treatment, but does not itself set a standard for domestic treatment. By contrast, the intergenerational equity principle, by stipulating that subsequent generations shall be under no greater disability than present ones, effectively prescribes a standard of national and international treatment. This may explain why states have been more reluctant to adopt the principle of intergenerational equity than that of nondiscrimination.[77]

---

74 See *Our Common Future, supra*, note 1 at 43.

75 See *Environmental Protection and Sustainable Development, supra*, note 18 at 44.

76 E.B. Weiss, "The Planetary Trust: Conservation and Intergenerational Equity" (1984) 11 Ecol. L.Q. 495. Weiss, the leading legal exponent of the principle, does not discuss the application of the principle in the context of utility regulation.

77 The principle of nondiscrimination now finds broad acceptance, although the Legal Experts Group referred to it as "an emerging principle of international environmental law." See *Environmental*

Although the principle of intergenerational equity takes an important position in the work of the group of experts, they concede that its status is somewhat uncertain. They acknowledge that, insofar as it deals with international or trans-boundary matters (rather than just national standard-setting, confined in impact to an individual state), it "*may* in many respects be deemed to find *substantial* support in existing general international law."[78] Perhaps the clearest reference to the obligation owed to future generations is the UNESCO World Cultural and Natural Heritage Convention, which, in Article 4, refers to the duty of states to ensure the "transmission to future generations of the cultural and natural heritage...."[79] The principle similarly finds a prominent place in the 1972 Stockholm Declaration,[80] and has also been recited in many preambles to conventions pertaining to the preservation of species diversity. These instances, however, are but a weak foundation on which to mount a case that the principle represents an existing norm of international law.

A stronger basis of support for the principle of intergenerational equity in international law can be found in its adoption as the underlying principle of many international agreements dealing with the harvesting of particular species or stocks. In effect, these agreements and their references to optimum or sustainable yield may be seen as an implementation of the broader equitable principle. Examples include fisheries agreements,[81] the Antarctic Marine Living Resources Convention,[82] and the Migratory Species Convention.[83] Support for the principle can also be found in some pollution conventions,[84] and is no doubt inherent in the general objectives (Article 2) and preamble to the Antarctic Minerals Convention.[85]

Protection and Sustainable Development, supra, note 18 at 88–89 (commentary on Article 13). In addition to the materials cited there (in the main UNEP and OECD), reference may be made to the ILC's work on liability and international rivers.

78   *Id.* at 44–45 (emphasis added).

79   See World Heritage Convention, *supra,* note 55.

80   UN Doc. A/Conf. 48/14/Rev. 1, especially Principles 1, 2, and 5.

81   See A.W. Koers, *International Regulation of Marine Fisheries: A Study of Regional Fisheries Organizations* (Surrey: Fishing News (Books), 1973); D.M. Johnston, *The International Law of Fisheries: A Framework for Policy-Oriented Inquiries* (New Haven: Yale University Press, 1965).

82   Canberra, 20 May 1980, (1980) 19 Int'l Leg. Mat. 937 (Article 2).

83   See Migratory Species Convention, *supra,* note 60, especially the preamble: "Aware that each generation of man holds the resources of the earth for future generations and has an obligation to ensure that this legacy is conserved and, where utilized, is used wisely...." The notion of a "legacy" resonates with domestic law analogies.

84   Convention for the Protection of the Mediterranean Sea Against Pollution, Barcelona, 16 February 1976, *supra,* note 61.

85   Wellington, 2 June 1988, (1988) 27 Int'l Leg. Mat. 859.

Even stronger support may be found, however, by referring to the general principles of law recognized by civilized nations. Legal systems generally recognize interests in land that are limited to one generation. For the common lawyer, the interest is represented by the life estate, which has many of the features of the civil law usufruct.[86] The life tenant[87] has disabilities in the form of an obligation not to commit waste, to maintain the property in repair, and not to misuse the capital. The remainderman has the right to seek damages from the estate of the life tenant, but also (and perhaps more important from our perspective) the right to restrain the tenant from committing waste.[88] The relative rights of successive generations also form the basis for both the common law rule on perpetuities and the statutory formulations of the rule: the dead hand of the past should not control the decisions of future generations.

In more modern, and perhaps more relevant, terms, widespread support for the principle of intergenerational equity can be found in the general principles of utility regulation. Indeed, utility regulators are very familiar with this precise term. To the utility lawyer, the principle means that the full costs of present services should be borne by the present generation of customers and should not be foisted onto future generations. Application of the principle has meant that future decommissioning costs for utility plants must be built into the present cost of service and thence into the rate structure.[89]

Utility regulators are forced, from time to time, to give concrete effect to these broad principles, and there is no more striking and relevant example of this than the decommissioning costs associated with nuclear power plants. The utilities, through their regulators, have had to accept plans calling for the establishment of some sort of trust fund based upon the total estimated cost of decommissioning.[90] These estimates, which are inherently uncertain (because, to date, there has been no experience in decommissioning a large, commercial nuclear plant), have been

---

86 W. Buckland, *A Textbook of Roman Law: From Augustus to Justinian* (3d ed., rev'd by P. Stein; Cambridge: Cambridge University Press, 1965) at 269.

87 R.E. Megarry & H.W.R. Wade, *The Law of Real Property* (5th ed.; London: Stevens, 1984) at 92.

88 A succession of life estates does have some consequences for the flexibility and range of options available to the present generation. At its worst, a chain of life estates may have the consequence that certain land uses are entirely precluded, because no one has the authority to authorize them: for example, the cutting of timber and the opening of mines. In practice, flexibility can be achieved by the terms of a settlement (the life tenant can be made dispunishable or unimpeachable for certain types of waste) or by the terms of settled lands legislation.

89 Utility law has also always recognized the principle of nondiscrimination, or at least a duty not to discriminate unduly. See J.C. Bonbright, *Principles of Public Utility Rates* (New York: Columbia University Press, 1961) at ch. 19.

90 The pattern is not totally consistent in the case of Ontario Hydro. Hydro has not established an external fund, a matter which has been the subject of comments by its regulator, the Ontario Energy Board (OEB), H.R. 17.

periodically revised upward to take into account new information. The U.S. Nuclear Regulatory Commission has suggested five criteria for evaluating alternative financing mechanisms for nuclear decommissioning:

1. Degree of assurance that funds will be available when needed
2. Cost
3. Intergenerational equity
4. Flexibility in responding to changed circumstances
5. Adaptability to different ownership and jurisdictional arrangements.[91]

The funds approved by utility boards are in some cases simply massive.[92] Approvals emphasize the need for regular reconsideration of estimates, to take into account a tendency to underestimate costs and to ensure that significant changes in valuation do not go unrecognized; to do otherwise might make such provisions inequitable between current and future customers.[93]

The principles that apply to decommissioning charges for nuclear plants also apply to costs associated with the safe disposal of irradiated fuels,[94] although trust funds have not always been established for this purpose.

Application of the Principle of Intergenerational Equity to the Atmosphere

The principle of intergenerational equity seems particularly appropriate to the problem of the atmosphere. Scientists have told us that there is a significant delay between the manufacture of CFCs and their release into the atmospheric ozone layer where the damage occurs. There are also significant delays from the release of GHGs until the consequences in the form of global warming are felt. It is unlikely that any present generation will suffer the full impact of its own delicts. How might the principle of intergenerational equity be operationalized in the context of the atmosphere, and what difference would it make to the drafting of an international agreement on the atmosphere?

---

91 Referred to and discussed in many American utility cases, including *Re Wolf Creek Nuclear Generating Facility* (1986), 70 P.U.R. (4th) 475 at 541.

92 The California Public Utility Commissioners, in approving trust funds for California utilities in order that they could obtain federal tax deductions, noted that "the asset value of the trust funds could reach $20 billion in the second decade of the 21st century." *Re Nuclear Facility Decommissioning Costs* (1987), 84 P.U.R. (4th) 13 at 30.

93 OEB Report, H.R. 11 at 62. The fund requirements for particular utilities are developed by reference to specific sites because of the variations in requirements and design differences. Cost estimates also vary with future plans for the site, and in particular will be extremely expensive if it is contended that the site be available for unrestricted use, if the plant is to be dismantled immediately. See OEB Report, H.R. 10 (1981) at 164–165.

94 OEB Report, H.R. 10 at 135–137. In the case of Ontario Hydro, repeated delays in finding a satisfactory method of disposal are a continuing source of concern for the Ontario Energy Board in determining what monies should be set aside. See OEB Report, H.R. 17 at para. 9.7.

Statement of principles, and objectives and definitions. It would be useful to have an explicit recognition of the principle of intergenerational equity. For example, the basic obligation might be stated as:

States have the obligation to protect and preserve the atmosphere for the benefit of present and future generations.

Insofar as an atmospheric convention is drafted around a definition of "atmospheric interference" or some other similar concept, some reference to intergenerational interferences may be apt.

Project assessment and the principle that those who take the benefit should assume the burden. There is a growing recognition that states should be required to conduct prior assessments of new projects or activities within their territory or under their control that may have transboundary consequences. Projects or activities, in the context of atmospheric preservation, would include such things as power plants and deforestation. The results of such assessments should be made available to affected states. More sophisticated versions of the obligation to conduct assessments require the host state not to discriminate between consequences within or without its territory. These versions also allow other countries equal access to the assessment process.

What is suggested here is, first, that host states should be required to conduct project/activity assessments that will particularize a project's intergenerational atmospheric effects. Second, a state should be required to take those intergenerational consequences into account when deciding whether or not to approve a project. Third, states should be required to make project approvals conditional on the adoption of mechanisms to ensure that the generation benefiting from the project is paying its full costs. Such conditions should apply to all projects and should not discriminate as to transboundary consequences. One of the aims here is to ensure that costs are fully internalized and taken into account in deciding whether or not to approve the project or activity. Fourth, in developing an assessment procedure, states should devise mechanisms to give subsequent generations equal access to the procedure. This might be achieved through the appointment of a special counsel or guardian; an analogy here would be the courts' practice of appointing counsel to speak for unborn generations in the context of the interpretation of wills, or to speak for an interest that a court believes should be represented. More generally, Weiss has suggested that states should consider the appointment of an ombudsman to advocate the interest of subsequent generations.[95] Finally, given the long-term implications of government policies for the atmosphere, states might be required to conduct a regular intergenerational assessment of, for example, their energy policies.

---

95   See Weiss, *supra*, note 76 at 572. There is a parallel here in the notion of a "supervisory authority" under the Nordic Environment Convention, *supra*, note 48 (Article 4). The authority has standing to appear before the courts and authorities of other countries.

States should undoubtedly be given ample discretion in crafting mechanisms to ensure that the recipients of the benefits bear the costs. However, one such strategy that, as noted, has found favor with utility regulators in the context of nuclear energy is the external trust. The monies paid into the trust represent an attempted calculation — albeit a perhaps uncertain one — of future costs, allocated to each generation of consumers for each rate year on the basis of the benefit received. By the same token, we could recognize that the consumption of fossil fuels may have an indirect cost for future generations — a cost that it is inappropriate to thrust entirely upon them. Hence, an atmospheric trust fund might be established so as to internalize costs within the benefiting generation. Disbursements[96] would be made at a future time, when expenses were incurred in adapting to global warming. Payments might be made for such adaptive strategies as the construction of sea walls and dikes, or the development of new plant and tree stocks appropriate to changed climates. Alternatively, monies might be used to pay for reforestation costs. The payments into the fund should be seen not as a tax, but simply as part of the real cost of fossil-fuel generation — just as disposal and decommissioning costs are seen as part of the real costs of nuclear generation. In order to facilitate disbursement on an international basis, the fund would ideally be administered externally, that is, by an international agency.

CONCLUSIONS

Although the Brundtland Report is now some two years old, its assessment of the basic problems facing the atmosphere has only been confirmed by succeeding events. If anything, the Commission erred on the conservative side in its predictions of global warming. It is apparent that there is also a significant and growing consensus among world leaders that the Brundtland analysis is correct. Scarcely a day passes without some announcement or speech reported in the media on the subject of global warming or on the need to adopt "green" policies to prevent a browning of the globe.

Public pronouncements, however, are not enough. The review in this paper indicates that we have a long way to go to develop international conventional law that will cope with problems of global warming. It is true that some steps have been taken within the Vienna Ozone Convention, and that the ECE Convention and protocols provide us with useful precedents. However, one of the key messages of the Brundtland Report is that technical precedents, based on past practice, are not sufficient to ensure an atmosphere that will sustain the earth. New solutions must be drafted with an eye to problems of equitable distribution, both geographically and intertemporally. In the latter part of this paper I have suggested that some of the

---

96 The UNESCO Convention, one of the few international analogies, is remarkably vague on the purposes for which expenditure may be made from the fund established by Article 15 of the Convention, *supra,* note 55.

goals of the Brundtland Commission could be furthered by the adoption of two basic principles within an international law of the atmosphere: the principle of inter-generational equity and the principle of equitable utilization of the atmosphere. Both suggestions have radical overtones for the traditional international lawyer; but then, as the Brundtland Commission so perspicaciously pointed out, we face a global crisis, and perpetuation of the status quo is unlikely to help us.

TOWARDS ECOSYSTEM INTEGRITY IN THE GREAT LAKES – ST. LAWRENCE RIVER BASIN

Henry A. Regier and Andrew L. Hamilton

SUSTAINABLE DEVELOPMENT: SO WHAT'S NEW?

Sustainable development is an old concept, or at least one version of it is. That version is comfortably traditional within circles that understand something about managing human interventions in ecological systems (Table 1). For example, commissioners representing Canada, Mexico, and the United States signed a Declaration of Principles following a North American Conservation Conference in Washington in 1909[1]; the contents of Table 1 are consistent with those principles of 1909. The old ideals are enjoying an international rejuvenescence and seem to be proliferating new and perhaps more radical implications.[2] Whether the result will be clever press releases rather than strong reform remains to be seen.

Development of renewable resources to serve the interests of the imperial motherland (or "metropolis") was a key theme of Harold A. Innis.[3] Innis focused on cod, furs, and forests. According to John H. Dales,[4] the studies of Innis and his peers applied not only to the imperial development of "staple industries" in Canda, but also to other areas of the world at that time. Their work was subsequently extended to the nonsustainable "imperialistic" resource development, within Canada, of the rural hinterland (especially the North).[5] More detailed ecosystemic studies of the causes underlying such nonsustainability in more recent decades have been reported for Canadian forests and fish.[6] Within modern political economies, development of renewable resources has generally occurred within a cultural context of polarization between some heartland and hinterland.

The nonsustainable exploitation of animals as valued resources or "amenities"

1   R. Van Hise, *The Conservation of Natural Resources in the United States* (New York: MacMillan, 1911) at 385–393.

2   World Commission on Environment and Development, *Our Common Future* (Oxford: Oxford University Press, 1987) (Chair: G.H. Brundtland).

3   H.A. Innis, *Essays in Canadian Economic History,* M.Q. Innis, ed. (Toronto: University of Toronto Press, 1956).

4   J.H. Dales, "Canadian Scholarship in Economics" in R.H. Hubbard, ed., *Scholarship in Canada, 1967* (Toronto: University of Toronto Press, 1968) at 82.

5   K.J. Rea, *The Political Economy of Northern Development* (Background Study No. 36) (Ottawa: Science Council of Canada, April 1976).

6   H.A. Regier & G.L. Baskerville, "Sustainable Redevelopment of Regional Ecosystems Degraded by Exploitive Development" in W.C. Clark & R.E. Munn, eds., *Sustainable Development of the Biosphere* (Cambridge: Cambridge University Press, 1986) at 75.

attracted widespread political interest in North America and Europe during the 1890s. The population collapses of the American bison and the passenger pigeon provided extreme examples of nonsustainability in action. Scientific, "rational" techniques of renewable resource management began to emerge at that time, applied to international exploitation of fur seals in the North Pacific and fish in the northeast Atlantic.

With respect to fisheries, a key political-scientific concept came into clear focus in the early 1950s: maximum sustainable yield (MSY). Major international-fisheries conventions were crafted around this concept, including the Great Lakes

---

TABLE 1
Excerpts From an Early Version of "Conservation"

But at the beginning of this twentieth century we have for the first time taken stock of our resources and find that they are not inexhaustible. (p. 376)

It is the aim of conservation to reduce the intensity of struggle for existence, to make the situation more favorable, to reduce mere subsistence to a subordinate place, and thus give an opportunity for development to a higher intellectual and spiritual level. (p. 364)

Conservation is not a simple subject which can be treated with reference to a single resource, independently of the others; it is an interlocking one. The conservation of one resource is related to that of another. (p. 362)

Thus, whatever subject we begin conservation with, before we have finished we pass into other of its branches. A complete treatment of any part of the subject in all of its ramifications of necessity repeats a portion of the treatment of another part of the subject. (p. 362)

The principles of conservation ... require for their practice a sense of social responsibility upon the part of the individual and corporation. They demand a self-denial which cannot be expected from the owners of private property. They require that the needs of mankind shall be placed before immediate results. Therefore it is too much to expect that these principles will be generally practiced except as they are embodied into law and the law enforced by the community. (p. 362)

Conservation means "the greatest good to the greatest number — and that for the longest time". (p. 379)

The new movement for conservation can no more be stilled than can the tides which depend upon the movements of the planets, because it rests upon as fundamental a cause, — severe limitation of the natural resources of the nation. The part of wisdom is to work with the movement, and not against it; it may be guided; it cannot be stayed. (p. 378)

It has been shown by the physicist Arrhenius that the carbon dioxide of the atmosphere serves as does the glass of a hothouse to save the heat of the sun. Says he, "if the carbon dioxide is increased 2.5 to 3 times its present value, the temperature in the arctic regions must rise 8 to 9° C and produce a climate as mild as that of the Eocene period".[1] (p. 33)

Source: R. Van Hise, *The Conservation of Natural Resources in the United States* (New York: MacMillan Co., 1911).

Notes:[1] Svante Arrhenius, "On the Influence of Carbonic Acid in the Air Upon the Temperature of the Ground" (1896) 41 Philos. Mag. 237 at 267–268.

Fishery Convention of 1954. Following two decades of great efforts to apply the concept, some of the most innovative MSY researchers/planners met to assess their progress and to develop advice for the negotiators of the U.N. Law of the Sea Convention. Their assessment of MSY — their own creation — follows:

> In sum, the concept of maximum sustainable yield as a simple function of stock size was developed to provide a generalized approximate description of the response of a stock or species to exploitation. It has served a useful evolutionary function, as a means of generalized description, and as an elementary teaching aid for students and for administrators. It has provided a preliminary conservation goal where it has been used to try to avoid or correct overexploitation. It has played a significant role in the evolution of understanding of wild populations. However, like some other simplified concepts, maximum sustainable yield has become institutionalized in a more absolute and precise role than intended by the biologists who were responsible for its original formulation. It is being expected to perform functions for which it was never intended, serving for example, as the sole conceptual basis for or goal of management in some cases. Once a concept has been adopted and institutionalized, it is difficult to change it. In this case, because of its institutionalization, the concept of maximum sustainable yield is now an obstacle to the acceptance of concepts that derive from present ecological knowledge, and that would provide a more adequate basis for management. A more adequate basis is especially necessary at this time when the overall impact of man on the biosphere is increasing and diversifying as never before.[7]

There is a somewhat similar story to tell with respect to the use of the natural system as a "resource" for accepting and deactivating our less noxious wastes, whether domestic, industrial, commercial, or other. Pollution problems also came into focus in the late nineteenth century in parts of the world that were urbanizing, commercializing, and industrializing. The concept of assimilative capacity — implicitly, maximum sustainable assimilation (MSA) — came to play a role in "environmentalist" science and practice similar to that played by MSY in "resourcist" science and practice. And in the 1970s it too was found wanting, for example, by Jorling:

> The earlier program [within U.S. federal legislation, prior to 1972] included a calculation of "the assimilative capacity" which can be defined as that volume of pollutants which could be processed, treated or otherwise disposed of in the receiving waters while still maintaining the designated use. ... Assimilative capacity became a rather rough, negotiated estimate ... of what waste treatment services could be rendered by a particular reach of water. This calculation, or more accurately negotiated agreement of assimilative capacity, coupled with a determination of acceptable beneficial use and an agreement on the specific numbers or criteria, created circumstances in which compromise and indefinite delay operated to frustrate enforceability.
>
> ... So, in addition to concepts such as ... assimilative capacity, the central program required further logical gymnastics such as the provision of mixing zones which, of course, are defined as those areas of greater or lesser distance around an outfall source in which measurements are not taken. Mixing zones are strictly for the purpose of allowing another layer of negotiation and compromise, always with the burden of proof on the government, the public and the environment.

---

7   S.J. Holt & L.M. Talbot, "New Principles for the Conservation of Wild Living Resources" in L.A. Krumholz, ed., *Wildlife Monographs* (No. 59) (Louisville: Wildlife Society, 1978). See also P.A. Larkin, "An Epitaph for the Concept of Maximum Sustainable Yield" (1977) 106 Transactions of the American Fisheries Society at 1.

The net effect of the program was the application of controls which were fully in accord with and acceptable to the interests of the discharge source.[8]

Within both MSY and MSA, sustainability was a constraint that specified the maximally permissible level of use or abuse, with the level of permissibility based on a political compromise in which winners and losers were not clearly identified. Thus, a concept of sustainability has been used in management practice for decades. But MSY, MSA, and related concepts discussed below have in practice failed to ensure sustainability. New converts to a commitment to sustainability should be made aware of that concept's history. The new criteria of sustainability must go far beyond the old, simplistic versions, and this must also be true for development, as is implied in Figure 1.[9]

FIGURE 1
A Schema to Illustrate the Meaning of Some Terms

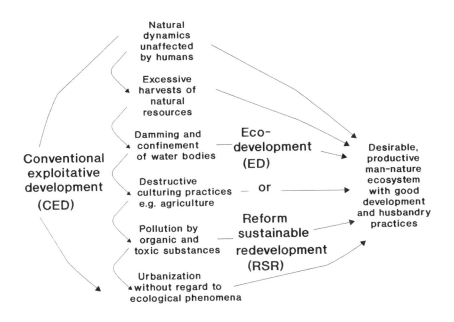

---

8   T. Jorling, "Incorporating Ecological Interpretation into Basic Statutes" in R.K. Ballentine & L.J. Guarraia, coordinators, *The Integrity of Water* (Proceedings of a Symposium convened by the U.S. Environmental Protection Agency) (Washington: U.S. Government Printing Office, 1977).

9   H.A. Regier *et al.*, "Rehabilitation of Degraded River Ecosystems" in D.P. Dodge, ed., *Proceedings of the International Large River Symposium* (Canadian Special Publication of Fisheries and Aquatic Sciences 106) (Ottawa: Dept. of Fisheries and Oceans, 1989).

SUSTAINABILITY SOPHISTRIES

A variety of policy options concerning sustainability may be examined with the help of the conventional bioeconomic model related, say, to a fishery for a particular stock of fish. The simple case treated here concerns a standardized form of commercial fishery used exclusively and consistently to harvest a homogeneous stock of fish within a habitat that is not being altered by external nature or cultural trends. The abstraction sketched here presupposes that fishermen do not exercise any communitarian rationality;[10] instead, they are assumed to be individualistic, economistic automatons of the kind presupposed by Hardin[11] in his fable about the "tragedy of the commons."

For the sake of simplicity, let the value of the catch to the fisherman be directly proportional to the physical amount landed; also, let the value (i.e., cost) of the fishing effort to the fishermen be directly proportional to a convenient physical measure of the effort. These simplifications do not affect the basic argument discussed in this section.

Figure 2 is a sketch of the conventional bioeconomic model. The dome-shaped curve shows the aggregated monetary returns, R_i, to the fishermen of a catch taken with the aggregated measure of physical effort, E_i, at an aggregated expense or cost to the fishermen of C_i. Here C_i includes "opportunity costs," taxes on property, interest on loans, and so forth. Any point on the curve or straight line denotes an equilibrium situation, that is, an equilibrium value attained after some years of stereotypical fishing practices at a particular level of effort. In other words, the stock of fish has adapted fully to the particular kind and intensity of the fishing practice.

Five sets of R, C, and E are of special interest in policy discussions:

1.   In some aquatic ecosystems no commercial fishery is allowed because all fish have been reserved for recreational angling fishery, or for viewing, as in a park. This is one extreme of "sustainability," as far as the commercial fishery is concerned!

2.   A fishery may be managed so as to maximize the difference between returns, R_i, and costs, C_i. In Figure 2, $R_1 - C_1$ is the maximal sustainable difference, and R_1 corresponds to the *maximal sustainable economic yield.* C_1 includes all costs of fishing. $R_1 - C_1$ is equal to the rent that the owner of the fish stock could charge the fishermen. If some or all of the rent is

---

10   F. Berkes, *Common Property Resources in Ecology and Community-based Sustainable Development* (London: Bellhaven Press, 1989); E. Pinkerton, ed., *Co-operative Management of Local Fisheries: New Directions for Improved Management and Community Development* (Vancouver: University of British Columbia Press, 1989).

11   G. Hardin, "The Tragedy of the Commons" (1968) 162 *Science* 1243.

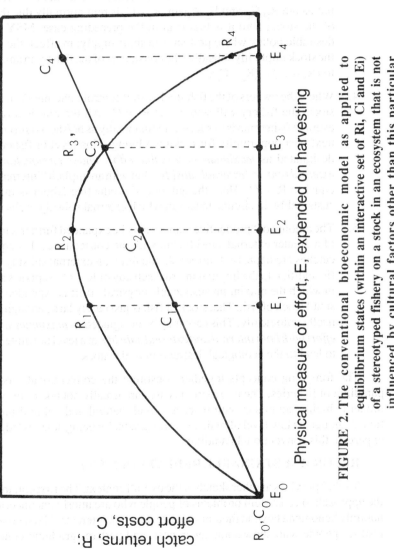

Physical measure of effort, E, expended on harvesting

FIGURE 2. The conventional bioeconomic model as applied to equilibrium states (within an interactive set of Ri, Ci and Ei) of a stereotyped fishery on a stock in an ecosystem that is not influenced by cultural factors other than this particular fishery, and not subject to secular trends in natural factors.

forgone, then the fishermen benefit financially from an implicit subsidy equal to the amount of rent forgone.

3.   A fishery may be managed so as to maximize the physical measure of the catch, that is, *maximum sustainable yield.* In Figure 2, the corresponding points are R_2, C_2, and E_2. Again, $R_2 - C_2$ is rent normally due the owners of the stock; here it is less than in the preceding case. MSY may be a desirable policy where protein is in short supply; in effect, the owners of the stock implicitly subsidize the consumers of the fish by an amount equal to $(R_1 - C_1) - (R_2 - C_2)$.

4.   Where the owners of the fish stock do not control fishermen's access to the stock, the fishery will stabilize at $R_3 = C_3$. All the rent is forgone. The average fisherman is as successful financially as he/she would be at his/her next-best opportunity for making a living. This level of fishery may be designated as *maximum sustainable effort under circumstances of no external rent or "external subsidy,"* but with an implicit "internal subsidy" equal to $R_1 - C_1$. Here the amount of productive labour is maximized, sustainably, in circumstances in which external subsidy is absent.

5.   The amount of "productive" labour may be expanded further with the help of a greater external subsidy, but with the consequence that equilibrium catches are depressed further. At the limit, an external subsidy of $E_4 - R_4$ (in addition to the implicit internal subsidy of $R_1 - C_1$) supports a situation in which the maximum sustainable physical effort is expended to catch a small stock of fish. That stock of fish is just barely large enough to sustain itself ecologically. This case may be designated as *maximum sustainable effort with both internal and external subsidy,* at a level not quite sufficient to lead to the ecological destruction of the stock.

The foregoing concepts together constitute the conventional bioeconomic paradigm of fisheries. The two extreme cases are usually not taken seriously. The model is highly simplistic with respect to both natural and cultural presuppositions,[12] though its low level of realism is only gradually being acknowledged by the experts in this conventional paradigm.

REFORM SUSTAINABLE REDEVELOPMENT

Table 2 provides another sketch of the overall context. The first column profiles the approach to ecosystem problems of people who are utterly unconcerned about natural phenomena beyond their immediate personal interests. The second column profiles people who show some awareness, and perhaps grudging concern. The

---

12   See Berkes and Pinkerton, *supra,* note 10.

TABLE 2
Comparison of Four Approaches to Resolving Ecosystem Problems

PROBLEM	APPROACH			
	EGOSYSTEMIC	PIECEMEAL	ENVIRONMENTAL	ECOSYSTEMIC
Infectious disease	Patent medicines, quarantine	Sewer conduits, pills	Public health programs	Personal hygiene
Organic waste	Hold your nose	Discharge downstream	Reduce BOD	Energy recovery
Eutrophication	Stay away	Discharge downstream	Phosphorus removal	Nutrient recycling
Acid rain	Deny it	Discharge permits	Use clean fuel on bad days	Alternative energy sources
Energy shortages	Hunt a scapegoat	Increase supply	Expand grid, conservation	Renewable energy
Toxic chemicals	Hide, disperse	Treat one-by-one, pollution havens	Recover, reuse	Nontoxic alternatives
Greenhouse effect	Ignore problem	Invest in air conditioners	Breed new crops	Carbon recycling, hydrogen fuel
Pests	Broad spectrum biocide	Selective pesticide	Integrated pest management	Ecological control
Traffic congestion	More roads through cities	More superhighways	Staggered hours	Public transport, decentralize
Demotechnic growth	Shift disbenefits	Technofix	Zoned development	Conserver society
Attitude to nature	Dominate, exploit	Cost/benefit	Environmental management	Ecosystem ethic
View of future	Egocentric	Linear, predictable	Wary of surprises	Emergent, adaptive, evolving

Source: Adapted from J.R. Vallentyne & A.L. Hamilton, "Managing Human Uses and Abuses of Aquatic Resources in the Canadian Ecosystem" in M.C. Healey & R.R. Wallace, eds, *Canadian Aquatic Resources* (Canadian Bulletin of Fisheries and Aquatic Resources 215) (Ottawa: Minister of Supply and Services, 1987) at 516..

third column displays the approach of conventional resourcists/environmentalists[13] who have employed concepts such as MSY and MSA, together with benefit/cost accounting, risk analysis, and so on. The fourth column includes some innovations of the present and, perhaps, realities of the future.[14]

Table 3 provides a sketch of some general attributes of the approaches outlined in the third and fourth columns of Table 2, here identified as technocentric utilitarian and ecocentric communitarian, respectively. Pepper[15] has discussed the contrast between these general concepts at length. There is a rough correspondence between our concepts and what Sagoff[16] has described as consequentialist and deontological ethics. "Communitarianism" as used here has somewhat broader application than as used by Bookchin.[17] He defines it as a leftist concept (that is, leftist within today's ideological spectrum), a stipulation that may result in its automatic dismissal by people of conventional rightist persuasion who find fault with anything that can be labelled "leftist." Instead, our concept of communitarianism includes the main connotation of the term "common" in the Brundtland Commission's *Our Common Future*.[18]

During the past two decades, within the Great Lakes Basin, the concepts and commitments of reform sustainable redevelopment (RSR) have gradually gained ascendancy over those of conventional exploitive development (CED).[19] RSR has recently been endorsed as a key concept, applicable in degraded ecosystems, within UNESCO's Man and the Biosphere Program. Within the reform movement in the Great Lakes region, "ecosystem integrity" is being explored as a goal for cultural/natural interactions at all levels, from local through regional to global. Ecosystem integrity is the goal to be served by sustainable development.

ECOSYSTEM INTEGRITY IN THE GREAT LAKES–ST. LAWRENCE RIVER BASIN

In the United States, the concept of an ecosystem implicitly entered federal legislation via the 1970 National Environment Policy Act (NEPA), in which Lynton Caldwell played a leading role. "Integrity" was invoked as a goal in the 1972 Federal Water Pollution Control Act Amendments, with Thomas Jorling and George Woodwell as the major innovators. American and, eventually, Canadian scientists

---

13   J.A. Livingston, *The Fallacy of Wildlife Conservation* (Toronto: McClelland and Stewart, 1981).

14   A. Rosemarin, ed., "Ecosystem Redevelopment" (1988) 17(2) Ambio 81.

15   D. Pepper, *The Roots of Modern Environmentalism* (London: Croom Helm, 1984).

16   M. Sagoff, *The Economy of the Earth: Philosophy, Law and the Environment* (Cambridge: Cambridge University Press, 1988).

17   M. Bookchin, *Toward an Ecological Society* (Montreal: Black Rose Books, 1980).

18   *Our Common Future, supra*, note 2.

19   T.H. Whillans, ed., "Saving the Great Lakes" (1986) 13(3) Alternatives 3.

TABLE 3
A Comparative Sketch of Two Approaches to Environmental Issues

Factors	Technocentric Utilitarianism	Ecocentric Communitarianism
DEVELOPMENT	Use by use, separately	Combined uses, interactively
	Oriented outward	Oriented inward
SUSTAINABILITY	Of priority uses, separately	Of cultural/natural ecosystem integrity
SOCIAL STRATEGY	Progress through sales or quotas	Prosperity through cooperation
ECONOMIC ETHOS	Constraints within mutual competition	Inducements within mutual aid
	Market mechanism dominant	Market mechanism subservient
SCIENTIFIC EMPHASIS	Linear reductionistic causality	Systemic mutual causality
TIME HORIZON	Years	Generations
USE OF NUMBERS, RE. EQUITY	Aggregated and fuzzy about winners and losers	Detailed, especially about winners and losers
EXPERTS	Resourcists, environmentalists	Stewards, husbandmen
POLITICS	Capitalist, socialist, communist	Green, bioregionalist

and planners strove to give the concepts operational meaning,[20] but with only moderate success. Then, in 1978, both terms were granted recognition and importance in the binational Great Lakes Water Quality Agreement (GLWQA). Prior efforts by the Great Lakes Research Advisory Board, and especially by J.R. Vallentyne and D.R. Rosenberger, contributed to the formal use of the term "ecosystem" in the 1978 Agreement.

---

20 For example, see Ballentine & Guarraia, *supra,* note 8; B.J. Lee, H.A. Regier & D.J. Rapport, "Ten Ecosystem Approaches to the Planning and Management of the Great Lakes" (1982) 8 J. of Great Lakes Research 505.

The GLWQA invokes the perspective of an "ecosystem approach" and the objective of "chemical, physical and biological integrity of the waters" with respect to water quality. At first blush, this might seem to imply that the GLWQA's perspective and objective do not apply to water levels and flows, fisheries, waterfowl, shore works, and so forth. But this conclusion would be mistaken. Concepts such as ecosystem and integrity are holistic, and must apply to the whole interconnected phenomenon in order to be effective for some feature(s) of it. In effect, then, the GLWQA invoked the perspective, goal, and methods of "ecosystem integrity" for all features of the Great Lakes Basin that relate to cultural/natural interactions. The Great Lakes Fishery Commission recognized this general application with a formal internal commitment in 1981.

When first introduced into U.S. federal legislation, the concepts of ecosystem and integrity were both intended to encompass the natural as well as the cultural attributes of a river basin, mountain range, plateau, and so on. They were primarily deontological rather than consequentialist concepts.[21] Such concepts were examined by an inter-agency task force of the Canadian government in the mid-1980s, and an appropriate strategy was developed.[22] The resulting strategy document apparently played a role in the binational negotiations that led to the 1987 Protocol amending the 1978 GLWQA.[23] With reference to the activities undertaken pursuant to the 1978 GLWQA (as amended in 1983 and 1987), the commitment to "ecosystem integrity" is apparent with respect to a number of issues, discussed below.

Consistent with U.S. federal legal commitments, it was recognized that a policy of zero discharge should apply to hazardous manufactured contaminants that are fundamentally alien to life processes. If one is serious about ecosystem integrity as a deontological principle, one cannot in good conscience accept the release into the environment of persistent toxic substances such as harmful radionuclides or congeners of DDTs, PCBs, PAHs, and the like. These contaminants are profoundly disintegrative in their effects on living systems, in that they interfere with the reproductive processes of organisms, and especially of species that play strongly integrative roles in the ecosystem (for example, large birds, fish, reptiles, and mammals). The release of mutagens, carcinogens, and teratogens into living systems is clearly inconsistent with the maintenance of ecosystem integrity, and such releases are increasingly being viewed as criminal actions.

Under the 1978 GLWQA, ecosystemic goals were to be specified for each of

21 See Sagoff, *supra,* note 16.

22 R.L. Thomas *et al.,* "The Ecosystems Approach: A Strategy for the Management of Renewable Resources in the Great Lakes Basin" in L.K. Caldwell, ed., *Perspectives on Ecosystem Management for the Great Lakes: A Reader* (Albany: State University of New York Press, 1988).

23 International Joint Commission, Revised Great Lakes Water Quality Agreement (Windsor: International Joint Commission, 1988).

the lakes. In the 1987 amending protocol, such goals were endorsed for Lake Superior. One goal, *inter alia,* specified a particular level of productivity for the lake trout, a salmonid. This species is an "integrative indicator" of both natural and cultural factors acting on and within Lake Superior.[24] The prospect now is that lake trout will be used to specify goals for the relatively cold, clear, and deep waters of other parts of the Great Lakes system. A comparable integrative indicator — walleye, a percid — has been proposed for the cool, turbid, shallower waters of the system. Some consideration has also been given to candidate integrative indicators for the coastal zone — for example, smallmouth bass or eagles — and even local pristine wetlands. When the next amending protocol is written, a more complete suite of indicators of ecosystemic integrity will presumably be incorporated for most of the waters of the Great Lakes, and perhaps also for the St. Lawrence River. Again, such goals relate to both the cultural and the natural polarities of ecosystem integrity.

Ecosystem integrity is also being addressed, under GLWQA, with respect to development of Remedial Action Plans (RAPs) for areas of concern. Of the many degraded locales around the lakes, some forty-two were identified as areas of concern. In 1985 Canada and the United States committed themselves to developing a RAP for each of these areas.[25] Water-quality planners and managers invoked a participatory process to integrate planning and action across different levels of government.

One particular planning process already underway in Green Bay, Wisconsin,[26] was consistent with the Great Lakes Water Quality Board's requirements, and in effect became the model process for all RAPs. The Green Bay RAP process exhibits integrity in several ways. Information on natural features of the degraded locale is interpreted within the conceptual context of ecosystem integration due to natural processes, and ecosystem disintegration due to cultural abuses — that is, in the context of stress-response ecology. The RAP involves stakeholders in a democratically fair process of learning, dialogue, and planning. The interdisciplinary concepts and methods of stress-response ecosystemic studies provide a "level playing field" for all stakeholder or actor groups[27] and the disciplinary specialists that serve

24 R.A. Ryder & C.J. Edwards, *A Conceptual Approach for the Application of Biological Indicators of Ecosystem Quality in the Great Lakes Basin* (Windsor: International Joint Commission — Great Lakes Science Advisory Board, 1985).

25 Great Lakes Water Quality Board, *Report on Great Lakes Water Quality* (Windsor: International Joint Commission, 1985).

26 H.J. Harris *et al., Green Bay in the Future — A Rehabilitative Prospectus* (Technical Report No. 38) (Ann Arbor: Great Lakes Fishery Commission, 1982); A.A. Bixby, *The Great Lakes Water Quality Agreement and Areas of Concern: A Program Audit For Assessing an Institution* (M.A. Thesis) (Toronto: University of Toronto, 1985).

27 G.R. Francis, "Toward Understanding Great Lakes 'Organizational Ecosystems' " (Editorial) (1987) 13 J. of Great Lakes Research 233.

the interests of each of those groups. The local goals that were eventually specified require modifications of cultural practices so that the natural ecosystemic processes can help to effect partial recovery.

The general commitment to ecosystemic integrity within the Green Bay RAP process is now also evident in some of the other RAPs. The International Joint Commission (IJC), through review of each draft RAP that involves peers inside and outside the IJC family of offices and boards, is encouraging formulators of RAPs to follow common guidelines.

The use of RAPs for degraded areas is now being assessed for possible application to other features of the Great Lakes–St. Lawrence River Basin. An interjurisdictional, transgovernmental network is forming to improve the degree of protection offered to highly valued pristine heritage areas of the coastal zone.[28] A system of parallel, site-specific Heritage Area Security Plans (HASPs) is being explored and an appropriate planning process is underway for Long Point, on the Ontario shore of Lake Erie.[29] As a prototype HASP process, the Long Point initiative resembles the prototype RAP process of Green Bay. This is not surprising, since both were fostered collaboratively by an inter-university group of researchers.[30]

The RAP process may also be a model for local areas in the coastal zone where fluctuations in water levels and flows cause major difficulties. An Inundation Zone Adaptive Plan (IZAP) may eventually be developed for each of these, with the involvement of the local municipality and other stakeholders. This possibility has been the subject of preliminary discussion by some participating experts in the current IJC Reference Board on Water Levels and Flows.

We have sketched some intergovernmental and transgovernmental initiatives now underway that are consistent with a commitment to ecosystem integrity. To us, these initiatives attest to a cultural shift towards ecocentric communitarianism and away from over-reliance on technocentric utilitarianism.

One implication of this shift may be broad disenchantment with harsh legal processes to reduce cultural abuses of the natural system. American opinion leaders are suggesting that the United States' highly litigious approach to environmental issues, when compared to the approaches of other western countries, may have been misguided or may now be outdated.[31] Planning and decision-making for major

---

28   P.G. Smith, "A Guide to Great Lakes Natural Heritage" (1987) 27(3) *Seasons* (Insert).

29   G.R. Francis *et al.*, *A Prospectus for the Management of the Long Point Ecosystem* (Technical Report No. 43) (Ann Arbor: Great Lakes Fishery Commission, 1985).

30   See Harris *et al.*, *supra*, note 26; Francis *et al.*, *supra*, note 29.

31   D.L. Hawk, *Regulation of the Non-rational* (M.S. Report) (New Jersey: School of Architecture, Institute of Technology, 1984); R.A. Kagan, "What Makes Uncle Sammy Sue?" (1988) 21(2) Law and Society Review 717.

Great Lakes waters (for example, the Niagara River and Lake Ontario degraded areas) is now apparently being conducted in more openly collaborative fashion. (With their RAP process, the Green Bay people demonstrated how to do this.) Although legal threats are still explicit, and "criminalization" of the more hazardous substances is progressing, reliance is placed more on negotiated agreements at particular sites and less on Procrustean uniform standards across the entire system. The latter approach could not be implemented readily in the United States, because polluters became highly defensive and stalled action indefinitely in the courts. In Canada, meanwhile, one wonders whether new legislation such as the Canadian Environmental Protection Act and Ontario's Municipal and Industrial Strategy for Abatement will foster a more adversarial climate.

A shift to a more collaborative approach would, perhaps, be consistent with ecocentric communitariansim — provided that the abuses could be thoroughly remedied through collaborative means. Increasing numbers of political leaders and chief executive officers now wish to be seen as possessing integrity on such matters.

AN OVERARCHING ECOSYSTEM CHARTER

We have sketched some of the political and practical innovations in the Great Lakes Basin that offer some hope for reform sustainable redevelopment's becoming the dominant commitment in the Basin. As Charles Ross, a long-time (now former) Commissioner of the IJC, has suggested,[32] this evolutionary process might be expedited by creating an "ecosystem charter" that would overarch all of the more specialized agreements now in place in the Great Lakes–St. Lawrence River Basin.

A recent proposal for such an ecosystem charter[33] emphasizes self-management of people as a more promising strategy than the attempted management of large natural structures and processes. The proposed charter would bring together legal and ethical principles concerning cultural/natural interactions, principles already endorsed to some extent in the Basin. It would use ecosystem integrity, in both the cultural and the natural meanings of the term, as a key goal and commitment. It could be supported by an appropriate institutional capability to mobilize relevant information for purposes of public information and general political accountability beyond the specialized agreements.[34] It might be aided by a transjurisdictional

---

32 W.J. Christie *et al.*, "Managing the Great Lakes Basin as a Home" (1986) 12 J. of Great Lakes Research 3.

33 Rawson Academy, *An Ecosystem Charter for the Great Lakes–St. Lawrence River Basin* (Ottawa: Rawson Academy, 1989).

34 A.E.J. Went, *Seventy Years Agrowing: A History of the International Council for the Exploration of the Sea, 1902–1972* (Copenhagen: ICES, 1972); ICES *Procès-verbal de la réunion 1988* (Copenhagen: ICES, 1989).

ombudsman[35] and other institutions.[36] Such an ecosystem charter should help to ensure the sustainable redevelopment of the Great Lakes–St. Lawrence River Basin. It should also help with the expeditious implementation of the environmental principles proposed by the Brundtland Commission.[37]

POSTSCRIPT ON THE BRUNDTLAND REPORT

Recall our sketch of the continuing tension between progress-oriented techno-centric utilitarians and integrity-oriented ecocentric communitarians (see Table 3). This tension is also apparent in the Brundtland Report. A superficial reading of the text might leave the impression that technocentric utilitarians dominated the World Commission on Environment and Development; technique-related numbers are found everywhere in the Report. But a closer reading shows that ecocentric communitarians were at work. There is evidence of their influence in the boxes of quotes from intervenors in the Commission's hearings, the Report's emphasis on empowerment of women and minorities, its support for integrated rural develop-ment, its indictment of militarism, and so on. The legal, deontological principles of Annexe I of the Report also go beyond the older conventions of technocentric utilitarians.

The contents of the Brundtland Report do not, in fact, go far beyond the general sense of the sectoral recommendations that flowed from the Food and Agriculture Organization's Second World Food Congress (convened at The Hague in 1970), the UN World Conference on the Human Environment (Stockholm, 1972), and the UN World Population Conference (Bucharest, 1974). On this basis, we surmise that reform was stalemated on these issues internationally, as it was within Canada and the United States, between the mid-1970s and the late 1980s. The major signifi-cance of the Brundtland Report lies less in its detailed contents than in the mem-bership of the Commission and in the list of countries that endorse it. However, we may have entered a period of more rapid reform, beyond press releases and sim-plistic technocentric utilitarianism, and may be moving towards more integrative ecocentric communitarianism. A global process to generate a sequel to the Brundtland Report — a sequel that would expedite a more thoroughgoing reform — may soon be in order.

---

35 NRC/RSC, *The Great Lakes Water Quality Agreement: An Evolving Instrument for Ecosystem Management* (Washington: National Academy Press, 1985).

36 L.K. Caldwell, *International Environmental Policy: Emergence and Dimensions* (Durham: Duke University Press, 1984); Caldwell, *supra*, note 22; P.R. Muldoon, *Cross-border Litigation: Environmental Rights in the Great Lakes Ecosystem* (Toronto: Carswell, 1986).

37 See *Our Common Future, supra*, note 2, at Annexe I.

3

SUSTAINABLE DEVELOPMENT AND ENERGY

SUSTAINABLE DEVELOPMENT: ITS IMPLICATIONS FOR ENERGY POLICY IN CANADA

Jack Gibbons, Paul Muldoon, and Marcia Valiante*

In recent years, international and Canadian policy-makers have recognized the need to rethink how economic growth can be reconciled with protection of the environment and conservation of natural resources. The history of efforts to reconcile these apparently conflicting goals is a long one, with the most recent attempt encompassed under the rubric of "sustainable development," particularly as enunciated by the World Commission on Environment and Development (the Brundtland Commission). Since the concept of sustainable development has, at least rhetorically, gained a degree of political acceptance, considerable efforts are now being devoted to investigating its meaning and implications for various sectors of society. The first major effort to analyse its implications for Canada's energy sector was the work of the Energy Options Advisory Committee (the Kierans Committee).

This paper analyses the Brundtland and Kierans concepts of sustainable development and their implications for Canadian energy policy. The first section briefly traces the history of thought on sustainable development. The second and third sections explore the generic implications of Brundtland's and Kierans' concepts of sustainable development, respectively. The fourth section analyses the implications of these concepts for the objectives of Canadian energy policy, and the fifth section discusses Brundtland's and Kierans' proposed means of achieving their energy policy objectives. The sixth section uses Ontario Hydro as a case study to examine

*   We are indebted to Anne Powell for her constructive comments and criticism.

the implications of Kierans' concept of sustainable development for Canada's publicly owned electric utilities. The seventh section offers some conclusions.

The paper's general thesis is that the Brundtland Commission's concept of sustainable development is much broader and more radical than that of the Kierans Committee. However, even the Kierans Committee's concept of sustainable development would require major reforms for our publicly owned electric utilities, such as Ontario Hydro.

HISTORY OF THOUGHT ON SUSTAINABLE DEVELOPMENT

The concept of sustainable development links the goals of human development and environmental quality. It arose from the widespread recognition that current development patterns could not continue into the future because of their increasingly significant environmental repercussions. The concept recognizes that development and environment are not in conflict, but are mutually reinforcing. This part of the paper reviews the evolution of the concept and describes its major elements.

Early Notions of Sustainability

In its most rudimentary form, the notion of sustainability is not new. John Stuart Mill proposed the concept of a sustainable economy in his 1857 work *Principles of Political Economy*,[1] and Thomas Malthus predicted widespread shortages of food and other resources if population growth was left unchecked. The biological sciences have employed such concepts for decades (for example, in the use of the terms "steady state" and "homeostasis").

The 1972 "Blueprint for Survival" published in the *Ecologist* noted that "[t]he principal defect of the industrial way of life with its ethos of expansion is that it is not sustainable."[2] The concept of sustainability also appeared in various books and papers.[3] The 1972 Declaration on the Human Environment (Stockholm Declaration) suggested a balance had to be struck between "economic development" and "environmental protection" through pollution control strategies and mitigation of the obvious adverse impacts of resource exploitation practices. The consequence of this approach, however, was that environmental concerns were treated as "add-on" considerations, to be taken into account once development decisions were made.

---

1   J.S. Mill, *Principles of Political Economy*, vol. 2 (London: John W. Pouker, 1857) at 320–326.

2   M. Allaby *et al.*, "Blueprint for Survival" (1972) 2(1) *The Ecologist* 1 at 2.

3   For example, D. Meadows, ed., *Alternatives to Growth I: A Search for Sustainable Futures* (Cambridge: Ballinger, 1977); J. Coomer, ed., *Quest for a Sustainable Society* (Toronto: Published in cooperation with the Woodland Conference (by) Pergamon Press, 1981); background papers such as "Development and Environment Report (Founex Report)" in U.N. Environment Programme, *In Defence of the Earth: The Basic Texts on Environment* (Nairobi: UNEP, 1981).

Following the Stockholm Conference, the United Nations Environment Programme (UNEP), non-governmental organizations, and academics made some gains in furthering the concept. These early efforts treated the concept expansively, and laid the foundation for a broad ethical or philosophical approach that drew together ecological, economic, political, social, and cultural components into a coherent, although somewhat vague, framework of thought. Sustainable development suggested more than a "balancing" of economic and environmental goals: the emerging view recognized that these goals are ultimately not in conflict, but that long-term economic and social development depends on environmental quality. It also demanded practices that would meld the two goals into ecologically sound development practices.

UNEP's concept of "ecodevelopment" is a good example of the attempts to articulate a coherent development framework that went beyond just balancing supposedly conflicting social, economic, and environmental goals. One of the central themes of ecodevelopment was equity — a recognition of the need for a more equitable distribution of wealth on a global basis. This theme is evidenced in many documents, declarations, and pronouncements, including several UNEP documents; the findings of the Report of the Independent Commission on International Development Issues, *North–South: A Program for Survival* (the Brandt Commission); statements in the context of the New International Economic Order; and the United Nations' International Development Strategy for the Third Development Decade. Another theme was equity between generations. As expressed in the Nairobi Declaration, a more comprehensive approach is needed that "can lead to environmentally sound and sustainable socio-economic development."[4]

The New Synthesis

By the 1980s, then, the general principles relating to a new development framework were emerging. This framework was supplemented by such initiatives as the UNEP-sponsored World Conservation Strategy,[5] the World Charter for Nature, and other international instruments that continued to stress the interdependence of humans and their environment, and the fragility of that relationship. The aim of the World Conservation Strategy, for example, is to advance international and national strategies for the conservation of living resources. According to the Strategy, sustainable development can only be achieved by

1.   maintaining essential ecological processes and life-support systems,

---

4   Nairobi Declaration, 18 May 1972, in United Nations Environment Programme, *Report of the Governing Council*, 37 U.N. GAOR Annex 2, Supp. (No. 25) at 49, U.N. Doc. A/37/25 (1982), reprinted in (1984), 19 *Texas International Law Journal* 361.

5   International Union for Conservation of Nature and Natural Resources, *World Conservation Strategy: Living Resource Conservation for Sustainable Development* (Gland: I.U.C.N.-U.N.E.P.-W.W.F., 1980).

2.   preserving genetic diversity, and

3.   ensuring sustainable utilization of species and ecosystems.

The emerging development framework was, therefore, a synthesis of many — heretofore assumed disparate — principles requiring a fundamental rethinking of various social, economic, political, and ecological values and priorities. The establishment and work of the United Nations' World Commission on Environment and Development represented an attempt to flesh out, and propose ways to achieve, this new vision for development. The resulting 1987 report, *Our Common Future,* was not the invention of the sustainable development concept, but a synthesis and renewal of it. Since then, governments and individuals have been attempting to grasp its full implications.

BRUNDTLAND'S CONCEPT OF SUSTAINABLE DEVELOPMENT

Our Common Future (the Brundtland Report) defines sustainable development as follows:

> Sustainable development is development that meets the needs of the present without compromising the ability of future generations to meet their own needs.[6]

For the purposes of this paper, this concept of sustainable development has at least four important implications.

First, it rejects maximization of the production of market-traded goods and services, or Gross National Product (GNP), as the single goal of human activity. According to the Brundtland Report, economic growth is necessary, but is legitimate only if subservient to immediate and long-term human needs. Thus a rise in GNP is not desirable if it increases inequality, reduces sustainability, or conflicts with our enjoyment of life. The Report states:

> Sustainable development involves more than growth. It requires a change in the content of growth, to make it less material- and energy-intensive and more equitable in its impact. These changes are required in all countries as part of a package of measures to maintain the stock of ecological capital, to improve the distribution of income, and to reduce the degree of vulnerability to economic crises....
>
> Income distribution is one aspect of the quality of growth, ... rapid growth combined with deteriorating income distribution may be worse than slower growth combined with redistribution in favour of the poor....
>
> Sustainability requires views of human needs and well-being that incorporate such non-economic variables as education and health enjoyed for their own sake, clean air and water, and the protection of natural beauty.[7]

---

6   World Commission on Environment and Development, *Our Common Future* (Oxford: Oxford University Press, 1987) (Chair: G.H. Brundtland) at 43.

7   *Id.* at 52, 53.

Second, development must be directed towards meeting the essential needs of all the world's people. This cannot be accomplished unless there is greater equity in access to resources, and in the distribution of costs and benefits between rich and poor and between men and women. Thus, "[d]evelopment involves a progressive transformation of economy and society."[8]

Third, sustainable development means that greater priority must be given to the needs of future generations:

> Many present efforts to guard and maintain human progress, to meet human needs, and to realize human ambitions are simply unsustainable — in both the rich and poor nations. They draw too heavily, too quickly, on already overdrawn environmental resource accounts to be affordable far into the future without bankrupting those accounts. They may show profits on the balance sheets of our generation, but our children will inherit the losses. We borrow environmental capital from future generations with no intention or prospect of repaying. They may damn us for our spendthrift ways, but they can never collect on our debt to them. We act as we do because we can get away with it: future generations do not vote; they have no political or financial power; they cannot challenge our decisions.
>
> But the results of the present profligacy are rapidly closing the options for future generations. Most of today's decision makers will be dead before the planet feels the heavier effects of acid precipitation, global warming, ozone depletion, or widespread desertification and species loss.[9]

Fourth, sustainable development requires that decision-making processes become more democratic. Increased effective participation in the decision-making process will, according to the Brundtland Report, lead to decisions that are more compatible with sustainable development:

> An industry may get away with unacceptable levels of air and water pollution because the people who bear the brunt of it are poor and unable to complain effectively.[10]

In addition, increased citizen participation will foster political support for sustainable development policies:

> Making the difficult choices involved in achieving sustainable development will depend on the widespread support and involvement of an informed public and non-governmental organizations, the scientific community, and industry. Their rights, roles, and participation in development planning, decision making, and project implementation should be expanded.[11]

Brundtland's definition of sustainable development is a moral imperative from which the above implications flow. Moreover, in addition to a concern for global and intergenerational equity, a fundamental tenet of sustainable development is the belief that there are ecological limits to growth. The Brundtland Report shares this concern:

> Growth has no set limits in terms of population or resource use beyond which lies ecological disaster. Different limits hold for the use of energy, materials, water, and land. Many of these will

---

8   *Id*. at 43.

9   *Id*. at 8.

10   *Id*. at 46.

11   *Id*. at 21.

manifest themselves in the form of rising costs and diminishing returns, rather than in the form of any sudden loss of a resource base.... But ultimate limits there are, and sustainability requires that long before these are reached, the world must ensure equitable access to the constrained resource and reorient technological efforts to relieve the pressure.[12]

KIERANS' CONCEPT OF SUSTAINABLE ECONOMIC DEVELOPMENT

From the perspective of Canadian energy policy, a second important interpretation of sustainable development is the one provided by the Energy Options Advisory Committee. The Committee was established in 1987 by the federal Minister of Energy, Mines and Resources, the Hon. Marcel Masse, to "review and assess Canada's energy prospects and options into the twenty-first century."[13] The vast majority of the Committee's members were business persons from the energy sector; the Committee's chair was Tom Kierans, an investment banker. The Energy Options Advisory Committee's Report, *Energy and Canadians: Into the 21st Century* (the Kierans Report) was published in 1988. It has been tabled in the House of Commons and is awaiting detailed consideration by a committee.

According to the Kierans Report, the operative concept is "sustainable economic development," which is the obligation to manage

all of our existing resources to enhance Canada's options, thereby favouring future generations with the capital, educated labour force, technology, environment and resource base that will generate the potential for per capita economic prosperity at least as great as that enjoyed today.[14]

Thus, the Kierans Report's view of sustainable economic development recognizes that the environment, like labour, technology, and capital, is an important factor in the production of economic goods and services. In addition, the Report notes, the quality of the environment has intrinsic importance for the nation's quality of life or living standards broadly defined. The Report states that

future Canadians should have a quality of life, environment and economic well-being equal or superior to what is currently enjoyed.[15]

In other words, the definition of sustainable economic development in the Kierans Report explicitly acknowledges that one's level of well-being is a function of the quality of one's environment as well as of one's standard of living. The Kierans Report also suggests that sustainable economic development can be achieved

within the context of a market-oriented economy by elevating environmental objectives to the same status as such goals as growth in per capita income and distributional equity.[16]

---

12   *Id.* at 45.

13   Energy Options Advisory Committee, *Energy and Canadians: Into the 21st Century* (Ottawa: Minister of Supply and Services, 1988) (Chair: T.E. Kierans) at Appendix A-3.

14   *Id.* at 12.

15   *Id.*

16   *Id.* at 59.

Despite the above statements of principle with respect to the equality of environmental and economic objectives, the spirit of the Kierans Report is that the goal of Canadian economic policy should be to pursue economic growth subject to certain environmental and other constraints:

> It [sustainable economic development] means development, but not at any cost: development that does not poison the atmosphere, destroy the environment, deal arbitrarily with people, or waste resources, thereby precluding future generations from realizing economic opportunities similar or superior to those enjoyed today.[17]

Thus Kierans' concept of sustainable economic development is a refinement of our post-war economic policy, namely, that the nation should maximize its per capita GNP subject to a number of constraints — reasonable price stability, a low level of unemployment, and an equitable distribution of income. Kierans has just added one more constraint: acceptable environmental impact. In short, the fundamental difference between Brundtland's and Kierans' concepts of sustainable development is that the former's goal is to meet global human needs, whereas the latter's is to perpetuate Canada's economic prosperity subject to certain environmental and other constraints.

THE IMPLICATIONS OF SUSTAINABLE DEVELOPMENT FOR THE OBJECTIVES OF CANADIAN ENERGY POLICY

Having reviewed the different interpretations of sustainable development found in the Brundtland and Kierans Reports, we face the next question: what are the implications of those interpretations for the objectives of Canadian energy policy?

The Brundtland Report

According to the Brundtland analysis, a number of fundamental problems arise with respect to the level and distribution of global energy consumption. First, the present level of energy consumption is ecologically unsustainable. For example, the carbon emissions that result from fossil fuel combustion are causing the global warming of the planet known as the "greenhouse effect"; this problem is especially serious because no currently available technology can reduce carbon dioxide emissions. Moreover, the sulphur dioxide and nitrogen oxide by-products of fossil fuel combustion contribute to acid rain and smog. Finally, the above emissions plus the carbon monoxide and particulate by-products of fossil fuel combustion are responsible for toxic air pollution.[18] The Brundtland Report also reveals serious concerns about the use of nuclear power to generate electricity: the release of

---

17 *Id.* at 60.

18 "Between 1959 and 1979, fossil fuel use worldwide quadrupled." L. Brown, *State of the World: 1980* (New York: W.W. Norton, 1984) at 11.

radiation as a result of a nuclear accident; the long-term storage of nuclear wastes; and the relationship between nuclear power, nuclear terrorism, and the production of nuclear bombs. The Report states that

> the generation of nuclear power is only justifiable if there are solid solutions to the unsolved problems to which it gives rise. The highest priority should be accorded to research and development on environmentally sound and ecologically viable alternatives, as well as on means of increasing the safety of nuclear energy.[19]

The second fundamental problem with the pattern of global energy consumption, according to the Brundtland Report, is that it is grossly inequitable. The developed nations are consuming more than their fair share of the world's energy resources. As Brundtland notes, per capita energy consumption in Western industrialized nations is more than eighty times that in sub-Saharan Africa.[20]

The above facts, combined with the principles of ecological sustainability and an overriding commitment to the "essential needs of the world's poor," lead to the Brundtland Commission's conclusion that the developed nations must substantially reduce their consumption of nonrenewable energy. According to the Brundtland Report, a significant reduction in the developed world's nonrenewable energy consumption could permit the developing nations to increase their energy consumption and living standards in a context that is globally sustainable.[21]

The Brundtland Report does not specifically address the issue of the appropriate level of nonrenewable energy exports by industrialized nations such as Canada. But its conclusion that developed nations must reduce their energy consumption in order to allow developing countries to increase theirs, in a context that is globally sustainable, does have implications for Canadian energy exports.

If those developed nations that import energy from Canada reduce their energy consumption in response to the Brundtland Report, then presumably Canada's energy exports to them will decline. But if they do not reduce their energy consumption sufficiently, does Canada have an obligation to reduce its energy exports to them? One could argue that Canada does, because the importing countries' high level of energy consumption will, at least in part, be the result of Canada's relatively low-cost energy exports (which reduce their incentive to conserve energy and use it more efficiently). On the other hand, increased energy exports to developing nations would be consistent with the Brundtland Report's recommendations.

The Kierans Report

The Kierans Report's conclusions regarding the appropriate objectives of Canadian energy policy are diametrically opposed to those of the Brundtland Report.

---

19   See *Our Common Future, supra,* note 6 at 14–15.

20   *Id.* at 14.

21   *Id.* at 173–174.

Rather than concluding that the level of nonrenewable energy consumption should be reduced, the Kierans Report suggests that a deliberate policy objective of energy conservation or "hoarding" is ill advised. Instead, the Advisory Committee recommends that the level of energy consumption be determined primarily by market forces:

> The Advisory Committee sees greater risk to present and future Canadian living standards from *artificially* constraining development and use of our energy resources than from developing and using them. [22]

This position is deducible from two fundamental premises of the Kierans Report: that the prime objective of development is to ensure a high standard of living for Canadians into the future, and that this will occur if economic decisions are made primarily by market forces.

In addition, the validity of the Kierans Report's conclusion that a conservation policy would artificially constrain development depends on its implicit rejection of the notion that the biosphere places absolute limits on our ability to consume energy. Instead of absolute limits to growth, the Kierans Committee used the concept of "scarcity," which means that as supplies decrease, prices increase and alternatives arise. Dr. David Brooks, a member of the Energy Options Advisory Committee, challenged the usefulness of this concept:

> [I]t is my view that sustainable development will ultimately be seen to preclude *any* increase in energy consumption, and thus *any* need for a larger energy industry. As the earth's atmosphere is now telling us, there are limits to growth, at least to growth as represented by materials throughput.[23]

Not surprisingly, the Kierans Report also opposes any restrictions on energy exports. It recommends that energy exports, like domestic energy consumption, should be guided by market forces in order to enhance Canadian living standards:

> [A]pproaches based on retarding the rate of development, trade and use of energy resources would not only limit present prospects and options but also limit those of the future. In contrast, developing trade and using our resources, guided by economic considerations and the operation of market forces, will increase the number of choices available both now and tomorrow....[24]

MEANS OF ACHIEVING SUSTAINABLE DEVELOPMENT

This section discusses and compares the Brundtland and Kierans Reports' proposed means of implementing a sustainable pattern of energy consumption in Canada. The discussion is organized around the following topics: the integration of economic and environmental decision-making and public participation, pricing, and public awareness and information.

---

22 See *Energy and Canadians, supra,* note 13 at 24 (emphasis added).

23 *Id.* at 121.

24 *Id.* at 33.

Integration of Economic and Environmental Decision-Making and Public Participation

The Brundtland Report

According to the Brundtland Report, government agencies that are responsible for economic decision-making must also be responsible and accountable for the ecological consequences of their decisions. As the Report states:

> [T]he major central economic and sectoral agencies of governments should now be made directly responsible and fully accountable for ensuring that their policies, programmes, and budgets support development that is ecologically as well as economically sustainable.[25]

In addition, citizen participation in the decision-making process is necessary to ensure that development is equitable and in the common interest. Participation is also necessary to gain public support for sustainable development policies. According to the Brundtland Commission, citizen participation can best be achieved by decentralized decision-making:

> This is best secured by decentralizing the management of resources upon which local communities depend, and giving these communities an effective say over the use of these resources. It will also require promoting citizens' initiatives, empowering people's organizations, and strengthening local democracy.[26]

For large-scale projects with a significant environmental impact, the Brundtland Report notes the need for public hearings where citizens have the resources to participate effectively. Indeed, when the environmental impact is especially high, there may be a need for a referendum:

> When the environmental impact of a proposed project is particularly high, public scrutiny of the case should be mandatory and, wherever feasible, the decision should be subject to prior public approval, perhaps by referendum.[27]

The Kierans Report

Like the Brundtland Report, the Kierans Report calls for the integration of economic and environmental decision-making. The proposed means of achieving this goal are two-fold. First, the Kierans Report supports the recommendation of the National Task Force on Environment and Economy for the establishment of a national, multisector roundtable on the environment and the economy to advise the federal Cabinet on the environment. In the Kierans Committee's opinion, such an initiative would make Canada "a world leader in integrating environmental with social and economic objectives."[28] Second, the Kierans Report states that energy regulatory boards should take full account of environmental costs when making their

---

25   See *Our Common Future, supra,* note 6 at 314.

26   *Id.* at 63.

27   *Id.* at 64.

28   See *Energy and Canadians, supra,* note 13 at 64.

decisions. It also endorses public participation at environmental assessment and electric-utility regulatory hearings. On the other hand, it believes that there could be less need for environmental assessment in the future if environmental standards are raised.[29]

Pricing Policy

The Brundtland Report

According to the Brundtland Report, the key to achieving energy efficiency is high energy prices:

> There is general agreement that the efficiency gains achieved by some industrialized countries over the past 13 years were driven largely by higher energy prices, triggered by higher oil prices. Prior to the recent fall in oil prices, energy efficiency was growing at a rate of 2.0 per cent annually in some countries, having increased gradually year by year.
>
> It is doubtful whether such steady improvements can be maintained and extended if energy prices are held below the level needed to encourage the design and adoption of more energy-efficient homes, industrial processes, and transportation vehicles.[30]

Not surprisingly, one of the most significant tools the Brundtland Report proposes for promoting sustainable development in the context of energy policy is conservation pricing — setting energy prices at levels that ensure a steady decline in nonrenewable energy consumption.[31]

The Kierans Report

According to the Kierans Report, energy prices should be determined by market forces (the laws of supply and demand):

> Because the energy economy is dynamic, with constantly changing supply and demand conditions, flexibility and resilience must characterize energy policy. Market mechanisms provide the information that makes it possible to anticipate and accommodate change, and allow the most efficient or least-cost energy choices.[32]

But the Kierans Committee recognizes that market forces will only lead to economically

---

29   *Id.* at 63, 78.

30   See *Our Common Future, supra*, note 6 at 200.

31   See *Our Common Future, supra*, note 6 at 200-201. The conservation price would presumably equal the pre-tax price plus a conservation tax or surcharge. The conservation tax, in turn, would presumably be a function of the pollutant content of the fuel; i.e., the dirtier the fuel, the higher the tax. This would encourage consumers to put greatest emphasis on reducing their consumption of relatively dirty fuels. This could be achieved by energy-efficient investments and/or by the substitution of relatively clean fuels (e.g., natural gas) for relatively dirty fuels (e.g., coal, oil).

    According to Article 903 of The Canada–U.S. Free Trade Agreement, a tax can be imposed on the export of an energy good to the United States if the tax is also imposed on the domestic consumption of the energy good. Thus, conservation pricing can be used to reduce our energy exports.

32   See *Energy and Canadians, supra*, note 13 at 65.

and environmentally appropriate energy production and consumption if the costs of environmental protection are internalized, and if energy development is constrained by environmental standards and regulations. Furthermore, the cost of achieving these standards must be borne by energy consumers. The Report notes:

> [E]nvironmental costs are not always quantifiable and ... market mechanisms on their own do not adequately account for environmental and social impacts of a project. But when these costs are known and quantifiable, they should be paid by the beneficiaries in an appropriate and timely manner.

> The Advisory Committee favours the use of performance standards whenever necessary, noting that many well-considered standards are embodied in existing laws and regulations. By instituting standards, government establishes the rules to guide industry and consumers in their decision-making. Industries can either develop technology to meet the standards in an economically efficient manner, or cease or reduce the act which is causing the problem. By setting standards, the government causes the environmental impacts of development and use to be internalized in market decision-making.[33]

Unfortunately, the Kierans Report provides no guidance as to how costs are to be accounted for and how standards are to be determined, other than recommending that the federal government take the lead and that standards be nationally consistent.[34]

Public Awareness and Information

Both the Brundtland and Kierans Reports strongly support proper energy pricing as a tool for achieving sustainable development. But proper pricing will only be fully effective if consumers have information about the energy efficiency of homes, cars, and appliances. As a consequence, both Reports support efforts to make energy-efficiency information widely available, including mandatory appliance-efficiency labelling.[35] It is noteworthy that, while electrical appliances (e.g., stoves, refrigerators, dryers) are subject to mandatory energy-efficiency labelling (Energuide), there is no such labelling requirement for gas appliances sold in Canada.

ONTARIO HYDRO: A CASE STUDY OF THE IMPLICATIONS OF SUSTAINABLE ECONOMIC DEVELOPMENT

Introduction

In previous sections we have noted that Brundtland's and Kierans' concepts of sustainable development, and their energy policy recommendations, are radically different. Nevertheless, in the case of Canada's publicly owned electric utilities,[36] the implementation of Kierans' proposals, at least in the short run, would promote Brundtland's energy policy objectives. That is, the results would be increased emphasis on conservation and renewable energy, and the substitution of natural gas

---

33   *Id*. at 60–61.

34   *Id*. at 63.

35   *Id*. at 102; *Our Common Future, supra,* note 6 at 197.

36   Canada's publicly owned electric utilities supply over 90 percent of Canada's electricity needs.

for coal-generated electricity.[37] The harmony between Brundtland and Kierans in the electricity sector is due to the fact that, at the margin, economically rational electric policies are also environmentally acceptable.

We will analyse the implications of Kierans' electric-utility reform proposals using Ontario Hydro as a case study. Ontario Hydro is, in terms of assets, Canada's largest non-financial corporation.[38] Its assets exceed $34 billion and its annual sales exceed $6 billion. Hydro wholesales power to over three hundred municipal electric utilities, and sells power directly to over eight hundred thousand rural customers and more than one hundred large industrial customers.

Ontario Hydro's generation mix in 1993 will be 61 percent nuclear, 22 percent hydro, and 17 percent coal. According to Hydro, its existing facilities and its committed new supply-and-demand-management programs will enable it to meet Ontario's electricity needs on a reliable basis until 1996. However, Hydro predicts that by 2010, given its most likely load growth, it will require another 8,000 megawatts (MW) of demand or supply resources. This 8,000 MW is equivalent to approximately 40 percent of Hydro's existing peak load. Assuming Hydro's high-growth load forecast, the additional requirement would be approximately 22,000 MW, or more than 100 percent of the existing peak load.[39]

Since large-scale coal and nuclear generation stations have a lead time of ten to fifteen years, the important public policy question facing Ontario Hydro and the Government of Ontario is whether to order a new large-scale coal or nuclear generating station or to put greater reliance on alternative supply sources (e.g., small-scale hydro, gas) and/or energy conservation.

Kierans' fundamental critique of Canada's publicly owned electric utilities is that they are not operated in a sufficiently business-like fashion. Specifically, Kierans proposes that electric utilities should

1. adopt least-cost planning principles,

2. ensure that their rates fully reflect their costs of service, and

3. be regulated by independent regulatory boards.[40]

Ontario Hydro's achievement of the first two objectives, least-cost planning and full-cost pricing, is frustrated by government subsidies, the Power Corporation Act, and/or Hydro's interpretation of that Act.

---

37 See *Our Common Future, supra*, note 6 at 176–177.
38 *The Financial Post 500* (Summer 1989) at 84.
39 Ontario Hydro, *Meeting Future Energy Needs: Draft Demands/Supply Planning Strategy* (December 1987) at S3, 5–6.
40 See *Energy and Canadians, supra*, note 13 at 78.

Least-Cost Planning

According to the Power Corporation Act, Hydro's mandate is to produce power at cost.[41] Hydro has interpreted "power at cost" to mean that it must select the generation and energy-conservation options that minimize its financial costs. Unfortunately, Hydro's financial costs are less than the true economic costs of power generation. As a consequence, the Act creates artificial biases in Hydro's generation selection process. In addition, the Act artificially limits Hydro's demand-management options.

Bias in Capital Intensivity

Ontario Hydro's required rate of return on its assets or capital is less than that of a private corporation. This lesser rate is the result of a number of factors: Hydro's debt is guaranteed by the Province of Ontario,[42] its liability in the event of a nuclear accident is limited to $75 million by the Nuclear Liability Act, it is not required to pay dividends, and it is exempt from federal and provincial corporate income tax. Thus, the financial cost to Ontario Hydro of obtaining a dollar of capital (the interest rate on its bonds) is less than the economic cost to society of transferring the capital from the private sector to Ontario Hydro (foregone output in the private sector).[43]

Since Hydro's financial cost of capital is lower than the true cost to the economy, capital-intensive generation options[44] will appear more attractive than they really are. As a consequence, Hydro's generation selection process is biased in favour of capital-intensive generation options. Thus, the nuclear option is artificially favoured over coal; and coal, in turn, is artificially favoured over gas.

Bias in Generation

Ontario Hydro will buy power from a privately owned generating station only if the cost of the private power is less than or equal to the annualized cost to Hydro of building a new generating station. As already noted, the financial cost of capital to Ontario Hydro is less than its true economic cost to the economy as a whole. Thus,

---

41 R.S.O. 1980, c. 384, ss. 56, 75.

42 The benefit to Ontario Hydro of the debt guarantee has been reduced by the Ontario Budget of 17 May 1989, which levied an annual debt guarantee fee, equal to one-half of one percent of Hydro's total outstanding debt, on Ontario Hydro.

43 According to Glenn Jenkins, the average real rate of return on capital of Canada's publicly owned electric utilities between 1965 and 1973 was 3.46 percent, whereas the average real rate of return on capital in the private sector was 10 percent between 1965 and 1974. G.P. Jenkins, *Capital in Canada: Its Social and Private Performance 1965–1974* (Discussion Paper No. 98) (Ottawa: Economic Council of Canada, 1977) at 73, 138–140.

44 A capital-intensive generating option is one where capital costs as a percentage of the total costs of generating a kilowatt-hour of electricity are relatively high. For example, nuclear and hydro are the most capital-intensive generating options; coal is less capital intensive and more fuel intensive; natural gas, in turn, is more fuel intensive and less capital intensive than coal.

the financial cost to Hydro of building a new generating station is less than its real economic cost. Consequently, the maximum rate Hydro will offer for private generation is *less* than the true incremental cost of a Hydro-owned and -operated generating station. Given that privately owned generating stations are primarily small hydro dams and gas-fired generators, the consequence of this bias is that too much of Ontario's electricity is generated by coal and nuclear energy.

Bias in Energy Supply

There are two fundamental ways of meeting a rise in the demand for electrical services. The first is to increase one's generation, transmission, and distribution capacity. The second is to reduce existing customers' need for the electricity. When the latter occurs, existing customers' supply can then be dedicated to new customers.

Hydro's mandate was changed in 1981 to include the promotion of energy conservation. Unfortunately, the legislated scope of the energy conservation mandate is unnecessarily restrictive. For example, according to Section 56b(3) of the Power Corporation Act, Hydro is not allowed to meet an increase in the demand for electricity by providing financial assistance for the conversion of electrically heated homes to an alternative supply option (e.g., gas).

Full-Cost Pricing

According to Kierans, electricity rates should reflect the cost of electricity service, in order to encourage economically rational energy-efficiency investments and to prevent excessive electricity consumption:

- To the extent that regulated prices understate the real market costs of energy, they encourage excessive energy use.

- This also weakens the incentives to use more energy-efficient processes or to substitute less costly energy sources, leading to sluggish adaption and inefficient energy use in the economy.[45]

According to Section 75 of the Power Corporation Act, Hydro is required to sell power at cost.[46] Hydro has interpreted this to mean that it must set the price of electricity equal to its average financial costs. This interpretation of the Act implies that Hydro's rates will understate the true economic cost of electricity supply for two reasons. First, as was noted in the section on least-cost planning, because Hydro's capital costs are subsidized, its financial costs will understate the economic cost of power supply. Second, average-cost pricing means that high-cost incremental supply (coal and nuclear) is rolled in with the low-cost hydraulic generating stations built before 1960. As a result, the price of electricity does not even equal the full financial cost of incremental supply.

---

45   See *Energy and Canadians, supra,* note 13 at 67.

46   The obligation to *sell* power at cost is distinct from the previously noted obligation to *produce* power at cost.

The full economic cost of power supply could be included in the price of electricity by amending the Power Corporation Act to require Ontario Hydro to earn a rate of return on its incremental supply investments equal to that of a comparable private-sector corporation. Hydro's resulting increased revenues could be used to finance dividend payments to its owner, the Government of Ontario.

Full-economic-cost pricing as defined above is equivalent to marginal-cost pricing, and appears to be consistent with the thrust of the Kierans Report. However, the Report does contain the cryptic statement that "strict marginal cost pricing ... could be damaging at the present time."[47] The caveats "strict" and "at the present time" can be interpreted to mean that Kierans believes electricity rates should be gradually raised to their marginal costs.

The Need for Regulation

Kierans' third major recommendation for publicly owned electric utilities is that they should be regulated by independent regulatory boards:

> A more appropriate approach would be to impose or strengthen regulatory control, with the aim of making the utilities more responsive to market forces and separating their regulated mandates from other government influences."[48]

This recommendation is especially appropriate for Ontario Hydro, as a brief review of its regulatory framework — the Ontario Energy Board Act,[49] the Power Corporation Act,[50] and the Environmental Assessment Act[51] — will reveal.

According to Section 37 of the Ontario Energy Board Act (OEBA), Ontario Hydro cannot raise its rates before its proposal has been reviewed by the Ontario Energy Board (OEB). Unfortunately, in every review hearing but one, the OEB has been directed by the Minister of Energy, under Section 37(2) of the OEBA, not to examine the main cause of Hydro's rising rates — that is, its system-expansion program.

In its September 1987 report with respect to Hydro's 1988 rate proposal, the OEB stated that this restriction may be *ultra vires:*

> The Board's concern is that a reference under subsection 37(2) containing restrictions by the Minister may invalidate, in law, the Board's Report in that the directions of the Minister may be ultra vires.[52]

Furthermore, the OEB only reviews Hydro's rate proposal; it does not regulate

---

47   See *Energy and Canadians, supra,* note 13 at 78.

48   *Id.*

49   R.S.O. 1980, c. 332.

50   R.S.O. 1980, c. 384.

51   R.S.O. 1980, c. 140.

52   Ontario Energy Board, *In the Matter of a Reference Respecting Ontario Hydro* (H.R. 16), vol. 1 at 1/6.

Hydro's rates. After the OEB has held its review and issued its recommendations, Ontario Hydro can ignore all of those recommendations and set its rates at whatever level it pleases. This state of affairs has led the OEB to question the value of the review process:

> In recent times the Hydro hearings have involved in excess of 8,000 person-hours by this Board and its staff alone, and aggregate cost in excess of $3,000,000 including the direct and indirect costs of Hydro and the intervenors.
>
> *In recent Reports the Board has made important recommendations* concerning, among other things, the inappropriateness of Hydro's pricing policies, in particular: its failure to include the full cost of equity in net income and its propensity to defer recovery of other costs; its inability to control costs generally, the inappropriateness of the moratorium on rate design; and its tardiness in making public its system development plans.
>
> *Hydro has, in the main, rejected these recommendations and, as a consequence, the Board is seriously concerned whether the hearings are any longer cost effective.* [53]

The lack of a regulator with teeth will hamper sustainable development if Ontario Hydro's management is biased against the options that are most consistent with sustainable development (i.e., energy conservation and small-scale hydro and gas-fired generation). Unfortunately, this bias appears to be in place. As the OEB has noted with respect to Hydro's conservation program:

> The external evidence is not consistent with Hydro's claim to a commitment to conservation. The Board is particularly concerned that Hydro is taking an inordinately long period of time to screen, test market, and implement its conservation programs.[54]

The Report of the Electricity Planning Technical Advisory Panel to Ontario's Mnister of Energy has reached similar conclusions:

> [W]e believe, Hydro tends to understate the full potential of demand options. No doubt there is an institutional aspect to this. Experience suggests that the development and execution of demand options require different structures, different skills, different attitudes, perhaps different people, than the marketing side of a generation-oriented utility. Conservation represents something that has never previously been a central thrust of the organization, and there is a contrast in mindset between selling electricity and promoting conservation.[55]

The OEB also noted that there is opposition within Ontario Hydro to the development of independent or parallel generation:

> However, the Board also heard evidence by Mr. Palmer, of Hydro, that other departments are not always willing to help in the process and that there is a certain amount of "internal opposition" to the development of parallel generation by some groups within the Corporation. Additional constraints imposed by other groups within Hydro are unnecessary and undesirable impediments to the effective development of parallel generation in the Province.[56]

---

53   *Id.* at 1/6–1/8 (emphasis added).
54   *Id.* at 5/7.
55   Electricity Planning Technical Advisory Panel to the Minister of Energy, *Review of Ontario Hydro's Draft Planning Strategy* (Toronto: Minister of Energy, 1988) at 27.
56   See *In the Matter of a Reference Respecting Ontario Hydro, supra,* note 52 at 6/11.

Finally, a well-accepted principle within the context of sustainable development is that a preventive approach to environmental protection is imperative. In the case of Ontario Hydro, there is a statutory framework, the Environmental Assessment Act (EAA), that takes such an approach. All new undertakings by Ontario Hydro, including all generating and transmission projects, are subject to approval under the EAA. Yet, since the EAA was proclaimed, all of Hydro's generating projects have been exempted from its application. Because of this exemption process, there has been no regulatory public review of Hydro's generating projects, no regulatory forum to discuss the need or alternatives to these undertakings, and no opportunity for the public to test and challenge the assumptions and findings Hydro used in arriving at its decisions.[57] On the other hand, according to Section 51 of the Power Corporation Act, Ontario Hydro must receive approval from the Lieutenant Governor in Council in order to borrow money. Because Ontario Hydro's capital expenditures are financed primarily by debt, Section 51 gives the Ontario Cabinet control over Hydro's system-expansion program. Unfortunately, this type of regulation does not allow for public participation in the decision-making process.

In addition to the previously noted specific weaknesses of the OEBA and the EAA, there is an obvious lack of integration of economic and environmental regulation. So-called environmental decisions (when reviewed) are considered by the Environmental Assessment Board and/or the Ontario Municipal Board, while so-called economic or financial decisions (which often have environmental impacts) are reviewed by the OEB. Hence, some thought should be given to a more comprehensive and coherent regulatory structure. The Kierans Report suggests that one regulatory authority be established with respect to all environmental matters:

> The Advisory Committee believes that the Environmental Assessment Review Process should be streamlined. In cases of joint mandates and jurisdictions, only one review should be conducted, taking into account the requirements of all the affected jurisdictions.[58]

CONCLUSIONS

In its *First Annual Review*, in 1964, the Economic Council of Canada identified five basic economic and social goals for the Canadian economy:

- full employment
- a high rate of economic growth
- reasonable stability of prices
- a viable balance of payments, and
- an equitable distribution of rising incomes.[59]

---

57   In 1974 the OEB reviewed Ontario Hydro's system expansion program; however, as already noted, the OEB's recommendations are not binding on Ontario Hydro.

58   See *Energy and Canadians, supra,* note 13 at 63.

59   Economic Council of Canada, *First Annual Review: Economic Goals for Canada to 1970* (Ottawa: Queen's Printer, 1964) at 1.

While the Economic Council of Canada considered all of the above goals to be important, it appears that it put prime emphasis on a high rate of economic growth. In other words, the aim seems to have been to maximize economic growth subject to the constraints of achieving reasonable success in fulfulling the other goals:

> Success, on the other hand, would bring great benefits. The increase in total output to 1970 would be almost double the rate of the last seven years. The improvement in average personal incomes would be even larger.[60]

It is submitted that Kierans' concept of sustainable economic development is a refinement of the 1964 goals of the Economic Council of Canada. That is, GNP should be maximized subject to the 1964 constraints, but with the added constraint of maintaining a reasonably healthy environment.

A fundamental difference between the Kierans Report on the one hand, and the Brundtland Report and mainstream thought on sustainable development on the other, is that the latter do not view economic growth as an end in itself, but merely as a means to the fulfillment of human needs. In addition, the Brundtland school of thought believes that there are ecological limits to energy consumption, whereas Kierans — implicitly at least — does not accept this. A commitment to human needs implies a commitment to equity, because the needs of the poor take priority over the wants of the rich. A concern for human needs also implies a concern for the welfare of future generations. This concern, when combined with the knowledge that the biosphere places limits on our ability to consume material and energy resources, leads to a rejection of growth mania. As Herman Daly has written:

> Growth chestnuts have to be placed on the unyielding anvil of biophysical realities and then crushed with the hammer of moral argument. The entropy law and ecology provide the biophysical anvil. Concern for future generations and subhuman life and inequities in current wealth distribution provide the moral hammer.[61]

The Kierans Report's concept of sustainable economic development would be relatively easy to implement, since it would merely fine-tune the status quo. But will it lead to development that is consistent with global sustainability? Furthermore, is Kierans' concept of sustainable economic development more desirable than Brundtland's concept of sustainable development? The Brundtland Report claims that its vision of sustainable development can be attained, but that it will require significant changes in public values and institutions:

> A safe, environmentally sound, and economically viable energy pathway that will sustain human progress into the distant future is clearly imperative. It is also possible. But it will require new dimensions of political will and institutional co-operation to achieve it.[62]

---

60   *Id.* at 5.
61   Herman Daly, ed., *Economics, Ecology, Ethics: Essays Toward A Steady-State Economy* (San Francisco: W.H. Freeman, 1980) at 11.
62   See *Our Common Future, supra,* note 6 at 202.

However, even the Kierans Report's concept of sustainable economic development implies significant changes for Ontario Hydro's regulatory framework. Implementing sustainable economic development would require, at least as a first step, the following Ontario Hydro reforms:

1. Amending the Power Corporation Act to require Ontario Hydro to provide electric services at the lowest long-term economic cost consistent with safety, flexibility, reliability, and acceptable environmental impact

2. Amending the Power Corporation Act to require Ontario Hydro to sell electricity at a price equal to its marginal economic cost

3. Subjecting Ontario Hydro to comprehensive binding public regulation by one or more independent regulatory boards[63]

If these three institutional reforms are made, Ontario's incremental electric service needs for many years to come will be provided by a combination of energy conservation, small-scale hydro plants, and gas-fired generation, not the status quo options of coal and nuclear power.

---

63   Virtually the same reform recommendations have been made by the Electricity Planning Technical Advisory Panel. See *Review of Ontario Hydro's Draft Planning Strategy, supra,* note 55 at 7, 32, 49.

A LEGAL PERSPECTIVE ON THE NUCLEAR OPTION: THE AMERICAN EXPERIENCE

Joseph P. Tomain

A few seconds after 4:00 a.m. on March 28, 1989, the United States recognized — celebrated is entirely the wrong word — the tenth anniversary of the "incident" at Three Mile Island. By now it is a truism that the nuclear industry is dead, and analysts and commentators can argue over the culprits. The usual suspects can be rounded up: bad utility managers, unsophisticated contractors, annoying antinuclear activists, negligent government officials, and poor financial analysts, among others.[1] Note that human intervention, not technology, is listed as the cause of nuclear power's demise. Indeed, the Kemeny Commission agreed with other investigators that a primary cause of TMI was "operator error."[2]

Blaming human error as the cause of technological failure is ironic — and with irony comes more than a little bit of truth. In order to maintain mastery over our environment, we must claim control over our technology, and we cannot give in to the lie that technology has outstripped our ability to deal with it. It may well be that we cannot completely own our own technology, yet ultimately there is no one else to accept responsibility. All of this may sound obvious, yet I suggest that any good analysis of commercial nuclear power demonstrates that the causes of nuclear failure run deep into the structure of the political economies of countries that have exercised the nuclear option.

Nuclear power is the first and most notable example of "big science."[3] The Manhattan Project[4] did not fit the classical picture of scientific discovery in which a scientist or two sit in a small lab, usually attached to a great university, and run experiments until that moment when Eureka strikes. Rather, the successful design, testing, and execution of the atom bomb was the product of hundreds of scientists, thousands of technicians, multiple laboratory facilities, and, most significant of all,

---

1   For example, see J.L. Campbell, *Collapse of an Industry: Nuclear Power and the Contradictions of U.S. Policy* (Ithaca: Cornell University Press, 1988); L.S. Hyman, *America's Electric Utilities: Past, Present and Future,* (3d ed.; Arlington: Public Utilities Reports, 1988) c. 14; J. Tomain, *Nuclear Power Transformation* (Bloomington: Indiana University Press, 1987). See also *infra,* note 55.

2   United States, President's Commission on the Accident at Three Mile Island, *The Need for Change: The Legacy of TMI* (Washington: Government Printing Office, 1979) at 10 [hereinafter "Kemeny Commission Report"].

3   For example, see J. Trefil, "Beyond the Quark: The Case for the Supercollider," *New York Times* (30 April 1989) Section 6 at 24.

4   R. Rhodes, *The Making of the Atomic Bomb* (New York: Simon & Schuster, 1986).

a joint government/industry partnership without which there would be no commercial nuclear power industry in the United States — and, most probably, in any part of the world.[5]

Ostensibly, there seems to be no significant connection between nuclear power and the concept of sustainable development.[6] Indeed, the two ideas seem antithetical. Nuclear power is the quintessential example of the hard path[7] while sustainable development can be seen as antinuclear and transitional to the soft path. Not all advocates of sustainable development believe in the antinomy.[8] Still, it is unfortunately unrealistic to ignore both the structure of commercial nuclear power and its relation to sustainable development. Nuclear power policy and a program of sustainable development have attributes in common. Both involve "big science," both require public/private-sector cooperation, and both rely on sophisticated technologies and analyses.

---

5   One story about the necessary connection between government and industry involves the Price-Anderson Act, 42 USC §§2210 (1982 and West Supp. Dec. 1988), which is legislation that limits the liability of nuclear power operators in the event of an accident. Westinghouse executive Charles Weaver recalls:

> We knew at the time that all questions [about safety risks] weren't answered. That's why we fully supported the Price-Anderson liability legislation. When I testified before Congress, I made it perfectly clear that we could not proceed as a private company without that kind of government backing.

M. Hertsgaar, *Nuclear Inc.: The Men and Money Behind Nuclear Energy* (New York: Pantheon Books, 1983) at 33.

6   See, for example, C. Flavin, "Creating a Sustainable Energy Future" in L.R. Brown, ed., *State of the World 1988* (New York: W.W. Norton, 1988) at 22:

> The question that comes up among policymakers again and again is: If not coal, and if not nuclear, then what? It is the central energy question today, and it does *have* an answer. The key to resolving the coal-nuclear conundrum is simple but potentially revolutionary: greatly improved energy efficiency in the short run, complemented by renewable energy in the long run.

In the 1989 edition of the same book, Christopher Flavin answers the question even more directly:

> Our conclusion is that the simultaneous pursuit of renewables and efficiency — and the abandonment of the nuclear power "option" — is the only safe and cost-effective way to slow global warming.

L.R. Brown, C. Flavin & S. Postel, "Outlining a Global Action Plan" in L.R. Brown., ed., *State of the World 1989* (New York: W.W. Norton, 1989) 174 at 176.

See also Environmental and Energy Study Institute, *Energy Policy Statement: A Call to Action for the Next President and Congress* (5 October 1988) (Bipartisan group of U.S. politicians, environmental leaders, and corporate executives favoring sustainable development with no role for nuclear power outlined in their proposal).

7   See A.B. Lovins, *Soft Energy Paths: Toward a Durable Peace* (San Francisco: Friends of the Earth International, 1977) at c. 2.

8   See, for example, World Commission on Environment and Development, *Energy 2000: A Global Strategy for Sustainable Development* (London: Zed Books, 1987). Safer nuclear power can play a role in a program of sustainable development.

The deep irony of sustainable development is that, in response, nuclear power may well re-emerge as a transitional technology. The nuclear industry will respond to changes in politics (law) and markets (the economy), rather than completely abandon its multi-billion-dollar forty-year investment. The nuclear power establishment — i.e., government *and* industry — is responding by streamlining licensing as well as standardizing design and construction in order to reduce the cost of nuclear plants below that of coal-fired generating stations. In the age of acid rain and growth of demand for electricity, the nuclear corpse may surprise us all.

THE INSTITUTIONAL STRUCTURE OF NUCLEAR POWER

Any discussion of the future of nuclear power depends on an understanding of the industry's institutional structure and its regulation. Without the encouraging hand of government, there would be no nuclear power industry. Interdependencies and interrelationships between government and industry therefore need to be understood before talk of alternative policies can make sense. Similarly, any discussion of the role of nuclear power in a program of sustainable development also requires an understanding of the institutional structure, because that structure is embedded in the policy-making process. In the United States, the structure is so fully embedded that a dominant model of energy law and policy can be identified. Reforms intended to develop alternative energy policies, including reforms to incorporate sustainable development, cut across the grain of that model. This section elaborates the dominant model and prefigures a discussion of an alternative model in which nuclear power plays a role, even if unwittingly, in sustainable development.

The Dominant Model of U.S. Energy Policy

The dominant model of U.S. energy policy is familiar. Starting with a preference for market ordering, the model supports a limited number of conventional resources, while recognizing that segments of some energy industries possess market power requiring government regulation. The prevailing market view is that OPEC is not able to hold the supply line in oil, that the Natural Gas Policy Act has opened up natural gas supplies, and that the demand for electricity is more price-elastic than analysts had previously thought. Oil, natural gas, and electricity supplies are more abundant than many dire predictions in the mid-1970s anticipated, and thus present a competitive environment for nuclear power.

An abundance of resources can be traced to market forces that were stabilized by government oversight. The abundance was no more a product of Reagan's deregulation politics than it was a result of Carter's central planning. Rather, stable energy production, distribution, and consumption occur as a consequence of the interplay of government and industry within relatively narrow limits of a mixed-market political economy.[9] The United States has an industrial policy of sorts

---

9   See generally C.E. Lindblom, *Politics and Markets: The World's Political-Economic Systems* (New York: Basic Books, 1977).

regarding energy production, distribution, and consumption. The key to understanding the political economy of energy lies in recognizing the tight interrelationship between government and industry.[10]

This symbiotic relationship between government and industry is manifested by four characteristics. First, in some segments of the industry energy resources are complementary so that the regulation of one does not necessarily adversely affect the other. Oil and electricity, for example, divide the energy pie into more-or-less equal halves that do not greatly overlap. Electricity does not occupy much of the transportation sector and oil is not the most economic resource for producing electricity. Therefore, federal energy policy can support both oil and electricity production. Second, energy resources are susceptible to inter-fuel competition. A federal policy that promotes the use of coal to generate electricity simultaneously discourages the use of nuclear power for the same purpose. Third, industry and government depend on each other for the distribution and allocation of benefits and burdens. The federal government, for example, controls most of the new oil reserves but depends on private industry for their development. In like fashion, the oil industry is not above asking for the helping hand of government in the form of oil import quotas, regardless of its frequent laissez-faire posturing. Finally, both business and government are stimulated to act by market disequilibria. Oil price controls were the response to the 1973 Arab oil embargo, and increased exploration for natural gas was the reaction to a loosening of federally established prices. This interplay between government and industry has produced a dominant model of domestic energy policy.

Domestic energy policy favors large-scale, high-technology, capital-intensive, integrated, centralized producers of energy from fossil fuels.[11] These archetypal energy firms are favored over alternatives such as small solar or wind firms, because energy policy-makers believe that larger firms can continue to realize economies of scale. Policy-makers gamble that greater energy efficiencies can be achieved by archetypal firms, rather than by alternative firms, technological innovation, or discovery of new reserves or energy sources.

The preference for traditional forms of energy production over alternative sources and new technologies is based on the assumption that there is a positive correlation between energy use and economic growth,[12] referred to as the energy–GNP

---

10   See R.H.K. Vietor, *Energy Policy in America Since 1945: A Study of Business-government Relations* (Cambridge: Cambridge University Press, 1984) at 1–12. See also J. Clark, *Energy and the Federal Government: Fossil Fuel Policies, 1900–1946* (Champaign: University of Illinois Press, 1987).

11   See Lovins, *supra,* note 7 at 1–31.

12   See, for example, E.R. Berndt & D.O. Wood, "Energy Price Shocks and Productivity Growth: A Survey" in R.L. Gordon, H.D. Jacoby & M.B. Zimmerman, eds., *Energy: Markets and Regulation — Essays in Honor of M.A. Adelman* (Cambridge: MIT Press, 1987) at 305; S.H. Schurr *et al.,*

link.[13] Although the correlation is not perfect,[14] economic productivity is thought to increase with an increase in energy production. These beliefs may or may not be true. Nevertheless, they persist, and the favoritism will continue as long as alternative firms carry the burden of persuading policy-makers otherwise. To restate the point, the embedded policy will continue as long as energy production, consumption, and prices remain stable.

The resulting energy policy has the following general goals:

1. To assure abundant supplies[15]

2. To maintain reasonable prices[16]

3. To limit the market power of the archetype firms[17]

Energy in America's Future: The Choices Before Us (Baltimore: Johns Hopkins University Press, 1979) c. 3; Council on Environmental Quality and State Department, *The Global 2000 Report to the President* (Washington: U.S. Government Printing Office, 1980); J.L. Simon & H. Kahn, *The Resourceful Earth: A Response to Global 2000* (Oxford: Blackwell, 1984). But see Lovins, *supra*, note 7 at 7–11.

13   The statement that there is an energy-GNP link is not meant to imply that greater economic productivity and more energy production necessarily mean an improvement in general welfare. Bigger may be better; however, that is a normative claim that I am not prepared to make, let alone defend. The energy-GNP link is intended as a positive, not a normative, assertion.

14   D. Yergin, "Conservation: The Key Energy Source" in R. Stobaugh & D. Yergin, eds., *Energy Future* (New York: Random House, 1979) 136 at 141–142.

15   Today, a healthy availability of energy resources means that the lights go on when the switch is flipped, the car starts when the key is turned, and the air conditioning works. See also Yergin, *id*. at 144–148.

16   A corollary of the energy-GNP link is stability in energy prices. As long as the real price of energy is stable, then productivity is stable, because a larger portion of income is not expended on energy. With the exception of, approximately, the decade 1973–1983, energy prices have been stable since the beginning of the century. See United States, Department of Commerce, *Historical Statistics of the United States: Colonial Times to 1957* (Washington: Department of Commerce, 1960) at series G 244-330 and 353-426; *Statistical Abstract of the United States: 1984* (Washington: Department of Commerce, 1983) Table 985 at 577; *Statistical Abstract of the United States: 1987* (Washington: Department of Commerce, 1986) Table 941 at 547; Energy Information Agency, *Annual Energy Review — 1987* DOE/EIA-0384 (87) (May 1988) (Table 22).

17   "Market power" can be variously defined:

> [T]he ability of a firm (or a group of firms, acting jointly) to raise price above the competitive level without losing so many sales so rapidly that the price increase is unprofitable and must be rescinded.

W.M. Landes & R.A. Posner, "Market Power in Antitrust Cases" (1981) 94 Harvard L. Rev. 937. See also R. Schmalensee *et al.*, "Comments — Landes and Posner on Market Power: Four Responses" (1982) 95 Harvard L. Rev. 1787. "Monopoly power is the power to control prices or exclude competition." *United States v. E.I. du Pont de Nemours & Co.*, 351 US 377 (1956) at 391. "[T]he abilities of firms to influence the prices of their products either through independent actions or through actions coordinated with others." W. Baldwin, *Market Power, Competition, and Antitrust Policy* (Homewood: Irwin, 1987) at 3.

Today, market power is threatened by natural gas pipelines and electric transmission facilities. See R.J. Pierce, "A Proposal to Deregulate the Market for Bulk Power" (1986) 72 Va.

4.   To promote inter- and intra-fuel competition[18]

5.   To support a limited number of conventional fuels (oil, natural gas, coal, hydropower, and nuclear power)[19]

6.   To allow energy decision-making and policy-making to develop within an active federal/state regulatory system.[20]

This loose policy can be contrasted with a comprehensive national energy plan. Although Congress requires the president to submit to it a biennial national energy plan (which is done through the Department of Energy[21]), the United States has never had a single, end-state energy plan with articulated and coordinated goals and objectives. Instead, the country has a series of policies pertaining to individual industries.[22] Combined, these separate policies share the characteristics noted above, and together they are consistent with the traditional and prevailing market-oriented pluralism, or the democratic capitalism, of the U.S. political economy.

Federal energy regulation aspires to attain the benefits of a competitive market, including wealth maximization, efficient and fair allocation and distribution of resources, and technological innovation, while promoting individual liberty and

L. Rev. 1183 (electricity transmission retains market power); "Reconstituting the Natural Gas Industry From Wellhead to Burnertip" (1988) 9 Energy L.J. 1 at 16–18 (natural gas transmission retains market power).

18   See generally Vietor and Clark, *supra,* note 10.

19   Most of the fuels produced and consumed domestically consist of fossil fuels like coal, natural gas, and oil. These fossil fuels are used either directly or in the production of electricity. Nuclear power and hydropower supplement fossil fuels in the production of electricity. "Alternative fuels," such as solar, wind, geothermal, or even synthetic fuels such as oil shale, do not play a major role in the country's energy picture, as the following figures demonstrate.

      The United States consumed 76 quads (one quad equals one quadrillion BTUs) of energy in 1987. The 76 quads are divided among the following resources: coal (18.00), natural gas (17.18), oil (32.63), hydropower (3.04), nuclear power (4.92), geothermal (0.23), and other (wood, waste, wind, photovoltaic, and solar connected to electric utilities; these sources producing energy for direct consumption are not included) (0.02). See Energy Information Agency, *supra,* note 16 at 11. Production figures are similar, although somewhat lower, indicating that the country is a net importer of energy. In 1987, the country produced 64.55 quads of energy divided among the following resources: coal (20.12), natural gas (16.84), oil (17.59), natural gas liquids (2.23), hydropower (2.61), nuclear power (4.92), geothermal (0.23), and other (0.02). See Energy Information Agency, *supra,* note 16 at 9.

20   See *infra,* section on "Energy Federalism."

21   42 USC §7321 (1982).

22   See generally J.E. Chubb, *Interest Groups and the Bureaucracy: The Politics of Energy* (Stanford: Stanford University Press, 1983) c. 1, 7; B. Commoner, *The Politics of Energy* (New York: Alfred A. Knopf, 1979); D.H. Davis, *Energy Politics* (2d ed.; New York: St. Martin's Press, 1978); Ford Foundation, *A Time To Choose: America's Energy Future* (Cambridge: Ballinger, 1974); W.A. Rosenbaum, *Energy, Politics and Public Policy* (Washington: Congressional Quarterly Press, 1981); J.P. Tomain, "Institutionalized Conflicts Between Law and Policy" (1985) 22 Houston L. Rev. 661.

equality.[23] It should come as no surprise that energy industries do not operate in such a rarified market. Instead, government regulation is necessary to reduce market imperfections and approach a state of at least workable competition.[24]

Starting from the market baseline, energy policy-makers (state and federal) aim at mimicking the market as they resist inter-fuel competition and planning in favor of inter-fuel and intra-fuel competition among a limited number of conventional resources. The embedded hard energy path favors conventional fuels such as oil, coal, natural gas, hydropower, electricity, and nuclear power, while de-emphasizing both conventional and unconventional alternative energy sources.[25] Simply put, it is unrealistic to assume that a radically different energy policy will emerge from this entrenched system. Thus, neither President Carter's attempt to coordinate and formulate a comprehensive and centralized national energy plan nor President Reagan's attempt to deregulate energy on a broad scale was likely to stray far from the model. Nor is it likely that federal energy policy will be transformed greatly during the new presidential administration.

The existence of a dominant energy policy does not preclude new regulatory initiatives, but those initiatives occur along a fairly narrow spectrum. Indeed, it is precisely because of interactions between government and industry, between federal and state governments, and between markets and politics, that energy regulation is a continuous process. Sometimes the policy that emerges from these interactions tilts in favor of government, and sometimes in favor of the market. Nevertheless, government and industry participation in energy policy-making stays in rough equilibrium. In other words, the impact of a program of sustainable development on U.S. domestic energy policy is likely to be slight. Any greater expectations must be accompanied by years of education, politicking, and public relations. The burden of transforming the dominant model of energy rests with those advocates who wish to alter the status quo.

The Role of Nuclear Power in U.S. Energy Policy

Given the explicit preference for large-scale, high-technology producers of conventional fuels, commercial nuclear power seems particularly suited to play a major role in U.S. energy policy. Today nuclear power generates about 18 percent

---

23 See, for example, F.M. Scherer, *Industrial Market Structure and Economic Performance* (2d ed.; Boston: Houghton Mifflin, 1980) c. 1.

24 See, for example, Bailey & Baumol, "Deregulation and the Theory of Contestable Markets" (1984) 1 Yale J. on Reg. 111.

25 "Alternative energy sources" can be divided into conventional substitutes and renewable resources. Conventional substitutes would include such resources as oil shale, tar sands, and coal gas, which are intended to supplement and substitute for oil and natural gas. Renewable resources would include solar, wind, and biomass.

of domestic electricity,[26] even though the industry is stalled, for a variety of factors alluded to earlier. Nevertheless, the nuclear power industry is so entrenched in U.S. energy policy that neither industry nor government will abandon this energy source.

Unfortunately, the continued presence of government/industry support for nuclear power is not unproblematic. Structurally, government and industry are so intertwined that the presence of the nuclear "option" will continue to be felt for the foreseeable future. What follows, then, is a partial list of the institutional dimensions of commercial nuclear power. While not all of the items promote nuclear power, the list reveals how deeply institutionalized nuclear power is in the political economy of the United States.

Ratemaking

The most subtle incentive promoting the use of nuclear power — in fact, promoting the use of all electricity generation in the United States — is the formula used to set electricity rates. The formula is simple to state, and although its application is quite complex, its effects are also easy to ascertain.

The simplest formulation is $R = O + (V - D)\, r$. The elements of this traditional formula are defined as:

R   is the utility's total revenue requirement or rate level. This is the total amount of money that a regulatory agency allows a utility to earn.

O   is the utility's operating expenses.

V   is the gross value of the utility's tangible and intangible property.

D   is the utility's accrued depreciation; combined, $V - D$ constitutes the utility's rate base.

r   is the rate of return that a utility is allowed to earn on its capital investment or on its rate base.[27]

This elementary equation yields the result that the more money a utility invests in capital expansion, the more revenue the utility will generate.[28] Until the mid-1960s, electric utilities could continue to invest in capital plant and still realize economies of scale — i.e., lower per-unit cost — making shareholders and ratepayers happy. More notably, billions of dollars of that capital investment were in nuclear power because it promised so much. Nuclear power was touted as a safe, clean, and modern technology that would produce electricity "too cheap to meter."

---

26   See Energy Information Agency, *supra,* note 16 at 211.

27   See J.P. Tomain, J.E. Hickey & S.S. Hollis, *Energy Law and Policy* (Cincinnati: Anderson, 1989).

28   The tendency to over-invest is known as the Averch-Johnson effect. See H. Averch & L.L. Johnson, "Behavior of the Firm Under Regulatory Constraint" (1962) 52 Am. Econ. Rev. 1052.

The 1960s are referred to as the "Great Bandwagon Market," during which 40,000 megawatts of capacity were ordered.[29]

The happy marriage of more plant and lower cost could not continue indefinitely, and the electricity industry took a turn for the worse beginning in 1965. At that time, production costs began to rise but prices remained stable. To make matters worse, rates were designed to encourage consumption, thus putting a further cash squeeze on utilities.[30] By the time utilities and their regulators reacted to the fundamental shift in the electricity market, the "real" cost of electricity had risen significantly and consumers voiced their protest: the change in the market evoked a political response. Throughout the 1970s, utilities' requests for rate increases met increasing opposition from ratepayers and regulators.[31]

Nuclear power hit the upturn in the cost of production at exactly the wrong time. After utilities had committed funds for new plant construction, the rate formula dictated that they continue to invest. Like poker players with a losing hand, utility managers found it difficult to make the heroic decision to fold and cut their losses rather than ante up one more time. The results of staying in the nuclear game too long were cash-flow problems as construction was delayed up to twenty years; excess capacity of high-priced electricity; and nuclear-plant cancellations, abandonments, or conversions. In other words — huge financial losses.

Back-end Costs

The federal government adopted a pronuclear, promotional posture early on in the course of regulation. In 1946 the first Atomic Energy Act[32] was passed with the explicit intent of moving nuclear power away from weaponry and toward commercial use. Later, in 1954, the first Act was dramatically amended[33] in order to move commercial power closer to the private sector. The 1954 Act, together with the Price-Anderson Act[34] and some 1964 amendments[35] authorizing private ownership of nuclear materials, greatly facilitated private-sector involvement. All of this legislation, however, was directed at front-end investment, with no attention paid to the back-end of the fuel cycle.

---

29 See Tomain, *supra*, note 1 at 10.

30 See Hyman, *supra*, note 1.

31 See P. Navarro, *The Dimming of America: The Real Costs of Electric Utility Regulatory Failure* (Cambridge: Ballinger, 1985); D.D. Anderson, *Regulatory Politics and Electric Utilities: A Case Study in Political Economy* (Boston: Auburn House, 1981).

32 Pub. L. No. 79-585, 60 Stat. 755 (1946).

33 Atomic Energy Act of 1954, Pub. L. No. 83-703, 68 Stat. 919 (1954).

34 Anderson-Price Atomic Energy Damages Act, Pub. L. No. 85-256, 71 Stat. 576 (1957). See also *supra*, note 5.

35 Pub. L. No. 88-489, 78 Stat. 602 (1964). (The Acts referred to in notes 32–35 are codified (with other amendments) at 42 USC §§2011-2296 (1982).

Attention was directed to the back-end as a result of two major events — the enviromental movement and Three Mile Island (TMI). After the National Environmental Policy Act[36] (NEPA) went into effect on January 1, 1970, its requirements were soon tested against the then Atomic Energy Commission (AEC) and were found to be applicable.[37] The application of NEPA to nuclear power meant that the industry had a public watchdog in the form of environmentalists who were also concerned with safety. NEPA provided some entrée into the formidable administrative processes of nuclear regulation.[38] This entrée, together with the schizophrenia of the AEC/NCR's[39] mandate — that is to say, that the federal agency was simultaneously to promote the development of nuclear power and to monitor the safe construction and operation of plants — broke apart the nearly uniform promotional nuclear policy during the mid-1970s. At that time, a rift developed between NRC technical staff and appointed decision-makers. Ironically, the technocrats exercised caution on safety issues at the risk of delay, while the politicians exhibited nuclear boosterism as they pushed for speedier licensing. This rift raised the level of internal and external criticism of the agency and increased public dissatisfaction with nuclear power.[40]

Three Mile Island signalled another downturn for the nuclear market. Even though TMI is the largest nuclear accident in U.S. history, and even though it did cause a severe negative public reaction to the industry's safety claims, TMI's more significant signal was financial. After TMI, phrases such as "plant shut-down," "clean-up costs," "temporary decommissioning," and "replacement power" became part of the nuclear-industry lexicon. The common denominator of this language was money. Each of these terms imposed unanticipated costs on the industry, thus greatly increasing the costs of doing business in the nuclear market.

Other costs also followed TMI. Emergency off-site evacuation became synonymous with, and forced the closure of, Shoreham. Bankruptcy became synonymous with Public Service Co. of New Hampshire because of that firm's inability to get Seabrook funded and up and running. And "backfitting" threatens to impose additional construction and operation costs.[41]

---

36   42 USC §§4331 et seq. (1982).

37   Calvert Cliffs' Coordinating Committee v. U.S. Atomic Energy Comm'n, 449 F. 2d 1109 (D.C. Cir. 1971).

38   Professor Harold Green, former AEC attorney and a proponent of nuclear power, once wrote that public participation in nuclear regulation was "at best a charade and at worst a sham." Quoted in Tomain, supra, note 1 at 57.

39   In 1974, the Atomic Energy Commission was reorganized into the Nuclear Regulatory Commission, in part to separate the promotional/safety roles of the agency. See The Energy Reorganization Act of 1974, Pub. L. No. 93-438, 88 Stat. 1233 (1974) (codified at 42 USC §§5801-91 (1982)). The NRC has not divested itself of these dual and conflicting roles.

40   See Campbell, supra, note 1 at c. 4.

41   See 10 CFR §50.109 (1988). Backfitting occurs when the NRC requires a modification or addition

The most significant back-end cost yet to be fully accounted for is the disposal of nuclear waste. Although scientists have known about the dangers of radioactive waste since the beginning of the century, it was not until 1982 that the federal government passed legislation addressing disposal. The Nuclear Waste Policy Act of 1982[42] set out a system for designating sites for waste disposal facilities. That system was both cumbersome and politically unacceptable, and had to be drastically amended in 1987 when Congress designated one site — at Yucca Mountain in south central Nevada — as the first depository. As it turns out, geological difficulties make this an unlikely site and, currently, there are no viable alternatives.[43] The most likely solution to the waste dilemma will involve financial payments to the host state. The problem is that the compensation cannot be set in anything like a market because the good being valued (nuclear waste) is unique, it is not traded in a market. Moreover, the costs (environmental and health) associated with the good cannot be fully realized for decades, and with some forms of waste they cannot be realized for thousands of years.

Energy Federalism

The United States has a federal structure, which means the federal government in Washington shares political power with the fifty states. Energy regulation is a joint federal–state enterprise because of two realities.

The first is the geophysical reality that a large portion of natural resources are privately owned and fall under state jurisdiction. Also, because the federal government owns one-third of the country's land, and has jurisdiction over the outer continental shelf, the natural resources used for energy production necessarily involve dual jurisdictions.

The second reality of energy federalism is economic. Energy is sold in national and international markets. These markets benefit from coordination of supply and demand (and pricing) to maximize the efficiency of production, distribution, and consumption, while keeping the United States an active player in global markets. The states, however, see things slightly differently. Natural resources provide the states with substantial revenue and, not unexpectedly, the states are extremely protective of their resources. Consequently, energy policy in the United States is developed in an active federal system: the federal government tends towards centralization in Washington in order to avoid balkanization of energy markets by

---

to a nuclear plant after a construction license has been issued and before the issuance of an operating license.

42   42 USC §§10101 (1982) *et seq.* as amended by Pub. L. No. 100-203 (1987), 101 Stat. 1330 §§5001-5065.

43   See L.J. Carter, *Nuclear Imperatives and Public Trust: Dealing With Radioactive Waste* (Washington: Resources for the Future, 1987); J.P. Tomain, Book Review of *Nuclear Imperatives and Public Trust* (1988) 29 Jurimetrics Journal 97.

the states, while the states — particularly producing states — prefer local controls in order to protect their resources, revenues, and citizens.

Nuclear power is not immune to these tensions. Centralized regulation makes sense given the magnitude of investment, and the high technology and scientific sensitivity of nuclear power. Decentralization also makes sense because of nuclear power's political sensitivity — residents resist the placement of nuclear power plants in their backyards, and they resist rate hikes caused by cost overruns and imprudent management. Not surprisingly, nuclear regulation has attempted to accommodate this centralization–decentralization tension by according the federal government a near-exclusive role in safety regulation and the states a large role in financial regulation.[44]

Regulatory Reform

In 1974, the Atomic Energy Commission was broken into two agencies, the Energy Research and Development Administration (ERDA) and the Nuclear Regulatory Commission (NRC), ostensibly to divide the agency's functions between promotion and regulation.[45] A recent study of the NRC's first decade by the Union of Concerned Scientists concludes that the Congressional desire has not been realized:

> The goal of Congress in establishing the NRC was to alter the institutional dynamics of the regulation of civilian nuclear power by freeing the regulators from the inherent conflict posed by being both regulators and promoters of the technology. The NRC's performance during its first decade indicates that the approach has not succeeded. The act of dividing the Atomic Energy Commission in two has not had the results hoped for.
>
> . . .
>
> The Union of Concerned Scientists believes that the record of the first decade demonstrates that the NRC's primary and instinctive allegiance is still to the industry it regulates.[46]

This conclusion, evocative of captured agency theory,[47] reiterates the theme that

---

44   *Pacific Gas & Electric Co.* v. *State Energy Resources Conserv. & Develop. Comm'n,* 461 US 190 (1983), 103 S. Ct. 1713 (1983).

     States do not have a completely free hand in financial regulation. Although states set the rates at which nuclear-generated electricity can be sold at retail, the Federal Energy Regulatory Commission (FERC) sets wholesale rates, and thus affects the price of nuclear-generated electricity and the financial viability of the industry. Compare *Mississippi Power & Light Co.* v. *Mississippi ex rel. Moore,* 487 US (1988), 108 S. Ct. 2428 (1988) (FERC sets rates under "filed contract" doctrine) with *Duquesne Light Co.* v. *Barasch,* 57 USLW 4083 (US 11 January 1989), 109 S. Ct. 609 (1989) (states can set retail rates that reasonably balance the interests of investors and consumers).

45   See text, *supra,* note 39.

46   Union of Concerned Scientists, *Safety Second: The NRC and America's Nuclear Power Plants* (Bloomington: Indiana University Press, 1987) at 159.

47   Compare the accounts of the captured agency in T.J. Lowi, *The End of Liberalism: The Second*

regulatory reform is needed and that promotion and regulation are not compatible.

Although the regulatory apparatus surrounding nuclear power was overhauled as recently as 1974, the calls for dramatic reorganization of the NRC have been constant since TMI. The Kemeny Commission recommended a major restructuring of the NRC, reporting in 1979 that "as presently constituted, the NRC does not possess the organizational and management capabilities necessary for the effective pursuit of safety goals."[48]

While the NRC structure remains as it was ten years ago, the Kemeny Commission recommendations did not fall on deaf ears. Its specific recommendations have become the focus of NRC reorganization legislation, and the political prognosis seems to be that the agency will be reformed. The heart of the Kemeny Commission recommendations is that the NRC, as a five-member agency, be abolished and replaced by a single administrator to oversee the agency's operation. Moreover, the NRC's dual mandate to promote and monitor safety must be more clearly delineated; a safety-oversight body outside the administrator's office would therefore be necessary.[49]

Current legislative proposals move in these directions. Regulatory reform measures reveal the Kemeny Commission's influence in their proposals to replace the NRC by a Nuclear Safety Agency headed by a single administrator accountable to the President, with a strengthened inspections and investigations component.[50] Other legislation proposes the creation of an Office of Investigations, reporting directly to the Commission, to examine evidence of illegalities by nuclear licensees.[51] Legislation has also been introduced to streamline the licensing process and encourage standardization through early site permits, standard design approvals, and one-step licensing that combines licensing procedures for construction and operation.[52]

Concrete reform proposals are based on assumptions about the purpose of nuclear regulation and about future energy projections. If policy-makers see energy policy as adhering to the traditional model of large-scale, high-technology power

Republic of the United States (2d ed.; New York: W.W. Norton, 1979) and R.A. Posner, "Theories of Economic Regulation" (1974) 5 Bell J. Econ. Mgmt. Sci. 335 at 341–343.

48 Kemeny Commission Report, *supra*, note 2 at 61. See also Rogovin *et al., Three Mile Island: A Report to the Commissioners and to the Public* (Washington: Government Printing Office, 1980).

49 The Commission made more detailed recommendations directed at a clearer definition of the agency's substantive safety mandate, improved operator training, and procedural changes. Similarly, the Union of Concerned Scientists recommended increased attention to the agency's safety mandate, the creation of an independent safety board, and increased public participation; *supra*, note 46 at 160–163.

50 Senate Committee on Environment and Public Works, S. Rep. No. 100-364 (1988).

51 House Committee on Energy and Commerce, H. Rep. No. 100-878, Part 2 (1988).

52 See H. R. 2078, The Nuclear Powerplant Standardization Act of 1989; 54 F.R. 15, 372 (1989).

production, then one set of reforms will follow. If policy-makers see energy from the perspective of sustainable development, then another set of reforms will be generated. Reforms also depend on one's view of the future.[53] What will the demand for electricity be over the next two decades? What type of generation plants will be needed? Will nuclear power play a large role? Will the electricity market change so much that traditional public utilities (nuclear power among them) must compete for a share of the market against "qualifying facilities" and "independent power producers"?[54] Once these basic assumptions are made, reforms make sense.

Specific reforms at the federal level would include abolishing the NRC; creating an independent safety body; establishing a separate licensing agency with a separate appeals board (or eliminating administrative appeals); relying on "hard-look" judicial review; repealing or greatly modifying the Price-Anderson Act; and creating a federal Office of Public Advocate to provide expertise and funding for intervenors. At the state level, concrete reforms would include restructuring the ratemaking formula to avoid cost-plus pricing; extending legislative initiatives into the non-radiological side of nuclear regulation; funding intervenors; and encouraging inter-state and state–federal participation in such issues as waste disposal, nuclear transportation, and emergency planning. These proposals are based on increased participation and increased decentralization, and favor a post-industrial nuclear policy not inconsistent with sustainable development.

A set of reforms consistent with the dominant and traditional model can also be fashioned. At the federal level, traditional model reforms would include streamlining licensing; renewing Price-Anderson; circumscribing public participation; supporting standardization; and promoting development of a national grid. At the state level, reforms would encompass continuing cost-based ratemaking; lowering the prudency standard; and increasing the technical and economic expertise of Public Utility Commission staff.

This list of institutionalized elements of U.S. nuclear policy reveals contradictory attitudes towards nuclear power. First, nuclear policy- and decision-making are no longer singularly promotive of the industry. Rather, the industry enjoys its supporters as it suffers its detractors. Regulatory authority is fractured only slightly less than public appreciation of the resource. The second lesson contained in the list is the "embeddedness" of nuclear power in the U.S. energy program. Nuclear power resides deeply within the structure and is more likely than not to stay there. The interesting issue before us is nuclear power's compatibility with sustainable development.

---

53 See Technology Futures, Inc. & Scientific Foresight, Inc., *Principles for Electric Power Policy* (Westport: Quorum Books, 1984) at c. 2 (developing six scenarios for future electricity markets, including "nuclear resurgence").

54 See E. Kahn, *Electric Utility Planning & Regulation* (Washington: American Council for an Energy-Efficient Economy, 1988) c. 6, 9; J.P. Tomain, "Energy Policy Advice for the New Administration" (1989) 46 Wash. & Lee L. Rev. 63.

NUCLEAR POWER AND SUSTAINABLE DEVELOPMENT

Given the structural relationships in the nuclear industry between private and public sectors, between federal and state governments, and, ultimately, between markets and politics, what does the foregoing tell us about nuclear power and sustainable development? Essentially, the ratemaking process, back-end costs, and energy federalism indicate that there is no monolithic support for nuclear power.

Nuclear politics at the end of the 1980s is a mirror image of nuclear politics at the beginning of the 1950s. In the 1950s, public and private, military and civilian, investors and consumers, all supported the commercialization of nuclear power as a safe, clean, cheap source of electricity that would help us forget the nightmare of the Bomb. Thus, the 1950s witnessed a united front promoting nuclear power production. In the 1980s, the only consensus is that nuclear power is too expensive and too risky an investment. No money is being spent on new plants, although R&D is being invested in new designs, and the present stock of nuclear plant is being operated and monitored at considerable cost.

Although the industry is inactive, it is not moribund. The sleeping giant can revive under two conditions. The first is political: public acceptance of nuclear power must increase. The second is economic: the cost of nuclear power must decrease. These two conditions are not unrelated, and the future of nuclear power may lie in the hands of the craftsman behind sustainable development programs. If we assume that the demand for electricity continues to grow, nuclear power will see a re-emergence precisely when the costs of coal-fired electricity become comparatively prohibitive.[55] When the private and social costs attributable to acid rain, the greenhouse effect, and more direct injuries to human health and the environment caused by coal become greater than the private and social costs of nuclear power, then nuclear power will gain ascendancy.

Admittedly, the cost-benefit analysis necessary to do the comparative calculation is not susceptible to effortless arithmetic solution. While it is relatively easy to calculate the private costs of constructing a coal-fired plant versus a nuclear power station, the identification and calculation of social costs involve political assessments as much as, if not more than, they involve economic analyses. Such cost-

---

55   Financial analyst Leonard Hyman of Merrill Lynch Pierce Fenner & Smith Inc. is less sanguine:

> Nuclear power will not play its hoped-for role in the energy market, but it should produce about one-fifth of our electricity.... The nuclear option appears to have been killed off, a victim of cost overruns, technical difficulties, loss of public confidence, lack of political backing, the fall in fuel prices and slower than expected growth in demand in electricity. Loss of that option could become a problem if fuel prices rise, or foreign nations embargo their energy exports, or if fossil fuel combustion must be reduced in order to prevent damage to the climate. Otherwise, it appears as if most utilities in the United States could find replacements for cancelled nuclear projects.

See Hyman, *supra,* note 1 at 269.

benefit analysis must venture into difficult and non-quantifiable matters such as intergenerational effects, citizen disaffection, long-term health and environmental effects, future power demands and supplies, new technologies, transnational markets, and the like.

Clearly, the nuclear industry is not oblivious to the simple conclusion that nuclear power must be perceived as "safe enough," and that "safe enough" is a comparative, socio-political standard, not an exclusively positive economic one. Indeed, the industry movement toward smaller, standardized plants is an investment strategy aimed at lowering the cost and increasing the safety of new plant, in an attempt to restore public faith in the nuclear option. This attempted restoration of faith will be done primarily through an appeal to the consumer's pocketbook. If the nuclear industry can demonstrate both lower financial costs of construction and operation (lower private costs), and the relative safety of nuclear power (lower social costs), especially compared with coal, then nuclear power can become an active participant in future energy programs. This future role, however, does not mean that nuclear power is compatible with sustainable development.

CONCLUSION — THE FUTURE

Thus, the question is rightly posed: Is nuclear power compatible with a program of sustainable development? Theoretically, the presence of nuclear power in such a program is neither necessary nor desirable. It is not necessary because it is not as benign a technology as that demanded by the more environmentally sensitive aspirations of sustainable development. Nor has nuclear power proven itself to be an efficient technology. Somewhat more subtly, nuclear power is undesirable because, as the paradigmatic hard-path energy source, it contradicts the transitional goals of sustainable development.

In practice, though, nuclear power will play a role in any program of sustainable development now being planned. First, and at the most pragmatic level, neither industry nor government will walk away from their multi-billion-dollar investment.[56] The structural integrity of the government/industry joint venture guarantees political power to the industry and, *a fortiori*, brings economic power as well. At a

---

56 The love/hate relationship of the residents near Lilco's Shoreham nuclear power station on Long Island, New York, is a perfect example of the difficulty of moving out of nuclear power. The completed plant has not come on line because of problems in evacuating the area should a nuclear accident occur. Now the plant is slated to be dismantled, and consumers will be required to pick up a large part of the tab. More problematic is the fact that power shortages are predicted for the Northeast, and replacement power will burden consumers with even more costs. If costs rise too much, major industrial consumers will relocate rather than pay exorbitant rates. With large industrial customers leaving the local utility, smaller customers, and residential and small commercial users, will have to pick up an even larger portion of the tab. This inflation-like spiral will not continue indefinitely, nor is it likely that the scenario will be repeated around the country, precisely because the costs to consumers are too difficult to absorb.

minimum, the venture will continue to support the more than one hundred plants in operation, both because the United States has a growing need for power and because alternative fuels, especially coal, are all highly problematic. In addition, government will continue to regulate these plants, and billions of dollars must be committed to the back-end of the fuel cycle for waste disposal and decommissioning.

The practical realization that nuclear power will continue to play a role in future energy planning does not resolve the theoretical tension between nuclear power and sustainable development. A deeper look at the two is necessary before some compatibility can be found.

In the foregoing discussion of regulatory reforms, it was noted that reform options depended on the energy model and future scenario used by policy-makers. Put slightly differently, the accommodation of a role for nuclear power in a program of sustainable development depends on a change in attitude or mindset. Energy production (nuclear power) and environmental protection (sustainable develop-ment) must find a common language before nuclear power can fit comfortably into a program of sustainable development. That common language might be found in a broad application of welfare economics, with an attentive eye to the externalities (social costs) and long-term effects of policies.[57]

Until the 1980s, it seemed that energy law and policy, and environmental law and policy, utilized qualitatively different languages, and, not surprisingly, devel-oped qualitatively different policies and programs. Energy law and policy relied, and continue to rely, exclusively on the neo-classical version of the microeconomic model. With this model, supply and demand and price drive policy-makers. This model can function only with hard, positive, quantifiable data that can be easily translated into costs. Environmental law and policy, by contrast, were initially based on an ethos of stewardship. Spaceship Earth was seen as a fragile complex of ecosystems, the protection of which was placed in human hands. Consequently, the development and analysis of environmental laws and policies resisted the hard quantifiable world of economic analysis, even of the loose cost-risk-benefit form. Instead, environmental analysts and policy-makers relied on "softer" political variables such as safety, preservation, and conservation, which do not lend them-selves well to quantification.

The economic downturn of the late 1970s and early 1980s, and the future threats posed by global climatic shifts and changes in world markets, challenge both energy and environmental policy-makers. Neither can proceed with business as usual.

---

57   M. Sagoff, *The Economy of the Earth: Philosophy, Law and the Environment* (Cambridge: Cambridge University Press, 1988). Social regulation, like sustainable development, should be based on philosophy, politics, and/or aesthetics, and not on economics, whether neo-classical or welfare.

Energy policy-makers must anticipate the long-term and social costs (environmental and health, *inter alia*) associated with large-scale projects, even as they set policy for short- and medium-term energy needs. Likewise, environmental policy-makers must factor into their more ambitious programs the short- and medium-term energy needs of active and productive national economies.

One senses that energy and environmental policy-makers are beginning to talk to each other rather than continuing to treat each other as adversaries. The current discourse is more politically sensitive and asks more technically difficult questions of economists. Perhaps the common language will look to safety, intergenerational effects, democratic political participation, and environmental care as much as it looks to efficiency, productivity, and wealth creation. The common language should be a rich language of political economy rather than a narrow language of either the short-term satisfaction of individual needs (economics) or the long-term creation of utopias (politics). Both extremes are likely to fail. The great promise of sustainable development is that it can serve as the bridge between these two formerly isolated worlds, and that energy production and environmental protection can reach a common ground through the common language of sustainable development.

SUSTAINABLE ENERGY PATHS: THE POSSIBILITIES AND THE CHALLENGES

David B. Brooks and Ralph D. Torrie

The societal goal of sustainable development presents formidable and fundamental challenges to the way in which we utilize natural resources — renewable as well as nonrenewable. This paper presents an overview of the Canadian energy economy and of federal energy policy, past and present, and a discussion of possibilities for a sustainable energy future for Canada.

Our analysis begins with a brief historical and statistical review of the energy economy in Canada, from the pre-OPEC era of presumed unlimited supply to the present period of moderating prices and escalating alarm over the environmental implications of the current energy trajectory. This is followed by a description of key elements of federal energy policies over this same period and of the challenges to those policies. The following section contains a description of some of the analytical work that has been done in support of the alternative positions, not as a definitive statement, but merely to show that the alternatives implicit in the challenges to conventional policies have been analyzed and shown to be viable. We will suggest that, while least-cost energy policies would represent an enormous improvement over current attempts to resuscitate the conventional paradigm, only a soft energy path based on social goals is fully compatible with sustainable development. A final section summarizes our major conclusions.

We must preface this analysis with a comment on the difference in perceptions of the fundamental nature of the energy economy. The way in which one defines the energy problematique will determine the approach one takes to energy policy; we will refer to what might be called the "conventional" and "emerging" paradigms. The conventional paradigm is commodity-oriented, the commodities being fuels and electricity. In this framework, "energy demand" is the demand for fuels and electricity, and "energy policy" is energy resource and commodity (i.e., fuels and electricity) policy. In this framework, the so-called demand-side options (i.e., conservation and efficiency) are perceived and evaluated as measures for alleviating the commodity supply problem.

The emerging paradigm is end-use oriented and starts with the realization that demands for fuels and electricity are derived from more fundamental demands for the services these fuels can help provide, and that the energy economy is a system for the provision of these services and not just a commodity market. In this framework, energy policy is concerned with the manner in which the entire system, including the resource and commodity components, operates to provide the

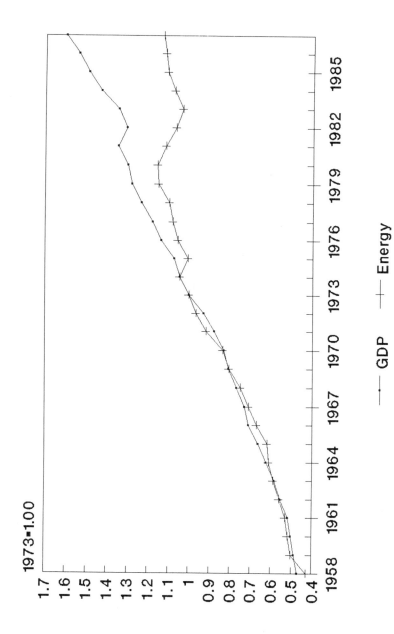

FIGURE 1
Fuel and Electricity Demand vs.
GDP in Canada, 1958–1987

underlying demand for services. In this framework, the demand-side options are actually seen as part of the supply system for energy services.

Environmental issues are also perceived and responded to quite differently under the two paradigms. Under the conventional paradigm, environment is relegated primarily to the end-of-the-pipe issues — that is, mitigation of impacts or "externalities," in economic jargon. In contrast, under the emerging paradigm, ecological sustainability is (or at least can be) a key aspect of the end-use service, and can be integrated with policy options so as to anticipate and avoid environmental problems.

We believe only the emerging paradigm offers a framework that is both adequate and preferable for understanding and addressing the issues that are raised by current and projected levels of energy resource production and commodity consumption. Indeed, our central purpose in this paper is to elaborate on this essential thesis.

ENERGY AND THE ECONOMY:
A HISTORICAL REVIEW, 1958–1987

Our analysis of Canadian energy demand draws on a data base that tracks the production of energy resources and the consumption of energy commodities in Canada from 1958 to 1987.[1] In this paper, we can only present a few basic facts about the Canadian energy economy; for a more detailed description the reader is referred to the literature.[2]

In Figure 1, we show the final demand for fuels and electricity in Canada from 1958 to 1987.[3] Between 1958 and 1973, Canadian consumption of fuels and

---

1   This is a database that has been developed by Torrie Smith Associates and Marbek Resource Consultants Limited and draws on the standard Statistics Canada and Energy, Mines and Resources sources, as well as numerous supplementary sources.

2   For a general discussion of the subject, see J. Darmstadter, J. Dunkerley & J. Alterman, *How Industrial Societies Use Energy: A Comparative Analysis* (Baltimore: Johns Hopkins University Press, 1977). For a specific treatment of Canadian energy use, see Marbek Resource Consultants and Torrie Smith Associates, *Energy Demand in Canada, 1973–1987: A Retrospective Analysis* (Ottawa: Energy, Mines and Resources, 1989); and D.B. Brooks, *Zero Energy Growth For Canada* (Toronto: McClelland and Stewart, 1981). Statistical information can be found in Energy, Mines and Resources, *Energy Statistics Handbook,* which is updated regularly.

3   More precisely, the data used in this report refer to the end-use or secondary energy demand (fuels and electricity, not primary resources) for energy purposes by energy users (as opposed to energy producers). The corresponding total domestic demand for primary energy resources (e.g., crude oil, coal, natural gas, hydropower) is about 125 percent of final demand for secondary energy. The difference is composed of (in decreasing order of importance) the use of energy resources for non-energy purposes (e.g., petrochemical feedstock), the primary energy resource losses that occur in the conversion to electricity and other secondary fuels, and the energy requirements of the energy industry itself (producer consumption). While the ratio of resource consumption to final demand for energy commodities has been fairly constant in the past, growth in non-hydro electricity production and heavy oil developments could make the Canadian primary/secondary efficiency

electricity doubled, with a corresponding rise in Gross Domestic Product (GDP). This was the pattern of energy development that characterized all the industrial nations, and was also the pattern to which developing nations aspired. By 1973 Canadian secondary energy demand had reached 5,600 petajoules:[4]

During this period, there was a very direct and remarkably stable correspondence between growth in the economy and growth in the use of fuels and electricity. Reliable forecasts of fuel and electricity demand could be based on this highly aggregate correlation. In effect, the demand for fuels and electricity during this period was a dependable surrogate for the underlying demand for energy services. Fuel and electricity represented a very small part of the total cost of industrial production, or owning and operating a motor vehicle, house, or commercial establishment.

Energy economists, policy-makers, and producers planned for exponential growth in the economy and in energy resource extraction and commodity production as if high-quality supplies were unlimited and demand were insatiable — and with very little regard for the environment.

Before we describe the very profound changes that began to occur in the energy economy in the 1970s, it is worth noting a few other facts about energy use in Canada:

1. In terms of the major end-use sectors — industrial, transport (including all modes of commercial freight and passenger transport, as well as private automobiles and trucks), residential, and commercial (including governments and other institutions) — the relative shares of the total final demand for fuels and electricity have been fairly stable over time. Industry has always been the largest consuming sector, accounting for 35–40 percent of secondary energy demand, followed by transportation, for about 24–26 percent, residential, for 20–22 percent, and commercial/institutional, for about 15–18 percent.

2. A handful of very energy-intensive industries account for a disproportionately large share of industrial energy use. Taken together, pulp and paper, primary metal refining, nonmetallic mineral production, industrial

---

of the Canadian energy economy deteriorate significantly in the years ahead. From an environmental perspective, it will become increasingly important to realize that the impact of growth or decline in final demand will be multiplied at the power plant or the mine in the form of waste production, acid gas emissions, carbon dioxide production, and thermal and other types of pollution.

4   A petajoule is a very large unit of energy. It represents the direct consumption (in the form of space and water heating fuels, electricity and gasoline) of 4,000–5,000 households. It is equivalent to 278 million kilowatt-hours of electricity, or about 29 million gallons of gasoline or home heating oil, or 950 billion cubic feet of natural gas, or 51 thousand tonnes of wood.

chemicals, and the food and beverage industries account for over 70 percent of all mining and manufacturing energy use.

3. A subtle, but in some ways more powerful, disaggregation of energy use is according to end-use categories. Nearly 60 percent of Canada's use of fuels and electricity is for the provision of heat, and more than half of this is for the low-temperature requirements of space heating, the remainder being for higher-temperature industrial heat processes. Transport fuels represent the next largest component at 30 percent of secondary energy demand, and the proportion of total energy end-use services that is "electricity-specific" (e.g., electronics, appliances, motors, lighting, electro-chemistry) is a relatively minor, albeit strategically critical, 12 percent of total secondary energy demand.

4. By 1973, when the ground beneath the energy economy began to shift, petroleum products represented some 54 percent of total secondary energy use, natural gas 20 percent, coal 5 percent, biomass 7 percent, and all forms of electricity about 14 percent.

Two very dramatic trends in the energy economy began to develop in the mid-1970s. First, oil's share of the energy pie began a steep decline, from 54 percent in 1973 to less than 40 percent by 1987, with natural gas and electricity picking up about equal portions of the 14 percent decline. This move "off oil" was greater in Canada than in most other nations, reflecting the availability of low-priced alternatives and active government encouragement.

The second (and much more profound) trend that emerged in the 1970s was that the energy pie itself virtually stopped growing in spite of continued strong (although somewhat erratic) growth in the GDP. As can be seen in Figure 1, the energy intensity of the Canadian economy (as measured by the ratio of secondary energy demand to GDP), which had been virtually constant for twenty years, dropped a phenomenal 30 percent between 1973 and 1987.

There are only two causes for a decline in the ratio of fuels and electricity use to GDP: first, a decline in the amount of energy required to produce particular goods or services (i.e., energy conservation); and second, changes in the relative composition of the GDP toward activities and production that use less energy per dollar of output. Space does not permit much elaboration on these complex phenomena, but energy conservation and structural chånge have been of roughly equal importance in the rise of Canadian energy productivity. Energy conservation has been particularly important in the household sector, in transportation, and in the energy-intensive processing industries. On the structural side, growth in the services sector and the relative decline in the GDP share of energy-intensive processing industries have been major factors in deflating the energy/GDP ratio.

The salient point here is that the decline in the energy/GDP ratio of the Canadian economy goes far beyond a simple demand response to higher energy prices, and reflects deep-seated and irreversible structural changes occurring throughout the industrial world that are not caused (at least directly) by changes in energy commodity prices. Conversely, little more than half of the 30 percent improvement that has occurred in the energy productivity of the Canadian economy can be attributed to energy conservation; analyses that typically show untapped technical and economic energy conservation potential in the 30–60 percent range must be viewed in this context.

ENERGY POLICY: CONVENTIONAL PARADIGMS AND NEW CHALLENGES

Energy Policy in Canada

For the purposes of this paper, the history of federal energy policy can be divided into three periods: the years prior to the first Energy Crisis in 1973, the years from 1973 until the election of the new government in 1984, and the years since 1985.

Until the first Energy Crisis, energy policy in Canada was concerned with little but ensuring adequate supplies of fuels and electricity at reasonable cost, for the growth of Canada and for exports. Energy resources were seen as essentially limitless in supply, so regulation could be very limited — applied only to the extent necessary to ensure a measure of competition and functioning markets. Moreover, it was assumed — and, as shown above, statistical analysis seemed to corroborate — that trends in economic growth and in the consumption of fuels and electricity would parallel one another. Thus, any suggestion of restricting energy demand growth was seen as tantamount to suggesting the curbing of economic growth.

Secondary attention during the pre-1973 period was given to regional development, and support to this end was provided, mainly through favorable tax treatment. The federal government was also mindful that modest tax revenues could be obtained from energy resource production and consumption. However, the federal government neither was nor wanted to be a major actor in the energy policy scene. (So-called water-and-power socialism was almost entirely a provincial phenomenon.) Only where no other alternative was available, as in the North, or where a nation-building goal came to the fore, as in the pipeline debate, did federal energy policy become more interventionist.

Starting with the first Energy Crisis in 1973, and particularly after the second in 1978–79, the federal government began to take a much more active role in energy policy. This was an era in which considerable scope was granted for economists to manage the economy (and not just in Canada), and senior bureaucrats began to recognize how great an economic role was played by energy resource development.

They believed that investments in exploration, production, and delivery represented a significant source of growth in Canada's GDP, and that low-cost fuels and electricity could give Canadian industry a significant advantage in increasingly competitive world markets. They also believed that higher energy commodity prices could provide a major source of revenue to finance the social programs favored by the Liberal government of the day — and that appropriate application of tax and subsidy policies could shift the focus of investment (and, ultimately, of production and revenue) from provincial to federal lands.

The era of federal energy intervention climaxed with the National Energy Program (NEP). However, even prior to the NEP, another strand had become evident in federal energy policies: demand management. An Office of Energy Conservation (and later, with somewhat different objectives, an Office of Renewable Energy) was created, and by 1976 government reports referred specifically to opportunities to improve Canada's energy economy through conservation. The NEP went much further. It suggested that demand management should have a policy role equal to that of supply management, and either confirmed or extended a number of conservation policies and programs that had been established by the Office of Energy Conservation.

Federal energy intervention and the NEP came to be major issues in the election campaign of 1984. The new Conservative government was elected with the mandate to reduce the role of government throughout the economy and, in particular, to dismantle the NEP.[5] This they did with a vengeance, including most if not all portions of the conservation program. Federal supports to the energy resource sector (notably frontier oil) were also eliminated, as was the complex price structure erected to give Canadians a better deal on energy commodity prices.

It seems, therefore, that the period from 1985 onward represents a return to pre-1973 policies. However, this is not really the case. In contrast with its apparent distaste for any intervention on the demand side, the federal government has found new ways to offer support for energy resource development. Particularly in the election campaign of 1989, it made commitments to provide federal funding for an array of energy mega-projects, including some of highly questionable economic value. Ironically, those projects were justified on the basis of security of supply and of regional development, both of which had been explicitly rejected as appropriate criteria for energy development by a commission specifically appointed by then Minister of Energy Marcel Masse to review federal energy policy.

Assumptions Inherent in Canada's Energy Policy

With the partial exception of some activities between 1973 and 1985, the gyrations in federal energy policy mask two dominant thrusts: primarily, the attempt

---

5   The success of the NEP was always dependent on rising oil prices, which, the presumption was, would have provided enough revenue to keep everyone, including provincial governments, content.

to treat energy as a commodity; and secondarily, a policy focus on the supply aspects of that commodity. The federal perspective can be summed up as follows: Energy may be a difficult commodity to manage from an economic point of view because of certain geological characteristics, because of the potential for monopoly in distribution (electricity and natural gas), and because of the annoying tendency of other governments to subsidize exports, but it can nevertheless be treated for policy purposes as a commodity, and those purposes can most conveniently be served by appropriate policy directed toward increases in energy supply. In particular, there is no need for, nor would it be appropriate to promulgate, social objectives for energy policies other than those implicit in sound economic management. Therefore, energy policy can be reduced to oil, gas, coal, or electricity policy, where private corporations or public utilities will operate on market principles (as adjusted to ensure adequate supply) for domestic or foreign customers.

Unfortunately, the key assumptions underlying Canadian energy policy are questionable from both an economic and an ecological perspective. Among other things, the conventional paradigm ignores several characteristics of energy: first, the pervasive environmental impacts; second, thermodynamic laws; and third, the scale of energy operations.

Conventional economic analyses have not been unmindful of the adverse effects associated with energy resource development and consumption, at least not over the past couple of decades. The standard economic approach is to treat environmental impacts as "externalities" — that is, system costs that do not appear on the right account books. This approach is perfectly appropriate when the impacts are small and scattered. It is less so when they are large and pervasive, which is precisely the case with energy. There is no practical economic analysis that can truly allow for the effects of global warming, nor is there any evident way to determine the "external effects" of policies favoring single-family homes or automobiles, even though both have significant energy and environmental implications. What one can say is that, with some minor exceptions, energy policy that allows for environmental effects and uncertainties will almost surely place most of its emphasis on demand reduction — where environmental impacts tend to be light — rather than on increasing supply — where they are almost invariably heavy.

A second problem is that economics treats resources as throughput, with little or no attention to the source from which they come or the sinks into which they go. On a small scale, this is reasonable; in today's world, it is disastrous. In effect, economics recognizes the First Law of Thermodynamics (the quantity of energy is always the same) but neglects the Second (its quality is always declining). While technical development has masked the effect, the human economy is essentially drawing down its energy capital, with implications for both resource management and environmental pollution. Clearly, demand-oriented policies offer important scope to avoid thermodynamic losses, with gains at both the source and the sink. More important, although all commodities are subject to the influence of thermodynamics, it is questionable whether energy as a whole, which is the explicit focus of the discipline, can be treated as a commodity when the policy focus should be less on delivery or conservation of *quantities* of energy than of *qualities* of energy.

Third, the sheer scale of energy resource development and delivery should raise questions as to the appropriateness of treating energy as just another commodity. Throughout the industrial world, energy firms tend to be the largest and most powerful in the economy. They command enormous amounts of capital, and their investments play a great role in macroeconomic development. Typically integrated from production through delivery, they are critical to the smooth operation of industrial and urbanized economies, which have come to depend on steady deliveries of vast quantities of high-quality energy. There is simply no countervailing bloc of economic power on the side of consumers (nor, in many cases, of political power on the part of governments).

These weaknesses in the assumptions underlying conventional energy policies led to a number of challenges that, cumulatively, have all but destroyed the rationale for those policies.

Regional Development and Nuclear Power: Exceptions in Federal Energy Policy

Before looking directly at the challenges to Canadian energy policies as a whole, one should recognize that two exceptions exist to the general reluctance to attach social objectives to energy policy: a general one involving regional development, and a specific one involving the nuclear industry. The general exception originates in the purported links between energy production or use and the health of the economy. The older view that the health and growth of the economy depend upon continued additions of energy has been discarded, as western economies have been shown to be quite capable of growing with no or only slow additions to energy use. However, the link between energy and economy may have some merit at the regional level. Energy *production* can be a source of strength to the regions where that energy is produced — just like any other income-producing activity. The point is not the truth of this link, which is undeniable, but the question whether support for specific regional economies is truly part of energy policy. Wherever placed, this rationale has been responsible for enormous federal expenditures over the decades, very few of them justified on the basis of economics.

The specific exception to the absence of social goals in federal energy policy involves the sustained and heavy federal commitment to nuclear power. The rationale was varied, but always included the goal of moving Canada into a high-tech industrial economy. However, the nuclear industry has always been — and remains — a special case in so many ways that it makes no sense to treat it as merely another source of energy.

Nationalist, Economic, and Environmental Challenges

The conventional paradigm for federal energy policy has never been free from criticism. Indeed, federal energy policy has, throughout the past several decades, been one of the more contentious and partisan areas of debate. For our purposes, we can divide the critique into three components, although in much of the debate the three overlap. The earliest critique came from a nationalist perspective. This was followed by an environmental critique, which in turn came to be almost subsumed by an economic critique. Recently, however, the environmental critique has returned to the fore, so that the three components reflect four phases.

The earliest critique came from Canadian nationalists, who wanted to see Canadian energy resources developed mainly for Canadian use, or at least in such a way as to maximize benefits within Canada. Some of these nationalists were motivated by old conservationist fears of absolute exhaustion; others wanted to use our energy wealth to build a modern manufacturing economy; still others felt that the absence of Canadian ownership and control in the energy industry meant that the federal government lacked critical levers in managing the economy. Whatever the motivation, Canadian nationalism has presented a long-standing challenge to the absence of social goals for Canadian energy policy. Depending upon how it is expressed, however, the nationalist challenge may or may not be compatible with sustainable development, and for the purposes of this article can be put to one side.

The environmental movement began to gather strength in the early 1970s, and much of the movement has focused on energy policy. With recognition of the full extent of Canada's energy resources, early concerns about literal exhaustion came to be replaced by concerns about the widespread and serious environmental damage commonly associated with energy supply. Suddenly, smoke plumes, fouled water courses, acid rain, strip coal-mining, oil spills, tanker wrecks, mine tailings, and even access to wilderness areas emerged as issues. Still, these were not very fundamental challenges *per se*. Taken alone, they represented merely an insistence on more care for the environment during the exploration, production, and delivery of energy resources.

A shift of the environmental critique to a more radical perspective came with the recognition that the most effective way to achieve environmental goals lay not in improvements to energy supply processes, but in reduction of energy demands — that is, in energy conservation. Environmentalists quickly came to the position that energy conservation was the best form of environmental protection. Moreover, energy conservation resolved another troubling issue that had been taken up by the environmental movement: nuclear power. From a narrow perspective, nuclear power presents only relatively minor problems, but in the larger view it raises a host of other issues, as much social and political as environmental. If it could be shown, however, that the additional electricity was not necessary, the whole nuclear debate would become irrelevant.

But how could it be shown that conservation was sufficient to obviate the need for additional energy, and particularly additional electricity? Almost as if on cue, the economic component of the challenge to conventional energy policy arrived on the scene. Originally on an end-use by end-use basis, and later more systematically, calculations showed that it was simply cheaper to conserve than to supply energy. When expressed most carefully, the issue was not strictly one of energy conservation, but of economic efficiency; that is, even when energy is treated as a commodity, the cost of becoming more efficient in the use of energy commodities is, in almost every case, less than that of producing enough energy to perform the same service.

The economic challenge to conventional energy policies was very powerful indeed, and for much of the 1980s subsumed and even superseded the environmental challenge. Analyses demonstrated powerfully that greater energy efficiency (possibly supplemented with renewable sources of energy) would all but eliminate the need for new energy supplies, and particularly for new energy mega-projects. (The growing need for light oil represented a modest exception.) Least-cost energy policies, as they came to be called, were shown to be sufficient to eliminate many of the most environmentally questionable aspects of conventional energy policy. Moreover, the remarkable technical progress in energy efficiency, and notably in electricity efficiency, kept expanding the economic potential — and, in most cases, with little or no environmental penalty. In many areas the economically efficient level of energy savings moved from 20–25 percent in the mid-1970s to 50–60 percent (90 percent in some end-uses) by the late 1980s. Not surprisingly, environmentalists were gradually joined by academics and such bodies as the Economic Council of Canada in putting forward the economic case for much more conservation in federal (and provincial) energy policies.

A recent analysis of the potential for electricity conservation in Ontario exemplifies this approach.[6] This study developed "supply curves" of electricity conservation in Ontario by analyzing the application of numerous energy-efficiency improvement measures, using the same conventions used by Ontario Hydro for costing new power plants. The results revealed a potential for more than 8,000 megawatts of peak-capacity savings that could be achieved by the year 2000 with investments of less than $1,000 per peak kilowatt, and that would "supply" saved electricity for a unit cost between 0.1 and 4.0 cents per kilowatt-hour.

6   Marbek Resource Consultants and Torrie Smith Associates, *Electricity Conservation and Acid Rain in Ontario* (Toronto: Ministry of Energy, March 1989, rev'd May 1989).

Properly seen, however, the economic challenge to the conventional paradigm is only a partial challenge. It insists that the conventional paradigm must logically be extended from an exclusive focus on energy supply to an equal and opposite focus on energy demand. It does not insist that energy policy move away from the commodity orientation, with its implication that the lowest-cost source (whether demand or supply) is best.

The last third of the 1980s has seen a revival of the environmental challenge to energy policy. In contrast to earlier concerns, this challenge is rooted less in local damages or land use than in growing scientific evidence of broad-scale environmental damage, and particularly global climate change. Concern about acid rain, later joined by concerns about ozone depletion, greenhouse gases, and other problems, has put environment firmly back on the federal energy policy agenda — indeed, on its international political agenda.

The shift back towards an environmental challenge may have profound implications for energy policy. Most people accept that links exist between environment and economics, but it has become difficult to argue convincingly that least-cost strategies would be sufficient to achieve all environmental goals. No matter that, as some argued, it would be cheaper to allow coal to be burned in the American Midwest, and to have mining and electrical firms pay for the damages caused by acid rain in Canada, than to shift to alternative fuels. Canadian simply did not want acidified lakes and artificial maple syrup.

Finally, the conventional energy policy paradigm was challenged sharply by growing international attention to the concept of sustainable development. The Brundtland Report put forward a strong case for establishing economic policies that would preserve the environmental base on which the economy depended. In many ways, the Report reversed the major cause-and-effect linkages: rather than focusing on how the economy affects the environment, the Report suggested that, at least after a point in development, we should look at how the environment affects the economy.

The association of economic and environmental challenges to energy policy has by no means come completely unravelled. To a considerable degree, greater economic efficiency in delivery of energy services still serves environmental goals. However, the two are not the same, and it is not at all clear to what extent sustainable development in any country can be achieved by following economic signals alone. Of more immediate concern for those who have to make energy policy, there is no reason to assume that least-cost energy policies can limit acid rain to the extent demanded by the public, and even less to think that they can achieve the carbon dioxide emission reductions deemed necessary to avoid climate change.

LEAST COST AND SOFT PATH:
QUANTIFYING THE CHALLENGE

A strong analytical foundation for alternative energy policies in Canada has been developed, evolving from an economic to an environmental — or, to use the jargon, from least cost to soft paths. (Ironically, the original alternative energy analyses were termed soft paths, but their analytics were almost entirely within a least-cost framework.)

While a number of alternative energy studies had been done in the 1970s, the most complete study originated with a 1981 contract between Friends of the Earth (FOE) and the federal Department of Energy, Mines and Resources to produce a study of alternative directions for energy policy in Canada — directions that would emphasize energy efficiency and reliance on renewable forms of energy. A team of analysts was assembled, and the resulting twelve-volume report — *2025: Soft Energy Futures for Canada* — was published in February 1983.[7]

The results of the FOE study can be summarized briefly as follows: under conditions of strong economic growth (an increase of more than 200 percent in GDP) and moderate population growth (an increase of over 50 percent), it would be technically feasible and cost-effective to operate the Canadian economy in 2025 with 12 percent less energy than in 1978, and, over the same 47-year period, to shift from a 16 percent reliance on renewable sources to 77 percent. In the lower-growth scenario (economic growth of 140 percent over the 47-year period), assuming the real cost of soft technologies drops slightly, it would be feasible and cost-effective to use 34 percent less energy in 2025 than in 1978, with 82 percent of that energy provided by renewable sources. (Technical feasibility is defined in terms of the availability of either off-the-shelf or prototype technology. Cost-effectiveness is defined in terms of the long-run marginal costs of alternative ways of supplying energy in Canada.) Over the study period, energy use per capita falls to between one-half and two-fifths of its level in 1978, and energy use per dollar of GDP to just over one-quarter of its 1978 level.

The environmental dimensions of the original FOE study were largely restricted to the *a priori* elimination of sources of supply deemed inappropriate — Arctic oil, nuclear electricity, and coal-based liquids. The economics alone took care of what were then seen as the remaining problems, through the virtual elimination of petroleum as an important energy source in Canada, the emergence of biomass solids (pellets) and liquids (methanol) as major new energy

---

7   Analysts and authors of provincial reports include H. Boerma, K. Brown, L. Ehrlich, A. Gallant, J. Harrison, T. Hodge, S. Holtz, H. Lajambe, R. Lalonde, J. Lewis, Y. Penning, B. Pond, W. Ross, G. Stiles, and R.D. Torrie. See D.B. Brooks, J.B. Robinson & R.D. Torrie, eds., *2025: Soft Energy Futures for Canada* (Report prepared on behalf of Friends of the Earth Canada) (Ottawa: Energy, Mines and Resources and Environment Canada, February 1983).

commodities, the restriction of coal use to only a couple of provinces, and little or no growth in the use of electricity (although, as a share of total demand, a greater role for electricity was projected).

The FOE report remains the definitive national study on the long-term potential for energy conservation and renewable energy in Canada. However, in the few years since it was published, a number of important changes have occurred in the world's energy and environmental situation. Partly in response to these changes, and partly as a result of constructive review of the FOE study itself, the study was updated in 1988.[8] Three sets of questions made this update particularly relevant:

1.   Given the lower oil and gas price projections that now prevail, what is their impact on the cost-effectiveness of the conservation and efficiency measures adopted in the original study, and to what extent is the cost-effectiveness of new and renewable sources of energy affected?

2.   Given the indications that a technological revolution is taking place in all forms of energy-using equipment and processes (particularly those using electricity), how should the original analysis be modified to reflect the greater cost-effectiveness and high rates of adoption of energy-saving techniques? More accurately, how do the costs of these emerging technologies compare with the supply costs of electricity and fuels in Canada?

3.   Finally, and perhaps most important from a conceptual point of view, how can environmental concerns be incorporated directly into the analysis? Will such incorporation accord with the Brundtland Commission's call for the urgent adoption of energy efficiency, with the objective of cutting in half the per capita primary energy consumption in all industrial countries by the end of the century?

The simple answer to the first two questions is "not very much at all." That is, the updated analysis of the FOE study showed that the technical and economic feasibility of conservation and efficiency have not been significantly affected by the decline in oil and gas prices. It is still true, as it was in 1983, that under conditions of strong economic growth and moderate population growth, it would be technically feasible and cost-effective to operate the Canadian economy in 2025 with less energy than in 1978. In the updated analysis of the FOE consumer-saturation scenario, secondary energy use drops by 27 percent by 2025, per capita use by over 50 percent, and energy intensity of the economy by 66 percent. Per capita use of primary energy resources (including feedstocks) drops from about 340 gigajoules

8   R.D. Torrie & D.B. Brooks, *2025: Soft Energy Futures for Canada – 1988 Update* (Report prepared for Canadian Environmental Network Energy Caucus for submission to Energy Options Policy Review) (Ottawa: Energy, Mines and Resources, February 1988).

in 1978 to approximately 160 gigajoules in 2025, thus meeting the goal of a 50 percent reduction in primary energy intensity suggested by the Brundtland Commission.

The effects are more important on the supply side. In general, the new and renewable forms of energy (wind, photovoltaics, active solar) are not cost-effective under the new price projections, and both oil and natural gas continue to make significant contributions to the supply mix throughout the study period. Wood fuel and grain-based ethanol are included in the updated scenario, but their combined contribution to secondary energy is still relatively small by 2025. There is less diversity of supply in the updated scenario than in the original FOE scenario, but the overall efficiency of the energy system is much higher. The use of electricity stagnates, as opposing trends for the greater use of electricity and the more efficient use of electricity tend to cancel each other.

The answer to the third of the three questions that led to the updated alternative energy study is more difficult, for reasons that require some understanding of the ways in which environmental and social criteria have been incorporated into alternative energy analyses. Three separate but related approaches have generally been employed (all three were adopted in both the original and the updated studies).

First, the future scenario that is developed is made up of assumptions about population levels and the amount and kind of economic activities — including income and leisure activities, kinds of services available, and so forth. To an important extent, these are related to environmental and other social values. For example, a deliberate choice can be made of income levels that grow more slowly — in effect, a trade-off for more time for family and leisure. This value trade-off, translated into the aggregate effect of many individuals' decisions, will reduce society's energy demand. Similarly, a transportation scenario could be developed to incorporate more emphasis in city planning on pedestrian activity and mass transit, with the intention of improving urban air quality and reducing congestion.

Second, environmental values are built in through the central stress on matching both the *scale* and the *quality* of energy sources to those required by end-use demands. This introduction of what is essentially a thermodynamic concept adds another dimension to energy efficiency. By minimizing the use of high-quality fuels and electricity to meet end-uses of lower thermodynamic quality (such as heating or cooling the interior of a building a few degrees above the outside temperature), primary energy resources can be conserved for those applications for which they are essential.

Finally, environmental values are incorporated in a soft-path scenario by explicitly choosing or restricting the use of certain supply technologies or resources for environmental reasons. Other values, such as concern about culture or community impacts, can also be built in through this method. Postulating that coal-fired electric generation is only acceptable if acid emissions are controlled, or keeping certain rivers wild, or capping nuclear energy expansion: all are choices that can be made in developing a soft-path scenario. The task of the soft-path analyst is then to see if other resources suffice for that society's energy demand. Similarly, the analyst can phase in certain technologies more rapidly than economic criteria alone would permit, as part of a deliberate policy for environmental protection.

The strength of these three approaches, especially in combination, can be seen by reviewing the results from the updated FOE study. The most important environmental implication of the updated scenario, as with all soft-energy-path scenarios, is the reduced level of demand for energy commodites required to provide a given level of services. The reductions in energy use described above translate into a significant reduction in ecosystem stress caused by energy conversion technologies and primary energy resource extraction.

Second, conversion losses in the shift from primary to secondary energy are much lower in the updated analysis than in the original scenario, so much so that the absolute level of primary energy production in 2025 is down even though secondary energy use is up. The elimination of methanol as a transportation fuel (which has very high energy costs in its production) and the reduced role of nuclear and coal-fired electricity combine to make the energy system in the updated scenario much more efficient. Although fossil fuel use is still quite significant in 2025, it is well below current levels, and there is a relative shift away from the carbon-rich fuels and their amplified environmental impacts.

Third, the application of electricity conservation technology and the reduced role of electricity in the space-heating market more than offset higher electricity intensities for industrial production and residential appliances, and the fairly rapid penetration of the electric car. The results are a lower level of coal-fired power generation than in the original FOE scenario and the continued feasibility of a complete phasing out of nuclear power. Primary hydroelectricity production is also down in the updated scenario, with no new capacity additions after 2000.

Fourth, the biomass scenario in the updated analysis represents a more manageable rate of growth for biomass energy than was the case with the original FOE scenario. For one thing, the high primary biomass harvest required to support the assumed levels of methanol production — the major environmental problem associated with the original FOE scenario — has been eliminated in this scenario. Further, after an initial period of strong growth as wood pellets and ethanol develop their niches in the energy economy, continuing gains in end-use efficiency allow the primary biomass harvest to remain fairly stable, and even decline slightly, between 2000 and 2025. Properly managed, the wood energy harvest can make a positive contribution to both regeneration of Canada's forest lands and revitalization (on a sustainable basis) of some parts of our rural economy.

In sum, the updated analysis confirms that energy futures that place much less stress on the environment are both technically and economically feasible, even in the face of lower oil and gas price projections. In fact, the re-opened analysis is preferable to the original from an environmental perspective, despite lower energy prices. However, against this confirmation one must issue two caveats. First, such a demonstration of potential does not ensure that those futures will come about. It only means that they could do so without a concomitant need to develop new technologies or incur higher economic costs than conventional alternatives. Which future does finally come about also depends on political choices. Second, neither the original nor the updated analysis represents "best-case" energy futures from the perspective of environmental sustainability — far from it. The best sustainable future would require a reconsideration of many social and economic factors that were beyond the scope of either study. Primary-materials recycling, the reuse and recycling of consumer goods, deliberate choices to live more conserving lifestyles, a move to energy-conserving settlement patterns, industrial strategies that de-emphasize the energy-guzzling primary industries (paper, steel, chemicals): these are all factors that would go into a true "conserver society" scenario, but that were not considered in the updated analysis.

CONCLUSIONS

The preceding sections lead us to three major conclusions.

First, almost no matter what one's perspective, federal energy policies in Canada have been far from satisfactory. Whether one approaches policy formulation from the perspective of market solutions or of environmental (to say nothing of social) goals, it is evident that neither economic efficiency nor environmental protection has been served. The emphasis on the supply side of energy policy to the exclusion of demand has doomed economic objectives, and the emphasis on treating energy as a commodity has doomed environmental objectives. For either or both of these reasons, Canadian federal energy policies are neither on nor moving toward a sustainable course.

Second, given the need for new federal energy policies, it remains necessary to determine whether to challenge both the supply and the commodity tenets of conventional policies. The least-cost approach would challenge the former but not the latter; the soft-path approach would challenge both. Granted that there is considerable overlap in results between the two, there is also a great need to determine the extent to which the two approaches diverge. In analytical terms, we must identify the extent to which a soft-path energy supply curve with explicit attention to specific environmental goals, such as reduced carbon dioxide emissions, overlaps with a least-cost energy supply curve.

Finally, we contend that sustainable development implies energy policies based on soft-path and not merely least-cost principles. We make this contention in both a weak and a strong form. The weak form suggests that the goals of environmental policy will increasingly take precedence over those of conventional economic or energy policy. Therefore, energy policy will require that energy options first be defined by how well they satisfy certain environmental criteria (specific levels of sulfur or carbon dioxide reduction). Once so defined, the options would be selected on the basis of least-cost criteria, provided only that the environmental criteria are satisfied.

In its stronger form, the basis for a focus on soft-path approaches rests on the objectives of sustainable development. In the immediate future the thrust for change will come from (1) the growing consensus within the scientific community that current development patterns around the world constitute a serious and urgent threat to the stability of global ecosystems, and (2) the recognition that only extensive reforestation and significant reductions in energy consumption offer any immediate hope for offsetting adverse effects and avoiding climate change. At this level, there is little expectation that least-cost policies will suffice. Given additional criteria for sustainability, and particularly when equity is introduced as a criterion, there is even less of a role for purely economic policies, no matter how much attention they give to demand. Instead, soft-path policies, with their deliberate focus on social and environmental goals, will be required.

In conclusion, we believe it is necessary to caution against either of two misconceptions. First, emphasis on a soft-path approach does not and must not imply that economics and economic efficiency are irrelevant. They remain essential objectives of energy policy, without which little else is possible, but they are now coupled with other objectives that cannot usefully be brought within the economic paradigm. Second, notwithstanding our conclusion that the soft-energy path represents a feasible way to achieve a sustainable energy policy in Canada, we do not maintain that attaining sustainability will be easy. The political, economic, and social obstacles are formidable. Even achieving the first proximate goal for sustainability — a 20 percent reduction in carbon dioxide emissions by the year 2005 — requires a much greater effort at energy conservation than anything seen to date. The task is anything but easy. However, it is also essential, for, if with all our advantages, we in Canada cannot move toward sustainable energy policies, what expectations can we have for the remainder of the world?

4

SUSTAINABLE DEVELOPMENT IN NORTHERN REGIONS

NORTHERN INDIGENOUS CULTURES IN THE FACE OF DEVELOPMENT

Adrian Tanner

This paper raises the question of the relevance that "culture" and "values" have for "sustainable development."[1] The Brundtland Report,[2] in addressing such development-related problems as environmental degradation, population growth, resource depletion, debt crisis, urbanization, and militarization, passes over this matter with no more than a brief acknowledgement.[3] In part, this is owing to the Report's macro-level approach to development, which necessarily bypasses any details of particular local social and cultural conditions. Perhaps such details are left to more specialized studies of the causes of and solutions to specific local problems. However, even in its own macro-level terms, the Report offers no conception of development as a social process within which cultural ideas or values have a place.

---

1   Although the term "sustainable development" is popularly used in the limited sense of development that avoids ecological crises, the Brundtland Report (to its credit, in my view) uses the term to include development that avoids both economic and ecological crises. The forms of human economic behaviour are part of our species' relations with the ecosystem. The two (i.e., economy and ecosystem) are to be seen as intimately connected and thus in need of being dealt with in a single analytic framework.

2   World Commission on Environment and Development, *Our Common Future* (Oxford: Oxford University Press, 1987) (Chair: G.H. Brundtland).

3   *Id.* at 38. Of course, this book is not alone; most texts dealing with development in general overlook social and cultural factors.

Moreover, the solutions it offers, though described in terms of moral "oughts," and as "socially desirable,"[4] are otherwise treated in universalistic and culture-free terms.

An example of a development-related problem is population growth, which, according to the sustainable development approach, calls for campaigns "to strengthen the social, cultural and economic motivations for couples to have small families."[5] The relevance of culture to this question goes beyond public relations; for some peoples it is linked to the value placed on having at least one child of the appropriate gender to inherit, on having enough children to support parents in their old age, on religious barriers to population planning, or on the political desire for an expanding population.[6] Furthermore, at the macro level, one of the simplest ways for development as a general process to occur is through a continually growing market; because an obvious source of such growth is population increase, developing economies therefore have an incentive to support those cultural values in favour of population growth.

To cite another case, the Brundtland Report suggests that resource depletion in the Third World is in part caused by the need for foreign exchange.[7] However, this "need" is in itself cultural, and can be shown to be an intricate link in the development process itself, which includes changes in the cultural institutions of property. Prior to starting on the road to development, many non-Western societies have no open market in land and resources. Instead, a variety of tenure and usufructuary institutions distribute rights to resources in perpetuity. Moreover, many of these cultures have ideologies of land, animals, or nature that in general inhibit large-scale development and resource depletion. In the process of development, the cultural institutions of the market and private property, and the ideology of individual freedom from social constraints underlying these institutions, are applied not only to land, but to virtually any exploitable resource. Even such representatives of collectivities as national governments, whether capitalist or communist, use the privatization of natural resources to buy, sell, and use resources as if they were private property. In some Third World states where this notion has been introduced, one can observe the breakdown of earlier social forms in which there were recognized communally based rights to resources. Change in non-industrial cultures towards the privatization of resources, while facilitating development, makes control of resource depletion increasingly difficult.

There are many other examples of the significance of culture, both for the progress of development, and for the emergence of development-related problems.

---

4   *Id.* at 47.

5   *Id.* at 106.

6   For example, recently bonuses specifically aimed at increasing the population, in addition to Family Allowance, have been paid to mothers in Quebec.

7   See *Our Common Future, supra,* note 1 at 67–68.

Modern "development," while its origins and process may make it effectively a unitary, worldwide, multinational phenomenon, has a specific historical context and a specific set of economic and cultural correlates. Development problems can be solved, if at all, only through an understanding of this "culture" of development, and of how this process is bound to create new cultural situations out of previous ones.

DEVELOPMENT THEORY AND DEVELOPMENT IDEOLOGY

Much of the contemporary writing about development, economic crises, and ecological crises is written from a moralistic and ideological perspective. By "ideology" I refer to a form of thinking whose main organizing principle is the drawing of conclusions about recommended forms of human behaviour in order to solve what is presented as a problem, or to bring about a desired state of affairs. Development theories frequently look remarkably like pure ideologies. While there is nothing wrong with this kind of thinking, it is an anathema to a scientific approach, as it tends to interfere with the process of verifying such conclusions on the basis of factual evidence. Despite my desire to avoid preaching a particular ideology, I accept that it is hardly possible for humans to think without introducing a framework of understanding to the facts, and (at least when thinking about human affairs) such a framework is usually inspired by an ideology. Whether we intend them or not, most thought has ideological implications.

Underlying this paper is a generalized opposition to the sustainable development movement, a rejection based on theoretical positions and empirical observations that (because they are tangential to my main subject matter) cannot all be spelled out, and for which I do not claim there exists in all cases final proof. To give an indication of my general approach, "sustainable development" seems to me to be an oxymoron. While I concede that it is possible in certain cases to foresee and minimize the impacts of some development-caused crises, I hold that, in general, development-oriented economies have cultural values and institutional forms that are inseparable from patterns of boom and bust, and from ecological crisis; these phenomena are not accidents, but are generated by the development process itself. I certainly hope I can be proved wrong in this.

I therefore question whether development is the planned, controlled phenomenon it is made to appear in the writings of many development specialists. One way of utilizing my general approach in this paper is to include what might be called a "limiting" case to the foregoing view of development. The example I use is the subarctic fur trade, in which boom and bust and ecological crisis were to a remarkable degree avoided over a three-hundred-year period.

IS DEVELOPMENT SUSTAINABLE IN PRINCIPLE?

Before looking at the northern fur trade, I will critically examine the concept of sustainable development, and in particular will suggest that social disruptions and economic instability have always been part of the development process. This generalization about the nonsustainability of development is a hypothesis, but one for which there is considerable evidence, both in recent history and today. Moreover, as discussed below, the notion that economic growth or development is endemically crisis-ridden is not new, but is a conclusion that has been arrived at independently by several theorists. It is, however, a view that in Canada is not as yet universal; indeed, the concept of managing development so as to avoid such crises is widely discussed as a serious possibility.

Theories of development frequently distinguish between the development process within the developed or industrialized world and that within the underdeveloped or Third world, and apply themselves exclusively to the understanding of one or the other. But the two processes are clearly closely connected. Moreover, both are historically based on similar social conditions: the introduction of new forms of legitimation by which some persons could utilize the work of others. The division of labour by means of the class system and colonialism has a parallel sociological basis within the two development processes.

There is, in fact, a long tradition of theories of development, including those of Marx, Lenin, Baran, Frank, and Wallerstein, demonstrating that capitalist economies, as part of their development, must move outside their centres of origin to insert themselves within non-capitalist economies, not only because initial industrial expansion causes shortages of raw materials at home, but also because the inherent need to expand production leads to the continual search for new markets. For example, underdevelopment, far from being based (as the Brundtland Report assumes) on Third World demand for improved living standards (even though such demands are part of the condition of underdevelopment), or simply being the state of affairs prior to capitalist development, is a condition of economic subordination brought about as a result of the development process itself — that is, through the penetration of capitalism into the non-capitalist hinterland.[8] Moreover, as Wallerstein has argued, this "development of underdevelopment" is not confined merely to capitalist states; one can speak of the Soviet Union, for example, as a core power in the capitalist world economy.[9]

Marxist theory also presents us with a more precise way of approaching "economic sustainability," by defining its opposite, "economic crisis," as "an interruption in the normal reproduction process."[10] In other words, sustainability

8   A.G. Frank, "Sociology of Development and Underdevelopment of Sociology" (1967) 3 Catalyst 20.

9   I. Wallerstein, *The Capitalist World-Economy* (Cambridge: Cambridge University Press, 1979) at 33.

10   E. Mandel, *Marxist Economic Theory*, trans. B. Pearce, vol. 1 (New York: Monthly Review Press, 1968) at 342.

can be seen as the process of putting the necessary social and economic conditions in place to ensure the continuity of the particular existing mode of production. While there is an extensive debate over the causes of continual economic crises within capitalism, including the phenomenon of business cycles, many economic theorists from all parts of the ideological spectrum accept the occurrence of these crises as a given. (Indeed, a specialty called "crisis theory" has recently developed within economics.[11]) As regularly occurring phenomena, economic depressions, recessions, technological changeovers, the flight of capital to sources of cheap labour, global changes in the economic centre of gravity, and so forth are incompatible with the notion of sustainability within a developing economy.

A number of authors have also suggested that, in addition to the periodic crises faced by development-oriented economies, there are more serious limits to the development process in general. These authors, who include Schumacher,[12] Hirsch,[13] Meadows et al.,[14] Commoner,[15] and the Canadian Broadcasting Corporation,[16] have suggested that development cannot continue indefinitely, arguing the existence both of external environmental and technological limits, and of internal social or cultural limits.

A society that is characterized by sustainable forms of economic production has such an economy not by chance, but because it has an integrated set of institutions and values — in short, a culture, which (among other things) is oriented towards the goal of long-term stability. Societies characterized by development exist also not by chance, but because they have a cultural orientation towards innovation and expansion. Although Levi-Strauss is frequently credited with insisting on this division, as, for example, in his references to "hot" and "cold" societies, it is clear he intends these terms to be used in a relativistic sense.[17] Thus, some earlier societies did have many of the same dynamic characteristics as modern industrial ones, but their development was not sustained. Moreover, the line between a development-oriented and a non--development-oriented society must be somewhat arbitrary. Polanyi has spoken of the historical turning point in the full adoption of this kind of society as the "Great Transformation,"[18] to refer to the development of the abstract

11 For example, see S. Bowles, D. Gordon & T. Weisskopf, *Beyond the Wasteland: A Democratic Alternative to Economic Decline* (Garden City: Doubleday, 1983); J. O'Connor, *The Meaning of Crisis: A Theoretical Introduction* (New York: Basil Blackwell, 1987).

12 E.F. Schumacher, *Small is Beautiful* (London: Blond & Briggs, 1973).

13 F. Hirsch, *The Social Limits to Growth* (Cambridge: Harvard University Press, 1976).

14 D.H. Meadows et al., *The Limits to Growth* (New York: Universe Books, 1972).

15 B. Commoner, *The Closing Circle: Nature, Man and Technology* (New York: Alfred A. Knopf, 1971).

16 Canadian Broadcasting Corporation, *A Planet for the Taking* (Television Series) (Toronto: Canadian Broadcasting Corp., 1986).

17 C. Levi-Strauss, *Race and History* (Paris: UNESCO, 1952).

18 K. Polanyi, *The Great Transformation* (Boston: Beacon Press, 1944).

concept of the market and of all-purpose money. The twin concepts of market and money, in turn, assume the existence of other institutions of the modern state, particularly record-keeping, communications, and, most important, the law of contract and the mechanisms necessary to enforce it.

Industrial society is characterized not merely by development, but by the continual process of launching newer and newer development projects. This plurality of projects is significant because of the basic fact of competition between projects. A project initially involves capital investment, which requires a certain level of return. Competition between projects implies a continual tendency to expand production up to the physical ecological limits. While states can place restrictions (in the form of regulations) on projects to limit the latter's growth to less than environmentally imposed limits, this is usually a futile exercise. For one thing, states are in competition with each other to attract new projects; for another, these developments have unintended consequences. The frequent result is ecological crisis in some form.

A second result of competition between projects (existing and potential) is the continual drive for technological innovation to produce more at lower cost. Whenever the search for new technology produces a major successful innovation, this leads to new projects, which put existing ones out of business. Such periodic sectoral declines adversely affect large sectors of the population, who are unable to adapt quickly enough to the new competing projects.

NORTHERN DEVELOPMENT AND
CULTURAL DEVASTATION

I now focus on the relationship between development and the indigenous people of the Canadian North, from a historical perspective. There is an abundance of evidence worldwide that the development process has in general had, and continues to have, a devastating effect on indigenous minority peoples.[19] Among Native peoples of Canada, even with the social welfare net, development is the cause of numerous serious social problems. For example, the impact of oil exploration on the Lubicon Cree of Alberta was described by the World Council of Churches delegation in 1984 as having "genocidal consequences." The impact on the Grassy Narrows Ojibwa of community relocation and mercury pollution from a nearby pulp mill was equally destructive.[20]

The Grassy Narrows case is significant because, Shkilnyk argues, it was not economic development as such that undermined the community, but the government's relocation scheme, which was undertaken in order that the community could be

---

19   J.H. Bodley, *Victims of Progress* (2d ed.; Palo Alto: Mayfield, 1982).

20   A.M. Shkilnyk, *A Poison Stronger Than Love: The Destruction of an Ojibwa Community* (New Haven: Yale University Press, 1985).

"modernized"— that is, provided with a local school, medical facilities, electricity, water, and sewage. But most of all, the relocation was done to end the community's geographic isolation, by placing it in road communication with the rest of the country. Unless we assume that the relocation introduced modernization as a "good" in itself, we must conclude that these innovations were actually *preparations* for some unspecified potential future economic development; therefore these preparations were, in this case, the destructive factor, rather than development itself. Other recent studies confirm that social problems arise when the government extends bureaucratic control over isolated communities, even in advance of any actual extensive economic development schemes.[21]

I mention these cases because they are recent, well known, and well documented; they are also *typical*. The factors underlying such development-related problems are commonplace in the experience of Canadian Native communities, as is their aftermath. Many formerly isolated northern Native communities have, following the impact of development, exhibited to a greater or lesser degree a linked series of symptoms of social and cultural breakdown: alcohol abuse, interpersonal violence, child neglect, very high rates of incarceration, and very high suicide rates. Moreover, the pattern of social breakdown following northern development appears to be part of the same process that has previously affected more southern Native communities after they felt the impact of development. Consequently, the destructive aftermath of development, or of the introduction of its infrastructure, can be said to be the predominant factor accounting for the shared social characteristics of most Canadian Native communities today.[22]

While the process of cultural breakdown in Native communities of the Canadian North affected by development differs from case to case, the process typically involves the following: (1) increasing barriers to the group's pursuit of its subsistence economy (e.g., ecological degradation, land alienation, resource competition from newcomers, game laws, sedentary pressures); (2) barriers to the group's participation in the unstable development wage economy; (3) placement of the group within a sedentary settlement for bureaucratic control and administrative convenience; (4) mandatory schooling, using the dominant culture's curriculum, leading to high dropout rates; and (5) proliferation among Native youth of the dominant group's values and ideology, through films, television, music, and videos. Along with these changes is an apparent undermining of the basis of the group's existing culture, values, and social order, and the introduction among the youth of

21 R. Paine, ed., *The White Arctic: Anthropological Essays on Tutelage and Ethnicity* (Toronto: University of Toronto Press, 1977); P. Driben & R.S. Trudeau, *When Freedom is Lost: The Dark Side of the Relationship Between Government and the Fort Hope Band* (Toronto: University of Toronto Press, 1983).

22 Department of Indian and Northern Affairs, *Indian Conditions: A Survey* (Ottawa: Department of Indian and Northern Affairs, 1980).

new expectations, without the possibility of satisfying them either through participation in the dominant group's economic system or through economic development
within the group itself. The group instead is reduced to living in poverty on social
assistance, and adopts pathological self-destructive behavior and/or a political
ideology of militant ethnic nationalism.

SUSTAINABILITY AND FUR TRADE DEVELOPMENT

It might be objected that these problems are not relevant to the issue of
sustainable development, that what these illustrate is the nonsustainability of a
people in the face of development, because they are not development-oriented. I
propose therefore to look at the opposite kind of case, where development was
brought to a non-development-oriented group without causing social and cultural
breakdown. I will use a historical example, the introduction of commercial fur
trapping among the northern Native peoples of Canada. This may appear to be an
odd choice, for two reasons. First, it is taken from the early imperial period of
European colonialism, which is usually considered to have been a particularly
immoral phase in the history of development, and especially destructive to non-
Western peoples. Second, the fur trade in particular is frequently thought of as an
especially extreme case of the exploitation of a non-Western people, an exploitation
that made them dependent on the whims of the fashion market and tied them to the
trader by bonds of debt dependency. As I will show, however, while in many regions
the fur trade had a disastrous impact on Native people, in much of the Arctic and
subarctic it spanned a remarkably stable period lasting up to three hundred years,
and left Native people with a considerable degree of autonomy.

It is sometimes assumed that development and the market embody universal
natural processes, rather than those of a particular cultural group. Thus, when
considering the history of development in frontier regions, such as the Canadian
North, we often pay little attention to the adaptive role played by the cultures of the
aboriginal peoples of the region. If we have seen the aboriginal peoples as playing
predominantly reactive rather than proactive roles in northern development, it is in
part because we have failed to see that they have been pursuing goals that differ from
ours. It also follows from the insignificant political voice that these peoples, the
long-term inhabitants of the region, have so far had in the formal decision-making
process.

The initial confrontation between Europeans and Canadian Native people,
which occurred primarily within the context of the fur trade, was between one group
with values and a world view oriented towards expansion, and another with values
and a world view oriented towards long-term stability. In many of the northern
regions this confrontation did not lead to either the destruction of aboriginal cultures
or the reorientation of aboriginal people in the direction of development, nor were
Europeans influenced to change direction away from development. Thus, the North

today is still an interesting place to view the continuing interaction between a culture focussed on sustainability and a culture focussed on development. It is not yet clear whether the Canadian propensity to seek compromises between irreconcilable positions will be able to generate an accommodation between aboriginal desires to retain the natural environment and Eurocanadian needs for development.

The nature and severity of the impact of the fur trade in northern Canada on aboriginal peoples remains controversial among scholars. Some see it as having had an early and devastating impact on the aboriginal and as exemplifying the worst excesses of colonial exploitative development, made more destructive by the cut-throat tactics of rival traders and the encouragement of intertribal warfare.[23] According to other scholars, the aboriginal peoples who were drawn into the trade used it to their own advantage, and maintained to a remarkable degree the continuity of their own cultures, with minimal disruption.[24]

Any attempt to generalize about the effects of the fur trade overlooks the fact that the impact varied significantly in different parts of Canada. I will not try to summarize the range of impacts here, but will try to demonstrate the diversity by looking at the impact of the fur trade on two groups, the Mistassini Cree living to the east of James Bay, and the Innu of Labrador.

In discussing sustainable development in this context, I propose to deal with the "sustainable" and "development" aspects separately, following my hypothesis that each is characteristic of a different kind of society. On the basis of these two terms, two ideal types of society have been identified. The first of these, which I will call a *subsistence-oriented* society, is non-expansionary and has economic institutions and ecological adaptations that sustain the social form over the long run. The second, which I will call a *wealth-oriented* society, is expansionary and embraces notions of development and progress, but faces continual crises and the need to reorganize itself. The aim of the economy in the former is focussed on enabling small groups, such as extended families, to produce so as to satisfy most, if not all, of their own needs, for which they have a relatively low but inflexible demand. They use sharing and gift exchange to maintain egalitarian living standards.

Prior to European contact, the aboriginal societies of North America and many other parts of the world were predominantly of the subsistence-oriented type. Despite changes to aboriginal societies brought about by the pressures of colonialism, nationalism, and international industrial development, many such societies, both in Canada and elsewhere, have been able to retain at least a sector of their

---

23 For example, see C. Yerbury, *Subarctic Indians and the Fur Trade* (Vancouver: University of British Columbia Press, 1986).

24 For example, see M. Asch, *Home and Native Land: Aboriginal Rights and the Canadian Constitution* (Toronto: Methuen, 1984).

culture and economy that is subsistence-oriented, alongside a wealth-oriented sector. This tendency for the sustainable subsistence sector to resist incorporation into the development, market-oriented sector is frequently referred to as the "dual economy."

In the context of the confrontation between Europeans and aboriginal peoples, the dual economy can be seen as the attempt to embrace the two poles of sustainability and development within a single society. Markets as such did not undermine such societies, but changes in cultural needs and values, and especially the adoption of new inflationary values, the loss of control over population growth, and long-term or irreversible ecological damage, could do so. Thus, in Canada, aboriginal sustained subsistence-oriented societies were not undermined by colonial fur trade contact alone.

Mistassini

Such a continuity can be illustrated by a very brief description of the hunting/trapping economy of one regional sub-group of the Mistassini, the Nichicun, as observed by me in 1971, or roughly 370 years after fur trade relations had been established with Europeans. The main sources of monetary income were furs trapped between October and April, wages earned primarily in the three or four months of summer, and transfer payments such as Family Allowance, pensions, and Social Assistance. However, the largest single source of income, in terms of value of the store-bought equivalent, was the meat harvested in addition to trapping activities.

The inherent instability of the productive base for individual hunter/trappers was compensated for by the rigorous ethic and practice of sharing, using generalized reciprocity. Sharing between families was not confined to meat from hunting, but included even store-bought supplies, if one family happened to run low. Each year a major monetary outlay was needed to finance the coming winter. In the past, under assured monopoly conditions, a whole winter's outfit of hardware, clothing, and luxury foods was obtained on credit from the Hudson's Bay Company (HBC). Credit limits were later reduced to enough for supplies for only part of the winter, and by 1971 additional credit was needed to finance the flight to the hunting territory, in place of the arduous canoe and portage journeys. The HBC underwrote the credit for these flights, but used expected transfer payments as well as the expected fur catch as security. The function of credit was essentially to isolate hunting group economics from the economics of the market, leaving the group in total control of production, using non-market values and organizational forms.

I was especially struck by the way the HBC had shifted its trading methods at Nichicun away from normal market practices and towards something much closer to Cree cultural ideas of sharing and reciprocity. For various periods during the nineteenth century, and up to the period after the Second World War, the Nichicun were a group separate from the Mistassini, and had their own staffed HBC post. After the effective amalgamation of the Nichicun into the Mistassini group, the HBC had opened an unstaffed store for the Nichicun next to a small Department of Transport weather station, centrally located with respect to the Nichicun hunting territories. This store was stocked with essentials every summer, and during the following winter individuals took what supplies they needed, leaving lists to be later collected by the Mistassini HBC manager and added to each individual's account. This honour system of trade is for me symptomatic of the continuity of a sustainable, non-market economic ethic. The system, and the willingness of Cree hunter/trappers to allow the HBC manager the equivalent of power of attorney to manage their accounts (including permission to credit their government cheques to their store accounts) may seem like an open invitation to exploitation, but was actually conflict-free, as the success of the system at the Nichicun store indicates.

The point here is that the Mistassini hunters do not trap fur for money as such; they do so for more complex reasons. In part they do so because many of the trapped species — particularly their staple furbearer, the beaver — provide high-quality edible meat. They trap also because it is part of a lifestyle that is an end in itself. I do not suggest that they trap because of a romantic love of communing with nature; their motive is far more specifically a Cree notion of religious love, which surrounds their relationship with game animals—a relationship that includes within the single activity food harvesting, spiritualism, and aesthetics. As long as the HBC-managed market sector of the total exchange system continued to supply needed store goods, there was no impetus to accumulate more. In this way, all other sources of cash were fed into, and used by, the essentially non-market, gift-exchange-based economy of the hunter/trapper household.

Of course, when the households of hunter/trappers were not in the bush but living in the village, the household economy changed direction toward that of mainstream society, with some casual wage work. An entirely different market-oriented economic sphere would take effect, in which the HBC was merely one retailer in competition with others, including those in the nearest town and the mail-order houses. The two spheres were not entirely separate; surpluses from the summer/village economic sphere could be transferred into the winter/bush economic sphere, and meat from the bush was consumed in the village.

At the time of my research, the struggle between the Cree and the Quebec government over the building of the James Bay hydroelectric project began. This project can be seen as one of a number of northern frontier developments designed for the benefit of the south, and which threaten the ecology of the region, and thereby the sustainability of the aboriginal economy. The Cree were more fortunate than most, since a court victory gave them the clout to obtain some modifications to the project and some protection from it. The initial phase of the project appears to be the least destructive, so there may well be further problems ahead. In my view, the main advantage the Cree had was a well-established two-sector economy, that of hunting/trapping and that of wage work. Although the project will reduce the hunting/trapping sector, the Cree fought hard to retain hunting/trapping as a significant option for a large percentage of the population for a large part of the year. The challenge for the Cree is to modify their culture without destroying it, so as to incorporate these two sectors based on essentially antagonistic values. Contradiction within a culture is not uncommon; the question is whether the contradiction will divide the community or not.

The specific challenges facing the Cree as they try to balance sustainability and development are ecological and economic. Among the threats to the ecology are a number of large-scale forestry projects in the southern part of the territory, over which the Cree would like to have greater control. There is also the imminent building of additional hydroelectric projects, which will be far more damaging than the one already built, and for which Hydro-Quebec appears unwilling to undertake normal environmental impact assessments. Finally, the Cree themselves are undergoing something of a population explosion, which places them in the position of needing economic expansion. The economic threats include the possibility that the Guaranteed Annual Income to hunters and trappers (a subsidy acquired as part of the James Bay Agreement) may introduce market pressures and motives into the hitherto non-market hunting/trapping sector.

Labrador

My encounters with the Innu of Labrador, a people closely related to the Cree of Mistassini, began in 1974 and have continued to the present. It may be because my research with them overlapped to some extent my work with the Mistassini that I am drawn by the contrast between the two groups. Although 1974 was approximately the beginning of what amounts to a nativistic and nationalistic political movement among the Labrador Innu, my first impressions were of a group suffering from an almost total social breakdown. In contrast to the Mistassini, the Innu of Labrador do not appear to have achieved a conflict-free accommodation with the European fur trade. In part this is because of different ecological conditions. In Labrador the primary food animal is the caribou. Since the caribou are extremely nomadic, and gather together at certain times of the year, there proved to be a conflict between the requirements of fur trapping and those of hunting. Although the Mistassini also had some caribou, their main sources of meat were moose, bear, and beaver, animals that are spread fairly evenly across the territory; a dependence on beaver, moose, and bear therefore need not conflict with the requirements of trapping. However, when the HBC first tried to initiate trapping among the northern Innu, many of them starved in attempting to follow the directives of the traders and live on trapping in areas where there were no caribou to hunt. Although apparently independently of the arrival of traders, the northern caribou herd suffered a collapse early in the twentieth century, causing further starvation among the Innu.

In part because the Innu were unwilling to devote themselves full-time to trapping, the HBC, which did not establish a post in Labrador until 1836, turned to Labradorians of mixed European and Inuit descent, known as "settlers," as trappers and salmon fishermen. These people, who had a significant market-oriented sector in their economy, and did not depend on hunting for their subsistence while they trapped, effectively competed with the Innu for the most lucrative trapping areas, and by 1900 had reached far into the interior, leading to some hostility between the two groups. This competition lessened after 1942 with the building of the Goose Bay military air base, where jobs attracted the settlers but not the Innu. In 1960 the Newfoundland government, which had refused to recognize the Innu as registered Indians under federal jurisdiction when Newfoundland entered Confederation in 1949, began a series of moves to force the Innu to settle in two villages — Sheshatshiu, near Goose Bay, and Davis Inlet, on the northern coast. Schools were built, but unlike most northern Native communities, these villages had no arrangements for student residences, forcing parents to remain in the villages. Hunting and trapping were made more difficult with the implementation of game laws, which were applied to Innu and non-Innu alike — again in contrast to the practice elsewhere in northern Canada, where aboriginal people hunting for their own food are not subject to game laws.

At the same time, a series of industrial developments that would drastically reduce Innu hunting lands began in Labrador without the knowledge of the Innu. Several large mines linked by a railway were opened in western Labrador, and the Churchill Falls hydroelectric project created a vast shallow reservoir, which, because it was totally unexpected, flooded a significant amount of Innu hunting and trapping equipment. The reservoir also significantly reduced the traditional hunting lands of the Sheshatshiu Innu. The increased population in the Goose Bay area (which was further added to as the result of new forestry projects), many of whom use snowmobiles, all-terrain vehicles, and aircraft, has had the effect of reducing the game available in the area to the Innu. With a population whose main cultural values were related to hunting, and yet who were largely deprived of this activity and were sustained by nothing more than Social Assistance cheques, the predictable result was a decline in health and an epidemic of alcohol abuse, interpersonal violence, and suicide.

Some changes have subsequently taken place, including a number of attempts by the Innu to re-establish their hunting-based way of life. A number of camps are established every year, but, like those of the Mistassini, they are dependent on aircraft; they are, however, without a dependable economic base with which to pay for them. The most significant development among the Innu has been the initiation of a series of demonstrations and confrontations with the government, mainly centred on opposition to the use of low-flying jets in military training and the plans to establish a NATO tactical weapons training centre. These are merely the best-publicized examples, however; the Innu have also engaged in demonstrations concerning the delivery of social services in their villages and the application of provincial game laws to them. Underlying these demonstrations is an ideology of Innu cultural nationalism that is among the most radical of any aboriginal group in Canada.

CONCLUSION

Even societies dependent on renewable resources must face limits to the expansion they can achieve. For example, the amount of land available to an agricultural society for cultivation is to some degree limited. Once expansion into all available land has occurred, further increases in productivity can be achieved using techniques of intensification, but an upper limit to productivity must eventually be reached. Absolute limits on the development of any particular resource base must exist, even if we may not know where future technology will set those limits.[25]

The hypothesis that no form of development can possibly be indefinitely sustainable follows from the assumption that development involves, by definition, an expansion of economic production, either to satisfy an increase in population or to permit a net per capita increase in consumption. It might be questioned, however, whether the concept could reasonably be modified to include not only economic expansion, but also what we might call "optimization." In other words, can the concept of development embrace economic changes in the direction of satisfying human needs in new ways that require *less* material consumption, and less energy expenditure per capita? Another attempt to salvage the concept would be to limit it to new projects that themselves represent new additions to production, and are thus developments, but, once they are underway, are non-expansionary and do not depend on nonrenewable resources. An example might be a hydroelectric project. In evaluating whether a project is sustainable in these terms, one would need to recognize that the energy and raw and manufactured materials required to build the project weigh against a claim to sustainability, as do any negative environmental impacts and the destruction of the previous uses of the land displaced by such a project. Moreover, while an individual project might pass such a sustainability test, the need for economic expansion would require a continuing addition of new projects, which would ultimately have the same effects as one expansionary project.

25   Kenneth Boulding, "Can There be Models for Sustainable Development?" in A. Davidson & M. Daence, eds., *The Brundtland Challenge and the Cost of Inaction* (Halifax: Institute for Research in Public Policy, 1988).

The difficulty with these attempts to redefine our way around the contradiction inherent within "sustainable development" is (amongst other things) that they overlook the economic context within which the call for sustainable development has been raised, in our particular society and in the industrial world in general. That reality is that our economic system is dependent upon continual expansion of production, so that if this year's production does not increase over last year's, we face a crisis. Even if individuals could be more satisfied with less (something that would require a radical shift in cultural values), there are serious doubts whether the present economic system could adjust. Thus, however desirable the utopian concept of development that would meet increased satisfaction of needs through decreased material consumption, for the time being we are left with the need for development in the more traditional sense of continuing increases in material production.

How, then, do we account for the serious discussion apparently being given to this concept? It might be argued that the current popularity of sustainable development must be interpreted in the context of the problem of economic instability. At one time the opening and closing of whole towns was seen as an inevitable part of a frontier reality. The typical case of this instability would be the social disruption caused by the closing of a community's single-industry enterprise, such as a mine, after it had been operating for a number of years. As the frontier of rugged individualists is replaced by real communities, resistance to closures and labour migration grows. Moreover, there is a new aspect to the problem of socially disruptive industrial closures, which are increasingly no longer confined to the frontier. Current economic instability is as much due to technological and world market changes as it is to the depletion of resources. If such is the background to the current concern for sustainable development, then the phrase must be seen not as the expression of an absolute principle that it first appears to be, but as the advocacy of a policy in which, by selecting the right kind and mix of industries, one gives relatively more attention to long-term viability over short-term advantage, with an attempt thereby to avoid some of the worst parts of the boom and bust cycle.

Much of the rhetoric of sustainable development advocates paying attention to the long-term ecological viability of development projects. The assumption here is that, through an environmental impact assessment process, we have the ability to accurately predict long-term ecological effects. As difficult as this task often turns out to be, there are even greater difficulties in predicting how one development will mesh with others in a region to generate combined impacts, and what the social impact of a development or combination of developments will be. The doubtful assumption is made that the biological and social sciences are able to identify ecologically and socially sustainable forms of development over nonsustainable ones.

I am not particularly hopeful that, as a consciousness-raising exercise, the sustainable development debate will change development policy. Thirty years ago, when I was an undergraduate at the University of British Columbia, we learned about the sustained-yield management policy in the forest industry, meaning that each year enough new trees are planted to replace those cut, thus assuring a sustained level of harvestable timber in future years. The idea seemed at the time self-evidently sensible, and — since all the forests were controlled by a single jurisdiction, the province — a simple matter to implement. Despite this, a sustained-yield management policy is still only a dream. As in the case of deficit financing, the temptation for government and industry, faced with the choice between taking present benefits and planning for the future, seems always to be to choose the former. Moreover, a sustained-yield policy is unambiguous and achievable; what chance has a policy like sustainable development, which is ambiguous and which ultimately can never be achieved (since to choose only sustainable projects would make development as required by our economic system impossible)?

Development is a continuing requirement of market-oriented economies. Throughout the colonial and post-colonial encounter, development has come up against societies and cultures based on economies that are non-expansionary. The fur trade provides one example where an accommodation of development was possible under certain circumstances. As a result of such compromises, Canada still has aboriginal populations with living cultures. The framework by which that accommodation was achieved — the dual economy — provides a possible mechanism for sustaining northern aboriginal cultures in the face of other kinds of development. The successful accommodation between development and sustainability evidenced by some specific regional examples of the fur trade came about because the aboriginal peoples were in charge of their half of the exchange — the production of fur in the context of a communal subsistence-based family-centred way of life, which was able to draw on aboriginal knowledge and tradition. While I am personally pessimistic, the evolution of further mechanisms of accommodation can likewise occur only if aboriginal peoples have power over the significant decisions. The alternatives are either the social breakdown of whole communities or an increasing level of political confrontation.

LEGAL ASPECTS OF IMPLEMENTING SUSTAINABLE DEVELOPMENT IN CANADA'S NORTHERN TERRITORIES

*Constance D. Hunt**

Canadians conceive of themselves as a northern people. Yet often the consciousness of our "northern-ness" lies below the surface: the North is always there, wild and pristine, cold and sparsely populated. In the process surrounding the Meech Lake Accord, for example, the profound implications the Accord would have for the political development of the two northern territories were largely ignored, and northern political leaders were excluded from the negotiations.

While we value our "northerness" at least at a subliminal level, only recently have we begun to recognize the vulnerability of the North to the global environmental problems outlined in the Brundtland Report.[1] Although some scientists have long pointed out that global warming is likely to have a more serious impact in northern regions than elsewhere, only in the past few months has significant publicity been given to the assertion that the hole in the ozone layer is expanding over the Arctic Circle. Similarly, the sensitivity of northern ecosystems to environmental degradation has been emphasized for decades by northerners and others, but public concern over such issues as the high levels of contaminants in Arctic species has been slow to develop. Mercury contamination in local fish supplies, oil spills in northern waters, proposals for nuclear submarines in the Arctic, reports of "Arctic haze," and worries about the impact of industrial activities on migratory wildlife species are a few examples demonstrating the importance of the concept of sustainable economic development in the Canadian North.[2] Recent proposals for oil and gas and mining projects have reminded us, too, of the continuing potential of northern nonrenewable resource development. The fact that the North is the homeland of a number of aboriginal populations with strong links to the land and wildlife adds a unique dimension to any discussion of northern sustainable development.

This paper begins with a brief review of selected themes from the Brundtland Report that, in a northern context, take on special significance, followed by an overview of some recent developments that have major implications for efforts to achieve sustainable development in the Canadian North. The paper then considers

* Research assistance by Cecilia Low and Holly Prus is gratefully acknowledged.

1 The World Commission on Environment and Development, *Our Common Future* (Oxford: Oxford University Press, 1987) (Chair: G.H. Brundtland).

2 The term "the North" is not used in any specific geographical sense in this paper, but refers generally to the political jurisdictions of the Yukon and Northwest Territories as well as the northern regions of the provinces, including Labrador.

examples from northern Canada that illustrate imaginative ways in which sustainable development is being pursued. While other parts of Canada and the world have much to learn from the northern experience in this regard, there are also major barriers that will need to be overcome if sustainable development is to become a reality in the North. Some of these barriers are identified and discussed in the paper's penultimate section. Finally, some conclusions are offered.

THE BRUNDTLAND REPORT:
ITS SPECIAL SIGNIFICANCE FOR THE NORTH

No attempt is made in this section to provide a general overview or critique of the Brundtland Report.[3] Instead, themes and ideas from the Report that are particularly relevant in a northern context are outlined briefly. Among these are the following:

- Most institutions facing the challenge of responding to global environmental problems tend to be "independent, fragmented, [and] working to relatively narrow mandates with closed decision processes." Policies and institutions must change so that those responsible for managing resources become interlocked with those responsible for managing the economy (p. 9).

- "Tribal and indigenous peoples will need special attention as the forces of economic development disrupt their traditional life-styles — life-styles that can offer modern societies many lessons in the management of resources ... [T]heir traditional rights should be recognized and they should be given a decisive voice in formulating policies about resource development in their areas" (p. 12).

- "A first priority is to establish the problem of disappearing species and threatened ecosystems on political agendas as a major economic and resource issue ... The network of protected areas that the world will need in the future must include much larger areas brought under some degree of protection ... Governments should investigate the prospect of agreeing to a 'Species Convention', similar in spirit and scope to other international conventions reflecting principles of 'universal resources' " (pp. 13-14).

- There must be increased energy efficiency as a bridge toward a future in which we use low energy paths based upon renewable resources. Market pressures alone will be insufficient to achieve this. "A safe, environmentally sound, and economically viable energy pathway that will sustain

---

3   For a critical assessment, see *Perspectives of Sustainable Development: Some Critical Issues Related to the Brundtland Report* (Stockholm: Stockholm Group for Studies on Natural Resources Management, 1988). See also M. Redclift, *Sustainable Development: Exploring the Contradictions* (London: Methuen, 1987).

human progress into the distant future is clearly imperative. It is also possible. But it will require new dimensions of political will and institutional co-operation to achieve it" (p. 15).

• The rights, roles, and participation of an informed public, nongovernmental organizations, the scientific community, and industry in development planning, decision-making, and project implementation should be expanded (p. 21).

• Governments "need to fill major gaps in existing national and international law related to the environment, to find ways to recognize and protect the rights of present and future generations ... and to strengthen procedures for avoiding or resolving disputes on environment and resource management issues" (p. 21).

As will be seen, many of these ideas have already been reflected in initiatives taken in northern Canada. At the same time, there are barriers to be overcome if these goals are to be achieved in the North.

RECENT DEVELOPMENTS IN THE NORTH
OF SPECIAL SIGNIFICANCE TO THE
ATTAINMENT OF SUSTAINABLE DEVELOPMENT

Although rapid change is a characteristic of our times, change is nowhere more apparent than in the North. The following section describes some of the key developments of the past decade that provide the particular context for northern sustainable development, including aboriginal land claims, devolution, other political developments such as aboriginal self-government and the possible division of the Northwest Territories, and conservation initiatives. For the purpose of analysis, each topic is treated separately, but they are closely interrelated.

The Settlement of Aboriginal Land Claims

Since 1973,[4] the federal government has pursued a policy of negotiating the settlement of land claims with aboriginal groups in the so-called comprehensive claims areas (roughly, those areas that have not been subject to treaty). Arguably, this policy initiative has become even more imperative since 1982, when existing aboriginal rights were given recognition in the Constitution of Canada.[5] In the first decade of the claims process, agreements were reached with aboriginal groups in northern Quebec (the James Bay and Northern Quebec Agreement and the

---

4   The 1973 policy was prompted by the Supreme Court of Canada's decision in *Calder et al. v. A.G. B.C.* (1973), [1973] S.C.R. 313. The policy itself is reproduced in B.W. Morse, ed., *Aboriginal Peoples and the Law: Indian, Métis and Inuit Rights in Canada* (Ottawa: Carleton University Press, 1985) at 629.

5   Constitution Act, 1982, s. 35. For a discussion, see N. Lyon, "Constitutional Issues in Native Law" in Morse, *id.* at 408.

Northeastern Quebec Agreement[6]) and in the northwestern portion of the N.W.T.[7] Recently, agreements in principle have been signed with the Dene-Métis of the N.W.T. and the Indians of the Yukon,[8] and an agreement in principle with the Inuit of the Eastern Arctic is reportedly near completion.[9] Negotiations have recently begun with the Inuit of Labrador.

Details of these agreements will be discussed in the next section of this paper. For present purposes, it may be noted that the arrangements made to date share several features. First, they involve the extinguishment of the aboriginal claims.[10] Second, they mandate the transfer of considerable amounts of land (both subsurface and surface rights) to the communal ownership of aboriginal groups. Third, they require the establishment of various institutions to ensure the involvement of aboriginal peoples in a variety of decisions, including those related to resource use and management. Fourth, they provide for the establishment of protected areas such as parks.[11] Fifth, some of the agreements contemplate aboriginal groups' sharing in royalties generated from nonrenewable resource development.[12] Sixth, while the agreements permit the participation of aboriginal groups in many decisions, they have failed to come to grips with expansive claims to "self-government" articulated by aboriginal Canadians for at least the past decade.[13]

As a result of these agreements, large tracts of northern lands are being reclassified from Crown lands to special forms of private ownership governed by the complex provisions of the various agreements. Many of these provisions may have constitutional protection[14]; at the least, some of them override the requirements

---

6   The James Bay and Northern Quebec Agreement (Québec: Éditeur officiel, 1976) (hereinafter "JBNQA"); The Northeastern Quebec Agreement (Ottawa: Dept. of Indian and Northern Affairs, 1978).

7   The Inuvialuit Final Agreement (Ottawa: Minister of Indian Affairs and Northern Development, 1984) (hereinafter "IFA").

8   Dene/Métis Comprehensive Claim Agreement in Principle Between Canada and the Dene Nation and the Métis Association of the Northwest Territories (Ottawa: Minister of Indian Affairs and Northern Development, 1988) (hereinafter "D/M AIP"); Yukon Indian Land Claim Framework Agreement (February 1989) (hereinafter "YFA").

9   *News/North* (23 January 1989) 4.

10   For example, IFA, *supra*, note 7, ss. 4, 5; JBNQA, *supra*, note 6, s. 2.1; D/M AIP, *supra*, note 8, s. 3.1.9; YFA, *supra*, note 8, Sub-Agreement on General Provisions, s. 4.0.

11   For example, the IFA, *supra*, note 7, requires the establishment of a national park on the Yukon North Slope and a territorial park on Herschel Island. The D/M AIP, *supra*, note 8, also contains provisions relating to parks and other protected areas.

12   For example, the D/M AIP, *supra*, note 8, s. 10, requires government to pay the Dene/Métis 50 percent of the first $2 million of resource royalty it receives and 10 percent of any additional resource royalties it receives.

13   See discussion accompanying note 22, *infra*.

14   For a discussion of this topic, see J.M. Keeping, "The Inuvialuit Final Agreement" (Calgary: Canadian Institute of Resources Law, The University of Calgary, 1989).

of other laws.[15] Moreover, while the agreements signed to date share several characteristics, they are by no means identical; and the complexity of the arrangements often makes it difficult to comprehend the rules that govern these aboriginal lands and the implications of those rules for industry, government, and others.[16]

On the one hand, Canada's approach to northern aboriginal claims moves toward the Brundtland Commission's exhortation to national governments to recognize and protect traditional rights to land and other resources, to protect local institutions that enforce responsibility in resource use, and to give local communities a voice in decisions about resource use in their areas. As will be seen later, however, the agreements also create new challenges for achieving institutional coordination and cooperation.

Devolution of Responsibilities to Territorial Governments

The Yukon and N.W.T. governments are creatures of federal statutes,[17] lacking the independent constitutional status enjoyed by the provinces. This simple fact has many ramifications. First, the law-making authority of the territorial governments is constrained by federal legislation. Second, aside from lands transferred to aboriginal groups pursuant to the land claims agreements, most lands in the territories are owned and controlled by the federal Crown.[18] As has often been pointed out,[19] this creates serious problems of resource management; for example, although the territorial governments have jurisdiction over wildlife, they lack the power to protect wildlife habitat. Third, in frustration over a perceived lack of federal sensitivity to the political and other aspirations of northerners, territorial governments have sometimes sidestepped legal niceties and asserted authority over important matters[20]; such actions can lead to overlap, duplication, and lack of coordination. Fourth, for a number of years the federal government has pursued a policy of "devolving" control over certain matters to the territorial governments. The recent agreements in principle concerning the territorial role in energy

---

15   For example, s. 3(3) of the IFA, *supra,* note 7, provides that, in the event of inconsistency or conflict between the IFA or its implementing legislation and other laws, the IFA shall prevail.

16   For a detailed analysis of the implications of the IFA for oil and gas activities, see Keeping, *supra,* note 14.

17   Yukon Act, R.S.C. 1985, c. Y-2; Northwest Territories Act, R.S.C. 1985, c. N-27.

18   For example, one report suggests that less than one-tenth of one percent of land in the N.W.T. has been transferred to the administration and control of the Government of the Territories. R.M. Larson, "The Administration of Restricted Lands in the Northwest Territories" (Yellowknife: Dept. of Renewable Resources, n.d.).

19   See, for example, *Report of the Task Force on Northern Conservation* (20 December 1984) at 34.

20   For example, the Government of the N.W.T. has issued policies concerning resource development and renewable resource compensation, which have dubious validity given the Territories' constitutional status. For a discussion, see C.D. Hunt, "Knowing the North: The Law and Its Institutions" (1986) 4 C.N.L.R. 1 at 40. A more recent example is the Northwest Territories Environmental Protection Policy, which is currently under discussion.

management[21] provide a good illustration of this approach. Fifth, as discussed below, aboriginal groups in the territories have been suspicious of the concept of devolution, fearing that it could conflict with their own political aspirations.

The devolution of control over resource management to the territorial governments may be seen as in harmony with the Brundtland Report's recommendation that local communities should play a larger role in decisions about resource management in their areas. Like the aboriginal claims agreements, however, this devolution creates new challenges for the attainment of sustainable development.

Other Political Developments in the Territories

The devolution of authority over certain matters by the federal government to the territorial governments is, at least in part, a response to the aspirations of territorial residents to have more control over their own lives. One way for this to be accomplished, of course, would be for the territories to move gradually toward provincehood: based on the model of the rest of the country, this would eventually give them control over their resources and legislative authority on a roughly equal footing with the federal government. The move toward provincehood would, in almost any circumstances, be fraught with difficulties; in the North, however, it has been considerably complicated by other issues, including aboriginal aspirations to self-government and, in the N.W.T., the prospect of division. Although some of these dynamics may seem of marginal relevance to the attainment of sustainable development, together they form an important backdrop against which the prospects for the future must be considered.

Reference has been made earlier to the fact that, in 1982, aboriginal rights received formal recognition in the Canadian Constitution. Although the rights were recognized, they were not defined; one of the requirements of the amendments was that meetings be held between aboriginal leaders and provincial and federal first ministers in order to attempt to flesh out the meaning of the new constitutional provisions. When a series of first ministers' meetings failed to provide a consensus upon which the definition of self-government could be based,[22] the federal government chose to pursue self-government initiatives with individual Indian bands.[23]

---

21   Northern Accord Agreement in Principle, 6 September 1988, Canada–Northwest Territories; An Enabling Agreement Between the Government of Canada and the Government of the Yukon Respecting Oil and Gas Resource Management and Revenues, 22 September 1988. The Agreements are discussed in C.D. Hunt, "Northern Oil and Gas Agreements in Principle" (1989) 25 Resources 1.

22   A review of the 1983, 1984, and 1985 conferences is found in B. Schwartz, *First Principles, Second Thoughts: Aboriginal Peoples, Constitutional Reform and Canadian Statecraft* (Montreal: The Institute for Research on Public Policy, 1986).

23   This policy is referred to in *Living Treaties: Lasting Agreements* (Report of the Task Force to Review Comprehensive Claims Policy) (Ottawa: Department of Indian Affairs and Northern Development, December 1985) at 22.

Although northern aboriginal groups had participated in the first ministers' meetings, they also sought to have self-government issues dealt with in the context of their comprehensive claims agreements. This strategy, however, has had only limited success.

For example, the question of self-government was not resolved in the IFA, although the following section was included:

> Canada agrees that where restructuring of the public institutions of government is considered for the Western Arctic Region, the Inuvialuit shall not be treated less favourably than any other native groups or native people with respect to the governmental powers and authority conferred on them.[24]

The Dene/Métis of the N.W.T. were possibly the most vociferous advocates of self-government, but they too have apparently failed to resolve this issue within the context of claims negotiations, at least at the agreement-in-principle stage. Section 3.1.24 of the D/M AIP[25] provides that nothing in the final agreement shall affect the ability of the Dene/Métis to negotiate self-government agreements with government; thus, the matter has temporarily been put aside in order to permit movement from agreement in principle to final agreement.

In some respects, the YFA[26] goes further than the other two, although its provisions may be viewed as a mere application of the general federal policy on self-government. The YFA's "Sub-Agreement on Yukon Indian Self-Government" envisages negotiations on a band-by-band basis "appropriate to the circumstances of the concerned Yukon First Nation."[27] Powers negotiated by the Yukon First Nations through this process may include the authority to "enact laws and regulations of a local nature for the good government of their Settlement Lands and the inhabitants of such lands."[28] Moreover, guaranteed representation for Yukon First Nations on public government commissions, councils, boards, and committees may be negotiated.[29] Perhaps most important is the following provision:

> cl. 7.1 Yukon First Nations with the Government of Canada, Government of the Yukon and Yukon municipalities may develop common administrative or planning structures within a community, region or district of the Yukon ....

It has recently been reported that the Inuit are continuing to pursue the matter of self-government in their claims negotiations.[30]

The relationship between self-government, land claims, and possible division

---

24   *Supra*, note 7, s. 4(3).
25   *Supra*, note 8.
26   *Supra*, note 8.
27   *Supra*, note 8, s. 1.1.
28   *Supra*, note 8, s. 1.2.1.
29   *Supra*, note 8, s. 4.1.
30   K. Jackson, "Minister won't solve boundary fight," *News/North* (27 February 1989) 3.

of the N.W.T. can only be understood by reverting briefly to some recent history.[31] In 1982 the Constitutional Alliance was formed as an independent body with representation from the Legislative Assembly and the aboriginal organizations, and with the responsibility for developing recommendations on the shape of government in the North. A plebiscite held in the N.W.T. had found a majority of voters in favour of the concept of dividing the N.W.T. A major part of the Alliance's work, then, related to discussion of new shapes of government in two territories. In 1987 the Legislative Assembly endorsed the Iqaluit Agreement concerning a boundary between the two territories, but it proved impossible to move forward on this because the Inuit and Dene/Métis failed to agree on a boundary for the purposes of land claims agreements.[32]

A paper recently released by the Government of the N.W.T. graphically illustrates some of the problems that arise from the changing political scene in the N.W.T.[33] It describes four options for territorial evolution: division, creation of a province, creation of autonomous federal territories, and reassertion of federal authority. It then outlines four options for the future shape of government: the current consensus approach, the development of a party system, guaranteed representation in the Legislative Assembly for aboriginal people, and partnership or consociation. To complicate matters further, the paper points out the need to address the question of the authority of different levels of government: communities, regions, and possibly aboriginal self-government.

Although there continues to be wide public discussion of these matters, the absence of consensus is demonstrated by recent submissions made by two aboriginal organizations to the Legislative Assembly. The Dene Nation and Métis Association has pointed out that it perceives a conflict between aspirations of aboriginal self-government on the one hand, and devolution of powers to the territorial government and the move toward provincehood on the other:

> [A]boriginal self-government ... requires a sharing of power between aboriginal and public institutions such as does not exist in our present system of government. If the present government continues to take on more powers to itself, without having in place the necessary structures and agreements for redistributing these powers, it will soon cease to recognize the need for aboriginal self-government at all.[34]

---

31   The overview that follows is a summary of what appears in Government of the Northwest Territories, *Political and Constitutional Development in the Northwest Territories* (Discussion Paper) (November 1988) at 6.

32   The division movement is still alive in the Eastern Arctic, despite the fact that the Dene/Métis and Inuit boundary issue remains at an impasse. K. Jackson, "Inuit group promoting division," *News/ North* (13 February 1989) 10.

33   *Supra,* note 31 at 7.

34   Dene Nation and Métis Association of the Northwest Territories, "Devolution of Powers to the Government of the Northwest Territories: Provincehood and Aboriginal Self-Government" (1 November 1988) at 2.

For these reasons, the Dene/Métis and other aboriginal groups have insisted that they be entitled to participate fully in arrangements for the transfer of power to the N.W.T. government — for example, in the context of the northern accord on devolution of power over oil and gas resources.[35] Moreover, despite the extinguishment clause in the IFA, the Inuvialuit continue to assert that they maintain an aboriginal right to self-government, to ensure that their interests are protected in the event that institutions of public government make decisions that are not effective from the point of view of aboriginal populations.[36]

These dynamics have important implications for the application of principles of sustainable economic development in the N.W.T. Obviously, the shape and content of government institutions are in a state of fluidity, making it difficult to predict who will have power over which matters, and which policies are likely to be pursued. Moreover, as the government's discussion paper points out:

> The proliferation of regional and local special purpose bodies has led to confusion in responsibilities and costly duplication ... [T]he Assembly may want to discuss the role of regional councils and other regional bodies as it relates to the proliferation of these groups, the cost and, as well, the shape of institutions arising out of final land claims agreements.[37]

The debate initiated on these complex matters in November 1988 by the Legislative Assembly is meant to lead to recommendations on the process, framework, and form for shaping public government.[38] In the meantime, as we will see below, some possible solutions to these matters may already be emerging in the N.W.T.

Recent Conservation Initiatives

As has been explained elsewhere,[39] work on the development of a comprehensive conservation policy for northern Canada began in earnest in 1982, following ten years of limited success in dealing with proposals to establish protected areas north of 60°. One result of the process was the establishment, in 1983, of a Task Force on Northern Conservation, which reported in December 1984.[40] Although the Task Force had been charged with the responsibility of advising on conservation

---

35   *Id.* at 3; and Hunt, *supra,* note 21.

36   Inuvialuit Regional Corporation, *Submission to the Legislative Assembly of the Northwest Territories on the Principles of Devolution* (Yellowknife, 1 November 1988) at 6.

37   *Supra,* note 31 at 10.

38   *Id.* at 12.

39   R. Schwass, J.T. Inglis & J.K. Naysmith, "Northern Conservation Strategy" in J.G. Nelson, R. Needham & L. Norton, eds., *Arctic Heritage: Proceedings of a Symposium* (Ottawa: Association of Canadian Universities for Northern Studies, 1987) at 337.

40   *Report of the Task Force on Northern Conservation, supra,* note 19. The recommendations of the Task Force are reviewed *id.* at 339 and in R. Revel, "Task Force on Northern Conservation Report: An Evaluation from the Perspective of the Canadian Sub-Arctic International Biological Programme" in Needham, Nelson & Norton, *id.* at 345.

targets that could be met over a two-year period, it declined to do so on the grounds that this would interfere with the arrangements for a land use planning process that had been entered into between the federal and territorial governments.[41] Its mandate was further complicated by the fact that, during the course of its work, land claims negotiations were still at a relatively early stage. Notwithstanding these difficulties, the Task Force was able to identify six major problems relevant to conservation:

1. A narrow, reactive regulatory system

2. Institutional competition among governments and government agencies

3. Failure to consider adequately resource values (social, cultural, and economic) and alternative choices as they apply to both development and conservation initiatives prior to making land use decisions

4. Insufficient opportunity for the participation of northerners in resource utilization decisions

5. Resources disposition legislation that is deficient with respect to conservation measures

6. Lack of sustained political commitment to conservation.

Among the Task Force's specific recommendations were an in-depth review and updating of existing legislation to provide for active management of the resources, and pursuit of an integrated resource management strategy.[42]

Since the completion of the Task Force Report, both the territorial and federal governments have undertaken other conservation initiatives. For example, in December 1987 the Department of Fisheries and Oceans issued a discussion paper on a Canadian Arctic Marine Conservation Strategy.[43] Intended to provide a basis for an eventual strategy, the discussion paper states that its purpose is "to provide for an integrated regime which will foster the well-being of renewable resources and their sustained consumptive and non-consumptive use, along with the development of nonrenewable resources in harmony with that of renewable resource development."[44] Among the principles outlined in the discussion paper are that conservation requires an ecosystems approach and integrated management of renewable and nonrenewable resource activities; and that the implementation of an Arctic Marine Conservation Strategy will use existing institutions and processes wherever possible.[45] As the paper notes:

---

41   *Report of the Task Force on Northern Conservation, id.* at 3. The land use planning process is discussed *infra* in the text accompanying note 72.

42   *Id.* at 34 and 15.

43   *Canadian Arctic Marine Conservation Strategy Discussion Paper* (Ottawa: Minister of Supply and Services Canada, Fisheries and Oceans, December 1987).

44   *Id.* at 10.

45   *Id.* at 11.

Methods must be found to reconcile differences in objectives and to optimize use of resources, with due consideration given to all resource values — economic, social and cultural. This will require cooperation and consultation among resource managers and with natural resource users, including their participation in resource management decisions (p. 13).

Despite these and other statements about the need for coherent frameworks to ensure effective and efficient coordination, for improvements to the northern regulatory system, and for institutional and legislative reviews to ensure effective integration of ocean management, the discussion paper is thin on specific proposals. Since it was issued, consultations have been pursued with industry, aboriginal groups, and other interested parties. These consultations were completed in the fall of 1988, and final policy proposals are being prepared for submission to Cabinet.[46] In the meantime, some steps have been taken to pursue the kinds of initiatives suggested in the discussion paper, including the development of a coordinated response to environmental emergencies in Arctic waters.[47]

Another federal initiative of relevance to the North was the Task Force on Park Establishment,[48] set up in 1986 by the Minister of the Environment. Among its specific terms of reference was the role of native claims and native peoples in parks. The main recommendation made with respect to the North was that officials be encouraged to pursue vigorously the establishment of national parks, park reserves, and Canadian Heritage Lands, through aboriginal claims and cooperative approaches with territorial governments.[49] The Task Force supported the notion of aboriginal involvement in management. It also noted that it would be necessary to work in harmony with the newly established land use planning process, and that existing regulatory mechanisms should be used to protect areas prior to their final designation as conservation areas.

Both territorial governments have also pursued conservation initiatives. In the Yukon, a public discussion paper has been released as a result of the joint efforts of the Department of Renewable Resources and the Public Working Group on the Yukon Conservation Strategy.[50] Noting that the devolution of authority to the Yukon government, and the settlement of aboriginal claims, will encourage the

---

46   Information on the status of the Canadian Arctic Marine Conservation Strategy was provided by Brian Wong, Program Officer, Arctic and Inland Fisheries, Department of Fisheries and Oceans, 25 April 1989.

47   This information was provided by Bill Stephen, Northern Affairs Program, Northwest Territories Region, Department of Indian and Northern Affairs, Yellowknife, 25 April 1989.

48   The Task Force reported in December, 1986. See *Our Parks — Vision for the 21st Century* (Waterloo: Environment Canada, Parks, and Heritage Resources Centre, University of Waterloo, 7 November 1986).

49   *Id.* at 52.

50   *Building a Conservation Strategy for the Yukon* (Public Discussion Paper) (Yukon: Public Working Group on the Yukon Conservation Strategy and the Department of Renewable Resources, October 1988).

integrated management of renewable and nonrenewable resources in the territory, the discussion paper suggests that a conservation strategy can help clarify the issues and decisions needed to promote constitutional development.[51] Given such ambitions for a conservation strategy, it is disappointing that the discussion paper does not concretely address how nonrenewable resource use can be integrated with renewable resource use. The only relevant suggestions on this point are that a management plan should be established for such purposes, that mechanisms should be developed to resolve conflicts between renewable and nonrenewable resource uses, and that an environmental impact assessment process should be established for all resource developments.[52] The discussion paper also proposes that legislation should ensure equitable treatment for all resource users and allow for integrated management; that land and water management should be integrated within one government agency; and that a board might be established to advise government on conservation and related issues.[53]

The approach of the Northwest Territories government has shifted from developing a conservation strategy to endorsing a sustainable development policy.[54] A draft policy was prepared by an interdepartmental working group and endorsed by the Executive Council in May 1989. The policy, which is to address such issues as ensuring long-term benefits from resource development, establishing an efficient review process for resource development projects, and controlling transboundary environmental contaminants, will be further developed through public consultations and the preparation of an action plan. Final drafting will be coordinated by the Department of Renewable Resources, working with the Departments of Energy, Mines and Petroleum Resources, and Economic Development and Tourism. Among the draft principles under discussion are that initiatives taken under the policy are to be consistent with, or complementary to, those aspects of aboriginal land claims that relate to conservation and resource development; and that, as far as possible, the policy should be implemented through existing mechanisms and processes, or those being developed through land claims or other processes.

As this brief overview indicates, there have been many initiatives taken over the past decade relating to northern conservation. This fact seems to demonstrate a strong commitment to conservation on the part of both levels of government as well as many government departments. I will return further on in this paper to the

---

51   *Id.* at 4.

52   *Id.* at 9.

53   *Id.* at 11.

54   Personal communication, Jamie Bastedo, Senior Policy Analyst, Department of Renewable Resources, Government of the Northwest Territories, 25 May 1989; and Press Release 89-086, Government of the Northwest Territories, "Government Makes Commitment to Sustainable Development."

question of how well-coordinated these initiatives have been and how they fit with other northern developments.

NORTHERN SUSTAINABLE DEVELOPMENT: SOME EXAMPLES

As noted above, the issue of sustainable development has special significance in the North because of the sensitivity of the northern ecosystem, the heavy reliance of the aboriginal population (from cultural and other perspectives) on the land and its products, and the existence in the North of important nonrenewable resources. This section of the paper explores some lessons that the northern experience can offer other parts of Canada and other countries that are struggling to come to grips with the legislative and policy changes required by the concept of sustainable development. Given the complexities of today's North, it might be asserted that if sustainable development is attainable there, it is attainable almost anywhere. The approaches discussed below are selective rather than comprehensive. The topics examined are the management of migratory species; the land use planning process; land claims agreements; industry's interaction with local communities; and local, regional, and circumpolar initiatives by aboriginal people to promote conservation and sustainable development.

Management of Migratory Species

The northern experience includes the challenge of managing migratory species in a multi-jurisdictional context, both nationally and internationally. One result has been the development of novel institutional arrangements, many of which now involve local users. Three international examples, dating from 1916, illustrate approaches to managing migratory species that have had varying degrees of success.

The Migratory Birds Convention Treaty

In tracing the history of the negotiations between Canada and the United States that led to this 1916 treaty, Foster emphasizes the important role played by the provinces, but notes that "through an unfortunate oversight ... copies of the draft proposal were not sent to the Yukon and Northwest Territorial governments, nor were Indian and Inuit people consulted on the issue."[55] These "unfortunate oversights" have had dire consequences. The treaty's closed-season dates ignore the northern context: in parts of the North, many migratory species have already left for the South by the time hunting season opens there (September 1).[56] The treaty also ignores Crown guarantees of Indian hunting and fishing rights made in treaties throughout Canada.

---

55   J. Foster, *Working for Wildlife: The Beginning of Preservation in Canada* (Toronto: University of Toronto Press, 1978) at 134.

56   *Id.* at 148.

The treaty has been an irritant in aboriginal-government relations in both countries,[57] and in Canada has led to a series of court cases that have challenged the extent to which the treaty binds aboriginal people.[58] Repeated requests for federal action have had no concrete results.[59] A policy of not enforcing treaty breaches against aboriginal offenders was struck down on the grounds that prosecutorial discretion cannot be exercised on a racial basis.[60]

Northern aboriginal communities' continuing concerns about the treaty have prompted specific governmental attempts, within land claims agreements, to resolve the difficulties. For example, section 14(37) of the IFA obliges Canada "to explore means to permit the Inuvialuit to legally hunt migratory game birds in the spring" and to consult with the Wildlife Management Advisory Council (established under the IFA) when implementing amendments to the Migratory Birds Convention Act. Similar provisions are found in the JBNQA, the D/M AIP, and the YFA.[61] In 1979 Canada and the United States entered into a protocol permitting them to "authorize by statute, regulation or decree the taking of migratory birds and the collection of their eggs by the indigenous inhabitants of the State of Alaska and the Indians and Inuit of Canada for their own nutritional needs ... during any period of the year ... so as to provide for the preservation and maintenance of stocks of migratory birds."[62] The protocol, however, was never ratified by the United States and is thus not in force.

---

57   For a discussion of the effect of the treaty in Alaska, see J. Sissons, *Judge of the Far North* (Toronto: McClelland and Stewart, 1973) at 153.

58   Almost all the decisions have gone against the aboriginal challengers. See *R. v. Sikyea* (1964), [1964] S.C.R. 642, (1965) 44 C.R. 266; *R. v. George* (1966), [1966] S.C.R. 267, 55 D.L.R. (2d) 386; and *R. v. Daniels* (1968), 2 D.L.R. (3d) 1, 64 W.W.R. 385 (S.C.C.). The one exception is *R. v. Flett* (1987), [1987] 5 W.W.R. 115 (Man. Prov. Ct.), where it was held that to the extent that the legislation implementing the treaty, the Migratory Birds Convention Act, purports to infringe the rights of treaty Indians to hunt for food in all seasons, it is of no force and effect because of s. 35 of the Constitution Act, 1982.

59   See P. Cumming & R. Mickenberg, eds., *Native Rights in Canada* (2d ed.; Toronto: The Indian-Eskimo Association of Canada in association with General Publishing, 1972) at 220–221. One reason why the federal government may have been reluctant to act concerns the likelihood that, if the treaty were reopened, individual provinces would also demand changes and perhaps raise questions about federal authority to enter into a treaty that concerns resources in the provinces. The issue was litigated in the Supreme Court of Prince Edward Island shortly after the treaty was signed, with the result that the federal authority was upheld. See Foster, *supra*, note 55 at 147. Legal developments since that case was decided, however, would not necessarily guarantee the same result today. For a discussion relevant to this point, see J.O. Saunders, "Canadian Federalism and International Management of Natural Resources" in J.O. Saunders, ed., *Managing Natural Resources in a Federal State* (Toronto: Carswell, 1986) at 267.

60   *R. v. Catagas* (1977), 81 D.L.R. (3d) 396 (Man. C.A.).

61   *Supra*, note 6, s. 24.14.2; *supra*, note 7, s. 13.3.6 and s. 3.6 of Sub-Agreement 13, respectively.

62   Protocol Amending the Convention of August 16, 1916 for the Protection of Migratory Birds in Canada and the United States of America (Ottawa, 30 January 1979).

The migratory birds experience demonstrates the rigidities, litigation, and disregard for law that can result when international agreements are entered into without the participation of users. Interestingly, some steps toward resolving problems that seem virtually insoluble at an international level have been taken through cooperation between user groups in distant areas.[63] In 1984 the Yupik of the Yukon–Kuskokwim Delta area of Alaska reached agreement with the State of California, acting on behalf of sport hunters, to limit bird hunting for sport in California and for subsistence in the Yukon–Kuskokwim in order to protect a bird population that had suddenly declined. This example demonstrates how sustainable development of renewable resources can be promoted even in the absence of a suitable legal framework.

Management of the Porcupine Caribou Herd

The Porcupine Caribou herd, one of the largest populations of caribou in the world, has traditionally been harvested by the aboriginal people of both Canada and the United States. Concerns about its management came to public attention when, during the Berger hearings on the Mackenzie Valley gas pipeline, residents of Old Crow, Yukon, and elsewhere stressed the need for a cooperative caribou management agreement administered by a board.[64] Such a board was also proposed in 1978 when the Canadian Department of External Affairs began negotiating a bilateral agreement concerning the herd with the United States. Although these negotiations reached an impasse in 1980, efforts to reach agreement on management arrangements continued between the federal government and the governments and aboriginal organizations of the Yukon and N.W.T. The Canada–U.S. negotiations were reactivated in 1983, based upon a 1982 agreement that had been reached between the Indian and Inuit communities in Alaska and the Yukon. In 1985 a Porcupine Caribou Management Agreement was signed between the Canadian interest groups; an agreement between the Canadian and American governments followed in July 1987.[65] Thus, it took nearly ten years for the Canadian and American governments to finalize negotiations, the underlying concept of which had been proposed by local users.

The preamble to the Agreement recognizes the importance of this herd as a resource for aboriginal people in both countries. Section 2(a) sets out as one

---

63   The situation described here is outlined in Inuit Circumpolar Conference, *Towards An Inuit Regional Conservation Strategy* (Framework Document Adopted By the Inuit Circumpolar Conference General Assembly, Kotzebue, Alaska, 1986) at 56.

64   Background concerning the Porcupine Caribou Treaty is found in Porcupine Caribou Management Board, *1st Annual Report,* 1986–87; (1979) 3(2) Northern Perspectives; (1983) 1(11) Northern Decisions. Helpful information has also been provided by Art Martell, Director, Pacific and Yukon Region, Canadian Wildlife Service.

65   Agreement between the Government of Canada and the Government of the United States of America on the Conservation of the Porcupine Caribou Herd (Ottawa, 17 July 1987).

objective of the Agreement "[t]o conserve the Porcupine Caribou Herd and its habitat through international co-operation and co-ordination so that the risk of irreversible damage or long-term adverse effects as a result of use of caribou or their habitat is minimized." "Conservation" is defined in Section 1(b) as

> the management and use of the Porcupine Caribou Herd and its habitat utilizing methods and procedures which ensure the long-term productivity and usefulness of the Porcupine Caribou Herd.

The obligations of the parties, set out in Section 3, are relatively modest. They include taking appropriate action to conserve the herd and its habitat; giving effective consideration to the herd, its habitat, and its users in evaluating proposed activities within its range; notifying the other country of proposed activities likely to cause significant long-term adverse impact on the herd or its habitat, so that there can be consultation; and prohibiting the commercial sale of meat[66] from the herd.

Section 4 provides for the establishment of the International Porcupine Caribou Herd Board. This advisory body consists of four members appointed by each party, and is to provide advice on aspects of the conservation of the herd that require international coordination, "seeking, where appropriate, information available from management agencies, local communities, users of Porcupine Caribou, scientific and other interests." While the Board's advice is not binding on the parties, both agree (in Section 4(e)) to support the operation of the Board, in particular by notifying it of activities that could significantly affect the conservation of the herd or its habitat and providing the Board with an opportunity to make recommendations; by considering and responding to the Board's recommendations; and by providing written reasons for any rejection of the recommendations.

It is now almost two years since the treaty came into effect, but the Board has yet to meet. Despite this slow progress, an *ad hoc* technical committee, in operation since 1978, has facilitated the exchange of cooperative information. Moreover, the United States has complied with the treaty by providing notification of proposed activities such as oil exploration in the Arctic National Wildlife Range. The treaty's relatively weak provisions, however, mean that disputes about the anticipated impact of proposed activities will not necessarily be resolved to the satisfaction of the notified party.

Polar Bear Management

In 1973 Canada entered into an agreement with several other circumpolar countries concerning the management of polar bear populations.[67] In contrast to the

---

66   Since the term "commercial sale" is not defined, it is unclear whether this is intended to include methods of barter commonly practised with country food in aboriginal communities.

67   Agreement on the Conservation of Polar Bears (Oslo, 15 November 1973) Canada-Denmark-Norway-USSR-United States. The Agreement became effective on 26 May 1976.

arrangements for the Porcupine Caribou herd, but like the treaty arrangements for migratory birds, the negotiations leading up to this agreement had little, if any, Inuit involvement.[68] Article I of the treaty prohibits the taking of polar bears except as provided for in Article III, which protects the taking of bears "by local people using traditional methods in the exercise of their traditional rights and in accordance with the laws of that Party" and "wherever polar bears have or might have been subject to taking by traditional means by its nationals." Other provisions in the treaty are intended to promote habitat protection and research.

Within the framework of this treaty, polar bear hunting in the N.W.T. has continued to be regulated pursuant to the provisions of the Wildlife Ordinance.[69] Under this system, the annual quota is allocated on a community basis, with local hunters' and trappers' committees making decisions as to quota distribution. In Alaska, the Marine Mammal Protection Act of 1972 protects the right of subsistence hunters, but there is no regulation of the subsistence hunt.[70]

In 1983 scientific evidence began to indicate that Canadian and Alaskan aboriginals were harvesting the same polar bear population in the Beaufort Sea. Concerns developed in Canada about the effect on the population of the unregulated subsistence hunt in Alaska. The experience of the caribou negotiations made Canadian Inuvialuit reluctant to have this problem dealt with on a government-to-government basis lest, during lengthy negotiations, the population become jeopardized. Discussions undertaken in 1985 between the Canadian Inuvialuit and the Alaskan Inupiat (through the Inuvialuit Game Council and the North Slope Borough Fish and Game Management Committee, respectively) quickly led to a resolution by the Inupiat concerning the hunting of female and young bears. Although the relevant governments supported the discussions, actual arrangements were pursued by the aboriginal user groups themselves. By September 1986 a Memorandum of Understanding had been initialled by both aboriginal groups, and by January 1988 a polar bear management agreement had been entered into. Lawyers were not involved until the final drafting stages.

The preamble to the Agreement notes that it shall not be read as abrogating the responsibilities of federal, provincial, or state authorities under existing or future

---

68   As a result of concerns expressed by the Inuit of Tapirisat of Canada at the time, questions were asked in the House of Commons of the Minister responsible for the Canadian position on the Agreement on 7 November 1973, by Conservative Member of Parliament Flora MacDonald. Commons Debates at 7626.

69   O.N.W.T. 1978, c. 8 (3d). Polar bear harvesting is dealt with specifically in the Hunting and Possession of Wildlife Regulations, R-038-84, passed pursuant to the Act.

70   P.L. 92-522 21 October 1972. Much of the information that follows has been helpfully provided by Ian Stirling, Research Scientist, Canadian Wildlife Service, and Leslie Treseder of the Inuvialuit Joint Secretariat. See also Polar Bear Management in the Southern Beaufort Sea — An Agreement Between Inuvialuit Game Council and North Slope Borough Fish And Game Management Committee (January 1988), especially the preamble.

statutes. The Agreement provides for the establishment of two groups, a Technical Advisory Committee and a Joint Commission. The Commission, which appoints the Technical Advisory Committee, is made up of two appointees of each of the signing parties. The former met in October 1988, and the latter is expected to meet in April 1989.

The first "Guidelines for Harvesting" achieved through this Agreement set allowable takes that, for the most part, reflected current harvesting. In Canada, quotas continue to be administered as they were before. The situation in Alaska is more complex due to the absence of a pre-existing regulatory system for the subsistence harvest; at present, the North Slope Borough itself administers the take.

As this is the first year the management agreement has been in effect, it is premature to evaluate its success. Nevertheless, it stands as an example of the results that can be achieved when local users are committed to conservation and set out to resolve the management of a shared migratory resource, within the umbrella of national and international laws. In contrast to government-to-government arrangements, epitomized by the caribou treaty, this approach can have quick results; and in contrast to arrangements that ignore users, epitomized by the migratory birds treaty, this approach can garner the support of user groups with correspondingly greater likelihood that its provisions will be adhered to.

The Land Use Planning Process

The earlier analysis has revealed one constantly recurring theme about northern resource management: it must be integrated. But how can this be achieved? One emerging mechanism is land use planning, long advocated but only recently realized through the signing of letter agreements between the federal government and other interested parties.[71]

Northwest Territories

The land use planning process in the N.W.T. seems to have originally been conceived of as a territory-wide Commission based in Yellowknife with representation from the two levels of government and from the native organizations, combined with a Land Use Policy Advisory Committee to advise ministers on the planning process throughout the territory. The N.W.T. Commission was established in 1986, with regional commissions for Lancaster Sound and the Mackenzie Valley Beaufort Sea areas set up in 1986 and 1987, respectively, and later followed by a

---

71   For background information, see T. Fenge, "Development in the Beaufort Sea Region: From EARP to Regional Planning" (1983) 11(3) Northern Perspectives 6; "Planning for Lancaster Sound: Where to Now?" (1986) 14(3) Northern Perspectives 10; Governments of Canada and the NWT, "Overview and Organization of Northern Land Use Planning" (16 September 1985). The process has moved more slowly in the Yukon than in the N.W.T., since the former has been underway only since October 1987.

regional commission for Denendeh. Late in 1988, it was decided that the N.W.T. Commission and the Advisory Committee would be replaced by a management steering committee made up of representatives from the aboriginal groups and the two levels of government, with the management committee giving directions to regional planning programs.[72]

The process has already had an interesting interaction with N.W.T. land claims negotiations. For example, although subsections 7(82)–(84) of the IFA had provided for the establishment of a land use planning mechanism within the Inuvialuit Settlement Region, the Inuvialuit agreed to participate in the Mackenzie Delta Beaufort Sea Regional Commission, set up in 1987. The Regional Commission consists of two commissioners each appointed by the N.W.T. Commission, the Inuvialuit Game Council and Inuvialuit Regional Corporation, and the Mackenzie Delta Tribal Council,[73] and has focused on a community-based process. A working group has been established in each community to advise the Commission on local and regional priorities to be addressed in the land use plan, and to prepare a map of the community's land use. The Regional Commission has also met with other interest groups, such as representatives of the petroleum industry.

In its interim report, the Regional Commission emphasized that many land use problems can be resolved through existing mechanisms. In regard to nonrenewable resource use, the Commission sees the role of land use planning as ensuring that such activities are undertaken in the context of integrated resource management, that is, planning developments so that they avoid critical areas but still support the local economy. The Commission has also pointed out the need for new management systems grounded in law, noting that while legislative backing might be premature at this point, it will be required in the future to ensure that workable and necessary actions are taken. Emphasis has been placed on the need for innovation in resource management mechanisms:

> [G]overnments must retain the ultimate authority and responsibility for management of publicly-owned resources. However, the structure of government departments, usually segmented to permit expertise to be brought to bear on single issues, or groups of like issues, does not lend itself to effective integrated resource management ... Existing resource management bodies created under the IFA offer new approaches to joint management ... Such extensions of proven techniques, however, will require policy decisions by both federal and territorial governments.[74]

In its conclusions, the Commission identified two important issues. First, there is a need for more liaison with governments and industry. Second, there is a need for a policy statement on what will happen when a land use plan for the region is

---

72   Mackenzie Delta–Beaufort Sea Regional Land Use Planning Commission, *Newsletter,* No. 3 (December 1988).

73   Mackenzie Delta–Beaufort Sea Regional Land Use Planning Commission, *Interim Report* (12 August 1988) at 2.

74   *Id.* at 29–30.

completed. Workshops conducted in the region in late spring 1989 were intended in part to facilitate interaction between industry and communities.

The D/M AIP also emphasizes the need to involve communities and regions in the land use planning process.[75] It contemplates the establishment of a planning board with equal membership provided by the Dene/Métis and government, as well as the possible establishment of regional planning boards. These provisions envisage that land use planning will be grounded in legislation, which will "provide for the relationship between land use plans and those authorities with jurisdiction to grant licences, permits, leases or interests relating to the use of land and water in the settlement area, including the issue of conformity with such plans."[76] While the details remain to be worked out in the final agreement, it is encouraging to note that the D/M AIP has addressed such important issues as the relationship between land use planning and other legislation, and has recognized the desirability of clarifying the legal status of the planning process.

The Yukon

Land use planning has also received attention in the YFA. The Sub-Agreement on Land Use Planning identifies the objectives, among others, of creating a single land use planning process for the Yukon and avoiding duplication in the public processes for land use planning.[77] Section 2 of the Sub-Agreement states that the land use planning process shall serve as a frame of reference for decisions and activities involving resource use, facilitate integrated resource management, and reflect the principles of "balanced and sustainable development." This phrase is defined in Clause 2.2.8 as

> environmentally and economically sound development that meets the needs of the present while having due regard for the ability of future generations to meet their own needs.

While this vague definition seems to have been largely "lifted" from the Brundtland Report, its appearance in the YFA is significant because it is one of the first attempts in Canada to define sustainable development in a quasi-legal document.[78]

The land use planning concept in the YFA is for regionally based planning commissions, with one-third representation by nominees of Yukon First Nations, one-third by government, and one-third "based on the demographic ratio of Yukon Indian People to the total population in a planning region."[79] While the process will

---

75   D/M AIP, *supra,* note 8, s. 28.2.4.

76   *Id.,* s. 28.2.11.

77   YFA, *supra,* note 7, at 45, ss. 1.1, 1.6.

78   A recent Government of Northwest Territories document defines "sustainable development" as "a form of social and economic growth which harmonizes conservation and development goals." See Northwest Territories Environmental Protection Policy (3 January 1989).

79   YFA, *supra,* note 7 at 46, s. 3.1.

not necessarily be based in law (except, of course, to the extent that the enabling legislation for the settlement is itself legally and constitutionally based), the notion is that an appropriate minister will review plans developed by a regional commission and reject or modify them as he or she deems fit, but only after giving reasons for doing so. Clause 5.1 provides that plans will be implemented "on the basis of jurisdictional responsibilities as defined in Settlement Agreements," but the import of this phrase is not clear.

Although the YFA demonstrates that some thought has been given to land use planning and its interrelationship with claims matters, other government policy documents are nearly devoid of reference to land use planning. For example, in June 1988 the Government of the Yukon released its response to the Recommendations of the National Task Force on the Environment and the Economy.[80] While stressing the need for integrated resource management, this report mentions the land use planning process only in the context of taking steps to open environmental, resource, and economic development policy-making and planning to greater public input. Even more curiously, the recently released discussion paper on a Yukon Conservation Strategy makes no specific reference to the role that the evolving land use planning process might or should have, an omission that seems especially odd given the paper's emphasis on integrated resource management.[81]

Land Claims Agreements and Sustainable Development

Reference has already been made to several provisions of the IFA, the D/M AIP, and the YFA. The purpose of this section is to look at certain other aspects that are particularly relevant to the attainment of sustainable development. Because of its relatively advanced state, the IFA is the focus here, but for comparative purposes reference is also made to the evolving agreements.

The notion of conservation is, notably, intrinsic to the IFA. For example, one of the three goals specified in Section 1 is the protection and preservation of the Arctic wildlife, environment, and biological productivity (the other two goals are the protection of Inuvialuit culture and identity, and the meaningful participation of the Inuvialuit in the economy and society). This emphasis on conservation is reflected in many parts of the IFA, including sections that deal with wildlife harvesting. The same point can be made about the D/M AIP and the YFA. Although neither contains a general "objectives" section, both have extensive provisions concerning wildlife, which specifically note the objective of ensuring wildlife conservation.[82]

---

80 *Response of the Government of Yukon to the Recommendations of the National Task Force on Environment and Economy* (Whitehorse: Department of Renewable Resources, June 1988).

81 *Supra*, note 50.

82 D/M AIP, *supra*, note 8, s. 13.1.1(b) states the objective of conserving and protecting wildlife and wildlife habitat and applying conservation principles and practices through planning and

Preceding sections have referred to some of the provisions relating to land use planning in these agreements. All three also contain requirements for environmental or development assessment. For example, Section 11 of the IFA provides for the establishment of two bodies, an Environmental Impact Screening Committee and an Environmental Impact Review Board, both of which have representatives appointed by government and the Inuvialuit. Four types of developments are subject to this procedure: proposed developments of consequence to the Inuvialuit Settlement Region (ISR) and likely to cause negative environmental impact, developments in the Yukon North Slope region, developments in the ISR in respect of which the Inuvialuit request environmental impact screening, and certain developments in areas that overlap with Dene/Métis harvesting regions. Section 11(12) puts the onus on the proponent of a "screenable" proposed development to submit a project description to the Screening Committee, along with sufficient information to permit a preliminary assessment. The Screening Committee can take into account the suitability of assessments pursuant to other assessment processes or can refer the proposal to the Review Board. Section 11(27) gives the relevant government authority the power to decide whether or not to permit a proposal to proceed, after that authority has received the advice of the Review Board, but Section 11(31) prohibits the issuance of any development licence or permit unless there has been compliance with the provisions of the IFA.

In the period between May 1, 1987, and April 30, 1988, the Screening Committee rendered decisions on thirty projects, four of which were referred to the Review Board.[83] No hearings have yet been held by the Board, however; in one case, the applicant later revised its proposal and the Screening Committee chose to refer it to a body other than the Review Board, while in the other three cases the proponents have yet to submit necessary documentation to the Board.

Although the later stages of the IFA's environmental assessment process thus remain untested, in the Review Board's first report the then Chairman, Carson Templeton, made several critical observations about the IFA's operation.[84] He stressed the need to formalize the review process with related functions of the federal and territorial governments; the need for long-range planning on the funding of the IFA's various committees and of the Board itself; the need for annual performance assessments of the committees and the Board; and the need to sort out

management; the YFA, *supra,* note 8, Sub-Agreement on Fish and Wildlife Conservation and Use at 67, s. 1.1 states the objective of ensuring that conservation is the basic principle governing the management of all fish and wildlife resources and their habitats.

83   The information that follows is derived from "Environmental Impact Screening Committee Comes of Age" (1988/89) 11 Arctic Petroleum Review 44; Environmental Impact Screening Committee, *1986–88 Annual Activity Report* (Inuvik: August 1988); Environmental Impact Review Board, *Annual Report 1986/87* (Inuvik: May 1988).

84   *Id.* at 6–7.

the relationship between the compensation provisions of the IFA and other compensation arrangements contained in various government policies and laws.

At least some of the problems Mr. Templeton identified seem to have been addressed in the provisions of the D/M AIP that deal with environmental impact assessment.[85] A development proposal may be referred to the Environmental Impact Review Board that is to be established; after examination, the Board can recommend to the Minister that the proposal be reviewed by it or by another body of which at least one-quarter of the members are to be nominees of the Dene/Métis. Reviews must include public consultation or hearings in affected communities, and must lead to a report to the Minister. While the Minister may reject recommendations, written reasons must be given; if he or she accepts the recommendations, clause 2.8.3.16 provides that they must "be implemented by each department and agency of government responsible for issuing a licence, permit or other authorization ... to the extent of the legislative authority of each department and agency." Similar rules apply to independent regulatory agencies such as the National Energy Board.

The YFA's envisaged "development assessment" process goes even further in integrating it with other processes.[86] Among the objectives identified in clause 1 is the establishment of a process that "where possible, ensures complementarity, integrates, simplifies and unifies the existing environmental and socio-economic processes of Government" and "that is clearly linked to land use planning and all other land and water management processes, avoiding and where possible reducing an overlap or redundancy in these processes." The process is to include formal opportunities for effective public participation in all appropriate phases of development assessment. It is to be implemented by appropriate federal and territorial legislation, including necessary modifications to existing laws.

Interestingly, the YFA development assessment procedures require that any boards established be institutions of public government. This approach helps to meet one commonly expressed concern about the N.W.T. land claims arrangements — that they create a multitude of new institutions and processes, many of which overlap and have duplicative functions. In the context of the IFA, we will see below one example of how cooperative action between such institutions is helping to overcome this difficulty. Moreover, a Joint Secretariat has recently been established to provide technical and administrative support to the various renewable resource committees, boards, and councils established by the IFA.[87] Unlike some of the bodies set up pursuant to the IFA, this Joint Secretariat is not strictly an Inuvialuit

---

85   D/M AIP, *supra,* note 8, s. 28.3.

86   YFA, *supra,* note 8, Sub-Agreement on Development Assessment at 49.

87   Letter dated 22 December 1988 from Gary Wagner, Resource Person, Environment, Joint Secretariat, Inuvik, to Janet Keeping of the Canadian Institute of Resources Law.

organization, but is responsible to the Inuvialuit and the Government of Canada, with the participation also of the Yukon and N.W.T. governments. While such an organization obviously has an important role to play in the overall arrangements, its existence raises a question about the extent to which the Inuvialuit can continue to control the processes that are fundamental to the IFA's design.

Industry Interaction with Other Interest Groups

An underlying theme of sustainable development is the need to integrate environmental issues with development plans. When development plans concern nonrenewable resources, this implies the necessity of close interaction between industrial proponents and residents of communities likely to be affected by their activities. Land claims agreements will set out the process whereby industry and aboriginal landowners will interact. For example, under the IFA, the Inuvialuit seem to have developed a satisfactory working relationship with the oil and gas industry.[88]

Until final agreements are achieved throughout the North, however (and thereafter on non-aboriginal lands), industry will need to carefully consider its interactions. In this regard, the sort of relationship that has developed between Chevron and the community of Fort Good Hope helps to demonstrate that, with high-level corporate commitment, it is possible for nonrenewable resource activities to proceed in a way that meets local concerns.[89] Another member of the petroleum industry had initiated contacts with the community in order to overcome a federally imposed moratorium on the issuance of oil and gas rights in the Mackenzie Valley. When the government accepted Chevron's bid for the rights despite Fort Good Hope's preference for the competitor company, Chevron embarked on lengthy negotiations with the community in order to reach mutually satisfactory plans. The resulting joint venture agreement gives Fort Good Hope the option of acquiring a working interest in an eventual production project on specified lands. While Chevron, as operator, has overall control of safety, technical, and most financial matters, in other respects the project is to be overseen by a system of committees composed of one representative from each party. This structure includes a subcommittee that assesses and monitors operations with respect to their impact on the environment, and a subcommittee to adjudicate compensation claims in accordance with an agreed policy. Decisions made by such subcommittees are to be by unanimous vote, failing which they will be determined by the main operating committee or an arbitrator. Because much of the future interaction between industry

88   For a general description of the way in which new oil and gas rights are issued on Inuvialuit lands, see Keeping, *supra*, note 14.

89   The following information is based on F. Cassidy & N. Dale, *After Native Claims? The Implications of Comprehensive Claims Settlements for Natural Resources in British Columbia* (Lantzville: Oolichan Books and the Institute for Research on Public Policy, 1988) at 147, and a summary of the Fort Good Hope Joint Venture Agreement provided to the author by H. Gaudet, Vice President, Land Department and Public Affairs, Chevron Canada Resources.

and northern communities will take place in the context of the land claims agreements, the Chevron–Fort Good Hope experience may be of greatest interest elsewhere as an example of a mechanism whereby industry and local communities can work together.

Local, Regional, and Circumpolar Initiatives to Promote Conservation and Sustainable Development

One commentator on northern sustainable development has emphasized the need for all levels of society to understand the concepts of sustainable development; to incorporate these goals, policies, and objectives; and to think globally while acting locally.[90] A few examples follow of northern initiatives to promote conservation and sustainable development at the local, regional, and circumpolar level.

Local Initiatives

The community of Old Crow in the northern Yukon has completed a comprehensive community socio-economic development plan emphasizing further development of the renewable resource base on a sustainable basis.[91] In addition to addressing use and management of water, wood, fish, fur, caribou, and waterfowl, Old Crow has identified concerns about other possible activities, including hydroelectric developments, pipelines, highway crossings, sewage disposal, and Northern Warning System projects. The community's study emphasizes the need for more and better linkages among the community, the land use planning process, and the Yukon Water Board, and the need to follow a philosophy of "maximize our input, minimize their impact" in relation to development projects.

Observers of the Old Crow process have noted that the institutional context in which it has taken place is changing as a result of such forces as land claims agreements and devolution. They suggest that the result will be the rationalization of management activities within one agency and a significant reduction in the uncertainty faced by the people of Old Crow.[92] One would hope that this would be the case over the long term, but, given the complexities described earlier, it is difficult to see how it can be true over the short term.

Regional Initiatives

An example of an initiative taken at a regional level is the Renewable Resource Conservation and Management Plan prepared jointly by the Wildlife Management Advisory Council (N.W.T.) and the Fisheries Joint Management Committee, both bodies set up pursuant to the IFA.[93] Although Section 14(60)(b) of the IFA had

---

90   P. Duffy, "Achieving Sustainable Development in the North" (1988) 14(8) Information North 1.

91   Described in S. Fuller & T. Mctiernan, "Old Crow and the Northern Yukon: Achieving Sustainable Renewable Resource Utilization" (1987) 14(1) Alternatives 18.

92   Id. at 24.

93   Wildlife Management Advisory Council and Fisheries Joint Management Committee, Inuvialuit

required the former body to prepare a wildlife conservation and management plan for the Western Arctic Region for recommendation to the appropriate authorities, it was decided to prepare the Plan cooperatively with the Fisheries Joint Management Committee "in an effort to bring together the different planning activities in the region which are concerned with renewable resources."[94] Other bodies involved in this process were the Inuvialuit Game Council (also established by the IFA) and the Regional Land Use Planning Commission (discussed earlier).

The document prepared envisages the development of Community Conservation Plans for the six communities in the Inuvialuit Settlement Region, defining goals and objectives that are consistent with the overall Plan, the regional land use plan, and species management plans prepared by the responsible management authorities. A legal review is to be conducted to make territorial and federal legislation consistent with the IFA and the Plan. Important natural resources are to be protected from the negative impact of development by the environmental impact bodies set up under the IFA and by the provision of special long-term protection to areas where development is undesirable. To accomplish this, communities will be encouraged to provide input into the regional land use planning process.

This renewable resource management plan represents a laudable attempt to coordinate the mandates of a number of bodies and to influence decisions taken by government officials. Since the bodies involved are only advisory, however, the Plan does not appear to have any legal status. Moreover, the Plan itself identifies a serious problem in the North: the existing resource management statutes have not been amended to take account of the changing institutional framework.

Circumpolar Initiatives

The Inuit Circumpolar Committee (ICC), established in 1977, includes the northern aboriginal peoples of Canada, the United States, and Greenland. In 1986, as a result of a framework document adopted by the Inuit Circumpolar Conference General Assembly in Kotzebue, Alaska, the ICC set out to develop an Inuit Regional Conservation Strategy, the first such activity to be undertaken by an indigenous group at a regional level.[95] The development of such a strategy was seen to be important for several reasons, including the Inuit's heavy reliance on Arctic resources, and the many threats to such resources.

Renewable Resource Conservation and Management Plan (Northwest Territories, 25 April 1988).

94   Id. at 1.

95   Supra, note 62. The philosophy of the ICC towards sustainable development is described in R.F. Keith & M. Simon, "Sustainable Development in the Northern Circumpolar World" in P. Jacobs & D.A. Munro, eds., Conservation with Equity: Strategies for Sustainable Development (Proceedings of the Conference on Conservation and Development: Implementing the World Conservation Strategy) (Gland: International Union for Conservation of Nature and Natural Resources, 1987) 209 at 222.

The framework document outlines several approaches that could be taken. One is the formulation and promotion of guidelines for institutions of Inuit self-government. Noting that the division of resource and environmental management responsibilities among many separate agencies is a major obstacle to conservation and sustainable development, the document suggests that Inuit institutions should reflect Inuit needs and a more integrated approach to environmental management, and that government should organize itself so that Inuit do not have to deal with a multitude of agencies. The document also suggests that models for community management systems be developed to promote the restoration of control at the local level, with one or more model projects that combine conservation and development being devised and promoted.[96] Since the framework document was adopted, changes have been made to reflect new developments and issues. This continuing process will be the subject of discussion at the ICC's meeting in July 1989.[97]

BARRIERS TO NORTHERN SUSTAINABLE DEVELOPMENT

As the previous review has indicated, an enormous amount of activity relating to resource management is taking place in the northern territories, much of which offers excellent ideas to be emulated. Despite some of the achievements that have been canvassed, there are also serious problems that require attention. Coping with such problems will be a daunting challenge, especially in the face of emerging proposals for nonrenewable resource developments such as oil and gas production and transportation, and uranium mining. The purpose of this section is to identify some of those problems and suggest possible ways of addressing them.

One overriding problem is the growing gap between law and policy. This is not a new problem,[98] nor should its identification as a "problem" be taken to suggest that "policies" need always be translated into "laws." Indeed, certain subjects are better dealt with in policy than in law. On occasion, moreover, what some have considered to be mere policy not giving rise to legal rights can be treated as law by the courts.[99] But the gap between law and policy in the North, identified more than a decade ago, has been exacerbated by developments of the past five years. This period has seen an explosion of activity by all levels of government and by diverse government departments (at both the federal and territorial level) in relation to matters such as land use planning, conservation, compensation for damage to renewable resources,

---

96   The notion of demonstration projects also appears in *Building a Conservation Strategy for the Yukon, supra,* note 50 at 12.

97   Personal communication, Nancy Doubleday, ICC, 25 May 1989.

98   See A.R. Lucas & E.B. Peterson, "Northern Land Use Law and Policy Development: 1972–78 and the Future" in R.F. Keith & J.B. Wright, eds., *Northern Transitions,* vol. 2 (Ottawa: Canadian Arctic Resources Committee, 1978) at 63.

99   A case in point is the recent Federal Court decision regarding the environmental assessment review process (EARP). See *Canadian Wildlife Federation Inc.* v. *Canada (Minister of the Environment)* (1989), [1989] F.C.J. No. 301, Action No. T-80-89, 10 April 1989.

and management of renewable resources. During the same period, the IFA's implementation has led to the establishment of many new bodies that have only advisory status but are themselves embarking upon policy development. The translation of the D/M AIP and the YFA into final agreements may add new layers of complexity. Very few of these developments have resulted in legislative change.[100] Oil and gas, mining, land and water use, and environmental management continue to be governed by legislation that, for the most part, is as resource- and site-specific as it was a decade ago.

There are several dangers that emerge from this widening gap. One is that those with interests in resource management will find it increasingly difficult to know what the rules are and who is in charge of them. When policies issued by a myriad of governments, departments, agencies, and groups conflict, overlap, or are unclear, the natural tendency is to rely upon the clearly binding legislative rules. Yet, increasingly, these rules no longer reflect the "reality" in which northern resource management decisions are made. Another danger is that, to the extent that policies conflict or are ignored, local communities that have helped to shape them will become disenchanted with the process in which they have participated. The N.W.T. land use planning process, the Old Crow socio-economic development plan, and the Inuvialuit Renewable Resource Conservation and Management Plan all illustrate this point. Where is the link between the issuance of oil and gas rights on non–Inuvialuit land and the Renewable Resource Conservation and Management Plan? What is the status of the Old Crow plan in National Energy Board hearings? What is the relationship between community land use plans and decisions on ocean dumping in the Beaufort Sea?

A related problem is that, for the most part, the various conservation initiatives have not dealt well with the issue of how to integrate nonrenewable resource decision-making with the protection of renewable resources such as wildlife. As we have seen, most policy and similar documents either ignore this issue or treat it superficially. Yet the resolution of the almost inevitable conflicts between non-renewable and renewable resources lies at the root of what sustainable development must mean in the North. If this issue is not confronted, the achievement of sustainable development will be impossible. More surprising, perhaps, is the fact that some of the conservation initiatives do not themselves take account of related initiatives, such as the evolving land use process. If there is nobody in a position of authority who can see the "big picture" (and, given the current situation, it is hard to believe that there is), there is a strong likelihood that the *status quo* will prevail, and that resource decisions will be made according to the dictates of the prevailing legal framework.

---

100   A major exception to this observation is the IFA, which has legislative and, at least to some degree, constitutional status. See *Western Arctic (Inuvialuit) Claims Settlement*, S.C. 1984, c. 24.

Much of the initiative for conservation and renewable resource protection has come, in the past, from those most reliant on such resources — the aboriginal residents of the territories. More recently, the territorial governments have also focused on renewable resources, at least in part because of their commitment to generating economic development that is based on such resources. This cohesiveness of purpose, it is suggested, is beginning to break down. The population of the territories is growing rapidly, and there are increasing concerns about wage employment opportunities for young people. The territorial governments are looked to for the provision of social services but have little capacity to generate revenue. Devolution and the land claims agreements will provide both aboriginal groups and the territorial governments with strong vested interests in nonrenewable resource development. Traces of potential conflicts are already beginning to appear.[101] When the views of those who have been largely responsible for promoting decisions and developing policies that are compatible with the notion of sustainable development become fractured, who will represent environmentally sound planning and decision-making? And how will the national and international interests in such approaches be protected?

The litany of problems identified here should not, however, be cause for despair. Rather, their recognition should be considered a first but necessary step in devising ways of responding to them. Some of the earlier analysis, moreover, points to the fact that some solutions are already beginning to take shape. It should be noted in this respect that devolution offers all interested parties a wonderful opportunity to move toward a new and better resource management system. Consider, for example, the recent northern energy accords. Rather than simply copy the resource-specific oil and gas legislation found in other jurisdictions, the territorial governments should consider developing a new legislative framework that is not fragmented but is based on the notion of sustainable development. Recent initiatives in this direction in New Zealand may offer helpful models. Pursuing this path will not be easy, but it is an opportunity that will arise only once: it will be much easier to promote "integrated resource management" with fresh legislation than it will be to alter well-established laws that are familiar to interested parties.

In the meantime, and as part of the process, a broad review of current legislation is needed as acutely as it was when called for by the Task Force on Northern Conservation and the discussion paper on an arctic marine conservation strategy. The process of devolution will be long, and a more coherent resource management legislative framework (that takes into account the role of land use planning and conservation strategies) is desperately needed now.

---

101   See C. Harper, " Inuvik Chief Breaks with Dene Nation Hearing," *News/North* (24 April 1989) 1, describing the different aboriginal positions on proposed northern natural gas exports that are emerging in the National Energy Board hearings.

It is encouraging to note that both the Dene/Métis and Yukon land claims agreements are more sensitive than was the IFA to the need to integrate their processes and institutions with existing ones. As we have seen, for example, the YFA's provisions concerning the development assessment process contemplate the establishment of institutions of public government, while the D/M AIP's provisions on land use planning contemplate a legislative base for the process. The N.W.T. government's draft policy on sustainable development emphasizes the need to build upon existing mechanisms and coordinate initiatives with land claims processes. It is also encouraging to note that, despite the multitude of organizations established in the Western Arctic both in and out of the IFA, there seems to be some movement toward cooperative initiatives that minimize duplicative efforts.

As for the protection of the national interest in northern sustainable development, the land claims agreements accomplish this on aboriginal lands by providing that such lands are normally subject to the laws of general application from time to time in force.[102] The national interest in those laws, and in the management of non-aboriginal lands, will, of course, be protected through the normal political process.

CONCLUSIONS

Canada's northern territories offer much hope for the attainment of sustainable development. Northern experience in managing wildlife across jurisdictions shows us the dangers of doing so without involving local users, and the ways in which sustainable development can be promoted both within and without the legal system. The evolving land use process demonstrates the utility of community participation and the possibility of integrating land use planning with land claims arrangements. The land claims agreements themselves provide useful ideas about promoting conservation and, in some cases, about moving towards integrated resource management. Northern examples illustrate ways that industry and affected communities can work together in harmony, as well as the importance of local, regional, and international commitment to sustainable development.

The heightened interest in the northern environment, however, has caused other difficulties. Among the problems identified are the growing gap between policy and law, the apparently uncoordinated policy activity that is taking place both inside and outside governments, the failure to effectively integrate renewable and nonrenewable resource planning, the likelihood that groups with previously cohesive views will face internal conflict, and the possibility that some of the traditionally conservation-oriented interests may develop vested interests in nonrenewable resource development. These forces undeniably pose a great challenge for the attainment of sustainable development in the North. Yet there are reasons for optimism, including the possibility that devolution will be looked upon as providing

---

102   See IFA, *supra*, note 6, s. 7(97).

an opportunity for creative legislative solutions to old problems. If this challenge is taken up, it augers well for the future of sustainable development elsewhere, for if sustainable development can be achieved in the North, it is likely that it can be achieved anywhere.

ALASKAN AND CANADIAN TRUST FUNDS AS AGENTS OF SUSTAINABLE DEVELOPMENT

Michael Pretes and Michael Robinson

"Sustainable development" is a phrase that freely falls from many lips. Ever since it entered the public domain on page 8 of the so-called Brundtland Report — *Our Common Future*[1] — it has taken on a host of meanings. The authors of this paper have heard the term used in Alaska to describe the gathering of musk oxen wool (kiviut) for cottage-industry production of toques; in the Yukon it has been used to describe zinc production at the Faro mine; in the Northwest Territories it has been applied to non-consumptive, special-market-niche tourism development. In short, it is a malleable phrase. In this paper, "sustainable development" refers to a holistic process including employment creation, income generation, cultural enrichment, and the promotion of ecological harmony — terms stemming from the 1969 United Nations Stockholm Conference on Social Policy and Planning in National Development.[2] The paper describes the role trust funds can play in achieving sustainable development. Trust funds are a mechanism for retaining and protecting large sums of cash, including compensation received by native beneficiaries of land claims settlements, royalties paid to beneficiaries under the new Northern Accord, and potential severance and land taxes levied by governments on megaproject development.

The first section of the paper presents a brief overview of existing Alaskan and Canadian trust instruments, including both classic trust funds and trust-like mechanisms. The second section describes the current state of the economies of the Yukon and the Northwest Territories, and explores the development of a model trust fund to promote sustainable development. The paper concludes with a list of specific means by which trust fund income can improve the northern economy.

AN OVERVIEW OF ALASKAN AND CANADIAN TRUST INSTRUMENTS

In comparing the trust fund experiences and investment strategies of Alaska and Canada, we will consider both trust funds *per se* and trust-like mechanisms. Two cases are drawn from Alaska, three from northern Canada, and one from southern Canada. Each of these examples provides a foundation for the development of future northern trusts in the Northwest Territories and the Yukon.

---

1   World Commission on Environment and Development, *Our Common Future* (Oxford: Oxford University Press, 1987) (Chair: G.H. Brundtland).

2   B. Higgins & J.D. Higgins, *Economic Development of a Small Planet* (New York: W.W. Norton, 1979) at 151–152.

Trust funds are distinct investment accounts, established to provide a dependable and continuing source of revenue. Fund principal is often derived from government royalties or severance taxes levied on nonrenewable resource extraction. By depositing a portion of these rents in a trust fund, the government can extend the benefits of the resource across many generations or in perpetuity. In this sense, the money saved in the trust funds serves to indemnify future generations for the depletion of public resources.

Trust funds can also produce a significant income for government. In Alberta, for example, about 13 percent of the provincial budget is derived from income produced by the Alberta Heritage Savings Trust Fund.[3] In many resource-extracting regions, rents from natural resources constitute a large component of the government budget. Some regions are in fact highly dependent on resource export earnings. Barring additional discoveries or major shifts in world markets, the earnings potential of such regions therefore weakens as production declines and resources are depleted. The dire "boom and bust" consequences that stem from resource dependence can be mitigated by preserving a portion of resource rents for use during "bust" periods. If sufficient principal is retained, the income generated by the fund can in some cases replace, or at least offset, the decline in resource rents.

Another aspect of trust funds is their potential role in sustainable development. Large pools of capital can be invested in many ways; some funds have chosen to use part of their principal to support sustainable initiatives such as small-business development or environmental restoration and conservation. Both fund principal (in the form of certificates of deposit in local banks) and interest income (in the form of grants and small-business loans) can help to promote sustainable development, especially in isolated settings where there is limited investment potential.[4]

The three aspects of trust funds noted above — extending resource benefits, replacing resource rents, and functioning as development instruments — are also present to some degree in the trust-like mechanisms adopted by groups in some areas. Development corporations, while not trusts in the strict sense, share some of their features. Development corporation management, for example, is less concerned with retention of principal than with the stimulation of the local economy. Often this involves investment in industrial megaprojects such as refineries, canneries, and processing plants, though megaprojects are not the only investment opportunities pursued by development corporations. Airlines, hotels, construction, maintenance, and retail and wholesale marketing operations are a few of the

---

3   Government of Alberta, *Budget Address 1988* (Edmonton: Treasury Department, 1988).

4   For more detail on trust fund investment strategies and their contribution to sustainable development, see M. Pretes & M. Robinson, "Beyond Boom and Bust: A Strategy for Sustainable Development in the North" (1989) 25(153) Polar Record 115; and M. Robinson, M. Pretes & W. Wuttunee, "Investment Strategies for Northern Cash Windfalls: Learning from the Alaskan Experience" (1989) 42(3) Arctic 265.

enterprises established by development corporations in the North. Small businesses have also received assistance from them. What distinguishes development corporations from trust funds is that while the former emphasize business creation and maintenance, the latter emphasize portfolio investment.

Confusion often arises because of the name given to a trust fund or development corporation, and because these entities often combine aspects of both. Of the six cases presented below, the Alaska Permanent Fund Corporation is the only true trust fund. The Inuvialuit have divided their entities into separate development and investment corporations, while the Alberta Heritage Savings Fund is one entity with both a trust and a developmental purpose. The Cree Regional Authority Board of Compensation operates as a trust, but holds a development corporation as a subsidiary. Makivik Corporation, owned by the Inuit of northern Quebec, is a development corporation with a trust division. Finally, the Alaska native regional corporations have operated primarily as holding companies with a developmental purpose, with almost no emphasis on portfolio investment.

Alaska Native Regional Corporations

The Alaska Native Claims Settlement Act of 1971 was the United States government's response to the problems posed by the proposed construction of the Alyeska pipeline; native people in Alaska were able to block construction pending settlement of their land claims. In exchange for relinquishing historic claims to land, the Alaskan natives received title to certain designated lands and cash compensation in the amount of U.S. $962.5 million, which was paid over the decade 1972–1981. The Act also created twelve regional corporations that administered subsurface land rights, received the cash compensation, and operated for-profit businesses. A thirteenth corporation was created for natives not resident in the state; it received cash but no land. Each corporate beneficiary — defined as Alaskans of at least one-quarter native blood recognized by a native community and born before December 18, 1971 — received one hundred shares of stock in a regional corporation. Only shareholders could be elected to the board of directors of a corporation, which requirement created a heavy ongoing reliance on a small number of educated and experienced shareholders.

The corporate mandate contained in the Act encouraged the native corporations to pursue business investments in their region. In this sense, the native corporations were not true trusts, but rather development corporations. Collectively, investments were made in resource-related industries, including petroleum exploration, sand, gravel, timber, minerals, and fishing. Some additional investments were made in service industries such as trade, banking, real estate, and construction. In nearly all cases these investments were made within the state of Alaska, and usually within the settlement region.

It is now apparent that the regional corporation investments have been only marginally successful. Two striking problems were the lack of adequate investment opportunities in Alaska and the conflicting goals of the corporations. On the one hand, the corporations were to generate profits, while on the other hand, they were to provide social services within their region and increase living standards among the beneficiaries. The latter objective precluded investment outside the state, where returns were higher and risk lower.

Collectively, the return on assets of eleven of the corporations (complete data were missing for the two others) averaged minus one percent for the period 1974–1987, while the return on equity averaged minus four percent for the same period.[5] Some corporations performed better than others. Cook Inlet Regional Corporation, for example, had a seven percent return on assets for the given period, while others, such as Bering Straits Regional Corporation, have filed for bankruptcy.

Overall, business investment has not brought the expected prosperity to the regional corporations. While it is difficult to assess the social impact in terms of employment and education, the performance and current status of the corporations suggest that they have not achieved their developmental objectives. This is especially true given that the corporate goal of social responsibility has been insignificant in comparison to the profit-oriented goals.[6]

Alaska Permanent Fund Corporation

The Alaska Permanent Fund Corporation was created in 1976 after a statewide referendum entrenched the fund in the state constitution. Alaskans had been concerned for some time over the disposition of petroleum resource rents derived from state-owned land in Prudhoe Bay. U.S. $900 million was received from the first sale of oil leases in the late 1960s and early 1970s; this money was quickly spent by the state. Alaskans recognized the need for some mechanisms to limit state spending and to preserve some of the oil wealth for the future. In 1976 a special appropriation from the general fund created the Permanent Fund, with the provision that at least 25 percent of certain state resource revenues (mainly oil royalties) be deposited into it.[7] The fund balance now stands at over U.S. $10 billion.

The Alaska Permanent Fund has three stated objectives: to save a portion of the state's oil wealth, to protect these savings from loss of value, and to invest these

5   M. Robinson *et al., Coping with the Cash* (Yellowknife: Special Committee on the Northern Economy, 1989).

6   W. Wuttunee, *Competing Goals and Policies of Alaska's Native Regional Corporations* (M.A. Thesis) (Calgary: The University of Calgary, Faculty of Management, 1988).

7   Alaska Permanent Fund Corporation, *Annual Report* (Juneau: Alaska Permanent Fund Corporation, 1988).

savings to produce an income.[8] These objectives clearly indicate the trust focus of the fund. The Permanent Fund is predicted to become a major contributor to the state budget, and increasingly so as petroleum royalties decline.

Although the Fund is administered by the state of Alaska for the benefit of all present and future Alaskans, there are several mechanisms that prevent its abuse by the government. First, the principal of the fund is constitutionally protected, and may not be spent without the approval of a majority of Alaskans as expressed through a referendum. The principal must also be invested according to strict guidelines that emphasize low levels of risk. Because high returns and low risk are required, most Permanent Fund investments are located outside of Alaska, in the continental United States. The second check on Fund misuse is its management by a board of six trustees — two from the Alaska government and four private members selected on the basis of financial experience. Private directors have included prominent businessmen and bankers, as well as directors of native corporations. Investment policy is shaped by the board, while day-to-day investments are handled by private investment corporations such as the Bankers Trust Company of New York.

The 1987 allocated target for Permanent Fund investments was about 83 percent in bonds, 12 percent in stocks, and 5 percent in real estate. Most of the bond investments are high-grade United States government instruments, such as treasury bills. The stock component is a diversified blue-chip portfolio, while the real estate investments are distributed across several regions in the continental United States and across several types of properties.

The Alaska Permanent Fund, being a strict trust fund, is not directly concerned with stimulating the Alaskan economy or funding sustainable development initiatives. However, it does provide an indirect input to the economy through dividend payments from fund income to each Alaskan resident. Perhaps more important, the Alaska Permanent Fund provides an example of a successfully managed trust fund that could serve as the basis for a model trust fund for northern Canada.

Alberta Heritage Savings Trust Fund

The Alberta Heritage Savings Trust Fund (AHSTF) was established in the same year as the Alaska Permanent Fund, and with a similar purpose. The AHSTF was intended to save a portion of Alberta's oil royalties, and to use these saved funds to diversify and strengthen the Alberta economy and improve the quality of life for Albertans.[9] Since fiscal year 1987–88 no new money has been deposited into AHSTF; it stands capped with a financial balance of approximately $12.7 billion.

---

8   *Id.*

9   Alberta Heritage Savings Trust Fund, *Annual Report* (Edmonton: Treasury Department, 1988).

The AHSTF differs from its Alaskan counterpart in its emphasis on development rather than on savings. The fund also differs in management and control. The AHSTF is the direct responsibility of the Alberta Treasury, and all investment decisions are vested in the provincial Cabinet (except capital projects, which are limited to 20 percent of total fund investments and which must have approval of the Legislature).

Many of the AHSTF investments have been made within the province of Alberta; these include equity investments in oil sands projects, debentures of provincial Crown corporations, mixed stocks and bonds, and a small venture capital firm. The major external investments are a number of loans to other provinces. The AHSTF also has a number of "deemed assets" — an additional $2.7 billion — in such things as grain hopper cars, irrigation projects, provincial recreation areas, and medical facilities. While the AHSTF is able to fund many special items for the province through these capital investments, they reduce its ability to generate an income. In this sense, the sustainable element of the fund is diminished, since principal, and not interest, is used to fund projects.

Inuvialuit Development Corporation

The Inuvialuit Final Agreement of 1984 gave the Inuvialuit of the Northwest Territories title to designated lands and cash compensation of nearly $162 million, to be paid over fourteen years in annual installments of various sizes. With the funds from this settlement, the Inuvialuit established the Inuvialuit Trust, an accounting entity for various investment subsidiaries. The Inuvialuit Trust is directed by a board selected from members who have served on the community boards. The Inuvialuit have divided their portfolio and business investments into two separate bodies. The Inuvialuit Development Corporation (IDC) invests in businesses, while the Inuvialuit Investment Corporation (IIC) invests in stocks and bonds.

The IDC is a widely diversified company, both sectorally and regionally. Investments have been made inside as well as ouside the settlement region, and have included retail and wholesale marketing outlets; oil exploration and production companies; real estate development; and air, ground, and marine transportation companies. The IDC has also participated in several joint ventures. The IIC is responsible for portfolio investment, which consists of a diversified selection of stocks and bonds. The Inuvialuit have divided their compensation money into developmental and portfolio components, with a distinct mandate for each. This separation of mandates helps to avoid some of the Alaskan problems, and specifically the conflictual nature of the investment mandate.

Cree Regional Authority Board of Compensation

The Cree Regional Authority Board of Compensation (CRABC) stemmed from the James Bay and Northern Quebec Agreement of 1975. This agreement gave the James Bay Cree designated lands and cash compensation in return for relinquishing aboriginal title. Cash compensation for the Cree was approximately $136 million, to be paid over twenty years. The CRABC is the legal entity receiving the compensation funds, and is responsible for fund management and investment. This body is composed of the chiefs of the eight Cree communities, one member from each community, and three additional members. CRABC does not issue shares, but all eligible Cree are beneficiaries of the settlement and "members" of CRABC. Hence they are entitled to participate and to receive such benefits as the directors of CRABC shall determine.

The CRABC, as directed by the James Bay and Northern Quebec Agreement, pursues a conservative investment policy. Most investments are in North American stocks and bonds, and emphasize high yield with low risk. Principal is retained, while fund interest is used in a variety of ways. About 25 percent of the income is reinvested, while the remaining 75 percent is allocated to communities to fund local projects and hunter and trapper support programs, and to cover legal expenses.

A subsidiary of CRABC, the Cree Regional Economic Enterprises Company (CREECO), is responsible for business investment. CREECO was established with CRABC income and outside loan capital. The company holds a regional airline (Air Creebec) and a construction company (Cree Construction), and also has investments in real estate, fur brokerage, arts and crafts, and a skate-sharpener manufacturer. The Cree entities indicate one possible blending of trust and development purposes. The Cree have saved their principal and invested it conservatively, while using investment income to fund medium- and small-scale enterprises. This is a highly sustainable arrangement, and one that should be examined in light of its potential contribution to northern fund models.

Makivik Corporation

Makivik Corporation is the legal entity that received the compensation monies paid to the Inuit of northern Quebec as part of the James Bay and Northern Quebec Agreement of 1975. The Inuit received title to designated lands and about $88 million in compensation. Makivik has a similar mandate to its Cree counterpart — preservation of compensation capital with concomitant social and financial development in the settlement region. Like CRABC, Makivik was incorporated without share capital. All eligible Inuit are "members" and are entitled to benefit from the compensation monies. While compensation monies are administered collectively, the Inuit have noted that there is a need to promote individual initiative.

Makivik is divided into two functional components. The first of these manages the compensation monies, which are invested in high-yield, low-risk portfolio investments. The second component encompasses business activities and is divided into a number of subsidiary companies, such as a regional airline and a fishing company. Two other subsidiaries — a construction company and a maintenance company — were recently liquidated because they were not generating profits over an extended period. Like other northern entities, Makivik faced the problem of the lack of investment opportunities within the region. This lack leaves unanswered the vexing problem of where to invest: investment in the region is risky, but provides social benefits such as local employment; investment outside the region can produce a high rate of return at lower levels of risk, but does not stimulate the local economy.

LINKING DEVELOPMENT TRUST FUNDS
TO LOCAL ECONOMIC STRENGTHS

The fundamental economic problem of Canada's North is unbalanced, uneven growth.[10] Ever since the onset of the industrial economy in the North, the Yukon and the Northwest Territories have been viewed as storehouses of nonrenewable resources by the industrial, metropolitan South. Periodic outbursts of northern development activity, initiated in the South, have served to fuel the mythology surrounding megaprojects, to the point where they are now often touted as the only hope for an economically viable North. In reality, very few megaprojects have been built (in the 1940s and 1950s the Alaska Highway, the CANOL project, and the DEW Line might qualify; in the 1980s the IPL Norman Wells Pipeline comes closest), yet a sustained and sophisticated southern public relations effort has created a broadly held popular notion that the North's economy is derived from their construction and operations.

In 1986 the public administration sector contributed 46 percent of the total Yukon payroll and 36 percent of the total Northwest Territories payroll (see Figure 1). In the Yukon, small business accounted for 45 percent of total payroll; in the Northwest Territories, 41 percent. All other payroll sources account for 8 percent in the Yukon and 24 percent in the Northwest Territories. Clearly, megaprojects are subservient to government and small business in today's North.

In promoting the species *megaproject* as the economic foundation for tomorrow's North, proponents should be more candid about the long-term employment benefits associated with their plans. While it may take 5,000 workers three years to build a Mackenzie Valley gas pipeline, the whole system (from Inuvik to northern Alberta) will require only about 213 employees to operate.[11] Of these 213 positions, technicians, maintenance workers, utility men, and operators account for 140 positions, while highly skilled management, scientific, and professional occupations account for the balance of positions (some 73 jobs). It is likely that most of the 73 highly skilled positions will be filled by relocated southerners. Consequently, a

---

10   Special Committee on the Northern Economy, *Special Committee on the Northern Economy* (Yellowknife: Government of the Northwest Territories, 1988).

11   Polar Gas, *Polar Gas Training Program* (Discussion Paper) (Calgary: Polar Gas, 1985).

$5 billion megaproject will create roughly 140 operations and maintenance positions, all of which will last for the operating life of the pipeline, approximately thirty years.

This analysis is admittedly simplistic. It does not account for gas-plant operations jobs (to gather feedstock for the pipeline) in the Mackenzie delta or for indirect job creation in the support sectors. All told, perhaps another 500 jobs will be created to provide the operators of the pipeline with both gas and supplies. The basic point, however, still stands — megaprojects will not create the thousands of needed jobs in tomorrow's North. In the words of the Northwest Territories Special Committee on the Northern Economy:

FIGURE 1.
Northern Employment and Payroll Statistics

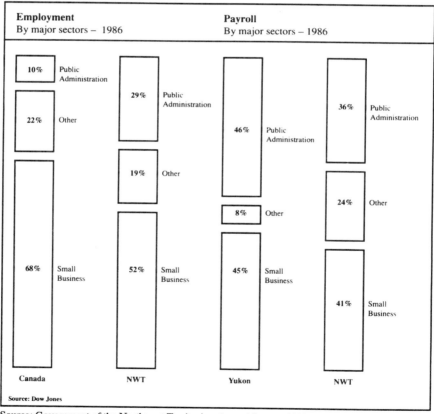

Source: Government of the Northwest Territories, *Annual Report,* 1989.

Our population is growing faster than anywhere else in Canada. If our young people entering the work force between now and the year 2000 are to find work, we must create 400 to 500 new jobs every year.[12]

In planning for a more balanced and sustainable northern economy, we must not succumb to a kind of *cargo cult* mentality, continually renewing our lust for the next megaproject in the immediate wake of the last. By focusing on current economic statistics, however, we can see the strength of northern small business. In the Northwest Territories it is clearly the leading employer (see Figure 1), providing 52 percent of total employment in 1986, as compared with government at 29 percent and "other" at 19 percent. Given the evident strength of small business, we should work towards maximizing the contributions of this sector.

Interestingly enough, the same tradition of local small-business strength persists in Canada's Atlantic provinces, and a recent Royal Commission on Employment and Unemployment has strongly recommended a balanced approach to economic development in Newfoundland. The Royal Commission report, entitled *Building on Our Strengths,* advocates

> medium- and small-scale enterprises, and ... modern forms of communication and technology, in order to build upon the latent strengths of all parts of our society, including our small outports, our resource towns and our regional service centres.[13]

In essence, the Newfoundland authors argue for realism in the construction of an economy that builds on local strengths, and at the same time maximizes the spin-offs from the locally active metropolitan industrial interests. In particular, *Building on Our Strengths* emphasizes the importance of developing new resource industries, tourism opportunities, and information- and service-sector jobs. The service sector is now the leading job creator in Canada,[14] and has been the fastest growing part of the Newfoundland economy in recent years. The Royal Commission recommends a major role for information and service in Newfoundland's future — "this sector remains our best hope for increased employment."[15]

The North can benefit from Newfoundland's foresight. Both regions are peripheral to mainstream markets and centres of commerce, and both are characterized by isolation from — and yet dependence on — Ottawa and massive transfers. Both are in the forefront of assessing economic futures in a world where the linkage between environment and economy is ever more important. In the revitalization of the inshore fisheries and the land-based bush economy, Newfoundland and the North are confronting the twin dilemmas of increasing population and environmental

---

12 See Special Committee on the Northern Economy, *supra,* note 10.

13 Royal Commission on Employment and Unemployment, *Building on Our Strengths* (Final Report) (St. John's: Queen's Printer, 1986) (Chair: D. House) at 446.

14 Clarkson Gordon/Woods Gordon, *Tomorrow's Customers* (Toronto: Clarkson Gordon, 1986).

15 See Royal Commission on Employment and Unemployment, *supra,* note 13 at 449.

limits to growth. In outport Newfoundland and northern bush camps, the challenge of creating sustainable economic development is well understood.

When one moves beyond talk to action, crafting the balanced and sustainable economy so needed in the North is perhaps the major challenge facing northerners today. In the recently concluded *Yukon 2000* planning exercise,[16] the Yukon Conservation Strategy, and the current work of the Special Committee on the Northern Economy, territorial governments are developing long-term strategies to guide economic development to the year 2000. Both territories now acknowledge that government can no longer grow and develop as it has in the past,[17] and are aware that changing global trade conditions leave limited opportunities for a continued reliance on oil and gas, minerals, and furs. Again in the words of the Northwest Territories Special Committee on the Northern Economy:

> Our economy won't improve by itself. We have to take the initiative. We want to present the Government of the Northwest Territories with some fresh, practical ideas for improving the economy.[18]

Fresh, practical ideas are available for northerners to act upon, and these can be allied with existing economic strengths to produce a more balanced economy. To begin with, the imminent settlement of the Northern Accords with the territories, and the Dene/Métis and Tungavik Federation of Nunavut land claims, will provide significant pools of new cash for investment. If a suitable developmental trust fund model is utilized, these new cash assets can contribute hundreds of millions of dollars per year in interest and dividends to northern beneficiaries, both native and non-native. With the existing strength of the small-business sector in the northern economy as base, there is significant potential for new growth.

The *Yukon 2000* process, the Special Committee on the Northern Economy, the Newfoundland Royal Commission on Employment and Unemployment, and a growing body of development literature[19] advocate special support programs for promoting small-scale enterprise in appropriate technology, renewable resource development, special-market-niche tourism, and information- and service-sector

---

16 *Yukon 2000* (Yukon Territorial Government, 1988).

17 See Special Committee on the Northern Economy, *supra,* note 10.

18 *Id.*

19 See G. Woodcock, *Gandhi* (London: Fontana, 1972); E.F. Schumacher, *Small is Beautiful* (London: Sphere Books, 1974); T.R. Berger, *Northern Frontier, Northern Homeland* (Ottawa: Ministry of Supply and Services, 1977); T.R. Berger, *Village Journey* (Report of the Alaska Native Review Commission) (New York: Hill & Wang, 1985); P. Hawken, *The Next Economy* (New York: Ballantine Books, 1983); P. Hawken, *Growing a Business* (Don Mills: Collins, 1987); M. Robinson & E. Ghostkeeper, "Implementing the Next Economy in a Unified Context: A Case Study of the Paddle Prairie Mall Corporation" (1988) 41(3) Arctic 173; M. Robinson & E. Ghostkeeper, "Native and Local Economics: A Consideration of Economic Evolution and the Next Economy" (1987) 40(2) Arctic 138; C. Irwin, *Lords of the Arctic, Wards of the State* (Ottawa: Health and Welfare Canada, 1988).

occupations. By combining the short-term, high-intensity economic benefits of megaprojects, the cash compensation awards of land claims settlements, and the money management techniques of developmental trust funds with a clear plan for balanced development, the North can achieve the sustainable employment and economic development it currently seeks.

MODEL DEVELOPMENTAL TRUST FUNDS FOR THE NORTH

Several recent papers[20] have argued the need for northern developmental trust funds, both for native beneficiaries of land claims settlements and for governments in receipt of Northern Accord cash flows. We will not retrace those arguments here, except to stress that trust funds have the potential of creating continuing financial support for many northern developmental needs. By investing and inflation-proofing principal, and harvesting interest and dividends, beneficiaries will have the means to create new (and enhance existing) scholarship and bursary programs for northern youth, to provide grants and loans to aspiring small-business entrepreneurs, to invest in prudently managed banks and trust companies (with the effect of increasing locally available loan capital), to create hunter support programs that enable recipients to remain actively on the land in the bush economy, and to enable per capita distribution of interest income to stimulate local purchasing power. All of these potential actions are developmental in the broadest sense and will shift the impetus for development from government to individuals and small-scale enterprises. In itself, this shift is not a radical move, and indeed it plays to the existing strength of entrepreneurs and small business in the Yukon and Northwest Territories economies.

Determination of the ultimate legal structure, developmental assistance philosophy, management philosophy, investment mix, dividend philosophy, and beneficiary information, review, and education processes for northern developmental trust funds is best left to beneficiaries and their elected representatives. Cautious preservation of the bulk of fund principal is extremely important, however, since in the quest for sustainable development, the funds must themselves be sustained. Given the experience of the native Alaskan regional corporations, the next generation of native beneficiaries should be extremely cautious about placing large portfolio investments at risk in the northern economy. Future beneficiaries can benefit from Alaskan hindsight, and spread their risk broadly in both geographic and investment terms. The authors also recommend avoiding the development of excessive "deemed assets" as part of trust fund principal. Here the beneficiaries can benefit from the experience of the Alberta Heritage Savings Trust Fund, which currently harbours several billion dollars worth of grain hopper cars, a golf course,

---

20   See Pretes & Robinson, *supra*, note 4; M. Robinson, M. Pretes & W. Wuttunee, *supra*, note 4; Robinson *et al.*, *supra*, note 5.

a grain terminal, and a large block of Alberta home mortgages. Clearly, the beneficiaries must set careful objectives for liquidity, rate-of-return, and risk. The authors advise a judicious blend of government bonds and treasury bills, comprising at least 60 percent of the principal, as the investment core of any new trust fund. Blue chip stocks, select parcels of real estate, and corporate debentures are recommended to balance the portfolio, and to enable the fund to benefit from international market forces. In this way, beneficiaries' money, held in trust, should provide guaranteed dollars in perpetuity to fund sustainable initiatives.

CONCLUSIONS

Megaprojects alone are not enough to provide the balanced growth that northern economies require. With its annual aggregate demand of four hundred to five hundred new jobs, the Northwest Territories has an obvious imbalance between job demand and job supply. New northern cash windfalls from the Northern Accords and the Dene/Métis and Tungavik Federation of Nunavut land claims settlements offer the best means of creating sustainable employment, if they are used to create developmental trust funds. Utilizing the interest and dividends from trust fund principal investment, the next generation of beneficiaries should be able both to broaden the economic base of the North and to build upon the existing strengths of the small-business sector and the local economy. An added benefit of this approach would be a subtle but continuing move away from government as the principal agency of northern development, in favour of individual initiative attuned to local patterns of environmental stewardship and culture.

5

INTERNATIONAL ECONOMIC RELATIONS AND SUSTAINABLE DEVELOPMENT

THE EVOLUTION OF ENVIRONMENTAL FACTORS IN AID PROGRAMS

David Runnalls

The last four or five years have seen a flurry of interest in the environmental policies and activities of international aid agencies. Hearings before various committees of the U.S. Congress, television programs about the environmental bankruptcy of Brazilian forestry and settlement programs, and frequent articles in the press have raised serious questions about the effects of large-scale interventions on the natural resource base of the Third World. This interest and pressure has rapidly changed at least the cosmetics of the way in which large agencies evaluate the environmental consequences of their lending and grants programs.

In response to this interest, many agencies have pointed out that such concerns are not new. Indeed, many have had procedures and practices for environmental impact analysis in place for a number of years. They also point out that they are not their own masters; it is the governments of developing countries who make the final decisions on location, design, and implementation of projects. The multilateral agencies, in particular, emphasize that they are also the prisoners of their own systems of finance and governance. They depend for their revenues on the private bond markets, and these markets place a high premium on maintenance of creditworthiness, soundness of economic appraisal, and speed and efficiency of disbursement. Their Boards of Directors are composed not of environmentalists or natural scientists, but of Ministers of Finance and their representatives, the latter sharing many of the concerns of the financial markets.

The bilateral agencies are instruments of national foreign policy, usually at least responsive, if not subordinate, to foreign ministries. Their policies are determined by foreign policy concerns as well as by the influence of a number of domestic pressures, both public and private. The latter range from the desire to promote domestic industries and encourage exports, the building up of the small-business sector, and urban industrialization all the way to the safeguarding of human rights, enhancement of the role of women in a society, and preservation of the environment. This paper examines the interplay of these forces and their effect on agency policy, and concludes with some speculations on where we go next.

It seems to me that, like Gaul, the relationship between the natural environment and foreign assistance agencies can be divided into three parts: first, the end of the age of innocence; second, the beginning of the age of environmental enlightenment; and, third, the transition to sustainable development. The first phase lasted throughout most of the 1970s; the second spanned the 1980s and is still continuing. The third phase is, I hope, now underway in at least a few agencies.

THE END OF THE AGE OF INNOCENCE

A number of developments throughout the 1970s shaped the relationship between the agencies and the environment. In 1968 the U.S. Conservation Foundation and Washington University of St. Louis convened a conference at Airlie House, near Washington, D.C. The conference and the subsequent publication of its proceedings as *The Careless Technology*[1] marked the first systematic attempt to document the relationship between development assistance projects and environmental deterioration. The conference had an effect on the World Bank. According to the late William Clark, the results of the conference, augmented by a lively meeting between eminent British environmentalist E.M. Nicholson and Robert McNamara, helped to persuade the latter of the need for systematic incorporation of environmental factors into the Bank's procedures and policies.

Accordingly, in 1970 the World Bank established the Office of Environmental Advisor. In his address to the Stockholm Conference, McNamara described the reason for the change:

> The question is not whether there should be continued economic growth. There must be. Nor is the question whether the impact on the environment must be respected. It has to be. Nor — least of all — is it a question of whether these two considerations are interlocked. They are.

---

1   M.T. Farvar & J.P. Milton, eds., *The Careless Technology: Ecology and International Development* (Garden City: Natural History Press, 1972).

The solution of the dilemma revolves clearly not about whether, but about how.[2]

The United Nations Conference on the Human Environment had been proposed in the General Assembly by Sweden, backed by most of the other members of the Organisation for Economic Co-operation and Development. Almost from the outset, the developing countries were at best lukewarm, and at worst hostile, toward the exercise. They feared that environmental rules and regulations would slow down their development, that stringent health regulations aimed at carcinogens or toxic substances would be used to block their exports, and that their attempts to exploit their forest and mineral wealth would be curtailed. Finally, many of them feared that these new-found environmental concerns would add substantially to the costs of their development projects and would prolong those projects' execution, without making additional financial resources available to cover these costs.

This skepticism on the part of the Third World was one of the reasons for the appointment of Maurice Strong as Secretary-General of the Conference. Strong, then President of the Canadian International Development Agency (CIDA), was highly regarded by many officials of developing countries. He resolved to change the political climate so that the upcoming Conference would devote a substantial portion of its time to problems facing the Third World, and took two major steps to advance the intellectual debate. First, he convened a meeting at Founex in Switzerland, chaired by Gamani Corea, of Sri Lanka, and Mahbub ul Haq, a Pakistani economist from the World Bank. The meeting examined all of the issues and set forth a number of recommendations for a more complete incorporation of environmental aspects into the development process. Because Third World intellectuals dominated the Founex meeting,[3] the resulting recommendations rapidly gained credibility within the governments of many developing countries. Founex made the environment/development debate credible in the Third World. Second, Strong commissioned British economist and writer Barbara Ward and American microbiologist Rene Dubos to write a book synthesizing the need for development with the necessity for minimizing adverse environmental effects. The result, *Only One Earth*,[4] was published in 1972, and Ward's reputation as a long-time advocate of the Third World ensured that it was read at the highest levels in governments and aid agencies.

The developing world, led by Mrs. Gandhi, attended the Conference in force and played a major role in its deliberations. Stockholm made environmental plan-

---

2   R.S. McNamara, *Address to the United Nations Conference on the Human Environment*, 8 June 1972 (Washington: International Bank for Reconstruction and Development) at 4.

3   "Development and Environment Report (Founex Report)" in UN Environment Programme, *In Defence of the Earth: The Basic Texts on Environment* (Nairobi: UNEP, 1981).

4   B. Ward & R. Dubois, *Only One Earth: The Care and Maintenance of a Small Planet* (Middlesex: Penguin Books, 1972).

ning and management a respectable part of the 1970s debate about development, basic needs, and the International Economic Order. It accomplished this by exploring the relationships between environmental decay and poverty, and by stating that development would better achieve its goals only if environmental factors were fully taken into account. It also led to a stream of literature, both popular and scientific, and a wealth of studies on the relationship between development and environmental deterioration.

In 1975 the U.S. Agency for International Development (USAID) was sued by four American environmental groups for failure to prepare an environmental impact statement on the uses of pesticides in its projects. The suit also concerned USAID's failure to establish project-review procedures under the National Environmental Policy Act (NEPA). This suit led to the preparation of new regulations for implementing the intent of NEPA in the foreign assistance program, and to new pesticide regulations. By 1977–78, USAID was the only development assistance agency with regular, legally enforceable procedures for assessing the environmental impacts of development projects.

In 1977 the United Nations Environment Program (UNEP) and CIDA financed a study by the International Institute for Environment and Development (IIED) of the environmental procedures and practices of nine multilateral development finance agencies. Published as *Banking on the Biosphere,*[5] the study pointed out that only the World Bank had "shown ... a unique practical concern over the environmental impact of its lending" in addition to "intellectual leadership in environmental matters in the international development community."[6] The report also stressed that the Bank's procedures and practices were far from perfect — they looked good only in comparison with those of other agencies, who had done very little. The report concluded that most of the institutions lacked clear procedures for the environmental assessment of their projects, criteria for assessing environmental impact, alternative forms of analysis and accountancy that include long-term social and environmental effects of development projects, and personnel trained to ensure proper consideration of the environmental dimensions of developing projects.

Banking on the Biosphere contained eleven recommendations,[7] most of which are incorporated into the "Declaration of Environmental Policies and Procedures Relating to Economic Developments." The Declaration, prepared under the auspices of UNEP, was signed by the nine agencies in 1980, and commits those agencies to five broad lines of policy:

---

5   R.E. Stein & B. Johnson, *Banking on the Biosphere? Environmental Procedures and Practices of Nine Multilateral Development Agencies* (Toronto: Lexington Books, 1979).

6   *Id.*

7   *Id.* at 137.

1. Institution of procedures for the systematic examination of development activities to ensure that appropriate measures are prepared to minimize environmental problems

2. Cooperation to ensure that appropriate environmental measures are incorporated into project design, and provision of technical assistance to developing countries to develop their indigenous capabilities

3. Development of project proposals that are designed to protect, rehabilitate, manage, or otherwise enhance the human environment and quality of life

4. Training of their operational staff

5. Conducting of studies leading to improved project-appraisal methodologies, and dissemination of information about their activities in this area.

The signatories also agreed to the establishment by UNEP of a Committee of International Development Institutions on the Environment (CIDIE). CIDIE has met six times (on an annual basis) since the Declaration was signed.

This affirmation of the need to incorporate environmental considerations into the policies of multilateral donor agencies was accompanied by the publication of a major statement by the community of environmental nongovernmental organizations (NGOs). The *World Conservation Strategy*,[8] produced by the International Union for Conservation of Nature and Natural Resources (IUCN), highlighted a major shift in the attitudes of conservation groups. Rather than concentrate on the preservation of individual species, the IUCN strategy seeks to preserve ecosystems through land use planning and to ensure the sustainable utilization of species and ecosystems. It recognizes that this can be accomplished only by integrating these concepts into national development strategies.

The third event of significance in 1980 was the IIED's publication of the results of its two-year study of the environmental policies of six of the bilateral development assistance agencies: those of Canada, the Federal Republic of Germany, the Netherlands, Sweden, the United Kingdom, and the United States. This study, entitled *The Environment and Bilateral Aid*,[9] concluded that, largely because of the litigation mentioned earlier, USAID was much further advanced than the other agencies. There was an urgent need in the other agencies for almost the entire repertoire of environmental tools: high-level policy statements, better data, enforceable assessment procedures, guidelines and checklists, and project evaluation techniques.

8   International Union for Conservation of Nature and Natural Resources, *World Conservation Strategy: Living Resource Conservation for Sustainable Development* (Gland: IUCN-UNEP-WWF, 1980).

9   International Institute for Environment and Development, *The Environment and Bilateral Aid* (London and Washington, IIED, 1980).

In sum, the motivating factors for the modest changes that took place up until 1980 are quite clear. The Stockholm Conference represented the first great wave of international concern for the environment and, as such, it generated immense publicity and enthusiasm. It also created a UN agency concerned with the environment, which continued to ask questions of the rest of the system. The continued questioning by two international NGOs (IIED and IUCN) helped to keep the questions on the table. Additionally, the USAID case marked the beginnings of a trend that would drive and dominate the next phase of the transition — the involvement of the conservation NGOs, led by the large, relatively well financed U.S. environmental groups. Finally, it is significant that the changes made by the banks and bilateral agencies (with the exception of USAID) during this period could be accommodated within the organizations with minimum bureaucratic disruption and little challenge to the agencies' missions.

THE BEGINNING OF THE AGE OF ENVIRONMENTAL ENLIGHTENMENT

The decade following the Stockholm Conference saw a flurry of activity on the environmental front. More than 120 governments created environmental ministries or agencies equipped with the usual panoply of laws, regulations, environmental impact assessment procedures, and the like. Yet the picture presented by the report that ushered in the 1980s was sombre indeed. *The Global 2000 Report to the President,*[10] published in the dying days of the Carter administration, painted a picture of a world whose natural systems were in desperate trouble. The so-called renewable resource bases of many Third World countries were beginning to look as if they were not only nonrenewable, but disappearing at terrifying rates. The conference in Nairobi, organized by UNEP to celebrate the ten years since Stockholm, was dominated by similar considerations.

The United States environmental community, hitherto very parochial in its outlook, now began to turn its attention to international environmental issues. The establishment of the World Resources Institute, the emergence of Worldwatch as a public information force, and the unlikely collaboration of the Reagan administration helped to focus this concern initially on the multilateral banks and USAID.

In 1983 a series of congressional hearings on the policies of the multilateral development banks began. The initial testimony by the Treasury Department on behalf of the administration tended to brush aside the criticism and to defend the status quo. The environmental community countered with what has by now become a familiar list of misguided and misplanned projects: Polonoreste in Brazil—a huge road-building and forest colonization project; the Narmada dam scheme in India— which would, upon completion, displace several hundred thousand people; the

---

10   Council on Environmental Quality, and the State Department, *The Global 2000 Report to the President* (Washington: U.S. Government Printing Office, 1980).

Indonesian transmigration scheme — a plan to resettle thousands of Javanese peasants to the outer islands; and the Botswana livestock project — a plan to fence thousands of acres of open savannah for cattle raising.

The response of Congress and the Treasury (which was in its early ideological phase and did not like the multilateral agencies on principle) was to send a detailed questionnaire to the banks inquiring about their environmental procedures and practices. The responses to this questionnaire provided the first detailed view of the agencies' performance available to outsiders. The banks appeared defensive, overly secretive, and unprepared to admit to any of their mistakes. This finding led to more congressional hearings, more fact-finding tours by environmental groups, and a proliferation of both money and staff resources within the environmental community. The Reagan Treasury, seeing a cheap way to appease an environmental community that was constantly taking it to task for its domestic performance, assigned a full-time staff person to the issue. Conservative senators who disliked the banks and USAID on principle, and yet were under attack by some of their constituents for their own environmental performance, became unlikely bedfellows of the Sierra Club. The Club's publication of a hard-hitting pamphlet, *Bankrolling Disasters*,[11] distributed to many of its 250,000 members, helped to raise the political temperature still further.

At the same time, the realization that the so-called African drought was in fact the breakdown of the environmental infrastructure of an entire continent led European governments and NGOs to question many of the large-scale development schemes of the continent. Several analyses by both the World Bank staff and some of the other agencies confirmed these impressions. The criticism of the agencies centered on eight major areas:

1. The lack of clear policies for environmental assessment at an early stage of the project cycle, well before substantial resources have been committed to the project

2. The lack of mandatory environmental guidelines and procedures

3. Tremendous understaffing of environment departments when they exist, or complete lack of environmental staffing

4. The lack of procedures for continual assessment and monitoring of environmental factors, not only in early stages but throughout the implementation phase of projects (Use of pesticides is a clear example where some monitoring capacity should be built into projects.)

5. The absence of environmental concerns and planning at the policy-making level in country and sector strategy documents

---

11   Sierra Club, *Bankrolling Disasters* (Washington: Sierra Club, 1986).

6.   The low priority given to environmental and natural-resource-related projects

7.   The lack of adequate consideration of environmental performance in post-project evaluation

8.   The lack of public environmental accountability in both developing and developed countries. (Indeed, many criticized the almost pathological secrecy of the agencies as the single greatest obstacle to change.)

The appointment of Barber Conable as President of the World Bank, the debate over the replenishment of the International Development Association (IDA), and the reorganization of the Bank served to bring these issues to a head. In a speech to the World Resources Institute before his appointment, Conable, a former Congressman, sought to reassure his critics by promising the creation of an environmental department within the Bank, greatly increased staffing, more open relations with the NGO community, and increased funding for projects aimed at the environment and natural resource sector. Since that speech, much progress has been made. The Bank now has an environmental department with more staff. The operational units also have far more (and far better qualified) staff to assess the impacts of Bank projects. Finally, much more attention is being paid to natural resource management projects, particularly forestry.

Many of the other agencies have also moved to increase both staff and resources available to deal with environmental problems. Procedures have been revised at the Inter-American Development Bank, and the Bank has a new president with an excellent background in the environment, dating back to the Stockholm Conference. Environmental staff are in place at the African Bank, and the Asian Bank now has a full division devoted to this problem with an annual budget of $10 million. It also claims an environmental lending portfolio of about $400 million per year.

The bilateral agencies have followed suit, with USAID again leading the way. USAID's enabling legislation has been amended by Congress to give it a legal mandate to deal with tropical forestry and biological diversity. Its environmental staffing has been increased, and the various regional bureaus are preparing their own overall strategies. Similar changes are underway at most of the European foreign assistance agencies. The changes within CIDA are dealt with in detail in this volume by François Bregha.

In sum, there has been progress in an astonishingly short period of time. Yet not all the problems of incorporating environmental considerations into development projects have been solved, by any means. Recent documents produced by both Canadian and other environmental groups are eloquent testimony to that conclusion. The current furor over the World Bank and IDB involvement in Amazonian development is but one example. In the multilateral agencies an additional political problem has arisen. Many of the developing-country members of the boards of these agencies still feel that these issues are being imposed upon them by the developed countries in general, and by the United States in particular. They already feel that the conditionality increasingly attached to multilateral lending is an affront to their sovereignty. Attempts to introduce environmental conditionality are therefore not welcome.

THE TRANSITION TO SUSTAINABLE DEVELOPMENT

At the conference convened to commemorate the tenth anniversary of the Stockholm Conference, Canada suggested the creation of a global commission to examine the relationships between environment and development. The World Commission on Environment and Development (the Brundtland Commission) produced its report, *Our Common Future*,[12] in May 1987. This report has fundamentally changed the terms of the debate over environment and development. After reviewing the dismal state of the world, the Commission concluded that the five- to ten-fold increase in world production needed to provide for the basic needs of the ten billion people who will live on the globe by the year 2040 will be impossible with our current patterns of production and consumption.

The Commission points out graphically that the degree and speed of change are such that we should no longer be talking simply about the influence of economic growth on the environment. Instead, we should focus on the fact that the natural environment has in many countries become a significant constraint on development. The Brundtland solution for this is the now familiar cliché of sustainable development. Sustainable development involves a very difficult marriage of environment and ecology — a marriage that we are only now trying to arrange in Canada.

Although debate about the definition of sustainable development is rapidly assuming the dimensions of a theology, I find the Brundtland definition quite adequate for our purposes: "new paths of progress which meet the needs and aspirations of the present generation without compromising the ability of future generations to meet their own needs."[13] The adoption of sustainable development as a (or, one hopes, the) major policy goal of aid agencies does not negate the progress made so far. Indeed, it requires that the new measures for environmental assessment, lending for natural resources projects, and the like be continued and strengthened. It requires more effective measures to preserve and protect prized ecological assets such as coastal resources, national parks and protected areas, and watershed management areas.

---

12   World Commission on Environment and Development, *Our Common Future* (Oxford: Oxford University Press, 1987) (Chair: G.H. Brundtland).

13   *Id.*

More important, however, it requires that sustainable development become a mainstream economic issue, central to the national planning and decision-making process, and not something to be handed to a politically weak, underfunded, and understaffed department of the environment and natural resources. It similarly requires pride of place in the planning documents and country strategies of foreign assistance agencies. It can be argued that the locus of environmental decision-making in the World Bank, for instance, should be situated not within the environment division, but within the line departments and those responsible for economic analysis, because sustainable development requires the reform of a whole series of ecologically perverse policies that often degrade and deplete a country's ecological capital. Recent research has indicated that certain kinds of economic policies, often designed for perfectly logical political or economic reasons, but with no thought of the environment at all, are of overwhelming importance in creating and driving unsustainable patterns of development. Two recent examples illustrate this with great clarity. One is the increasing conversion of good cropland, previously devoted to food production for domestic consumption, to cash crops for export in order to generate foreign exchange. This conversion can force small farmers onto more and more marginal lands, with all the potential that implies for deforestation and soil erosion and degradation. The second is a study recently completed for the World Bank,[14] which illustrates that much of the deforestation in Amazonia is driven by large companies seeking to develop pasture for raising cattle. The study concludes that none of these enterprises has ever shown a profit or is likely to show a profit. These investments are made almost solely to take advantage of favorable Brazilian tax treatment. Under Brazilian law, agriculture pays almost no tax, but expenses incurred by farmers can be written off against expenses incurred in other enterprises. Regional development subsidies and other tax write-offs, designed to stimulate employment and economic growth in the region, provide incentives for investments in what otherwise would be unprofitable enterprises. The Bank concludes that these policies are costing Brazil at least $2 billion per year in lost revenues alone, let alone the enormous costs of the destruction of rich biological resources.

Sustainable development also requires major reform of the development financing system. I am convinced that we will not succeed in persuading hard-pressed governments to devote more resources to environmental and natural resources management without substantial relief from the tremendous debt-servicing burden. Recent events in Venezuela and Argentina have shown the hazards of reducing standards of living to meet debt-servicing payments.

Meanwhile, ways must be found to utilize the existing mechanisms provided by the structural adjustment process to reshape the natural resource sectors of many countries. Structural adjustment packages, usually assembled by the World Bank

14   D.J. Mahar, *Government Policies and Deforestation in Brazil's Amazon Region* (Washington: The World Bank, 1989).

and concerned bilateral donors, always contain conditions that must be agreed to by recipients before they come into force. Historically, these conditions have related to "standard" economic issues such as revaluing exchange rates, changing agricultural pricing policies, or reforming the civil service. There is no reason, however, why this conditionality cannot in some cases be devoted to the restructuring of those sectors of the economy concerned with the use and management of natural resources — forestry, energy production and use, agriculture, and the like.

This kind of macroeconomic approach to sustainable development places a number of new demands on aid agencies and governments:

1. Both agencies and their clients must develop the capacity to analyze the consequences of a whole range of "ecologically perverse" policies, such as agricultural subsidies, distorted trade policies, inequitable patterns of landholding, and road building and other infrastructure schemes.

2. They must develop new techniques of economic analysis, including a new approach to national accounts that treats stocks as well as flows of resources and materials. This is essential if countries are to assess whether they are increasing or decreasing their ecological capital.

3. Agencies and their clients must develop country program strategies that incorporate sustainable development as their ultimate goal.

This "top down" approach will not, however, be sufficient in itself to achieve sustainable development. As Brundtland points out, development will only be sustainable if it involves the people of the Third World to the maximum extent in the planning and executing of their own development. The agencies must therefore insist that the development of local NGOs become one of their top priorities, even at the expense of occasionally antagonizing the host government. They must insist that environmental impact assessments and other similar documents be prepared with local participation. They need to develop special strategies for particularly disadvantaged groups, such as women and indigenous groups. Finally, education and human resource development for sustainability must have far greater play in the programs of the foreign aid agencies.

This is a very tall order for both the governments of the developing world and their funders in the North. It involves reorienting many of the strategies for foreign assistance with which we have become comfortable over the past two or three decades. It also involves greatly increased financial transfers, against the backdrop of the budget austerity that is now sweeping the developed world. Finally, it involves coming to grips with the debt crisis now paralyzing much of Latin America and Africa. What leads us to believe that all this might happen?

The answer, briefly, is global change, and particularly climate change, linked with a new definition of national and international security. We now have irrefutable evidence that we are profoundly altering the world's climate through the production of carbon dioxide and other so-called greenhouse gases, and through the destruction of portions of the earth's ozone shield by CFCs. If we proceed on our present course, it is likely that we will have very substantial warming by the third or fourth decade of the next century, accompanied by considerable increases in sea levels and potentially catastrophic shifts in rainfall patterns, with untold implications for agricultural production. This is a threat from which no one will escape. The degree of overall disruption will be such that there will be no "winners" or "losers." This threat is becoming known to senior politicians with sometimes dramatic results. The Soviets have described climate change as the single greatest threat to their national security. Mrs. Thatcher, that well-known Green, was so alarmed by the ozone problem that she convened a ministerial-level conference in London to discuss it.

Many of the solutions are known, although they are not simple — either politically or technologically. We must dramatically decrease our use of fossil fuels at the same time as we undertake massive reforestation projects to increase the area of carbon sinks. Initially, most of this burden will and should fall upon the shoulders of the developed countries. They are mainly responsible for the problem in the first place (for example, the United States and the Soviet Union in tandem produce close to 40–45 percent of the world's carbon dioxide). Yet all the savings made by years of effort could easily be lost if India and China proceed with their plans for rapid increases in the number of coal-fired power plants (up to two hundred in China alone).

But the politics of telling the developing world that, because we have created a problem, they must cut back on their plans to produce the most meager standard of living for their people simply will not work. Many are now calling for the development of a "global bargain," in which the developed world bears the brunt of the cutbacks in energy consumption and provides substantial financing for the developing world to pursue a path that is more sustainable and less energy-intensive. The terms would involve, over a period of years, substantial debt relief for countries who agree to maintain their existing tropical forests, and major efforts at reforestation of other lands. It would also involve transforming the traditional rules for patents and licenses, at least for non-polluting energy technology. Such a bargain might well prove to be beyond our reach. But many believe it stands a chance as superpower tensions ease, and the world's leaders increasingly realize that climate change is a problem from which none of us can escape.

AID AND THE ENVIRONMENT: THE CANADIAN APPROACH

François Bregha

In 1987–88, Canada spent $2.624 billion in official development assistance (ODA), an amount equivalent to almost half a percent of the gross national product (GNP).[1] Although foreign aid's share of GNP was cut in the April 1989 budget, Canada remains one of the principal donors among the industrialized countries.[2] Canada disburses its development assistance through several channels: bilaterally in government-to-government projects; multilaterally by funding sixty-five international organizations, such as UN agencies, development banks, and humanitarian organizations; and through nongovernmental organizations and development-oriented Crown corporations, such as the International Development Research Centre and Petro-Canada International Assistance Corporation.

The Canadian International Development Agency, or CIDA, is the principal instrument of Canada's foreign aid policy, accounting for about three-quarters of Canada's ODA budget. This paper focuses on CIDA in reviewing the Canadian approach to aid and the environment and, more particularly, on the challenges the Agency must resolve to meet the environmental objectives it has set itself.

BACKGROUND

Although CIDA claims that it "has long been at the forefront of incorporating environmental concerns into the development process,"[3] only in 1983 did it begin to take the institutional steps required to formally integrate environmental considerations into its planning cycle. Two independent reviews of CIDA's environmental performance conducted in the late 1970s concluded that at that time the Agency lacked a strong commitment to incorporating environmental concerns in regular program planning and project activities, systematic assessment of the environmental consequences at the project proposal stage, procedures by which to single out projects for special environmental attention, and adequate monitoring of the environmental effects of projects.[4]

CIDA's recent awakening to the importance of environmental issues should,

---

1   CIDA, *Annual Report 1987–1877* (Ottawa: Minister of Supply and Services, 1987).

2   Budget Papers tabled in the House of Commons by the Honourable Michael Wilson, 27 April 1989.

3   CIDA, Environmental Sector, *From Policy to Practice* (Internal Document, June 1988).

4   R.B. Ehrhardt *et al., Canadian Aid and the Environment: The Policies and Performance of the Canadian International Development Agency* (Ottawa: North-South Institute/The Institute for Resource and Environmental Studies, Dalhousie University, 1981). See also Johnson & Blake, *The Environmental and Bilateral Development Aid* (International Institute for Environment and Development, 1980).

of course, be judged in the context of the federal government's overall environmental record. When seen in this light, CIDA's performance is better than most: the Agency boasts that it is one of only three departments whose procedures the Federal Environmental Assessment and Review Office (FEARO) has approved, and the only one whose procedures are comprehensive. CIDA's own critics also concede that the Agency's environmental strategy "puts CIDA in a class above most aid donors, and second only to USAID in terms of environmental requirements."[5] They nevertheless see much room for improvement in the Agency's environmental performance.

In 1983 CIDA established an Office of Environmental Advisor to develop an environmental strategy for the Agency and to provide technical and policy assistance on individual projects. As its name implies, the Office had a staff of only one to advise CIDA on the environmental implications of disbursing several hundred million dollars in over one thousand projects in more than one hundred countries. Even when this Office was upgraded to a Sector in October 1987 and given a staff of six, these resources remained remarkably modest for the task at hand. Indeed, as most of this staff increase was the result of a reassignment of existing personnel who took their existing responsibilities with them, it overstated the staff resources CIDA had reallocated to environmental issues. More recently, the appointment of a vice president with a strong interest in environmental issues has increased the profile of the Environment Sector and led to further hiring. The Environment Sector nevertheless remains small and faces a daunting task in delivering on the policy commitments in CIDA's new ODA charter (discussed further on in this paper).

It was only three years ago, in 1986, that CIDA adopted a comprehensive environmental policy.[6] This policy, which was reaffirmed in CIDA's new ODA Charter in 1988, has five elements:

1. The conducting of environmental impact assessments on all proposed projects that are likely to involve environmental risks, including projects delivered by NGOs and the private sector

2. Priority on projects to improve the environment and restore natural resources

3. Greater stress on informing the Canadian public of the many aspects of environmental protection

4. Support for the creation of Third World institutions concerned with designing development projects in harmony with the environment

---

5   J. Ferretti, P. Muldoon & M. Valiante, "CIDA's New Environment Strategy" (1987) 9(4) Probe Post 25 at 30.

6   CIDA, *Environment and Development: The Policy of the Canadian International Development Agency* (Ottawa: CIDA, 1987).

5.   Greater emphasis on developing local capacity to collect, interpret, and use environmental data.

THE NEW ODA CHARTER

CIDA is now rightly placing environmental policy within the broader context of sustainable development. The term "sustainable development" was popularized by the World Commission on Environment and Development (the Brundtland Commission), which defined sustainable development as development that "meets the needs of the present without compromising the ability of future generations to meet their own needs."[7] CIDA was instrumental in creating the Commission and contributed $1 million to its $7 million budget.

In March 1988, after the first comprehensive review of Canada's foreign aid policies since the mid-1970s, the Minister responsible for CIDA, the Honourable Monique Landry, tabled Canada's new Official Development Assistance Charter entitled *Sharing Our Future*. The title was deliberately chosen to echo the title of the Brundtland Commission report, *Our Common Future,* and represents a conscious commitment by CIDA to sustainable development.

The Official Development Assistance Charter is designed to guide Canada's aid effort to the year 2000. Mme Landry has described it as "our 'coming of age' by showing that we know where we want to go, and how we intend to go about it."[8] The Charter is based on four principles:

1.   Put poverty first: the primary purpose of Canada's development effort is to help the world's poorest countries and people.

2.   Help people to help themselves: Canada's aid policies must strengthen the human and institutional capacity of developing countries to solve their own problems in harmony with their natural development.

3.   Developmental priorities must prevail in setting objectives for development assistance; as long as these priorities are met, aid objectives may take into account other foreign policy goals.

4.   Partnership is the key in strengthening the links between Canadian citizens and institutions, and those in the Third World.

With these principles as the foundation of its policy, CIDA has identified the environment as one of six priorities for its bilateral programmes and a factor to be considered in every project. It is important to note that several of CIDA's other priorities complement the Agency's emphasis on environmental issues. For

---

7   World Commission on Environment and Development, *Our Common Future* (Oxford: Oxford University Press, 1987) (Chair: G.H. Brundtland) at 8.

8   See CIDA, *supra,* note 1 at 5.

example, inasmuch as poverty has been decried as the worst form of pollution, the Agency's decision to make the alleviation of poverty a priority will yield environmental benefits. Similarly, the priority CIDA is placing on enhancing the role of women in development is justified not only in its own right; it will also pay environmental dividends because of the direct link between the role of women in developing societies and the use that is made of forests, fields, and water.

As a result of a gradual reorientation over the years, CIDA is taking a more proactive approach to environmental issues, and now devotes a substantial proportion of its bilateral assistance funds to projects and programmes designed to improve the management of renewable and nonrenewable resources, conservation and damage control, and rehabilitation. The exact proportion of CIDA money allocated to these ends, however, is unclear: a 1986 CIDA estimate places it at between 20 and 25 percent, double an Agency estimate made only four years before. As the 1982 estimate may already have been exaggerated by its reliance on a very broad definition of "environmental projects," the more recent figure should be treated with caution.[9]

In order to help it implement fully the new principles of its Charter, CIDA recently commissioned the Institute for Research on Public Policy (IRPP) — whose director of sustainable development, Jim MacNeill, served as secretary to the Brundtland Commission — to advise it on how Canada's aid programmes can more effectively support sustainable policies in developing countries. Through five public forums held in early 1989 across the country, the Institute received a wide sampling of views from academics, nongovernmental organizations (NGOs), industry, and others. At the time of writing, the Institute had submitted an interim report. It will be up to CIDA to translate the IRPP's many specific recommendations into operational terms over the next few years.

In developing new approaches to implement the environmental policies and strategies in *Sharing Our Future,* CIDA is also likely to benefit from two recent initiatives to create Canadian centres for policy analysis. In September 1988, the Prime Minister announced before the United Nations General Assembly that Canada would establish in Winnipeg a centre for the international promotion of the concept of sustainable development. CIDA will contribute $5 million over the next four to five years to this centre. The centre's programmes are not expected to be defined much before the end of 1989. Depending on its overall budget and the mandate it receives — the Manitoba government has strongly supported the establishment of such a centre — the Winnipeg centre could make an important contribution to CIDA's implementation of sustainable development strategies.

---

9   M. Gawn, *Donor Agencies and the Environment* (M.A. Thesis) (unpublished, December 1985) at 73. Cited in P. Muldoon, "The International Law of Ecodevelopment: Emerging Norms for Development Assistance Agencies" (1987) 22 Texas International Law Journal 1.

In addition, CIDA has announced its willingness to provide financial support to Canadian universities that wish to establish a centre of excellence in their area of specialization in international development. CIDA plans to make available up to $10 million a year for five years to assist in the creation of eight to ten such centres, the roles of which may include teaching, training, research, services to governments, a clearing-house function, conference organization, and publications. CIDA has already received several environmentally related proposals under this programme.

THE CHALLENGE AHEAD

In the environmental field, CIDA must now move from the policy-development to the implementation stage. The latter is clearly the more challenging of the two, as CIDA will have to translate its environmental policy into operational terms at every level of the organization: the corporate, the regional, and the national program levels. CIDA's new orientation represents a substantial shift in policy, a fact that CIDA's claim to earlier environmental enlightenment should not be allowed to obscure. The difficulties inherent in effecting institutional change on such a scale should not be underestimated: issues must be redefined, new objectives set, and attitudes changed. Even with strong leadership, it will take time before environmental values become imbued in CIDA's corporate culture.

Indeed, it is not clear whether CIDA fully understands the magnitude of the policy shift to which it has committed itself. CIDA today is essentially a project agency: almost all of its bilateral budget is allocated to funding individual projects. Yet, as is becoming increasingly evident in Canada, government policies often lead to greater environmental impacts than do projects. A sustainable development strategy must therefore ensure not only that projects are environmentally sound but that environmental considerations are integrated into broad government economic policies as well. In the words of the Brundtland Commission,

> the ability to choose policy paths that are sustainable requires that the ecological dimensions of policy be considered at the same time as the economic, trade, energy, agricultural, industrial, and other dimensions — on the same agendas and in the same national and international institutions.[10]

CIDA's commitment to sustainable development will require it to improve its internal macroeconomic analytical capability and broaden its focus from project management to influencing the policies of the countries receiving Canadian aid. A policy shift of such magnitude is not easily made. Nevertheless, until CIDA reallocates a significant share of its resources away from project implementation and towards improving policy formulation in developing countries, its efforts at promoting sustainable development are likely to fall short of their intended effect.

The Environment Sector will obviously have to play a major role in effecting

---

10   See *Our Common Future, supra,* note 7 at 313.

this change. This role is likely to be difficult: as a horizontal agency within CIDA, the direct influence the Sector can exert on projects is limited; as the purveyor of a new philosophy of development, it cannot expect to be popular in line departments whose policies it seeks to change; and as a very small group of professionals, it is overworked. It must therefore choose its grounds for battle carefully. The major institutional and attitudinal challenges CIDA faces in giving a greater role to environmental issues are described briefly below.

Environmental Assessment

An indication of the administrative difficulties CIDA will encounter in implementing the more far-reaching elements of its new ODA Charter can be gleaned from internal documentation leading to the adoption of the 1986 environmental assessment procedures. This documentation is written in reassuring tones meant to soothe the fears of alarmed colleagues, and therefore minimizes the administrative burden and policy changes the new procedures imply.

Until 1986, CIDA's environmental assessment work had been conducted in an *ad hoc* manner rather than on a formalized or standardized basis. In stating the rationale for the application of an environmental assessment policy, an internal description of the assessment framework pointed out that "the likelihood of abandonment of projects due to environmental assessment is remote," and then explained that

> experience to date indicates that approximately 10% of all projects may have environmental impacts which might require some degree of attention, and less than 1% may require separate detailed study (Initial Assessment). Of that 1%, an Environmental Impact Statement (EIS) will only be required in the case of megaprojects or projects with transboundary impacts.[11]

The cornerstone of the Environmental Assessment Review Process (EARP), and therefore of CIDA's environmental assessment procedures, is self-assessment: every branch is responsible for ensuring that the process is properly applied to projects within its jurisdiction. Self-assessment, however, can only be considered a satisfactory technique to incorporate environmental factors in project planning where measures to ensure compliance are present. The Environment Sector manifestly cannot ensure such compliance. Since the implementation of the 1986 environmental policy, several hundred projects have been screened and three environmental impact statements prepared. With very limited resources, the Sector is understandably hard-pressed to control the quality of the screening decisions made by desk officers. Nevertheless, as the environmental assessment and review process is legislated, the demands on the Environment Sector are likely to increase even further.

The fact that environmental assessment has been conducted in secrecy has

---

11   See CIDA, *supra,* note 3.

reinforced the suspicions of environmental groups that CIDA's procedures are not being enforced rigorously. Probe International, CIDA's most persistent critic on this point, has written:

> [S]elf-assessment and exemptions from disclosure not only robs the process of any credibility, it severely undermines the very purpose of foreign aid. By blocking scrutiny of local projects by the people of the Third World, our government is condemning them to second-class environmental review procedures and thereby taking greater chances with the environment on which they depend.[12]

The Disbursement Problem

In its new Charter, CIDA is making a substantial shift in its priorities and expenditures away from large-scale capital projects and towards human resource development programmes, such as basic education, improved health care, and skills training. This new policy thrust is inherently more labour-intensive. Training and institution-building are nonlinear processes; they require not only different skills than capital projects, but sometimes also prolonged nurturing. Moreover, they cannot be planned as easily, and depend much more on a supportive political climate. They may go against the established pattern of development and be more difficult to implement. They may also entail coordination with a larger number of government agencies and NGOs. The assistance funds required are unlikely to be as large but may have to be spent in smaller increments, and may thus cost proportionately more to administer.

Together, these characteristics complicate planning and spending, yet project officers are under considerable pressure to "move money" and prevent their budgets from lapsing. In a recent article, Runnalls notes that

> in periods of government staff cutbacks and restraints, a successful aid official bureaucrat is someone who moves money through the "pipeline" as quickly and as cheaply as possible. Woe to him or her who introduces a lengthy delay and costly consultancy for an unwanted environmental impact assessment.[13]

The efficiency with which project officers budget and spend the money allocated to them constitutes an important criterion in project and personal appraisal, because it is easy to quantify and has become an accepted measure of performance. Until equivalent criteria can be devised to evaluate the environmental strategy, the pressure to spend may undermine the strategy's implementation.

The disbursement problem is exacerbated by the difficulties CIDA may face in forging the new linkages necessary to implement its environmental strategy. In many cases CIDA's traditional contacts in recipient countries are with planning boards and sectoral departments, which can be expected to resist the loss of foreign

---

12 P. Adams, *Secrecy at Canada's Foreign Aid Institutions* (1988) INFOETOX.

13 D. Runnalls, *Environment and Development: A Critical Stocktaking* (Ottawa: North-South Institute, 1986).

aid money and influence to upstart environmental agencies, let alone to NGOs.

Tied Aid

Closely related to the disbursement issue is the problem of tied aid. Philanthropic motives seldom constitute the only justification for a foreign aid programme; more often than not, political and commercial interests also play an important role. Tied aid, under which a recipient country is obliged to spend a specified percentage of the funds it receives in the donor country, is perhaps the best-known manifestation of such commercial interests. Until last year, when it was relaxed, Canada's policy had been that 80 percent of bilateral allocations (which amount to roughly one-third of Canada's total aid budget) had to be used to purchase Canadian goods and services.

Tied aid does not always deliver the most appropriate goods or services to the recipient country. Muldoon notes that

> tied aid may be contrary to the goals of ecodevelopment since recipient countries must then structure their development in line with what the commercial sector of the donor country supplies, rather than its own social, cultural, or ecological needs.[14]

Over the years, tied aid has led to the growth of a business clientele with a vested interest in exporting its products and services through Canada's foreign aid programme. This clientele can be expected to lobby hard for the maintenance of the status quo.

Training

Perhaps the biggest constraint to the rapid implementation of CIDA's environment strategy is that there are not enough trained people to carry it out. There are not enough officers within CIDA itself who can recognize and address environmental issues; there are not enough Canadian environmental consultants able to work in tropical regions; and there are not enough scientifically trained professionals in many developing countries. A review of CIDA's environmental performance conducted by the North-South Institute and Dalhousie University's Institute for Resource and Environmental Studies had noted in 1981 that

> CIDA has not put a strong effort in building a cadre of international environmental specialists.... Until there is such a cadre, and until there is in CIDA both a mechanism to make sure that terms of reference for consultants include environmental factors when appropriate, and also specially designed environmental training programs ... there will not be a fruitful matching of environmental awareness and technical competence.[15]

The need for training is pervasive. The staff of CIDA's Professional Services Branch is composed predominantly of sectoral technicians, many of whom are not familiar with the integrated approaches underlying sustainable development. Some

---

14   See Muldoon, *supra,* note 9 at 51.

15   See Ehrhardt *et al., supra,* note 4 at 63.

Canadian NGOs do not know how to meet the environmental requirements that CIDA is imposing on them. In the absence of training, project officers will naturally tend to go for the obvious and do what is easiest, not what is most important. All of them will require some form of training. These needs will vary by organization, country, and programme, and will require careful and individualized attention, whether directed to environmental impact assessment, integrated resource management, environmental economics, or so on.

GLOBAL CONTEXT

CIDA's environmental strategy needs to be placed in the context of global environmental change. More people are being adversely affected by such change than ever before. It is now widely realized that soil erosion, deforestation, climatic warming, the depletion of the ozone layer, the accelerating extinction of wild species, the spread of deserts, the disappearance of tropical forests, the acidification of waters and soils in many regions of the globe, the accumulation of toxic chemicals and nuclear wastes, and growing population pressures on the land all threaten the economic development of many countries.

This list only tells part of the story. Current trends indicate that the world's population of five billion could double over the next thirty to forty years. That doubling in itself will place enormous demands on the Earth's resources. But if world poverty is to be reduced and the needs and aspirations of this growing human population are to be met, economic activity must not only double but increase five- to ten-fold. It is clear that such growth is impossible if it rests on a continuing depletion of the Earth's ecological capital.

In its latest annual report on the state of the world, the Worldwatch Institute warns that

> as the world enters the twenty-first century, the community of nations either will have rallied and turned back the threatening trends, or environmental deterioration and social disintegration will be feeding on each other.[16]

The Institute identifies global climatic warming, persistent poverty, and unchecked population growth as the greatest threats to environmental health and economic progress in the near term. Addressing these threats transcends CIDA's mandate, but must constitute an integral part of Canada's foreign environment and development policy. CIDA is now poorly equipped to identify and analyse the impact of such broad trends on its programmes and on the needs of developing countries. It should consider establishing an internal long-term socio-economic scanning capacity if it wishes to enhance the effectiveness of its programmes.

Canada has played a leading role in mobilizing international action on

---

16   L. Brown *et al., State of the World 1989* (New York: W.W. Norton, 1989) at 194.

atmospheric issues, the first threat listed by the Worldwatch Institute. In 1987 it hosted in Montreal the last round of negotiation on a protocol to protect the Earth's ozone layer. In 1988 it hosted in Toronto an international conference on the security threat posed by the changing atmosphere. Canada is now following up these efforts by promoting the negotiation of a "law of the air," modelled in part on the Law of the Sea.

One of the most difficult issues that industrialized countries, including Canada, will have to confront in obtaining the cooperation of the developing world in this effort concerns the allocation of costs. Put bluntly, should China's objective of placing a refrigerator in every home be jeopardized by international restrictions on chlorofluorocarbons (CFCs), which have been found to damage the ozone layer? In a related vein, scientists now agree that the burning of fossil fuels is one of the main contributors to global climatic change. Will developing countries have to bear the added costs of new energy technologies because industrialized nations have already emitted too much carbon dioxide into the atmosphere?

As the protection of the Earth's environment becomes recognized as an integral element in the definition of national security, answers to the foregoing questions will become increasingly important in the formulation of foreign aid programmes. As Canada's main ODA instrument, CIDA will be called upon to address these issues in its policies.

The objective of Canada's foreign aid programmes is, of course, to alleviate poverty, the second major threat to global environmental health and economic progress identified by the Worldwatch Institute. Canada has led the way in forgiving its Official Development Assistance loans to the poorest countries in sub-Saharan Africa. As noted earlier, Canada contributed about half a percent of its GNP to development assistance in 1988. Until the 1989 federal government budget, this proportion was to rise to .7 percent by the year 2000. The achievement of this target has been postponed yet again as a result of the government's budgetary restraint. The cuts announced in the 1989 budget will reduce planned ODA cash levels by $360 million in 1989–90 to $2.443 billion, or .43 percent of GNP. The environmental implications of these cuts, if any, remain unclear.

CONCLUSION

Sustainable development means much more than avoiding adverse environmental effects: it also includes raising the standard of living of the poorest of the poor; it means empowering local people to provide for themselves and their families through education and training; it means strengthening the natural resource management capabilities of recipient countries. This is an ambitious undertaking, and CIDA will therefore need time to effect the fundamental policy shift outlined in *Sharing Our Future.*

Several of CIDA's recent initiatives deserve praise: the creation of an Environment Sector and the adoption of the environmental strategy, the policy thrust of *Sharing Our Future,* model projects such as EMDI (Environmental Management Development in Indonesia), and the move to decentralize decision-making. All of these are examples of the Agency's new sensitivity to environmental issues.

CIDA will undoubtedly encounter obstacles on the road to sustainable development. Some recipient countries, for example, already argue that the practice of adding conditions to foreign aid encroaches upon their sovereignty. The implementation of CIDA's new development strategy necessarily raises the difficult issue of conditionality, inasmuch as it implies policy reform on the part of recipient countries. In another vein, the Agency's decentralization will consume much managerial energy and may make CIDA introspective, to the detriment of the implementation of the environmental strategy. CIDA will also have to establish a balance between adding environmental safeguards to sectoral initiatives and promoting integrated projects in the pursuit of sustainability. This balance will be difficult to strike: too much emphasis on programme integration may be as internally disruptive as too much on the policing role.

CIDA can take comfort, however, in the fact that the international environment is more supportive of its new policy thrust than ever before. Multilateral agencies are more sensitive to environmental issues, and developing countries themselves are realizing that the degradation of their environmental resources is curtailing their development prospects. This increased environmental awareness and the widespread acceptance of the Brundtland Report internationally should help CIDA in confronting the challenges inherent in the implementation of its environmental strategy.

LEGAL ISSUES IN DEVELOPMENT ASSISTANCE: THE CHALLENGE OF SUSTAINABLE DEVELOPMENT

*Phillip M. Saunders**

For many less-developed countries the pursuit of sustainable development, whether through improved management of resource exploitation or through enhancement of environmental protection, is inextricably linked to the impact of external development assistance. This relationship has been recognized for many years,[1] and that recognition has extended to the disproportionate effects of environmental degradation on those who are intended as the primary beneficiaries of many development assistance programmes:

> [I]f environmental dimensions [of development funding] are disregarded there will be not only unexpected ecological costs, but additional social and economic costs — which generally tend to fall most heavily upon the poor.[2]

The linkage between development assistance and sustainable development operates in at least two important ways. First, external assistance is often a major source of the capital funding required to permit resource development projects to proceed.[3] As a result, the criteria applied in project selection can influence whether or not such activities will be conducive to sustainable development.[4] Second, technical assistance and training are often required to help define and implement policies that promote the sustainable development of a country's resources or the protection of its environment.

---

* The views expressed in this paper are those of the author and do not necessarily reflect the policies of the International Centre for Ocean Development.

1 See, for example, "Development and Environment: The Founex Report" reprinted in United Nations Environment Programme, *In Defence of the Earth: The Basic Texts On Environment* (Nairobi: UNEP, 1981) at 3 (hereinafter referred to as "The Founex Report").

2 K.A. Dahlberg, "Ecological Effects of Current Development Processes In Less Developed Countries" in A. Vann & P. Rogers, eds., *Human Ecology and World Development* (London: Plenum Press, 1974) at 76–77.

3 P. Muldoon, "The International Law of Ecodevelopment: Emerging Norms for Development Assistance Agencies" (1987) 22 Tex. Int'l L.J. 1 at 2. One-third of net external capital receipts for developing countries is derived from development assistance.

4 Reviews of multilateral development bank activities over the past three decades have shown the effects of *failing* to implement environmentally sound criteria. These include adverse impacts resulting from projects in agriculture, cattle production, population resettlement, and water development. B.M. Rich, "The Multilateral Development Banks, Environmental Policy, and the United States" (1984-85) 12 Ecol. L.Q. 681 at 688-702.

Legal structures and systems play a critical role in both resource management and environmental protection. At the supranational level, the development of international law can be employed in the creation of new obligations to manage and protect the environment. Domestically, policies promoting the sustainable development of natural resources often rely upon the introduction or improvement of legislative and regulatory schemes. This paper examines the role of law, at both the national and the international level, in the interaction between development assistance and the environment. It reviews particular shortcomings in the application of law to economic development, and suggests some steps to increase the effectiveness of the legal sector's contribution.

INTERNATIONAL LEVEL

International law's primary contribution to the promotion of sustainable development in less-developed countries has been the establishment of new principles and standards for environmental protection and resource management. Obligations to manage and protect the environment are defined and agreed to at the international level, and are thus made binding on states (or at least on those that agree to be bound). From the early 1970s through to the 1980s this was clearly one of the most important areas of growth in international law. The watershed of this emerging international law of the environment, the Stockholm Declaration,[5] provided both political impetus and substantive guidance for legal advances in a number of sectors. New multilateral treaty obligations[6] filled the obvious gaps left by the customary international law of the environment.[7]

The new environmental principles were also changing the face of international law. New *types* of obligations could be discerned, going beyond traditional rules, which regulated state behaviour in a *negative* sense (in that states were primarily obliged *not* to take certain actions and were subject to sanctions for breaches). New, more positive obligations were established, such as requirements to cooperate in the furtherance of scientific research and environmental monitoring. These obligations were clearly more difficult to "enforce" than more familiar rules of international law, but they also provided more sophisticated means for international action on the environment.

---

5   See "Declaration of the United Nations Conference on the Human Environment" in United Nations, *Report of the United Nations Conference on the Human Environment*, UN Doc. A/Conf. 48/14 (hereinafter referred to as the *Stockholm Declaration*).

6   The examples of this growth in international environmental law are both numerous and wide-ranging in impact. For a review of relevant global and regional agreements, see United Nations Environment Programme, *Register of International Treaties and Other Agreements in the Field of the Environment* (Nairobi: UNEP, 1985) UNEP/GC/Information/11.

7   On the scarcity of effective customary international law relating to environmental protection, see United Nations Environment Programme, *Environmental Law: An In-Depth Review* (UNEP Report #2) (Nairobi: UNEP, 1981) at 5-6 (hereinafter referred to as *Environmental Law*).

The complexity of the new obligations is illustrated by the environmental management provisions of the 1982 Law of the Sea Convention (LOS).[8] The Convention contains a myriad of provisions[9] with direct environmental and resource management implications, provisions that go far beyond straightforward rules. It is possible to discern in the Convention at least four main types of obligations — some previously familiar to international law, and some not.[10] First, there are articles that *prescribe behaviour,* in that they dictate specific or general responsibilities of states.[11] Second, some articles *establish* or *affirm jurisdiction,* by either creating or confirming the right of a state to take jurisdiction over a resource,[12] or over a geographic area for management purposes.[13] A third category consists in articles that *establish criteria or standards* — either setting standards to be implemented, or establishing general criteria that subsequent international action can transform into specific standards.[14] Finally, some provisions are intended to *establish mechanisms,* by promoting or requiring the creation of international institutions or avenues for cooperation and management.[15]

This range of obligations is more flexible and complicated than were traditional approaches to international law, and also provided for post-Convention development and refinement of areas that were inadequately dealt with, whether for lack of technical information or lack of consensus. Critical to this further definition, in the Convention and elsewhere, were the associated new institutional mechanisms. Of

---

8   1982 United Nations Convention on the Law of the Sea. Done at Montego Bay, 10 December 1982. Not in force. UN Doc. A/Conf.62/122 (hereinafter "1982 LOS").

9   At least fifty-nine distinct provisions of the 1982 LOS can be seen to have environmental significance. See D.M. Johnston *et al., Conservation and Management of the Marine Environment: Responsibilities and Required Initiatives in Accordance with the 1982 UN Convention on the Law of the Sea* (IUCN: 1984). Chart prepared by Dalhousie Ocean Studies Programme under the auspices of the Commission for Environmental Policy, Law and Administration of the International Union for Conservation of Nature and Natural Resources.

10   *Id.* at "Introductory Note."

11   See, for example, Article 62(2), 1982 LOS, which requires states to take measures to ensure conservation of anadromous species within their EEZs.

12   Article 67(1), 1982 LOS, for example, *establishes* jurisdiction over catadromous stocks by the state in whose waters the majority of the life-cycle is spent. Article 65, on the other hand, affirms continuing coastal state (and international organization) authority to regulate marine mammal exploitation in the EEZ.

13   As is provided in Article 234, 1982 LOS, which creates special environmental jurisdiction for the coastal state over ice-covered areas of the EEZ and territorial sea.

14   Article 119 (1), 1982 LOS, for example, establishes criteria respecting allowable catches and other conservation measures on the high seas, criteria that states are meant to incorporate in national legislation.

15   See, for example, Article 118, 1982 LOS, which mandates states to cooperate in the creation of subregional and regional organizations for the conservation and management of high-seas living resources. Not all of these "mechanisms" are institutional in nature; some (such as Article 61(5) on sharing of fish stocks data) simply establish channels of communication.

greatest relevance was the United Nations Environment Programme (UNEP), established with a broad mandate to promote the aims of the Stockholm Declaration and Action Plan, including the advancement of international environmental law.[16] Thus, concomitant with the emergence of new types of obligations, the world community created institutions intended to ensure both practical implementation and further agreement on specific rules beyond the broad principles that had been stated.

Throughout this period of change and expansion in international law, the special problems of developing countries were given particular attention. The Stockholm Conference itself reflected the awareness that environment and underdevelopment were linked issues, and that principles of environmental law must reflect this fact:

> The Stockholm Declaration and Declaration of Principles emphasized two primary themes stressed at the Conference: 1) most environmental problems in developing countries are caused by, or related to, poverty and underdevelopment, and 2) development will better achieve its goals if it adequately takes into account environmental and natural resource concerns.[17]

It has been suggested that international law may now be evolving an obligation more directly relevant to development assistance — an obligation on donor nations to observe certain principles of environmental responsibility in the projects that they fund:

> The international law of ecodevelopment merges environmental and development concerns to create a framework for the rational use, allocation, and management of natural resources.... It obliges all states, international development agencies, and other development actors to integrate environmental considerations into their development activities...[18]

Even a proponent of such an approach would acknowledge, however, that most of these "norms" are not "hard" law, but rather "emerging law or 'soft' law that carries a strong moral and practical effect."[19] At this stage it is difficult to carry through even the case for "emerging" law: most of the relevant international resolutions and other documents are mainly recommendatory in nature.[20] It is in any event difficult to imagine rules of this kind being accepted and applied in any rigorous sense. Such rules imply an obligation on one state (the donor) to abide by certain rules within a second state (the recipient) that the second state, albeit a "bene-

---

16 See *Environmental Law, supra,* note 7 at 11.

17 See Rich, *supra,* note 4 at 704.

18 See Muldoon, *supra,* note 3 at 8.

19 *Id.* at 8.

20 Examples include the *Stockholm Declaration, supra,* note 5; the *Cocoyoc Declaration,* 1974 (UNEP/UNCTAD Symposium on Patterns of Resource Use, Environment and Development Strategies, UN Doc. A/X.2/292); UN General Assembly Resolution adopting *The International Development Strategy* (GA Res. 35/56, 35 UN GAOR Supp.-no. 48); the *Nairobi Declaration,* 1982 (UN Doc. A/37/25); and International Union for Conservation of Nature and Natural Resources, *World Conservation Strategy: Living Resource Conservation for Sustainable Development* (Morges: IUCN, 1980).

ficiary" of enlightened policies, might not wish to apply. The logic is more compelling where a third state is involved (where, for example, identifiable transboundary pollution or other damage might result from a project), but beyond this particular problem it is doubtful that any rule of general application will materialize. Perhaps more important is the "moral and practical effect" already referred to, which has resulted in the stated desire of most development assistance agencies to pursue environmentally sound policies, regardless of any "hard" international law obligation to do so. Whether they have succeeded or even intend to succeed is still debatable,[21] but it appears that many agencies have made significant improvements in recent years.

Despite the substantial responses of international law principles and mechanisms to the challenges of sustainable development in the less-developed countries, a number of difficulties remain. The following are some of the major issues that, while they may never truly be resolved, at least require attention if international law in this area is to be effective on a global basis.

The "Affordability" Issue

Although it is well accepted that environmentally unsound development is not development at all,[22] some still fear that, by adhering to relatively new standards of responsibility, developing countries may forgo some of the long-term benefits that developed countries have already reaped from less-controlled behaviour.[23] The underlying fear is that the economies of developing countries may slide further back if those countries agree to be bound by environmental standards that are really a "luxury," affordable only for developed states. This reasoning may be fallacious, but the fear is real and must be dealt with if international law is to progress in this area — particularly if that progress is to include less-developed states. Some allowances must be made for the special needs of developing countries, allowances that do not permit underdevelopment to be used as a convenient blanket excuse for environmental disasters.[24] This *desideratum* can be given concrete form by linking

---

21 Rich, *supra*, note 4 at 688, notes that there is evidence that multilateral development banks have continued to pursue environmentally unsound projects long after the "acceptance" of environmental guidelines.

22 See, for example, this statement from the Founex Report, *supra*, note 1 at 4–5: "In the past, there has been a tendency to equate the development goal with the more narrowly conceived objective of economic growth as measured by the rise of the gross national product.... A new emphasis is thus being placed on the attainment of social and cultural goals.... The recognition of environmental issues is an aspect of this widening of the development concept."

23 *Id.* at 26–27.

24 The most extreme example of this phoenomenon is the "export" of environmental problems to developing countries, whether through transfer of obsolete technologies and products, or the "rental" of areas in developing countries for the disposal of hazardous wastes. For a discussion, see R. Clarke & J. Palmer, *The Human Environment — Action or Disaster: An Account of the Public Hearing Held in London, June 1982* (Dublin: UNEP, 1983) at 51–54.

progress on new legal principles with assistance to those countries for which implementation may mean economic hardship.[25]

Assumptions of Capacities

Most international environmental law principles must be followed by implementation at the national level if they are to have any practical effect.[26] If implementation is to extend to all affected parties, then the standards should be within the realistic grasp of states. It is not particularly helpful to establish global standards that are not within many states' domestic regulatory or scientific capacities, and then to decry the lack of compliance. Again, external assistance linked directly to the implementation of new principles may provide one solution.

Nor is the problem simply one of standards — the same difficulty arises with respect to the *means* designated for the attainment of objectives. Developed countries often possess a distinct advantage in negotiations on technical issues of this type, and so may gain acceptance for criteria or approaches that may be inappropriate for less-developed states. There is often more than one route to a given objective, and the choice of one over another can have serious implications for the implementing state in terms of the financial and other resources needed to achieve compliance. In the LOS Convention, for example, states assume a number of obligations with respect to the management of fishery resources, including, *inter alia:*

Article 61
Conservation of the Living Resources of the EEZ

1. The coastal State shall determine the allowable catch of the living resources in its exclusive economic zone.

2. The coastal State, taking into account the best scientific evidence available to it, shall ensure through proper conservation and management measures that the maintenance of the living resources in the exclusive economic zone is not endangered by over-exploitation...

Taken at face value, the full implementation of such a system, which implies a capacity to undertake expensive stock assessments and thus set allowable catches,[27] might well be beyond the financial and technical capacities of many developing states. A similar problem arises with respect to the determination of

---

25 This approach was strongly supported by recommendations in the Stockholm Declaration Action Plan, in *In Defense of the Earth, supra,* note 1 at 25–26, recommendations 102, 103.

26 For a survey and analysis of the special problems facing developing countries in the enactment and, more important, the *implementation* of environmental law (including that mandated by international conventions) see J. Mayda, "Environmental Legislation in Developing Countries: Some Parameters and Constraints" (1984–85) 12 Ecol. L.Q. 997.

27 Further to this point, Article 62(2), 1982 LOS, calls on a state to determine its own capacity to harvest and allocate surpluses for foreign use. Given that some states have a greater capacity than others to carry out such assessments, the combined effect of these provisions may give a technical advantage to more developed states in fisheries access negotiations.

jurisdiction (and thus management control) over the continental shelf beyond two hundred nautical miles:

Article 76
Definition of the Continental Shelf

4.a)   For the purposes of this Convention, the coastal State shall establish the outer edge of the continental margin wherever the margin extends beyond 200 nautical miles from the baselines from which the breadth of the territorial sea is measured, by either:

   i)   a line delineated ... by reference to the outermost fixed points at each of which the thickness of sedimentary rocks is at least 1 per cent of the shortest distance from such point to the foot of the continental slope; or

   ii) a line delineated ... by reference to fixed points not more than 60 miles from the foot of the continental slope.

All of this assumes that a country wishing to maximize the benefits of continental shelf jurisdiction will have available highly technical information, which would be extremely expensive to obtain. For many developing countries that assumption is not valid, and the result is a potential disadvantage, relative to more-developed states, in the establishment of claims under these criteria.

Adoption of "Established" Legal Approaches

As there is a tendency to move with the "mainstream" on technical matters, so the definition and interpretation of international law has been susceptible to domination by a small number of states. This was, of course, especially true when many of today's states were colonies, with no effective voice in the creation of international law. Many of the principles that comprise international law were established during that era[28] — a problem that did not simply disappear with independence. The basis for future legal development was in large measure established in that earlier period, and in any event developed countries continued (by inclination and expertise) to dominate the processes by which new law was developed.

This trend was by no means universal,[29] and developing countries have increasingly assumed an activist role in international law. The problem remains, however, and is most acute when international law based on established (mainly Western) norms must be implemented in a local setting where it is irrelevant, or even

---

28   E. McWhinney, *United Nations Law-Making* (Paris: UNESCO, 1984) generally at 3–7, 37–38, and the following statement at 37: "It is on this basis that so much of 'classical' international law ... is now rejected or questioned by the 'new' countries of the Third World as 'Western' or 'Eurocentric' in character and hence as no longer authoritative and binding in the new, more richly pluralistic and inclusive world community of today...."

29   See *id.* at 213–235 on the nature of the transition in international law-making, as reflected by the 1982 LOS and the movement in the 1970s towards a New International Economic Order. On the increasing role of Africa and Asia in the development of international law, see T.O. Elias, *New Horizons in International Law* (The Netherlands: Sijthoff and Noordhoff, 1979) at 21–34.

destructive. For example, the accepted notion of "freedom of the seas" was imposed by colonial governments in Oceania—in full accordance with the international law of the period. That step directly contributed to the destruction of the marine tenure system in parts of the region,[30] and the tenure system was the basis of marine resource management in many areas (see discussion below). Post-independence governments largely accepted the concept of freedom of the seas, as well as its later erosion in favour of gradual "enclosure" of the oceans for Exclusive Economic Zones (EEZs) and other forms of jurisdiction enunciated in the Law of the Sea. These new forms of *state* jurisdiction did not, however, substitute for the *local* jurisdiction that had existed prior to the colonial period; nor were they a panacea for the problems of inshore fisheries.[31]

Inadequate Attention to Other Levels

The difficulty in dealing with localized approaches has broader implications. International law is by its nature state-centric; the state is the normal subject of international law,[32] and it is state behaviour that international law seeks to regulate. It is inevitable, therefore, that international environmental and resource law is based on the state's responsibility to take certain actions and refrain from others. In cases where authority is decentralized, it is possible for international legal expectations to be at odds with the most effective method of resource management. A state may be required, for example, to permit foreign fishing under generally accepted terms and conditions.[33] This requirement may not leave room for a local management authority that wishes to apply local rules.[34] International law strives for the valid

---

30   R.E. Johannes, "Traditional Marine Conservation Methods in Oceania and their Demise" (1978) 9 Annual Review of Ecology and Systematics 349 at 358.

31   On the low priority accorded small-scale fisheries in international legal negotiations, see J. Cordell, "Defending Customary Inshore Sea Rights" in K. Ruddle & T. Akimichi, eds., *Maritime Institutions in the South Pacific*, No. 17 Senri Ethnological Series (Osaka: National Museum of Ethnology, 1984) at 301–326. As Cordell notes at 303: "Small-scale fishermen have never been protagonists in the series of United Nations Law of the Sea Conventions...."

32   There are, of course, some exceptions to this general rule, such as the treatment of international organizations and "peoples" (without statehood) illustrated in the following International Court of Justice cases: "Reparation for Injuries Suffered in the Service of the United Nations" (1949) *ICJ Reports* 182; "International Status of South West Africa" (1950) *ICJ Reports* 146.

33   Article 62(2), 1982 LOS.

34   See below, section entitled "National Level." The protection and enforcement of local marine resource rights is recognized, for example, in the Solomon Islands. See G.B.K. Baines, "A Traditional Base for Inshore Fisheries Development in the Solomon Islands" in K. Ruddle & R.E. Johannes, eds., *The Traditional Knowledge and Management of Coastal Systems in Asia and the Pacific* (UNESCO, 1985). The fisheries law of Fiji also recognizes the rights of local resource "owners" to regulate and/or benefit from outside access to a fishery, with rights allocated as a component of the "mataqali" system of land tenure. See S. Iwakiri, "Mataqali of the Sea—A Study of the Customary Right on Reef and Lagoon in Fiji, South Pacific" (1983) 4(2) *Memoirs of the Kagashima University Research Center for the South Pacific* 133–143 at 134–136 and 142. On the role of traditional fishery rights in Fijian society, see also A. Ravuvu, *The Fijian Way of Life* (Suva: Institute of Pacific Studies, 1983) at 75.

objectives of predictable and widespread rules for interactions between states (and between a state and nationals of another state), but this very characteristic can be counterproductive for resource management, where the general rules are inapplicable or unacceptable. As a result, some accommodation must be made for local flexibility within general principles.

Another level of great potential importance to resource management is the region — a grouping of states bound by common interests on one or more issues.[35] Regional interpretation and application of international principles have been extremely important to the development of resource and environmental law; the regional level can be a crucial interim step between global generalities and specific measures.[36] While international law has proved more amenable to the regional than to the subnational level, there is still a tendency to view global agreement on an issue as inherently superior; and where the regional level conflicts with the global, international lawyers accord precedence to the latter. The regional level, closer as it is to national situations, deserves more attention for its law-creating possibilities.

NATIONAL LEVEL

At the national level, as was noted earlier, law has the potential for involvement in almost every aspect of policies for the promotion of sustainable development. From the perspective of donors, and, perhaps more important, from that of recipients, a number of issues arise concerning the effectiveness and appropriateness of development assistance as it relates to legal structures and systems in less-developed countries. There are two general types of problems involved: first, the nature of assistance given specifically for the development of legislative and regulatory schemes to promote sustainable development; and second, the impact of legal structures on the planning of projects not directly concerned with legal development. Some of these issues are explored below, in the context of examples from different development sectors and geographic areas.

Law and the Recognition of Local Structures

It is axiomatic that any assistance given in legal development must be cognizant of local laws and practices.[37] The problem can, however, be far more subtle and

---

35   It is important to bear in mind that the term "region" can have many different meanings and that a region can be defined on the basis of any number of criteria. For a survey of regional classifications and approaches, including those relating to environmental management, see D.M. Johnston & P.M. Saunders, "Ocean Boundary Issues and Developments in Regional Perspective" in D.M. Johnston & P.M. Saunders, eds., *Ocean Boundary-Making: Regional Issues and Developments* (London: Croom Helm, 1988) at 313–320.

36   See McWhinney, *supra,* note 28 at 8–11 for a discussion of the "regionalization" of international law.

37   This need for compatibility extends to recognition of "each nation's capability for policy development, institutional structures, administrative competence, and ability to train manage-

difficult than a simple review of formal legal sources would indicate. In many cases the "visible" legal structures will be carry-overs, perhaps with few or no changes, from the colonial period. There is a wealth of subnational practices, often with local authority equal to any legislative instrument, that may not appear in any statute book or compilation of cases. These practices can affect issues as fundamental to development as the nature of credit or the concepts of ownership of land or personal property.[38] In Oceania, this problem arises in the context of marine resources management — a sector that is either presently or potentially critical to national economic well-being in many Pacific Island Nations. If we leave aside the offshore tuna stocks, which are managed under different regimes,[39] the inshore resources of the reefs and lagoons offer substantial protein and employment possibilities, and raise a variety of management problems.[40]

The management of multispecies fisheries presents significant difficulties under the best of circumstances,[41] but becomes even more problematic when overlaid with unrecognized social factors and competing management systems. In the West, marine fisheries management generally proceeds from two related assumptions: the existence of a "common resource" with unlimited or relatively unlimited entry, and the need to modify that situation to reflect some form of property rights as a tool in the control of the fishery.[42] These assumptions lead directly to what have been termed "two institutional alternatives" for the managers of the resource:

---

ment, monitoring and enforcement personnel." See Mayda, *supra,* note 26 at 998. On the general problem of transferability of legal approaches in a development context, see J.A. Gardner, *Legal Imperialism* (Madison: University of Wisconsin, 1980) at 239–246.

38   For a discussion of the complexities involved in such elements as land tenure, credit, and capital formation in traditional societies — and particularly their integration with other aspects of the societal structure, such as religion— see R. Firth, "Capital, Saving and Credit in Peasant Societies: A Viewpoint From Economic Anthropology" in R. Firth & B. Yamey, eds., *Capital, Saving and Credit in Peasant Societies* (Chicago: Aldine, 1964) at 15.

39   The offshore tuna fishery operates under a range of bilateral and multilateral access arrangements. On the efforts at regional cooperation and control, see D. Doulman, "Distant-Water Fleet Operations and Regional Fisheries Cooperation" in D. Doulman, ed., *The Development of the Tuna Industry in the Pacific Region: An Analysis of Options* (Honolulu: East-West Center, 1987) at 33–52.

40   For a discussion of the cash income and protein contributions of small scale inshore fisheries in Fiji, see Iwakiri, *supra,* note 34 at 141.

41   "Unlike the stable single-species systems of accepted bioeconomic theory, fisheries tend to be highly variable, multiple-species systems with biological and social dynamics that are imperfectly understood and parameters that are extremely difficult to measure." J.A. Wilson, "The Economical Management of Multispecies Fisheries" (1982) 58 Land Econ. 417 at 417.

42   In essence, the reasoning reflects an underlying concern to avoid a "tragedy of the commons" as described by Hardin. See G. Hardin, "The Tragedy of the Commons" in G. Hardin & J. Baden, eds., *Managing The Commons* (San Francisco: W.H. Freeman, 1977) at 16.

1) [T]he establishment of sole-owner resource property rights, or 2) the simulation of the market outcomes ... through the application of taxes and subsidies or quasi-property rights (limited licenses, resource shares and so on).[43]

The alternatives are, however, predicated on the validity of the two assumptions — a common resource and unlimited entry. There are numerous instances in which other resource ownership patterns (neither completely "common" nor sole ownership) pre-existed the introduction of "modern" fisheries law. In Oceania, Johannes and others[44] have documented the existence of marine tenure systems dating back hundreds of years before colonial intervention:

> The most widespread single marine conservation measure employed in Oceania, and the most important, was reef and lagoon tenure. The system was simple: the right to fish in a particular area was controlled by a clan, chief or family, who thus regulated the exploitation of their own marine resources.[45]

Imposition of a legal structure based on Western notions of common fishery resources and *ferae naturae*[46] would be at odds with a system in which a form of ownership of these resources, or some right to the benefits of their exploitation, was a long-standing and accepted practice. This was acknowledged in some colonial and post-independence legislation, which preserved aspects of the traditional tenure systems,[47] but in many cases the existing tenure was destroyed in the colonial era.[48]

Further, it is not sufficient to assume that the marine tenure system itself replicated the functions of sole-owner property rights. The tenure system was normally based upon *groups* as the beneficiaries of such tenure, with an array of limited-use rights which might not be recognized by a Western legal system as property rights, and which would require very careful definition prior to protection by formal laws.[49]

---

43   See Wilson, *supra,* note 41 at 418.

44   In addition to the examples cited here, for a survey of the literature on "informal" property rights as they relate to fisheries, see A.T. Charles, "Fishery Socioeconomics: A Survey" (1988) 64 Land Econ. 276 at 282–283.

45   See Johannes, *supra,* note 30 at 350. Properly viewed, this tenure was not so much a "measure" as the institutional *basis* for the development and enforcement of measures.

46   The concept of *ferae naturae* as applied to fisheries would define fish as a common resource, not subject to individual ownership or property rights until captured or controlled.

47   Baines, *supra,* note 34 at 43–45, outlines the protection accorded traditional rights (including rights to marine resources) by legislatures and courts in the Solomon Islands. This extends to the general statement of the Provincial Government Act, 1981, s. 3(7): "Nothing in this section shall be construed as affecting traditional rights, privileges and usages in respect of land and fisheries in any parts of the Solomon Islands." He also notes at 48 that the courts have tempered such resource rights by refusing to extend them to control over right of passage through the affected area.

48   See Johannes, *supra,* note 30 at 356.

49   These rights are often non-geographical in nature, focusing rather on a particular species. Additionally, there may be various categories of rights "layered" upon each other and defined

Law and Value Choices

The choice of a regulatory or legislative approach to the implementation of a particular policy may appear to be "value-neutral," in that the key decisions are presumed to have been made in the earlier process of policy development. Such a choice can, however, carry with it important implications (whether positive or negative) for values of many types in the affected society. The *method* employed in regulation is more than a mechanistic or technical choice — it can have broader ramifications, which are not the direct concern of the technical advisor but are nonetheless critical to the success or failure of a scheme. Problems of this kind are encountered in the application of external values to the problem of range degradation and desertification through overgrazing. Range degradation is an issue of global scope, and of surprising intractability in many areas:

> There are few sectors of the environment that have been more badly damaged by man's activities than the grazing lands of the world. There are few fields of economic development characterized by greater or more destructive blunders than those involving attempts to improve the productivity of grazing lands and the domestic animals depending on them.[50]

One direct approach to the problem of overgrazing is the imposition of some control on the number of livestock permitted for a given area of land. This can be done by economic incentives or disincentives, or by the use of simple numerical limits and associated penalties. In either case, the assumption is that "rational" economic behaviour will ensure numbers decline to levels that permit long-term use of the grazing lands. The basic assumption is not, however, valid in cases where livestock ownership carries significance beyond its normal commercial value. Thus, cattle may provide income or economic security in ways not usually calculated as a direct benefit from the industry. In Botswana, for example, cattle not only provide important informal employment and self-employment opportunities,[51] but can also be essential to arable agriculture insofar as they are used for ploughing and transport.[52] These secondary economic aspects must be included in any assessment or prediction of responses to a given regulatory option.

Moreover, cattle in many societies possess a separate symbolic significance as a prime indicator of wealth and social prestige. Again, this is true of Botswana, where the traditional value accorded to cattle has survived the introduction of

---

partly by area, partly by season, and partly by purpose and mode of exploitation. See Baines, *supra,* note 34 at 45–46 and 48–49 on the complexity of the rights and their application.

50   R.F. Dasmann, J.P. Milton & P.H. Freeman, *Ecological Principles for Economic Development* (London: John Wiley and Sons, 1973) at 78.

51   Although agriculture in Botswana in the late 1970s and early 1980s provided "only 7% of formal employment ... the number of people informally or self-employed in agriculture far exceed[ed] the total in all sectors of formal employment." Livestock accounted for 80 percent of agricultural employment. See Government of Botswana, *National Development Plan V: 1979–1985* (Gaborone: Government Printer, 1980) at 133, 19.

52   D. Curtis, "The Social Organization of Ploughing" (1972) 4 Botswana Notes and Records 67.

commercial ranching and beef export on a large scale. Throughout the late 1970s and early 1980s, when attempts were made to improve control of grazing land, it was never possible to introduce significant stock control measures, especially in communal areas.[53] Here, as in other sectors, the "obvious" technical solution runs up against societal mores that would make its legal application impossible.

Law and Non-formal Inputs

Modern legal structures tend to rely on what might be termed "formal" sources for their definition and implementation. In order to gain the benefits of consistency and predictability, it is necessary to ensure as wide a geographic scope as possible (often the nation), and to base expectations of behaviour on rules that are clearly stated and widely disseminated in written form. The information base for most resource management systems is found in the scientific information provided by government agencies or others operating on their behalf.[54] Enforcement is assumed to take place, again, through the "legitimate" agencies of the state, or its delegates where necessary. These and other characteristics of "developed" legal systems have been exported to developing countries both during and after the colonial period, and in many cases have proven inappropriate to local conditions.

It is possible to identify at least five general stages in the development and implementation of environmental and resource management policies. First, a period of *problem identification* and *policy initiative* is required. During this phase, basic information gathering and research may take place, political direction and will must be stimulated, and, if possible, general criteria and standards must be established. The second stage involves further *focus* and *planning,* including more detailed research, definition of the scope of a problem, and, perhaps, drafting of legislative approaches. Third, a phase that might loosely be termed *legislative* would confirm criteria and standards in law, as well as institute necessary management schemes (licensing, etc.) and penalties for breaches. The first three stages encompass the development and initial implementation of a policy, but at least two more phases are essential. *Enforcement* must be carried out to prevent or punish breaches, and to improve the data available on the environmental problem or the resource. Finally, results must be *monitored* in order to evaluate the success or failure of a response and to provide data for any re-initiation of research and planning.

---

53   The communal lands of Botswana (approximately 70 percent of the total land area) fall under a system of communal ownership by a tribe. Traditionally, the chiefs could allocate *use rights* (e.g., grazing, housing), but not ownership. This system was continued with administrative changes by the Tribal Land Act of 1968, which vested control in Land Boards. The fundamental difficulty of imposing any rigid management control on this common resource remained. See T. Greenhow, "The Tribal Grazing Land Policy and Integrated Land-use Planning: A District View" (1978) 10 Botswana Notes and Records 159 at 161.

54   Charles, *supra,* note 44 at 289, notes this concentration on the "acquisition and use of biological data," and the extent to which it tends to exclude other disciplines from the management equation; the situation for non-formal inputs is only exacerbated.

Given the continued existence of the necessary institutional structures (whether as village authorities or in some other form),[55] "non-formal" systems can have productive inputs at a number of these stages. Traditional structures have often proven their capacity to provide information of great value to resource management systems. Pre-colonial knowledge of the environment (land and marine) was, in many societies, both broad and functionally related to exploitation activities, but this information was generally accorded little weight by colonial administrations, being lumped together with other "superstitions" as non-scientific and largely unusable.[56] Even modern writers can dismiss the possibility of integrating a region's traditional knowledge in management systems because it is based on superstition, without reference to the validity of the information.[57]

In many geographic areas, the traditional capacity extended beyond information to another function suggested earlier — creation of schemes or systems to manage a resource. In Oceania, at least eleven specific resource management approaches were employed by rights holders under the marine tenure systems.[58] Some of these approaches, in different forms, would be familiar today: closed areas, species size limits, protected areas for special purposes (e.g., turtle breeding), and closed seasons. In some instances, there was even a version of the modern Canadian practice of shifting resource "quotas," in that rights holders might voluntarily reallocate some of their rights to a disadvantaged group or village.[59] It is perhaps overstating the case to say that "[m]ost island peoples observed a complex set of rules governing fisheries which ensured sound management of the resource."[60] However, even if such rules did not always ensure sound management, it is true that they existed and in many cases served the purposes of resource management and protection for which they were devised.

It is in the general area of enforcement that traditional systems still display their most distinct advantages, especially for developing countries. Artisanal fisheries, in comparison with industrial fisheries, "consist of many more units ... and they land at many more points along the coast."[61] Added to this is the lower value of each

---

55   The traditional structure may find administrative expression and cohesion in new bodies, such as the Tribal Land Boards in Botswana, *supra,* or the Native Lands Trust Board in Fiji. See Iwakiri, *supra,* note 34 at 20.

56   A.L. Dahl, "Traditional Environmental Management in New Caledonia: A Review of Existing Knowledge" (1985) 18 SPREP Topic Review (Noumea: South Pacific Regional Environment Programme) at 1.

57   R. Lawson & M. Robinson, "Artisanal Fisheries in West Africa: Problems of Management Implementation" (1983) 7(4) Marine Policy at 288.

58   See Johannes, *supra,* note 30 at 352.

59   *Id.* at 351. The voluntary aspect does not seem to have been replicated in the modern version.

60   See A.L. Dahl, *supra,* note 56 at 7.

61   See Lawson & Robinson, *supra,* note 57 at 279.

catch, making intensive management efforts uneconomic. To a fisheries department in a developing country, with already stretched resources, local authority structures — with vested interests in the fishery — may be an attractive means of ensuring enforcement of conservation or other management measures. These structures, when supported by the additional authority of the legal system, can provide much more effective sanctions against violators than the police and courts alone:

> The result is a regime in which cultural rules are backed by the legal apparatus of the state.... The formal rules of law need to correspond with existing cultural rules unless the state is willing to devote considerable resources to enforcement. Illegality is rarely a significant deterrent in and of itself.[62]

The alternative to the use of local authority is often both less effective and more costly. In the extreme case, it will result in a management structure that fails simply for lack of resources to implement it properly:

> Legislation that weakens or nullifies marine tenure laws increases the government's responsibilities and places additional burdens on typically understaffed and underfunded fisheries departments.[63]

The final phase noted above is that of monitoring. Some attempt must be made to map the results of management efforts, so that the approach can be corrected and improved, if necessary. This requirement is directly tied to that of enforcement, as enforcement agencies will be in the best position to gather (although perhaps not to analyse) data on the resource. For this reason, the advantages of traditional structures in enforcement also apply to monitoring, at least with respect to the data-gathering role.

The systems described here are not restricted to small islands in the Pacific. One source of similar examples is the Mediterranean, where it was found that "[l]ocal-level management provides a relevant and feasible set of institutional arrangements for managing some coastal fisheries."[64] In Atlantic Canada and elsewhere, there is further evidence of the capacity for local management using accepted, albeit informal or unwritten, rules:

> There are many ethnographic studies ... which show how fishermen, through informal arrangements, are regulating their fishery. They control access to fishing grounds and monitor each other's behaviour at sea. Thus, the fishery does not always resemble a game like Hobbesian anarchy when Common Property Theory is applied.[65]

---

62 C. Dahl, "Traditional Marine Tenure: A Basis for Artisanal Fisheries Management" (1988) 12(1) Marine Policy at 45.

63 See Johannes, *supra,* note 30 at 360.

64 F. Berkes, "Local-level Management and the Commons Problem: A Comparative Study of Turkish Coastal Fisheries" (1986) 10(3) Marine Policy at 228.

65 S. Jentoft, "Models of Fishery Development: The Cooperative Approach" (1985) 9(4) Marine Policy at 327.

Examples are not confined to fisheries, but extend to agriculture, environmental control,[66] and other sectors. In a discussion of South Pacific environmental legislation, Venkatesh and Va'ai noted that for predominantly rural countries, environmental management is likely to rely quite heavily on traditional structures:

> [E]nvironmental control programmes must not only, as far as possible, blend in with customary practices but must also depend to a large extent on customary institutions to enforce them.[67]

Law and Costs and Capacities

Adoption of a particular regulatory approach will normally have financial and other implications that, particularly for developing countries, will directly affect the viability of a particular scheme. Administrative capacity in general has been identified by Hardin and others[68] as an important factor in the selection of responses to environmental problems. What cannot be afforded, or what cannot be supported by available technical resources, will probably not be implemented. Assumptions about the availability of budgets, trained staff, and other resources can be extremely dangerous when the validity of an approach depends upon the existence of those elements. Just as "appropriate technology" has become widely accepted as a fundamental need for many development activities, so there is an argument for the use of "appropriate bureaucracy." This issue arises in a number of contexts, as is illustrated by the following examples.

The development of methodologies for assessing marine fish stocks has been a major advance in the management of these resources, and has enabled the adoption of regulatory approaches such as quota management. It must be recognized, however, that the application of these theories (and therefore of the associated regulatory schemes) requires substantial inputs of government money and expertise — inputs of a magnitude that many developing countries may be unwilling or unable to devote to one resource sector. The difficulty is particularly acute in the case of the information upon which these systems depend for their operation. It is clear that the application of the statistical methods that underlie stock assessment is dependent upon reliable and extensive raw data on the fishery — data that are expensive and difficult to obtain. Without this fundamental input, the entire approach may be rendered invalid; therefore, caution must be exercised in exporting management schemes that, although theoretically valid, are practically inapplicable.

---

66   See A.L. Dahl, *supra,* note 56 for descriptions of the traditional knowledge base relating to both agriculture and environment in pre-colonial New Caledonia.

67   S. Venkatesh & S. Va'ai, "An Overview of Environmental Protection Legislation in the South Pacific Countries" (1983) 13 SPREP Topic Review (Noumea: South Pacific Regional Environment Programme) with update by M. Pulea at 43.

68   See Hardin, *supra,* note 42 at 23. See also D.H. Henning, *Environmental Policy and Administration* (New York: American Elsevier, 1974) at 36. Note that this issue is often discussed in terms of administrative capacity required to *solve* problems, whereas it can also arise as a *cause* in itself through lack of monitoring or other capabilities.

A further example is found in the use of environmental impact assessment (EIA) as a tool for managing environmental impacts of major development projects — a practice that has been widespread for many years.[69] EIA, in a number of forms, has played a fundamental role in attempts by development assistance agencies to ensure the environmental validity of projects they fund.[70] In some of its many permutations, however, EIA can be a complex, time-consuming, and expensive process, which depends for its success on extensive governmental capacities. Again, this raises fundamental questions with respect to "appropriate bureaucracies":

> It is now quite evident that detailed, expensive, time-consuming and sophisticated EIA techniques used in many developed contries at present are unlikely to be of much practical value for use in developing countries in an operational sense.[71]

To identify this problem is not to say that EIA is necessarily inappropriate or ineffective for developing countries. Rather, it must be adapted to local conditions and capacities, particularly through critical examinations of the choices of methodology and institutional arrangements, which can greatly influence cost and complexity.[72]

A problem that exists as a corollary to the costs/capacities issue is the creation of new dependency relationships through the imposition of particular environmental requirements on development projects. If a development agency insists upon a certain *methodology* of environmental assessment (as opposed to establishing *objectives* for the project), it may force developing countries to continually rely on consultants and other "experts" from the donor nations to implement the mandated schemes. The problem is exacerbated when a number of donor agencies adopt separate approaches to assessment, making it impossible for any one recipient country to maintain the expertise to meet all of the varying requirements. Although an assessment under these conditions may be successful as a "one-off" exercise, the long-term developmental impact is less positive than if an approach within the capacities of the recipient nation were evolved or adapted — thus leaving behind the ability and experience to apply the techniques to other projects.

Law as a Causal Factor

A final point to be kept in mind regarding law's application to sustainable development is the potential for legal structures to function as one of the *causes* of

---

69   For a survey of the application of EIA in developing countries, see A.K. Biswas & Q. Geping, eds., *Environmental Impact Assessment for Developing Countries* (Natural Resources and the Environment Series Vol. 19) (London: United Nations University, 1987).

70   See Rich, *supra,* note 4 at 713–714 on the United States' use of environmental impact statements in development projects; and Muldoon, *supra,* note 3 at 46–47 on CIDA's Environmental Assessment Framework.

71   A.K. Biswas & Q. Geping, "Guidelines for Environmental Impact Assessment in Developing Countries" in Biswas & Geping, *supra,* note 69 at 192.

72   *Id.* at 217–218.

environmental or resource management problems. Lawyers are accustomed to thinking of the law as primarily a tool for the *solution* of problems, and it is important to be aware that the reverse can be true. Land tenure systems associated with communal overgrazing are a familiar example of this relationship: the very nature of a country's land law can contribute to the degradation of grazing lands.[73] Similarly, legal systems imposed in Oceania have been identified as one significant source of the breakdown of marine tenure and its associated management structures.[74] In cases such as this, the "legal factor" rarely operates alone,[75] but it is nonetheless instructive for the legal advisor to observe that past legal approaches have been capable of contributing greatly to environmental degradation, and that there is no reason to suppose it cannot happen again. In proposing the latest solution, the lawyer runs the risk of creating tomorrow's problem.

CONCLUSIONS

The foregoing examination of some issues associated with law in the context of development assistance highlights a number of important challenges for the future. First, many would argue that the progress made in international environmental law has slowed considerably in recent years. This is of concern to all states, but nowhere more so than to less-developed countries. These states still rely to a greater extent than others on the direction afforded by international law in establishing their environmental and resource management standards. Whereas some developed countries might decide that they possess the internal capacity to initiate their own regulatory approaches, many developing states will continue to find guidance in uniform principles evolved at the international level. If that level is weakened as a reference or starting point, these states will be the most affected.

A related challenge, and one that has been recognized and taken up to some extent, concerns the need for assistance programs that follow directly from new international obligations. If such obligations are to have any real chance of implementation in large parts of the world, there will have to be substantial assistance aimed directly at helping developing countries meet the new

---

73 This relationship was, of course, central to Hardin's analysis of the commons problem — it hinged on a land tenure system that was not adequate to the management demands it was required to support. See Hardin, *supra,* note 42. The case of Botswana, discussed *supra,* provides an excellent example of this causal relationship between the land tenure system and mismanagement of grazing lands.

74 See Johannes, *supra,* note 30 at 356. Johannes identified three main causes of this collapse: the introduction of cash economies, the deterioration of traditional authority, and the introduction and imposition of new laws and practices.

75 The most common interaction of this type will be with some new technology that, when introduced, "overloads" the capacity of the existing legal and other systems to regulate exploitation of the resource. See C. Dahl, *supra,* note 62 on this problem in the inshore fisheries context. With respect to land use and the impacts of new technologies and methods, see G. Hardin, "The Ethical Implications of Carrying Capacity" in Hardin & Baden, *supra,* note 42 at 113–122.

requirements. Particular attention should be given to identified issues of global concern. Where possible, discussions on the structure and quantity of this assistance should be initiated as close in time as possible to the establishment of the obligations, in order to maintain momentum and to ensure that the assistance is relevant to the objectives of the international community.

At the level of national legal systems and the assistance provided for their development, there is clearly a need for further efforts at integrating traditional, subnational resource management systems into "modern" management structures. This task extends to other disciplines as well,[76] but the final step in any integration of this source of information and authority will be legal in nature; otherwise it will not achieve the recognition and acceptance of government agencies or of those from outside the local area who wish to exploit a resource.

The problem is made more difficult by the fact that it is not necessarily possible to adopt traditional systems in their entirety and assume that this will bring success. In too many instances, technological innovations have thrown the system out of balance — management measures that were adequate to a canoe fishery confined to one lagoon will not meet all the problems encountered when a trawler is introduced. The very institutions on which traditional authority was based may have been irretrievably weakened over the years, to the point that they cannot provide effective management. In addition, many of the traditional approaches are flawed in one or more respects[77] that would prevent their complete adoption. A careful evaluation will be needed in each case to determine what will and what will not serve to strengthen a country's overall resource management capabilities. A number of potential factors have been suggested as central to such an analysis, including resource scarcity, economic structure of the community, and the type of exploitative technology applied.[78] It has also been suggested that some rights-holding patterns are too complex or too fragmented to sustain management of any but the simplest

---

76   At the very least, this effort involves fisheries biologists and managers, anthropologists, economists, and administrators.

77   These "flaws" are partly the product of interaction between an existing system and some new factor — whether it be technological (e.g., the introduction of poison for fishing, more efficient gear types) or economic (e.g., the new cash value for turtle products). The result is a system that is no longer in balance. See Johannes, *supra,* note 30 at 355, for a survey of abuses within traditional management regimes (some pre-existing the introduction of new forces).

78   See C.L. Dahl, *supra,* note 62 at 40:

Five social conditions appear to be important to the functioning of [traditional marine tenure systems]. They are: resource scarcity; the ability to define resource boundaries; group/territorial identification; the type of technology used to exploit the resource; and the economic structure of the society.

See also Lawson & Robinson, *supra,* note 57 at 288, where it is noted that fishermen who range widely in search of migratory species (although remaining within one country) will be almost impossible to control under localized management schemes.

fishery.[79] Given the present state of knowledge, one of the initial needs will be the development of an acceptable methodology, and practical process, for establishing an inventory of traditional rights claimed in a particular area.[80]

The challenge of sustainable development will continue to be partly a challenge for legal development, nationally and internationally. The problems discussed here, and the future tasks suggested, will require the close attention of both developing countries and development assistance agencies if appropriate legal approaches are to be defined and applied on a global basis.

---

79 See Cordell, *supra,* note 31 at 309.

80 On the complexity of this issue, see R. Pollnac, "Investigating Territorial Use Rights Among Fishermen" in Ruddle & Akimachi, *supra,* note 31, 285–300 at 294–296. Consideration must be given to such factors as boundaries, size and composition of rights-holding units, the recognized legality of the claims, and problems of equity in allocating *within* the group holding rights.

CANADIAN GAS EXPORT POLICY: PART OF THE PROBLEM[1]

Janet Keeping

This paper examines the deregulation of natural gas in light of the principles of sustainable development. The paper will focus on the deregulation of gas exports and conclude with some recommendations about how Canadian gas export policy might be reformulated in a manner more consistent with the goal of achieving sustainable development.

NATURAL GAS DEREGULATION

From the early 1970s to the mid-1980s, the Canadian governments' approach to the natural gas industry was marked by heavy and complex regulation. During the 1980s, pressure increased to relieve the natural gas industry of this regulatory burden. There were two main sources of this impetus: great dissatisfaction with the National Energy Program[2] in the producing provinces (especially Alberta) and industry, and an ideological swing in business and government that put greater faith in the market. Other, more specific motivations were also at work.[3]

Government initiatives to deregulate petroleum and natural gas got substantially underway with the Western Accord, an agreement concluded in March 1985 amongst the federal government and the governments of the three producing provinces, British Columbia, Alberta, and Saskatchewan. As regards natural gas, the Accord was largely an agreement to agree, and provided that

> [a] task force of senior officials from the federal government and the producing provinces will work with all interested parties, including consuming provinces and industry, to develop a more flexible market-sensitive pricing mechanism on or before November 1, 1985.

That deadline was reached, albeit barely, when on October 31, 1985, the Agreement on Natural Gas Markets and Prices was signed by the governments of Canada,

---

1   The maxim "If you're not part of the solution, you're part of the problem" is credited to Eldridge Cleaver, American black-power activist and author. His remark has reappeared in recent, mainstream environmental literature. See Craig McInnes, "Can We Save This Planet?" in *Globe and Mail* (15 April 1989) D1.

2   The National Energy Program consisted in a series of federal legislative and policy initiatives first announced on 28 October 1980. The three primary objectives of the program were to increase the security of Canada's energy supply, to promote opportunities for the participation of Canadian individuals and companies in the energy industry, and to promote fairness in that industry: *Canadian Energy Program Reporter* (Don Mills: CCH Canadian, 1982) at 507.

3   For example, one objective of deregulation was to allow central Canadian industries the opportunity to acquire, for delivery to themselves, their own reserves of gas in the producing provinces. For background to this aspect of deregulation, see the report of the Ontario Energy Board on the use of natural gas as a feedstock in Ontario, E.B.R.L.G. 26 (Toronto, 10 February 1984) (Chair: R.H. Clendining).

British Columbia, Saskatchewan, and Alberta. The Agreement, as its name suggests, addressed two main issues: the pricing and the marketing of natural gas. The significance of these provisions of the Agreement will be briefly summarized. However, the Agreement also had implications for the export of natural gas. This aspect of the Agreement, and the regulatory response to it, will be examined in greater detail in this paper.

Essentially, the parties to the Agreement undertook to deregulate the price of Canadian natural gas. And, true to their word, the elaborate administrative structure pursuant to which gas prices had been fixed since the mid-1970s has been put into a state of suspended animation. Although the legislative scheme is still largely intact, governments no longer apply it so as to regulate the price of Canadian gas.[4] The marketing of natural gas was also radically changed. No longer would consumers of gas be confined to buying their gas supplies from local distribution companies. Direct purchases from western producers were to be possible. These have indeed materialized, although their limitation to primarily large-volume — that is, industrial — consumers has been, with very good reason, controversial.[5]

But what about deregulation's implications for gas exports? Early on it was recognized that market forces would not be able to take firm hold on the gas sector unless restrictions on the flow of exports were loosened. The regulation of short-term[6] gas exports had already been partially liberalized by the time the 1985 Agreement was concluded.[7] Governments' concern in the Agreement was, in this context, largely to ensure the relaxation of restrictions on long-term[8] gas export arrangements. To that end, Clause 16 of the Agreement anticipated that

> reviews of surplus tests underway or shortly to be initiated by the National Energy Board and by the appropriate provincial authorities will result in significantly freer access to domestic and export markets and thus will contribute to the achievement of the market-oriented pricing system contemplated in the Agreement.

As is clear from this clause, there is a provincial component to gas export regulation, and the Agreement went on to address specifically provincial jurisdiction in this area:

> The producing provinces shall retain their right to condition the removal of natural gas from the province to protect provincial public interest. Notwithstanding this basic right of ownership, the

---

4   For a detailed description of how this was accomplished, see "Alberta Petroleum Marketing Commission — Commentary — Natural Gas Pricing" in *Canada Energy Law Service*, vol. 3 (Don Mills: Richard DeBoo, 1989).

5   See, for example, J. Keeping, "Righteous Indignation, The Public Interest and Deregulation of Natural Gas" (1988) 21 Resources 5.

6   These are exports with a term of up to twenty-four months.

7   See "National Energy Board — Commentary — Export and Import of Oil, Natural Gas and Electricity — Natural Gas — 'Spot' Sales" in *Canada Energy Law Service*, vol. 1, *supra*, note 4.

8   Gas export arrangements may have terms of up to twenty-five or thirty years.

producing provinces do not intend to use this right to frustrate the intent of this Agreement. Specifically:

> (i) Alberta and British Columbia will initiate a review of their respective surplus tests to ensure that the tests will contribute to the achievement of the market-oriented pricing system contemplated in this Agreement.[9]

Although this paper is concerned with the National Energy Board's response to this aspect of the Agreement, two comments on the provincial role in regulating gas exports are in order. First, both Alberta and British Columbia reviewed their surplus determination procedures as contemplated by the Agreement, with the predictable result that surplus determination criteria were liberalized.[10] (Some interesting observations could be made at this juncture, especially on Alberta's handling of this issue, but they are beyond the scope of this paper.) Second, as seems so often to be the case, issues relating to the division of powers loom as potential obstacles to effective policy formulation and implementation.

When the 1985 Agreement was signed, the National Energy Board (NEB) was already reconsidering its surplus determination procedures—specifically, it was in the throes of a re-evaluation of the criteria according to which it decides how much gas is available for export. This process had been launched shortly after the signing of the Western Accord. The procedures in place at the time employed a formula related to gas reserves: this was the "25A1 Reserves Formula," which "required the setting aside of reserves equal to 25 times the current year's Canadian requirements plus the maximum quantities exportable under existing export licences before new exports could be licensed."[11]

Among the Board's reasons for conducting a review of the 25A1 Reserves Formula was the change to "a market-sensitive domestic pricing regime as contemplated by the Western Accord."[12] Hearings were held in November and December 1985, and in April 1986 the Board issued a decision that adopted a reserves-to-production ratio as the method of assessing gas available for export.[13] This method aimed at ensuring that gas would be exported from Canada only when the Canadian natural gas reserves-to-production ratio was at least fifteen—that is, when evidence could establish that a fifteen-year Canadian supply was assured.

---

9   Agreement among the Governments of Canada, Alberta, British Columbia and Saskatchewan on Natural Gas Markets and Prices, 31 October 1985, Clause 23(i).

10   Energy Resources Conservation Board, *Gas Supply Protection for Alberta: Policies and Procedures* (Proceeding 860226) (Calgary: ERCB, March 1987); Ministry of Energy, Mines and Petroleum Resources, *Review of the B.C. Natural Gas Surplus Determination Procedures: Reasons for Decision* (July 1987).

11   National Energy Board, *Reasons for Decision in the Matter of Phase 1, The Surplus Determination Procedures Phase of the Gas Export Omnibus Hearing, 1985* (Ottawa: Minister of Supply and Services, April 1986) at 23.

12   *Id.* at 3.

13   *Id.*

In rejecting the continued appropriateness of the 25A1 Reserves Formula and substituting the reserves-to-production ratio, the Board state that

the large inventories of natural gas associated with the 25A1 Reserves Formula are not required in a market-sensitive pricing environment. Such inventories could result in excessive inventory carrying costs and national economic inefficiency. The Board believes that the new market-sensitive pricing policy should, increasingly over time, assist in the balancing of supply and demand. The Board expects to be able to place increasing reliance in the future on the responsiveness of supply and demand to price and less reliance on the size of currently established reserves in protecting future Canadian requirements.[14]

This retreat from the 25A1 Reserves Formula was not, however, good enough. In late October 1986, the Minister of Energy, Mines and Resources wrote to the Chairman of the Board, essentially inviting the NEB to rethink its conclusions regarding the determination of surplus for export. The Board accepted that invitation, and the matter was once more set down for public hearings. In July 1987, the Board abandoned the reserves-to-production ratio, in its place adopting what is now in force — an approach referred to as a Market-Based Procedure. As the Board stated in its decision:

With respect to the existing procedures, ... it would now be anomalous and contrary to free market operation if the level of gas supply to Canadians were to be determined by other than market forces. For this reason, the Board finds the existing procedures to be no longer appropriate....

The new procedure, which will be referred to as the Market-Based Procedure, is founded on the premise that the marketplace will generally operate in such a way that Canadian requirements for natural gas will be met at fair market prices.[15]

The Board's abandonment of the reserves-to-production ratio was achieved over the objections of some participants in the hearing, who argued that that procedure remained appropriate. There was, on the other hand, a great deal of support for a change, most of which was quite strongly in favour of greater reliance on the market. A handful of participants opposed both the existing and proposed market-based mechanisms, arguing that "the current procedures did not give adequate protection and proposed a longer protection period."[16] For example, the Consumers' Association of Canada proposed that Canadian natural gas requirements be protected for at least thirty years,[17] and the Sierra Club of Western Canada recommended that exports be terminated altogether since, in its view, "any discussion of surplus determinations is superfluous. With finite resources there can be no surpluses."[18]

---

14 *Id.* at 23.

15 National Energy Board, *Reasons for Decision in the Matter of Review of Natural Gas Surplus Determination Procedures* (Ottawa: Minister of Supply and Services, July 1987) at 24.

16 *Id.* at 3.

17 See the submission and final argument of the Consumers' Association of Canada, dated 27 February and 19 May 1987, respectively.

18 See the submission of the Sierra Club of Western Canada, dated 9 March 1987 at 8.

Section 118(a) of the National Energy Board Act states:

On an application for a licence, the Board shall have regard to all considerations that appear to it to be relevant and, without limiting the generality of the foregoing, the Board shall

(a) satisfy itself that the quantity of oil, gas or power to be exported does not exceed the surplus remaining after due allowance has been made for the reasonably foreseeable requirements for use in Canada having regard, in the case of an application to export oil or gas, to the trends in the discovery of oil or gas in Canada ...[19]

The NEB's decision adopting the Market-Based Procedure recognizes this statutory obligation to ensure that proposed exports are surplus to reasonably foreseeable Canadian requirements for gas:

The Board will act in two ways to ensure that natural gas to be licensed for export is surplus to reasonably foreseeable Canadian requirements: one will be in the context of public hearings to consider applications to export natural gas; the other will be by monitoring Canadian energy markets on an ongoing basis.[20]

There are three components to the public hearing process referred to by the Board. The first is a complaints procedure. The Board observed in its decision that "gas should not be authorized for export if Canadian users have not had an opportunity to buy gas for their needs on terms and conditions similar to those of the proposed export."[21] Accordingly, "[w]hen an application for export is filed with the Board, interested parties will have an opportunity to examine the various elements of the proposal. It will be open to domestic users of natural gas to come forward and object to the export on the grounds that they cannot obtain additional supplies of gas under contract on terms and conditions, including price, similar to those in the export proposal."[22] The second component of the hearing process is consideration of the applicant's "export impact assessment." These assessments are to address "the ability of the Canadian gas producing sector to satisfy Canadian needs, given the proposed export."[23] The third component is a public-interest determination by the Board. The Board recognizes in this context its obligation to ensure that gas exports are in the Canadian public interest.

The Board's decision identifies two aspects to its undertaking to monitor Canadian energy markets on an ongoing basis. The first is a role it has played previously: it will continue to produce assessments of Canadian energy supply and demand at approximately two-year intervals. Second, it undertakes to produce, from time to time, analyses of Canadian natural gas supply, demand, and prices.

---

19   National Energy Board Act, R.S.C. 1985, c. N-7, s. 118(a).

20   National Energy Board, *supra*, note 15 at 24.

21   *Id.* at 24.

22   *Id.* at 24–25.

23   *Id.* at 25.

SUSTAINABLE DEVELOPMENT

This section attempts to identify the principles of sustainable development most applicable to Canadian natural gas policy. What guidance can be found in sustainable development literature for the determination of exportable surplus and, more generally, for the granting of export licences?

The central tenet of sustainable development seems to be that present citizens of the world should act in a way that leaves future generations with at least as wide a range of options as that enjoyed today. The Brundtland Commission Report defines sustainable development as development that "meets the needs of the present without compromising the ability of future generations to meet their own needs."[24] The report by the Experts Group on Environmental Law, which advised the Brundtland Commission, nicely encapsulates this duty to consider future needs in Article 2 of its General Principles Concerning Natural Resources and Environmental Interferences. Article 2 addresses "[c]onservation for present and future generations," and provides that "[s]tates shall ensure that the environment and natural resources are conserved and used for the benefit of present and future generations."[25]

There are, then, two aspects to the broad notion of "intergenerational equity"[26] advanced by both the Commission itself and its group of legal experts: conservation of resources and environmental protection. Both are applicable to reflections on natural gas export policy.

Conservation of natural gas is of clear importance. Natural gas is a fossil fuel that, while now plentiful in Canada and some other countries, is nonrenewable and thus finite in supply. The implications of the consumption of natural gas for the environment are more equivocal. On the one hand, the environmental degradation caused by the burning of fossil fuels has been documented beyond dispute. On the other hand, it is widely recognized that natural gas is environmentally superior to either oil or coal as a fuel: "Of all of the fossil fuels, natural gas has the least harmful environmental impact."[27] As a result, natural gas has been said to have a major role

---

24 World Commission on Environment and Development, *Our Common Future* (Oxford: Oxford University Press, 1987) (Chair: G.H. Brundtland) at 8.

25 Experts Group on Environmental Law of the World Commission on Environment and Development, *Environmental Protection and Sustainable Development: Legal Principles and Recommendations* (London: Graham & Trotman/Martinus Nijhoff, 1987) (Chair: R.D. Munro) at 42.

26 The concept of intergenerational equity is well known in the literature on, and jurisprudence relating to, public utility regulation. For an example of its application in a Canadian context, see the discussion of how income tax is to be accounted for in "British Columbia Utilities Commission — Commentary — Cost of Service — (d) Income Taxes" in *Canada Energy Law Service*, vol. 2, *supra*, note 4.

27 Standing Senate Committee on Energy and Natural Resources, *Natural Gas Deregulation and Marketing* (12th Report) (September 1988) (Chair: E.A. Hastings) at 1.

to play in the achievement of an environmentally sound energy strategy. Even some of those who see the "pursuit of renewables and efficiency ... [as] the only safe and cost-effective way to slow global warming" recognize the significance of natural gas "as a transition fuel since it produces less carbon per unit of energy than do the other fossil fuels."[28] There is, then, some tension between the need to conserve natural gas for future generations and the possibility that very great quantities of natural gas will be needed to bridge the gap between present energy consumption patterns and those that will ultimately prove sustainable.

Another important theme of the Brundtland Commission Report, and work derivative from it, is that sustainable development must be achieved worldwide, or it will not be achieved at all. In the Commission's words:

> Poverty is not only an evil in itself, but sustainable development requires meeting the basic needs of all and extending to all the opportunity to fulfil their aspirations for a better life. A world in which poverty is endemic will always be prone to ecological and other catastrophes.[29]

It should be noted that, at least in passages such as these, the Commission's assertion that sustainable development must be accomplished globally, or not at all, is an empirical rather than a normative claim — although, in either case, the accuracy of the claim may be disputed. But assuming its truth, it follows that the goal of Canadian natural gas policy should not be to conserve natural gas just for Canadians, or perhaps only for future North Americans.[30]

It is sometimes said that natural gas is at its broadest a continental resource, but this is not, strictly speaking, true.[31] Natural gas can be compressed, liquified, and then transported by other means than pipeline. This is already being done to some extent, and is being contemplated by countries that have no markets for gas delivered by pipeline.[32] And, as the Brundtland Commission stated in its report, "traditional fuels ... are most needed to enable developing countries to realize their growth potential...."[33]

Nor should Canadian concerns about the environmental consequences of energy consumption be confined to Canadian energy strategies. It is not just the

---

28   L.R. Brown, C. Flavin & S. Postel, "Outlining a Global Action Plan" in L.R. Brown, ed., *State of the World 1989* (New York: W.W. Norton, 1989) at 176.

29   See *Our Common Future, supra,* note 24 at 8.

30   If the assertion is a true, empirical one, then it follows that what is called for on the part of Canadians in order that sustainable development be achieved is not altruism, but self-interest, albeit of a well-informed kind. This observation is intended not as an attack on either the desirability or the possibility of altruism, but only to call attention to the fact that the problems associated with the concept of altruism may not be germane in the circumstances.

31   See Department of Energy, Mines and Resources Canada, *Energy in Canada, A Background Paper* (Ottawa: Minister of Supply and Services Canada, 1987) at 22.

32   Nigeria is said to be considering such a move for lack of any other market for its gas.

33   See *Our Common Future, supra,* note 24 at 201.

environmental consequences of our own energy consumption patterns that should inform our energy policy. Canadian consumption of the particularly offensive fossil fuels — oil and coal — must be of concern, but so too must that of the Americans. As well, it is possible that North American gas will assist in the transition of other economies to more sustainable energy strategies.

EVALUATING THE DEREGULATION OF GAS

Energy seems to present especially difficult problems for sustainable development. The Brundtland Commission observes that "[a] generally acceptable pathway to a safe and sustainable energy future has not yet been found."[34] For example, a vexing debate continues as to whether nuclear energy forms an integral part of a sustainable future or whether it is, as many had already concluded some time ago, anathema to the sustainability of anything (other than nuclear waste). But despite this lack of consensus, it still seems possible to say something meaningful about Canadian natural gas policy in the context of sustainable development. As has been said elsewhere, "[a]ccepting the absence of 'generally accepted pathways' towards sustainable energy futures, the question is then to find policies and institutional arrangements which at least point in the right directions, which do not foreclose the desired final outcome, and try to identify a number of signposts ... to guide us along the road."[35]

Has the deregulation of natural gas pointed us in the right direction? No. A number of observations are in order. First, generally speaking, the deregulation of natural gas has to be seen as inherently suspect if the achievement of sustainable development is accepted as a goal. One of the implications of the Brundtland Report is that the variables critical to sustainability will have to be regulated much more carefully. One such variable is the supply of strategic resources, such as natural gas. The notion that market forces will get us to where we have to be is, at best, farfetched:

> Energy is not so much a single product as a mix of products and services, a mix upon which the welfare of individuals, the sustainable development of nations, and the life-supporting capabilities of the global ecosystem depend. In the past, this mix has been allowed to flow together haphazardly, the proportions dictated by short-term pressures on and short-term goals of governments, institutions, and companies. Energy is too important for its development to continue in such a random manner. A safe, environmentally sound, and economically viable energy pathway that will sustain human progress into the distant future is clearly imperative. It is also possible. But it will require new dimensions of political will and institutional co-operation to achieve it.[36]

---

34 *Id.* at 169.

35 L. Kristoferson, "Energy and Environment — How to Implement Sustainable Futures" in *Perspectives of Sustainable Development: Some Critical Issues Related to the Brundtland Report* (Stockholm: Stockholm Group for Studies on Natural Resources Management, 1988) 91 at 95.

36 See *Our Common Future, supra,* note 24 at 202.

As the Commission says, achieving sustainable development will require greater cooperation — locally, nationally, globally. It is unlikely to mean less regulation, although it may mean that some existing regulatory measures are replaced by others.

Second, some comments should be made on the consequences of deregulation for the supply of Canadian gas. In 1986 natural gas constituted about 25 percent of Canadian primary energy consumption, and that share is expanding. Indeed, the ready availability of natural gas has slowed moves in Canada toward greater energy efficiency:

> In Canada ... the widespread availability of substitutes for oil (particularly natural gas) led consumers and governments to place relatively more emphasis on substitution than on conservation in responding to the "oil crisis." As a result, decreases in overall energy consumption have lagged somewhat behind other OECD countries ... while reductions in oil consumption *per se* compare favourably.[37]

In 1987 the overall Canadian reserves-to-production ratio was 34 years (although the ratio for Alberta was only 25 years).[38] More recent data, however, show that the national reserves-to-production ratio is now lower: in 1988 the "estimated life index" of Canadian gas was 30.1 years.[39] Evidence from other sources also supports the claim that Canadian gas is being "over-produced." It is estimated that Canada has about 2.5 percent of the world's gas reserves, but in 1987 Canada was third in terms of world output. "This indicates that Canada is overproducing its natural gas reserves relative to other major gas producing nations (with the notable exception of the United States, which held 4.9% of world proved reserves at year-end 1987 but produced 25.1% of the world's gas [in that] year)."[40]

Recent figures also show that exports of gas constitute an increasing proportion of Canadian production. In 1987 about 36 percent of Canadian production was exported. Estimates are that 40 percent of production was exported in 1988, with the percentage predicted to rise to 44 percent in 1989. All exports are currently to the United States.

It is difficult to isolate the exact extent to which recent trends can be attributed to deregulation as opposed to other developments, such as the drop in oil and gas prices experienced during the past decade. It seems clear, however, that deregulation has contributed to both the accelerated rate at which Canadian reserves are being depleted and the increase in the proportion of that production that is going to export.

As a third point, it must also be appreciated that the deregulation of natural gas

---

37   See *Energy in Canada, supra,* note 31 at 10.

38   See *Natural Gas Deregulation and Marketing, supra,* note 27 at 18.

39   "Gas Producers Cope With Change as Free Market Becomes Complex" 39(50) *Oilweek* (23 January 1989) 5 at 6.

40   See *Natural Gas Deregulation and Marketing, supra,* note 27 at 17.

has been but one manifestation of governmental determination to put greater reliance on market forces. Not only have oil and gas prices and markets been deregulated: electricity exports are undergoing deregulation as well. Yet over the same period, government support for research and development related to alternative and renewable energy sources has been reduced.[41] As Roland Priddle, Chairman of the NEB, has said, the last few years have been marked by "a reduced level of policy concern in North America over conservation and renewable resources."[42] Priddle has also observed that

> [o]n balance, ... the changed environment for conservation and renewable energy has made the job of selling these alternatives to fossil fuels much tougher. Their relative economics are now less favourable than before and a public made complacent by surpluses of oil and gas may be less likely to seek alternatives, particularly when the payback period of any investment is now longer than before.[43]

It is obvious from Priddle's remarks that the "discipline" of the market is to be extended to renewable and alternative energy sources as well:

> The challenge for conservation and renewable energy resources is clear: it is to be, and to be seen to be cost-competitive with fossil fuels, to take advantage of larger markets, and to continue to innovate.[44]

For those not entranced by the market, it is difficult to fathom why decision-makers would put so much faith in a policy approach that is so unlikely to succeed in achieving the necessary. As the Standing Senate Committee on Energy and Natural Resources states in its 1988 report, *Natural Gas Deregulation and Marketing:*

> The regulatory system ... [has] a continuing role to play ... in protecting the long-term interests of the producer, transporter, distributor and consumer when it is evident that the free operation of a complex and highly specialized commodity market is unable to do so.[45]

But if deregulation does not point to a solution, in what direction should policy-makers be looking? Almost assuredly, not backwards. It seems that it would be no solution at all to go back to a fixed formula for determination of exportable surplus. And it clearly seems a mistake to ban the export of Canadian gas altogether. One should have nothing less than a profound respect for those (such as the Sierra Club and the Consumers' Association of Canada) who, in the face of overwhelming odds, opposed the liberalization of surplus determination procedures in the interests of conservation. But it does not follow that the views they advanced in the past now constitute the best available policy alternative. Gas export levels should be determined in light of the need to achieve sustainable development, not by a fixed

---

41 See *Energy in Canada, supra,* note 31 at 79–80.

42 R. Priddle, "The Challenge for Conservation and Renewable Energy Sources" (Address to the Solar Energy Society of Canada Conference, 23 June 1988) at 4.

43 *Id.* at 5.

44 *Id.* at 9.

45 See *Natural Gas Deregulation and Marketing, supra,* note 27 at 3.

formula or on the basis of what now looks to be an overly nationalistic view of conservation.

The right direction may not require the lowering of export volumes — indeed, perhaps just the opposite.[46] What it certainly does require is the imposition of end-use constraints on those exports. Arguably, sustainability is increased, not diminished, by Canadian exports of gas, but this is so only if those exports are used to lessen consumption of the more offensive fossil fuels by the importing economies, and to move the importing economies closer to sustainable energy futures. An acceptable gas export policy would, as well, have to ensure that appropriate Canadian needs for gas were adequately taken into account.

As noted earlier in this paper, natural gas has a critical role to play as a bridging fuel in the achievement of sustainable development. Thus, the export of Canadian gas for use in a facility that would otherwise consume oil or coal constitutes a step in the right direction. But gas exports should not only serve as substitutes for the more offensive fuels; they should be used, and be seen to be used, to move the country importing the gas closer to a sustainable energy path. Natural gas consumption is not, at the end of the day, such an energy strategy. As mentioned earlier, natural gas is a fossil fuel and contributes to the environmental problems associated with the burning of those fuels; moreover, it is a nonrenewable resource. Canada should, therefore, use its capacity for gas export to reward non-Canadian efforts to move towards sustainability. For example, where two American utilities are competing for volumes of Canadian gas, the export could be approved for the firm that had shown the greatest progress in this area.

Finally, an acceptable gas export policy will, of course, respect appropriate domestic needs for gas. The significant word here is "appropriate," for it is clear that Canadians, along with the rest of the developed world, currently consume far more than their share of the world's fossil fuels. According to the Brundtland Commission, "Sustainable global development requires that those who are more affluent adopt life-styles within the planet's ecological means — in their use of energy, for

---

46   This paper focuses on the implications of sustainable development for gas export policy, but one must not lose sight of the thesis' significance for gas exploration and production. The suggestion that sustainability might require the export of greater volumes of gas is premised on the assumption that, should such a move require higher levels of exploration and production, these increased activity levels would themselves be environmentally acceptable. An overall energy policy has to take both into account:

Environmental awareness has strengthened the market for natural gas because it produces fewer emissions than other fossil fuels. "The same environmental awareness must be applied to the production and export of natural gas. The implications of not doing so will be far longer lasting than the life of the natural gas reserves in the Mackenzie Delta Beaufort Sea Region."

Mackenzie Delta–Beaufort Sea Regional Land Use Planning Commission, *Newsletter* (April 1989) at 2.

example."[47] It should be noted here that the various surplus-determination procedures employed by the NEB have never been anything other than predictive of future Canadian needs for natural gas.[48]

The rest of this paper briefly considers three possible objections to the recommendation that Canadian gas not be exported unless the indicated criteria are met. First, might it be said that the NEB lacks the jurisdiction to impose the recommended requirements on gas exports? Second, what about conservation pricing? Might that not do? And, third, do our international obligations under the General Agreement on Tariffs and Trade and the Free Trade Agreement with the United States not preclude such an approach?

Two possible jurisdictional points are presented by Section 118(a) of the National Energy Board Act, which was recited earlier.[49] First, do the end-use criteria advocated in this paper go beyond the Canadian public-interest inquiries mandated by the Act? For example, is an inquiry into the extent of an American utility's attempts to conduct its affairs in a sustainable manner a matter relevant to the Canadian public interest? On one view, it is not, given that the utility is American — physically located in the United States and serving American customers and shareholders. But surely the global nature of environmental problems should leave us with a broader concept of the Canadian public interest. The energy consumption patterns of other countries, and especially those of the United States, are clearly significant to the well-being of Canadians (for a particularly painful example, consider acid rain), and thus should be seen as falling within the scope of the NEB's inquiry.

A more technical but in some ways more interesting jurisdictional objection focuses on the word "surplus" in Section 118(a) of the National Energy Board Act. As the Sierra Club has argued before the Board, it is nonsense to speak of surpluses of hydrocarbons; there is no *surplus* of natural gas in Canada. It does not follow, on the analysis used in this paper, that gas exports should be terminated. But it is arguable that the Act should be amended and the reference to "surplus" deleted, if only to preclude future semantic arguments.

The second objection raised above relates to conservation pricing: Why resort to the regulation of gas exports by the imposition of end-use constraints when conservation pricing might do? The brief answer is that conservation pricing will not do. It has been argued in this paper that the achievement of sustainable development requires not only that serious consideration be given conservation of natural gas (because it is a finite resource), but also that, in the transition to

---

47 See *Our Common Future, supra,* note 24 at 9.

48 For a description of the "Evolution of NEB Surplus Determination Procedures" see National Energy Board, *supra,* note 15 at 49.

49 See text accompanying note 19, *supra.*

sustainable energy strategies, natural gas be used to replace the more environmentally offensive fossil fuels. That is, natural gas policy must be concerned not only with the amount of gas consumed (both domestically and through export) but also with how that gas is to be used. Conservation pricing could be an effective tool in limiting the amount of gas consumed, but it is difficult to see how it could be useful as a means to direct the uses to which gas is put. These observations are not offered as arguments against a conservation pricing policy per se, but are only intended to suggest that such pricing cannot be viewed as a policy alternative to the kind of end-use regulation called for here. In all likelihood, a responsible energy policy would involve both techniques, and others as well.

Finally, what of our international obligations in energy trade? Here, too, only a few comments can be made. In general, our international obligations in this sphere can be summed up as a requirement not to discriminate between the conditions imposed on export and those applicable to domestic use of the resource. At this level, there should be no conflict between the recommendations made in this paper and international obligations, since the conclusions herein reached regarding gas export policy apply with equal force to Canadian consumption of natural gas.

A more detailed examination of the Free Trade Agreement (FTA) provisions on energy[50] might, however, pose some problems for implementation of the recommendations made here. The FTA allows for the imposition of restrictions in the interests of conservation and "critical shortages," but only where three conditions are met.[51] The FTA's prohibition of discriminatory pricing is not problematic in this context, but the other two criteria could be. One requires that any such restriction "not reduce the proportion of the total export shipments of a specific energy good made available to the other Party relative to the total supply of that good of the Party maintaining the restriction" over a specified period of time. If export volumes were to go down as a result of the imposition of restrictions argued for in this paper, this provision might be violated. However, as suggested earlier in this paper, natural gas export volumes might well increase as a result of the approach advocated here. The third requirement under the FTA is that the imposition of such restrictions "not require the disruption of normal channels of supply to the other Party of normal proportions among specific energy goods supplied to the other Party ...." This provision might become problematic were natural gas exports to supplant exports of crude oil in a way thought prejudicial by Americans. Overall, however, it looks as though neither the FTA nor the General Agreement on Tariffs and Trade presents insuperable obstacles to the adoption of this paper's recommendations for gas export policy.

---

50 See The Canada-U.S. Free Trade Agreement (Ottawa: Department of External Affairs, December 1987) c. 9.

51 *Id.*, Article 904.

In conclusion, the search for simplistic solutions to energy policy must end soon. As the Brundtland Commission Report makes clear, the imperatives of the future are unavoidably complex:

> [I]n the end, sustainable development is not a fixed state of harmony, but rather a process of change in which the exploitation of resources, the direction of investments, the orientation of technological development, and institutional change are made consistent with future as well as present needs. We do not pretend that the process is easy or straightforward. Painful choices have to be made. Thus, in the final analysis, sustainable development must rest on political will.[52]

---

52 See *Our Common Future, supra,* note 24 at 9.

LEGAL ASPECTS OF TRADE AND SUSTAINABLE DEVELOPMENT

J. Owen Saunders

One of the great services performed by the Brundtland Commission was to challenge directly the popular equation that environment and economic health are antithetical goals — that in order to have "more" of one, it is necessary to give up some of the other. This fallacy is also often reflected in discussions on the relationship between world trade and environmental health. Stringent environmental standards are sometimes seen either as measures that will decrease the competitive abilities of a nation's industries or as insidious attempts to discriminate unfairly against competitors.

Concern over the possible negative effects of environmental measures on trade has been evident in both developing and industrialized states. Indeed, some of the earliest expressions of concern were voiced in one of the landmarks of the modern environmental movement, the 1972 United Nations Conference on the Human Environment (the Stockholm Conference). Despite the Stockholm Conference's undoubted achievements in setting an international environmental agenda, the concern that developing countries especially might suffer from increased environmental standards is clearly detectable in some of the Conference's recommendations. For example, with specific reference to the implications of environmental regulations for trade, the Conference included, *inter alia,* recommendations

that Governments take the necessary steps to ensure:

(a) That all countries present at the Conference agree not to invoke environmental concerns as a pretext for discriminatory trade policies or for reduced access to markets and recognize further that the *burdens* of the environmental policies of the industrialized countries should not be transferred, either directly or indirectly, to the developing countries ...

(b) That where environmental concerns lead to restrictions on trade, or to stricter environmental standards with *negative effects on exports,* particularly from developing countries, appropriate measures for compensation should be worked out ...

(e) That all countries agree that uniform environmental standards should not be expected to be applied universally by all countries with respect to given industrial processes or products except in those cases where environmental disruption may constitute a concern to other countries.... Environmental standards should be established, at whatever levels are necessary, to safeguard the environment, and *should not be directed towards gaining trade advantages;*[1]

and

that the General Agreement on Tariffs and Trade, the United Nations Conference on Trade and Development [UNCTAD] and other international bodies, as appropriate, should, within their

---

1   *Report of the United Nations Conference on the Human Environment* ("Stockholm Declaration"), New York, 1972, UN Doc. A/Conf. 48/14, (1972) 11 Int'l Leg. Mat. 1416, Recommendation 103 (emphasis added).

respective fields of competence, consider undertaking to monitor, assess, and regularly report the emergence of tariff and non-tariff *barriers to trade as a result of environmental policies.*[2]

This concern that increased environmental standards might adversely affect the trade opportunities of developing countries is reflected in a subsequent joint UNCTAD/UNEP report.[3] That report also strikes another frequently sounded note: the possibility that higher environmental standards in industrialized countries might pose a trade "opportunity" for developing countries, which arguably possess a "competitive advantage ... because of relatively greater 'assimilative capacity'."[4] One expressed concern in the report was that this advantage might be undercut by various types of subsidies in developed countries.[5]

This scenario of environmentalism as protectionism is not a concern restricted to developing countries. It can also be found as a primary thrust of the work on trade and environment carried out by the Organisation for Economic Co-operation and Development (OECD). The OECD's interest in this subject dates from approximately the same time as the Stockholm Conference, although its focus has been much more restricted. The concern that higher environmental standards might lead to trade distortions is reflected in the OECD's adoption in 1972, and subsequent refinement, of the "polluter pays principle"(PPP) as "the principle to be used for allocating costs of pollution prevention and control measures to encourage rational use of scarce environmental resources and to avoid distortions in international trade and investment."[6] PPP is defined as follows:

This principle means that the polluter should bear the expenses of carrying out the above mentioned measures decided by public authorities to ensure that the environment is in an acceptable state. In other words, the cost of these measures should be reflected in the cost of goods and services which cause pollution in production and/or consumption. Such measures should not be accompanied by subsidies that would create significant distortions in international trade and investment.[7]

As discussed further on, PPP in itself raises some difficult questions with respect to implementation. More generally, however, it must be questioned whether the principle can generate an adequate response to some of the broader environmental concerns raised by more recent work on sustainable development. It must also be

---

2   *Id.,* Recommendation 105 (emphasis added).

3   United Nations Conference on Trade and Development, *Report of the UNCTAD/UNEP Informal Meeting of Experts on Trade Aspects of Environmental Policies and Measures* (February 1977), UN Doc. UNCTAD/ST/MD/II (1978).

4   *Id.* at 4.

5   *Id.*

6   Organisation for Economic Co-operation and Development, *Guiding Principles Concerning International Economic Aspects of Environmental Policies,* Recommendation of 26 May 1972, C(72) 128, Annex, A(a)(4), reproduced in Organisation for Economic Co-operation and Development, *OECD and the Environment* (Paris: OECD, 1986) 23 at 24.

7   *Id.,* Annex, A(a)(5).

asked whether the existing trade law structure and institutions are appropriate for dealing with environmental concerns as they relate to trade.

In this paper I begin by discussing the traditional approach towards environment and trade, an approach that has as its primary focus the possible use of environmental measures as devices for trade distortion. I also discuss this approach's consistency with the major multilateral agreement and institution governing international trade relations: the General Agreement on Tariffs and Trade (GATT). The work of agencies more closely identified with particular groups of states — the OECD and UNCTAD — will also be reviewed. Beyond these formal institutions, however, the global community has recognized — albeit in somewhat *ad hoc* fashion — the need to place constraints on trade in the interests of legitimate environmental objectives. I discuss two major examples of such an approach: the Convention on International Trade in Endangered Species of Wild Fauna and Flora (CITES) and the recent Montreal Protocol with respect to protection of the ozone layer. Finally, I shall suggest some implications of this experience for the future relationship between trade law and the environment, a relationship that holds special interest for concerns that have become associated with sustainable development.

ENVIRONMENTAL PROTECTION AS A TRADE DISTORTION

Basic Concerns

The primary concern of the literature on trade law and economics with respect to environmental protection is the distorting effect that environmental standards may impose on trade relations. At its simplest level, this "distortion" might take one of two forms — a distortion of consumption decisions by restrictions on the availability of certain goods, because of their inherent environmental attributes (for example, beef with residues of growth hormones, or fruit with residual pesticides present); or a distortion of production decisions by measures aimed at encouraging or discouraging certain types of production methods on environmental grounds (for example, smelters or refineries with inadequate control of sulphur dioxide emissions).

Clearly, however, it is not always easy to decide what constitutes a trade-distorting measure and what constitutes a *bona fide* attempt to protect the environment. Moreover, one's perspective may be heavily influenced by one's position as an exporter or a domestic competitor. Taking, for example, the case of measures directed at the consumption of particular goods, one need only refer to the recent incident of Chilean grapes contaminated by cyanide to appreciate how far apart states may stand on even such fundamental environmental considerations as human health. Suppose, however, that the environmental interest in question is not human health, but a more controversial consideration — for example, the appropriateness of harvesting a resource at all because of the danger of exhaustion or because of some ethical consideration. Here there may be even greater scope for debate — witness the sharp disagreement over the Canadian cull of seal pups — and accordingly greater difficulty in resolving whether a trade measure is in some sense an unfair distortion.

The same is true of trade measures directed at production processes: in distinguishing between valid and invalid measures to protect the environment, providing a "neutral" perspective on what is a level playing field is not always easy. Take, for example, the case of exports of copper from a state with relatively low emission-control standards to a state with relatively high standards. Should the importing state be able to impose trade restrictions (whether through tariffs or quantitative restrictions) on the copper, on the ground that the exporting state's failure to impose equivalent environmental standards amounts to, in effect, an unfair export subsidy? The answer depends largely, again, on the appropriateness of the standards in question. Suppose, for example, the exporting country has an assimilative capacity significantly greater than that of the importing country. The exporter might well argue — and developing countries have argued — that the real trade distortion results from the attempted imposition of inappropriate pollution-control standards on the exporting state. One could go further and ask whether emission standards are appropriate at all in such situations; perhaps a comparison of ambient standards would be more revealing.

Environmental Protection and the GATT

If an *a priori* resolution of whether a particular trade measure relating to the environment is fair seems difficult to achieve, what guidance is provided by the major existing multilateral framework for trade relations, the GATT? The brief answer is that while the GATT provides some assistance in establishing general principles for defining trade distortions, it is far less helpful in discerning whether a specific environmental protection measure is valid. For example, although the GATT does impose certain requirements on the conduct of trade relations, such as the imposition of national-treatment standards for internal taxation and regula-tions,[8] and the elimination of quantitative restrictions on imports and exports,[9] these principles are subject to a host of exceptions. While there is no specific reference to exceptions based on environmental grounds, some aspects of the environment are captured in two of the general exceptions in Article XX, namely, measures

(b)   necessary to protect human, animal or plant life, or health; ...
      [and]

(g)   relating to the conservation of exhaustible natural resources if such measures are made
      effective in conjunction with restrictions on domestic production or consumption....

---

8   General Agreement on Tariffs and Trade, T.I.A.S. No. 1700, 55 U.N.T.S. 194, Art. III. (The
     current version of the GATT may be found in IV GATT, *Basic Instruments and Selected
     Documents* (1969).)

9   *Id.*, Art. XI.

These exceptions do not, of course, give a state *carte blanche* to except itself from the GATT: even those measures justified by invoking the above exceptions must meet the general requirements in Article XX that they not be "applied in a manner which would constitute a means of arbitrary or unjustifiable discrimination between countries where the same conditions prevail, or a disguised restriction on international trade." This language is, however, subject to widely differing interpretations, and begs the question of what is arbitrary, unjustifiable, or a disguised restriction.

Even were Article XX amenable to some definitive interpretation, the exceptions contained therein might well prove inadequate in providing guidance as to the acceptability of trade-oriented environmental measures. Article XX(b), for example, would embrace most traditional pollution concerns through its emphasis on health, but would health be broad enough to capture wider environmental interests such as climate change and desertification? Possibly, but it is by no means certain that trade tribunals would allow such scope.[10] As to Article XX(g), conservation of *exhaustible* natural resources, one might conceivably argue that air and water are in some sense exhaustible — at least with respect to quality — but the provision seems obviously intended to be much more restricted in coverage. As such, even with respect to the issue of resource conservation, the Article is seriously deficient in its scope.[11]

Quite apart from the issue of whether environmental concerns are adequately recognized in the GATT framework is the question of whether or not the policy tools available under the GATT are likely to lead to sound environmental policies. Let us take, for example, the case of an industry that, without controls, is heavily polluting in its production process. Some states respond to this with stringent pollution controls; other states, because of the need to attract industry, respond with only modest requirements for pollution abatement. State Z is an importer of the product, while state Y is an exporter with virtually no pollution legislation. State Z wishes to impose a tax on the exports in question from state Y on the ground that they are produced through environmentally unsound methods. Would the GATT allow this, and, if so, on what grounds?[12]

If the argument for such a tax[13] is based, for example, on the health exception,

---

10   It has been noted that the health exception "is generally recognized to be necessary, but susceptible to abuse." See Frederic L. Kirgis, Jr., "Effective Pollution Control in Industrialized Countries: International Economic Disincentives, Policy Responses and the GATT" (1972) 70 Michigan L. Rev. 859 at 892.

11   See G.P. Verbit, *Trade Agreements for Developing Countries* (New York: Columbia University Press, 1969) at 221–222.

12   For a much more detailed consideration of a number of such scenarios, see Kirgis, *supra,* note 10.

13   Different considerations would apply depending upon whether the charges were structured as an import duty (and particularly one not currently subject to a tariff "binding") or an internal tax (as

one is immediately confronted by the argument that the pollution in question is suffered not by the inhabitants of state Z, but by the inhabitants of state Y, and, as such, state Z can hardly invoke the excepting provisions of Article XX as justification for its actions. While it is true that Article XX does not refer specifically to the health of citizens of the acting state, this is certainly what must be inferred; otherwise the GATT could be read as implicitly justifying far-reaching intrusions on the territorial sovereignty of other states, an interpretation that is unsupported on a reading of the Agreement and on the basis of state practice.

There is, admittedly, another justification that could be constructed for a tax on Y's exports. The argument might go that unilateral (or even restricted multilateral) application of new and expensive environmental technology is economically impossible.[14] That is, it would be impossible for Z to impose this technology upon its industry unless other states imposed equivalent requirements on their industries (or at least on their export-competing sectors). Y's failure to impose such controls thus justifies an off-setting tax on its exports to Z. The better view, however, is probably that this application of the health exception would be unacceptable under the GATT. Given that the health exception is already viewed with some suspicion by the GATT Contracting Parties, a stronger link between the tax and the health of Z's population would almost certainly be required to justify the invocation of Article XX(b).

As well, it is by no means clear that such a measure would in practice lead to the imposition of adequate pollution control measures in Y. Factors such as availability of technology and foreign exchange considerations may dictate in favour of Y's (and Y's producers') simply swallowing the tax, particularly if other customers of Y do not impose similar requirements. In the end, there may be little effect other than a rise in consumer prices in Z and some increased taxation revenue accruing to the government of Z, but no effective impact on the central environmental concern.

Even if one were to accept the validity of such a tax, its imposition could pose some difficult administrative issues. If the tax is truly aimed at the polluting characteristics of the production process, it presumably varies from state to state, depending upon the standards applied. Even if this approach were assumed to be

---

assumed here). See *id.* at 897 *et seq.* Art. III:1 and III:2 of the GATT effectively prohibit discriminatory use of internal taxes "to afford protection to domestic production." Thus, in a recent GATT panel decision, the U.S. "Superfund" statute — which, *inter alia,* imposed excise taxes on petroleum to fund U.S. clean-up of hazardous wastes — was found to contravene Art. III:2 because it was imposed at a higher (i.e., discriminatory) level for imported oil than for domestic. The United States did not, however, contest that the discrimination had any valid purpose. See GATT, "Dispute Settlement Panel Report on United States Superfund Excise Taxes," adopted 17 June, 1987, (1988) 27 Int'l Leg. Mat. 1596.

14   This scenario is discussed in Kirgis, *id.* at 901.

consistent with the most-favoured-nation requirements of Article I of the GATT, it could present almost insurmountable problems in ascertaining what levels of tax should be set for individual exporters, particularly where there is a large number of suppliers. This is complicated even more if one takes into account the often very important distinction between theoretical standards and enforced standards. It also ignores a possibility referred to earlier — that similar emission standards may have significantly different effects on health (which is presumably the primary concern here), depending upon the assimilative capacity of the particular state.

An alternative invocation of the excepting provisions of Article XX is for Z to treat the matter as one involving a subsidy. That is, by failing to impose upon its industry a cost that must be borne by society as a whole, Y could be construed as conferring a benefit upon the industry in question, which subsidy should be subject to countervailing duty. There are, however, serious problems inherent in such an approach. Firstly, while Article XVI of the GATT (the key article on subsidies) does not define subsidies, the general wording of the article — which refers to "any subsidy, including any form of income or price support, which operates ... to increase exports of any product" — suggests that some positive government intervention in the market process is required before a subsidy can be found. This suggestion is confirmed by subsequent practice, and specifically by the Subsidies Code[15] negotiated during the Tokyo Round of trade talks. A perusal of the Annex to the Code provides an illustrative list of subsidies, all of which refer to provision of financial benefits — whether through grants, remissions, or specific exemptions from taxes. The Code clearly does not anticipate a situation where a state has merely adopted generally lower environmental standards — any more than it would prevent a state from "failing" to impose "acceptable" standards for wages, health, or education.

There might, of course, be some instances where failure to impose pollution controls could be characterized as a subsidy. For example, if a particular export industry were granted special exemptions from air-emission requirements that applied to all other industries — or, more obviously, were exempted from pollution *charges* applied to other sectors — then this might be construed as a benefit attaching to that particular industry, and thus as a subsidy. Such a specific bestowal of benefits, however, is likely to be the exception rather than the rule.[16]

---

15   GATT, *Agreement on Interpretation and Application of Articles VI, XVI, and XXIII of the General Agreement on Tariffs and Trade*, BISD, 26th Supp. 56 (1978–79).

16   Considerable debate attaches to the question of what constitutes "specific bestowal," particularly with respect to natural resources subsidies. Is it enough, for example, that any benefits (say, from relaxed pollution control standards) be generally available *as a matter of law* to defeat a charge of specific bestowal? Alternatively, can one ask whether *as a matter of fact* such nominally generally available subsidies operate so as to disproportionately favour some industries, and are thus specifically bestowed and liable to countervailing duties? The better view is that GATT speaks to the former test; however, recent U.S. jurisprudence (reversing past practice) and

Another limitation of the subsidy approach to the problem of dealing with differential environmental standards is the additional requirement of injury to the domestic industry as a precondition for the imposition of countervailing duties. Moreover, in the case of developing countries (which are often criticized for their unsatisfactory environmental standards) the Subsidies Code stresses the need for positive proof of such injury:

> There shall be no presumption that export subsidies granted by developing country signatories result in adverse effects, as defined in this Agreement, to the trade or production of another signatory. Such adverse effects shall be demonstrated by positive evidence, through an economic examination of the impact on trade or production of another signatory.[17]

Many of the problems noted earlier for Article XX with respect to quantifying differential environmental standards apply with equal force here. Additionally the *ad hoc,* typically slow and cumbersome nature of domestic countervail actions makes this approach inappropriate for dealing with the general issue of trade and environment, even if one could characterize a particular measure as a subsidy.[18]

In sum, although the GATT contains some elements that are relevant to the issue of environment and trade, on the whole it provides neither useful guidance on the substantive rules that should apply in this area nor an appropriate mechanism for dealing comprehensively with the question of environmentally acceptable trade practices. Even relevant provisions are largely restricted to more narrow concerns such as the direct effects of traded products on health, and have little to offer in dealing with broader long-term environmental problems. If one agrees that the GATT is indeed an inappropriate — or at least insufficient — forum for dealing with the environmental aspects of trade, the question remains, where can these issues most usefully be addressed?

Other International Economic Organizations: OECD and UNCTAD

Two other international economic organizations that have displayed an interest in environmental aspects of trade have been referred to earlier: the OECD and

---

legislation take the latter view. See *Preliminary Affirmative Countervailing Duty Determination; Certain Softwood Lumber Products from Canada,* 51 Fed. Reg. 37, 453 (1986); Omnibus Trade and Competitiveness Act of 1988, P.L. 100-418, §1312, amending 19 U.S.C. §1677 (5). For an economic/legal analysis — and criticism — of the changing U.S. position in this regard, see M.B. Percy & C.G. Yoder, *The Softwood Lumber Dispute and Canada–U.S. Trade in Natural Resources* (Halifax: Institute for Research on Public Policy, 1987).

17 See GATT, *supra,* note 15, Art. 14(4). Article 14 deals generally with the issue of subsidies and less-developed countries.

18 The OECD has also opposed the use of border measures as a means of dealing with differing environmental standards.

UNCTAD. While the OECD's membership is composed of what are commonly considered the advanced, industrialized market economies,[19] UNCTAD is a United Nations body that in trade matters is generally perceived as reflecting the interests and perspectives of developing countries.[20] Of the two, it seems fair to say that the primary initiative in trade and environment has come from the OECD, with its work on the polluter pays principle. UNCTAD's work in this area lacks the thematic unity of a principle such as PPP, and to some extent is a response to that principle.

The strengths of PPP are also its weaknesses. PPP represents a consensus of the leading actors in foreign trade[21] on how the costs of pollution should be allocated; whether an environmental measure is "fair" can thus be judged, at least from a trade perspective, by whether or not it conforms to this principle. If, for example, the cost of air pollution is borne by government through subsidization of pollution control expenditures, this is a contravention of PPP, and to the extent that the products of the polluting industry ultimately enter international commerce, this subsidization amounts to an unfair trade practice. PPP's weakness is reflective of its sponsors: it represents the industrialized world's view of the pressing trade/environment issue of the day.

Two other important limitations on PPP should also be noted. First, the language of the 1972 OECD recommendation adopting PPP is precisely that: recommendatory. Specifically, the OECD Council

> RECOMMENDS that the Governments of Member countries should, in determining environmental control policies and measures, observe the "Guiding Principles Concerning the International Economic Aspects of Environmental Policies" set forth in the Annex to this Recommendation.[22]

Second, even the guiding principles that flesh out this recommendation are open to significant exceptions and national variations. For example, with reference to a factor noted earlier in this paper, it is accepted that

> [d]iffering national environmental policies ... are justified by a variety of factors including among other things different pollution assimilative capacities of the environment in its present state,

---

19 But not yet such emerging industrial powers as South Korea and Singapore.

20 And, indeed, it was set up with this orientation in mind, reflecting developing countries' dissatisfaction with the Economic and Social Council, the UN organ originally entrusted with economic development issues: D.W. Bowett, *The Law of International Institutions* (3d ed.; London: Stevens, 1975) at 65.

21 And the leading actors in some significant polluting activities also. The OECD noted in 1986:

> Although OECD countries account for only 17 per cent of the world's population and less than a quarter of its land mass, they generate about 70 per cent of world Gross Domestic Product and 70 per cent of world trade. Moreover, they account for 60 per cent of the total atmospheric pollution generated by man.

See *OECD and the Environment, supra,* note 6 at 5.

22 See *Guiding Principles, supra,* note 6.

different social objectives and priorities attached to environmental protection and different degrees of industrialization and population density.[23]

The OECD expanded upon these exceptions in a 1974 recommendation on the implementation of PPP,[24] where it recognized the legitimate possibility of government assistance for easing the transition to more stringent pollution control regimes in cases where significant socio-economic problems might ensue,[25] and for pollution-related R & D.[26] The recommendation also anticipated an exception of potential significance to countries such as Canada, where regional economic considerations are important:

> Where measures taken to promote a country's specific socio-economic objectives, such as the reduction of serious inter-regional imbalances, would have the incidental effect of constituting aid for pollution-control purposes, the granting of such aid would not be inconsistent with the Polluter-Pays Principle.[27]

In sum, even taken on its own terms, PPP does not constitute a major addition to OECD members' legal obligations with respect to the environment. Not only is PPP highly restricted as a general principle for environmental regulation; its binding force is negligible given both its recommendatory nature and the exceptions it allows. This does not mean, however, that PPP is unimportant; what it does mean is that PPP should be seen as only one step in the evolution of law in this area, rather than as an end in itself.

Indeed, the OECD has always recognized the limitations of PPP and has moved beyond the principle in its own work on environment regulation. The 1972 recommendation marks the beginning of a long, and still continuing, series of OECD recommendations and studies on the environment — some of a general nature, but many dealing with specific areas of concern, such as air, water, energy, wastes, and chemicals.[28] Much of this work has relevance to trade law, perhaps most notably for transfrontier movements of hazardous wastes. Moreover, recent OECD pronouncements clearly indicate that the organization takes a much broader view of environmental issues than one restricted merely to questions of pollution control. For example, a 1982 OECD report on environmental and resource issues conceded that PPP did not then apply to two important cases:

> First, it does not apply in the case of investment within an OECD country that gives rise to spillovers into the global commons, unless an international agreement to reduce pollution from the source exists;

---

23 *Id.*, Annex, A(b)(6).

24 Organisation for Economic Co-operation and Development, *The Implementation of the Polluter-Pays Principle*, Recommendation of 14 November 1974, C(74) 223, reproduced in *OECD and the Environment, supra*, note 6 at 26–27.

25 *Id.*, II (2).

26 *Id.*, II (3).

27 *Id.*, II (4).

28 Most of these are reproduced in *OECD and the Environment, supra*, note 6.

> Second, it does not apply in the case of investment abroad that gives rise to spillovers from the country hosting the investment into countries neighbouring it or into the global commons, where the country hosting the investment does not apply the PPP.[29]

The first of these exceptions takes on special importance given the growing recognition of global environmental concerns; the second is of particular interest to developing countries, an audience that was left virtually unaddressed by much of the OECD's early work on the environment.

A broader agenda of emerging concerns is represented by the OECD's 1985 Declaration on Environment Resources for the Future,[30] where the member states declare that they will, *inter alia.*

> 7. Strengthen control over the generation and disposal of hazardous wastes and establish an effective and legally binding system for control of their transfrontier movements, *including movements to non-Member countries; ...*

> 9. Improve the management of natural resources, using an integrated approach, with a view to ensuring long-term environmental and economic sustainability....

> 11. Strengthen their efforts to contribute to environmentally-sound development in developing countries;

> 12. Address newly emerging environmental issues such as possible climatic change resulting from human activities and the environmental problems and promises of new, advanced technologies such as biotechnology.[31]

This declaration clearly anticipates a very wide range of environmental concerns, and foreshadows in a general way the issues raised by the Brundtland Report[32] — most obviously with respect to the emphasis on environmental sustainability and the need to preserve the global commons. What it lacks, of course, is any clear articulation of the international obligations attaching to such concerns, let alone any suggestion of how trade-related measures might be employed to enforce such obligations.

Compared to the work of the OECD, the effort expended on trade and environment by the major voice for trade concerns of developing countries has been disappointing, though perhaps understandable. The major document produced by UNCTAD in this area is the 1977 report of an UNCTAD/UNEP informal meeting

---

29 Organisation for Economic Co-operation and Development, *Economic and Ecological Interdependence* (Paris: OECD, 1982) at 69.

30 Organisation for Economic Co-operation and Development, *Declaration on Environment Resources for the Future,* adopted by Member Governments during the meeting of the Environment Committee at Ministerial level, 20 June 1985, reproduced in *OECD and the Environment, supra,* note 6 at 19–20.

31 Emphasis added.

32 World Commission on Environment and Development, *Our Common Future* (Oxford: Oxford University Press, 1987) (Chair: G.H. Brundtland).

of trade experts.[33] As such, it does not, of course, represent the official position of UNCTAD. Moreover, in the twelve years since the report appeared, the developing countries have undoubtedly become much more attuned to the negative long-run environmental consequences of unrestricted development. One need only refer to their recent interest in regulating "trade" in hazardous wastes to recognize how attitudes in this area have changed.[34] Nevertheless, the UNCTAD/UNEP report reflects an approach that has probably not entirely disappeared from the thinking of developing nations: that environmental standards applicable to developed nations are not necessarily appropriate to, and may even inhibit the growth of, developing countries.

Indeed, it is instructive to note that the meeting that gave rise to the above-noted report was convened pursuant to an UNCTAD/UNEP project entitled "Study on Trade Barriers and Restrictions Resulting From Environmental Policies." Similarly, the terms of reference for the meeting begin with the following mandate:

(1) To examine the relevant trade aspects of environmental policies and measures, in particular their implications for access of exports of developing countries and their likely or potential effects on the redeployment of industries to developing countries ...

(2) To consider measures for offsetting the *adverse effects of trade-related environmental policies and measures,* as well as those for assisting developing countries in complying with environmental measures of concern to them and applying measures in the context of their own environmental policies.[35]

While it is certainly true that developing countries have in general become more sensitive to environmental issues since the UNCTAD/UNEP report, and have also taken a somewhat different view of the environmental consequences of trade (at least with respect to hazardous materials), as yet there has been no consensus among trade-oriented bodies — and specifically UNCTAD — on a new agenda of concerns for the Third World with respect to the trade/environment relationship.

CONVENTIONS ON TRADE AND ENVIRONMENT

If the major intergovernmental bodies with a mandate for trade issues have not yet dealt in a comprehensive way with the implications of international environmental obligations for trade, we must ask whether there are any other mechanisms that will address such issues. The answer is that such mechanisms exist, but are not directly associated with trade institutions and are *ad hoc* in nature. Perhaps the primary example of the international development of "hard" environmental/trade law is provided by the evolution of norms with respect to hazardous materials, a subject addressed in another paper in this volume. However, one can point to the emergence of such obligations in at least two other areas of global interest: the

33 See *Report, supra,* note 3.

34 For a discussion of which, see the contribution by Leonard and Vallette in this volume.

35 See *Report, supra,* note 3, Annex I (emphasis added).

protection of endangered species of flora and fauna, and the protection of the atmosphere.

CITES

The Convention on International Trade in Endangered Species of Wild Fauna and Flora of 1973 (CITES)[36] traces its formal origins to the Stockholm Conference (although some had called for such a conference much earlier[37]), and specifically to Resolution 99.3:

> *It is recommended* that a plenipotentiary conference be convened as soon as possible, under appropriate governmental or intergovernmental auspices, to prepare and adopt a convention on export, import and transit of certain species of wild animals and plants.[38]

The preamble to CITES recalls two themes noted earlier — first, the assertion of a *global* (and intergenerational) interest in such species, in its recognition that "wild fauna and flora ... are an irreplaceable part of the natural systems of the earth which must be protected for this and the generations to come"; and, second, the emphasis on *state sovereignty* as a fundamental principle of international law, in the recognition that "peoples and States are and should be the best protectors of their own wild fauna and flora...."

The Convention strikes a balance between these interests in the way in which it regulates the trade in such species. Rather than impose an international regulatory system *per se,* CITES opted for national regulation, but subject to international standards as established in the Convention. A major function of CITES is the establishment of a classification system under which endangered species may be allocated to one of three categories: first, "all species threatened with extinction *which are or may be affected by trade*";[39] second, all species that may become threatened unless trade in them is strictly regulated, as well as species the control of which is necessary to maintain effective regulation of the potentially endangered species;[40] and, finally, species identified by an individual party to the Convention that are subject to national regulation to prevent or restrict exploitation, but where the cooperation of other parties is needed with respect to trade.[41]

---

36   Convention on International Trade in Endangered Species of Wild Fauna and Flora, Washington, 3 March 1973, (1973) 12 Int'l Leg. Mat. 1088.

37   The U.S. Congress called for such action in 1969: P.L. 91-135, §5(b), (c) (1969). The International Union for Conservation of Nature and Natural Resources (IUCN) had called for such a conference as early as 1963; the background of IUCN involvement is described in Legislative Developments, "Convention on International Trade in Endangered Species of Wild Fauna and Flora" (1974) 6 Law and Policy in Int'l Bus. 1211 at 1218.

38   See *Report, supra,* note 1.

39   See Convention, *supra,* note 36, Art. II (1) (emphasis added). Trade is defined by Art. I(c) to include "export, import and introduction from the sea."

40   *Id.,* Art. II (2).

41   *Id.,* Art. II (3).

The degree of protection accorded a species — or, more specifically, the stringency of the regulatory standards for trade in the species — varies according to the group, with the most stringent safeguards attached, not surprisingly, to species in the first group. It is important to note that even trade in the first group of species is not banned outright as a matter of international law. However, all parties permitting such trade must condition it on the obtaining of a certificate. Moreover, the certificate may only be issued when certain conditions are met.[42] (The certificates and conditions vary somewhat, depending on the type of trade engaged in — export, import, re-export, or introduction from the sea.) For example, an export permit is conditioned on, *inter alia,* a designated national scientific authority's advice that the export "will not be detrimental to the survival of that species," as well as a state management authority's confirmation that the taking and delivery of the specimen is in accordance with certain standards.[43]

This structure illustrates a fundamental tenet — and a potential weakness — of the Convention; its success depends crucially on the willingness of individual parties to enforce the trade rules set out therein. If parties are not willing to act, there is little legal recourse available — and certainly less room for exerting pressure than is found in the GATT (itself not regarded as a body with strong remedial legal provisions). There is provision for communicating concerns regarding the Convention's ineffective implementation to the parties involved,[44] but the appropriateness of any remedial action, and even the desirability of having an inquiry carried out, are matters left to the discretion of the individual state concerned. Similarly, in the event of a dispute over the Convention's application, disputants are only required to negotiate the matter; if the dispute cannot be resolved, the Convention provides only that the parties "*may,* by *mutual consent,* submit the dispute to arbitration."[45]

The weakness of the Convention's compliance provisions should not be overstated; such reluctance to include in the treaty a binding dispute-resolution mechanism is typical of international agreements — and particularly of multilateral agreements. This omission was certainly the price that had to be paid in order to achieve any treaty in this area. The Convention has other weaknesses, however; two in particular should be noted, both of which flow from the fact that this is a *trade* treaty. First, as a trade treaty, the Convention deals only with species endangered by trade; it provides no help for species that are not subject to trade. Second, the Convention protects designated species only *when* they are endangered by trade. Obviously, many factors other than trade affect species' survival — for example,

---

42 *Id.,* Art. III.
43 *Id.,* Art. III (2).
44 *Id.,* Art. XIII.
45 *Id.,* Art. XVIII.

the destruction of habitat.[46] Moreover, even if habitat destruction is itself partially the result of trade — as, for example, with much of the destruction of tropical forests — there is no requirement to in any way restrain or regulate such related trade.

Montreal Protocol

If the convention on trade in endangered species was phrased as a trade agreement, but with environmental impacts, the Montreal Protocol[47] is structured as an environmental agreement, but with impacts on trade. This agreement on substances that deplete the ozone layer is a protocol to the 1985 Vienna Convention for the Protection of the Ozone Layer,[48] and is designed to provide regulatory teeth to the latter. The Vienna Convention (which explicitly recalls Principle 21 of the Stockholm Declaration in its preamble) by itself establishes very little in the way of "hard law." For example, the basic obligation with respect to protecting the ozone layer is highly qualified, committing the parties only to

> take appropriate measures *in accordance with the provisions of this Convention* and of those protocols to which they are party to protect human health and the environment against adverse effects resulting or likely to result from human activities which modify or are likely to modify the ozone layer.[49]

There is not, then, a general obligation to protect the ozone layer (let alone the atmosphere generally); there is only an obligation to protect it to the extent required by the Convention and its protocols (in which the parties may or may not decide to participate). The additional obligations in the Vienna Convention are hardly onerous, and consist mainly in setting an agenda for research and formalizing arrangements for cooperation and the exchange of legal, scientific, and technical information amongst parties — in other words, the type of "soft law" that characterizes many multilateral environmental treaties.

The Montreal Protocol is significant precisely because it does impose some specific quantifiable obligations on parties with respect to consumption of certain controlled substances. Monitoring of the success of the Protocol is facilitated by a requirement that parties provide annual data to the secretariat of the Vienna Convention (Article 7), and, while mechanisms for ensuring compliance are not provided for specifically, the general problem of non-compliance is at least anticipated in Article 8, which sets this as an agenda item for the first meeting of parties to the Protocol.

---

46 Legislative Developments, *supra,* note 37 at 1226.

47 Protocol on Substances that Deplete the Ozone Layer, Montreal, 16 September 1987, (1987) 26 Int'l Leg. Mat. 1541.

48 Vienna Convention for the Protection of the Ozone Layer, Vienna, 22 March 1985, (1987) 26 Int'l Leg. Mat. 1529.

49 *Id.,* Art. 2 (emphasis added).

Of most interest for this paper is Article 4, which is directed at control of trade between parties and non-parties to the Protocol. This article is, in effect, a recognition of the particular problems presented by the "tragedy of the commons"[50] — in this case, the global commons. Rather than attempting the far more difficult task of establishing international environmental obligations as a form of *jus cogens*, or of characterizing endangerment of the ozone layer as an international crime,[51] the Protocol instead attempts to isolate non-parties, at least with respect to their import and export of certain controlled substances. This is accomplished by, *inter alia*, phasing in bans on imports from non-party states of controlled substances and products containing those substances (Art. 4(1), (3)); by discouraging the export to non-parties of technology for producing and using such substances (Art. 4(5)); and by requiring parties to refrain from extending new financial assistance for exports of related production technology to non-parties (Art. 4(6)). Of potentially even broader reach, the parties shall determine the feasibility of banning or restricting imports from non-parties of products produced with controlled substances, even though those products may not contain such substances (Art. 4(4)).

Like CITES, the Montreal Protocol does not reach all uses of controlled substances, but it does move beyond the former in limiting parties' domestic use of those substances. It also addresses the problem of non-party compliance by introducing measures that go beyond mere trade in the particular substances to strike at the capacity of non-parties to produce and use the substances.

This penalization of non-parties — regardless of what controls they may actually have in place to protect the ozone layer — has an added benefit. It encourages universality of participation in the Protocol, and thus increases the possibility that the standards set therein will be regarded not merely as treaty obligations, but also as indicative of general customary international law, and therefore binding on non-parties as well. Admittedly, the scope of the obligations in the Protocol is limited insofar as it deals with only a few controlled substances (chlorofluorocarbons and halons). Nevertheless, the Protocol provides a potentially useful structure for dealing with other problems of the global commons — particularly in its use of trade obligations as leverage against dissenting polluters.

---

50 G. Hardin, "The Tragedy of the Commons" in G. Hardin & J. Baden, eds., *Managing the Commons* (San Francisco: W.H. Freeman, 1977) at 16.

51 The possibility of "international crimes" against the environment has been raised by the International Law Commission in its work on codifying principles of state responsibility. In its draft articles, the ILC refers to the possibility that an international crime may result, *inter alia*, from

(d) a serious breach of an international obligation of essential importance for the safeguarding and preservation of the human environment, such as those prohibiting massive pollution of the atmosphere or of the seas.

International Law Commission, "Draft Articles on State Responsibility" [1979] Yrbk. Int'l L. Comm. II, 91; (1979) 18 Int'l Leg. Mat. 1568, Art. 19 (3).

CONCLUSIONS

The recognition of the "environmental factor" in trade law (or the trade factor in environmental law) dates roughly from the beginnings of the modern era of environmentalism in the late 1960s and early 1970s. As we have seen, the primary interest in this relationship has focused — at least in the trade-oriented institutions — on the dangers of environmental measures as possible trade-distorting actions. This caution towards environmentalism has been shared by both developing and developed states. In the case of the former, the primary concern has been possible reliance on such considerations as a disguised means of raising protectionist barriers against imports from developing countries. An additional concern of developed countries has been the possibility that failure to adequately capture pollution costs from producers may represent a disguised export subsidy.

There has, however, been some recognition of another aspect to the environment–trade interface: the use of trade measures as a means of protecting the global commons — particularly with respect to endangered species and the atmosphere. This may be the feature that distinguishes the success of the measures to date. Limited though they are, they address matters that are generally perceived as having *global* effects rather than merely local ones. We all suffer with the depletion of the ozone layer; we are all poorer when the earth's biological heritage is diminished.

What does this tell us about the likely course of other trade/environment issues? First, it is unlikely that GATT or other trade-oriented institutions will be significant forums for initiating measures aimed at the environmental consequences of trade. This is certainly true for significant multilateral environmental issues such as the greenhouse effect, but it may also prove true for more narrow issues such as PPP: there is now evidence, for example, to suggest that "pollution shopping" by multinationals may not prove to be the important factor in investment/trade decisions that it was once suspected of being. Second, the use of trade-oriented measures might well be applied to other environmental concerns — but this will probably be accomplished on an *ad hoc* basis. The evidence of the past suggests that issues involving sustainability of global resources are particularly amenable to such an approach, both because they are more likely to generate the requisite political will in the world community and because they often involve trade as an important element. Two examples of the type of issue that might be open to such an approach are the greenhouse effect and the increasing use of drift gill net fishing practices — both very directly involving the question of global sustainability.

THE INTERNATIONAL WASTE TRADE: A GREENPEACE REPORT

Ann Leonard and Jim Vallette

In the aftermath of huge toxic disasters, such as those at Love Canal in the United Sates and Seveso in Italy, industrialized countries have adopted increasingly strict and costly regulations for the disposal of solid and hazardous wastes. In attempts to avoid these regulations, many waste generators have been on the lookout for cheap and easy ways to get their wastes off their hands. One increasingly popular method is to ship wastes to less-developed countries. Such waste-trade schemes are either arranged covertly or accompanied by cash payments large enough to entice countries to accept the dangerous cargoes.

The international trade in wastes has soared in recent years. Between 1986 and 1988 alone, over 3.1 million tons of wastes were shipped from industrialized to developing countries. If the waste traders are not stopped soon, many more millions of tons of waste will be dumped, buried, or burned in developing countries.

EXAMPLES OF THE INTERNATIONAL WASTE TRADE

As the examples in Appendix A indicate, attempts to dump waste in foreign countries are varied and numerous. At least seventy-three developing nations around the world have been proposed as dumpsites for wastes from industrialized countries. Last year, toxics from the United States were dumped as far afield as Haiti, Guinea, and South Africa. Wastes from Europe have been discovered in war-ravaged Beirut, in a Venezuelan port, and in the tiny village of Koko, Nigeria. These waste-trade schemes involve every type of waste imaginable — radioactive wastes, toxic wastes, municipal solid wastes, incinerator ash, asbestos wastes, sewage sludge, and old tires.

In our research into the international waste trade, Greenpeace has identified two types of waste-trade schemes. There are the outrageous one-time shipments, like the infamous Khian Sea loaded with U.S. incinerator ash, and the highly toxic wastes from Italy dumped in Koko, Nigeria. This type of waste trade has received most of the recent media attention. There are also, however, long-term waste-trade schemes. Although these schemes have avoided publicity, they are potentially much more damaging than the one-time shipments.

For a number of reasons, long-term schemes are difficult to publicize and defeat. Many of them exploit the politics of poverty in a much more subtle manner than one-time shipments. Waste traders involved in long-term schemes commonly offer benefits beyond cash — such as electricity or "land reclamation" — to developing countries in critical need of these commodities.

Most long-term schemes involve the construction of incinerators to burn foreign wastes in less-developed countries. Incinerators, in addition to producing toxic emissions and even more toxic ash, can produce electricity. In many developing countries, electricity is a scarce and desperately needed commodity. There are currently plans to burn foreign hazardous waste for electricity generation in Bangladesh, Paraguay, Haiti, Angola, Tunisia, Sierra Leone, Honduras, and elsewhere. The combined capacity of these proposed incinerators is over one million tons per year. Already, China currently imports tens of thousands of tons of waste each year for burning in an incinerator.

Equally seductive are schemes to import wastes for use as land-reclamation materials in countries where land is scarce or unusable. Many U.S. firms are trying to ship solid wastes, such as sewage sludge, incinerator ash, or household garbage, to Central America and the Caribbean to fill in ecologically vibrant, but unusable, wetlands.

One U.S. firm, Admiralty Pacific, has received the preliminary approval of the President of the Marshall Islands to import garbage from the West Coast of the United States. Admiralty Pacific plans to dump millions of tons of municipal refuse on a tiny South Pacific atoll in the Marshalls, thus increasing the surface area and altitude of the island. The company claims that the increased size of the islands will protect the Marshallese citizens from flooding as sea levels rise due to the greenhouse effect caused by atmospheric pollution. In addition, the Marshallese government will be paid millions of dollars for accepting U.S. garbage.

PROBLEMS WITH THE INTERNATIONAL WASTE TRADE

Waste Trade Threatens the Populations and Environments of Importing Countries

All waste-disposal facilities, including high-temperature incinerators, landfills, and "detoxification plants," will eventually release contaminants into the environment. The hazards of industrial wastes are well documented.[1] Throughout the developed world, hazardous wastes have contaminated the air, soil, and water, and contributed to environmental degradation and human suffering. Rates of cancer, birth defects, and other health problems are alarmingly high in areas contaminated by hazardous wastes.

Municipal, or household, waste also poses severe risks to human health and the

---

1   For information on the hazards of industrial wastes, see S.S. Epstein, L.D. Brown & C. Pope, *Hazardous Waste in America* (San Francisco: Sierra Club Books, 1982); United States, Environmental Protection Agency (EPA), "Report to Congress on the Discharge of Hazardous Wastes to Publicly Owned Treatment Works," EPA 530-SW-86-004 (1986).

environment.[2] Although household waste is commonly referred to as "non-toxic," many extremely toxic materials are routinely discarded in the municipal waste stream. Items such as used batteries, paints, cleaning solvents, automobile oil, and garden pesticides combine with hazardous wastes that are illegally disposed of, or exempted under various "small-quantity generator" provisions, to increase the toxicity of municipal waste. A recent study at A&M University concluded that the leachate from municipal landfills is, in many cases, equally as hazardous as leachate from industrial waste landfills.[3]

If wastes are too dangerous to dispose of in the generating countries, they are too dangerous to dispose of in other countries. Most of the countries targeted for waste-trade schemes lack the environmental regulations and facilities necessary to handle industrial or municipal wastes. For this reason, these wastes pose even greater threats to less-developed countries. When wastes are exported, the populations and environments of the receiving countries are forced to suffer for the unhealthy and unsustainable production processes of the industrialized world.

Waste Trade is a Disincentive for Waste Reduction

The export of wastes allows industrialized countries to avoid the only real solution to the waste crisis — changes in production processes to eliminate harmful wastes at the source. As long as waste can be shipped abroad, there is less incentive for industries to implement existing, or develop new, technologies for minimizing waste at the source.

The waste trade delays the real solution to the waste problem by perpetuating the myth that safe disposal options exist for hazardous wastes. Once the waste is packed up and exported, developed countries believe the disposal dilemma is solved. However, waste trade merely shifts the most direct problem to another country. By polluting the global environment, the waste always eventually returns through contaminated air, soil, food, and water.

Waste Trade is Bad Foreign Policy

Developing countries have branded the waste trade as "toxic terrorism" and "toxic imperialism." At least forty-four developing countries have banned the import of wastes. The industrialized countries must recognize the rights of developing countries and stop dumping waste on them.

All landfills and incinerators, even when constructed and operated with the best

---

2   For information on municipal wastes, see United States, EPA, "Report to Congress: Solid Waste Disposal in the United States," EPA 530-SW-88-011 (1988); H. Belevi & P. Baccini, "Long-Term Behavior of Municipal Solid Waste Landfills" (1989) 7 Waste Management and Research 43.

3   K.W. Brown & K.C. Donnelly, "An Estimation of the Risk Associated with the Organic Constituents of Hazardous and Municipal Waste Landfill Leachates" (1988) 5(1) Hazardous Waste and Hazardous Materials.

available technology, create both real and perceived threats to public health and the environment. In light of the tremendous opposition such sites arouse within the borders of industrialized countries, it is clear that exporting waste also has serious implications for foreign relations. It is only a matter of time until contaminants are released from waste-disposal operations abroad; then all fingers will point to the industrialized countries as generators and exporters of "toxic time-bombs."

Waste Trade is an Ethical Issue

Developing countries that are considering or have accepted proposals to import foreign wastes are often swayed by the huge cash payments that accompany those wastes. These payments are often large enough to tempt developing nations to consider mortgaging their public health and environmental integrity for much-needed currency. Unethical business deals like these force developing nations to make the unfair choice between poison and poverty. The practice of industrialized countries exploiting developing nations by paying them to accept hazardous wastes is absolutely unjustifiable on scientific, political, or ethical grounds.

APPROACHES TO REGULATION

The United States

The current U.S. law regulating hazardous waste exports relies on the notion of "prior consent." The procedure for exporting waste, except to Canada and Mexico (with whom the United States has bilateral agreements), simply requires the United States to notify the receiving country of the proposed export and to obtain from them written consent to the shipment. There are major flaws in the use of prior consent to permit waste exports:

1. The receiving country is given only a very brief description of the waste. Developing countries often lack the technical expertise to fully evaluate the impacts of waste-trade proposals. The Environmental Protection Agency (EPA) does not provide any critical review of the export proposal or the final disposal method in the recipient country.

2. The validity of the notification procedure is questionable, since the government officials agreeing to import wastes are rarely the people directly affected by the disposal facilities.

3. The theory of prior consent implies voluntary acceptance of imported wastes. However, the concept of "voluntary" loses its meaning in the arena of international waste trade. No country really *wants* another country's waste, but the economic situation in developing countries makes it difficult for them to reject an offer that will bring them millions of dollars.

Wastes that are in fact dangerous, but are not legally defined as "hazardous" (such as sewage sludge, incinerator ash, and household waste), may now be exported with no controls whatsoever. In addition, the EPA does not have the authority to refuse an export permit, even when it is clear that the waste will be handled in an environmentally unsound manner in the country of import.

In congressional testimony last summer, the Inspector General of the EPA blasted his agency's efforts to monitor the export of wastes from the United States, describing them as "a shambles." The EPA's waste-export program, he noted, is staffed by only two people. In fact, more people work for Greenpeace to stop waste exports than work for the EPA to regulate these exports.

Currently, Congress and the Senate are considering legislation regarding waste exports. The Waste Export Control Act has been devised as an amendment to the Resources Conservation and Recovery Act, the major U.S. law regulating hazardous waste disposal. The bill was introduced May 31, 1989, sponsored by Congressmen Synar, Conyers, Porter, and Wolpe. Senators Kasten, Lautenberg, and Baucus were also involved in the drafting process, and are expected to introduce a similar bill in the Senate. The basis of the bill is the establishment of a permitting process for waste exports. The criterion for approval of applications to export waste is that the waste be destined for disposal facilities that are constructed and operated under standards comparable to those required in the United States.

While Greenpeace agrees that waste-export legislation is necessary, we find this bill inadequate. By regulating rather than preventing waste exports, the United States will legitimize this deadly business. The permitting system will allow waste exports to continue, thereby creating a business out of what should be a crime.

Allowing waste exports in cases where the waste is destined for disposal facilities comparable to those in the United States is inappropriate for a number of reasons:

1. Waste traders would be able simply to cross the borders to Mexico to take advantage of lower land and labor prices than those of the United States. Potentially, a string of toxic-waste disposal facilities would be constructed along the border, and exploitation of less-industrialized countries would continue.

2. It is highly unlikely that the EPA will be able to constantly monitor all foreign-waste disposal facilities. Many countries targeted for waste export have limited resources; it is unfair and unrealistic to expect importing countries to monitor and enforce U.S.-operated facilities disposing of U.S. waste. U.S. regulations alone, without the agency infrastructure existing in the United States, will not guarantee that waste will be handled as required domestically.

3. The recent loss of the highly toxic pesticide, Lindane, in the English Channel and the tragic Exxon oil spill are examples of the dangers involved in transporting hazardous materials. Disposal in comparable facilities does not justify the risks involved and the energy consumed in the international transport of wastes.

4. Most important, U.S. regulations are inadequate to protect public health and the environment. Landfills and incinerators all over the United States have leaked contaminants into the air, soil, water, and food supplies. The Waste Export Control Act, in its present draft, condones the export of flawed and dangerous technologies.

Tightening up the loose points in the bill is not sufficient; the entire focus of the bill must be changed. Because Greenpeace is adamantly opposed to the export of U.S. wastes, we believe that if it is allowed at all, it should be permitted only under the most exceptional circumstances.

Waste exports must be prohibited unless, at minimum,

1. no waste-prevention techniques could have been used,

2. the waste is destined for a disposal method that is more environmentally benign than any available or feasible in the United States, and

3. citizens of the recipient country—not just its government officials—have been provided both the necessary information to evaluate the proposed waste trade and the opportunity to testify during the permitting process.

United Nations Environment Programme's Global Convention

Last March, the Global Convention on the Transboundary Movement of Hazardous Wastes, sponsored by the United Nations Environment Programme (UNEP), was signed in Basel, Switzerland, by over thirty countries. This Convention was a potentially valuable vehicle to curb the international waste trade. Unfortunately, it failed to address the demands of the majority of the world's nations for a global ban on waste trade. To understand why the eighteen months of negotiations produced such a weak treaty, we must look at the roots of the Basel Convention.

In 1985, before the international waste trade became an issue of great concern in the Third World, wastes were traded widely between European countries. That year, the huge Swiss chemical firm Hoffmann Laroche was embarrassed when it lost forty-three barrels of highly toxic dioxin-contaminated wastes from its plant in Seveso, Italy. It was even more embarrassed when Greenpeace helped discover the barrels in a farmhouse near Paris.

Hoffmann Laroche is based in Basel, Switzerland. Soon after the Seveso embarrassment, another Basel-based firm suffered an even more serious public relations disaster. Tanks loaded with highly toxic chemicals exploded one winter's night at a plant in Basel run by the chemical giant Sandoz. Sandoz's poisons filled the air of three countries, and destroyed stretches of the Rhine River downstream in Germany, France, and the Netherlands. The Basel chemical industry had lost its image of purity. In an effort to cleanse this sullied image, the Swiss chemical industry strongly encouraged and underwrote negotiations on what was to be the Basel Convention. Switzerland and its chemical industry hoped that the Convention would be viewed as a great step forward by industry, government, and environmentalists, in combatting a common enemy — the uncontrolled movement of hazardous wastes.

It is important to understand that the pressure to create and sign the Basel Convention came from the chemical industry in Europe, and not from the developing world. Industry and industrialized countries have not questioned the need for the international waste trade — they just do not want to be embarrassed by the loss of any more barrels of extremely toxic wastes. The convention they envisioned would be a duplication of recently adopted laws and directives in the United States and the European Community, which require waste exporters to notify the governments of any exporting and importing countries before any shipment takes place.

But events occurring during the Convention negotiations last year highlighted the fact that mere notification systems are ineffective means of controlling the international waste trade. A notification system does not restrict the international waste trade; it simply sets up a global tracking system for wastes. It became obvious last year that the Basel Convention's highest priority should have been to prevent the Third World from becoming the industrialized world's waste dump, by an outright prohibition on waste shipments from industrialized to developing countries. Industrialized countries had the power to stop waste exports to the Third World; instead, they opted to legalize them. While attending four negotiation sessions as official "observers," Greenpeace witnessed the industrialized countries' systematic dismantling of the Convention's environmental safeguards.

As the waste-trade issue heated up through 1988, more and more developing countries attended the negotiations, demanding that this Convention ban waste shipments to their territories. These countries also demanded a number of mechanisms that would attack the heart of the international waste trade. Developing countries demanded tough enforcement measures, the free and public flow of information about every waste-trade scheme, and the imposition of liability on exporting countries for future damages caused by their waste shipments. Just about every demand by a developing country was ignored. And those that had been adopted in earlier negotiations were stripped away from the Convention in the final week of negotiations.

Entering the final week of negotiations in Basel, we still had some hope that industrialized countries would be persuaded to use the Convention to ban an obvious injustice. Throughout the week, Greenpeace and many developing countries pointed out numerous flaws and loopholes in the draft Convention. One glaring omission was the exclusion of radioactive wastes from its scope. The International Atomic Energy Agency (IAEA) urged negotiators to exclude radioactive wastes from the Convention because, allegedly, they were covered by existing IAEA international control systems. However, after researching the relevant international law, Greenpeace discovered that — excluding fissile radioactive wastes — no such regulations exist; therefore, Greenpeace demanded that the Convention include non-fissile radioactive wastes.

We also urged delegates to delete a loophole in the Convention that allows bilateral and multilateral treaties for waste trade between contracting parties and non-contracting parties. These treaties do not need to conform to the provisions of the Convention. If a convention allows contracting parties to ship wastes to non-contracting parties, then the provisions of that convention will, of course, be easily circumvented.

Nevertheless, the loopholes and omissions pointed out by Greenpeace and developing countries were either expanded or ignored in the final hours, despite the strong objections of many Third World countries. Throughout the final week, negotiations on the Global Waste Trade Convention degenerated into squabbles between the Swiss chair of negotiations and many developing countries. It became surprisingly clear that industrialized countries would not sign the Basel Convention unless it was a weak, loophole-ridden vehicle with which they could justify and expand their involvement in the international waste trade.

Industrialized nations ultimately succeeded in limiting the scope of the Convention to a simple waste-trade notification system. Power politics prevailed in the final week of negotiations, at the worst possible time. If any convention should not be tailored to the demands of industrialized countries, this one is it. But pressures to sign the Convention in Basel, coupled with the unified efforts of waste-trading nations to dismantle the Convention's protective measures, led to a document that threatens to legitimize and expand this deadly trade.

The Basel Convention was not drafted in the spirit of compromise. The developing countries' demands for protection from the international waste trade were almost entirely ignored. In the end, when the Convention was signed in Basel on March 22, 1989, it neither banned waste exports from industrialized to developing countries nor included radioactive wastes. It also allows free trade in wastes between contracting and non-contracting parties. The biggest danger generated by the implementation of the Convention is that it creates the illusion that the international waste trade is now under control. It will do more to institutionalize waste trade than it will to prevent it.

Some delegates to the negotiations hailed the Convention as a major step toward solving the problems created by waste trade. Some have ventured even further into the realm of illusion: the Swiss Environment Minister made the remarkable statement that, because of this document, the international waste trade would be extinct in three years. On the contrary, of course, by posing as a solution to the international waste trade, the Basel Convention actually delays any real, long-term solutions by a matter of months if not years. Its provisions are no stronger than those already in place in industrialized countries, and these existing regulations have proven incapable of curtailing either legal or illegal waste traffic.

The heart of the Convention is the requirement that importing countries be notified of, and consent to, waste shipments before they occur. Waste traders around the world must be relieved that their business is threatened by little more than some minor paperwork. Indeed, some waste traders were openly enthusiastic as the convention was signed. One prominent waste trader is Gianfranco Ambrosini, an Italian businessman who masterminded a shipment of wastes from Italy to the tiny African country of Djibouti. On the eve of the signing of the convention, Ambrosini pointed out that, compared to other hurdles he faces in shipping wastes to developing countries, getting the signature of one government official, as the Convention requires, is no problem. Ambrosini said that the Basel Convention does absolutely nothing to prevent him from engaging in waste trade. Ambrosini's analysis was echoed by another waste trader, Andreas Kunstler. Kunstler, a resident of Basel, is trying to build an incinerator for European toxic wastes in Angola. Kunstler scoffed at the Convention, and labeled the negotiators "hypocrites."

Greenpeace has been following dozens of long-term plans to build incinerators, landfills, and other waste-import facilities in developing countries. None of these schemes has been withdrawn following the signing of the Basel Convention. That is a clear signal that waste traders do not feel threatened by it.

A Global Ban on the International Waste Trade

The only solution to the political and environmental problems that arise from the international waste trade is to ban this practice worldwide. All countries, all companies, and all individuals should be preventing the production of toxic waste at the source — rather than dumping these pollutants elsewhere.

International organizations, national governments, and nongovernmental organizations around the world are calling for a ban on the international waste trade. A ban, backed up with strict enforcement mechanisms, is the only way to protect the global environment. A ban on waste trade is also a necessary step in forcing industries to reduce the production of toxic wastes, through the utilization of clean technologies and safe materials — the only real solution to the waste-disposal problem.

APPENDIX A

The following are case studies of specific international waste-trade schemes. They are excerpts from The International Trade in Wastes: A Greenpeace Inventory, *which describes scores of examples of proposed, rejected, completed, or current waste-trade schemes. The complete inventory has been omitted due to space constraints, but is available from Greenpeace's International Waste Trade Project at 1436 U St., N.W., Washington, D.C., 20009, U.S.A., or by calling (202) 462-1177.*

Examples of International Waste Trade Schemes

1.   An Epic Journey: The KHIAN SEA

The journey of the renegade ash ship, KHIAN SEA, which carried almost 14,000 tons of incinerator ash from the city of Philadelphia, U.S.A., for 27 months, ended in late 1988. During its epic voyage, the KHIAN SEA carried its toxic cargo to five continents before unloading it somewhere in the Indian Ocean region.

The vessel's incredible journey began in August 1986, when it unsuccessfully attempted to dump its cargo on a Bahamian island. The ash ship then began wandering around the Caribbean Sea, looking for a welcoming port.

The KHIAN SEA dumps part of its cargo in Haiti

On October 26, 1987, the Haitian Department of Commerce issued an import permit to the KHIAN SEA. The permit was issued for "ingrais pour du sol" — fertilizer. The ship's real cargo, however, was 13,476 tons of toxic municipal incinerator ash from Philadelphia.

The deal was arranged by a Haitian company called "Cultivators of the West." This company was headed by brothers of Haitian Col. Jean Claude-Paul.

On December 31, 1987, the KHIAN SEA sailed into Gonaives, Haiti. Three weeks later, on January 21, 1988, some 100 Haitian laborers began unloading ash from the ship.

On January 29, 1988, the Haitian government ordered the ash out of the country. Haiti's minister of commerce, Mario Celestin, said, "All means will be taken so that all quantities dumped will be reloaded and the boat will be dealt with according to the law."

Six days later, the KHIAN SEA departed Gonaives in the middle of the night, leaving behind an estimated 2,000 to 4,500 tons of Philadelphia's incinerator ash. Many months and two coups d'états later, the ash remains on the Gonaives beach.

On February 15, 1988, a Greenpeace investigative team documented the ash pile on a remote peninsula outside Gonaives. A portion of the ash pile abutted the Bay of Gonaives and some ash has entered the salt water bay. Investigators also viewed strong oceanic breezes carrying the ash toward the city of Gonaives.

Environmental and political activists in Haiti and in Miami have held repeated protests urging the U.S. and Haitian governments to return the ash in Gonaives to Philadelphia.

The people of Gonaives organized protests last March 25th and May 7th against the presence of the waste. According to the J.O.C. [a Haitian organization of young Christian workers], Haitian Colonel Gambetta Hippolyte intervened "by force of arms," and prevented both demonstrations from taking place. Then-Haitian president, Leslie Manigat, responded to public pressure and promised to remove the wastes.

During his brief tenure in power, on June 16, 1988, former Haitian president Leslie Manigat referred to the clean-up efforts underway as follows: "The work is being done by a team of experts. The operation is under way and I wish to inform proudly and gratefully that the firm in question is doing the Haitian people a favor. It is doing it for free." Unfortunately, local environmentalists were not impressed by the man's clean-up efforts.

In October 1988, the J.O.C. released a report about the ash pile. In the early summer of 1988, according to the J.O.C., 655 barrels of ash were packed, but were still on the beach in Gonaives through October 1988. The group found that at least 268 barrels were poorly closed, 28 were partially covered with plastic, and 61 were completely open with no protection at all.

The unbarreled ash remained piled on the beach. The wastes were located only 3.5 meters from the sea and no warning signs or fences were erected to protect the population from entering the area.

The J.O.C. made a number of demands on October 17th, including: an immediate prohibition of entry into the contaminated area, return of the wastes to the United States, evaluation of health and environmental damages, compensation to victims, and prosecution of responsible individuals.

Philadelphia's ash presents both acute and chronic threats to human health and the marine and terrestrial environment in Gonaives and the Gulf of Gonaives. Based on earlier analyses by Greenpeace, the ash currently on the Gonaives beach may contain as much as 210,000 pounds of toxic heavy metals, including legally hazardous levels of lead and cadmium and high levels of mercury and arsenic. The ash also carries significant levels of the most potent toxic chemicals known — dioxins and furans.

The Journey Continues

After the KHIAN SEA left Haiti, it sailed up the U.S. east coast and anchored near

Philadelphia in March 1988, but, unfortunately, did not receive permission to offload the remaining ash in Philadelphia. The ship left the Philadelphia area in May 1988, disobeying U.S. Coast Guard orders to remain at anchorage.

Still loaded with over 10,000 tons of Philadelphia's ash, the KHIAN SEA crossed the Atlantic in June 1988, and passed the west coast of Africa.

The ship arrived at a shipyard in Bijela, Yugoslavia for repairs in early July. While in Yugoslavia, the vessel changed its name to the FELICIA. The owners of the KHIAN SEA, Amalgamated Shipping of the Bahamas, claim that they also sold the vessel to a firm named Romo Shipping. Romo Shipping was incorporated in the Caribbean island of St. Nevis shortly before the alleged transaction took place.

The vessel's movements have been controlled by a consortium of brokerage firms headed by U.S. businessman Robert Dowd. These firms are Coastal Carriers of Annapolis, Maryland, Amalgamated Shipping of the Bahamas, Marcona Shipping of Florida, and Lily Navigation of Liberia.

The Ash Disappears

In late September 1988, the FELICIA passed through the Suez Canal, still loaded with its two-year old cargo, and reported its next destination as the Philippines. Greenpeace subsequently alerted the governments of every country in or bordering the Indian Ocean about the threat posed by the ash ship.

During the fall, the FELICIA planned to land in Sri Lanka, the Philippines, Indonesia and Singapore. Each of these governments denied entry to the vessel.

The government of Sri Lanka informed Greenpeace that the vessel had attempted to unload its toxic cargo in a landfill in Bangladesh, but could not after heavy floods made the landfill inaccessible. Soon thereafter, the vessel requested, but was denied, permission to dump its cargo in Sri Lanka.

The FELICIA also was denied entry in Indonesia. Emil Salim, Population and Environment Minister, rejected an offer by a foreign broker to take wastes for "a large sum of money." "Indonesia will never allow any country to dump its industrial waste here," Salim promised.

Finally, in November, the FELICIA appeared off the Singapore coast, with its hold empty, and with a new name — the PELICANO. Somewhere between the Suez Canal and Singapore, in October and/or November, the ash ship discharged its cargo. According to the captain of the PELICANO, Captain Arturo Fuentes, "the ash was never dumped at sea. We brought it to a country and barges with cranes came alongside to scoop the ash out." The captain's claim has not been substantiated. Fuentes admitted: "Greenpeace really did us in."

In the course of the KHIAN SEA's journey, countries on five continents rejected its cargo. These countries included the Bahamas, Bermuda, Cape Verde Islands, Chile, Costa Rica, Dominican Republic, Guinea, Guinea-Bissau, Haiti, Honduras, Indonesia, Philippines, Senegal, Sri Lanka, and Yugoslavia.

The Vessel's Owners Go To Court

Although the ship's holds are empty, the story is far from over. Players involved in the saga have taken the battle to court to try to recover the huge financial losses (over U.S. $3 million) resulting from the 27 month ordeal.

The generator of the ash, the City of Philadelphia, denies any responsibility for the final disposal of the ash. According to Philadelphia officials, the issue is between the waste disposal firm contracted, Joseph Paolino & Sons, and the companies Paolino hired. However, Philadelphia has refused to pay Paolino until it is proved that the ash was disposed of legally.

While the ship crossed the Atlantic last summer, Paolino & Sons obtained a federal injunction which required Amalgamated Shipping, the supposed owners of the vessel, to notify Paolino, the U.S. Environmental Protection Agency, and the U.S. District Court at least three days before disposing of the ash.

In late December, the U.S. District Court held a preliminary hearing on Amalgamated Shipping's alleged violation of this injunction. Amalgamated argued that the sale of the KHIAN SEA to Romo Shipping cleared their firm from adhering to the federal injunction. The federal judge said that he would "probably" find Amalgamated in contempt of court.

2. Admiralty Pacific's Proposal to Dump U.S. Wastes in the Marshall Islands

A U.S. company, Admiralty Pacific, is currently proposing to export millions of tons of municipal garbage from the U.S. west coast to be used as landfill in the South Pacific Marshall Islands. According to Admiralty Pacific's proposal, the benefits for the Marshall Islands in the first 5 years of importing waste include U.S. $140 million in cash, more land area for development and agriculture, and higher elevation to offset the rising sea levels expected from global warming.

Under the firm's proposal, up to 3,500,000 tons would be dumped in the first year and over 17 million tons would be dumped by the end of the fifth year. Admiralty Pacific hopes to continue the operation for at least 15 years. Eventually, if Admiralty Pacific has its way, the Marshall Islands will become the dumping ground for one-third of California's solid waste and over 10% of all the waste produced on the U.S. west coast.

Although the Marshallese government has not given final approval to the proposal, Admiralty Pacific is anxious to get the green light on their plan because it claims to have signed contracts to dispose of U.S. waste. Dan Fleming, of

Admiralty Pacific, told a reporter: "If we're not hauling garbage to the Marshalls by June 1990, we'll be sued." Admiralty Pacific claims to have hired the Radian Corporation, a California-based engineering firm, to conduct a technical feasibility study of their proposal. The study, at a cost of U.S. $2–3 million, will not be completed until the end of 1989.

Despite Admiralty Pacific's claims that all metals will be removed from the municipal waste before it is shipped, thereby rendering it non-toxic, Greenpeace is concerned about the environmental impact of disposing of 34 million pounds of garbage in the small South Pacific atolls. Admiralty Pacific has not explained how it will remove metals from the huge volume of garbage in question. Even if it were able to remove metal objects, metal residue and other toxics would be present in inks, dyes, cleansers, polishes, automobile supplies, pesticides and other harmful products in everyday garbage.

3. Incineration Rejected in Guyana

In September 1988, the president of Guyana, Desmond Hoyte, announced that his government has rejected a proposal by two California partner firms to burn over 60,000 tons of waste a year in Guyana.

Earlier in the year, the government had entered into a joint venture with the firms, Pott Industries and Teixeira Farms. The joint venture, called the Guyana Resource Corporation, had announced plans to construct an industrial waste incinerator somewhere along Guyana's Demerara River by early 1989, at the edge of the South American rainforests.

The plan was met with heavy opposition from Guyanese opposition parties, which held numerous protests in Guyana, at the Potts Industry headquarters in Culver City, California, and at the Guyanese High Commission in London.

Anglican Bishop Randolph George called the proposal "a money deal — like drugs." Eusi Kwayana of the opposition party, the Working People's Alliance, added, "I place no reliance whatsoever on people who are agents of waste disposal." Other opponents of the scheme included the People's Progressive Party, the Guyana Human Rights Association, the Guyana Medical Association, and the United Republican Party of Guyana.

The chair of Pott Industries, Finn Moller, also heads Oasis Petroleum, a bankrupt oil company in which Esam Khashoggi, brother of the Saudi arms trader, Adnan Khashoggi, is a major investor. Moller has faced a number of government probes and lawsuits for alleged financial abuses.

In September 1988, President Hoyte said, "The investors ... have been going around making completely unauthorized statements. They have not supplied us with the information we required in order to enable us to judge the safety of this project. We have reached the stage now where I can definitely state that the project is a non-starter."

INSTITUTE PUBLICATIONS

Following is a complete list of CIRL publications currently available:

The Offshore Petroleum Regimes of Canada and Australia, by Constance D. Hunt. 1989. ISBN 0-919269-29-X. $24.00

The Inuvialuit Final Agreement, by Janet M. Keeping. 1989. ISBN 0-919269-28-1. $24.00

Toxic Water Pollution in Canada, by Paul Muldoon and Marcia Valiante. 1988. ISBN 0-919269-24-9. 117 p. $22.00

Interjurisdictional Issues in Canadian Water Management, by J. Owen Saunders. 1988. ISBN 0-919269-27-3. 130 p. $22.00

The Framework of Water Rights Legislation in Canada, by David R. Percy. 1988. ISBN 0-919269-21-4. 103 p. $20.00

Maritime Boundaries and Resource Development: Options for the Beaufort Sea, by Donald R. Rothwell. 1988. ISBN 0-919269-24-9. 61 p. $15.00

A Reference Guide to Mining Legislation in Canada (Second Edition), by Barry Barton, Barbara Roulston and Nancy Strantz. 1988. ISBN 0-919269-25-7. 123 p. $30.00

Aboriginal Water Rights in Canada: A Study of Aboriginal Title to Water and Indian Water Rights, by Richard H. Bartlett. 1988. ISBN 0-919269-23-0. 231 p. $30.00

Liability for Drilling- and Production-Source Oil Pollution in the Canadian Offshore, by Christian G. Yoder. Working Paper 12. 1986. ISBN 0-919269-20-6. 84 p. $17.00

A Guide to Appearing Before the Surface Rights Board of Alberta (Second Edition), by Barry Barton and Barbara Roulston. Working Paper 11. 1986. ISBN 0-919269-19-2. 124 p. $17.00

Crown Timber Rights in Alberta, by N.D. Bankes. Working Paper 10. 1986. ISBN 0-919269-17-6. 128 p. $17.00

The Canadian Regulation of Offshore Installations, by Christian G. Yoder. Working Paper 9. 1985. ISBN 0-919269-18-4. 116 p. $17.00

The Assignment and Registration of Crown Mineral Interests, by N.D. Bankes. Working Paper 5. 1985. ISBN 0-919269-11-7. 126 p. $17.00

Oil and Gas Conservation on Canada Lands, by Owen L. Anderson. Working Paper 7. 1985. ISBN 0-919269-16-8. 122 p. $17.00

Canadian Maritime Law and the Offshore: A Primer, by W. Wylie Spicer. Canadian Continental Shelf Law 3; Working Paper 6. 1984. ISBN 0-919269-12-5. 65 p. $13.00

Public Disposition of Natural Resources, Essays from the First Banff Conference on Natural Resources Law, April 12-15, 1983; Nigel Bankes and J. Owen Saunders, eds. ISBN 0-919269-14-1. 366 p. hardcover. $47.00*

Fairness in Environmental and Social Impact Assessment Processes, Proceedings of a Seminar, The Banff Centre, February 1-3, 1983; Evangeline S. Case, Peter Z.R. Finkle and Alastair R. Lucas, eds. Proceedings 2. ISBN 0-919269-08-7. 125 p. $17.00

Canadian Electricity Exports: Legal and Regulatory Issues, by Alastair R. Lucas and J. Owen Saunders. Working Paper 3. 1983. ISBN 0-919269-09-5. 40 p. $9.50

The International Legal Context of Petroleum Operations in Canadian Arctic Waters, by Ian Townsend Gault. Canadian Continental Shelf Law 2; Working Paper 4. 1983. ISBN 0-919269-10-9. 76 p. $9.00

Acid Precipitation in North America: The Case for Transboundary Cooperation, by Douglas M. Johnston and Peter Finkle. 1983. ISBN 0-919269-05-2. 75 p. $10.00

Petroleum Operations on the Canadian Continental Margin — The Legal Issues in a Modern Perspective, by Ian Townsend Gault. Canadian Continental Shelf 1; Working Paper 2. 1983. ISBN 0-919269-02-8. $10.00

Environmental Regulation – Its Impact on Major Oil and Gas Projects: Oil Sands and Arctic, by C.D. Hunt and A.R. Lucas. 1980. ISBN 0-919269-00-1. 168 p. $12.95

Resources: The Newsletter of the Canadian Institute of Resources Law. ISSN 0714-5918. Quarterly. Free

1988-89 Annual Report. Free

DISCUSSION PAPERS

Successor Liability for Environmental Damage, by Terry Davis. 1989. $10.00

Surrounding Circumstances and Custom: Extrinsic Evidence in the Interpretation of Oil and Gas Industry Agreements in Alberta, by David E. Hardy. 1989. $10.00

Views on Surface Rights in Alberta, Papers and materials from the Workshop on Surface Rights, Drumheller, 20-21 April 1988; Barry Barton, ed. $10.00

Classifying Non-operating Interests in Oil and Gas, by Eugene Kuntz; presented at a seminar sponsored by the Faculty of Law and The Canadian Institute of Resources Law, The University of Calgary, 7 April 1988. $10.00

Publications are available from: Canadian Institute of Resources Law, 430 BioSciences Building, Faculty of Law, The University of Calgary, Calgary, Alberta, Canada T2N 1N4. Telephone (403) 220-3200. Telex 03-821545. Facsimile (403) 282-6182.

Orders from outside Canada please add $2.00 per book.

OTHER PUBLICATIONS

Canada Energy Law Service.
ISBN 0-88820-108-7, 5 v.
available from Richard De Boo Publishers
    81 Curlew Drive
    Don Mills, Ontario, Canada
    M3A 3P7

INSTITUTE PUBLICATIONS AVAILABLE FROM CARSWELL LEGAL PUBLICATIONS

Trading Canada's Natural Resources, Essays from the Third Banff Conference on Natural Resources Law, Banff, Alberta, May 6-9, 1987. J. Owen Saunders, ed. 367 p. (hardcover) $75.00*

Managing Natural Resources in a Federal State, Essays from the Second Banff Conference on Natural Resources Law, Banff, Alberta, April 17-20, 1985. J. Owen Saunders, ed. 372 p. (hardcover) $70.00*

Call Carswell Legal Publications TOLL FREE 1-800-387-5164 (Canada only)

*20% off if you order two or more volumes of Essays from the Banff Conference on Natural Resources Law sponsored by The Canadian Institute of Resources Law